Download Forms on Nolo.com

To download the forms, go to this book's companion page at:

 www.nolo.com/back-of-book/PAT.html

Checking the companion page is also a good way
to stay informed on topics related to this book.

More Resources from Nolo.com

Legal Forms, Books, & Software
Hundreds of do-it-yourself products—all written in plain English, approved, and updated by our in-house legal editors.

Legal Articles
Get informed with thousands of free articles on everyday legal topics. Our articles are accurate, up to date, and reader friendly.

Find a Lawyer
Want to talk to a lawyer? Use Nolo to find a lawyer who can help you with your case.

△△ NOLO The Trusted Name
(but don't take our word for it)

"In Nolo you can trust."
THE NEW YORK TIMES

"Nolo is always there in a jam as the nation's premier publisher of do-it-yourself legal books."
NEWSWEEK

"Nolo publications…guide people simply through the how, when, where and why of the law."
THE WASHINGTON POST

"[Nolo's]…material is developed by experienced attorneys who have a knack for making complicated material accessible."
LIBRARY JOURNAL

"When it comes to self-help legal stuff, nobody does a better job than Nolo…"
USA TODAY

"The most prominent U.S. publisher of self-help legal aids."
TIME MAGAZINE

"Nolo is a pioneer in both consumer and business self-help books and software."
LOS ANGELES TIMES

22nd Edition

Patent It Yourself

Your Step-by-Step Guide to Filing at the U.S. Patent Office

**Patent Attorneys David E. Blau
and David Pressman**

TWENTY-SECOND EDITION	AUGUST 2025
Editor	GLEN SECOR
Cover Design	SUSAN PUTNEY
Book Design	SUSAN PUTNEY
Proofreading	IRENE BARNARD
Index	MELISSA STEARNS HYDE
Printing	SHERIDAN

ISSN: 1554-9925 (print)
ISSN: 2371-9966 (online)
ISBN: 978-1-4133-3268-1 (pbk)
ISBN: 978-1-4133-3269-8 (ebook)

This book covers only United States law, unless it specifically states otherwise.

Copyright © 1985, 1995, 1996, 1997, 1998, 2000, 2002, 2003, 2004, 2005, 2006, 2008, 2009, 2011, and 2012 by David Pressman. Copyright © 2014, 2016, 2018, 2020, 2022, and 2025 by David Pressman and MH Sub I, LLC dba Nolo.

All rights reserved. The NOLO trademark is registered in the U.S. Patent and Trademark Office. Printed in the U.S.A.

No part of this publication may be reproduced, stored in a retrieval system, or transmitted in any form or by any means, electronic, mechanical, photocopying, recording, or otherwise without prior written permission. Reproduction prohibitions do not apply to the forms contained in this product when reproduced for personal use. For information on bulk purchases or corporate premium sales, please contact tradecs@nolo.com.

> ### Please note
>
> Accurate, plain-English legal information can help you solve many of your own legal problems. But this text is not a substitute for personalized advice from a knowledgeable lawyer. If you want the help of a trained professional—and we'll always point out situations in which we think that's a good idea—consult an attorney licensed to practice in your state.

MH Sub I, LLC dba Nolo, 909 N. Pacific Coast Hwy, 11th Fl., El Segundo, CA 90245.

Acknowledgments

Thanks go to all who read this book, especially those who have reached out to me with questions, comments, and feedback. Each time I undertake a new revision of this work, I keep you in my thoughts, because you are the reason I do this.

Thanks also to David Pressman for his insight and hard work making this book possible and keeping it relevant, and to the staff at Nolo, including Janet Portman and David Goguen at Nolo for their helpful feedback in previous editions. Thanks also to Elizabeth de Armond for teaching me to be an organized writer, and to Timothy Holbrook for teaching me the importance of patent law.

Finally, thanks to my parents Peter and Evelyn Blau for their unfailing love and support.

—Dave Blau

My deep thanks go to my clients, and other inventors whose creativity and genius I so greatly admire and envy. My readers have given me much valuable feedback and suggestions, and I am grateful to them as well.

I also thank the staff at Nolo, including Richard Stim, Steve Elias, Stephanie Harolde, and Ralph Warner for their ideas, contributions, and support, and, especially, Terri Hearsh for substantially improving the look and feel of the book.

Finally, I thank my wife Roberta for her unflagging support and contributions.

—David Pressman

About the Authors

David E. Blau is a patent attorney at Daly, Crowley, Mofford & Durkee in Quincy, Massachusetts (working remotely from North Carolina), and is a member of the U.S. Patent and Trademark Office and Massachusetts bars. Dave received his B.S. from the California Institute of Technology, with majors in both Mathematics and Engineering & Applied Science. Prior to law school, he worked for the government as a mathematician, for a number of private companies writing software to perform scalable content storage and distribution and back-office online commerce functions, and co-founded a web design business. He received his J.D. from the Chicago-Kent College of Law with a certificate in Intellectual Property, and has practiced patent law in the Boston area ever since. Outside the practice of law, Dave is a scuba diver and a licensed private pilot who hopes to get his instrument rating someday.

David Pressman is a member of the California and Patent and Trademark Office bars. He has more than 45 years' experience in the patent profession, as a patent examiner for the U.S. Patent Office, a patent attorney for Philco-Ford Corp., Elco Corp., and Varian Associates, as a columnist for *EDN* Magazine and Entrepreneur. com, and as an instructor at San Francisco State University. He contributed the Patent, Trademark and Copyright entries to the *World Book Encyclopedia*. He's also an inventor, with two patents issued. When not writing, dabbling in electronics, programming, inventing, or playing his trumpet, he practices as a patent lawyer in San Francisco. Originally from Philadelphia, he has a B.S. in Electrical Engineering from Pennsylvania State University. He spent his first year in law school at the University of Pennsylvania and completed his second and third years at George Washington University, where he served on the *Law Review* and received a Juris Doctor degree. He is also active in the general semantics and vegetarian movements. His mother, Mildred Phillips, was also a writer, having composed lyrics for numerous published songs, including Bill Haley's "Mambo Rock."

Table of Contents

Your Legal Companion 1

   A. You Don't Have to Use a Patent Attorney 2

   B. A Layperson Can Do a Quality Job 2

   C. Using an Attorney 2

   D. Should You Do It Yourself? 2

   E. How to Use *Patent It Yourself* 4

1 Introduction to Patents and Other Intellectual Property 5

   A. Intellectual Property—The Big Picture 7

   B. How Intellectual Property Law Provides "Offensive Rights" (and Not Protection)
       to Inventors 9

   C. Alternative and Supplementary Offensive Rights 9

   D. Patents 10

   E. Trademarks 19

   F. Copyrights 23

   G. Trade Secrets 28

   H. Unfair Competition 32

   I. Acquisition of Offensive Rights in Intellectual Property—Summary Chart 33

   J. Summary of Legal Remedies for Misappropriation of Various Types of
       Intellectual Property 33

   K. Invention Exploitation Flowchart 35

   L. Summary 35

2 The Science and Magic of Inventing 37

   A. What We Mean by "Invention" 38

   B. Inventing by Problem Recognition and Solution 39

   C. Inventing by Magic (Accident and Flash of Genius) 42

   D. Making Ramifications and Improvements of Your Invention 43

   E. Solving Creativity Problems 44

   F. Contact Other Inventors 47

   G. Beware of the Novice Inventor's "PGL Syndrome" 47

   H. Don't Bury Your Invention 48

   I. Summary 48

3 Documentation and the PPA 49

- A. Introduction 51
- B. Documentation Is Vital to the Invention Process 51
- C. Documentation Has Legal Implications 52
- D. Trade Secret Considerations 52
- E. Record Conception and the Building and Testing of Your Invention 53
- F. How to Record Your Invention 54
- G. Another Way to Record Conception or Building and Testing—The Invention Disclosure 60
- H. Don't Sit on Your Invention After Documenting It 62
- I. Don't Use a "Post Office Patent" to Document Your Invention 62
- J. The Provisional Patent Application—A Substitute for Building and Testing, With Some Disadvantages 62
- K. Summary 83

4 Will Your Invention Sell? 85

- A. Why Evaluate Your Invention for Salability? 86
- B. Start Small But Ramp Up 86
- C. You Can't Be 100% Sure of Any Invention's Commercial Prospects 87
- D. Take Time to Do a Commercial Feasibility Evaluation 87
- E. Check Your Marketability Conclusions Using the Techniques of Consultation and Research 94
- F. Now's the Time to Build and Test It (If Possible) 96
- G. The Next Step 98
- H. Summary 98

5 Is It Patentable? 99

- A. Patentability Compared to Commercial Viability 101
- B. Legal Requirements for a Utility Patent 101
- C. Requirement #1: Subject Matter Eligibility 103
- D. Requirement #2: Utility 107
- E. Requirement #3: Novelty 110
- F. Requirement #4: Nonobviousness 115
- G. The Patentability Flowchart 126
- H. Don't Make Assumptions About the Law 129
- I. Summary 129

6 Search and You May Find 131

- A. Why Make a Patentability Search? 133
- B. When Not to Search 135
- C. The Two Ways to Make a Patentability Search 136
- D. The Quality of a Patent Search Can Vary 136

E. How to Hire a Patent Professional 137

F. How to Prepare Your Searcher 139

G. Analyzing the Search Report 139

H. The Scope of Patent Coverage 151

I. Do-It-Yourself (DIY) Computer Searching 153

J. Classification Searching 158

K. How To Computer Search 169

L. Summary 172

7 What Should I Do Next? 173

A. Fig. 7A—Invention Decision Chart 174

B. Drop It If You Don't See Commercial Potential (Chart Route 10-12-14-X) 174

C. File an Application and Sell or License It If You See Patentability
(Chart Route 14-16-18-20-22-C) 176

D. Manufacture and Distribute Your Invention Yourself, Keeping It as a Trade
Secret (Chart Route 20-32-D) 177

E. File Patent Application and Manufacture and Distribute Your Invention
Yourself (Trade-Secret Protectable Invention) (Chart Route 20-32-34-E) 178

F. File Patent Application and Manufacture and Distribute Invention Yourself
(Non-Trade-Secret Protectable Invention) (Chart Route 20-32-34-E) 179

G. Try to Sell Invention to Manufacturer Before Obtaining a "Regular" Patent
Application (Chart Route 10-12-14-16-18-B) 179

H. If You Have Commercial Potential Without Patentability, License or Sell Your
Invention to a Manufacturer Without Filing (Chart Route 16-24-26-28-30-B) 179

I. Make and Sell Your Invention Yourself Without a Utility Patent Application
(Chart Route 16-24-26-28-30-A) 182

J. Summary 182

8 How to Draft the Specification and Initial Drawings 183

A. Lay Inventors *Can* Do It! 185

B. What's Contained in a Patent Application 185

C. What Happens When Your Application Is Received by the PTO 187

D. Do Preliminary Work Before Preparing Your Patent Application 189

E. Flowchart 191

F. Your Written Description Must Comply With the Full Disclosure Rules 191

G. Software, Computer-Related Inventions, and Business Methods 195

H. First Prepare Sketches and Name Parts 197

I. Drafting the Specification 201

J. Review Your Specification and Abstract Carefully 215

K. Use of Artificial Intelligence (AI) To Draft the Specification 215

L. Checklist for Your Patent Application Draft 216

M. Specification of Sample Patent Application 216

N. Summary 216

9 Now for the Legalese—The Claims 233

- A. What Are Claims? 235
- B. The Law Regarding Claims 236
- C. Some Sample Claims 239
- D. Common Misconceptions Regarding Claims 244
- E. One Claim Should Be as Broad as Possible 245
- F. The Effect of Prior Art on Your Claim 247
- G. Technical Requirements of Claims 248
- H. Drafting Your Main (Independent) Claim 255
- I. Other Techniques in Claim Writing 259
- J. Drafting Dependent Claims 261
- K. Drafting Additional Sets of Claims 267
- L. Checklist for Drafting Claims 268
- M. Use of Artificial Intelligence (AI) To Draft Claims 269
- N. Summary 270

10 Finalizing and Filing Your Application 275

- A. The Drawings 277
- B. Finalizing Your Specification for Paper Filing 289
- C. Finalizing Your Specification for Patent Center Filing 309
- D. File the Information Disclosure Statement Within Three Months 314
- E. Assignments 320
- F. Petitions to Make Special—Getting Your Application Examined Faster ... 322
- G. Filing a Design Patent Application 328
- H. Summary 330

11 How to Market Your Invention 331

- A. Perseverance and Patience Are Essential 333
- B. Overview of Alternative Ways to Profit From Your Invention 333
- C. Be Ready to Demonstrate a Working Model of Your Invention to Potential Customers 337
- D. Finding Prospective Manufacturers/Distributors 338
- E. "NIH" Syndrome 339
- F. The Waiver and Precautions in Signing It 339
- G. The Best Way to Present Your Invention to a Manufacturer 341
- H. Presenting Your Invention by Correspondence 343
- I. Making an Agreement to Sell Your Invention 343
- J. Manufacturing and/or Distributing the Invention Yourself 343
- K. Summary 346

12 Going Abroad 347

A. Don't File Abroad Unless Your Invention Has Very Good Prospects in Another Country 348

B. Foreign Filing: The Basics 349

C. The Paris Convention and the One-Year Foreign-Filing Rule 350

D. The World Trade Organization and TRIPS 350

E. European Patent Office/Europäisches Patentamt/Office Européen des Brevets (EPO) 350

F. The Patent Cooperation Treaty (PCT) 354

G. Non-Convention Countries 356

H. The Hague Agreement 356

I. The Early Foreign-Filing License or Mandatory Six-Month Delay 357

J. The Patent Laws of Other Countries Are Different 357

K. Ways to File Abroad 358

L. Rescind Any Nonpublication Request 363

M. Foreign-Filing Resources 364

N. Summary 365

13 Getting the PTO to Deliver 367

A. What Happens After Your Patent Application Is Filed 370

B. General Considerations During Patent Prosecution 376

C. A Sample Office Action 388

D. What to Do When You Receive an Office Action (OA) 394

E. Format for Amending the Specification and Claims 415

F. Drafting the Remarks 417

G. Drawing Amendments 425

H. Typing and Filing the Amendment 426

I. If Your Application Is Allowable 428

J. If Your First Amendment Doesn't Result in Allowance 429

K. Derivation Proceedings 434

L. Defensive Publication 435

M. If Your Application Claims More Than One Invention 435

N. The Public May Cite Additional Prior Art Against Your Published Patent Application 436

O. NASA Declarations 436

P. Design Patent Application Prosecution 437

Q. What to Do If You Miss or Want to Extend a PTO Deadline 437

R. Summary 439

14 Your Application Can Have Children 441

A. Available Supplemental Cases 442

B. Continuation Application 444

C. Request for Continued Examination (RCE) 446

D. Divisional Applications 448

E. Continuation-In-Part and Independent Applications 450

F. Reissue Applications 453

G. Defensive Publications 453

H. Substitute Applications 454

I. Double Patenting and Terminal Disclaimers 454

J. Summary 455

15 After Your Patent Issues: Use, Maintenance, and Infringement 457

A. Issue Notification 459

B. Press Release and Marketing 459

C. Check Your Patent for Errors 459

D. Patent Number Marking 460

E. Advertising Your Patent for Sale 461

F. What Rights Does Your Patent Give You? 462

G. Be Wary of Offers to Provide Information About Your Patent 464

H. Maintenance Fees 466

I. Legal Options If You Discover an Infringement of Your Patent 467

J. What to Do About Patent Infringement 468

K. Product Clearance (Can I Legally Copy or Make That?) 474

L. How to Cite Prior Art and Other Information in Patent Applications and Patents 477

M. Injunctions 479

N. Jury Trials 479

O. Arbitration 479

P. Court Appeals 480

Q. How Patent Rights Can Be Forfeited 480

R. Tax Deductions and Income 481

S. Patent Litigation Financing 481

T. Summary 481

16 Ownership, Assignment, and Licensing of Inventions 483

   A. Inventor, Applicant, Owner 484

   B. The Property Nature of Patents 485

   C. Who Can Apply for a Patent? 485

   D. Joint Owners' Agreement 487

   E. Special Issues Faced by the Employed Inventor 487

   F. Assignment of Invention and Patent Rights 490

   G. Record Your Assignment With the PTO 492

   H. Licensing of Inventions—An Overview 492

   I. Universal License Agreement 495

   J. How Much Should You Get for Your Invention? 499

   K. Summary 500

Appendixes

1 Abbreviations Used in *Patent It Yourself* 501

2 Resources: Government Publications, Patent Websites, and Books of Use and Interest 503

   A. Government Publications 504

   B. Patent Websites 504

3 Glossaries 507

   A. Glossary of Useful Technical Terms 508

   B. Glossary of Legal Terms 514

4 Fee Schedule 521

5 Mail, Telephone, Fax, and Email Communications With the PTO 523

   A. Patent and Trademark Office Mail Addresses 524

   B. Patent and Trademark Office Telephones and Faxes 525

6 Quick-Reference Timing Chart 527

7 Downloadable Forms 529

   A. Editing RTFs 530

   B. List of Forms 530

Index 533

Your Legal Companion

A. You Don't Have to Use a Patent Attorney 2

B. A Layperson Can Do a Quality Job 2

C. Using an Attorney..2

D. Should You Do It Yourself?..2

E. How to Use *Patent It Yourself* 4

Patent It Yourself allows you, the inventor, to patent and commercially exploit your invention by yourself. It provides:

- instructions for documenting an invention, and how and when to file a Provisional Patent Application
- step-by-step guidance for obtaining a U.S. patent, together with all downloadable forms necessary for each step of the process
- an overview of the procedures and requirements for getting patent protection abroad, and instructions for finding the necessary resources to do this
- an explanation of alternative and supplementary forms of protection available for inventions, such as trade secrets, copyrights, trademarks, and unfair competition law, and
- detailed information and advice on how to commercially evaluate, market, and license your invention.

One purpose of this book is to save you money. According to the American Intellectual Property Law Association, the *average* cost of preparing a minimally complex patent application is approximately $8,500; preparing a relatively complex application—for example, an application for a chemical, biotech, mechanics, electronics, or data processing invention—may cost between $11,500 and $15,500. You might not be able to afford these fees, and even if you can, it still pays to do it yourself. By following the instructions set out in this book, you'll not only save on attorneys' fees, you'll be personally involved in every step of the patenting process. After all, you know your invention better than anyone else!

A. You Don't Have to Use a Patent Attorney

The laws contain no requirement that you must have a patent attorney to file a patent application, deal with the patent office concerning the application, or obtain the patent. In fact, the patent office offers an assistance program for *pro se* (no lawyer) cases, and specifically requires patent examiners to help inventors in *pro se* cases in many areas. Many hundreds of patent applications are filed and successfully prosecuted each year by pro se inventors. More information can be found on the patent office website: www.uspto.gov/patents/basics/using-legal-services/pro-se-assistance-program.

B. A Layperson Can Do a Quality Job

Keep in mind that the quality of a patent usually depends on four basic factors:

1. whether the patent application contains a full, clear, and accurate description of how to make and use the invention
2. whether the reach of the patent (technically covered in the patent "claims") is as broad as possible, given the state of prior developments in the field
3. whether the application "sells" the advantages of the invention, and
4. how an applicant handles correspondence with the patent office.

Fortunately, it takes no special legal expertise to excel in all four of these areas, especially if you utilize the many checklists we have provided throughout this book.

C. Using an Attorney

Even if you do choose to work with an attorney, you'll find that this book allows you to take an active role in the patent process, do a better job of monitoring your attorney (no trivial consideration), and better understand the ways in which the law is willing to protect your invention. No matter how competent an attorney is, a client who understands what's going on will always obtain better service. Indeed, many corporate legal departments use this book to prepare their inventors and support personnel for dealing with patent attorneys, and to protect their inventions more effectively.

D. Should You Do It Yourself?

Even though many (if not most) inventors can file and handle their own patent application, the big question is should you do so on your own or hire an expert? The cost factor alone may dictate your decision if you can't afford the $5,000 to $15,000 most attorneys now charge to prepare a patent application on a simple invention.

Patent It Yourself—Quick-Start Guide

If you don't have the time to read *Patent It Yourself* from cover to cover,
this Quick-Start Guide will tell you where to look to accomplish a specific task.

Task	What to Read or Do
You've invented something and you want to protect it.	Read Chapter 1, which introduces the basic tasks—that is, recording the invention (by filing a Provisional Patent Application, or "PPA" for short), evaluating the commercial potential, searching for patentability, applying for a patent, and marketing it.
You have a patent and want to license or sell it.	Read Chapter 11 on marketing.
You have a patent that may be infringed.	Read Chapter 15 to learn how to determine whether it's infringed and how to go after the infringer.
You have a patent and want to make sure it stays in force.	Read "Maintenance Fees" in Chapter 15.
You have a patent and want to sell or license it.	Read Chapter 16 on assignments and licensing.
You want to learn about all forms of intellectual property.	Read Chapters 1 and 7.
You want to determine whether your invention will sell.	Read Chapter 4 on evaluating commerciality.
You want to see if your invention is patentable.	Read Chapters 5 and 6 on patentability and searching.
You want to get a monopoly on your invention abroad.	Read Chapter 12 on foreign patenting.
You have a pending patent application and want to learn how to deal with the Patent Office.	Read Chapter 13 on patent application prosecution and Chapter 14 on branches of your application.
You want to see more reference sources for inventors.	See Appendix 2, "Resources: Government Publications, Patent Websites, and Books of Use and Interest."
You need a name for something or a definition of a patent-legal term.	See Appendix 3, "Glossaries."
You need to determine a time limit.	See Appendix 6, "Quick-Reference Timing Chart."
You need a patent form.	See Appendix 7, "Downloadable Forms."

On the other hand, if you can afford an attorney and you don't have enough time to do it yourself, don't think you'll be able to write a detailed description of your invention in conjunction with drawings, aren't diligent and committed enough to complete projects in a reasonable time (or in a fairly high-quality manner), then it might make sense to use an attorney in conjunction with *Patent It Yourself*. Here again, at the very least you'll be in a much better position to monitor and enhance the attorney's work.

The above can be expressed by the following equation:

$$\text{DIY} \ \alpha \ \frac{\text{AT} \cdot \text{WA} \cdot \text{D} \cdot \text{DC}}{\text{AF}}$$

which means you should be inclined to *Do It Yourself* (DIY) in direct proportion to your *Available Time* (AT), your *Writing Ability* (WA), your *Diligence* (D), and your *Desire to Control* things (DC), and in inverse proportion to your *Available Funds* (AF). While this formula isn't an attempt at precision, it illustrates the appropriate criteria when making the "do-it-yourself versus hire-an-attorney" decision.

The best answer for some inventors may be to do some of both. Using this approach, diligent inventors will do much of the patent work themselves, only consulting with an attorney at an hourly rate if snags develop, or to check the patent application before submission.

E. How to Use *Patent It Yourself*

The book is organized primarily for chronological use, starting with an overview of the entire intellectual property field (which includes patents, trademarks, copyright, and trade secret law). Then it sequentially covers the steps most inventors will take to monopolize and profit from their inventions.

We refer throughout to intellectual property laws and rules. Laws passed by Congress form the United States Code (U.S.C.), and are organized by topic into titles and sections. These laws define your rights. Title 35 contains the federal patent laws—you might become very familiar with it while reading this book!

Using legal citation, title 35, section 102 of the Code is written "35 U.S.C. 102." (See what comes up if you type this citation into your favorite search engine.)

Regulations or rules provide the procedures that must be followed to secure your rights. These rules are issued by government agencies, including the United States Patent and Trademark Office (PTO) and the Copyright Office, and are organized in the Code of Federal Regulations (CFR). Title 37 of the CFR includes the regulations relating to patents, trademarks, and copyrights. Part 1 of this title is concerned specifically with patent rules. Using legal citation, title 37, section 1.111 is written "37 CFR 1.111."

Some government agencies, including the PTO, go further and provide written guidance to the public and to PTO employees on how to comply with the laws and regulations. While this guidance does not have the force of law, and does not create or modify any rights, it can be useful to understand how the agency operates and how it will react to the actions you take. In the PTO this guidance is called the *Manual of Patent Examining Procedure* (MPEP). www.uspto.gov/web/offices/pac/mpep.

Many abbreviations are used throughout *Patent It Yourself* to save space and spare you the tedium of repeatedly reading long phrases. If at any time you need to refresh your memory about an abbreviation, please refer to Appendix 1, "Abbreviations Used in *Patent It Yourself.*"

Appendix 3 provides two dictionaries. The first is a list of technical terms used in the preparation of patent applications ("Glossary of Useful Technical Terms"). The second list provides definitions for many of the terms used throughout this book ("Glossary of Legal Terms").

Throughout the book we'll discuss numerous patent-related forms, and a few example forms are provided as reference. Appendix 7 includes instructions for downloading all forms discussed in the book, plus a few more.

The law is constantly changing. We try to update the important changes in each printing, but in the meantime you can get updates at www.nolo.com.

Welcome to the world of intellectual property! Good luck and successful inventing!

CHAPTER

1

Introduction to Patents and Other Intellectual Property

A. Intellectual Property—The Big Picture 7

B. How Intellectual Property Law Provides "Offensive Rights" (and Not Protection) to Inventors 9

C. Alternative and Supplementary Offensive Rights 9

D. Patents 10

   1. What Is a Patent? 10

   2. Patents Are Like Property 10

   3. What Can Be Patented—The Three Types of Patents 10

   4. What Can't Be Patented 12

   5. The Novelty and Nonobviousness Requirements 13

   6. Patent Filing Deadlines 15

   7. Patent Fees 15

   8. How Long Do Patent Rights Last? 16

   9. How Patent Rights Can Be Lost 17

   10. What Rights a Patent Grants, and the Prior-Art Reference Value of a Patent 17

   11. Some Common Patent Misconceptions 18

E. Trademarks 19

   1. What Is a Trademark? 19

   2. Monopoly Rights of a Trademark Owner 20

   3. Relationship of Trademark Law to Patent Law 21

   4. Overview of How Offensive Rights to Trademarks Are Acquired 21

   5. What Doesn't Qualify as a Trademark (for the Purpose of Developing Offensive Rights) 23

F. Copyrights 23

   1. What Is Copyright? 24

   2. Copyright Compared With Utility Patent 24

   3. Areas Where Patent and Copyright Law Overlap 25

   4. Areas Where Trademark and Copyright Law Overlap 27

   5. When and How to Obtain Copyright Coverage 28

G. Trade Secrets 28

    1. What Is a Trade Secret? 28

    2. Relationship of Patents to Trade Secrets 29

    3. Advantages of Trade Secret Protection 30

    4. Disadvantages of Trade Secret Versus Patenting 30

    5. Acquiring and Maintaining Trade Secret Rights 31

H. Unfair Competition 32

    1. When Unfair Competition Principles Create Offensive Rights 32

    2. How Does the Law of Unfair Competition Affect You? 33

    3. Comparison of Unfair Competition With Design Patents 33

I. Acquisition of Offensive Rights in Intellectual Property—Summary Chart 33

**J. Summary of Legal Remedies for Misappropriation of Various Types
of Intellectual Property** 33

K. Invention Exploitation Flowchart 35

L. Summary 35

Inventor's Commandment 1

Prior to deciding how to proceed with any creation, you should learn and be familiar with the various forms of intellectual property, including utility patents, design patents, trademarks, copyright, and trade secrets, as well as unfair competition law, so that you will be able to select and employ the proper form(s) of coverage for your creation.

In this chapter we'll introduce you to the world of "intellectual property" (IP) law, including not only patents, but trademarks, copyright, trade secrets, and so on. Although you may think that a patent is the only form of protection available for your creation, there are many other forms of IP that may be available to help you. We strongly recommend that you become familiar with and consider all forms of IP, since you may find that you can use one or more of the other forms of IP in addition to or instead of a patent.

This chapter presents an overview of the different types of IP, including patents. Of course, we'll honor the title of this book in later chapters, which focus on how to obtain and profit from a patent.

Before we start, to show the importance of patents to a society, consider what Mark Twain said about patents way back in 1889:

> *"That reminds me to remark, in passing, that the very first official thing I did, in my administration—and it was on the very first day of it, too—was to start a patent office; for I knew that a country without a patent office and good patent laws was just a crab, and couldn't travel any way but sideways or backwards."*

> **—A Connecticut Yankee in King Arthur's Court, Chapter IX, "The Tournament."**

Have you ever thought about why the standard of living in the United States is so high? We believe it's due in part to the U.S. patent system, which stimulates creativity and industry in the United States. As Abraham Lincoln said, "The patent system added the fuel of interest to the fire of genius."

Now, let's begin!

A. Intellectual Property—The Big Picture

"Intellectual property" (sometimes called "intangible property" or "IP") refers to any product of the human mind or intellect, such as an idea, invention, expression, unique name, business method, industrial process, or chemical formula, which has some value in the marketplace, and can ultimately be reduced to a tangible form, such as a computer, a chemical, a software-based invention, a gadget, a process, and so on. Intellectual property law, in turn, covers the various legal principles that determine:

- who owns any given intellectual property
- when such owners can exclude others from commercially exploiting the property, and
- the degree of recognition that the courts are willing to give to such property (that is, whether they will enforce the owner's rights).

In short, intellectual property law determines when and how a person can capitalize on a creation. In recent decades the role of IP has expanded greatly, and it will continue to do so as society relies more and more on technology and information.

Over the years, intellectual property law has fallen into several distinct subcategories, according to the type of "property" involved:

- **Patent law** provides rights with regard to technological inventions. As we'll see later in this chapter, there are three types of patents: utility, design, and plant. Each type covers a different kind of invention.

- **Trademark law** provides rights related to certain symbols (for example, a word, design, or sound) used to identify a source of goods or services. Examples of trademarks are *Ivory, Coke, Nolo,* the *Mercedes-Benz* star, and the *NBC* chimes. With regard to advertising slogans, while the courts generally do not regard them as trademarks, they will give them trademark rights as long as their owners have used them consistently as brand names, and not just in the media. Slogans are primarily covered by copyright law and unfair competition (see below).
- **Copyright law** provides rights related to expressive works, such as books, songs, and movies. It grants authors, composers, programmers, artists, and others the right to prevent others from copying or using their original expression without permission, and to recover damages from those who do so. Copyright law gives me offensive rights against anyone who copies this book without my permission.
- **Trade secret law** covers rights with regard to private knowledge that gives the owner a competitive business advantage—for example, manufacturing processes, magic techniques, and formulae. Methods of producing laser light shows and fireworks are trade secrets. Unless its owner makes substantial efforts to keep the knowledge secret, any trade secret rights will be lost.
- **Unfair competition law** gives rights to owners of nonfunctional mental creations that don't fall within the rights offered by the four types of law just discussed, but that have nevertheless been unfairly copied by competitors. For example, "trade dress" (such as the shape of a *Heinz* Tomato Ketchup bottle), a business name (such as *Procter & Gamble Co.*), a unique advertising slogan (for example, "Roaches check in but they don't check out"), or a distinctive packaging label (such as *Duracell*'s copper-top energy cells) may all enjoy rights under unfair competition principles.

Outside of extremely specialized areas, such as semiconductor mask works (17 U.S.C. §§ 901 to 914) and passenger vessel hull and deck designs (17 U.S.C. §§ 1301 to 1332), all intellectual property falls into one of the above broad types. All of these forms of intellectual property law are shown and briefly depicted in Fig. 1A—The Intellectual Property Mandala.

* One must obtain a governmental certificate (patent or registration) to enforce any offensive rights.

‡ Timing is crucial: Application must be filed within one year after public exposure.

Fig. 1A—The Intellectual Property Mandala

At one point, patents were the most significant part of IP law, so most attorneys who handled trademarks, copyright, trade secrets, and unfair competition, as well as patents, called themselves "patent attorneys." Nowadays, the nonpatent forms of IP law have become far more significant, so most patent attorneys who also work with those other forms of IP now call themselves IP attorneys. This term has led to some confusion, because many attorneys who aren't licensed to practice patent law (they only do trademark, copyright, and so on) also call themselves "IP attorneys." To practice patent law before the U.S. Patent and Trademark Office (PTO), one must pass a separate "agent's exam" given by the PTO that covers patent laws, rules, and agency operation. So if you need someone to represent you before the PTO and you encounter an attorney who is merely identified as an "IP attorney," it's a good idea to ask the attorney (or check the PTO's site) to see if they're licensed to practice before the PTO.

Many clients have come to us with an invention or idea, asking if there was some easier and quicker way to protect their invention than the seven methods shown in the IP mandala, above. Alas, we always have to disappoint them. We have included in this chapter all of the IP techniques that exist. There are no additional or secret weapons in the IP arsenal, so you'll have to work with what we have.

B. How Intellectual Property Law Provides "Offensive Rights" (and Not Protection) to Inventors

Many people speak of a patent as a form of "protection." The fact is that an intellectual property right is an offensive weapon (an attacking sword), rather than "protection" (a defensive shield). To properly benefit from a patent, as we'll see in Chapter 15, the patent owner must sue or threaten to sue anyone who trespasses on the right, and the same holds true for the other forms of IP. The patent doesn't provide any "protection" in its own right, and does not give its owner a defense if he or she infringes someone else's patent. Although the word "protection" is in common usage for all types of intellectual property, it's more accurate to say that a patent—as well as a copyright, trade secret, and trademark—gives its owner "offensive rights" against infringers. In other words the patent, copyright, trade secret, or trademark provides a tool with which you can enforce a monopoly on your creation.

The distinction between protection (a defense) and offensive rights is as important in intellectual property law as it is in football or basketball: while a good defense may be valuable, you'll need a powerful offense to win the game or stop the infringer. To help you keep this distinction in mind, we try consistently to use the term "offensive rights" instead of "protection." However, if we slip up from time to time, please remember that by protection we only mean that inventors have the right to affirmatively come forward and invoke the court's help in preventing infringement by others.

Important Definitions

While these definitions may seem elementary, we provide them here because many inventors confuse these terms, and so that you will know exactly what we mean when we use these terms later.

Also, in the patent world, a single word or comma can make the difference between allowance or rejection of a set of claims, or whether a court will hold that a device infringes a patent. All patent practitioners consider it important and usually essential to use words and punctuation precisely and accurately.

An **invention** is any new and useful process, machine, manufacture, or material composition, or an improvement to one of these, developed by a human.

A **patent application** is a set of papers that describe an invention, suitable for filing in a patent office to apply for (or in the case of a Provisional Patent Application, establish a date to apply for) a patent on the invention.

A **patent** is a grant from a government that confers upon an inventor the legal right to exclude others from making, using, selling, importing, or offering an invention for sale for a fixed duration. (We encounter many beginning inventors who refer to a patent application as a "patent." If we feel they won't take offense, we usually correct them gently to start them on the path of accurate word usage.)

C. Alternative and Supplementary Offensive Rights

As you probably realize after getting this far, there are several alternative and often overlapping ways to acquire offensive rights on your intellectual property. Let's think of these as different roads to the same destination. While the immediate filing of your patent application is one of these roads, it is just one route you might take. The purpose of this chapter is to provide you with a map of the other roads and to help you decide which is the best way to travel, given your circumstances.

The value of your invention can sometimes be better served by using one of the other forms of intellectual property and can almost always be enhanced by simultaneously using a patent with one or more of these other forms—such as unique trade dress, a good trademark, and copyright-covered labels and instructions—and by maintaining later improvements as a trade secret.

D. Patents

1. What Is a Patent?

A patent is a grant, given by the government to an inventor for a limited time, of the right to exclude others from making, using, selling, and importing an invention. You can use this right to exclude others by notifying infringers of your patent, or if that fails, by filing a patent infringement lawsuit in federal court. The "limited time" you have to exclude others is typically about 17 to 18 years, as long as maintenance fees are paid. (See Chapter 15 for more on these fees.) The invention itself is defined in the patent by one or more claims. (See Chapter 9 for more on patent claims.)

Who can apply for a patent? Anyone, regardless of age, nationality, mental competency, state or history of incarceration, or any other characteristic, so long as he or she is a true inventor of the invention. Even dead or insane persons may apply through their personal representative. (See Chapter 16 for more on patent ownership.)

2. Patents Are Like Property

According to the law (35 U.S.C. § 261), patents have the attributes of personal property. That means, among other things, that a patent is transferable by sale or gift, by will, or through probate. Patent rights can also be licensed; that is, you can retain ownership of the patent but grant anyone else, including a company, the right to make, use, or sell your invention in exchange for the payment of fees, called "royalties" (more on licensing in Chapter 16).

As we've mentioned, patent rights are granted by the federal government, acting through the Patent and Trademark Office (a division of the Department of Commerce), in Alexandria, Virginia. These rights are recognized and enforced by the U.S. (federal) courts, and extend throughout the entire United States, including its territories and possessions.

3. What Can Be Patented— The Three Types of Patents

There are three types of patents—utility patents, design patents, and plant patents. Let's briefly look at each.

- **Utility patents (35 U.S.C. §§ 100–157).** As we'll see in Chapters 8 to 10, a utility patent, the most applied-for type of patent, covers inventive *function*. Examples of utility inventions are Velcro® hook-and-loop fasteners, new drugs, electronic circuits, improvements to computers and the internet, semiconductor manufacturing processes, lab-created bacteria, newly refined genes, useful plants, automatic transmissions, and virtually anything else under the sun that can be made by humans.

  To get a utility patent, one must file a patent application that has a detailed description teaching others how to make and use the invention, together with claims (formally written sentence fragments) that define the invention, drawings of the invention (if warranted), other formal paperwork, and a filing fee. Again, only the actual inventor can apply for a utility (or any other) patent. The front or abstract page of a typical utility patent is illustrated in Fig. 1B.

- **Design patents (35 U.S.C. §§ 171–173).** As discussed in more detail in Chapter 10, a design patent (as opposed to a utility patent) covers inventive appearance: the unique, decorative shape or visible surface ornamentation of an article of manufacture. So, if a lamp, a building, a computer case, or a desk has a truly unique shape or pattern, its design can be patented. Even computer/phone screen icons and an arrangement of printing on a piece of paper can be patented.

United States Patent [19]
Holmes

[11] Patent Number: **4,949,887**
[45] Date of Patent: **Aug. 21, 1990**

[54] INSULATED MULTI-USE SEAT CUSHION WITH CLOSABLE HAND AND FOOT OPENINGS

[76] Inventor: William A. Holmes, 209 Highland Ave., Piedmont, Calif. 94611-3709

[21] Appl. No.: 132,982

[22] Filed: Dec. 15, 1987

Related U.S. Application Data

[63] Continuation-in-part of Ser. No. 867,453, May 28, 1986, abandoned.

[51] Int. Cl.[5] A61G 1/00
[52] U.S. Cl. 224/151; 224/205; 224/236; 2/66; 2/202; 126/204; 297/188
[58] Field of Search 224/151, 153, 202, 205, 224/257, 206, 207, 236, 237; 2/66, 91, 93, 108, 202, 203; 383/61, 110, 98, 99, 8; 128/382; 190/107, 102; 5/417–421; 297/230, 188, 192, 219; 126/204, 207, 208

[56] **References Cited**
U.S. PATENT DOCUMENTS

273,523	3/1883	Havasy	190/102
1,137,049	4/1915	Bushwick	190/107
2,835,896	5/1958	Giese	2/66
3,460,740	8/1969	Hagen	383/110
3,793,643	2/1974	Kinoshita	2/66
4,423,834	1/1984	Rush	224/151
4,604,987	8/1986	Keltner	5/421

Primary Examiner—Linda J. Sholl
Attorney, Agent, or Firm—David Pressman

[57] **ABSTRACT**

An insulated hollow cushion has a neck strap (30), an interior portion (72) sufficiently large to accommodate a portable heating source and/or hot and cold foods (74, 76), two side slits through which hands can be inserted for warmth, sealable flaps (16, 20) for closing the side slits when insulation is desired, a slit (36) at the top of the cushion for insertion of items into the cushion's interior, a closeable top flap (28) to seal the top opening for insulation purposes, and a closeable top small flap (56) to insulate the gap between a user's ankles when such user's feet are inserted through the top slit. The side flaps can be insulated so that they can be tucked into the side openings to narrow these openings to provide a tight seal when small hands are inserted into these openings. The insulating layer within the front (10) or the back panel can have multiple perforations (92) over an area thereof and this area can be covered, uncovered, or partially covered by a releasably closable flap (84), thereby to provide a "heat window" which allows maximum transmission of heat (or cold) from an internal hot (or cold) source, or partial transmission, or no more transmission than would occur through an intact insulated wall.

20 Claims, 6 Drawing Sheets

Fig. 1B—Utility Patent Abstract Page

The design must be for an article that is different from an object in its natural state; thus, a figure of a man would not be suitable for a design patent, but if the man is an unnatural position, this can be patented. For an example, see design patent Des. 440,263 (2001). (Chapter 6 describes how to find patents.)

A design patent application consists primarily of drawings and a single, formal claim to the article of manufacture "as shown," along with formal paperwork and a filing fee.

- **Plant patents (35 U.S.C. §§ 161–164).** A plant patent covers inventive *plant cultivation*. Since plants change characteristics through cross-breeding, a plant patent covers only plants that can be reproduced asexually (that is, using grafts, cuttings, or spores). Sexually reproducible plants (that is, those that use pollination), tuber-propagated plants, and varieties of asexually reproduced plants (other than fungi or bacteria) can be protected under the Plant Variety Protection Act (7 U.S.C. §§ 2321 to 2583). If a plant also has a useful function (for example, it is medicinal), it may be protected by a utility patent, no matter how it reproduces. A plant patent application has the same filing requirements as a utility application, but has a single, formal claim to the plant "as shown and described."

  Plant patents are a comparatively recent innovation (1930). Luther Burbank, the great botanist of Santa Rosa, California, goaded Congress to act, stating, "We plant inventors cannot patent a new plum, though the man who makes an automobile horn can get a patent and retire to Southern California and wear silk underclothes the rest of his life." Although Burbank died in 1926, his widow Elizabeth obtained several patents in his name, the first of which was Plant Pat. 12, issued April 5, 1932 for a plum (appropriately enough) "characterized by the ripening period of its fruit and the freestone characteristic of its seed."

At some point you may question whether it is better to seek a utility patent or a design patent for an invention with a pleasing shape. Keep in mind that for a design patent, the uniqueness of the shape must be purely ornamental or aesthetic, not functional. If the design is functional, then only a utility patent is proper, even if the shape also is aesthetic. A useful way to distinguish between a design invention and a utility invention is to ask yourself, "Were the novel features added to make the device *work* better or *look* better?" Or, ask, "Will removing the novel features substantially impair the function of the device?"

Three examples will illustrate the difference between a design invention and a utility invention. The first is a jet plane with a constricted waist for reducing turbulence at supersonic speeds. Although the novel shape is attractive, its functionality makes it suitable for a utility patent only. The second example is a woodshop wall clock that is shaped like a circular saw blade. Changing the shape of this invention does not change how it functions, so a design patent is indicated. The third example is a uniquely shaped wearable watch-phone. The wearable functionality of the phone is suited to a utility patent, while the appearance of the watch is suited to a design patent, and the inventor may apply for both kinds of patent.

Sometimes the state of the art, rather than the nature of the novelty, will determine whether a design or utility patent is proper for an invention. If a new feature of a device performs a novel function, then a utility patent is proper. However, if the state of the art is such that the general nature of the feature and its function is old, but the feature has a novel shape that is an aesthetic improvement, then only a design patent will be proper.

4. What Can't Be Patented

Despite the large number of things that can be patented, there are some "inventions" that the law will not allow to be patented for reasons of public policy.

The Supreme Court explained in the 1972 case *Gottschalk v. Benson* that, "Phenomena of nature, though just discovered, mental processes, and abstract intellectual concepts are not patentable, as they are the basic tools of scientific and technological work." In the 2012 case *Mayo Collaborative Services v. Prometheus*

Labs., Inc., the Court elaborated that "monopolization of these tools through the grant of a patent might tend to impede innovation more than it would tend to promote it," as the Constitution gives government the power to grant patents only "to promote the progress of science and useful arts." Since then, the lower courts, the patent office, patent attorneys, and inventors have struggled to understand what falls into this "judicial exception" to invention eligibility for patenting.

In October 2019, the U.S. Patent and Trademark Office (PTO) issued updated "subject matter eligibility" guidelines that group unpatentable inventions into three categories: mathematical concepts, methods of organizing human activity, and mental processes. The examples below are taken from the PTO guidelines, and while they are informative, they are also incomplete, since the courts regularly add new "noninventions" to the list.

Pure mathematics is the most basic "abstract intellectual concept" that cannot be patented. In this category, the PTO includes mathematical relationships between quantities (however described), formulas or equations, and pure calculations (however performed, including by a computer).

Certain methods of organizing human activity are also unpatentable, since they are seen as representing social progress rather than technological invention. "Fundamental economic practices or principles" such as financial hedging, insurance, mitigating risk, processing payments, and placing orders in a market are unpatentable, as are "commercial or legal interactions," including contracts, legal obligations, advertising, marketing and sales activities, and business relationships. Also unpatentable is "managing personal behavior or relationships between people," such as rules for playing a dice or board game, and voting.

Finally, mental processes are unpatentable because they can be performed without any technology at all, and courts cannot limit how people think. Mental processes include observations (including data gathering), evaluations, judgments, and opinions, and are especially relevant in fields like diagnostic medicine where these processes are much of what professionals do on a daily basis. The PTO considers an invention to be a mental process if it is at all possible to perform in the human mind—even if the inventor intends it to be performed using a computer, or with mechanical aids like a pen and paper.

Other inventions that are not patentable include those that cannot be reduced to tangible form, human beings (including unmodified DNA, genetic clones, and the like), and tax-avoidance schemes. (See Chapters 5, 8, 9, and 13 for more information.)

Computer program note. Computer programs cannot be patented per se. The reason is that running a program, however smartly designed or written, is considered merely using the computer for its intended purpose of running programs, which is not inventive. However, processes that are performed (in part) by software can be patented as long as they don't run afoul of the above exceptions, and this can be made more likely if the invention encompasses changes to the physical world that cannot be considered pure mathematics, mere human activity, or mental processes. This was the rule of the 1981 case *Diamond v. Diehr*, in which the time for curing synthetic rubber in a press was calculated using a computer. Computer programs and algorithms per se (without hardware) alternately can be protected by copyright law, and sometimes by trade secret law. See Sections F and G below for more on this point.

With respect to designs, the PTO won't grant design patents on:

- any design whose novelty has significant functional utility (use a utility patent for this kind of invention)
- ornamentation that is on the surface only, rather than forming an integral part of a device, or
- any device that has a shape that exists in nature.

5. The Novelty and Nonobviousness Requirements

An invention, whether a jet plane, wall clock, or plum, is not really an invention unless it is new. But workers sometimes engage in workmanlike or routine problem-solving, and their creations, even though they are technically new, are "obvious" developments and shouldn't earn the strong protection of a patent monopoly—at least, according to Congress!

The Life of an Invention

Although most inventors will be concerned with the rights a patent grants during its monopoly or in-force period, the law recognizes four "rights" periods in the life of an invention. These four periods are as follows:

1. **Patent application not yet filed.** Since March 2013, if two inventors file patent applications on the same patentable invention, the Patent and Trademark Office (PTO) will award a patent to the first inventor to file, even if the other inventor conceived and built and tested the invention first. There is an exception: if the second inventor to file (Sally) can prove that the first inventor to file (Fred) "derived" (stole, acquired, or misappropriated) the invention from Sally, then the patent will go to Sally.

   During this period, the invention should be treated as a "trade secret"—that is, kept confidential. This gives the inventor the legal right to sue and recover damages against anyone who illegally learns of the invention—for instance, through industrial spying. For this reason, inventors should document their inventions properly. Good documentation practice is covered in Chapter 3.

2. **Patent pending—patent application filed but not yet issued.** After a patent application is filed, the invention is "patent pending." During the patent pending period, including the one-year period after a Provisional Patent Application (PPA) is filed, the inventor's rights are the same as described in Period 1 above, with one exception noted below.* Otherwise, the inventor has no rights whatsoever against infringers—only the hope of a future monopoly, which doesn't commence until a patent issues.

   Most companies that manufacture a product that is the subject of a pending patent application will mark the product "patent pending" in order to warn potential copiers that if they copy the product, they may have to stop later (and thus scrap all their molds and tooling) if a patent issues. The Patent and Trademark Office (PTO) by law must keep all patent applications preserved in secrecy until the application is published or the patent issues

(whichever comes first). The patent pending period usually lasts from one to three years.

3. **In-force patent—patent issued but hasn't yet expired.** After the patent issues, the patent owner can bring and maintain a lawsuit for patent infringement against anyone who makes, uses, or sells the invention without permission. A utility patent's in-force period lasts from the date it issues until 20 years from the filing date of its first Regular Patent Application, provided maintenance fees are paid. (Chapter 14 provides more detail about filing multiple applications for an invention with several points of novelty.) Plant patents last just as long, but don't require maintenance fees. Neither does a design patent, however a design patent remains in force for 15 years from the day it was granted, regardless of when the application was initially filed.

   Nearly every initial utility or plant patent is guaranteed an in-force period of at least 17 years—20 years from filing, less three years that the PTO is granted to examine the application. To assure this 17-year term, the patent will be extended, if necessary, to compensate for delays resulting from failures by the PTO in processing the patent application. Also, once the patent issues, it becomes a public record or publication that can block others who file later from getting patents on the same or similar inventions—that is, it becomes "prior art" to anyone who files after its filing date.

4. **Patent expired.** After the patent expires (20 years after the filing date, or sooner if a maintenance fee isn't paid), the patent owner has no further rights, although infringement suits can be brought for any infringement that occurred during the patent's in-force period for up to six years afterward. An expired patent remains a valid "prior-art reference" (as of its filing date) forever.

---

* Under the 18-month publication statute (see Section Q2), an inventor whose application is published prior to issuance may obtain royalties from an infringer from the date of publication, provided the application later issues as a patent and the infringer had actual notice of the published application.

To uphold these policies, an examiner at the Patent and Trademark Office (PTO) applies these "novelty" and "nonobviousness" requirements of the patent laws to each patent application.

The novelty requirement is easy to satisfy: Your invention must be different from what is already known to the public. Any difference, however slight, will suffice. (Note: When we refer to your invention, we are referring to the way it is "claimed" in your patent. The claims, as we'll discuss later in Chapter 9, define your invention.)

Novelty, however, is only one hurdle to overcome. In addition to being novel, the examiner must also be convinced that your invention is "nonobvious." This means that at the time you came up with your invention, it would not have been considered obvious to a person skilled in the area of technology involved in your creation (called its "art," as in the phrase "state of the art"). As we'll see in Chapter 5, nonobviousness is best shown by new and unexpected, surprising, or far superior results, when compared with previous inventions and knowledge (the "prior art") in the particular area of the invention. (In addition to being novel and nonobvious, utility inventions must also be "in a statutory class" and be useful. More on this later.)

6. Patent Filing Deadlines

As we'll see in more detail in Chapter 5, under current law in the United States you must file your patent application within one year after you first publish, commercialize, or reveal without restriction details of the invention. However foreign countries don't have this one-year grace period, so there's some disadvantage if you sell or publish before filing. For this reason, your safest route is to file a complete U.S. patent application before you commercialize or publish your invention.

You are permitted to file a "provisional patent application" (PPA) describing your invention in detail, in accordance with the instructions in Chapters 3 and 8. (No claims, discussed in Chapter 9, are needed, but it can be helpful to include them.) This PPA can be used, under most circumstances, to defeat or block a patent application or invention of someone else who may subsequently file a patent application on the same invention. However, to obtain the benefit of the PPA's filing date, a regular patent application (RPA) must be filed within one year after the PPA's filing date—more on this in Chapters 7 and 8. Alternately, you may make your first filing an RPA, if you are able to meet its more stringent formal requirements.

Under the First-Inventor-To-File (FITF) law effective March 16, 2013, if anyone (except the inventor or someone who obtained details of the invention from the inventor) first discloses the relevant details of the invention to the public by commercialization, publication, or other means, then it is too late to file a valid patent application on the invention. That's because the disclosure will be considered "prior art" to the patent application. However, if the actual inventor or someone who obtained details of the invention from the inventor makes the disclosure, then the actual inventor may file a valid patent application up to one year after the disclosure. It is still a better idea to file a patent application (PPA or RPA) on your invention before any public disclosure in the United States. That's because a public disclosure before filing will destroy your foreign-filing rights (see Chapter 12), and anyone who sees your disclosure may file their own application on it before you file, thus requiring an expensive and uncertain derivation proceeding.

7. Patent Fees

How much will it cost to get a patent? Assuming you use this book and don't use any patent attorneys or agents, and not including costs of drawings, typing, photocopying, and postage, the only fees you'll have to pay are government fees.

The PTO has the authority to set fees to recover actual costs that the agency incurs. So, the fees change on an irregular basis. The amounts of these fees for the current year are listed on the PTO Fee Schedule in Appendix 4. The PTO always lists current fees on its website, www.uspto.gov.

As indicated in the Schedule, most PTO fees are three-part: large entity, small entity, and micro entity. The large entity fees are generally paid by large corporations, while the small entity fees, which are one-half of the large entity fees, are generally paid by start-ups and growing companies. Micro entity fees are typically for solo inventors. For more on these fees, see Chapter 10, Section E5.

The names of these fees and the circumstances when they're due are as follows:

- **Provisional filing fee.** To file a provisional patent application, you'll have to pay a *PPA Filing Fee*. A PPA cannot become a patent, but gives you a year to file a utility application that can.
- **Regular filing fee.** To file a nonprovisional utility, design, or patent application, you must pay a *Patent Application Filing Fee*. This fee has three components—filing fee, search fee, and examination fee—that are different for each type of patent, but all three must be paid before the PTO will begin examining your application.
- **Issue fee.** To have the PTO issue your utility, design, or plant patent, you must pay a *Patent Application Issue Fee*.
- **Maintenance fee.** To keep your utility patent in force for its full statutory term, you must pay the PTO three maintenance fees. These fees must be paid before 4, 8, and 12 years from the date your patent issued, and may be paid up to a year in advance of those dates, or up to six months in advance with a penalty. To recap:
  - *Maintenance Fee I*, payable 3.0 to 3.5 years after issuance without penalty
  - *Maintenance Fee II*, payable 7.0 to 7.5 years after issuance without penalty, and
  - *Maintenance Fee III*, payable 11.0 to 11.5 years after issuance without penalty.

Under the America Invents Act (AIA), if you file your application in paper form (not online) there is a paper-filing surcharge and if you are a "micro entity" you'll be able to get a 75% reduction on most fees. (See Chapter 10 for the definition of a micro entity.)

8. How Long Do Patent Rights Last?

How long can you, the patent owner, exclude others from infringing the exclusive rights granted by your patent? Utility and plant patents expire 20 years from the earliest date of filing a Regular Patent Application, while design patents last 15 years from the date of issuance. The terms of patents for certain products whose commercial marketing has been delayed due to regulatory review (drugs or food additives, for example) can be extended beyond the statutory period.

While the term of a patent is calculated from its filing date, the monopoly period it creates—its in-force period—doesn't start until the patent issues. Effective June 2000, every initial utility patent is guaranteed an in-force period of at least 17 years. The patent term will be extended for as long as necessary to compensate for any of the following:

- any delay caused by the PTO failing to examine a new application within 14 months from filing
- any delay caused by the PTO failing to take any of the following actions within four months:
  - reply to an amendment or to an appeal brief
  - issue an allowance or Office Action after a decision on appeal, or
  - issue a patent after the issue fee is paid and any required drawings are filed
- any delay caused by the PTO failing to issue a patent within three years from filing, unless the delay was due to the applicant filing a continuation application or buying a delay to reply to an Office Action, or
- any delay due to secrecy orders, appeals, or interferences.

The patent's in-force or enforceable monopoly period starts when the patent issues, usually about one to three years after the application is filed. From the date of filing to issuance (termed the "pendency period") the inventor has no rights, with one exception: If the patent application is published, an inventor will gain some "provisional" rights against an infringer. An inventor may obtain royalties from an infringer from the date of publication provided (1) the application later issues as a patent, and (2) the infringer had actual notice of the published application.

When, and if, the patent later issues—whether or not the application was published—the inventor will obtain the right to prevent, going forward, the continuation of any infringing activity that started during the pendency period. Relevant time periods are indicated in "The Life of an Invention," above, and in the chart in Appendix 6.

9. How Patent Rights Can Be Lost

The patent right isn't an absolute monopoly for the period that it is in force (from the date of issuance until the expiration date—20 years from date of filing).

It can be lost if:

- utility patent maintenance fees aren't paid
- it can be proved that the patent either (a) fails adequately to teach how to make and use the invention, (b) improperly describes the invention, or (c) contains claims that are legally inadequate
- one or more prior-art references (earlier patents or other publications) are uncovered that show that the invention of the patent wasn't new or wasn't different enough when the invention was made
- the patent owner engages in certain defined types of illegal conduct—that is, commits antitrust or other violations connected with the patent, or
- the patent applicant committed "fraud on the Patent and Trademark Office (PTO)" by failing to disclose material information, such as relevant prior-art references, to the PTO during the period when the patent application was pending.

In short, the patent monopoly, while powerful, may be defeated and is limited in scope and time.

10. What Rights a Patent Grants, and the Prior-Art Reference Value of a Patent

The patent grant gives its owner—one or more individuals, a partnership, corporation, or other entity to which an inventor has "assigned" (legally transferred) the invention—the right to file, maintain, and recover in a lawsuit against any person or legal entity (infringer) who makes, uses, or sells the claimed invention, or an essential part of it. If the patent owner wins the lawsuit, the judge will issue an injunction (a signed order) against the infringer, ordering the infringer not to make, use, or sell the invention any more. Also, the judge will award the patent owner damages—money to compensate the patent owner for loss due to the infringement. The amount of the damages is often the equivalent to a reasonable royalty (say 5%), based on the infringer's sales. However, if the patent owner can convince the judge that the infringer acted in bad faith—for example, infringed intentionally with no reasonable excuse—the judge can triple the damages and make the infringer pay the patent owner's attorneys' fees.

In addition to bringing in licensing income and enabling a manufacturer to charge more for a unique product, patents also have other uses. Some inventors file for and obtain patents mainly for vanity, or the prestige a patent brings. Others use patents to impress (and obtain financing from) investors. And many organizations obtain large portfolios of patents simply to assert them as a defense against any company that charges the organization with patent infringement.

The value of patents cannot be overestimated. As Dr. Edwin Land, the inventor and founder of Polaroid, stated, "The only thing that keeps us alive is our brilliance. The only way to protect our brilliance is patents." For a more concrete example, consider that in 2021 the PTO granted more than 8,600 patents to IBM, which now holds about 113,000 U.S. patents! And every year since 2016, inventors have filed about 650,000 patent applications in the PTO!

Since the patent defines the invention monopoly very precisely, the patent owner can use the patent only against supposed infringers who make, use, or sell things or processes that fall within the defined monopoly. This means that not everyone who makes something like your invention will be an infringer; you can validly sue only those whose products or processes fall within the scope of the claims in your patent. (See Chapters 9, 13, and 15 for more on claims.)

In addition to its above-described use as an offensive weapon, a patent also provides a prior-art reference that will block others from getting a patent on anything disclosed in the patent. In this respect, a patent is like a periodical (magazine) article or book. This dual nature of a patent is illustrated in Fig. 1C, below.

11. Some Common Patent Misconceptions

Over the years that we've practiced patent law, we've come across a number of misconceptions that laypersons have about patents. As part of our effort to impart what a patent is, we want to clear up a few of the most common here at the outset.

When I'm Used as an Offensive Weapon	When I'm Used as a Prior-Art Reference
1. My claims can be used to stop infringers and/or obtain damages from them.	1. My specification and drawings constitute prior art, just like any magazine article or book. They can be used to prevent others from getting a patent on what I disclose.
2. My offensive rights start when I issue (or when my application is published—See Section D(8), above), and expire 20 years from my filing date, provided my maintenance fees are paid.	2. I'm effective as prior art on my filing date, and I remain effective as prior art forever.
3. My powers are based solely upon my claims.	3. My claims are irrelevant. Think of me simply as a book, magazine article, website, or any other publication.

Fig. 1C—A Patent Can Be Used as an Offensive Weapon or as a Prior-Art Reference

Common Misconception: Once you get a patent, you'll automatically be rich and famous.

Fact: A patent is like a hunting license: It's useful just to go after infringers. If the invention isn't commercialized, the patent is usually worthless. You won't get rich or famous from your patent unless you or someone else gets the invention into widespread commercial use. In this connection, we've met many inventors who tell us that times are rough and they need to get a patent quickly to lift them out of poverty and make things better. We always have to throw cold water on their hopes by telling them that no one should ever depend on a patent to change their life since few patents ever make money for their inventors, and even when they do, it usually takes years for a patented invention to bear fruit. It's okay to pursue your invention and a patent so long as you realize that this path is usually a long shot to success, and requires significant business development and marketing skills.

Common Misconception: A patent gives its owner the right to practice an invention.

Fact: If you come up with an invention, you may practice (make, use, and sell) it freely, with or without a patent, provided that it's not covered by the claims of another's "in-force" patent; that is, a patent that is within its 20-year term. If you have a patent on an improvement invention such as a triode (three-element vacuum tube) and someone holds a patent on a basic invention such as a diode (two-element vacuum tube), your patent will not give you any defense if the owner of the basic patent charges you with infringement.

However, if the owner of the basic patent wants to use your improvement invention, you may be able to work out a cross-license to avoid having to stop using and selling your own invention.

Common Misconception: If you make or sell a device on which you have a patent, your patent will protect you against the infringement claims of others.

Fact: A patent is for offensive use only and has no value in defending against infringement charges from other patents, except that your patent sometimes will have value in a counterattack if the other patent owner infringes your patent.

Common Misconception: If a product, such as a tooth whitener, says "patented," no one else can make a product with a similar function.

Fact. Most patents cover only one specific aspect or version of a product, rather than the basic function of the product. For instance, the patent on the tooth whitener may cover only a specific composition, and many other compositions that perform the same function (albeit in an inferior—or superior—way) may exist that don't infringe the patent.

Common Misconception: If a product has been patented, it's bound to be superior.

Fact: Although many advertisers would like you to believe this about the products they sell, in reality a patent merely means the invention is significantly different, not necessarily superior.

E. Trademarks

Trademarks comprise the most familiar branch of intellectual property law. On a daily basis, everyone sees, uses, and makes many decisions on the basis of trademarks. For instance, you probably decided to purchase your car, your appliances, much of the packaged food in your residence, your magazines, your computer, and your clothes on the basis of their trademarks, at least to some extent. We believe that trademarks originated in 16th century Britain when silversmiths began putting their initials on their products. Naturally, disreputable competitors seeking to capitalize on a well-known silversmith's reputation soon came along and counterfeited the "trade mark" on copycat silverware. Judges were called upon to punish and stop the counterfeiters of the mark and lo, trademark law was born!

1. What Is a Trademark?

In its most literal meaning, a trademark is any word or other symbol that is consistently attached to, or forms part of, a product or its packaging to identify and distinguish it from others in the marketplace. In other words, a trademark is a brand.

An example of a word trademark is Fitbit®, a maker of wearable technology. In addition to words, trademarks can be designs or logos (the Nike swoosh), sounds (the NBC chimes), smells, and even colors. For example, the PTO granted a trademark registration on a specific color used for a line of dry-cleaning ironing pads. The shape of an object (such as the truncated, contrasting, conical top of A.T. Cross pens) can even be a trademark, provided (1) the shape doesn't provide a superior function, and (2) the shape has become associated in the minds of the purchasing public with the manufacturer (known in trademark terms as "secondary meaning").

Many patented goods or processes also are covered by trademarks. For example, photocopiers from the Xerox Corporation have many patents on their internal parts, and also are sold under their well-known trademark. Without the patents, people could copy the internal parts, but Xerox would still have a monopoly on its valuable and widely recognized trademark.

The term "trademark" is also commonly used to mean "service marks." These are marks (words or other symbols) that are associated with services offered in the marketplace. Examples of service marks include the letters "NBC" (broadcast network services), the Blue Cross–Blue Shield emblem (medical/insurance services), and the words, Café Gratitude (restaurant services).

Two other types of trademark are: "certification marks," the identifying symbols or names used by independent groups, boards, or commissions that certify the quality of goods or services—such as the Good Housekeeping Seal of Approval; and "collective marks," identifying symbols or names showing membership in an organization—for example, the FDIC symbol indicates that a bank is a member of the government-insured banking network.

An important third category of business identifier that is often confused with trademarks is called a "trade name." In the law, a trade name is the word or words under which a company does business, while a trademark is the word or other symbol under which a company sells its products or services. To understand this better, let's use "Procter & Gamble" as an example. The words "Procter & Gamble" are a trade or company name, while "Ivory" is a trademark—that is, a brand name for Procter & Gamble's Ivory® white soap. However, the media often refer to trademarks as trade names. Also, many companies such as Ford, use the same words as a trade name and a trademark, so the difference sometimes becomes academic.

Trademarks, such as Ivory, enjoy offensive rights under both federal and state trademark laws. The trade name Procter & Gamble, however, enjoys offensive rights primarily under state law (corporation registrations, fictitious name registrations, and unfair competition law). However, a federal law can also be used to slap down a trade-name infringement as a "false designation of origin" (15 U.S.C. § 1125).

2. Monopoly Rights of a Trademark Owner

Briefly, the owner of a trademark may or may not be entitled to legal offensive rights depending on how distinctive (or strong) the law considers the trademark. Trademarks that are arbitrary (Apple® computers), fanciful (Double Rainbow® ice cream), or coined terms (adidas® shoes) are considered strong, and thus entitled to a relatively broad scope of offensive rights. On the other hand, marks that describe some function or characteristic of the product (such as "RapidCompute® computers" or "RelieveIt® analgesic") are considered weaker and won't enjoy as broad a scope of offensive rights. Although the above differences may seem somewhat arbitrary, they really aren't. The courts give fanciful, coined, or other arbitrary marks a stronger and broader monopoly than descriptive marks because descriptive marks come close to words in common usage and the law protects everyone's right to use these. Also, the owner of a "famous" mark can prevent anyone from diluting the mark—that is, blurring or tarnishing its distinctiveness—even if the diluting mark is not used on similar goods or services.

Protection of Domain Names

A domain name is a unique "address" that connects your computer, phone, or other device with a website. But a domain name can be more than an address; it is often the identifier for a business. A domain name may even function as a trademark (and may infringe another company's trademark). Registering a domain name does not guarantee your exclusive use of that term in commerce and—because each domain name must be unique—it is impossible for two different businesses to have the same domain name.

Keep in mind that even if a company owns a federally registered trademark, someone else may still have the right to own a domain name that includes that trademark. For example, many different companies have federally registered the trademark Executive for different goods or services. All of these companies may want www.executive.com, but the first one to purchase it—in this case, a software company—is the one that acquired the domain name.

When registering a domain name, a company should be sure that nobody else is using it as a trademark for similar goods and services. If another business is selling similar goods or services with a similar name, the use of the domain name can be terminated under trademark law. In addition, a domain name can be challenged if the owner is a cybersquatter—someone registering, trafficking in, or using a domain name with the intent to profit in bad faith from the goodwill of a trademark belonging to someone else. Domain name owners can sue under the Anticybersquatting Consumer Protection Act (ACPA—15 U.S.C. § 1125(d)), or can arbitrate under ICANN's Uniform Dispute Resolution Policy (UDRP). While you can't recover damages from the infringer under a UDRP arbitration, the procedure is less expensive and less time-consuming (it usually takes about three to six months).

The easiest way to check if a domain name is available is at one of the dozens of online websites that have been approved to register domain names. A listing of these website registrars can be accessed at the ICANN site (www.icann.org). ICANN is the organization that oversees the process of approving domain name registrars. For more information, review *Trademark: Legal Care for Your Brand*, by Glen Secor (Nolo).

In addition to the strong/weak mark dichotomy, trademark owners may be denied offensive rights if the trademark becomes commonly used to describe an entire class of products; that is, it becomes "generic." For example, "aspirin," once a trademark that enjoyed strong offensive rights, became a generic word (no offensive rights) for any type of over-the-counter painkiller using a certain chemical. Why? Because its owner used it improperly as a noun (such as "Buy Aspirin") rather than as a proper adjective (such as "Buy Aspirin (brand) analgesic"), and the public therefore came to view it as synonymous with the product it described.

3. Relationship of Trademark Law to Patent Law

As indicated above, trademarks are very useful in conjunction with inventions, whether patentable or not. A clever trademark can be used with an invention to provide it with a unique aspect in the marketplace so that purchasers will tend to buy the trademarked product over a generic one. For example, consider the Crock-Pot® slow cooker, Ivory® soap, and the Hula-Hoop® exercise device. These trademarks helped make all of these products successful and market leaders even though they were not granted any basic patent. In short, a trademark provides brand-name recognition to the product and a patent provides a tool to enforce a monopoly on its utilitarian function.

Since trademark rights can be kept forever (as long as the trademark continues to be used), a trademark can be a powerful means of effectively extending a monopoly initially created by a patent.

4. Overview of How Offensive Rights to Trademarks Are Acquired

Here's a list of steps you should take if you come up with a trademark and you want to acquire offensive rights to it and use it properly. Because this is a patent book, we haven't covered this topic in detail.

a. Preserve Your Mark as a Trade Secret Until You Use It

As we explain in Subsection d, below, you must take certain actions before you can acquire offensive rights in a mark. This means that during the developmental stage you must treat your trademark as a trade secret so that others won't adopt your proposed mark and use it first. (See Section G, below, for an overview of acquiring offensive rights to trade secrets.)

b. Make Sure the Mark Isn't Generic or Descriptive

Ask yourself if the mark is generic or descriptive. A generic mark is a word or other symbol that the public already uses to designate the goods or service on which you want to use the mark. Thus you can't acquire offensive rights on "The Pill" for a birth-control pill, since it's already a generic term.

A descriptive mark is similar to a generic mark in that it describes the goods, but hasn't yet gotten into widespread public use. For instance, if you came up with a new electric fork, you cannot acquire offensive rights in the mark Electric Fork, since it merely describes the product.

c. Make Sure Your Mark Isn't Already in Use

It's essential to select a mark that is not in use by someone else. The goodwill you develop around the mark may go up in smoke in the event of a trademark infringement contest, and to make things worse, you may be liable for damages as well. Even if your proposed mark isn't identical to the already-used mark, the other mark's owner can prevent you from using it if, in the eyes of the law, there is a likelihood of customer confusion. Even if there's no such likelihood, the owner of a famous mark can block a mark that is likely to tarnish the reputation of the famous mark. To determine if your mark is already in use, you'll have to make a trademark search or hire someone to do it for you.

A complete trademark search should cover registered and unregistered (common law) marks. You can search all pending and registered trademarks for free using the PTO's Trademark Search (https://tmsearch.uspto.gov/search/search-information), and you can search all marks (registered and not) on a search engine, such as Google. For those interested in adopting a website or domain name, Network Solutions has an online search service (www.networksolutions.com/domains).

d. Use or Apply to Register Your Trademark

The first to actually use or file an intent-to-use (ITU) application to register the trademark owns it—that is, acquires offensive rights against infringers. Actual use means shipping goods or advertising services that bear the trademark (not just use in advertising). If an ITU application is filed, the trademark owner must actually use the mark before it can be registered.

As a trademark owner, you can validly sue a person who later uses a similar mark for similar goods in a context that is likely to mislead the public. Contrary to popular belief, trademarks do not have to be registered for offensive rights to be acquired: Any entity that uses a mark has common law (judge-made law) rights and has superior rights over infringers of the mark, provided the entity is the first to use the mark and it's a valid mark. However, as explained in Subsection e, just below, registration can substantially add to these offensive rights.

e. Use and Register Your Trademark

If you apply to register your mark federally on the basis of your intent to use it, you will, as stated, eventually have to actually use it on your goods to get it registered. You must thus follow through by actually using it and proving such use as part of your registration application. To federally register a trademark, use the online registration procedures at the PTO website (www.uspto.gov). All communication with the PTO in trademark matters (including registrations) is electronic, except in limited circumstances. Trademark registration certificates are issued electronically.

If you do adopt and use a trademark on your goods before applying for registration, you should register it in your state trademark office if it's used exclusively in your state, and/or the PTO if it's used across a territorial or international border. Once your mark is federally registered, it will be much easier to sue infringers. The federal registration will cause the court to presume that you have exclusive ownership of the mark and the exclusive right to use it. If you don't

register your trademark and it's infringed, you'll have much more difficulty when you go to court.

To register a trademark in your state, start with an online search for the Secretary of State's office in your state. Whether you complete the application process online or through the mail, the cost will usually be about $100 to $200.

> ### Trade Group Registration of Trademarks
>
> Instead of (or in addition to) registering your trademark with one or more state trademark offices and the U.S. Patent and Trademark Office (PTO), you can register it with an appropriate specific trade organization. Similarly, movie titles can be registered with a movie industry association, and websites and domain names can be registered with internet services. So if you intend to use a trademark in a given industry, check with the industry's main association to see if you can register your mark with them as an alternative or in addition to a PTO or state registration.

f. Use Your Trademark Properly

The law considers it very important to use a trademark properly once you've adopted it as a brand name for your goods. Before it's registered, you should indicate it's a trademark by providing the superscript "TM" after the mark—for example, LeRoy™ Shoes. If it's a service mark, such as a restaurant name or a name for a service business, use the "SM" superscript—for example, Alice's™ Restaurant. Once the mark is federally registered, provide the superscript "®" or indicate that the mark is registered in the PTO—such as "Reg. U.S. Pat. & TM. Off." (We have done this with registered trademarks in this book, out of respect for their owners.)

Word trademarks should always be used as brand names on any literature. That is, they should be used as adjective modifiers in association with the general name of the goods to which they apply, and shouldn't be used as a substitute for the name of the goods. For example, if you're making and selling can openers and have adopted the trademark *Ajax*, always use the words "*Ajax* can opener" or "*Ajax* brand can opener" and never refer to an *Ajax* alone. Otherwise, the name can become generic and be lost, as happened to "cellophane" and "aspirin."

5. What Doesn't Qualify as a Trademark (for the Purpose of Developing Offensive Rights)

The courts won't enforce trademark offensive rights, nor will the PTO or state trademark offices grant trademark registrations, on the following:

- lengthy written matter (copyright is the proper form of coverage here)
- slogans that are merely informational or laudatory, such as "Proudly made in the U.S.A."
- trade names not being used as a trademark or service mark
- deceptive or obscene matter
- governmental emblems, personal names, or likenesses without consent
- marks that they consider close enough to existing marks as to be likely to cause confusion
- pure surnames or purely geographical designations
- generic terms, or
- descriptive words that do not distinguish a company's products or services.

Recently, however, the Supreme Court has thrown out prohibitions against granting "disparaging" marks like "The Slants" for a band (*Matal v. Tam* in 2017) and "immoral or scandalous" marks like "FUCT" for a clothing brand (*Iancu v. Brunetti* in 2019) because those bans violated the First Amendment right to free speech. "Offensive rights" indeed!

F. Copyrights

A copyright is another offensive right given by law, this time to an author, artist, composer, or programmer. It empowers the holder of a copyright

registration to sue in federal court and to have the court issue an injunction ordering the defendant, if found liable, to cease publishing or copying the registered literary, dramatic, musical, artistic, or software works. While a patent can effectively provide offensive rights on a technological application of an idea, a copyright covers only the author's or artist's particular way of expressing an idea. Thus, while a copyright can provide offensive rights on the particular arrangement of words that constitute a book or play, it can't cover the book's subject matter, message, or teachings. Put otherwise, you are free to publish any of the ideas, concepts, and information in this (or any) book, provided that you write it in your own words. But if you copy the specific wording, then you'll infringe the copyright on this book.

Some specific types of works that are covered by copyright are books, poetry, plays, songs, catalogs, photographs, computer programs, advertisements, labels, movies, maps, drawings, sculpture, prints and art reproductions, game boards and rules, and recordings. One yogi has even filed a lawsuit for infringement claiming others have copied his yoga poses. Certain materials, such as titles, slogans, lettering, ideas, plans, forms, useful things, nonoriginal material, and noncreative material (such as a list of names and telephone numbers) can't be covered through copyright. U.S. government publications, by law, aren't covered by copyright and may almost always be freely copied and sold by anyone, if desired.

The 1998 Digital Millennium Copyright Act supplements the Copyright Act and provides criminal penalties for those who provide technology that can circumvent copyright protection. (It leaves a "safe harbor" for internet service providers who merely provide access to infringing materials.) It also provides a way to protect original boat hull designs.

While we provide a brief overview of copyright principles in the rest of this section, more complete discussions of this subject are available in *The Copyright Handbook: What Every Writer Needs to Know* (for written works), by Stephen Fishman (Nolo).

1. What Is Copyright?

Now that we've seen what a copyright covers, what exactly is a copyright? As stated, a copyright is the offensive right that the government gives an author of any original work of expression (such as those mentioned above) to exclude others from copying or commercially using the work of expression without proper authorization. Put simply, it is a "right to copy" an expressive work.

To obtain a copyright, the expressive nature of the work must be "original" to the creator, and not merely the result of extended effort. Thus, the Supreme Court held in a 1991 decision (*Feist Publications, Inc. v. Rural Telephone Service*) that a telephone company that compiled, through much work, an alphabetical directory of names and addresses could not prevent another publisher from copying the directory, since the names and addresses as such were not "original" to the company. Also, a copyright cannot cover any functional system, method, process, concept, principle, or device, although it can cover a specific explanation or description of anything.

The copyright springs into existence the instant the work of expression first assumes some tangible form, and lasts until it expires by law (the life of the author plus 70 years, or for works made for hire, 95 years from publication or 120 years from creation, whichever is shorter). A work made for hire is one made by an employee in the course of the employment or by an independent contractor under a written work-made-for-hire contract.

2. Copyright Compared With Utility Patent

The process involved in obtaining a patent differs significantly from that of registering a copyright. A copyright is deemed to exist automatically upon creation of the work, with no registration being necessary unless you want to sue an infringer. On the other hand, to obtain patent rights, an application must be filed with the PTO, and that office must review, approve, and issue a patent.

How to Secure Offensive Copyright Rights in a Work

While no longer necessary for works published after March 1, 1989, it's still advisable first to place the familiar copyright notice (for example, Copyright © 2025 Amanda Author) on each published copy of the work. This tells anyone who sees the work that the copyright is being claimed, who is claiming it, and when the work was first published. (The year isn't used on pictures, sculptures, or graphic works.) This notice prevents an infringer from later claiming that the infringement was accidental.

Next you should register the work with the U.S. Copyright Office. If done in a timely manner, registration makes your case better if and when you prosecute a court action (for example, you can get minimum statutory damages and may be awarded attorneys' fees). It's useful to distinguish between steps (a) and (b), placing the copyright notice on the work and actually getting a copyright registration. Thus we suggest that you don't say, "I copyrighted my program," but rather say, "I put a copyright notice on my program," or "I applied for (or received) a copyright registration on my program."

If a copyright is registered with the Copyright Office (which technically is part of the Library of Congress) on any copyrightable material, a certificate of registration will be granted without any significant examination as to the work's novelty. The PTO (part of the U.S. Department of Commerce), on the other hand, makes a strict and thorough examination of all patent applications and won't grant a patent unless it considers the invention novel and nonobvious.

Finally, with some exceptions, the two forms of offensive rights cover types of creation that are mutually exclusive. Simply put, things that are entitled to a patent are generally not entitled to a copyright, and vice versa. However, it's important to understand that there is a small gray area where this generalization isn't necessarily true. A few creations that are both functional and expressive may be eligible for both types of coverage.

3. Areas Where Patent and Copyright Law Overlap

Let's look at these principal areas where you may be able to obtain offensive rights on intellectual property under either patent or copyright coverage, or both.

a. Computer Software

Computer programs are the best example of a type of creative work that may qualify for both a patent and copyright protection.

Viewed in the abstract, a computer program is simply an algorithm: a sequence of steps that, if performed in the right order, produces an intended result. In this view, a program is an unpatentable abstract idea. However, from another perspective, a computer or other device programmed to implement the algorithm is a tangible thing that is functionally different from other computers and devices that do not perform the algorithm. And a CD or DVD that stores the program has a different physical pattern of pits or grooves than other CDs and DVDs. (More on this topic in Chapters 5 and 9.) That said, courts recently have been rejecting machines that physically embody abstract ideas in obvious ways, including software stored in computer-readable media using purely conventional techniques.

Why patent a program as opposed to simply registering a copyright on it? Because the patent affords up to 20 years of broad, hard-to-design-around offensive rights for the program, even if an infringing program is created independently.

What is the drawback? It takes about two to three years, a considerable amount of work, and a fair amount of money, even if you do it all yourself, to obtain a patent. And because much software becomes obsolete in a short time, your software may not be worth protecting by the time the patent issues. Thus, you often don't need the full term of coverage a patent offers, and money spent on obtaining one may well be wasted.

While copyrighting of programs is relatively inexpensive as well as easy to accomplish, the coverage gained isn't as broad as is offered by a patent. This is so because copyright covers only the particular way the program is written, not what it does. For instance, all major word processing programs accomplish pretty much the same tasks (such as cursor movement, screen and print formatting, search and find functions, and moving text from one location to another) but each does so through a differently expressed interface, and thus each is entitled to separate copyright status. Also, a copyright isn't available against independent creators—that is, those who write a similar or even identical program without copying it from the copyrighted program. Patents, on the other hand, can be used to sue independent creators of the patented invention—that is, even if the infringer never heard of or had access to the invention.

So when choosing whether to rely on copyright or a patent for software that is tied to or transfers hardware to a machine or apparatus, the software author must weigh the broader offensive rights that a patent brings against the expense and time in obtaining one, and its potentially limited business value once obtained. Likewise, the ease with which copyright is obtained must be counterbalanced by the narrow nature of its coverage.

There is one further drawback to copyright for programs: If you do choose to rely on copyright rather than a patent to cover your program, and you don't publicly use it, sell it, or make it otherwise publicly known, you take the risk that someone else may patent it in the meantime.

b. Shapes and Designs

The inventor may also have a choice of utility patent or copyright in areas where an object's shape or design is both functional and aesthetic. Consider, for example, a new alphabet with letters that are attractive, yet which also provide more efficient, unambiguous spelling (such as the efficient alphabet that Shaw used to write *Androcles and the Lion*), or which are easier to read in subdued light. Patent or copyright can be used. The former will afford broader coverage to whatever principles can be identified and the latter will be cheaper, quicker, and easier to obtain, but limited to the specific shapes of the letters. Note that unlike design patents, copyright can be used to cover some aesthetic shapes even if they also have a significant function.

In many areas, both forms of coverage can be used together for different aspects of the creation. Thus in parlor games, the game apparatus, if sufficiently unique, can be patented, while the gameboard, rules, box, and design of the game pieces can be covered by copyright. The artwork on the box or package for almost any invention can be covered by copyright, as can the instructions accompanying the product. Also the name of the game (for example, *Dungeons & Dragons*) is a trademark and can be covered as such.

If the invention can also be considered a sculptural work, or if it's embodied or encased in a sculptural work, copyright is available for the sculpture. However, copyright can't be used for a utilitarian article, unless it has an aesthetic feature that can be separated from and can exist independently of the article. This rule, known as the "separability requirement," is very important in copyright law.

Of course, to emphasize our earlier point, both copyrights and patents generally have their exclusive domains. Assuming they don't have any aesthetic components, patents are exclusive for machines, compositions, articles, processes, and new uses per se. On the other hand, copyrights are exclusive for works of expression, such as writings, sculpture, movies, plays, recordings, and artwork, assuming they don't have any functional aspects.

c. Copyright Compared to Design Patents

There's considerable overlap here, since aesthetics are the basis of both forms of coverage. Design patents are used mainly to cover industrial designs where the shape of the object has ornamental features and the shape is inseparable from, or meaningless if separated from, the object. For example, a tire tread design, a computer case, and the workshop clock shaped like a saw blade (see Section D3, above) are perfect for a design patent, but a surface decal, which could be used elsewhere, is not. In other words, if the work is purely artistic, a design patent is improper. Copyright, on the other hand, can be used for almost any artistic or written creation, whether or not it's inseparable from an underlying object, so long as the aspect of the work for which copyright is being sought is ornamental and not functional. This means copyright can be used for pure surface ornamentation, such as the artwork on a can of beans, as well as sculptural works where the "art" and the object are integrated, such as a statue. For instance, the shape of a toy was held to be properly covered by copyright since the shape played no role in how the toy functioned and since a toy wasn't considered to perform a useful function (although many parents who use toys to divert their children would disagree). The same principle should apply to "adult toys," provided they are strictly for amusement and don't have a utilitarian function.

What are the differences in the coverage afforded by design patents and copyright? Design patents are relatively expensive to obtain (the filing fee is higher, and an issue fee is required—see Appendix 4, "Fee Schedule"), formal drawings are required, a novelty examination is required, and the rights last only 15 years. However, a design patent offers broader rights than a copyright in that it covers the aesthetic principles underlying the design. This means that someone else coming up with a similar, but somewhat changed, design would probably be liable for patent infringement.

Copyright, on the other hand, provides relatively narrow offensive rights (minor changes in all of the artwork's features will usually avoid infringement), the government fee for registration is very small (see Appendix 4, "Fee Schedule"), the term is long (the life of the creator plus 70 years, or a flat 95 or 120 years for works classified as made-for-hire). And as no novelty examination is performed, you're virtually assured of obtaining a copyright registration certificate if you file.

It has been said that a design patent is basically a copyright with the teeth of a patent because it can cover similar areas as copyright but provides broader offensive rights.

	Design Patent	Copyright
Permissible for all of the following:	The aesthetic aspects of articles of manufacture, such as jewelry, furniture, musical and other instruments, and fabrics.	Literary and artistic content of written materials, lectures, periodicals, plays, musical compositions, maps, artworks, software, reproductions, photographs, prints, labels, translations, movies, sculpture.
Disadvantages:	Must prepare a formal application with ink drawings, must prosecute before the PTO with legal briefs, large filing fee and issue fees, lasts only 15 years, takes a long time (one to three years) to secure rights.	Gives a narrow scope of offensive rights, no doctrine of equivalents, no protection of concepts (only particular form of expression thereof), only good against proven actual copiers (not independent creators).
Advantages:	Broader scope of offensive rights, including doctrine of equivalents (see Chapter 15), can cover concepts, good against independent creators.	Only need fill out a simple form with samples of the actual work, no formal drawings needed, no need for legal briefs, only small filing fee, no issue fee, lasts a very long time (life + 70 years or 95–120 years), instant offensive rights.
Can't be used for:	Articles where the novel features have a utilitarian function (use utility patent); writings, flat artwork, photos, maps, drawings, programs, prints, labels, movies (use copyright); surface ornamentation, or objects with a shape that appears in nature.	Utilitarian articles, unless the aesthetic features are separable from and can exist independently of the article (toys aren't considered utilitarian), machines, processes, systems, concepts, principles, or discoveries.
Recommended for:	The aesthetic shape or layout of utilitarian articles.	Articles of manufacture that aren't utilitarian, or if utilitarian, have aesthetic aspects that can be separated and exist independently, jewelry, furniture, fabrics, literary content of written materials, lectures, periodicals, plays, maps, musical compositions, artworks, software, reproductions, photographs, prints, labels with artwork, translations, movies, sculpture.

Fig. 1D—Design Patents Compared to Copyrights

Because the distinctions between design patents and copyrights are especially confusing, we've provided a comparison chart to summarize the distinctions between these two forms in Fig. 1D, above.

4. Areas Where Trademark and Copyright Law Overlap

As described above in Section E1, trademarks can be creative designs or logos, or might combine designs with words, while original creative works can be protected by copyright. Therefore, in cases where trademarks or service marks are not simply letters or words, it may be appropriate to seek both trademark and copyright protection for them.

However, copyright only extends to expressive content that is "original" to the author, and some things that might make up a trademark or service mark design are not considered sufficiently original. These include words and short phrases such as names and titles; typeface, fonts, and lettering; and familiar symbols and common designs like circles and musical notes. (37 CFR 202.1.) If a design consists only of these elements, either alone or laid out in some fashion, the Copyright Office may refuse registration on the basis of insufficient original authorship.

5. When and How to Obtain Copyright Coverage

If you desire to obtain coverage for a copyrightable invention, program, creation, or for instructions, packaging, or artwork that goes with your invention, you don't need to do anything until the item is distributed or published. This is because, as mentioned, your copyright rights arise when your work is first put into tangible form. And, although there is no requirement for a copyright notice on your work before it's generally distributed to the public, we strongly advise you to put the proper copyright notice on any copyrightable material right away, since this will give anyone who receives the material notice that you claim copyright in it and they shouldn't reproduce it without permission.

When your material is distributed to the public, it's even more desirable (though no longer mandatory for works published after March 1, 1989) that you place a copyright notice on it to notify others that you claim copyright and to prevent infringers from claiming they were "innocent" and thus entitled to reduced damages. This notice should consist of the word "Copyright," followed by a "c" in a circle © (or a "p" in a circle ℗ for recordings and records), followed by the year the work is first published (widely distributed without restriction), followed by the name of the copyright owner. The copyright notice on this book appears as "Copyright © 2014, 2016, 2018, 2020, 2022, and 2025 by David Pressman and MH Sub I, LLC dba Nolo. All Rights Reserved."

If anyone infringes your copyright (that is, without your permission someone copies, markets, displays, or produces a derivative work based on your original work) and you want to go to court to prevent this from happening and collect damages, you first have to register your work with the U.S. Copyright Office. If you register the work within three months of the time your item is distributed or published, or before the infringement occurs, you may be entitled to attorney fees, costs, and damages that don't have to be proved by you (called "statutory damages").

All things considered, we strongly advise you to register your work as soon as it's published if you think you're entitled to copyright coverage. The Copyright Office, Washington, D.C. 20559, provides free information and forms on copyright. Visit www.copyright.gov or call 202-707-9100.

For more information on copyright law, consult Stephen Fishman's *The Copyright Handbook: What Every Writer Needs to Know* (Nolo).

G. Trade Secrets

This section provides a basic definition of trade secrets, distinguishes trade secret protection from patents, lists the advantages and disadvantages of trade secret versus patenting, and tells you how to acquire and maintain trade secret rights.

1. What Is a Trade Secret?

Thanks to the intense coverage of the tech industry by the media, the term "trade secret" has become virtually a household word. What are these trade secrets and why are they valuable enough to warrant corporations paying millions of dollars to high-priced attorneys to protect them?

In a sentence, a trade secret is any information, design, device, process, composition, technique, or formula that is not known generally, and that affords its owner a competitive business advantage.

Among the items considered as trade secrets are:

- chemical formulas, such as the formula for the paper used to make U.S. currency
- manufacturing processes, such as the process used to form the eyes in sewing needles and the process for adhering PTFE (sold under the trademark Teflon) to a frying pan
- "magic-type" trade secrets, such as the techniques used to produce laser light shows, magician's illusions, and fireworks, and
- chemical recipes that involve both formulas and processes, such as the recipes for certain soft drinks, cosmetics, chemicals, and artificial gems;

for example, Chatham, Inc., can actually make precious gems such as rubies, emeralds, and sapphires, and it relies almost exclusively on trade secrets to protect its valuable technology.

Even if the ingredients of a chemical are publicly known, the method of combining the ingredients and their sources of supply can still be a trade secret.

Obviously, since these types of information and know-how can go to the very heart of a business and its competitive position, businesses will often expend a great deal of time, energy, and money to guard their trade secrets.

When we refer to trade secrets in this book, we mean those that consist of technical information, such as in the examples given above. However, virtually every business also owns "business-information" type trade secrets, such as customer lists, names of suppliers, and pricing data. The law will enforce rights to both types of trade secrets, provided the information concerned was kept confidential and can be shown to be non-public knowledge and truly valuable.

More so than in any of the other intellectual property categories, the primary idea underlying trade secrets is plain common sense. If a business knows or has some information that gives it an edge over competitors, the degree of offensive rights that the law will afford to the owner of a trade secret is proportional to the business value of the trade secret and how well the owner actually kept the secret. If a company is sloppy about its secrets, the courts will reject its request for relief. Conversely, a company that takes reasonable measures to maintain the information as a secret will be afforded relief against those who wrongfully obtain the information. These central factors underlying trade secrets have profound implications for those who are seeking patents, as we discuss below.

2. Relationship of Patents to Trade Secrets

Assuming that you have kept your invention secret, you can rely on trade secret principles to enforce rights on the invention. If your invention is maintained as a trade secret and you put it into commercial use, you must file a patent application within one year of the date the invention was used commercially. If you wait over a year, any patent that you ultimately obtain will be held invalid if this fact is discovered (and you will lose trade secret protection because your invention will have been published during the application process).

The PTO treats patent applications as confidential, so it is possible to apply for a patent and still maintain the underlying information as a trade secret—at least for the first 18 months of the application period. The PTO will publish your patent application 18 months after the earliest claimed filing date, but they will not publish it if, at the time of filing, you include a nonpublication request (NPR), stating that it will not be foreign-filed. (The NPR is included by checking a box on the Application Data Sheet—see Chapter 10 for more information. The 18-month publication statute was enacted in order to make U.S. patent laws more like those of foreign countries.) If you don't request nonpublication, your application will be printed verbatim after 18 months and all of your secret "know-how" becomes public and the trade secret status of your application will be lost. If you file an NPR and later file the application in a foreign jurisdiction, you must rescind the NPR within 45 days of the later filing or you will lose your U.S. application.

If you file an NPR, the information in your patent application will become publicly available only if and when a patent issues. However, if a patent is refused so that your application is not published, the competition will still not know about your invention and any competitive advantage inherent in that fact can be maintained. The trade secret will remain intact. If the PTO allows your patent application, but you wish, instead of getting a patent, to preserve your invention as a trade secret, you can still choose not to pay the issue fee so that no patent will issue.

What happens if your application is not published after 18 months and a patent later issues? This public disclosure doesn't usually hurt the inventor, since the patent can be used to prevent anyone else from commercially exploiting the underlying information.

CAUTION

If you maintain an invention as a trade secret and put it into commercial use, you *must* file any patent application within one year of the date you first used it commercially. If you wait over a year, any patent that you do ultimately obtain will be held invalid if this fact is discovered. (More on the "one-year rule" in Chapter 5.)

The following material discusses the pros and cons of each form of offensive rights.

3. Advantages of Trade Secret Protection

Often we advise people to choose trade secret rights over those afforded by a patent, assuming it's possible to protect the creation by either. Let's look at some of the reasons why:

- The main advantage of a trade secret is the possibility of perpetual protection. While a patent is limited by statute to 20 years from filing and isn't renewable, a trade secret will last indefinitely if not discovered. For example, some fireworks and sewing needle trade secrets have been maintained for decades.
- A trade secret can be maintained without the cost or effort involved in patenting.
- There is no need to disclose details of your invention to the public for trade secret rights (as you have to do with a patented invention).
- With a trade secret, you have definite, already-existing rights and don't have to worry about whether your patent application will be allowed.
- Because a trade secret isn't distributed to the public as a patent is, no one can look at your trade secret and try to design around it, as they can with the claims of your patent.
- A trade secret can be established without naming any inventors, as must be done with a patent application. Thus no effort need be made to determine the proper inventor and a company needn't request its inventor-employee to assign (legally transfer) ownership of the trade secret to it, as is required with a patent application.

- A trade secret doesn't have to be a significant, important technological advance, unlike a patented invention. In particular, innovative (and nontechnical) business practices or insights that provide a competitive advantage are often better protected as trade secrets.
- A trade secret can cover more information, including many relatively minor details, whereas a patent generally covers only one, broad principle and its ramifications. For example, a complicated manufacturing machine with many new designs and that incorporates several new techniques can be covered as a trade secret merely by keeping the whole machine secret. To cover it by patent, on the other hand, many expensive and time-consuming patent applications would be required, and even then the patent wouldn't cover many minor ideas in the machine.
- Trade secret rights are obtained immediately, whereas a patent takes a couple of years to obtain, in which time rapidly evolving technology can bypass the patented invention.

4. Disadvantages of Trade Secret Versus Patenting

Before you stop reading this book, please understand that we spent three years writing it and thousands of hours updating it for a good reason. Or put more clearly, there are many circumstances in which trade secret rights have significant disadvantages. In these contexts, using the rights provided by a patent is essential.

The main reason that trade secrets are often a poor way to cover your work is that they can't be maintained when the public is able to discover the information by inspecting, dissecting, or analyzing the product (called "reverse engineering"). Thus, mechanical and electronic devices that are sold to the public can't be kept as trade secrets. However, the essential information contained in certain chemical compositions sold to the public (cosmetics, for example), and in computer programs (assuming they're distributed to the public in object code form), often can't be readily reverse engineered, and thus can be maintained as trade secrets. However, because very sophisticated analytic tools are now available, such as chromatographs, Auger analyzers, spectroscopes, spectrophotometers, scanning electron microscopes, and software decompilers, most things can be analyzed and copied, no matter how sophisticated or small they are. And remember, the law generally allows anyone to copy and make anything freely, unless it is patented or subject to copyright coverage, or unless its shape is its trademark (a historical example is the shape of "Fotomat" huts in the 1970s and 80s), or unless its shape has become so well-known or distinctive as to be entitled to trade dress rights. (See Section H, below.)

Strict precautions must always be taken and continually enforced to maintain the confidentiality of a trade secret. If your trade secret is discovered either legitimately or illegally, it's generally lost forever, although you do have rights against anyone who purloins your trade secret by illegal means. You can sue the thief and any conspirators for the economic loss you suffered as a result of the thief's actions. In practice this amount can be considerable, since it will include the economic value of the trade secret.

Since an individual who steals a trade secret rarely has sufficient assets to compensate for the loss, the trade secret owner will often pursue the thief's new employer or whatever business purchased the secrets—usually an entity with deeper pockets. Under this approach, the trade secret owner must demonstrate the employer or business knew or had a reason to know that the secret was acquired improperly. For example, when some Hitachi employees purloined some IBM trade secrets, IBM sued Hitachi as well as the individuals concerned and actually obtained millions of dollars in compensation from Hitachi. In addition, a trade secret is more difficult to sue on and enforce than a patent. A patent must be initially presumed valid by the court, but a trade secret must be proven to exist before the suit may proceed.

A trade secret can be patented by someone else who discovers it by legitimate means. For instance, suppose you invent a new formula, say for a hair treatment lotion, and keep it secret. Jane M., who is totally

unconnected with you and who has never even heard of your lotion, comes up with the same formula and decides to patent it, which she does successfully. She can legitimately sue and hold you liable for infringing her patent with your own invention!

There is one exception to this principle. If you are charged with infringement of a method patent, but you invented and were commercially using the method as a trade secret at least one year before the effective filing date of a patent, you will have what is known as "prior-user rights," a full defense to the infringement charge. This is also true (and may invalidate the interloper's patent) if you sold a product produced by the method before the patent's effective filing date.

What conclusion should you draw from this discussion? Because offensive rights connected with trade secrets continue as long as the trade secret itself is maintained, and because infringement of patents on "trade-secretable" inventions is difficult to discover, if you have an invention that can be kept as a trade secret for approximately 20 years, you may be better off doing so than obtaining a patent on it.

5. Acquiring and Maintaining Trade Secret Rights

After we explain the differences between trade secret and patents, inventors will often say to me, "I've decided trade secret is the way to go; how do I get one?" The inventor is pleased to learn that, as stated above, acquiring and maintaining trade secret rights involves only simple, commonsense procedures and doesn't require any governmental or bureaucratic paperwork. All that is necessary is that the inventor take reasonable precautions to keep the information confidential. Also, an employer should have all employees who have access to company trade secrets sign an agreement to keep the information confidential; see Fig. 16A (in Chapter 16) for a typical employment agreement regarding trade secrets and other employer rights. Over the years, the courts have devised a number of tests for determining what these reasonable precautions should be and whether a trade secret owner has taken them.

Most states now have a statute that makes the theft of a trade secret a criminal offense as well as a civil action (for instance, the Uniform Trade Secrets Act, a model law published by a private organization that has been adopted by all states except New York and North Carolina). Moreover, there is now a federal statute for the same purpose (the Economic Espionage Act, 18 U.S.C. § 1831 to 1839).

If you're interested in further reading on the subject, review Nondisclosure Agreement for Inventors, an eForm kit available for download at www.nolo.com. (Also, see Appendix 2, "Resources: Government Publications, Patent Websites, and Books of Use and Interest.")

H. Unfair Competition

The area of "unfair competition" is the most difficult to explain. Although anyone who is creative, or is in a competitive business, will encounter unfair competition problems or questions from time to time, any attempts to define this area are necessarily fraught with confusion. And no wonder! The scope of unfair competition law is nebulous in the first place and is regularly being changed by judges who make new and often contradictory rulings.

1. When Unfair Competition Principles Create Offensive Rights

Fortunately, this is a patent book rather than a law school course. And, for the purpose of this book, all you really need to understand about unfair competition law can be summarized in several sentences:

- An unfair competition situation exists when one business either (a) represents or offers its goods or services in such a way as to potentially cause the class of buyers who purchase the particular type of goods or services to confuse them with goods or services offered by another business, or (b) is

unjustly enriched as a result of using the fruits of the other business's labor or creativity.
- Unfair competition law is available as a source of offensive rights under common law (judge-made law) rights, the federal "false-designation-of-origin" statute (15 U.S.C. § 1125(a)), and state unfair competition statutes. One example of a state statute is California's Consumer's Legal Remedies Act (Civil Code 1750-1784 and Calif. Code of Civil Procedure 1770), which prohibits 20 categories of illegal acts, including passing off goods or services as those of another or with a deceptive representation, such as a false designation of geographical origin.
- Unfair competition can be used to cover such items as advertising symbols, methods of packaging, slogans, business names, "trade dress" (that is, anything distinctive used by a merchant to package or house its goods, such as the yellow container that came to be identified with Kodak® film for decades, starting in the 1970s), and titles. Also, Bette Midler successfully sued an advertising agency for using a singer whose voice sounded like hers. Fuddrucker's restaurants sued a competitor that copied their distinctive restaurant layout. And the owners of the Pebble Beach, California, golf course sued a golf course in Texas for copying Pebble Beach's distinctive layout. In other words, when the characteristics of a product or service aren't distinctive or defined enough to be considered a trademark, then unfair competition may be the appropriate way to cover it.
- If an injured party can prove that a business has engaged in unfair competition, a judge will issue an injunction (legal order) prohibiting the business from any further such activity or defining what the business can and can't do. Further, the court may award compensation (monetary damages) to the injured business (that is, the business that lost profits because of the public's confusion).

2. How Does the Law of Unfair Competition Affect You?

There are several ways in which the law of unfair competition can affect you.

- If you already have a product or service you find has been copied or pirated, and the methods described above (patents, copyrights, trademarks, and trade secrets) are no help (perhaps because it's not patentable or it's too late to patent it, it doesn't qualify under the copyright or trademark laws, or it doesn't qualify as a trade secret), you still may be able to get relief under the law of unfair competition.
- If you're contemplating coming out with a product or service, try to make it as distinctive as reasonably possible in as many ways as reasonably possible so that you'll easily be able to establish a distinctive, recognizable appearance (termed in the law as "secondary meaning"). For example, you would be wise to use unique and distinctive packaging ("trade dress"), unique advertising slogans and symbols, a unique title, a distinctive business name, and a clever advertising campaign. And the more you advertise and expose your product, and the more distinctive (different) it is, the stronger your unfair competition rights will be.

3. Comparison of Unfair Competition With Design Patents

Some inventors confuse the trade dress area of unfair competition law with design patents. Trade dress refers to the distinctive appearance of a business, a product, or product packaging, where the appearance distinguishes the product or business from other similar products or businesses but isn't significant or specific enough to be considered a trademark. The coloring of a package or label, or the layout of a business premises, are good examples of distinctive trade dress.

Patentable designs, on the other hand, relate to the appearance of an article that enhances its aesthetic appeal, which is more than mere surface ornamentation and which is novel and nonobvious. Examples are a modernistic lamp design and the pattern of a fabric. While trade dress can be mere coloring, surface ornamentation, or a general appearance, a design-patentable invention has to be a shape or appearance of a specific article which is more than a surface appearance, which relates to the overall appearance of the article, and which is different enough to be considered nonobvious.

I. Acquisition of Offensive Rights in Intellectual Property—Summary Chart

The "Acquisition of Offensive Rights in Intellectual Property" chart below summarizes how an inventor or creator should acquire offense rights in every type of intellectual property.

J. Summary of Legal Remedies for Misappropriation of Various Types of Intellectual Property

Now that you're familiar with all of the types of intangible property, the "Legal Remedies for Misappropriation of Various Types of Intellectual Property," chart below summarizes how to select the appropriate remedy for any type of intellectual property dispute.

The enforcement of an intellectual property right requires considerable knowledge and experience. For background on intellectual property disputes (and to save money when consulting an attorney), consult the Nolo texts below.

- **Copyright.** *The Copyright Handbook: What Every Writer Needs to Know,* by Stephen Fishman.
- **Trademark.** *Trademark: Legal Care for Your Brand,* by Glen Secor.
- **Trade Secrets.** *Patent, Copyright & Trademark: An Intellectual Property Desk Reference,* by Richard Stim.

Acquisition of Offensive Rights in Intellectual Property

If Your Creation Relates To:	Acquire Offensive Rights By:
An Invention. The functional aspect of any machine, article, composition, or process or new use of any of the foregoing—such as circuits, gadgets, apparatus, machinery, tools, devices, implements, chemical compositions, and industrial or other processes or techniques that one could discover from final product, toys, game apparatus, semiconductor devices, buildings, receptacles, and vehicles, scientific apparatus, abrasives, hardware, plumbing, parts, alloys, laminates, protective coatings, drugs,[1] timekeeping apparatus, cleaning implements, filters, or anything else made by humans where the novel aspects have a functional purpose.	Utility patent (use the rest of this book). File the utility patent application as soon as possible, but within one year of offer of sale or publication, and get a patent.
Design. Any new design for any tangible thing where the design is nonfunctional and is part of and not removable from the thing, such as a bottle, a computer case, jewelry, a type of material weave, a tire tread design, a building or other structure, any article of clothing, item of apparel, furniture, tool, or computer screen icon.	Design patent. File a design patent application as soon as possible, but within one year of offer of sale or publication, and get a design patent.
Plant. Any asexually reproduced plant.[2]	Plant patent (see 37 CFR 1.161–1.167).
Trademark. Any signifier, whether a symbol, sign, word, sound, design, device, shape, smell, mark, and so on, used to distinguish goods (trademark) such as "Ajax"™ tools or distinguish services (service mark) such as FedEx. The signifier cannot be generic—for example, "electric fork," and cannot be descriptive unless adequate sales or advertising demonstrate secondary meaning.	Using it as a trademark with "™" or "SM" superscript and then registering it in state and/or federal trademark offices. Also, you can apply to register federally before using, based upon your intent to use the mark.
Copyright. Any book, recording, computer program, work of art, musical work, dramatic work, choreographic work, graphic work, motion picture, videotape, map, architectural drawing, gameboard box and game instructions, and so on.	Placing a correct copyright notice on the work; for example, "© 2021 M. Smith"; apply for copyright registration, preferably within three months of publication.
Trade Secret. Any information whatever that isn't generally known that will give a business advantage or is commercially useful, such as formulae, ideas, techniques, know-how, designs, materials, or processes.	Keep it secret; establish standard operating procedures and keep good records so you can prove you kept it secret. Have employees sign "nondisclosure" or "keep-confidential" agreements and identify it as proprietary information or a trade secret (see Chapter 3) and limit its dissemination using appropriate means.
Unfair Competition. Any distinctive design, slogan, title, shape, color, trade dress, package, business layout, and so on.	Using it publicly as much as possible, in advertising and other uses, so as to establish a "secondary meaning" to enable you to win an unfair competition lawsuit. (See above.)

[1] Orphan drugs (those useful in treating rare diseases) can be covered under the Orphan Drug Act, 21 U.S.C. § 360; write to the Food and Drug Administration for details.

[2] Sexually reproduced plants can be monopolized under the Plant Variety Protection Act, 7 U.S.C. § 2321; write to Plant Variety Protection Office, National Agriculture Library, Room 500, 10301 Baltimore Boulevard, Beltsville, MD 20705. Also, both types of plants (sexually and asexually reproducible) can be covered by utility patent.

Legal Remedies for Misappropriation of Various Types of Intellectual Property

Underlying Mental Creation	Legal Remedy for Misappropriation
Invention (machine, article, process, composition, new use) —covered by federal utility patent law.	Patent infringement litigation in federal court.
Industrial or aesthetic design—covered by federal design patent law.	Patent infringement litigation in federal court.
Brand name for a good or service; certification or collective mark or seal—covered by common law, or state or federal trademark law.	Trademark infringement litigation either before or after registration in state or federal court. Also, trademarks can be recorded with U.S. Customs and Border Protection to prevent the importation of goods with infringing marks.
Writings, music, recordings, art, software, sculpture, photos, and so on—covered by federal copyright law.	Copyright infringement litigation, after registration, in federal court.
Confidential technical or business information, not known by competitors—covered by state and federal trade secret law.	Trade secret litigation in state or federal court.
Distinctive trade dress, informative slogans, novel business layout, and so on—covered by common law, state and federal trademark and unfair competition laws.	Unfair competition or trademark litigation in state or federal court.

K. Invention Exploitation Flowchart

To make it easier to use this book, we recommend you follow a five-step procedure after you invent something.

The procedure can be conveniently summarized by the initials RESAM (Record it, Evaluate commercial potential, Search it, Apply for a patent, and Market it). Fig. 1E below shows these steps and the other overall steps for exploiting your invention and where the chapter's instructions for these steps are found.

L. Summary

The law recognizes seven ways in which intellectual property can be monopolized or clothed with offensive rights: utility patents, design patents, plant patents, trademarks, copyright, trade secrets, and unfair competition.

Utility patents provide a government-sanctioned monopoly on utilitarian inventions. The monopoly lasts 20 years from filing, provided three maintenance fees are paid. The U.S. Patent and Trademark Office (PTO) will grant patents only on inventions that are (a) in a statutory class (machines, articles, processes, compositions, and new uses) and not a "judicial exception," (b) useful, (c) novel, and nonobvious. The PTO charges filing and issue fees and requires a formal description of the invention with drawings, forms, and claims (legal definitions of the invention). Patents provide offensive rights but are not needed to practice one's own invention and do not protect an inventor who infringes the patents of others. After a patent expires, its monopoly no longer exists.

Design patents provide a government-sanctioned monopoly on aesthetic or ornamental inventions; the monopoly lasts 15 years from issuance. No maintenance fees are required. The PTO will grant patents only on designs that are ornamental, involve more than mere surface ornamentation, are not a natural object, but are novel and nonobvious. The PTO charges filing and issue fees and requires a brief description of the design with drawings and forms.

Plant patents provide a government-sanctioned monopoly on asexually reproduced plants; the monopoly lasts 20 years from filing. No maintenance fees are required. The PTO will grant patents only on plants that are novel and nonobvious. The PTO charges filing and issue fees and requires a brief description of the plant with drawings and forms.

Fig. 1E—Patent Exploitation Flowchart

Trademarks are signifiers (such as brand names) for goods or services. Mere use of a mark confers the user with common law monopoly rights, but it's better to register the mark with a state trademark office (intrastate use) or the PTO (interstate use). Before using, make a search of the proposed mark, considering the goods or service and the strength of mark. If confusion is not likely and the mark is not generic, the government will register it. Descriptive marks are registerable provided that the user can demonstrate sufficient sales or advertising. Before federal registration, use the mark with a "TM" superscript (^{TM}) and as a proper adjective followed by common name of goods. After registration, use the "®" superscript. One can also apply to the federal government for an intent to use the mark, but one must show actual use before the PTO will register the mark.

Copyright covers works of authors, artists, photographers, composers, programmers, and so on. Copyright covers only a particular form of expression of an idea, but not an idea per se. Copyright is not good for forms, simple TMs, slogans, methods, lists, formulae, utilitarian articles (unless artwork is separable from article), and so on. On published versions of work, it's desirable to include a © notice. Copyrights last for life of the author plus 70 years, or 95 years from the date of publication in the case of a work made for hire. The work should be registered with the Copyright Office before or after publication to secure full rights.

Trade secrets cover novel information that has some commercial advantage and is not generally known. The information must be kept secret. Trade secret rights will be lost if the secret is discovered by reverse engineering from the final product. Usually only chemical formulae, industrial and commercial processes, and programs with controlled distribution are covered by trade secrets. Trade secrets have a theoretically perpetual term, incur little cost, and provide definite, immediate rights. Patents are preferable over trade secrets as they can be used against independent creators, can't be avoided by reverse engineering, and enjoy more respect in the business and scientific community.

Unfair competition is a catchall category based on judge-made law and "false-designation-of-origin" statutes to cover trade names, slogans, trade dress, unfair practices, unjust enrichment, "palming off," and so on.

CHAPTER
2

The Science and Magic of Inventing

A. What We Mean by "Invention"	38
B. Inventing by Problem Recognition and Solution	39
C. Inventing by Magic (Accident and Flash of Genius)	42
D. Making Ramifications and Improvements of Your Invention	43
E. Solving Creativity Problems	44
F. Contact Other Inventors	47
G. Beware of the Novice Inventor's "PGL Syndrome"	47
H. Don't Bury Your Invention	48
I. Summary	48

Inventor's Commandment 2

To invent successfully, be aware of problems you encounter and seek solutions. Also, take the time to study and investigate the practicality of new phenomena, whether they occur by accident or flash of insight. Persevere with any development you believe has commercial potential.

Before we get to patents, the primary subject of this book, we provide this chapter to discuss inventions and inventing. Why do this? To begin, you may be a first-time inventor with no real-world experience protecting and patenting inventions. We believe you'll be a better inventor if you understand and become familiar with some successful inventors and the invention process. We also believe that too many first-timers get discouraged too quickly.

To inspire you to hang in there, we include here some success stories. Hopefully, when you see that many other small, independent inventors have found their pot of gold, you'll be motivated to press on.

Inventing can be more than just profitable, it can enhance our lives, making them more interesting, pleasurable, exciting, rewarding, and educational. As the noted Swiss psychologist Jean Piaget, once said, "We learn most when we have to invent." Remember that everything of significance, even the chair you're probably seated in now, started with an idea in someone's brain. If you come up with something, don't dismiss it; it could turn out to be something great!

Common Misconception: The day of the small inventor is over; an independent inventor no longer has any chance to hit the jackpot with an invention.

Fact: As you'll see by the examples given later in this chapter, many small, independent inventors have done extremely well with their inventions. Billions of dollars in royalties and other compensation are paid each year to independent inventors for their creations. In fact, most inventions that have spurred new industries have come from individual inventors. So, don't be a victim of the "no-use-going-on-with-it-because-surely-someone-has-invented-it-already"

syndrome. While we recommend that you don't rush blindly ahead to patent your work without making a sensible investigation of prior inventions and your creation's commercial potential (in the ways we discuss later), we urge you not to quit without giving your invention a fair chance.

Another reason for this chapter is that many inventors come up with valuable inventions, but they haven't developed them sufficiently so that they can be readily sold. If their creations could be improved with further work, they'd have a far greater chance of success. So here we'll also give hints about things like improving your inventions, solving problems about workability, and drawbacks.

If you've already made an invention, or are even in the business of inventing, we believe the creativity-boosting techniques in this chapter will help you to make better inventions. On the other hand, we also recognize that the information in this chapter may not be particularly helpful to the experienced inventor or the corporate inventor—after all, you're already firmly entrenched in the inventing business. If you would rather skip this information for now, go to Chapter 3, where our discussion of record keeping should prove of value to even the most seasoned of inventors.

A. What We Mean by "Invention"

In its most general sense, an invention is a solution to a problem. For the purpose of this book, an invention is any idea, thing, or process that isn't generally and currently known; which, without too much skill or ingenuity, can exist in or be reduced to tangible form or used in a tangible thing; which has some use or value to society; and which you or someone else has thought up or discovered.

Note that under this definition, an invention can be a process or even an idea, so long as it can be made tangible in some way, "without too much skill or ingenuity." On the other hand, the definition eliminates fantasies and wishes, such as time-travel or perpetual motion machines, since these obviously (at least to us) can't be made tangible.

An invention must have some use or value to society; otherwise what good is it, and how will you sell it? It must be generally unknown anywhere in the world (at the time you invent it), and it must have been thought up or discovered by you or someone else—otherwise it doesn't really have inventive value.

While you may think that an invention must be a major development to be successful, the truth is that most successful inventions are evolutionary rather than revolutionary. For example, the basic concept of the transistor was invented in the 1930s, but was not feasible enough to be successful until Drs. Brittain, Bardeen, and Shockley made some evolutionary but successful improvements in the late 1940s.

Why do we bother to define the term invention in such detail? So you'll begin to understand it and have a better feel for it, as well as to define the limits of its usage in this book. As you'll see, our primary concern is with inventions that qualify for a patent (that is, patentable inventions). However, nonpatentable inventions can also be valuable as long as society finds them at least somewhat special and useful.

B. Inventing by Problem Recognition and Solution

Now that you know what an invention is, how do you make one? Most inventions are conceived by: (1) recognizing a problem, and (2) fashioning a solution.

Although it may seem trivial, recognizing a problem often amounts to about 90% of the act of conceiving an invention. As one wise person said, "To be an inventor is to perceive need." In these situations, once the problem is recognized, conceiving the solution is easy. Consider some of the Salton products—the home peanut butter maker, for instance, or the plug-in ice cream maker for use in the freezer. In both cases, once the problem was defined (the need for an easy homemade version of a product normally purchased at the store) implementing the solution merely involved electrification and/or size reduction of an existing appliance. Once the problem was defined, any competent appliance designer could accomplish its solution. True, during the implementation of the idea— that is, the design of the actual hardware—designers

and engineers often contribute the very aspects of the invention that make it ingenious and patentable. Still, the main ingredient leading to a successful outcome for most inventions consists of recognizing and defining the problem that needs to be solved. Although Edison seemed to contradict this when he said that inventing is 10% inspiration and 90% perspiration, he was referring to the whole experience of inventing, including conception, making a practicable model, and licensing or selling the invention. Here, we're referring just to the conception part of inventing—what Edison called "inspiration."

Of course, in some contexts, the recognition of a problem plays no part in the invention. Most "improvement inventions" fall into this category, such as the improvement of the mechanism of a ballpoint pen to make it cheaper, more reliable, stronger, and so on. But in general, you will find it most effective to go about inventing via the two-step process of identifying a problem and solving it. Or, as famed inventor Jacob Rabinow said, "You invent because something bothers you."

Let's look at some simple inventions that were made using this two-step process, and that have been commercially implemented. We delineate the problem ℙ and solution 𝕊 in each instance. Where we know an Independent Inventor was responsible, we add an 𝕀𝕀.

1. **Grasscrete.** ℙ Wide expanses of concrete or asphalt in a parking lot or driveway are unsightly. 𝕊 Make many cross-shaped holes in the paving and plant grass in the earth below so that the grass grows to the surface and makes the lot or driveway appear mostly green; grass is protected from the car's tires because of its subsurface position.

2. **Intermittent windshield wipers.** ℙ In drizzles, the slowest speed of windshield wipers was unnecessarily fast, and merely slowing the wipers was unsatisfactory, since a slow sweep was distracting for the driver. 𝕊 Provide a "drizzle" setting where the windshield wipers made normally fast sweeps but paused after each sweep. (Dr. Robert Kearns, 𝕀𝕀. Dr. Kearns's brilliantly ingenious solution earned him and his estate more than $50 million in royalties, after he sued Ford, Chrysler, and others, as dramatized in the movie *Flash of Genius*.)

3. **Buried plastic cable-locator strip.** P Construction excavators often damage buried cables (or pipes) because surface warning signs often are removed or can't be placed over the entire buried cable. S Bury a brightly colored plastic strip parallel to and above the cable; it serves as a warning to excavators that a cable is buried below the spot where they're digging. (This is a "new-use" invention since the plastic strip per se was obviously already in existence.)

4. **Magnetic safety lock for police pistols.** P Police pistols are occasionally fired by unauthorized persons. S A special safety lock inside the pistol releases only when the pistol is held by someone wearing a finger ring containing a high-coercive-force samarium-cobalt magnet.

5. **Wiz-z-zer™ gyroscopic top.** P Gyroscopes are difficult to get running: They require the user to wind a string around a shaft surrounded by gimbals and then pull it steadily but forcefully to set the rotor in motion. S Provide an enclosed gyro in the shape of a top with an extending friction tip that can be easily spun at high speed by moving it across any surface. (Paul Brown, II. Mr. Brown came up with this great invention because, while at a party, he had repeated difficulty operating a friend's son's gyro. His first royalty check from Mattel was five times his annual salary!)

6. **Dolby® audio tape hiss elimination.** P Audio tapes played at low volume levels usually have an audible hiss. S Frequency-selective companding (compressing and expanding) of the audio during recording and expanding of the audio during playback to eliminate hiss. (Ray Dolby, one of the most successful IIs of modern times.)

7. **Xerography.** P Copying documents required messy, slow, complicated photographic apparatus. S Xerography—the charging of a photosensitive surface in a pattern employing light reflected from the document to be copied and then using this charged surface to pick up and deposit black powder onto a blank sheet. (Chester Carlson, II. When Mr. Carlson, a patent attorney, brought his invention to Kodak, they rejected it, saying it could never

be commercially implemented. Undaunted, Carlson brought it to The Haloid Co., which accepted it and changed its name to Xerox Corporation; the rest is history.)

8. **Flip-top can.** P Cans of beverage were difficult to open, requiring a church key or can opener. S Provide the familiar flip-top can. (Ermal Fraze, II.)

9. **FM, CW, and AGC.** P Information wasn't conveyable by radio due to noisy, limited frequency response and fade-out of AM reception. S Provide CW, FM, and AGC circuitry, familiar to all electronic engineers. (Edwin Howard Armstrong, II, the genius of high fidelity.)

10. **Thermostatic showerhead.** P Shower takers sometimes get burned because they inadvertently turn on the hot water while standing under the shower. S Provide a thermostatic cut-off valve in the supply pipe. (Alfred M. Moen, II.)

11. **VCR Plus.** P In the days before streaming and "on-demand" movies, many people were too lazy or too put off by technical matters to learn how to enter a date, time, and channel into their VCR. S With VCR Plus, each program was assigned a special code number in the newspaper TV listings and the VCR owner needed merely enter the number and transmit it to the VCR.

12. **Organic production of acetone.** P During World War I, the U.K. desperately needed acetone to make explosives, since its normal source was cut off. S Use an anaerobic bacterium to produce acetone from locally available corn mash.

    (Dr. Chaim Weizmann, II. This invention helped save one nation and start a new one: It was instrumental in helping the U.K. and the Allies survive WWI and defeat the Germans. The U.K. rewarded Weizmann with the Balfour Declaration, which helped lead to the eventual formation of the State of Israel.)

13. **Grocery shopping cart.** P Shoppers in grocery stores used their own small, hand-carried wicker baskets and bought only the small amounts that they could carry in the baskets, thereby necessitating several trips to the grocery and causing sales to be relatively low per customer visit.

§ Provide a "grocery cart," that is, a large wire basket in a frame on wheels so that it can be rolled around and carry a large amount of groceries. (Sylvan Goldman, ▮. When Mr. Goldman first introduced his carts (about 1925), shoppers wouldn't use them and stores wouldn't buy them despite his extensive efforts. He eventually found a way to get his carts accepted: He hired crews of "shoppers" to wheel the carts around and fill them in his store, and also hired an employee to offer the carts to entering shoppers. Goldman then made millions from patents on his cart and its improvements (nesting carts and airport carts). This illustrates the crucial value of perseverance and marketing genius.

14. **Belt loops.** ▯ Until 1922, men's pants (then called "pantaloons") were held up by either unsightly suspenders or an awkward cinch at the rear of the waist fabric. § Provide "loops" at the top of the pants so that a "belt" could be inserted through the loops. (First sold by Levi Strauss & Co.)

The inventors of these inventions necessarily went through the problem-solution process (though not necessarily in that order) to make their invention. Even if an inventor believes the invention came spontaneously, you'll usually find that problem-solution steps were somehow involved, even if they appear to coalesce.

So, if you either don't have an invention or want to make some new ones, you should begin by ferreting out problem or "need" areas. This can often be done by paying close attention to your daily activities. How do you or others perform tasks? What problems do you encounter and how do you solve them? What needs do you perceive, even if they're as simple as wanting a full month's calendar on your scheduling app? Ask yourself if something can't be done more easily, cheaply, simply, or reliably, if it can't be made lighter, quicker, stronger, and so on. Write the problems down and keep a list. Make sure you take the time to think through the problems or needs you've discovered.

Sometimes the solution to the problem you identify will be a simple expedient, such as electrification or reduction in size. Generally, however, it will be more involved, as in some of the examples listed above.

But you don't have to be a genius to come up with a solution. Draw on solutions from analogous or even nonanalogous fields. Experiment, meditate, look around. When a possible solution strikes you, write it down, even if it's in the middle of the night. History records a great number of important scientific and conceptual breakthroughs occurring during sleep or borderline-sleep states.

Also, remember that sometimes the "problem" may be the ordinary way something has been done for years, and which no one has ever recognized as a problem. Consider showerheads. Although essentially the same device operated satisfactorily for about 50 years, the inventor of water-massaging showerheads recognized the deficiency of an ordinary constant spray that didn't create any massage effect. He thus developed the water-massaging head that causes the water to come out in spurts from various head orifices, thereby creating the massaging effect.

Don't hesitate to go against the grain of custom or accepted practice if that's where your invention takes you. Many widespread erroneous beliefs were just waiting to be shattered. The medical field, in particular, had numerous nonsensical practices and beliefs, such as the use of "poudrage" (pouring talcum powder onto the heart to stimulate it to heal itself), bloodletting, and blistering, and the belief that insanity could be cured by drilling holes in the head to let the demons out. In more recent times the medical establishment believed that ulcers were caused by stress and spicy foods, but Drs. Barry J. Marshall and J. Robin Warren of Australia discovered that a bacterium was the culprit, earning them a Nobel prize. As *Forbes* magazine noted (November 14, 2005) "great breakthroughs very often come from outsiders, entrepreneurial folk, not part of the establishment of mainstream thought."

You'll probably find the going easier if you invent in fields with which you're familiar. In this way you won't tend to "reinvent the wheel." Also, think about uncrowded fields or newly emerging ones where you will find ample room for innovation. But even if you work in an established area, you're likely to find plenty of opportunity for new inventions.

Many inventors have discovered problems (and come up with solutions) by observing current events in the media. A number of years ago there were problems with medical personnel being stuck and infected by hypodermic needles that slipped or were used against them by disturbed patients. The result—a rash of patents on safety needles. Current problem areas such as COVID-19, voting machines, "green" energy, identity theft, and credit card fraud are creating potential markets for inventive individuals. For example, a market exists for a simple, tamper-proof, easy-to-use voting machine or a foolproof way to vote online. If you have technical ability, another way to invent is to "follow the cutting edge." Biotechnology, nanotechnology, alternative energy, energy conservation, and water purification are current hot areas.

One important principle to successful inventing is to remember the acronym KISS (Keep It Simple, Stupid!). If you can successfully eliminate just one part from any mass-produced machine, its manufacturer (or a competing manufacturer!) will be overjoyed: The cost of the machine will be reduced, it will be lighter, and, of course, it will be more reliable. Another way to look at this is Sandra Bekele's (an inventor-friend) admonition to (figuratively) "eliminate the corners." Or, to quote jazz great Charlie Mingus, "Anybody can make the simple complicated. Creativity is making the complicated simple."

Lastly, says highly successful toy inventor Richard Levy, don't go into inventing for money alone; you've got to enjoy the game and the hunt to make it all truly worthwhile.

C. Inventing by Magic (Accident and Flash of Genius)

When we don't understand how something is done, we sometimes call it "magic." Inventions made by "magic" don't involve the problem-solution technique that we just described; rather, they usually occur by "accident" or by "flash of genius." The PTO and the courts really don't care how you come up with an invention, so long as they can see that it hasn't already been accomplished and it looks substantially different from what's been done before. In the hopelessly stilted language of the law, "Patentability shall not be negated by the manner in which the invention was made." (35 U.S.C. § 103.)

Many famous inventions have resulted from accident or coincidence. For example, Charles Goodyear invented rubber vulcanization when he accidentally added some sulphur to a rubber melt. In the late 1800s, a chemist supposedly left a crutcher (soap-making machine) on too long, causing air to be dispersed into the soap mixture. He found that the soap floated when it hardened, thus giving birth to floatable soap bars, such as Ivory® brand. In the 1890s the brothers W.K. and J.H. Kellogg, who ran a health sanitarium in Battle Creek, Michigan, accidentally left some of their health bread dough out overnight. They tried to salvage the stale dough by rolling it into loaves but found that it flaked into small pieces. Instead of discarding the flakes, J.H. fed them to his patients, who loved them, so they refined, ramified, and marketed them, eventually selling them as Kellogg's Cornflakes. In 1912, another chemist, Jacques Brandenberger, accidentally mixed some chemicals together and spilled them, finding they hardened to a flexible, transparent sheet (later known as "cellophane"). When Alexander Fleming accidentally contaminated one of his bacterial cultures with a mold, he was sufficiently alert and scientifically minded to notice that the mold killed the bacteria, so he carried this discovery forward and isolated the active ingredient in the mold, which later was named penicillin. (He chose not to patent it, so he got the fame, but not the fortune.)

And in 1948, Georges de Mestral, after taking a walk in the forest of his native Switzerland, noticed some cockleburs had stuck to his pants. Being of scientific mind, he removed and examined them and figured out why they adhered so well. He applied his newly discovered knowledge and as a result invented—and made a fortune from—hook-and-loop fasteners, which his company sold under the trademark Velcro.

In 1938 chemist Roy Plunkett, while experimenting with refrigerant fluids at a DuPont lab in New Jersey, left some fluorine-based gas in a freezer and came back to find a solid, slippery polymer that was extremely resistant to bonding and to which nothing would stick. Known initially as PTFE, it later earned billions for DuPont under the trademark *Teflon*.

The law considers the fact that these inventions came about by total accident, without the exercise of any creativity by their "inventors," legally irrelevant. All other things being equal, a patent on cellophane would be just as strong as one on nylon (another former trademark), the result of 12 years' intensive and brilliant work by DuPont's now-deceased genius, Dr. Wallace Carothers of Wilmington, Delaware.

Since we don't understand how the "magic" occurs, we can't offer any tips on inventing by accident. Please remember, however, that in case you ever come up with an accidental development, take the time and apply the effort to study, analyze, and try to "practicalize" it. If it has potential value, treat it like any other invention; the law will.

The other type of "magical" invention we'll refer to as the product of a "flash of genius." While "flash of genius" inventions inherently solve a need, the inventive act usually occurs spontaneously and not as a result of an attack on any problem. Some examples of this type are the electric knife and the previously discussed Salton inventions which actually created their own need, the Pet Rock (perhaps more clever trademark and marketing ploy than real invention, but highly profitable just the same), Bushnell's "Pong" game, the Cabbage Patch dolls, Ruth Handler's Barbie Dolls, and a client's Audochron® clock, which announces the time by a series of countable chimes for the hours, tens of minutes, and minutes. With these inventions, the inventor didn't solve any real problem or need, but rather came up with a very novel invention which provided a new type of amusement or a means for conspicuous consumption (showing off).

Although we can't capture how the creativity in these types of cases occurs, we suggest several techniques for stimulating and unlocking such creativity. Using these techniques, many inventors have come up with valuable inventions and profitable ideas and marketing ploys.

"Chance favors only the prepared mind."

—**Louis Pasteur**

D. Making Ramifications and Improvements of Your Invention

Once you've made an invention, write down the problem and solution involved. Then, try to ramify it—that is, to do it or make it branch out in other ways so it will be cheaper, faster, better, bigger (or smaller), stronger, lighter (or heavier), longer- (or shorter-) lasting, or even just different. Why ramify?

1. Most inventors usually find that their initial solution can be improved or made more workable.
2. By conceiving of such improvements first, you can foreclose future competitors from obtaining patents on them.
3. Even if you believe your first solution is the best and most workable, your potential producers or manufacturers may not see it that way. So, it's best to have as many alternatives or variations handy as possible.
4. When you apply for a patent, the more ramifications you have, the easier it will be to make your patent stronger.
5. Conversely, if the broad concept or initial embodiment of your invention is "knocked out" by a search of the "prior art" made by you, your searcher, or the examiner in the Patent and Trademark Office, you'll have something to fall back on, so you'll still be able to get a patent.
6. Ramifications often help you understand your basic invention better, see it in a new light, see new uses or new ways to do it, and so on.
7. Ramifications can be held back and introduced later, after the basic invention has been "milked" commercially, thereby prolonging the profits, as DuPont did with its Teflon® II. Be sure to try to patent the ramifications as soon as possible, however, to foreclose someone else from doing so.

In some situations, you'll find that you won't be able to ramify beyond your basic conception. But give it a try anyway, and make sure you record in writing any ramifications you do come up with as soon as possible.

One way to make ramifications is to pretend that a part of your device can't be made due to a law or crucial material shortage and then try to come up with a replacement.

In addition to making ramifications to your invention, after you've finished with filing a patent application or you've gotten it out on the market, try to make improvements—that is, more substantial changes. Why? There are several reasons: (1) To extend your monopoly and keep the gravy flowing longer; (2) To enhance your credibility as an inventor—if you have several patents it will make any infringer look worse in litigation and make it easier for you to win your lawsuit; (3) Improvement patents cut off avenues that another company can use to design around your base patent; (4) A bank or investor will be more likely to lend you money if you have several patents.

E. Solving Creativity Problems

Unfortunately, hardly any invention ever works right or "flies" the first time it's built. You need to build and test it to be aware of the working problems. If you don't, the first builder, whoever it is, will inevitably face them. If this is a corporation to which you've sold or licensed your invention, it's sure to create problems. If your first construction doesn't work, don't be discouraged; expect problems and expect to solve them through perseverance. If you don't believe me, consider Edison's views on this subject:

> *"Genius? Nothing! Sticking to it is the genius! Any other bright-minded fellow can accomplish just as much if he will stick like hell and remember nothing that's any good works by itself. You've got to make the damn thing work!… I failed my way to success…. Genius is one percent inspiration and ninety-nine percent perspiration."*

If you show your invention to someone and you get static in return, don't necessarily get discouraged; the history of invention abounds with quotes from naysayers who were proved to be disastrously wrong. The enlightening book *303 of The World's Worst Predictions*, by W. Coffey, is full of amusing and insightful erroneous quotes. Here are a few teasers:

> *"Everything that can be invented has been invented."*

> —U.S. Patent Office Director,
> urging President McKinley to abolish the Office (1899)

> *"What, sir? You would make a ship sail against the wind and currents by lighting a bonfire under her decks? I pray you excuse me. I have no time to listen to such nonsense."*

> —Napoleon Bonaparte to Robert Fulton, after hearing
> Fulton's plans for a steam engine–driven boat

> *"I think there is a world market for about five computers."*

> —Thomas J. Watson, IBM President (1956)

> *"Man won't fly for a thousand years."*

> —Wilbur Wright to Orville
> after a disappointing experiment in 1901

Many have analyzed the creative process, but so far no one has come up with a foolproof recipe or technique for innovating. However, almost all writers on the topic recommend that, unless you already have a "flash of genius," you first thoroughly prepare and familiarize yourself with the field, always keeping an open mind. After that, it's common advice to wait a while (allot an incubation period) to let your mind digest and work on the problem. Following incubation, work on the problem again and insight may come, sometimes in bits and pieces. "To discover something you've never seen before, walk the same path you walked yesterday." (R.W. Emerson.) Alternatively, some experts recommend that, after preparation, you make a concentrated effort, which may lead to frustration and withdrawal. But be patient, since the insight, which may be an image or a fantasy, will usually come. Of course, follow-through is necessary to implement and profit from the insight or fantasy.

If you have creativity problems, such as how to make that great idea work, here are some specific techniques you can use to enhance your creativity, and hopefully solve that problem.

Frame it differently. One of the most effective ways to solve a problem is to "frame" the problem properly. Framing is another way of describing the way in which one looks at a situation. A common example of framing a problem occurs when you try to move a bulky sofa through a small doorway. If the first way doesn't work, frame the problem differently by turning the sofa upside down and trying again. Or take another example: If you have an apparatus that includes a lever, and you can't find a design shape for the lever that the machine will accommodate, look at the situation another way; perhaps you can redesign the apparatus to eliminate the lever altogether!

Use your creative brain. In the course of trying to solve a problem with an invention, you may encounter a brick wall of resistance when you try to think your way logically through the problem. Such logical thinking is a linear type of process (that is, one step follows another), which utilizes our rational faculties. This works fine when we're operating in the realm of what we know or have experienced. However, when we need to deal with new information, ideas, and perspectives, linear thinking will often come up short. On the other hand, creativity by definition involves the application of new information to old problems and the conception of new perspectives and ideas. For this you will be most effective if you learn to operate in a nonlinear manner; that is, use your creative brain. Stated differently, if you think in a linear manner, you'll tend to be conservative and keep coming up with techniques which are already known. This, of course, is just what you don't want.

One way to engage your creative faculties in a search for a creative solution to your quandary is to pose the problem in clear terms and then forget about it and think of something completely different. For example, if you can't fit that lever in your apparatus, think of a different activity, or just take a break (how about a nice boating trip or a hike in the woods). Your subconscious will work on the problem while you're "away." Then come back to the problem and force your different activity onto your problem. In other words, try to think of the apparatus and your boating trip or hike simultaneously. You may find that a solution appears by magic (for example, you may realize a way to design the machine without the lever!).

Let go of assumptions. If you adhere to assumptions, you'll never innovate, since innovation, by definition, is the adoption of something new, the embarkation on an untrodden path. As Erich Fromm said, "Creativity requires the courage to let go of [assumed] certainties." So if you've got a problem, try to see what assumptions are boxing you in (they're usually hidden) and then let them go or try to cancel them—think "outside the box"—and see what you come up with.

Meditation or autonomous sensory meridian response (ASMR). Another way to bring out your creativity is to meditate on the problem or meditate merely to get away from the problem. Either will help. As strange as it seems, some experts say that creativity can be enhanced during reverie by listening to a largo movement from a baroque symphony or triggering the pleasure of ASMR. At least you'll enjoy it! Also, the use of biofeedback machines can induce or teach deep relaxation with enhanced alpha, or even theta brain waves, a very effective stimulus to creativity.

Dreams. Some creative people find dreams the most effective way of all to solve problems. Or as Edison said: "I never invented anything; my dreams did."

Elias Howe solved the basic problem of his sewing machine in a dream. He saw some tribal warriors who ordered him to come up with a solution or they would kill him. He couldn't make a solution, so the warriors then threw their spears at him. When the spears came close, he saw that each had a hole near its tip. He awoke from the nightmare in terror, but soon realized the symbology: He put a hole near the tip of his bobbin needle and passed the thread through. Again, the rest is history.

Similarly, Mendeleev came up with the periodic table of the elements in a dream.

To stimulate creative dreaming, first immerse yourself in the problem near bedtime. Then forget about it—do something completely different and go to sleep. Your subconscious will be able to work on the problem. You'll most likely have a dream with an inspiration or insight. Then remember the dream and evaluate the insight to find out if it's correct (sometimes it won't be!).

Note that you'll forget most dreams, so keep a dream diary, a notebook, or your smartphone handy, by your bedside. Before you go to bed, repeat fifteen times, "I'll remember my dreams." Whenever you do dream, wake up (you'll find it possible to do this if you intend to do so beforehand) and write your dreams down promptly. Once they are written down, forget about them, go back to sleep, and try to figure them out in the morning. Sometimes a week or more will pass before the meanings become clear. Or talk your dreams over with an equally inventive friend and see if he or she can get the meaning—sometimes talking about it helps.

While sleep dreams are usually the most productive, often daydreams will bring valued insight. So, don't dismiss your daydreams either!

Good luck. And pleasant dreams!

Computerized creating. As strange as it may seem, computer technology can be used to enhance creativity, solve problems, bust through conceptual roadblocks, and get into the recesses of your memory. Several "mindware" or "CAT" (computer-aided thinking software) programs and books for this purpose exist, and may be of significant value in this area. The programs work by first asking you to enter lots of details of your problem or area and then they rearrange the details and suggest lots of modifications and permutations for you to consider. To find these programs and books, simply search "idea generator" in any search engine.

The hot tub method. This has been used by many creative geniuses, starting with Archimedes, who discovered the principle of volumetric measurement while in his tub. It works like this: When you relax in a hot tub for a long period, the heat mellows you out and dilates your blood vessels so as to draw blood from your analytical brain, allowing your creative subconscious to come to the fore.

Unstructured fanaticism. As "excellence guru" Tom Peters states, structured planners rarely come up with the really great innovations; monomaniacs who pursue a goal with unstructured fanaticism often do. So let yourself go and become an unreasonable lunatic—it may do the trick!

Group brainstorming. If all else fails, get a group of friends or trusted associates together (or on a computer network) and throw the problem to the group. For some unknown reason, a group of people working together often come up with more good ideas than the same individuals working separately. This synergistic method is often used in corporations with great success. The use of others to help innovate has been called "leveraging knowledge," since one's knowledge and abilities are multiplied by others in a group. There is even brainstorming software available now.

Increase self-confidence. Those with more self-confidence and self-esteem tend to be more venturesome, and hence more creative. If you suffer from low self-confidence or low self-esteem, you may wish to explore local courses or read some self-improvement books.

20 questions. Dixie Hammond of Focus Works in Van Nuys, California, suggested 20 questions you can ask to encourage ideas:

1. What if …?
2. Can we improve …?
3. How will a customer benefit?
4. Are we forgetting anything?
5. What is the next step?
6. What can we do better?
7. What do you think about …?
8. How can we improve quality?
9. How can we streamline?
10. What should we modify?
11. What should we replace?
12. What should we add?
13. What should we eliminate?
14. Can we make any new assumptions?
15. What will make it work?
16. What other ideas do you have?
17. What issues should we explore?
18. What patterns can you see?
19. How can we simplify?
20. Why?

Idea tools. Most inventions don't work well as originally developed. Here are some suggestions for modifying your invention to make it work better:

- **Divide.** Divide it into smaller components or separate functions.

- **Combine.** Combine separate ideas, parts, or functions.
- **Simplify.** Simplify it—for example, by making it smoother, or streamlined.
- **Substitute.** Use different materials, parts, functions, or ingredients.
- **Add.** Add additional parts, movement, color, flavor, sound, functions, textures, or ingredients.
- **Subtract.** Remove parts or steps.
- **Reverse.** Reverse the mode of operation or position, or transpose cause and effect.
- **Minimize.** Make it smaller, lighter, or lower.
- **Maximize.** Make it bigger, stronger, better, higher, in multiples; exaggerate it.
- **Redesign.** Redesign the exterior or interior, change the symmetry, speed, shape, function, or perspective; give it new meaning.

F. Contact Other Inventors

Many inventors' organizations have developed or sprung up in order to provide inventors with information and ideas, model makers, lists of searchers, speakers, patent attorneys, and so on, as well as to sponsor various seminars and trade fairs where inventions can be exhibited. One or more of these organizations may provide you with invaluable assistance in your inventing efforts.

Inventors' organizations have a reputation for honesty and provide reasonable value for the membership or other fees charged, but check for yourself before investing a significant amount of your time or money. A listing of inventor organizations can be found at Inventors Digest Online, www.inventorsdigest.com. If you wish to subscribe to an online inventors' group, Inventors Groups of America (www.inventleader.org) is an excellent resource.

You can also find inventors' groups in your area by asking the Patent and Trademark Resource Center close to you. You can find a listing of PTRCs in Chapter 6, or by visiting the PTO website (www.uspto.gov) and clicking on the "Learning and Resources" tab, then "Patent and Trademark Resource Centers" under "USPTO near you."

G. Beware of the Novice Inventor's "PGL Syndrome"

As the late inventor Paul Brown discovered, many novice inventors have a very different attitude from experienced inventors. He called this attitude "PGL (Paranoia, Greed, Laziness) syndrome." Let's discuss the components of Mr. Brown's syndrome in more detail, since each usually is a significant hindrance for inexperienced inventors.

Paranoia. Extremely common with inexperienced inventors, paranoia (excessive suspicion of other people's motives) makes them afraid to discuss or show their invention to others—some even go as far as refusing to disclose it to a patent attorney. We do advise some measure of caution with unpatented inventions. However, once you record your invention properly (as discussed in Chapter 3), you can and should disclose it to selected persons, provided you take adequate measures to document whom you've disclosed it to and when. Don't be as paranoid as my friend Tom who invented a very valuable stereo movie invention but kept it totally to himself out of fear of theft, only to see it patented and commercialized by someone else.

Greed/overestimation. Most people have heard fabulous stories of successful inventors who've collected millions in royalties. For example Los Angeles orthopedic surgeon and independent inventor Dr. Gary Michelson was awarded $1.35 *billion* in a settlement with Medtronic, Inc. over some spinal fusion inventions. As a result, some novice inventors think that their invention is worth millions and demand an unreasonably large royalty or lump-sum payment for their creation. This is seldom wise. It is much better to set your sights at a reasonable level (see Chapter 16) so you won't miss out on commercial opportunities.

Laziness. Some novice inventors believe that all they need to do is show their invention to a company, sign a lucrative contract, and let the money roll in. Unfortunately it hardly ever happens so easily. To be successful, you usually have to record your invention properly, build and test a working model (desirable but not always necessary), file a patent application, seek out suitable companies to produce and market the invention, and work like crazy to sell the invention to one of these companies.

H. Don't Bury Your Invention

If you believe that you have what will turn out to be a successful idea, but you have doubts because it's very different, or you get negative opinions from your friends, consider that Alexander Graham Bell was asked by an irate banker to remove "that toy" from his office. The "toy" was the telephone. Or if that doesn't convince you, ponder these words of Mark Twain, Albert Einstein, and John Shedd:

> *"The man with a new idea is a crank—until the idea succeeds."*
>
> **—Mark Twain**

> *"For an idea that does not at first seem insane, there is no hope."*
>
> **—Albert Einstein**

> *"Opportunities are seldom labeled."*
>
> **—John Shedd**

And as a successful inventor, Nolan Bushnell, *(Pong)* said, "Everyone who's ever taken a shower has an idea. It's the person who does something about it who makes a difference."

Don't forget that, in addition to making money if you're successful, an invention can create jobs, make our lives easier and more interesting, and eliminate drudgery. Consider the Linotype® machine, where each machine eliminated 90 manual type-setters and their arduous task and spawned a new industry and profession. Then came the modern computer—one of which could do the work of nine Linotype machines—spawning another new industry and ushering in the smartphone era. If you still doubt the value of inventors and inventions, consider this: Without inventors and their inventions, we would still be living the way we lived 50,000 years ago!

We hope you've received our message in this chapter loud and clear. If you have a worthwhile invention, and you scrupulously follow all the advice and instructions given in this and the succeeding chapters, and persevere, we believe you'll have a very good chance of success.

> *"Each invention leads to new inventions and each discovery to new discoveries; invention breeds invention, science begets science, the children of knowledge produce their kind in larger and larger families; the process goes on from decade to decade, from generation to generation."*
>
> **—Alfred Korzybski**

I. Summary

The day of the lone inventor is not over; many successful inventions and industries have been started by independent inventors.

Most inventions are created after recognizing a problem and finding a solution. However, inventions are also made by "magic" (accident and flash of genius), the process of which is not easily analyzed.

If you make an invention, try to conceive of variations or ramifications to enhance its value. If you have trouble solving invention problems, persevere: Frame the problem differently, use nonlinear techniques, let go of assumptions, try meditation, employ your dreams or the computer, use brainstorming, correspond with inventors' organizations, and so on. Beware of the novice inventors' PGL Syndrome (paranoia, greed, laziness). Above all, persevere!

CHAPTER

3

Documentation and the PPA

A. Introduction	51
B. Documentation Is Vital to the Invention Process	51
1. Good Engineering Practice	51
2. Psychological Stimulus	51
3. Analysis Stimulus	51
C. Documentation Has Legal Implications	52
1. Proof in Case of Theft	52
2. Proof in Case of Confusion of Inventorship	52
3. Supporting Tax Deductions	52
4. Avoidance of Ownership Disputes	52
D. Trade Secret Considerations	52
E. Record Conception and the Building and Testing of Your Invention	53
1. Keep Good Records of Building and Testing Activity	53
2. Keep Your Building and Testing Activity Confidential	53
F. How to Record Your Invention	54
1. The Lab Notebook	54
2. How to Enter Technical Information in the Notebook	55
3. What Should Be Entered in the Notebook	55
4. How to Handle Digital Documents, Large or Formal Sketches, Photos, Charts, or Graphs Drawn on Special Paper	58
5. Witnessing the Notebook	59
6. What to Do With the Notebook	60
G. Another Way to Record Conception or Building and Testing— The Invention Disclosure	60
H. Don't Sit on Your Invention After Documenting It	62
I. Don't Use a "Post Office Patent" to Document Your Invention	62
J. The Provisional Patent Application—A Substitute for Building and Testing, With Some Disadvantages	62
1. What Is a Provisional Patent Application (PPA)?	62
2. What a PPA Is Not	62
3. What a PPA Accomplishes	63

4. Advantages of a PPA Over Building and Testing..63

5. Disadvantages of the PPA..64

6. PPA Misconceptions...65

7. How to Prepare and File a PPA..65

8. PPA Checklist...82

9. PPAs and Foreign Filing...82

10. What If You Make Changes to the Invention?...83

K. Summary..83

Inventor's Commandment 3

In case you later need to prove you are the inventor of something, and the date when you invented it, after you conceive of the idea, you shouldn't proceed to develop, build, or test it, or reveal it to others, until you (1) write in ink or type a clear description of your invention on paper (or create a digital document and print it out), (2) sign and date the same, and (3) have this document signed and dated by two trustworthy people who have "witnessed and understood" your write-up.

Inventor's Commandment 4

(1) For commercial evaluation reasons, and in case of an invention dispute, try to build and test your invention (if at all possible) as soon as you can, (2) keep full and true written, signed, and dated records of all the efforts, correspondence, and receipts concerning your invention, especially if you build and test it, and (3) have two others sign and date that they have "Witnessed and understood" your building and testing. (As an alternative—or in addition—to documenting, building, and testing in this manner, you can use the PTO's Provisional Patent Application program, but be aware of the disadvantages and limitations of the PPA.)

A. Introduction

There are two distinct and important reasons why all inventors should document all of their work. The first has to do with the inventing process itself. The second involves the possibility that you will need to prove that you are the inventor and when you made the invention.

B. Documentation Is Vital to the Invention Process

It takes more than a good idea to sustain the invention process. It is absolutely essential to keep good, sound, and complete records, for two reasons: to preserve the invention process (explained in this section) and to prove inventorship and date if ever necessary (which we'll cover in the next section).

1. Good Engineering Practice

Good engineers and technicians record their developments in chronological order so that they can refer back to their engineering diary at any time— days, weeks, months, or even years later. First, this enables them to avoid running up the same blind alley twice. Second, good records will shed light on subsequent developments, will allow the inventor to find needed data and details of past developments, and will provide a base for new paths of exploration and ramifications, especially if failures have occurred.

2. Psychological Stimulus

Many of us come up with great ideas, especially when we're engaged in some other activity (including dreaming), and we forget to write them down. If we could get into the habit of writing down our thoughts on a piece of paper or preserving them in a digital file, later on we'd find that note there to bug us, almost forcing us to do something about it. So, keep pen and paper or your phone with you at all times, and preserve your thoughts as soon as they occur.

3. Analysis Stimulus

WWII Admiral William Raborn once said, "If you can't write it down, you don't really know what you are doing."

Putting a description of your idea in writing forces you to think about it and crystallize it into communicable form. Note that no matter how great your idea, and no matter how much of the work you do yourself, you'll never be able to make a nickel from it until you can communicate it to others—for example, to get a patent, to license it, or to sell the product.

"Writing forces you to think and get your thoughts straight."

—*Warren Buffett*

C. Documentation Has Legal Implications

There are several reasons why it's legally important to promptly and properly record your conception of your invention.

1. Proof in Case of Theft

If someone sees or hears about your invention and attempts to "steal" it by claiming it as their own invention (in actuality, a rare occurrence), there will probably be a lawsuit or derivation proceeding (see Chapter 13, section K) in which the true and first inventor must be identified. In such a proceeding, the side with the earliest, best, and most convincing evidence will win. 'Nuff said!

2. Proof in Case of Confusion of Inventorship

Often several engineers or friends will be working on the same problem, and if inventorship isn't promptly recorded, memories could fade and there might be confusion as to who is (are) the actual inventor(s). Also, bosses and other supervisors have been known to claim inventorship, or joint inventorship, in an employee's invention. If all inventors promptly recorded their inventions, signed and dated them, and got them witnessed and dated, preferably by coworkers (including bosses), there would be very few cases of such confusion of inventorship.

3. Supporting Tax Deductions

Once you make an invention and spend any money on your creation, the IRS may consider you "in business," thus enabling you to file a "Schedule C" or "Schedule E" (Form 1040) with your tax return to deduct all expenditures you made for your invention, from even ordinary income that you received. The IRS will be far more inclined to allow these deductions (assuming you're audited) if you can support them with full, clear, and accurate records of all of your invention activities, including—but not limited to—conception, building, and testing, as well as expenditures for tools, plastics, other materials, models, and so on. For more information about tax implications of patenting, consult a tax professional.

4. Avoidance of Ownership Disputes

Suppose you make an invention in a specific area— say bicycles—and later you go to work for a company engaged in this area—say a bicycle manufacturer. If you haven't already filed a patent application on your bike, you'll have a very hard time proving you already made the invention before your employment with this company if you haven't kept a proper record. In this situation and in many others, the company (or an individual or other organization with whom you deal) will likely claim ownership of your prior invention under your employment (or other) agreement unless you have the "paper" to prove prior invention.

D. Trade Secret Considerations

An invention can qualify as a trade secret, at least for the first 18 months of the patent application period. After 18 months, the PTO will publish the patent application unless the applicant also simultaneously filed a nonpublication request (NPR). Applications that are not published after 18 months will remain as trade secrets until the patent issues. Keeping an invention secret can provide its owner with certain obvious commercial advantages, and the owner may have recourse in the courts against any person who improperly discloses the secret to others.

Whether your invention is to be patented or kept as a trade secret (you can decide later), you should first record it properly so that you can prove that you invented it and that you did so as of a certain date. Since you can keep your notebook confidential, at least for the time being, no loss of any potential trade secret protection will result from your making a proper record of your conception.

⚠️ **CAUTION**

Remember that while recording your invention can be vital in the situations outlined above, it provides only limited rights, since it won't give you any weapon to use if anyone independently comes up with something identical to your creation, or if anyone copies your invention once it's out on the market. To acquire full offensive rights in these situations, you need to obtain a patent on your invention. Only a patent will give you rights against independent creators whose work mirrors your invention, and those who copy it once it's out on the market.

E. Record Conception and the Building and Testing of Your Invention

After you conceive of your invention you should record the conception in a lab notebook or an invention disclosure as explained below. After recording conception, you should try to build and test your invention as soon as you can and keep detailed and adequate records of your efforts.

1. Keep Good Records of Building and Testing Activity

The building and testing of an invention can be as (or even more) important than its conception, and faithfully keeping a journal of those activities can be vital proof of your invention in case of theft, confusion of inventors, and the need to establish tax deductions. However, the recordation of your efforts to build and test your invention is no longer necessary to obtain a patent, except if a special situation occurs that requires you to prove your development efforts.

EXAMPLE: On March 23, 2013 (after the First-Inventor-to-File law took effect), Millie invents a new hands-free computer pointing device that uses eye motions, thereby eliminating the need for a mouse. She writes up the details of her creation, signs and dates it, and has two witnesses sign and date it, thereby documenting conception. She builds and tests it and then writes up a description of the device and its operation and documents this in the same way. Harry, a janitor in her lab, sees her invention while performing his duties. Harry tells his brother Jake, who files a patent application on the device in his name. A few months later Millie files her patent application. The PTO rejects Millie's application based on Jake's earlier filing date. Millie files a derivation proceeding against Jake and his earlier-filed application and shows her earlier records of conception and building and testing before Jake's filing date and also shows that Jake's brother Harry had access to her invention. The Patent Trial and Appeal Board finds that Jake derived the invention from Millie and can either order Millie's name to be substituted for Jake's in Jake's application or Jake's application to be rejected as anticipated by Millie's earlier work.

Note: It is not necessary to prove building and testing to win a derivation proceeding, although it will surely help. If you can't or don't build and test, your record of conception will be sufficient.

2. Keep Your Building and Testing Activity Confidential

If, as part of the testing of your invention, you have to order any special part or material, or if you have to reveal to or discuss your invention with anyone to get it built or documented, be cautious about how and whom you contact. And when you do make any specific revelation, have the recipient of the information about your invention (the receiving party) sign a Nondisclosure Agreement ("NDA"; downloadable Form 3-1; see Appendix 7).

Getting the Agreement Signed

Model makers and machine shops are accustomed to signing these agreements. When you make an appointment to show your invention and you wish to have the recipient sign the agreement before viewing, it's only courteous and proper business practice to advise the recipient that you are bringing along a nondisclosure agreement (NDA) before signing. Don't spring the agreement in a surprise manner.

The agreement is completed by specifically identifying the confidential materials (documents or hardware) (the "Confidential Information"), and the name of the recipient (the Receiving Party; you're the Disclosing Party). Have the Receiving Party fill in, sign, and date the bottom of the agreement. Give a copy of the signed NDA to the Receiving Party, as well as any extra copies that may be needed if any other persons in the Receiving Party's organization are to sign also.

Note that if you are lending confidential materials to the Receiving Party, the agreement refers to the delivery of materials to the Receiving Party as a "loan." This will give you maximum rights if the Receiving Party makes unauthorized use of or refuses to return the materials.

It's also desirable to document everything you transact with the receiving party by sending a confirmatory email after each transaction and getting receipts or acknowledgments for everything you do lend or deliver. In other words, get and make a full "paper trail" of your activities.

This agreement will cover almost all situations where you need to disclose your invention or deliver proprietary materials under an NDA. However, it isn't cast in stone: If, for example, you are making more than a loan of the materials, feel free to redraft the agreement; for example, by changing "loaned" to "delivered."

> ⓘ **CAUTION**
>
> **About NDAs.** While it's desirable to have receiving parties sign an NDA, note that if a receiving party steals or copies your invention (rare for uncommercialized inventions), your NDA will be of little value unless (a) you have the funds to hire an attorney to sue the invention thief, or (b) your case is strong and worthwhile enough that you can get an attorney to take it on a contingency fee basis (meaning the attorney only gets paid out of money you recover in court or through settlement). Even then the thief can (a) raise defenses that may defeat your suit (nothing is certain in the law), (b) show that you have no actual monetary damages, or (c) be judgment proof (that is, have no assets to pay you for your damages). It's best to investigate (or "vet") your receiving party beforehand by getting references and doing a little research.

F. How to Record Your Invention

There are several ways to record your invention, discussed below, together with examples.

1. The Lab Notebook

The best way to record inventorship is by using a blank or lab notebook. Preferably, it should have a thick cover, with the pages bound in permanently, such as by sewing, gluing, or closed spiral binding. Also, the pages should be consecutively numbered. Lab notebooks of this type are available at engineering and laboratory supply stores, and generally have crosshatched, prenumbered pages with special lines at the bottom of each page for signatures (and signature dates) of the inventor and the witnesses. As should be apparent, the use of a bound, paginated notebook that's faithfully kept up provides a formidable piece of evidence if your inventorship or date of invention is ever called into question. A bound notebook with consecutively dated, signed, and witnessed entries on sequential pages establishes almost irrefutably that you are the inventor—that is, the first to conceive the invention—on the date indicated in the notebook. Lab notebooks can be purchased through Fisher Scientific (www.fishersci.com) or the Scientific Notebook Company (www.snco.com).

If you don't have or can't get a formal lab notebook like this, a standard bound letter-paper-size crackle-finish school copybook will serve. Just number all of the pages consecutively yourself, and don't forget the frequent dating, signing, and witnessing, even though there won't be special spaces for this. Date each entry in the notebook as of the date you and your coinventor(s), if any, make the entries and sign your name(s). If you made the entries over a day or two before you sign and date them, add a brief candid comment to this effect, such as, "I wrote the above on July 17, 2022, but forgot to sign and date it until now." Similarly, if you made and/or built the invention some time ago, but haven't made any records until now, again state the full, specific, and truthful facts and date the entry as of the date you write the entry and sign it. For example, "I thought of the above invention while trying to open a can of truffles at my sister's wedding reception on

July 23 (2021), but didn't write any description of it until now when I read *Patent It Yourself*."

2. How to Enter Technical Information in the Notebook

Fig. 3A is an example of a properly completed notebook page showing the recordation of conception, and Fig. 3B shows recordation of building and testing.

The sketches and diagrams should be clearly written (preferably double-spaced) in ink to preclude erasure and later-substituted entries. Your writing doesn't have to be beautiful and shouldn't be in legalese. Just make it clear enough for someone else to understand without having to read your mind. Use sketches when and wherever possible since readers will find these far easier to comprehend than words. Many inventors have told me they put off writing up their invention in a notebook or invention disclosure because they didn't know the proper "legal" terms to use, or had writer's block. However, as indicated, legalese isn't necessary or desirable. However, as indicated, legalese isn't necessary or desirable, and there are two effective ways to bypass writer's block:

- Rely mostly on sketches, with brief labels explaining the parts and their functions.
- Make sketches, describing them orally to a friend, and record your oral description with a tape recorder. Then go back and transcribe your description.

Do not leave any large blank spaces on a page—fill the page from top to bottom. If you do need to leave space to separate entries, or at the bottom on a page where you have insufficient space to start a new entry, draw a large cross over the blank space to preclude any subsequent entries, or, more accurately, to make it clear that no subsequent entries could have been made in your notebook.

If you make a mistake in an entry, don't attempt to erase it; merely line it out neatly and make a dated note why it was incorrect. The notation of error can be made in the margin adjacent to the correct entry, or it can be made several pages later, provided the error is referred to by page and date. Don't make cumulative changes to a single entry. If more than one change

is required, enter them later with all necessary cross-references to the earlier material they supplement. Refer back to earlier material by page and date.

If possible, make all entries directly in the notebook, or copy them there from rough notes on the day the notes were made. If this isn't possible, make them as soon as you can, with a notation explaining when the actual work was done, when the entries were made, and why the delay occurred.

If you've made an invention several months ago, and are now going to record it because you've just read this book, you should date the entries in the notebook when you actually write them, but you should also write when you actually made the invention and explain the delay with honesty and candor! Since the notebook is bound, you will have to handwrite the entries in it. Again, don't worry about the quality of your prose—your goal is only to make it clear enough for someone else to understand; use labeled sketches or the tape recorder/transcription techniques given above if writer's block occurs. If handwriting is difficult for you, or if your handwriting is illegible, you can use an Invention Disclosure form, described below.

3. What Should Be Entered in the Notebook

Your notebook should be used as a "technical diary"—that is, you should record in it anything you work on of technical significance, not just inventions. The front of the notebook should have your name and address and the date you started the notebook. When you record the conception of your invention, you and anyone who later sees the notebook will find it most meaningful if you use the following headings:

- Title (what your invention is called)
- Purpose (what purpose the invention is intended to serve)
- Description (a functional and structural description of the invention)
- Sketch (an informal sketch of the invention)
- Ramifications (include all ramifications of the invention that you thought of; if you fail to include a ramification and one of your witnesses thinks of it, the witness may have to be named as a coinventor if you file a patent application)

TITLE: Self-Adjusting Can Opener   23

PURPOSE: To provide a can opener that self-adjusts to any size can.

DESCRIPTION: The can opener has a sliding clamp with a locking groove at its edge [etc.]

… I conceived of this while I was at my friend Roberta's wedding last Sunday and saw

the caterer having trouble opening small and large cans with several openers…

Locking groove   SKETCH   Sliding clamp

RAMIFICATIONS: Instead of the locking groove, a special notch could be used as follows:

Notch   SKETCH

POSSIBLE NOVEL FEATURES: The sliding clamp with a raised frammis arm is believed entirely

new. Also, [etc.]…

ADVANTAGES: This can opener would eliminate the need for separate can openers for

different sized cans, thereby providing economy, ease of use, [etc.]…

INVENTOR: DATED:

Irma Inventor   *20xx/8/25*

THE ABOVE CONFIDENTIAL INFORMATION IS WITNESSED AND UNDERSTOOD:

Wilfred Witness   *20xx/9/25*

Alberta Attestor   *20xx/9/25*

Fig. 3A—Properly Completed Notebook Page Showing Conception

TITLE: Self-Adjusting Can Opener — Building & Testing   27

REFERENCE: Conception recorded on page 23.

DESCRIPTION: A working model of this opener was made for me by Fred Smith of Model Makers, Inc., starting Sept. 1. It was finished Sept. 13. It was made of cold-rolled steel, 13 mm. thick, with brass bearings [etc.]…

Here is the photo we took on Sept. 15:

Locking groove   PHOTO   Sliding clamp

RAMIFICATIONS: We also tried a nylon hinge, but it did not work because…

TEST DESCRIPTION: We tried the opener on fifty different cans, from size __ to size __ …

TEST RESULTS: For the size __ cans, the opener worked as well as the Ajax brand, opening each can in an average time of 8.3 seconds, the same as we obtained with the Ajax brand. [etc.]…

INVENTOR: DATED:

Irma Inventor   *20xx/9/27*

THE ABOVE CONFIDENTIAL INFORMATION IS WITNESSED AND UNDERSTOOD:

Steve Elias   *20xx/9/27*

Fred Friendly   *20xx/9/27*

Fig. 3B—Properly Completed Notebook Page Showing Building and Testing

- Novel features (include all possible novel features of the invention)
- Closest known prior art (the closest known existing approach of which you're aware), and
- Advantages (of the invention over previous developments and/or knowledge—see the example in Fig. 3A).

Don't forget to sign and date your conception and have two witnesses also sign and date the record of conception.

To record the subsequent building and testing of your invention at a later page of the notebook, you will find it most useful to record the following items:

1. Title and Back Reference
2. Technical Description
3. Photos and/or Sketches
4. Ramifications
5. Test Description
6. Test Results, and
7. Conclusion.

Fig. 3B (above) shows a properly done lab notebook record of the building and testing of an invention. Don't forget to sign and date, and have your witnesses also sign and date, the building and testing record, as well as the conception record. (See Section 5, below.)

If you're skilled enough to conceive, build, and test your invention all at once, just combine all of the items of Figs. 3A and 3B as one entry in your notebook.

Record as much factual data as possible; keep conclusions to a minimum and provide them only if they are supported by factual data. Thus, if a mousetrap operated successfully, describe its operation in enough detail to convince the reader that it works. Only then should you put in a conclusion, and it should be kept brief and with an opinion. For example, "Thus this mousetrap works faster and more reliably than the Ajax brand." Sweeping, opinionated, self-congratulating, or immodest statements tend to give an impartial reader a negative opinion of you or your invention.

However, it's useful to include the circumstances of conception, such as how you thought it up and where you were. This makes your account believable and helps refresh your memory later.

Word all entries so that they're complete and clear in themselves—that is, so that anyone can duplicate your work without further explanation. While you shouldn't use the lab notebook as a scratch pad to record every calculation and stray concept or note you make or think about, you also shouldn't make your entries so brief as to be of no value should the need for using the notebook as proof later arise. If you're in doubt as to whether to make an entry, make it; it's better to have too much than too little.

Also, you'll find it very helpful to save all of your "other paperwork" involved with the conception, building, and testing of an invention. Such paperwork includes correspondence and purchase receipts. These papers are highly trustworthy and useful as evidence, since they are very difficult to falsify. For example, if you buy a thermometer or have a machine shop make a part for you, you should save receipts and canceled checks from these expenditures since they'll tie in directly with your notebook work.

4. How to Handle Digital Documents, Large or Formal Sketches, Photos, Charts, or Graphs Drawn on Special Paper

If you have any digital documents or any other items that by their nature can't be entered directly in the notebook by hand, you should print out or otherwise enter them on separate sheets. These, too, should be signed, dated, and witnessed and then pasted or affixed in the notebook in proper chronological order. The inserted sheet should be referred to by entries made directly in the notebook, thus tying them in to the other material. Photos or other entries that can't be signed or written should be pasted in the notebook and referenced by legends (descriptive words, such as "photo taken of machine in operation") made directly in the notebook, preferably with lead lines that extend from the notebook page over onto the photo, so as to preclude a charge of substituting subsequently made photos (see Fig. 3B). The page the photo is pasted on should be signed, dated, and witnessed in the usual manner.

If an item covers an entire page, it can be referred to on an adjacent page. It's important to affix the items to the notebook page with a permanent adhesive, such as white glue or nonyellowing (frosty) transparent tape. If you have to draw a sketch in pencil and want to make a permanent record of it (to put in your notebook) without redrawing the sketch in ink, simply make a photocopy of the penciled sketch: voilà—a permanent copy!

If you make any drawings, photos, or prints that are too large to paste in your notebook, then you have two choices. You can fold them to notebook size and glue them into the notebook so that they can be unfolded and examined without removing them from the notebook. Or you can leave them separate from the notebook, but refer to, and describe them in the notebook. In either case, be sure to sign, date, and get witnesses to sign and date these large documents.

5. Witnessing the Notebook

The witnesses chosen should be as impartial and competent as possible, which means they shouldn't be close relatives or people who have been working so closely with you as to be possible coinventors. A knowledgeable friend, business associate, or professional will make an excellent witness, provided he or she has the necessary technical ability or background to understand the invention. Generally, a witness who understands what the invention does and how it's made and used will be adequate. But if the invention is technically complex, it's best to get a witness who understands the invention's underlying theory. The witness should also be someone who's likely to be available later. Obviously, a person who's seriously ill, or of very advanced age, wouldn't be a good choice. Don't ask your patent attorney (if you are using one) to perform this function, since the courts and the PTO won't allow an attorney to represent someone and also be that person's witness.

If the invention is a very simple mechanical device, practically anyone will have the technical qualifications to be a witness. But if it involves

advanced chemical or electronic concepts, obviously a person with an adequate background in the field will have to be used. The witness need not understand the theory behind the invention, but should be knowledgeable enough to understand what it does and how it works. If called upon later, the witnesses should be able to testify to their own knowledge that the physical and/or chemical facts of the entry are correct. Thus they shouldn't just be witnesses to your signature, so you should not use a notary or a layperson who just witnesses your signature, as do witnesses to a will. Rather the witnesses should actually read or view and understand the actual technical subject material in the notebook, including the actual tests if they are witnessing the building and testing (Fig. 3B). Obviously, then, you should call in your witnesses to observe your final tests and measurements so that they can later testify that they did witness them.

Should You Have Your Notebook Entries or Disclosure Notarized?

Many inventors ask if they should sign their notebook or disclosure before a notary public and have the document notarized. While notarization is slightly better than no witnesses at all, notarization is far inferior to live witnesses. Why? In the U.S. system of jurisprudence, the triers of fact (judge or jury) base their decisions primarily on the testimony of live witnesses, who are subject to cross examination and who understand the document in question and are not merely a "signature witness."

While one witness may be sufficient, the law gives much greater credence to two. If both are available, your case will be very strong. Also having two witnesses will enhance the likelihood of at least one of them being available to testify at a later date. And if a dispute occurs between two inventors, the one with the greater number of witnesses will prevail, assuming all other considerations are substantially equal.

Some notebooks already contain, on each page, a line for the inventor's signature and date, together with the words "Witnessed and Understood" with lines for two signatures and dates. If your notebook doesn't already contain these words and signature lines, merely write them in as indicated in Figs. 3A to 3C. To really tie down the trade secret status of your invention, you should add the words "The above confidential information is" just before the words "Witnessed and Understood," as has been done on Form 3-2 and on Figs. 3A, 3B, and 3C. You and the witnesses should sign and enter the date on the appropriate lines at the end of your description of the conception of your invention and at the end of your description of your building and testing.

6. What to Do With the Notebook

Now that you've made those nice notebook records of conception and hopefully building and testing, what should you do with the notebook? Nothing, except to keep it in a safe place in case it's ever needed (hopefully not!).

G. Another Way to Record Conception or Building and Testing— The Invention Disclosure

Suppose you conclude that for some good reason it's too difficult or inconvenient for you to keep a notebook or technical diary. There's a second, albeit somewhat inferior, way for you to record the conception or building and testing of your invention. This is by using a document called an "Invention Disclosure."

Despite its formidable name, an Invention Disclosure is hardly different from a properly completed notebook entry of an invention. It should be a complete record of your invention, including a title, its purpose(s), advantages, a detailed description of it, in sufficient detail so that one having ordinary skill in the field of your invention will be able to make and use it, possible novel features, ramifications, details of its construction if you built it, and results obtained,

if any. As with the notebook, include sketches when and wherever possible. While it might better be called an "Invention Record," in the arcane world of patents it's called a "disclosure," since an inventor often uses it to disclose an invention to others to get their opinion, have them develop it, and show what progress is being made. These entries should be made on a separate sheet of paper that has no other information on it except details of your invention and your name and address. For your convenience, this book's online companion page provides a downloadable Invention Disclosure form, and Fig. 3C illustrates how the form should be completed to record conception.

Since an Invention Disclosure isn't bound, the writing on it can, and preferably should, be printed or typed. But if you do write rather than type, just make sure your handwriting is legible. A sheet of professional or personal letterhead (if you have it) is suitable for an Invention Disclosure. Otherwise print your name, address, and telephone number at the top (or bottom, after your signature). Business letterhead is okay if the invention is to be owned by your business. If the disclosure runs to more than one page, you should write the title of your invention on the second and each succeeding page, followed by the word "continued," numbering each page and indicating the total number of pages of the entire disclosure— for example, "Page 1 of 3."

As before, the description of your invention should be signed and dated by you, marked "The above confidential information is Witnessed and Understood," and signed and dated, preferably by two witnesses, who, as before, are technically competent to understand your invention and who actually do understand and have witnessed the subject matter you have entered on your Invention Disclosure. If you use more than one page, each should be signed and dated by both the inventor and the witnesses. Again, to guarantee the trade secret status of your invention, you should make sure the words "The above confidential information is" appear just before the words "Witnessed and Understood."

Invention Disclosure

Sheet 1 of 1

Inventor(s): Irma Inventor

Address(es): 1919 Chestnut St., Philadelphia, PA 19103

Title of Invention: Self-Adjusting Can Opener

To record **Conception**, describe: 1. Circumstances of conception, 2. Purposes and advantages of invention, 3. Description, 4. Sketches, 5. Operation, 6. Ramifications, 7. Possible novel features, and 8. Closest known prior art. To record **Building and Testing**, describe: 1. Any previous disclosure of conception, 2. Construction, 3. Ramifications, 4. Operation and Tests, and 5. Test results. Include sketches and photos, where possible. Continue on additional identical copies of this sheet if necessary; inventors and witnesses should sign all sheets.

I thought of this can opener while at my friend Roberta's wedding last Sunday. I saw the caterer having trouble opening small and large cans with several openers. Thinking there was a better way, I recalled my Majestic KY3 sewing machine clamp and how it was adjustable and thought to modify the left arm to accommodate a can opener head.

My can opener will work with all sizes of cans and is actually cheaper than the most common existing one, the UR4 made by Ideal Co. of Racine, Wisconsin.

My can opener comprises a sliding clamp 10, a pincer groove 12, [etc.] as shown in the following sketch:

Sketch:

10 → SKETCH ← 12

Operation: The user operates the can opener in the same way as any squeeze-and-turn opener for any size can.

Instead of sliding clamp 10, I can use a special notch as follows:

Notch → SKETCH

I believe that the combination of sliding clamp 10 and pincer groove 12 is a new one for can openers. Also I believe that it may be novel to provide a frammis head with my whatsit.

The Acme KZ122 can opener, mfgd. by Acme Kitchenwares of Berkeley, California, and p. 417 of "Kitchen Tools & Their Uses" (Ready Publishers, Phila. 1981) show the closest can openers to my invention, in addition to the devices already mentioned.

Inventor(s): Irma Inventor   Date: 20xx / Jul / 6

_____   Date: _____ / _____ / _____

The following understand, have witnessed, and agree not to disclose the above confidential information:

Griselda Hammelfarb   Date: 20xx / Jul / 10

Neonore Zimla   Date: 20xx / Jul / 10

Fig. 3C—Invention Disclosure (Downloadable Form 3-2; see Appendix 7)

As with the notebook, if you conceive of an invention on one date and build and test the invention later, you should make two separate invention disclosures. Also, as with the notebook, keep the disclosure in a safe place.

> 💡 **TIP**
>
> **If you've conceived of or have effectively built and tested your invention on a computer or other device,** you must print out a hard copy on paper so that you and your witness can sign it properly. Digital records (absent hard-copy printouts) are too impermanent to be given legal credibility.

H. Don't Sit on Your Invention After Documenting It

While documenting your invention and the building and testing of it are very important, obviously such documentation (no matter how thorough and carefully crafted) will be of no value whatsoever unless you follow through and take further steps to exploit your invention. Keep in mind that whatever method or methods you use to document are not as important as filing a patent application and getting the invention to market so that you can profit from your creativity.

I. Don't Use a "Post Office Patent" to Document Your Invention

There's a myth that you can document the date you conceived of your invention (or even protect your invention) by mailing a description of your invention to yourself by certified (or registered) mail and keeping the sealed envelope. In fact, the law regards the use of a "Post Office Patent" as practically worthless and no substitute for the signatures of live witnesses on a description of your invention. The PTO's Patent Trial and Appeal Board, which has great power in these matters, has specifically said that it gives a sealed envelope little evidentiary value because "inventors are individuals of consummate ingenuity" who may utilize "steam appropriately or other agent to skillfully unseal an envelope."

J. The Provisional Patent Application— A Substitute for Building and Testing, With Some Disadvantages

Suppose you don't have the facilities, skill, or time to build and test your invention, and you are not in a position to file a complete utility (or plant) patent application right away. In this case you may file a Provisional Patent Application (PPA) that will serve as a legal alternative to building and testing a utility invention. (The PPA is not available for design patents per 35 U.S.C. § 172.) This proves to the PTO that, at the very least, you conceived your invention on or before the day you filed the PPA.

1. What Is a Provisional Patent Application (PPA)?

A PPA is a less formal version of, and usually shorter than, a regular patent application. It is used to establish an early filing date for a later-filed Regular Patent Application (RPA). A PPA must contain:

1. a detailed description of the invention telling how to make and use it
2. drawing(s), if necessary to understand how to make and use the invention
3. a cover sheet, fee transmittal form (prepared automatically if the PPA is filed electronically), and Certification of Micro Entity Status (if paying the micro entity fee)
4. a fee (micro entity (ME), small entity (SE), or large entity—see Appendix 4, "Fee Schedule"), and
5. a return receipt postcard (not required if PPA is filed electronically).

In actuality the term "PPA" is a misnomer, since it is a simple document deposit, not an application (that is, a request for something). Since a PPA is not even a true application, it is not and should never be called a patent.

2. What a PPA Is Not

A PPA is not a regular patent application (RPA) and therefore cannot by itself mature into a patent. For those readers already familiar with the regular patent application process described in Chapter 8, the PPA, unlike an RPA, does not require:

- a Patent Application Declaration (PAD)
- an Information Disclosure Statement (IDS)
- patent claims
- an abstract or summary
- a description of the invention's background, or
- a statement of the invention's advantages.

Although claims are not required in a PPA, it may be advantageous to include some anyway, to help you focus the narrative in your detailed description and to remind you to write about all of your invention's technical features.

If you don't file an RPA within a year of your PPA's filing date, your PPA will go abandoned and will be of little value. Also, your PPA cannot provide a filing date for subject matter that is not disclosed in it. So if you make any improvements to your original invention, you must file another PPA (or an RPA) to obtain rights in those improvements. The PTO will not allow you to go back and make any changes to your earlier PPA.

3. What a PPA Accomplishes

Once you file a PPA, you will be considered to have acquired an "effective filing date" (essentially, a "date received" stamp) for all of the information in the PPA, assuming that:

- an RPA (and optionally one or more foreign patent applications) are filed on the invention within one year, and
- the PPA fully describes the invention claimed in the RPA.

Being able to claim the PPA's filing date allows you to overcome any prior-art reference that is cited in opposition to your application and has a publication or filing date that is after your filing date.

4. Advantages of a PPA Over Building and Testing

In addition to the benefits of an early filing date, the PPA gives you the right to claim that your invention has "patent pending" status. In common parlance this means that you can publish, sell, or show your invention to others without fear of theft or loss of any domestic rights. This is because anyone who sees and steals your invention after you file your PPA would have a later filing date than yours.

Assuming you prepare it properly, there are other advantages to using a PPA in place of actually building and testing the invention. These are:

- You need not keep meticulous records of whatever building and testing you do accomplish.
- You need not obtain witnesses.
- You can be certain that your PPA will provide excellent proof of inventorship.
- You will be certain that your PPA's early filing date can be relied upon, provided your description of the invention in the PPA is legally sufficient as described below.
- You can file a technical article (which you might have written anyway) as a PPA. But remember, the article, to be adequate for a PPA, must fully disclose how to make and use the invention claimed in the RPA. As stated, the RPA must be filed within one year.
- You can file a PPA, then within one year, file an RPA, which has the practical effect of delaying examination of the RPA and extending—up to one year—your patent's expiration date. In other words a PPA gives you a filing date that does not start your 20-year patent term. Pushing your patent monopoly term ahead a year can be profitable if your invention is ahead of its time and is likely to have its best sales 20 years from now—for example, as often happens with drugs.
- If you've filed an RPA and wish to restart your 20-year term, you can do so by converting the RPA to a PPA and then filing a second RPA. To make the conversion, file a petition (a simple request letter will do) with the prescribed conversion fee within one year of the RPA's filing date. The PPA will take the first RPA's filing date. Then file the second RPA, also within one year of the first RPA's filing date. The second RPA

should claim the benefit of the PPA's filing date. The second RPA will expire 20 years from its own filing date, so you've restarted your 20-year term about a year later, albeit at a price.

- You can refer to your invention as "patent pending" once you've filed a PPA. This can be a marketing advantage, especially with companies that will not discuss any invention that is not patent pending.

- Suppose you file a PPA and then, within a year, you file an RPA that claims the benefit of the PPA's filing date. If your RPA issues as a patent, it will be effective against RPAs filed by your competitors as a prior-art reference as of its PPA's filing date. (35 U.S.C. § 102(a)(2).)

- If you are able to license or sell your invention before it is time to file an RPA, your licensee or buyer will have the opportunity to prepare and file the RPA using their own lawyers.

- Preparing an RPA after you've prepared a PPA will give you a second opportunity to perfect your application.

- If you file a PPA and thereafter make any changes in the invention, you can file additional PPAs to cover the changes. You can claim the benefit of as many PPAs as you want in any RPA(s) you file, so long as all PPAs you claim priority from were filed within a year preceding the RPA's filing date.

- You can put multiple inventions in a single PPA and claim the benefit of these in separate RPAs, provided the RPAs are filed within a year after the PPA was filed.

5. Disadvantages of the PPA

Alas, every silver box seems to contain a cloud. The disadvantages of filing a PPA are as follows:

1. You may tend to forgo building and testing and lose the related advantages, such as determining whether the invention is operable, practical, or useful, and having a working prototype to demonstrate to prospective manufacturers.
2. Your PPA may fail to contain a full description of how to make and use the invention or any

embodiment of it. In this case, you won't be able to rely on the PPA's filing date for the invention or any embodiment.
3. You may unintentionally forgo foreign protection. This is because you cannot wait one year after filing the RPA, as is usually done, to foreign file. Instead you must make your foreign filing decision, as well as your regular U.S. filing decision, within one year after your PPA is filed. As I will discuss in Chapter 12, foreign filing is extremely expensive and few foreign filers ever earn their money back.
4. You may try to license or interest a manufacturer in your invention in the approximately ten-month period between the time you file the PPA and the time you must begin preparation of your RPA. Since ten months is usually too short a period to license an invention, you may get discouraged and fail to file an RPA and thus give up a potentially valuable invention.
5. If you file an RPA that claims the date of your PPA, and you do not file a nonpublication request (see Chapter 10), at the time you file the RPA, your RPA will be published 18 months after you file the PPA, or about six months after you file the RPA. You may not want your application published so early as it will end trade secret status.

Note that the PTO has published the following cautions regarding PPAs:

- PPAs are not examined on their merits.
- The date of a PPA cannot be claimed if an RPA has not been filed within one year.
- A PPA cannot claim the benefit of an earlier application (foreign or domestic).
- The disclosure of a PPA must be clear and complete enough so that an ordinary person skilled in the field of the invention can make and use the invention.
- All contributors to the inventive subject matter of the PPA must be named in the PPA.
- The RPA must name at least one inventor that was named in the PPA.

- In order for an RPA to claim the date of the PPA, the PPA must be filed with the proper fee and must be complete.
- If the basic fee is not paid with the PPA, the fee can be paid later, but the PTO charges a penalty.
- PPAs are not available for designs.
- No subject matter can be added once the PPA is filed.
- No patent will result from the PPA unless an RPA is filed within a year or the PPA itself is converted to an RPA.

6. PPA Misconceptions

There are many common misconceptions circulating about what a PPA can accomplish. Here are some.

Common Misconception: The PTO will read and examine and reject or approve your PPA.

Fact: The PTO will never examine or read your PPA unless you need to rely on its date and ask the PTO to do so in order to obtain the benefit of the PPA's filing date.

Common Misconception: After filing your PPA, the PTO will grant you a provisional patent.

Fact: The PTO will never "accept," "grant," or "reject" your PPA based on its contents. There is no such thing as a "provisional patent" and your PPA will be discarded if you don't file an RPA within one year that claims the benefits of the PPA's date.

Common Misconception: You can modify your invention after filing a PPA and still claim its benefits.

Fact: If you have an invention in your RPA that isn't in your PPA, you simply will not be able to obtain the benefit of your PPA's filing date for that invention, if you ever need it. If you have an invention in your PPA that isn't in your RPA, the PTO won't care. You can put any and all inventions you want into a PPA and you can do the same with your RPA. (However, if your RPA claims multiple inventions, the PTO will require you to restrict the claims to one invention.)

Common Misconception: Filing a PPA provides the right to stop others.

Fact: A PPA is a simple placeholder that confers no rights, except the right to rely on its date if it's prepared properly and you file an RPA within a year.

7. How to Prepare and File a PPA

Ideally, the more your PPA resembles the RPA you file within the following year, the more you can be assured that you will be able to claim the PPA's filing date. For that reason, my general recommendation is that you follow the basic rules for writing an RPA set out in Chapter 10. But, since your PPA will not be examined by the PTO unless and until you file an RPA—and then only to see whether it adequately describes the invention being claimed in the RPA—your description need not:

- be a polished presentation (but it should be clearly written and understandable)
- contain claims, or
- be typed in any particular format.

As explained below, there are two ways to file a PPA with the PTO: (a) electronically using the PTO's Patent Center procedures over the internet (preferred), and (b) by mail (includes personal delivery in case you live near the PTO in Alexandria, Virginia). Whether preparing a PPA for electronic filing or mail, you will need to:

- prepare drawings, if necessary (these need not be polished, but should be understandable)
- prepare a complete description of the structure and operation of your invention
- prepare a PPA cover sheet and (if filing by mail) a fee transmittal form
- prepare a Certification of Micro Entity Status (if paying the micro entity fee)
- (if filing by mail) prepare a receipt postcard and check or credit card authorization, and
- (if filing electronically) prepare an Application Data Sheet (ADS) (although it's desirable to include an ADS if filing by mail, as well).

Provisional Patent Application of

Robert H. Howe

for

TITLE: ADJUSTABLE SLEEPING BAG WITH DRAWCORDS

DESCRIPTION

FIG. 1 is a perspective view taken from the user's right side of a sleeping bag 11 constructed in accordance with the invention. An upper portion 12 of the bag has a drawcord 14, circumferentially mounted within a fabric casing sleeve 15, and secured by cord lock 16. Such cord arrangements are repeated at each of locations 19, 20, 21, and 22. Each sleeve 15 and each contained drawcord 14 extends only across the upper portion of the bag, from a zipper 17 on the right side of the bag, to a corresponding location 18 (FIG. 2) on the left side. The bottom portion of the bag (not shown) has no drawcords. The drawcords are made of stretchable elastic or nonstretchable material (nylon), while the sleeves are preferably made of the same material as the bag's outer shell; for example, nylon or rayon. Such sleeves may be sewed, glued, or thermally bonded to the outside of the outer shell.

FIG. 2 is a left perspective view of the bag, showing left-side seam 18 and showing drawcord 14 mounted within sleeve 15 and secured by cord lock 16 at locations 19, 20, 21, and 22. Note that each sleeve 15 and its contained drawcord extends only over the top portion of the bag, from seam 18 to zipper 17.

FIG. 3 is a lateral cross-section through bag 11 at location 19 showing zipper 17, side seam 18, and drawcord 14 relaxed and secured by cord lock 16 while mounted within fabric casing sleeve 15. Sleeve 15 is sewn to outer shell fabric 25. Inner lining fabric 24 and insulation 23 are not compressed since drawcord 14 is relaxed. An occupant 26 of the bag is shown in a horizontal position; note that the bag fits loosely around the occupant and that there is a lot of air space between occupant 26 and the bag. A conventional underlying insulating pad or mat 27; for example, of foam is used under the bag.

Fig. 3D—Provisional Patent Application Without Embellishments

FIG. 4 is a lateral cross-section through sleeping bag 11 at location 19 with drawcord 14 tightened and secured by cord lock 16. Inner lining fabric 24 and insulation 23 are gathered together where they are surrounded by tightened drawcord 14. Note that the bag now fits relatively closely or tightly around occupant 26 and that there is very little air space left between occupant 26 and the bag. Insulating pad 27 is again shown under the bag.

OPERATION

In operation one uses the bag in a normal manner with insulating pad 27 under the bag. The user can, when desired, increase the warmth of the bag by tightening the drawcords and securing them with cord lock 16 (FIGS. 3 and 4). When the drawcords are tightened, five effects increase the bag's warmth:

(1) Insulating layer 23 and the inner lining fabric 24 surrounding occupant 26 become thicker.

(2) This increase in thickness also makes the bag less susceptible to the user narrowing the insulation by body movement; for example, by poking the insulation with an elbow.

(3) The surface area of outer shell fabric 25 exposed to cold air is reduced.

(4) Since the drawcord extends only over upper portion 12 of the bag, lower portion 13 does not tend to be raised from pad 27 beneath the bag to be exposed to cold air.

(5) The air space between occupant 26 and the bag is reduced.

When the user wishes to increase the inner volume of the bag to provide greater freedom of movement (at some loss of insulating ability), it is only necessary to relax the drawcords (FIG. 3) and allow the bag to expand.

Fig. 3D—Provisional Patent Application Without Embellishments (continued)

Fig. 3D—Provisional Patent Application Without Embellishments (continued)

Provisional Patent Application of

Robert H. Howe

For

TITLE: ADJUSTABLE SLEEPING BAG WITH DRAWCORDS

CROSS-REFERENCE TO RELATED APPLICATIONS: None.

FEDERALLY SPONSORED RESEARCH: None.

SEQUENCE LISTING: None.

BACKGROUND

This relates to sleeping bags, specifically to insulated sleeping bags having means that allow users to adjust the insulating ability and internal volume of the bags. Sleeping bags can be uncomfortable, and when they're uncomfortable, they can deny their users much-needed rest. Sleeping bag comfort is largely a matter of warmth—that is, providing the bag's user with the correct amount of insulation to suit the existing conditions—and a matter of providing the user with adequate freedom of movement. These two aspects of sleeping bag comfort can work against each other. For similarly shaped bags, the more room there is inside a bag, the more freedom of movement its user has. However, the more room inside a bag, the more air space the user's body is required to heat and the more outer bag surface is exposed to the cold. Most sleeping bags provide comfort in only a rather narrow range of temperatures. So, sleeping bag manufacturers have long sought means of effectively adjusting the suitability of sleeping bags to fit a wider range of temperatures.

Both U.S. Patent 2,350,410 to Matthesius (1944) and U.S. Patent 1,583,419 to Perl (1926) show sleeping wraps for infants. These bags have side cords which are tied around the upper portion of each of the wraps after an infant is placed on top of the wrap and the flat sides of the wrap are folded around the infant. With both of these wraps the cords are primarily to allow one to complete closure of the wraps. Therefore, they should not be considered sleeping bags but rather, what they clearly are—sleeping wraps for infants. Perl states, "the straps 15 will serve to prevent the possible moving and kicking of the infant from dislodging the cover portion."

Fig. 3E—Provisional Patent Application With Embellishments

2

Both wraps are flat, it is presumed, because it is easier and safer to lay a sometimes struggling, usually writhing infant on a flat surface and fold and tie the sides around the infant than it is to insert the infant into a bag. While the cords of these two wraps may be drawn more or less tightly about the infant before tying, neither wrap is adapted for simple adjustment of its internal volume.

One method used to optimize the warmth and roominess of a sleeping bag is shown in U.S. Patent 5,473,779 to Kramer (1995), where nonadjustable, permanently attached bands of elastic material are incorporated into the portion of the bag surrounding the user's knees and legs. The object is to provide increased freedom of movement while still reducing the inner volume of the bag to optimize bag warmth. However the greater freedom of movement is provided only to the knees and legs. The bag cannot be adjusted to adapt it for cooler or warmer temperatures.

The lower portions of insulated sleeping bags are typically less insulated than the upper portions of the same bags because bag manufacturers rely on bag users to employ well-insulated mats under the sleeping bags. Bag manufacturers rely on such mats for good reasons—they are cheap, effective, and not as compressed by the weight of the user as is the insulation contained in the lower portion of a sleeping bag. If a good insulating mat is not placed under a sleeping bag, it is likely that more warmth will be lost to the ground by conduction than will be lost by convection to the air above the sleeper.

However even if a good ground pad is used with the bag shown in U.S. Patent 4,888,828 to Tatsuno (1989), its effectiveness will be reduced. This is because Tatsuno uses nonadjustable elastic members that are permanently sewn into the bag in circumferential rings spaced axially along the bag. These rings totally encircle the bag and the bag's user and this presents a problem. By totally encircling the bag, each elasticized member pulls an area of the lower portion of the bag up and away from the underlying insulated pad. Thus, these areas are no longer insulated by full contact with the underlying insulating mat as they would otherwise be, but are instead exposed to cold air.

Roach, in U.S. Patent 4,894,878 (1990) shows a bag with a liner whose circumferential dimension can be reduced by a zipper to create increased overlap of the bag's insulating batts and hence more insulation. However, it is difficult to reach an inside zipper to make the necessary adjustment.

Hunt, in U.S. Patent 3,857,125 (1974) shows an insulated bag with inner and outer shell layers that are differentially cut, except in a small portion of the bag, that provides more freedom of movement for the user's shoulders. This differential cut, Hunt claims,

Fig. 3E—Provisional Patent Application With Embellishments (continued)

3

minimizes compression of the insulation when body pressures are exerted against the outer shell. Hunt also claims that the inner shell provides self-adjusting inward lofting of the insulation in the shoulder and chin areas. Hunt's bag provides a hood that surrounds the user's face. Hunt positions the adjustable end of a drawcord used to tighten this hood at one side of the user's face and sews the drawcord to the bag at the other side of the user's face. This, it is claimed, allows the user to independently adjust the tightness of that part of the hood that is above the face. While the effectiveness of providing separate adjustability in areas that are so close together is debatable, one thing is certain: Hunt's bag in no way addresses the need for a bag with adjustability in the fit of the upper insulation.

Demini Sports, of Amsterdam, Holland, has sold a sleeping bag since the early 1970s with drawcords which encircle the bag at spaced locations along the bag. However these bags suffer from the same defect as Tatsuno's, above. That is, since the means for compressing the bag completely encircle it, they draw the lower portion of the bag away from the underlying insulating ground pad, which, as stated, users normally provide under this type of bag.

In conclusion, insofar as I am aware, no sleeping bag formerly developed provides volume adjustability to a user without the defect of drawing the lower portion of the bag away from the underlying insulating ground pad.

SUMMARY

An improved sleeping bag has adjustable drawcords attached to the outer shell fabric. These drawcords extend only over the top portion of the bag. Cord locks are provided to tighten the drawcords to any desired degree of warmth. The drawcords are encased in drawcord sheaths extending only across the upper portion of the bag. This allows a user to reduce the inner air space of the bag without reducing the effectiveness of the insulation of the lower portion of the bag and without the discomfort of inner encircling drawcords.

Accordingly, several advantages are to provide an improved sleeping bag, to provide means of increasing the warmth of a sleeping bag during cooler weather, to provide a bag with increased freedom of movement during warmer weather, and to provide a more user-friendly, yet economical sleeping bag. Still further advantages will become apparent from a study of the following description and the accompanying drawings.

Fig. 3E—Provisional Patent Application With Embellishments (continued)

4

DRAWINGS

FIG. 1 is a perspective right-side view of a sleeping bag constructed in accordance with the invention, showing the upper half of the bag.

FIG. 2 is a perspective left-side view of the sleeping bag of FIG. 1.

FIG. 3 is a lateral cross-sectional view of the sleeping bag of FIGS. 1 and 2 with the drawcord relaxed.

FIG. 4 is a lateral cross-sectional view of the sleeping bag of FIGS. 1 and 2 with the drawcord tightened.

FIG. 5 is a perspective view of the bag taken from above, showing its insulation.

DETAILED DESCRIPTION

FIG. 1 is a perspective view taken from the user's right side of a sleeping bag 11 constructed in accordance with one embodiment. An upper portion 12 of the bag has a drawcord 14, circumferentially mounted within a fabric casing sleeve 15, and secured by cord lock 16. Such cord arrangements are repeated at each of locations 19, 20, 21, and 22. Each sleeve 15 and each contained drawcord 14 extends only across the upper portion of the bag, from a zipper 17 on the right side of the bag, to a corresponding location 18 (FIG. 2) on the left side. The bottom portion of the bag (not shown) has no drawcords. The drawcords are made of stretchable elastic or nonstretchable material (nylon), while the sleeves are preferably made of the same material as the bag's outer shell; for example, nylon or rayon. **Such sleeves may be sewed, glued, or thermally bonded to the outside of the outer shell.**

FIG. 2 is a left perspective view of the bag, showing left-side seam 18 and showing drawcord 14 mounted within sleeve 15 and secured by cord lock 16 at locations 19, 20, 21, and 22. Note that each sleeve 15 and its contained drawcord extends only over the top portion of the bag, from seam 18 to zipper 17.

FIG. 3 is a lateral cross-section through bag 11 at location 19 showing zipper 17, side seam 18, and drawcord 14 relaxed and secured by cord lock 16 while mounted within fabric casing sleeve 15. Sleeve 15 is sewn to outer shell fabric 25. Inner lining fabric 24 and insulation 23 are not compressed since drawcord 14 is relaxed. An occupant 26 of the bag is shown in a horizontal position; note that the bag fits loosely around the occupant and that there is a lot of air space between occupant 26 and the bag. A conventional underlying insulating pad or mat 27; for example, of foam is used under the bag.

Fig. 3E—Provisional Patent Application With Embellishments (continued)

5

FIG. 4 is a lateral cross-section through sleeping bag 11 at location 19 with drawcord 14 tightened and secured by cord lock 16. Inner lining fabric 24 and insulation 23 are gathered together where they are surrounded by tightened drawcord 14. Note that the bag now fits relatively closely or tightly around occupant 26 and that there is very little air space left between occupant 26 and the bag. Insulating pad 27 is again shown under the bag.

REFERENCE NUMERALS

11 sleeping bag

12 upper portion of sleeping bag

13 lower portion of sleeping bag

14 drawcord

15 fabric casing sleeve

16 cord lock

17 zipper

18 side seam

19 sleeve location

20 sleeve location

21 sleeve location

22 sleeve location

23 insulation

24 inner lining fabric

25 outer shell fabric

26 occupant

27 insulating pad

Fig. 3E—Provisional Patent Application With Embellishments (continued)

6

OPERATION

In operation one uses the bag in a normal manner with insulating pad 27 under the bag. The user can, when desired, increase the warmth of the bag by tightening the drawcords and securing them with cord lock 16 (FIGS. 3 and 4). When the drawcords are tightened, five effects increase the bag's warmth:

(1) Insulating layer 23 and the inner lining fabric 24 surrounding occupant 26 become thicker.

(2) This increase in thickness also makes the bag less susceptible to the user narrowing the insulation by body movement; for example, by poking the insulation with an elbow.

(3) The surface area of outer shell fabric 25 exposed to cold air is reduced.

(4) Since the drawcord extends only over upper portion 12 of the bag, lower portion 13 does not tend to be raised from pad 27 beneath the bag to be exposed to cold air.

(5) The air space between occupant 26 and the bag is reduced.

When the user wishes to increase the inner volume of the bag to provide greater freedom of movement (at some loss of insulating ability), it is only necessary to relax the drawcords (FIG. 3) and allow the bag to expand.

CLAIM

1. A sleeping bag, comprising:

- an upper portion which will overlie the body of an occupant when said occupant is in a horizontal position in said sleeping bag,

- a lower portion which underlies the body of said occupant, said lower and upper portions being joined at opposite sides of said sleeping bag, and

- at least one drawcord attached to said upper portion of said sleeping bag, said drawcord not extending onto said lower portion of said sleeping bag, said drawcord having two ends which are attached to said respective opposite sides of said sleeping bag,

whereby (a) during cold weather, an occupant of said sleeping bag can tighten and clamp said drawcord so that the inner volume and the exposed outer surface area of said sleeping bag can be reduced in order to better insulate said occupant, (b) contact

Fig. 3E—Provisional Patent Application With Embellishments (continued)

7

between said lower portion and any underlying flat insulated pad will not be reduced when said drawcord is tightened, and (c) said occupant of said sleeping bag can relax the tension on said drawcord during warmer conditions and thereby increase the volume of air within said sleeping bag adjacent to said occupant of said sleeping bag in order to give said occupant more freedom of movement.

ABSTRACT

A sleeping bag (11) design for providing adjustability of the inner volume and outer exposed surface area of the bag comprises sheathed drawcords (14), preferably elastic, attached only to the top or upper portion of the bag and secured by cord locks (16). A user of the bag can tighten the drawcords during cold weather, thereby providing a warmer bag by reducing the inner volume and the exposed outer surface area of the bag without reducing the thermal protection provided to the lower portion of the bag by an underlying flat insulated pad, as would be the case with drawcords fully encircling the bag. During warmer weather, the user can relax the drawcord adjustment, thereby providing the user with more freedom of movement. Thus a considerably more versatile sleeping bag is provided—that can be adjusted to provide more warmth during cold weather or more freedom of movement during warmer weather.

Fig. 3E—Provisional Patent Application With Embellishments (continued)

Qualifying as a Micro Entity

Inventors paying patent fees at the U.S. Patent and Trademark Office (USPTO) can select a status from Column A (Regular, or Undiscounted Fee), Column B (Small Entity Status), or Column C (Micro Entity Status). If the filer qualifies for small entity status, the USPTO offers a 60% discount, and a filer that qualifies as a micro entity receives an 80% discount on most fees. The goal of this multi-tiered system is to provide a break for smaller companies and independent inventors, and to encourage innovation.

Qualifying as a Small Entity. To qualify as a small entity you must either be an individual, a small business concern having no more than 500 employees (or affiliates), a university, or a 501(c)(3) nonprofit organization.

If you qualify as a small entity, you need only verify that status by executing a declaration when paying the fee. If, however, you are obligated to license or assign the patent to a bigger entity that doesn't qualify as a small entity—for example, you license your patent to Microsoft—then you cannot claim small entity status. Improperly claiming small entity status is considered inequitable conduct (fraud for the purpose of obtaining a discount) and can result in the loss of patent rights.

Qualifying as a Micro Entity. To qualify as a micro entity, the filer must meet all small entity requirements and must also meet the following criteria:

(1) The applicant has not been named as the inventor on a total of more than four utility patents (RPAs, not PPAs), design patents or plant patents. This also does not include certain international PCT applications and applications owned by a previous employer. In addition, the applicant had to have had a gross income in the previous year of less than three times the median household income reported by the Bureau of the Census. (The PTO publishes this "gross income limit," which is $241,830 as of this writing.) In the event that the patent application has been assigned, the assignee had to have a gross (not net) income of less than this limit; or

(2) the majority of the patent filer's employment income is from an Institution of Higher Education, or the applicant has assigned, or is obliged to assign the patent to an Institution of Higher Education. An Institution of Higher Education is a public or nonprofit accredited institution that admits postsecondary students for programs of not less than two years; that is, in most cases, a college or university.

How Do You Determine Micro Entity Status for Multiple Inventors? The rules apply individually to each joint inventor. So, no joint inventor can have been named as an inventor on more than four applications, and no joint inventor can have a gross income (as defined by the IRS) exceeding the "gross income limit."

a. Preparing the PPA

In keeping with our recommendation that you make your PPA look as much like your RPA as feasible, prepare your drawings and description as described in Chapter 8. Although you legally don't need to include the Background, Advantages, Description of Drawing Figures, List of Reference Numerals, Summary, Conclusion, or Abstract parts of the specification, it won't hurt if you do, and including these parts will make your PPA that much more effective if it is later

relied upon. Your drawings can be informal; they need not be inked or done carefully with a computer-aided design (CAD) program, but they (and the description) must be in permanent form (no pencil).

You also don't need to include any claims (discussed in Chapter 9). However, if possible, it is a good idea to draft some claims before filing the PPA, since this exercise will help you determine whether your detailed description includes everything necessary about your invention. Also some foreign jurisdictions may require that the application contain a claim to obtain priority.

PPAs: The Long and the Short

You can fully describe your invention by supplying the information contained in the Description and Operation sections of the Specification in the RPA (and drawings, if necessary). In others words, if you follow the instructions for drafting these two sections in Chapter 8, you will have an adequate PPA.

Generally, a richer or more fulsome PPA is recommended. This should include information contained in other sections of the RPA (the Background, Objects and Advantages, Drawing Figures, Reference Numerals, Summary, Description, Operation, at least one Claim, and the Abstract). If you follow the instructions for drafting these sections in Chapters 8 and 9, you will have a more-than-adequate PPA.

To give you an idea of the difference between the bare-bones and recommended PPA, compare two PPAs on the same invention: Fig. 3D provides an example of the bare-bones approach; while Fig. 3E shows a preferred, fulsome PPA. (An RPA filed on this invention issued as Patent 6,018,830 on February 1, 2000 and is titled "Adjustable Sleeping Bag With Drawcords.")

CAUTION

Provide a full description of your invention. While it need not be well written or use any legalese, your "description" MUST comply with the full disclosure requirements—that is, it MUST clearly teach how to make and use the invention and it MUST disclose the best mode or version you currently prefer, if it has several modes or versions. To this end, carefully review and follow the material in Chapter 8.

Your description should be written in as simple terms as possible so that a lay judge can understand it or can be easily taught to understand it. If the invention is technical or abstruse, start your description from ground zero, assuming your reader knows nothing about the field, and then gradually move up to the minimum technical level necessary, defining all technical terms. In addition, your invention must be in a statutory class (see Chapter 5, Section C, for more on statutory classes). For software inventions, this means that the invention must be intimately involved with hardware.

If you have several inventions, you can put them all into the PPA, even if they're not related. If you know of several embodiments of any invention, put them all in, even if you have doubts about the operability of any embodiment. The PTO will never read your PPA unless they need to verify that it supports an invention or embodiment that you are claiming in an RPA that you file within one year after you file the PPA. As with the invention disclosure, include as many embodiments of your basic invention as you can think of, even if some may not work. For more information on preparing a Provisional Patent Application, review *Patent Pending in 24 Hours*, by Richard Stim (Nolo).

b. Preparing the other filing documents

Now that you've prepared your PPA (long or short) including the description, drawings, and optionally a claim, you need to prepare a Provisional Application for Patent Cover Sheet document (Cover Sheet).

Preparing the Cover Sheet is very easy. Go to the PTO's site (www.uspto.gov), click on the "Patents" tab, then under "Apply for a patent" click on "Forms."

From there you'll see a screen that lets you select forms to download, including form SB/16, "Provisional Application for Patent Cover Sheet."

(The PTO recommends using the Patent Center version of this form.) Scroll through the forms or use the "CTRL + F" or "⌘ + F" keyboard function to locate form SB/16. (While you're at it, if you qualify for micro entity fees also download and save the form SB/15A (gross income basis) or the form SB/15B (institution of higher education basis), and download form AIA/14 "Application Data Sheet" because you'll need this too.)

Open the SB/16 form and fill it out (using your computer) with your name, city, state, and country. Click "Add" to add any additional inventors. Then type the title. Leave "Attorney Docket Number" blank or just put a short reference to your invention if you have filed or plan to file other PPAs. If you have a PTO Customer Number type it in the box, but if not, click "Firm or Individual Name" and some blanks will appear where you fill in your name(s), mailing address, and phone. Click the appropriate button regarding a U.S. government contract. If you have assigned (legally transferred) or are legally obligated to assign the invention to a company with more than 500 employees, check "No" under "Entity Status."

If you haven't assigned and are not legally obligated to assign, or are assigning the invention to an entity with 500 or fewer employees, check, "Applicant asserts small entity status under 37 CFR 1.27." If you qualify as a micro entity (ME), check the box, "Applicant certifies micro entity status under 37 CFR 1.29" and complete and include Form SB/15A (for independent inventors) or SB/15B (for institutions of higher learning). (See "Qualifying as a Micro Entity," above.) Type your name and date in the blocks at the end (leave the attorney's Registration Number blank), and sign the form in the Signature block. If there are two or more inventors, only one inventor need sign. You can sign the form using your computer by typing an "S" (slash-sandwiched) signature such as follows: "/ Mildred Phillips/" or you can print the form, sign it in ink, and scan it back to PDF.

With your PPA, Cover Sheet (Form SB/16), and Certification of Micro Entity Status (Form SB/15A or SB/15B) prepared, let's now go on to filing the PPA electronically.

c. Filing Electronically

You file a patent application on the PTO's Patent Center (patentcenter.uspto.gov). Applications are filed as Microsoft *Word* documents, with an option to file a duplicate copy in PDF format.

As part of its ongoing efforts to modernize and streamline patent application systems, the PTO now allows applicants to file new patent specifications in DOCX format. There are obvious advantages to online filing. You can (1) file an application anytime and from anywhere that has internet access, (2) obtain instant confirmation of receipt of documents and a Serial Number and Filing Date from the PTO, (3) send an application to the PTO without having to go to the post office to pay for and get a Priority Mail Express receipt, or having to wait for a postcard receipt, and (4) file an application without having to prepare an Application Transmittal, a Fee Transmittal, receipt postcard, or check or Credit Card Payment Form (CCPF).

Become a Registered eFiler (If Time Permits)

If you can wait several weeks to file, become a registered eFiler. You'll have to fill out a form to obtain a customer number, and send a notarized certificate to the PTO, obtain access codes, but as a registered eFiler you'll be able to track your application's progress and file additional documents or corrections. To register, go to the PTO's Patent Electronic Business Center page (www.uspto.gov/learning-and-resources/support-centers/patent-electronic-business-center) and navigate from there to instructions for becoming a registered eFiler; that is, click on "New Users" under the "New to Patents?" section, and follow the detailed instructions. If you can't wait several weeks, you can use Patent Center to file an application as an unregistered eFiler and register later.

To file your PPA electronically (whether you're a registered eFiler or not):

• **Organize your application.** Create a separate Application Holding Folder with a suitable name (for example, Derailleur PPA) and put in that folder the computer files for: (1) the PPA (Drawings, and Specification and optionally including Claims and Abstract), (2) the Cover Sheet (Form SB/16), and (3) Certification of Micro Entity Status (Form SB/15A if an independent inventor).

- **Prepare a PDF Application Data Sheet.** When filing electronically, the USPTO gives you a choice to either prepare your ADS ahead of time or the USPTO will generate an ADS electronically when you file your EFS application. If you want to prepare the ADS ahead of time (recommended), and you have a PDF program that enables you to fill out PDF forms, download a fillable EFS Application Data Sheet (PTO Form AIA/14) from the PTO's site. The PTO provides detailed instructions (Instructions for Application Data Sheet 37 CFR 1.76) for completing the ADS, and you should download and use them. You can find this 16-page guide at the PTO's forms page (see above). Download and follow the instructions.

Whether you prepare your ADS ahead of time or online, leave the Publication Information, Representative Information, Domestic Benefit, and Foreign Priority sections blank because (a) PPAs are not published, (b) you're filing pro se (without an attorney), and (c) you can't claim benefit of any earlier domestic or foreign applications.

Leave the Assignee section blank unless you are assigning (legally transferring) the application to another entity. You can sign the form on the computer using an S-signature (see above guide). Check both of the Opt-Out boxes. Leave the attorney's Registration Number blank. The program will automatically fill in the header blanks. Then, if you are completing the ADS ahead of time, save the completed form using a suitable name, such as "ADS.pdf," in your Application Holding Folder with your other application forms. Otherwise, it will be automatically added to your online application filing documents.

 TIP

Before uploading your electronic filing documents, take a dry run using Patent Center's "Training Mode."

- **Sign on.** Go to patentcenter.uspto.gov, click on the "New Submission" menu, then click on "Utility-Provisional."
- **Application data.** On the "Application Data" page in Patent Center, you will be given your ADS. The first option is to create a Web ADS as mentioned earlier. The second option is to upload an ADS that you previously prepared from a fillable PDF. The third option is to complete the ADS at a later time, although you may be charged a late fee. We recommend using the first option (Web ADS) because it provides real-time error checking and data validation that is not done for an uploaded ADS.

  In either case, fill in the title of the invention, a docket number for the application of your choosing (optional, but a suitable docket number can be something like "Krypton Derailleur"), and your name and Customer Number or address. It's best to copy this data electronically from your Data Sheet so that everything will be consistent. Click "Continue."

- **Upload Documents:** In the Upload Documents page either drag and drop files directly onto the page from your Application Holding Folder that contains the files of your application, or press the "Browse files" button and navigate to your Holding Folder. Select one of your application files, e.g., the ADS file, click "Open," and you should see it listed. The file will be recognized automatically as an ADS. When you choose to upload your Certification of Micro-Entity Status PDF, Patent Center will recognize it as being a Form SB/15. Repeat the above steps for each of your other PDF application files (*CoverLetter.pdf*, *Drawings.pdf*, and *Specification.docx*).

Patent Center immediately uploads and validates file formats and data, identifies PTO forms and most other document types, and tells you whether you are missing any documents (like your Cover Sheet), or whether any documents have the wrong format. If Patent Center can't automatically detect what file type you uploaded, use the drop-down menu to select "Edit document description," then choose "Application Part," then choose the description of the file's contents that will appear. When finished with all documents, click "Continue."

- **Calculate fees.** On the "Calculate Fees" page, select your entity size, which will usually be "Micro Entity," check the "Provisional" box, enter the number of pages in your PPA in the "Application Size Fee" box, and click the "Calculate" button. Your subtotal and total filing fee will be entered in the applicable boxes. Click "Continue."

- **Review and submit application.** This page will list your Application Data, all of your uploaded files, and a summary of the filing fee(s). If everything is okay, enter your first and last name and an email address under the "eFiler information" section, and click the "Submit" button at the bottom to bring up a submission receipt page with an assigned Application Number, Confirmation Number, date and time of receipt, and Total Fees due. Click the "YES! I want to pay now" button at the bottom.

- **Review fees and select payment method.** Unless you have a PTO Deposit Account or are set up for EFT, select "Charge Credit Card," then "Start online payment process" to bring up the payment page. Fill out the blanks and click the "Confirm" button at the bottom.

- **Acknowledgment receipt.** If everything is okay you'll get an Acknowledgment Receipt, which is analogous to the receipt postcard which was used for mailed filings. The Acknowledgment Receipt will list the Application (Serial) Number, the Confirmation Number, the application data and parts that you've filed.

Congratulations! You've bypassed the post office, filed an application electronically, and have gotten an instant filing acknowledgment, including a Serial Number. Select "Print This Page" to print the page for your records. In several weeks you'll get an official filing receipt by mail.

d. Filing by Mail

If you plan to file by mail (not recommended), your PPA should contain the following parts assembled in this order:

- Receipt Postcard
- PPA Cover Sheet—PTO Form SB/16
- Fee Transmittal—PTO Form SB/17
- Certification of Micro Entity Status—PTO Form SB/15A or 15B (if paying micro entity fees)
- Filing Fee—check, or PTO CCPF Form 2038 (if paying by credit card)
- Application Data Sheet (ADS) Form AIA/14 (optional but desirable)
- Drawings, and
- Specification (optionally including Claims and Abstract).

Preparing the Cover Letter, ADS, and Fee Transmittal is not difficult. For the cover letter, fill out and print Form PTO/SB/16 (which you can download from the PTO's site). Then, fill out the Fee Transmittal (Form PTO/SB/17, also on the PTO's site). Fill out the ADS (PTO/AIA/14) as instructed above. You can find current fees at the PTO website.

Read the Cover Letter form and fill in the name(s) and legal residences of the inventor(s), a title, the number of sheets of specification, and the number of sheets of drawings. The title and name(s) of the inventor(s) are tentative and can be changed later, so long as one inventor named in the PPA is also named in the RPA and that inventor's invention is claimed in the RPA and fully disclosed in the PPA. However, if your RPA contains any essential information that isn't in your PPA, you may not be able to rely on your PPA.

So again, be sure your description is adequate and complete.

You can file as a micro entity (ME) if you are an independent inventor or institution of higher education that meets certain requirements (see "Qualifying as a Micro Entity"). If you file as an ME, you pay 20% of the fees of a large entity. Alternatively, if you don't qualify as an ME, you may be able to file as small entity (SE) and pay 40% of the fees of a large entity. Complete the "Check or Credit Card" line (the fee schedule is in Appendix 4). If there are coinventors, only one inventor's signature and address is required.

If you want to get an instant filing date, obtain a Priority Mail Express envelope and label from your post office and complete the Priority Mail Express section. File your PPA as soon as possible.

Make a complete copy of all papers of your PPA and mount them in a separate "legal" file.

Attach a check or Credit Card Payment Form for the appropriate filing fee and a stamped receipt postcard. Address the front of the postcard to yourself and list on the back all of the papers you're sending for the PPA. Fig. 3F provides an example of a completed postcard. If you don't have any postcards, just use a blank 4" x 6" card (preferably colored, so it can be spotted more readily if mixed with other mail) and a postcard-rate stamp.

Provisional Patent Application of Ignatz Inventor and Imogene Inventress for "[Title of Invention]" consisting of ten sheets of specification, three sheets of drawings, cover letter, ADS fee transmittal form, $65 check (or Credit Card Payment Form) for filing fee, and receipt postcard filed today.

Fig. 3F—Back Side of Exemplary Receipt Postcard for PPA

Mail all papers to the address on the cover letter— that is, Commissioner for Patents, P.O. Box 1450, Alexandria, VA 22313-1450. If you use Priority Mail

Express (advisable), you can consider your PPA filed as soon as you receive the Priority Mail Express receipt from the postal clerk. About two weeks after you have mailed the PPA, you'll receive your postcard back, stamped with its date of receipt in the PTO and a serial number that the PTO has assigned to your PPA. If you use regular mail, the date stamped on your postcard will be the filing date of your PPA. Clip your postcard to your PPA cover letter.

e. After You File Your PPA

About a month later, you'll receive an official filing receipt from the PTO for your PPA. The filing receipt will contain your PPA's serial number, its date, the names of the inventor(s), the title, and so on. It will usually contain the notation "Foreign Filing License Granted [date]," which means the PTO hasn't classified your invention as restricted due to national security. (If the PTO has classified your invention as restricted for national security reasons, you will need to speak with a lawyer, and you'll almost certainly not be able to get rights to your invention in other countries.)

After you get the official filing receipt, you will never hear from the PTO again regarding the PPA. The ball is now in your court to file a timely RPA and to refer to your PPA if you ever need to rely on its date. Mount this in the file with your PPA. Now determine the date that is ten months after your PPA's filing date and mark this date on your calendar to remind you to consider following through with an RPA and possible foreign patent applications. If you don't file an RPA referring to your PPA within a year of your PPA's filing date, the PTO will forever disregard it.

8. PPA Checklist

If you do decide to file a PPA, here is a checklist to go through before you file it electronically or by mail to make sure that you've done everything correctly. Many errors can be avoided if you assemble everything, wait a day, and check everything again before filing.

PPA Checklist

- [ ] The specification and drawings clearly teach how to make and use all embodiments of the invention that you might later want to claim.

- [ ] Although it's not strictly necessary, your PPA should be in the format of an RPA, insofar as possible, so that it includes all the parts of an RPA's specification and is written as well and as clearly as an RPA should be. For the same reason, your PPA should comply with the Drawings and Specification checklists in Chapter 8.

- [ ] It is recommended that your PPA contain at least one claim so that you will become familiar with claims and the scope of offensive rights they provide, and also prevent any challenge to your PPA by foreign patent offices for failure to claim the invention as of your earliest filing date. Chapter 9 contains full instructions for drafting claims and checklist for the claims.

- [ ] If filing by mail, the PPA Cover Letter is completed, including Priority Mail Express section, to avoid possibility of loss in the mail and to get an instant filing date. If filing electronically the PTO's Application Data Sheet is completed and saved as a PDF file where you can easily retrieve it.

- [ ] If filing by mail, you've included a return receipt postcard with all papers being sent listed on the back.

- [ ] You've completed an ADS if filing electronically. (Also desirable if filing by mail.)

- [ ] If filing by mail, you've included a completed Fee Transmittal and Certification of Micro Entity Status (if paying the lowest fees for independent inventors).

- [ ] If filing by mail, you've included a Check or Credit Card Payment Form for the filing fee. If a check is used, it is payable to "PTO." Ensure that adequate funds on deposit or adequate credit are available. If filing electronically you have typed the credit card number accurately and adequate credit is available.

- [ ] If filing by mail, the parts are assembled in the above order. If filing electronically or by mail, you've made hard copies for your file.

- [ ] If filing by mail, envelope is addressed to:
  Mail Stop PPA Commissioner for Patents
  P.O. Box 1450
  Alexandria, VA 22313-1450

(Again, it is not necessary to file an Information Disclosure Statement or any prior art with your PPA.)

9. PPAs and Foreign Filing

As you'll learn in Chapter 12, there are two types of foreign jurisdictions in the patent world: those that are members of the Paris Convention and those that are not. If you file a PPA and then file in any Convention jurisdiction (for example, the European Patent Office, the U.K., France, China, Japan, Canada, Mexico, Russia, and so on, or if you file a Patent Cooperation Treaty (PCT) application) within a year, your application in the Convention jurisdiction will be entitled to the priority of your PPA's filing date. Thus, after you file a PPA, you can then freely publish and sell your invention without loss of any rights in any foreign Convention jurisdiction, provided you file in the foreign Convention jurisdiction within a year.

Unfortunately, non-Convention countries (for example, Ethiopia, Eritrea, and Somalia, Myanmar, and various island nations including Fiji, Maldives, and Micronesia) do not provide any priority, so you must file in these countries before you publish or offer your invention for sale publicly, as fully explained in Chapter 12.

10. What If You Make Changes to the Invention?

Note that you're not allowed to amend or add anything to your PPA. Thus, if you make any changes or improvements to the invention after filing a PPA, you should file a subsequent PPA to record any changes (unless they are minor, such as a change in material). Also, if the date is close to the one-year limit from the filing date of the PPA, it probably isn't worth filing a second PPA; instead, put the changes in the RPA. Your RPA can claim the benefit of more than one PPA and several RPAs may claim the benefit of one or more PPAs. Also, if a PPA contains several inventions, the RPA need not contain them all. Conversely, the RPA may contain several inventions even if its PPA contains only one. In this case the RPA will be entitled to the benefit of the PPA's date for only the invention(s) disclosed in the PPA.

K. Summary

Documentation of an invention is important to protect your legal right to assist in your creation of the invention. You should record conception of the invention, then build and test it, if at all possible, and then record your building and testing. You may record conception and building and testing in a lab notebook or by means of an invention disclosure. In either case you, the inventor, should sign and date the document and have it witnessed and dated. You should not use a "post office patent" to document your invention.

You may also file a provisional patent application (PPA) to obtain patent pending status. The PTO will never read the PPA unless you need to rely on its date later to obtain an earlier date for a regular patent application (RPA). The filing fee for a PPA is relatively small and it need not have claims or the formality of an RPA, but to be effective, the PPA must clearly and fully teach how to make and use the invention. To obtain the benefit of the PPA's filing date, the RPA and any foreign applications must be filed within one year and claim the benefit of the PPA. You may convert an RPA to a PPA and vice versa. Your RPA may claim the benefit of several PPAs. A PPA can contain several inventions, but you can rely on only those that the PPA fully and clearly discloses.

CHAPTER

4

Will Your Invention Sell?

A. Why Evaluate Your Invention for Salability?...86

B. Start Small But Ramp Up 86

C. You Can't Be 100% Sure of Any Invention's Commercial Prospects.........................87

D. Take Time to Do a Commercial Feasibility Evaluation..87

    1. The Positive and Negative Factors Test...87

    2. Factors Affecting the Marketability of Your Invention...88

    3. Applying the Factors...93

E. Check Your Marketability Conclusions Using the Techniques of
Consultation and Research 94

    1. How to Go About It 94

    2. Precautions to Take During Consultation 95

F. Now's the Time to Build and Test It (If Possible) 96

    1. Why Do It?..96

    2. If You Use a Model Maker, Use a Consultant's Agreement..................................96

    3. What If the Consultant Invents? 97

G. The Next Step..98

H. Summary 98

Inventor's Commandment 5

Don't spend substantial time or money on your creation until you have thoroughly evaluated it for commercial potential. You should proceed only after you are convinced that your creation can be sold profitably for a significant period of time.

A. Why Evaluate Your Invention for Salability?

Congratulations! If you've gotten this far, you've made an invention and have properly recorded your conception by a notebook or disclosure. You may have filed a Provisional Patent Application (PPA) to obtain a PTO filing date for your invention.

Now it's time to do two more things before proceeding: (1) evaluate your invention for commercial potential and (2) make a patentability search. While you can do these in any order, we recommend that you do the commercial evaluation first, as it is usually easier or cheaper than the search.

Why is a commercial evaluation so important? Because you won't want to invest further labor or take on financial risks without a reasonable expectation that your efforts and expenditures will be justified. We recommend you be reasonably confident that your invention is likely to make you at least $100,000 in profits or royalties, or at least 20 times the cost of what you plan to spend for searching, building a model, and patenting.

Keep in mind that if you come up with a technical breakthrough in a high-tech field, or a highly novel invention, you should consider patenting it even if you don't think it has immediate commercial value. That's because you may be able to license or sell your early patent very profitably some years later, and it will block later inventors from patenting it.

Common Misconception: Anyone who gets a patent will be assured of fame and fortune.

Fact: Fewer than one out of ten patented inventions make any money for their owners, mainly because the inventor did not adequately assess the commercial prospects of the inventions at the outset and because the inventor did not promote and market the invention adequately.

"It is to be remembered, that the pursuit of wealth by means of new inventions is a very precarious and uncertain one; a lottery where there are many thousand tickets for each prize."

—Eli Whitney

 CAUTION

Test marketing may prevent you from obtaining a patent abroad. In the United States, an inventor has one year to file a patent application (PPA or RPA) starting from his or her first public disclosure of the invention, but most other countries do not have this "grace period." Test marketing before you file will destroy your right to file a valid patent application in these other countries. (More on this in Chapter 12.) If you have any desire to protect your invention outside the United States, you should file your application before selling your product.

B. Start Small But Ramp Up

When you evaluate your invention for commercial potential, try to do it on a small scale at first in order to avoid a wasted expenditure. For example, if you make metal parts as part of building a prototype to test operability, try to have them made of wood or cardboard by an economical prototyping technique. You may also be able to make a virtual (computer-simulated) prototype. Similarly, prior to conducting extensive interviews, try to consult with a single expert to be sure you're not way out in left field. If your initial, small-scale investigation looks favorable and you don't run into any serious impediments, we advise that you then do it carefully, completely, and objectively, using the techniques of this chapter.

If after you do the full evaluation your idea looks like it has great commercial potential, but some other factor such as patentability or operability doesn't look too promising, don't make any hasty decision to drop it. Continue to explore the negative areas. On the other hand, if after a careful evaluation you are truly convinced that your invention won't be successful, don't waste any further time on it. The sooner you move on, the sooner you might find the next invention that will be successful.

C. You Can't Be 100% Sure of Any Invention's Commercial Prospects

There's only one question you need to answer in commercially evaluating your invention: If my invention is manufactured and sold, or otherwise commercially implemented (for example, as a process that is put into commercial use), and assuming it's promoted properly, will it generate a significant profit? Unfortunately, no one can ever answer this question with certainty. The answer will always depend on how the invention is promoted, how well it's designed, how well it's packaged, the mood of the market, the timing of its commercial debut, and dozens of other intangible factors. For example, if the Pet Rock came out now, rather than in the 1960s, it might be a complete dud. Similarly, if probiotic water was marketed in the '60s, rather than in current times, it probably would not have had as much success. Most marketing experts say that five "P" factors must all be "right" for a new product to make it: Production, Price, Position (its place in the market), Promotion, and Perseverance.

In addition to the "Five Ps," the packaging (outer box as well as the shape of the device itself) can be crucial to its success. Consider the Audochron clock, which indicates the time by three successive groups of countable chimes. Given this technical feature only, the clock probably wouldn't have sold too well. But a talented designer put the works in a futuristic case shaped like a flattened gold sphere on a pedestal in which a plastic band at the center of the sphere lit with each chime. As a result, it became a status symbol and

sold relatively large quantities at a high price; it even appeared in *Architectural Digest* magazine, shown in a photo of a U.S. president's desk!

The trademark you select for your invention (Chapter 1) can also make a big difference as to whether it's a commercial success. If you doubt this, consider Vaseline® hand lotion. The lotion would very likely have been just another member of the bunch, consigned to mediocre sales, had not some clever marketing person come up with the trademark *Intensive Care*. This helped make it a sales leader. Ditto for the Hula-Hoop® exercise device and the Crock-Pot® slow cooker, both of which certainly weren't hurt by evocative names. Even a concept as dull as roach traps was blasted into marketing stardom by the trademark Roach Motel® roach trap and its brilliant ad campaign ("Roaches check in, but they don't check out").

D. Take Time to Do a Commercial Feasibility Evaluation

Despite the marketing uncertainties, most experts believe that you can make a useful evaluation of the commercial possibilities of an untested invention if you take the time to do some scientific and objective work in four areas:
- the positive and negative marketing factors attached to your invention
- consultation with experts, potential users of the invention, marketing people, and others
- research into prior developments in the same area as your invention, and
- the operability of an actual construction of the invention.

Let's take a look at each.

1. The Positive and Negative Factors Test

Every invention, no matter how many positive factors it seems to have at first glance, inevitably has one or more significant negative ones. To evaluate the positive and negative factors objectively, carefully consider each on the list below. Using Form 4-1, Positive and Negative Factors Evaluation Sheet (we provide a downloadable version on this book's companion page; see Appendix 7 for details), assign a commercial value or disadvantage weight to each factor on a scale of –100 to +100, according to your best, carefully considered estimate. If the factor is irrelevant to your invention, assign a weight of 0.

For example, if an invention provides overwhelming cost savings in relation to its existing counterparts, assign a +80 or higher to the "Cost" factor (#1) in the positive column. But if it requires a high capital expenditure (tooling) to build, a –50 would be appropriate for this factor (#45), and so on.

The following balance scale analogy will help you to understand the positive and negative factors evaluation: Pretend the positive factors are stacked on one side of a balance scale and the negative factors are stacked on the other side, as indicated in Fig. 4A.

Fig. 4A—Conceptual Weighing of Positive versus Negative Factors Here

If the positive factors (those given a weight from +1 to +100) strongly outweigh the negative (those from –1 to –100), you can regard this as a "go" indication that is, the invention is commercially viable. Obviously this balance scale is just an analogy. It can't be used with any true quantitative accuracy because no one has yet come up with a way to assign accurate and valid weights to the factors. Nevertheless, you'll find it of great help in evaluating the commercial prospects of your invention. Before you begin your evaluation, read through the following positive and negative factors.

You should consider each factor carefully, especially if you assign a negative value, even if the negative value is merely due to the need to change or design and produce new production equipment. I've seen inventions and developments that were better in every way than what already existed, but which weren't used solely because the improvement didn't justify the cost of replacing existing production equipment, or the cost associated with manufacturing and promoting the device.

The factors of your invention with negative values are generally more important and require more consideration than do those with positive values, since if your invention fails, it will obviously be one or more of the negatives that causes it. On the other hand, the positive factors will be of great value to you when convincing a patent examiner as to your invention's patentability, or when selling the invention to a potential licensee.

2. Factors Affecting the Marketability of Your Invention

1. **Cost.** Is your invention cheaper or more expensive to build or use than current counterparts? An example where making something more expensive to build would be an advantage is a credit or eligibility card; a more expensive card would be more difficult to counterfeit.
2. **Weight.** Is your invention lighter (or heavier) in weight than what is already known, and is such change in weight a benefit? For example, if you've invented a new automobile or airplane engine, a reduction in weight is a great benefit. However, if you've invented a new ballast material, obviously an increase in weight (provided it doesn't come at too great a cost in money or bulk) is a benefit.
3. **Size.** Is your invention smaller or larger in size or capacity than what is already known, and is such change in size a benefit?
4. **Safety/health factors.** Is your invention safer or healthier to use than what is already known? Clearly there's a strong trend in government and industry to improve the safety and reduce the possible chances for injury, harm, and product liability suits in most products and processes, and this trend has given birth to many new inventions. But beware, some safety devices cause more harm than they prevent: For example, antilock brakes have caused

more skids and accidents than conventional brakes, because users tend to pump them, although they are supposed to be pressed continuously.

5. **Speed.** Is your invention able to do a job faster (or slower) than its previous counterpart, and is such change in speed a benefit? This advantage is important in software inventions.

6. **Ease of use.** Is your invention easier (or harder) to use or learn to use than its previously known counterpart? An example of a product where an increase in difficulty of use would be a benefit is the childproof drug container cap. This advantage is also important if you have a software innovation.

7. **Ease of production.** Is your invention easier or cheaper (or harder or more expensive) to manufacture than previously known counterparts? Or can it be mass-produced, whereas previously known counterparts had to be made by hand?

8. **Durability.** Does your invention last longer (or wear out sooner) than previously known counterparts? Generally, a long-lasting invention is an advantage. However, keep in mind that many products, such as disposable razors, have earned their manufacturers millions by lasting for a shorter time than previously known counterparts.

9. **Repairability.** Is it easier to repair than previously known counterparts?

10. **Novelty.** Is your invention at all different from all previously known counterparts? Merely making an invention different may not appear to be an improvement per se, but it's often a great advantage: It provides an alternative method or device for doing the job in case the first method or device ever encounters difficulties (such as from government regulation), and in case the first device or method infringes a patent that you want to avoid infringing. It also provides something for ad people to crow about.

11. **Convenience/social benefit/mechanization.** Does your invention make living easier or more convenient? The electric knife, the remote-control TV, and the digital-readout clock have made millions of dollars for their creators because these gadgets save labor and time (even though the time required to earn the after-tax money to buy

the gadget is often greater than the time saved by using it). Even if the invention has one or more serious drawbacks, if it mechanizes a manual operation, it may still fly. Consider the original Epilady® leg-hair remover: Even though its rotating spring ripped out leg hairs in an extremely painful manner, it became a great success because it eliminated shaving and depilatories.

At the same time, many industries have been kick-started by making an existing invention easier and more convenient to use. For example, Henry Ford didn't invent the automobile; George Eastman didn't invent the camera; and Steve Jobs and Steve Wozniak didn't invent the computer. However, all of these individuals created new industries by making existing inventions much easier to use.

12. **Reliability.** Is your invention apt to fail less or need repair less often than previously known devices?

13. **Ecology.** Does your invention make use of what previously were thought to be waste products? Does it reduce the use of limited natural resources? Does it produce fewer waste products, such as smoke and waste water? If so, you have an advantage that is very important nowadays and that should be emphasized strongly.

14. **Salability.** Is your invention easier to sell or market than existing counterparts?

15. **Appearance.** Does your invention provide a better-appearing design than existing counterparts?

16. **Viewability.** If your invention relates to eye use, does it present a brighter, clearer, or more viewable image? For example, a color TV with a brighter picture, or photochromic eyeglasses that automatically darken in sunlight were valuable inventions.

17. **Precision.** Does your invention operate or provide greater precision or more accuracy than existing counterparts?

18. **Noise.** Does your invention operate more quietly? Does it eliminate or turn unpleasant noise into a more acceptable sound? (Noise-canceling headphones fit this bill.) Or does it make noise in a desirable situation—for example, a device that produces a warning sound when an air purifier filter needs changing might be desirable.

19. **Does your invention emanate fewer (or more) unpleasant fumes or odors?** For example, the public would benefit by adding an unpleasant odor to a poisonous or harmful substance (as when public utilities add mercaptan sulphur to heating and cooking gas to alert users when leaks occur).

20. **Taste.** If your invention is edible or comes into contact with the taste buds (for example, a pill or a pipe stem), does it taste better? Even a foul taste can be an advantage, such as for poisons to prevent ingestion by children, and for telephone cables to deter chewing by rodents.

21. **Market size.** Is there a larger market for your invention than for previously known devices? Because of climatic or legal restrictions, for example, certain inventions are only usable in small geographical areas. And because of economic factors, certain inventions may be limited to the relatively affluent. If your invention can avoid these restrictions, your potential market may be greatly increased, and this can be a significant advantage.

22. **Trend of demand.** Is the trend of demand for your device increasing? Of course you should distinguish, if possible, between a trend and a fad. The first will provide a market for your invention while the second is likely to leave you high and dry unless you catch it in the beginning stages.

23. **Seasonal demand.** Is your invention useful no matter what the season of the year? If so, it may have greater demand than a seasonal invention, such as one related to sailboat navigation.

24. **Difficulty of market penetration.** Is your device an improvement of a previously accepted device? If so, it will have an easier time penetrating the market and obtaining a good market share than a device that provides a completely new function.

25. **Potential competition.** Is your invention so simple, popular, or easy to manufacture that many imitators and copiers are likely to attempt to copy it or design around it, or try to break your patent as soon as it's brought out? Or is it a relatively complex, less popular, hard-to-manufacture device, which others wouldn't be likely to produce because of such factors as the large capital outlay required for tooling and production? However, don't assume that something that's easy to copy is not worth patenting, since patents on simple devices are upheld and enforced successfully all the time.

26. **Quality.** Does your invention produce or provide a higher quality output or result than existing counterparts? For example, Blu-Ray™ discs provide much better audio and video quality than VHS® recordings.

27. **Excitement.** (The Neophile and the Conspicuous Consumer/Status Seeker.) If your invention can provide consumer excitement, either through sheer newness or through evidence of a costly purchase, it has a decided advantage. That's because purchasing cutting-edge gadgets, such as a friendly robotic rug vacuum, excites some humans. These purchasers are "neophiles" (lovers of the new); their excitement comes from having and showing off their new "toy." At the same time, purchasers of expensive products exhibit "status seeking" behavior when they show off an expensive or unique item that they've acquired.

28. **Ability to acquire status.** Closely related to the preceding factor (Excitement), a product's ability to acquire a desirable or prestigious status will make it very successful and more profitable once it acquires a desired status among one or more groups. As Kevin Maney explains in his book, *Trade-Off: Why Some Things Catch On, and Others Don't* (Broadway), this is why some teens will pay $3 for a smartphone ring tone that announces their taste but will balk at paying 99 cents for the full song. Maney says that products like the iPhone®, Tiffany & Co.® jewelry, certain concert tickets, and first-class airline seats can command a larger profit because of their desired status. But bear in mind that a product's status can diminish if the product or service becomes too popular or convenient.

29. **Markup.** If your invention is in an excitement category (that is, if it's very different, novel, innovative, or luxurious), it can command a very high markup, a distinct selling advantage.

30. **Inferior performance.** Yes, we're serious! If your invention performs worse than comparable things that are already available, this can be a great advantage, if put to the proper use. Consider the 3M Company's fabulously successful Post-It® note pads: Their novelty is simply that they have a strip of stickum that is inferior to known adhesives, thus providing removable self-stick notes. Here the invention may not be so much the discovery of an inferior adhesive as the discovery of a new use for it.

31. **"Sexy" packaging.** If your invention is or comes in a "sexy" package, or is adaptable to being sold in such a package, this can be a great advantage. Consider the Hanes L'eggs® stockings, where the package (shaped like an egg) made the product!

32. **Miscellaneous/obviation of specific disadvantages of existing devices.** This is a catchall to cover anything we may have missed in the previous categories. Often the specific disadvantages that your invention overcomes will be quite obvious; they should be included here, nonetheless.

33. **Long life cycle.** If your invention has a potentially long life cycle; that is, it can be made and sold for many years before it becomes obsolete, this is an obvious strong advantage that will justify capital expenditures for tooling and conducting a big ad campaign.

34. **Related product addability.** If your invention will usher in new product lines, as did the personal computer, with disk drives, printers, and software, this will be an important advantage.

35. **Satisfies existing need.** If your invention will satisfy an existing, recognized need, such as preventing drug abuse, avoiding auto collisions, combating terrorism or crime, or preventing airplanes from catching fire upon crashing, your marketing difficulties will be reduced.

36. **Legality.** Does your invention comply with, or will its use fail to comply with, existing laws, regulations, and product and manufacturing requirements? Are administrative approvals required? If your invention carries legal difficulties with it, its acceptance will be problematic no matter how great its positive advantages are.

Also, if the legality of a product is questionable, its manufacturer, distributor, or retailer will have difficulty in obtaining product liability insurance.

37. **Operability.** Is it likely to work readily, or will significant additional design or technical development be required to make it practicable and workable? Usually problems of operability will become abundantly clear when you try to build a working model. Many great-looking inventions such as the turbine automobile engine turned out to be "techno-fizzle" when built and tested.

38. **Development.** Is the product already designed for the market, or is additional engineering, material selection, and appearance work required?

39. **Profitability.** Because of possible requirements for exotic materials, difficult machining steps, great size, and so on, is your invention likely to be difficult to sell at a profit, or at an acceptable price level?

40. **Obsolescence.** Is the field in which your invention is used likely to be around for a long time or die out soon? If the latter, most manufacturers won't be willing to invest money in production facilities.

41. **Incompatibility.** Is your invention likely to be compatible or incompatible with existing patterns of use, customs, and so on?

42. **Product liability risk.** Is your invention in a "safe" area, such as a ruler, or in a problem area, such as drugs, firearms, contact sports, and automobiles? If so, the risks of lawsuits against the manufacturer, due to product malfunction or injury from use, are likely to be greater than average. For example, a client of ours invented an ingenious, economical, and highly useful device for preventing a revolver from being accidentally fired. But, alas, though he tried everywhere, he couldn't get any company to take it on because they were afraid of product liability lawsuits if the device ever failed.

43. **Market dependence.** Is the sale of your invention dependent on a market for other goods, or is it useful in its own right? For example, an improved television tuner depends on the sale of televisions for its success, so that if the television market goes into a slump, the sales of your tuner certainly will fall also.

44. **Difficulty of distribution.** Is your invention easy to distribute, or is it so large, fragile, or perishable that it will be difficult or costly to distribute?

45. **Service requirements.** Is your invention free from service requirements or will it require frequent servicing and adjustment? If the latter, this is a distinct disadvantage.

46. **Production facilities.** Almost all inventions require new production facilities, a distinct disadvantage. This is because the manufacture of anything new requires new tooling and production techniques. But some inventions require only a modest change or no change, a tremendous advantage.

47. **Inertia need not/must be overcome.** There's a risk in introducing any new product. When any invention is radically different, potential manufacturers, users, and sellers manifest tremendous inertia, regardless of the invention's value. An example of a great invention that so far has failed because of user inertia is the Dvorak typewriter keyboard, which, although much faster and easier to use, was unable to overcome the awkward but entrenched Qwerty® keyboard.

48. **Minor/great technical advance.** In the '60s, we got a client a very broad patent on a laser pumped by a chemical reaction explosion. We were very pleased with this patent. However, it was so advanced at the time that the technology behind it was not implemented until a military program adopted it in the 1980s. Unfortunately, the patent expired in the meantime. The same goes for the computer mouse patent, which expired in 1980, just before the concept became popular, and the roller-blade skates, the patent for which expired in 1985, just before the roller-blade craze started. An FRB-Dallas survey found that major innovations like the telephone, radio, dishwasher, color TV, microwave oven, VCR, computer, and cell phone took an average of 11.4 years to be owned by 25% of all U.S. households. The moral? Even if you have a great invention, make sure it can be commercially implemented within about 17 years.

49. **Learning required.** If consumers will have to undergo substantial learning in order to use your invention, this is an obvious negative. An example: the early personal computers. On the other hand, some inventions, such as the automatically talking clock, make a task even easier to do and thus have an obvious strong advantage.

50. **Difficult/easy to promote.** If it will be difficult, expensive, or will require a long time to promote and market your invention; for example, because it's technically complex, has subtle advantages, or is very expensive, large, or awkward, you've got an obvious disadvantage. But if it solves an omnipresent problem and is cheap and easy to market, this is a clear advantage.

51. **Lack/presence of market.** If no market already exists for your invention, you'll have to convince the public that they need it—that is, that you have a "product in search of a market." While not a fatal flaw, and while this type of invention can be most profitable, you (or your licensee) will have to be prepared to expend substantial sums on promotion.

52. **Crowded/wide open field.** If the field is already crowded, you'll have an uphill battle.

53. **Commodities.** If you've invented a new commodity —such as a better plastic, solvent, or grain—you'll face stiff price competition from the established, already streamlined standards.

54. **Combination products.** If you've invented a "combination product"—that is, a product with two inventions that don't really groove together, like a stapler with a built-in beverage cup holder, people won't be beating a path to your door. On the other hand, the clock-radio was just the ticket.

55. **Entrenched competition.** Despite its overwhelming advantages, Edison had a terrible time promoting his lightbulb because the gas companies fought him bitterly.

56. **Instant anachronism.** A clever inventor in Oakland, California, invented a wonderful dictionary indexing device that made it much faster to look up any word. However, he was unable to sell it to any dictionary publisher because computerized

devices have nearly completely displaced the printed dictionary. His clever invention, the subject of U.S. Patent 4,813,710, was an "instant anachronism."

57. **Prototype availability.** Although the presence or absence of a prototype should not affect the marketability or commercial success of your invention, in reality it will! If you have a prototype available, or can make one, you'll find that your invention will be far easier to market.

58. **Broad patent coverage available.** Keep this factor in mind and come back to it after you evaluate patentability. Obviously, if you can obtain broad patent coverage on your invention, this will affect profitability, because if you're the only source for a device that performs a certain function you'll be able to charge more than you would in a competitive situation. A legal monopoly is a capitalist's dream!

59. **High sales anticipated.** If you can anticipate a high sales volume for your invention—for example, for a device like the Hula-Hoop® that is relatively simple, cheap, and easy to market—this will be a very positive factor.

60. **Visibility of invention in final product.** If your invention is highly visible in or essentially constitutes the entire final product—for example the sneakers with heels that light up when walking—this will be a distinct marketing advantage to entice buyers who love the new. On the other hand, if the invention is hidden in the final product, such as a stronger frame for an automobile, this factor will not be a plus in marketing to end purchasers. (But it might be a benefit to car makers looking to reduce liability from accidents—know your market!)

61. **Ease of packaging.** If your invention is easy to package—for example, a small gadget that can be put in a cheap blister package—this will be a great aid in marketing. However, if it's difficult and expensive to package, such as a bicycle or hockey stick, this will obviously be a negative factor.

62. **Youth market.** Young people have substantial discretionary income and tend to spend more in many product areas than the rest of the population. If your invention is something that will appeal to children or young adults, it may command more sales than something that is not attractive to this age group.

63. **Part of a trending activity.** If your invention is trending among consumers, it will be far easier to sell. For example, when the lottery was legalized in California, a spate of lottery-number selection products appeared and sold briskly until the public's interest simmered down.

64. **Will a contingent fee litigator take your case?** A contingent fee litigator is a lawyer or law firm that will take your case for a cut of the recovery, usually measured by lost profits/sales. But they will take on your case only if they are likely to be paid enough to make it worth their while. Before filing your patent application consider whether, if your issued patent is infringed, there will likely be enough sales of the infringing device to get a litigator to represent you on a contingent-fee arrangement. If there aren't enough sales, or if the infringers are fly-by-night, irresponsible operators, most litigators won't take your infringement case on a contingent fee basis. This is true even if you have a strong patent that is clearly infringed. In other words, the law is far more accessible when substantial amounts are likely to be recovered.

3. Applying the Factors

Now that you have a grasp of the factors that can influence the commercial viability of an invention, complete Form 4-1 by assigning a weight to each listed factor, either positive or negative. Also list and assign weights to any other factors you can think of which we've omitted. Then compute the sum of your factors and determine the difference to come up with a rough idea of a net value for your invention. We suggest that you continue to pursue inventions with net values of 50 and up, that you direct your efforts elsewhere if your invention has a net value of less than 0, and that you make further critical evaluation of inventions with net values between 0 and 50.

The list in the previous section has many other valuable uses:

- Using the list may cause you to focus on one or more drawbacks that are serious enough to kill your invention outright. While you might be disappointed to discover that your invention lacks a bright future, imagine how much more disappointed you would feel if you pursued it, only to discover the drawbacks after investing years of hard work and a great deal of money.
- The list can be used to provide a way of comparing two different inventions for relative value so that you'll know which to concentrate more effort on.
- It can be used to "sell" your invention to the PTO or a judge if your patent is ever involved in litigation. As we'll see, an invention must be nonobvious to be patentable, and nonobviousness is best proved by new and unexpected (superior) results of the type listed above.

You now should extract all factors on the list of Form 4-1 that have any value other than 0 and write these factors and their weights on Form 4-2, the Positive and Negative Factors Summary (we provide a downloadable version on this book's companion page; see Appendix 7 for details). This sheet, when completed, will provide you with a concise summary of the advantages and disadvantages of your invention. You can use it in at least four valuable ways:

1. To provide you with a capsule summary of your invention for commercial evaluation purposes
2. To help you prepare the "selling" parts of your patent application
3. To help you to sell or license your invention to a manufacturer, and
4. To help you to get the PTO to grant you a patent.

Don't hesitate to update or redo Forms 4-1 and 4-2 if more information comes to mind—especially if that information has a high value (either positive or negative).

E. Check Your Marketability Conclusions Using the Techniques of Consultation and Research

Once you reach some tentative conclusions about the commercial viability of your invention, it's time to get a reality check.

1. How to Go About It

If your evaluation is more positive than negative, we recommend that you extend your investigation by doing some consultation and research. If you continue to get positive signs, extend your search still further until you've learned all you can about the field of your invention. This knowledge will also be of great benefit when you make your patentability search, prepare your application, market your invention, and deal with the PTO.

> **TIP**
>
> **Don't disclose ideas and information without utilizing appropriate confidentiality safeguards as discussed below;** otherwise you may lose rights.

Start by asking both nonprofessionals and experts in the particular field of invention for an opinion, and by researching the relevant literature. Nonprofessionals can often be an excellent source of information and advice, especially if your invention is a consumer item that they are likely to have an opportunity to purchase if it's ever mass-produced. Consult your lay friends and associates; that is, those who have no special expertise in the field in which you are interested, but whose opinion you trust and feel will be objective. Often you may find it valuable not to tell them that you are the inventor so you'll get a more objective evaluation. You may also want to inquire as to what price they'd be willing to pay. It's especially helpful if you've built a working model so you can show it to them and ask if they'd buy it and for what price.

Experts to be consulted in the particular field of your invention include any and all of the following who can supply you with relevant feedback:
- salespeople and buyers in stores that sell devices similar to yours
- engineers, managers, or technicians in companies in the field of your invention
- scholars, educators, or professors who do research in the area of your invention, and
- friends who are "in the business."

Naturally you may not know all of these experts. Getting to them will require the creative use of the contacts you do have so as to arrange the proper introductions. Once you do, however, most people will be flattered that you've asked for their advice and pleased to help you.

If you can afford to pay for an evaluation, you may want to consider using an independent invention evaluation service. One university-based service we recommend is the Wisconsin Innovation Service Center (uww.edu/wisc).

After you show your invention—preferably a working model—note the initial reaction of whomever you show it to. If you hear a "Well, I'll be damned!" or "Why didn't I think of that!" you know you're on the right track. However if a consultant rejects your idea, don't blindly accept the rejection; try to find out the reason and whether it's valid. Some people don't like anything new, so develop a thick skin and an analytical approach. Keep in mind the words of Charles Brower: "A new idea is delicate. It can be killed by a sneer or a yawn; it can be stabbed to death by a quip and worried to death by a frown on the right man's brow."

For your literature search, we suggest that you start with an online search, or by locating a research librarian who's familiar with the area of your concern. Large technical and business libraries and those associated with major universities are obvious places to start. The library literature that you should investigate includes product directories, "how-to" books, catalogs, general reference books, and patents if they are available. Product catalogs are also helpful.

Remember that the purpose of the literature search isn't to determine whether your invention is new or patentable (that's covered in Chapter 5), but rather to give you additional background in the field so you can evaluate the positive and negative factors listed above. However, while you're doing your literature search, you may find that your invention was publicly known before you invented it: you'll either have to drop the invention, or try to make a new invention by improving your first effort. You'll be surprised how much better a feel you'll have for your invention once you've done some research and become familiar with the field.

 TIP

This search also isn't the equivalent of the "patent search" that occurs before you apply for your patent. Covered in Chapter 6 is the more formal patent search, which obviously will provide you with considerably more background in the area of your invention.

2. Precautions to Take During Consultation

If you do show your invention to others or discuss it with them to any extent, a degree of care is mandatory to preserve the trade secret status of your invention and to prevent theft of your ideas, or to prove it in case it occurs. (See Chapter 1 for more on trade secrets.) Remember that any of the agreements discussed below are only as good as the parties who have signed them. Thus you shouldn't disclose your invention to anyone you don't trust or who you feel will not be reliable. Suing someone for breaching a nondisclosure agreement is no substitute for picking a trustworthy person in the first place.

Here are some good alternatives that can be used to protect your invention from being misappropriated by others:
- Have others sign a receipt or logbook entry indicating that they have seen your invention. The logbook entry can be simply a page in your inventor's notebook that says at the top, "The

undersigned have seen and understood Tom Brown's confidential [name of invention] as described on pages ___ of this book, on the dates indicated. The undersigned agrees to maintain confidentiality."

- Ask those to whom you show your invention to sign and date your disclosure as witnesses. Witnesses can hardly ever claim that they invented independently of you if they're on record as having witnessed your invention.
- Get your consultants to sign the Nondisclosure Agreement (Form 3-1). However, it may be difficult for you to ask someone who's doing you a favor to sign this agreement.
- Although inferior to the other devices listed above, send a confirming or thank-you letter before and/or after your consultation so you'll have a written, uncontradicted record that you showed your invention to the person on a specific date and that you asked it to be kept confidential. A confirmatory after-the-fact letter can simply say, "Thanks very much for looking at my [name of invention] at your office last Wednesday, July 3. This letter is to confirm that you agreed that the details of my [name of invention] should be maintained in strictest confidence. Thanks for your cooperation. Sincerely, [your name]." Make a copy of any such letter and keep a copy for your records.

While care in disclosing your invention is necessary to prevent loss of its trade secret status and theft, don't go overboard with precautions. Many new inventors get such a severe case of "inventor's paranoia" (the "P" in the "PGL Syndrome" discussed in Chapter 2) that they're afraid to disclose their brainchild to anyone, or they're willing to disclose it only with such stringent safeguards that no one will want to look at it! In practice, most stolen inventions are taken only after they're out on the market and proven successful. This is because thieves are most interested in sure things.

F. Now's the Time to Build and Test It (If Possible)

Now that you have completed the conceptual process of your invention, it's time to build and test a working model (prototype), or engage someone who will do it for you for a fee.

1. Why Do It?

If you haven't already done so, it's very desirable to build and test a working model (prototype) of your invention, if at all possible. The reasons: A working model will give you something real to show your marketing consultants, plus valuable information about operability, cost, technical problems, and most of the other factors on the positive and negative factors list. If it's impractical to build a working model, often a nonworking model, or scale model, will give you almost as much valuable data. For some inventions it may be possible to build a "virtual prototype" (computer simulation).

 CAUTION

Publication may cause a loss of patent rights. An inventor who authorizes publication of his or her invention—for example, the inventor posts details of the invention on a website—has a one-year period to file a patent application. Nevertheless, it is unwise for an inventor to publish before filing because the inventor will lose foreign filing rights and another person may see the publication and file their own application on it before the true inventor files, thus requiring an expensive and uncertain derivation proceeding.

2. If You Use a Model Maker, Use a Consultant's Agreement

If you can't build and test it yourself, many model makers, engineers, technicians, and teachers are available who will be delighted to do the job for you for a fee, or for a percentage of the action. Also there may be a workshop in your area that will supply you with tools, space, and assistance for a fee. If you do use a model maker or consultant, you should take precautions to protect the confidentiality and proprietary status of your invention. There's no substitute for checking out your consultant carefully by asking for references (assuming you don't already know the consultant by reputation or referral).

In addition, have your consultant sign a copy of the Consultant's Work Agreement (Form 4-3, downloadable via this book's online companion page; see Appendix 7 for details). Note that this Agreement includes fill-in blanks to describe the names and addresses of the inventor and consultant, the name of the project or invention (such as "New Sweater-Drying Form"), detailed description of the work to be done (such as "build a wire-frame, plastic-covered, sweater-drying collapsible form in accordance with plans in attached Exhibit A—finished form to operate smoothly and collapse to 14" × 23" × 2" (or smaller) size"), and manner of payment (for example—⅓ at start, ⅓ upon construction, and ⅓ on acceptance by you, the Contractor), and which state's law should govern (pick the state where you reside if the Consultant is out-of-state).

Note that we've provided (see paragraph 7 of the Agreement) that any changes in the work to be performed or payment to be made shall be in writing. We've done this because we've been involved in many disputes where the Consultant does additional or more difficult work and wants more money, but the parties' memories differ as to what changes were agreed to, if any.

The Agreement also requires the Consultant to perform in a timely manner or you can void the Agreement and pay only 50%, or have the Consultant pay an agreed-upon penalty for every day he or she is delinquent.

3. What If the Consultant Invents?

Since many consultants are quite clever, they often come up with patentable improvements, ramifications, or even better versions of the basic invention that they're hired to build, test, or develop. This naturally brings up the issue of who will own and be able to use the Consultant's inventions. Having been involved in many disputes in this area, we know that an ounce of prevention—that is, a prior stipulation as to who will own any inventions the Consultant makes—can prevent many misunderstandings, arguments, and even lawsuits later on.

With this end in mind, we've written the agreement to require the Consultant to disclose all innovations made to you, to sign any patent applications that you choose to file on the Consultant's inventions, and also to assign such inventions to you. Note also that the inventions that belong to you (the Contractor) are those that arise out of the Consultant's work under the agreement, even if conceived on the Consultant's own time. This is a customary clause in employment agreements (see Chapter 16) and is provided so that the Consultant won't be able to claim that a valuable invention made under the agreement isn't yours because it was made on the Consultant's time. Generally the Consultant will be a sole inventor (who should be the only one named in the patent application if the Consultant's invention can exist independently of yours), and a joint inventor with you if the invention is closely related to or improves on yours. (More on inventorship in Chapter 10.) This is because all of the true inventor(s) must be named as inventor(s) in all patent applications no matter who owns the application. We provide a downloadable Assignment of Invention and Patent Application (Form 16-3) and a downloadable Joint Owners' Agreement (Form 16-2) on this book's companion page (see Appendix 7 for details).

G. The Next Step

If you decide to go ahead, your next step is to search for prior art and confirm your invention's patentability under the patent laws. To do this, you should first learn the basic four legal requirements for getting a patent. (See Chapter 5.) Then, if it meets the first two of these requirements (that is, if it's protectable under the law and useful), make a formal patent search (see Chapter 6) to determine if it's sufficiently novel to satisfy the other two requirements. When you make this search, you'll also obtain valuable commercial information about prior developments in the area of your invention. For example, if you've invented a new electric toothbrush, your search shows 30 patents on electric toothbrushes, and you've never seen any of these in the market, you should seriously question the commercial feasibility of this concept, even if it's patentable.

If, on the other hand, your commercial evaluation leaves you uncertain, though you feel there's good potential, wait a while before proceeding. The passage of time may give you a new perspective that can make your decision easier. If after a couple of weeks you still can't make up your mind, it's probably best to proceed to the next step (the determination of patentability, including a search). If this determination discloses that your invention is already known or otherwise unpatentable, that's the end of the road.

But if it shows that you have a patentable invention, you should probably attempt to patent and market it rather than let a potentially valuable and profitable idea die without being given its day in the sun.

H. Summary

You should carefully evaluate the salability of your invention before filing a patent application, because a patent alone will not make you rich or famous— the invention must also become a success in the marketplace. Test marketing is a valuable activity, but keep in mind that under the new patent law (FITF), marketing, use, sale, or showing before filing will destroy your foreign-filing rights and will place your U.S. rights in jeopardy. (An exception occurs if the inventor publishes the invention, in which case, such publication will destroy only foreign rights and the inventor can delay U.S. filing for up to a year after publication. In general, such publication is not recommended.) Also consult with experts and consumers, but take precautions against invention theft by using a nondisclosure agreement and other safeguards. Building a prototype is invaluable for obtaining commercial and technical information, but if you use a model maker, you must also take precautions by using the Consultant's Agreement.

CHAPTER 5

Is It Patentable?

A. Patentability Compared to Commercial Viability	101
B. Legal Requirements for a Utility Patent	101
C. Requirement #1: Subject Matter Eligibility	103
1. Processes, Including Software	104
2. Machines	105
3. Manufactures	106
4. Compositions of Matter	106
5. New Uses of Any of the Above	106
6. Examples of Inventions That Don't Fit Within a Statutory Class	107
D. Requirement #2: Utility	107
1. Unsafe New Drugs	108
2. Whimsical Inventions	108
3. Inventions Useful Only for Illegal Purposes	108
4. Nonoperable Inventions, Including Perpetual Motion Machines	108
5. Nuclear Weapons	109
6. Theoretical Phenomena	109
7. Aesthetic Purpose	109
8. Tax-Avoidance Schemes	109
9. Human Organisms	110
E. Requirement #3: Novelty	110
1. Prior Art	110
2. Any Physical or Method Step Difference Whatsoever Will Satisfy the Novelty Requirement	114
F. Requirement #4: Nonobviousness	115
1. Nonobvious to Whom?	116
2. What Does "Obvious" Mean?	116
3. Examples of Obviousness and Nonobviousness	118
4. Secondary Factors in Determining Nonobviousness	121
5. Secondary Factors in Determining Nonobviousness of Combination Inventions	123
6. How Does a Patent Examiner Determine "Nonobviousness"?	125
7. Weak Versus Strong Patents	126
8. The Inventor's Status Is Irrelevant	126

G. The Patentability Flowchart 126

H. Don't Make Assumptions About the Law 129

I. Summary 129

Inventor's Commandment 6

One-Year Rule: If you (or someone who obtained the details of your invention from you) disclose your invention, you have one year to file a provisional patent application (PPA) or regular patent application (RPA). If you miss that deadline, you have given away your invention to the public, and the prior disclosure will now be considered a bar to your patent application.

Inventor's Commandment 7

To evaluate or argue the patentability of any invention, use a two-step process. First, determine what novel features (§ 102) the invention has over the closest prior-art reference(s). Novelty can be a new physical (hardware) feature, a new combination or rearrangement of two separate old features, or a new use of an old feature. Second, determine if the novel feature(s) is nonobvious; that is, does it produce any new and unexpected results or otherwise indicate nonobviousness (§ 103).

Here we deal with the specific subject of what's legally patentable and what's not. Over many decades, both Congress and the courts have hammered out a series of laws and accompanying rules of interpretation that the PTO and the courts (and now you) must use to separate the patentable wheat from the unpatentable chaff.

A. Patentability Compared to Commercial Viability

If you assessed the commercial potential of your invention and your invention received a passing grade, your next question might be, "Can I get a patent on it?" The answer is important because you may have a difficult time commercially exploiting an invention that isn't patentable, despite its commercial feasibility. You may be able to realize value from an invention by selling it to a manufacturer as a trade secret (a difficult sale to make!), or by selling it yourself using a clever trademark, or in some cases by relying on copyright protection and unfair competition laws (as explained in Chapter 1). But such approaches are usually inferior to the broad offensive rights that a patent offers. If your invention fails to pass the tests of this chapter, reconsider its commercial prospects and whether other areas of intellectual property will provide adequate offensive rights in the absence of a patent. You should consider the commercial viability and patentability tests separately, since commercial success and patentability don't always coincide. Your invention should pass both tests before you file a patent application on it.

B. Legal Requirements for a Utility Patent

The legal requirements for a utility patent can be represented by a mountain having four upward sections (see Fig. 5A), each of which represents a separate test that every invention must pass to be awarded the patent. The PTO is required by statute to examine every utility patent application to be sure it passes each of these tests. If it passes, the PTO must award the inventor(s) a patent.

The four requirements and the pertinent respective statutes are:

1. **Statutory Class (35 U.S.C. § 101):** Will the PTO consider that the invention fits into one of five classes established by Congress? Or put specifically, will the PTO regard it as either a:
   - process or method, including a new use
   - machine
   - article of manufacture
   - composition of matter, or
   - improvement on one of the first four?
2. **Utility (35 U.S.C. § 101):** Can the invention properly be regarded as a useful one?
3. **Novelty (35 U.S.C. § 102):** Will the PTO consider that the invention is novel—that is, does it have any aspect or feature that is different in any way from all previous inventions and knowledge, called the "prior art"?

4. **Nonobviousness (35 U.S.C. § 103):** Will the PTO consider that the invention is nonobvious from the standpoint of someone who has ordinary skill in the specific technology involved in the invention—that is, does it provide one or more new and unexpected results? (When dealing with design patents, the question becomes: Will the PTO consider the design nonobvious in an ornamental or aesthetic sense?)

As Fig. 5A shows, the first three tests are represented by relatively short steps. The last one, nonobviousness, is relatively high. This reflects the challenge facing patent applicants. In other words, the PTO will find that most inventions (1) fit within at least one statutory class, (2) have utility (or ornamentality for designs), and (3) possess novelty. However, most patent applications that fail (almost half of all patent applications that are filed) are rejected by the PTO because of an objection that the invention is obvious.

Design and Plant Patents

Design patent applications must cover a new, original, and ornamental design for an article of manufacture, (35 U.S.C. § 171), and are examined in the same way and must pass the same novelty and nonobviousness tests as utility patent applications.

Plant patent applications are subject to the same legal requirements as utility patent applications (35 U.S.C. § 161), except that the statutory class requirement (first test) is obviously not relevant: plants provide their own statutory class. Since plant patents are relatively rare and are of very specialized interest, we don't go into detail except to set forth the additional legal requirements for getting one. They are: (1) the plant must be asexually reproduced; and (2) the plant must be a new variety. These may include cultivated spores, mutants, hybrids, and newly found seedlings, but should not be a tuber, propagated plant, bacterium, or a plant found in an uncultivated state. You may also obtain a monopoly on a sexually reproduced plant under the Plant Variety Protection Act. (For more information, see Chapter 1.)

Plants, if they are man-made (or elements of man-made plants), can also be covered by utility patents. These plants can be reproduced either sexually (by seeds) or asexually (by grafts, cuttings, or other human means). Utility patents have also been issued for elements of plants, such as proteins, genes, DNA, buds, pollen, fruit, plant-based chemicals, and the processes used in the manufacture of these plant products. To obtain a utility patent on a plant, the plant must be made by humans and must satisfy the statutory requirements (utility, novelty, and nonobviousness). The patent must describe and claim the specific characteristics of the plant for which offensive rights are sought. Sometimes the best way to meet this requirement is to deposit seeds or plant tissue at a specified public depository. Many countries have International Depository Authorities for such purposes.

Although a utility patent for a plant is harder and more time-consuming to acquire than a plant patent, a utility patent is a stronger form of offensive right. For example, a plant covered by a utility patent can be infringed if it is reproduced either sexually or asexually. By contrast, a plant patent can be infringed only if it is reproduced asexually from the actual plant protected by the patent.

Because the utility patent owner can thoroughly prevent others from making and using the invention, does this mean the buyer of a patented seed cannot sell the resulting plants to the public? No, because according to patent law's "first sale" or "exhaustion" doctrine, the seed's purchaser can sell the resulting plants but cannot manufacture the seed line.

PATENT #1,234,567

Is it nonobvious?
(Does the novelty produce any new and unexpected results?)

Does it have any novelty?
(Is there a new physical feature, a new combination of separate old features, or a new use of an old feature?)

Is it useful?

Is it in a statutory class?
(Process, machine, manufacture, composition, new use?)

Fig. 5A—Patentability Mountain: The Four Legal Requirements for Getting a Utility Patent

---

The Patent Laws

Congress derives its power to make the patent statutes from the broad wording of the U.S. Constitution (Art. 1, Section 8), which states:

"The Congress shall have power ... to promote the Progress of Science and useful Arts, by securing for limited Times to Authors and Inventors the exclusive Right to their respective Writings and Discoveries."

The patent statutes, passed by Congress to implement the rights bestowed by this Constitutional provision, can be found in Title 35 of the U.S. Code (35 U.S.C.).

The statutes, in turn, authorize the PTO to determine its own Rules of Practice (which are relatively broad, and are found in 37 CFR 1.1, and so on).

The PTO also publishes specific guidelines for patent examiners in the *Manual of Patent Examining Procedure* (MPEP; see Appendix 2, "Resources: Government Publications, Patent Websites, and Books of Use and Interest").

Fig. 5B illustrates the relationship between these authorities. The complete MPEP is available on the PTO's website and it includes the patent statutes and the PTO's Rules of Practice.

Fig. 5B—Patent Authorities

Let's now look at each of these requirements in more detail.

C. Requirement #1: Subject Matter Eligibility

Following the 2010 Supreme Court case *Bilski v. Kappos* and later decisions, the PTO has placed a careful focus on determining whether an invention constitutes "patent-eligible" subject matter. After much uncertainty in the courts, the PTO has adopted a two-step test for this purpose. In Step 1, the PTO determines whether the claimed invention is directed to one of the statutory classes listed in the patent law, 35 U.S.C. Section 101. If not, the invention is not patentable. If the invention falls under (or can be framed so that it falls under) a listed category, the PTO determines in Step 2 whether the invention nevertheless is unpatentable due to court-created exceptions. This is a two-part analysis. In Step 2A, the PTO asks whether the invention is a "judicial exception" to patentability: a law of nature, a natural phenomenon, or a purely abstract idea—in other words, whether it is not strictly limited to human-made creations or measurable changes in the world. If the invention is so limited, then it is "patent-eligible." If not, then the PTO asks in Step 2B whether the invention is "significantly more" than the judicial exception—that is, whether it is more than just the unpatentable subject matter alone, but an application of it to achieve a patentable end.

In Step 1 of this test, the PTO must consider your invention to fall into one of the five statutory classes for it to be patentable. Fortunately, the five statutory categories established are very broad and comprehensive. To give you an idea of how broad, when Congress passed the current version of the patent law in 1952, it intended that "anything under the sun that is made by man" falls within the classes.

So the statutory class requirement is rarely an issue. Accordingly, you'll usually be able to squeeze most inventions into at least one category. In many instances an invention will fit into more than one category, since they overlap. This isn't a problem, since you don't have to specify the category to which your invention belongs when you file your patent application.

Let's discuss the five statutory classes in more detail, and see how Step 2 of the test applies to each of them.

1. Processes, Including Software

Also termed "methods," processes are ways of doing or making things that involve more than purely mental manipulations. (The PTO views pure mental steps as being under the "abstract idea" judicial exception.) Processes always have one or more steps, each of which expresses some activity and manipulates or treats some physical thing. Thus patents have been granted on a method of gripping a golf club and a method of using a keyboard.

a. Conventional Processes

Examples of conventional processes are heat treatments, chemical reactions for making or changing something, and ways of making products or chemicals. The PTO has even granted patents on processes for combing the hair to cover a bald area, analyzing essays for plagiarism, and for feeding chickens a special diet that results in better eggs. Although surgical operations can still be patented, it no longer makes sense to take this step, since the law exempts medical practitioners from infringing any patent on a medical procedure per se.

b. Software

Software has fared poorly of late at the PTO. Software inventions typically pass Step 1 as statutory "processes," but fail Step 2A because they involve the "judicial exception" of abstract ideas. In its 2014 decision in *Alice Corp. v. CLS Bank International*, the Supreme Court ruled that a particular software claim was just

a conventional, computerized implementation of a financial technique, thus tantamount to claiming the technique itself as an abstract idea with the software merely a non-inventive tool to implement it. Since then, the PTO and the courts have been vigorous in denying software applications, especially those whose advance is simply a better or more efficient way to gather data, perform a particularized calculation or known task, and/or output a result.

But just because an invention uses software, that doesn't make it automatically unpatentable. Software and other computerized inventions, including internet-based inventions, are patentable as a process under Step 2B if they do "something more" than simply use a general-purpose computer (GPC) in a conventional way. The first hurdle that a software patent application must overcome: GPCs are designed to run generic software, and using a computer in its intended manner isn't inventive! They are also designed to gather, receive, store, and retrieve generic data, perform arbitrary computations, and communicate data with other GPCs, along with a host of other conventional functions. Taking an algorithm or noncomputerized process and saying "apply it on a GPC as software" is no longer patentable after *Alice*. This is true even for computer algorithms that you are the very first person to create, and even if a computer can perform the process much faster or more efficiently than was previously known. But the Supreme Court was very careful to say that some software could still be patentable. So how do the PTO and the courts resolve this apparent contradiction?

Software is patentable if it solves a technological problem or limitation in a GPC or the internet itself. Examples of this sort of software upheld by the courts as patentable since 2014 include improving how hyperlinks work, improving how a database stores data, improving how internet content is filtered, improving how distributed data are stored and retrieved, limiting how software runs based on its authorization, making complex electronic spreadsheets more accessible, and protecting a computer against malware. One way to think of the difference is to ask, "Does my invention improve how computers or internet technology work generally, not just for a particular task or computation?" If you can answer yes, then the software is likely patentable after Step 2B (although you may still run into stiff resistance trying to convince the PTO of this, and might have to resort to the courts to get your patent).

The other way software is patentable is when its use is unconventional. Recently, the Federal Circuit (the federal patent appeals court) ruled eligible a software process for animating lip movements synchronized to spoken dialogue, because the process used software animation "rules" not performed by human animators. So, the use of computer software did not merely implement a noncomputerized technique, but improved it in a nonconventional way. And, software is patentable on an unconventional or special-purpose computer, such as an embedded system (like an implanted medical device), or a distributed data storage or computational system (like a supercomputer). To avoid a PTO rejection for ineligibility, the claims should call out the unconventional nature of the process or the computer. (Claiming is discussed below in Chapter 9.)

c. Business Processes and Methods

In its 2010 *Bilski* decision, the Supreme Court stated that "a business method is simply one kind of 'method' that is, at least in some circumstances, eligible for patenting." However, as mentioned above, if the business method consists of purely mental steps or an algorithm, merely implementing that algorithm using software does not provide the "something more" needed in Step 2B to convert the method into a patentable process. Various courts have held as unpatentable "fundamental economic practices" including contract manipulation and mitigating risk, insurance-related activities, processing payments, and placing orders. Certain "methods of organizing human activity" are also nonstarters as the subject matter of patents, including managing business relationships, satisfying or avoiding legal obligations like contracts and taxes, marketing and sales practices, behavior management, and so on. Courts tend to view these types of activities (and their supporting systems, if merely conventional) as more social innovation

than technological, and routinely deny initial grants of patent applications, and overturn already-granted patents in these areas. So, while a business method patent is not prohibited by law, getting one in practice is very difficult.

If your invention stems from solving a business problem and you still believe a patent is the best road to follow, think about technological hurdles you had to overcome to make it work, and frame the invention in terms of overcoming those hurdles. Alternately, if your invention improves business performance in a way that is not easily discoverable to outsiders, consider keeping it as a trade secret. (See Chapter 1 for a discussion of trade secrets and their relation to patents.)

2. Machines

Machines are devices or things used for accomplishing a task. Like processes, they usually involve some activity or motion that's performed by working parts, but in machines the emphasis is on the parts or hardware, rather than the activity per se. Put differently, while a process involves the actual steps of manipulation of an item or work piece (the machine that does the manipulation is of secondary import), a machine is the thing that does the manipulating and the steps or manner of its operation, and the process itself, or material worked upon, are of lesser import.

Examples of machines are smartphones, cigarette lighters, robots, sewage treatment plants, clocks, all electronic circuits, automobiles, automatic transmissions, boats, rockets, TVs, computers, printers, lasers, photocopiers, and a layout for a bank. Many machine inventions can also be claimed as a process and/or as a machine. For instance, an electric circuit or a weaving machine can be claimed in terms of its actual hardware and/or as a process for manipulating an electrical signal or weaving fabrics.

While most software inventions are claimed and regarded as processes, they can usually also be claimed and regarded as machines. A computer whose operation is improved using software is a new machine, after all, and is thus patentable. You may claim patentable software as both a process or method, and as a machine.

Conversely, claiming "means for" carrying out a new computation is no longer good enough, since the PTO will try to interpret those "means" as covering a GPC. Unless you also disclose a nonconventional device to run the software (or more generally, perform the process), the PTO can and will reject your application--often referring to "abstract idea" rejections of the corresponding process, despite the fact that your machine is a tangible thing and not at all abstract!

> **TIP**
>
> **There are no clear lines among the five statutory classes.** The important thing to realize is that it doesn't matter as long as your invention fits into at least one of them. Put differently, you needn't be able to tell a machine from a process to qualify for a patent.

3. Manufactures

Manufactures, sometimes termed "articles of manu-facture," are items that have been made by human hands or by machines. This excludes naturally occurring things, like rocks, gold, shrimp, and wood, or slightly modified naturally occurring things, like a shrimp with its head and vein removed. But if you discover a new and nonobvious use for a naturally occurring thing, such as a way to use the molecules in a piece of gold as part of a computer memory, you can patent the invention as a new use (see below), or as a machine (the gold with the necessary hardware to make it function as a memory).

Manufactures are relatively simple things that don't have working or moving parts as prime features. Clearly, you will see some overlap between the machine and the manufacture categories. Many devices, such as wearable fitness trackers and electric toothbrushes, can be classified as either. Examples of manufactures are desks, houses, wires, tires, books, cloth, chairs, containers, transistors, dolls, ladders, envelopes, buildings, knives, hand tools, and boxes. Nevertheless, for purposes of Step 1 of subject matter eligibility, it is not important *which* category an invention falls in, only that it falls in *some* category.

4. Compositions of Matter

Compositions of matter are items such as chemical compositions, conglomerates, aggregates, or other chemically significant substances that are usually supplied in bulk (solid or particulate), liquid, or gaseous form. Examples are road-building compositions, all chemicals, gasoline, fuel gas, glue, paper, soap, drugs, microbes, animals (nonhuman), food additives, plastics, and even chicken eggs with high vitamin E (see U.S. Patent 5,246,717).

Although, as stated, naturally occurring things such as wood and rocks can't be patented, purified forms of naturally occurring things, such as medicine extracted from herbs, can be. One inventor even obtained composition of matter patents on new chemical elements he discovered. (U.S. Patents 3,156,523 and 3,161,462 to Nobel laureate and one-time chair of the Atomic Energy Commission Glenn T. Seaborg, for Americium and Curium.) And recently, genetically altered plants, microbes, and nonhuman animals have been allowed under this category. Although genes have been patented, the Supreme Court ruled in 2013 that naturally occurring DNA was unpatentable. In that case (*Association for Molecular Pathology v. Myriad Genetics, Inc.*), a Utah company was the first to extract and isolate two genes apart from the human body. The Supreme Court noted three things: (1) Myriad had not tried to patent a *process*, only the isolated DNA, (2) it had not tried to patent any *new* use of the isolated DNA (i.e., to perform a medical treatment; see section 5 below), and (3) the Court hypothesized that the creation of a synthetic version of the genes might be patentable.

Compositions are usually homogeneous chemical compositions or aggregates whose chemical natures are of primary importance and whose shapes are of secondary importance, while manufactures are items whose physical shapes are significant, but whose chemical compositions are of lesser importance.

5. New Uses of Any of the Above

A new-use invention is a new and nonobvious process or method for using an old and known invention, whether it be an old and known process, composition, machine, or article. The inventive act here isn't the creation of a new thing or process per se, but the discovery of a new use for something that already exists.

If you discover a new and nonobvious (unrelated) use of any old invention or thing, you can get a patent on your discovery. For example, suppose you discover that your Venetian blind cleaner can also be used as a seed planter. You obviously can't get a patent on the physical hardware that constitutes the Venetian blind cleaner, since you didn't invent it—someone already patented, invented, and/or designed it first—but you can get a patent on the specific new use (seed planting) of the old hardware. In other examples, one inventor obtained a patent on a new use for aspirin: feeding it to swine to increase their rate of growth. Another inventor got a patent on the new use of a powerful vacuum to suck prairie dogs out of the ground. Note, however, that if your invention has any new hardware, your invention probably should be claimed as new hardware, rather than (or in addition to) a new use of old hardware.

New-use inventions are relatively rare and technically are a form of a process. (35 U.S.C. § 100(b).) Indeed, they must be claimed as a process. (See Chapter 9 for a discussion of patent claims.) However, we list them as a distinct category to make them more prominent in your consideration of your invention.

6. Examples of Inventions That Don't Fit Within a Statutory Class

The following are examples of "inventions" that don't fit within any statutory class and hence are non-statutory subject matter that cannot be patented:

- Processes that could be performed solely within one's mind (such as a method of meditation or a method of speed-reading), even if they can also be performed with pen and paper.
- Naturally occurring phenomena and articles, even if modified somewhat, such as a shrimp with its head and veins removed.
- Laws of nature, including abstract scientific or mathematical principles (John Napier's invention of logarithms in 1614 was immensely innovative and valuable, but it would never get past the

bottom level of the patentability mountain. However, Napier's "bones" (rods used to multiply by adding) would clearly be statutory subject matter.)

- An arrangement of printed matter without some accompanying instrumentality (that is, letters or text in the abstract); printed matter per se isn't patentable, but a printed label on a mattress telling how to turn it to ensure even wear, or dictionary index tabs that guide you to the desired word more rapidly, have been patented as articles of manufacture.
- Computer programs per se, naked computer instructions, or algorithms that don't manipulate hardware such as an algorithm for computing π.
- Ideas per se. Thoughts or goals not expressed in concrete form or usage are obviously not assignable to any of the five categories above. If you have an idea, you must show how it can be made and used in tangible form so as to be useful in the real world, even if only on paper, before the PTO will accept it. For example, an idea for a burping doll can be effectively patented by patenting a doll with a burping mechanism.
- Electrical signals. The federal patent appeals court (the Federal Circuit) held in 2007 that transitory electrical signals, like radio waves, are not patentable subject matter since they are not a composition or manufacture.

D. Requirement #2: Utility

To be patentable your invention must be useful. Problems are seldom encountered with the literal utility requirement; any usefulness will suffice, provided the usefulness is functional, and not aesthetic. (For manufactures that have useful aesthetics, consider filing a design patent.) Utility is occasionally an issue in the chemical area when an inventor tries to patent a new chemical for which a use hasn't yet been found but for which its inventor will likely find a use later. If the inventor can't state (and prove, if challenged) a realistic use, the PTO won't grant a patent on the chemical. A chemical or mechanical intermediate that can be used to produce another useful chemical or useful hardware item is itself regarded as useful—for example, a novel paper blank that can be formed into an insulated cup is considered useful. Software-based inventions usually satisfy the utility requirement, since virtually all software has a utilitarian function, even if used to create aesthetic designs on an idle monitor or to evaluate golf scores or mutual fund assets. The main problem with software-based inventions is that they may fall under a "judicial exception," as noted in the previous section. Nonetheless, a software invention should be tested for utility just like any other invention.

Notwithstanding the fact that virtually all inventions are useful in the literal sense of the word, the courts and Congress have decided that some types of inventions are "not useful" as a matter of law, and patents on them are accordingly denied by the PTO. Let's look at this more closely.

1. Unsafe New Drugs

The PTO won't grant a patent on any new drug unless the applicant can show that not only is it useful in treating some condition, but also that it's relatively safe for its intended purpose. Put another way, the PTO considers an unsafe drug useless. Most drug patent applications won't be allowed unless the Food and Drug Administration (FDA) has approved tests of the drug for efficacy and safety, but drugs that are generally recognized as safe, or are in a "safe" chemical category with known safe drugs, don't need prior FDA approval to be patentable. For example, one inventor was able to patent the use of chili peppers to treat baldness since chilies were known to be safe.

2. Whimsical Inventions

Occasionally, the PTO will reject an application for a patent when it finds the invention to be totally whimsical, even though "useful" in some bizarre sense. Nevertheless, in 1937 the PTO issued a patent on a rear windshield for a horse with a tail-operated

wiper (U.S. Patent 2,079,053). They regarded this as having utility as an amusement or gag.

Most patent attorneys have collections of humorous patents. Below are several from our collection:

- a method of exercising a cat (U.S. Patent 5,443,036—1995),
- a lawnmower attachment for a child's tricycle (U.S. Patent 4,455,816—1984),
- animal ear protectors (U.S. Patent 4,233,942—1980),
- a figure-eight-shaped device to hold your big toes together to prevent sunburned inner thighs (U.S. Patent 3,712,271—1973), and
- dentures with individual teeth shaped like the wearer's head (U.S. Patent 3,049,804—1962).

3. Inventions Useful Only for Illegal Purposes

An important requirement for obtaining a patent, which Congress hasn't mentioned, but which the PTO and courts have brought in on their own initiative (by stretching the definition of "useful"), is legality. For example, inventions useful solely for illegal purposes, such as disabling burglar alarms, safecracking, copying currency, and defrauding the public, might be incredibly useful to some elements in our society, but the PTO won't issue patents on them. As mentioned above, tax-avoidance schemes are not patentable.

However, most inventions in this category can be described or claimed in a "legal" way. For example, a police radar detector would qualify for a patent if it's described as a tester to see if a radar is working or as a device for reminding drivers to watch their speed.

4. Nonoperable Inventions, Including Perpetual Motion Machines

Another facet of the useful requirement is operability. The invention must appear to the PTO to be workable before they will allow it. Thus, if your invention is a perpetual-motion machine, or a metaphysical-energy converter, or, more realistically, a very esoteric invention that looks technically questionable (it looks like it just plain won't work or violates some well-accepted physical law), your examiner will reject it as lacking utility because of inoperability. In this case you would either have to produce a logical, technical argument refuting the examiner's reasons (you can include affidavits or declarations of witnesses and experts and test results), or bring the invention in for a demonstration to prove its operability.

Operability is rarely questioned, since most patent applications cover inventions that employ known principles or hardware and will obviously work as described. If the examiner questions operability, however, you have the burden of proof. And note that all patent examiners have technical degrees (some even have Ph.D.s), so expect a very stringent test if the operability of your invention is ever questioned.

Despite the foregoing, the PTO occasionally issues a patent on what appears to be a perpetual-motion-like machine, as they did in 1979 (U.S. Patent 4,151,431). This raises an important point. The fact that a patent is granted doesn't mean that the underlying invention will work. It only means that the invention as described on paper appeared to a patent examiner to work (or that the examiner couldn't figure out why it wouldn't work).

The PTO, however, has become more careful about perpetual-energy or perpetual-motion machines. Some years ago, it denied an inventor a patent on a perpetual-energy machine. The inventor took the case to the courts, but lost after the National Bureau of Standards (the predecessor of the National Institute of Standards and Technology, NIST), acting as a court expert, found the machine didn't have an efficiency of more than 100%.

It's a common misconception that the PTO won't "accept" patent applications on perpetual-motion machines: The PTO will accept the application for filing since filing and docketing are clerical functions. They are also happy to accept the government fees you will have to pay! However, the examiner (a degreed professional) will almost certainly reject it later as inoperative (giving reasons) after a formal examination.

5. Nuclear Weapons

The invention must not be a nuclear weapon; such inventions aren't patentable because of a special statute. (42 U.S.C. § 2181.)

6. Theoretical Phenomena

Theoretical phenomena per se, such as the phenomenon of superconductivity, the transistor effect, or the discovery of logarithms aren't patentable per se. You must describe and claim a practical, realistic, hardware-based application of your invention for the PTO to consider it useful.

7. Aesthetic Purpose

If the invention's sole purpose or "function" is aesthetic, the PTO will reject it as lacking utility; such inventions should usually be the subject of a design patent application. A beautiful vase of unique design, a computer case whose unique shape does not make the computer operate better, and a computer program for producing a low-brightness design on an idle computer monitor, where the only novelty is the aesthetic uniqueness of the design, are examples of inventions that the law considers to lack statutory utility. However, if the design has a functional purpose then statutory utility would be present. For example, if the shape of the vase makes it easier and safer to lift, or if the shape of the computer case makes it cheaper to manufacture, or if an airplane has a unique type of fairing that enables it to fly at supersonic speeds without buffeting, then the PTO will hold there is utility.

8. Tax-Avoidance Schemes

Section 14 of the America Invents Act (AIA) reads as follows: "[A]ny strategy for reducing, avoiding, or deferring tax liability, whether known or unknown at the time of the invention or application for patent, shall be deemed insufficient to differentiate a claimed invention from the prior art." (35 U.S.C. § 102 note.) However, inventions for other aspects of taxation, such as facilitating preparation of tax returns, are considered to have utility.

9. Human Organisms

Section 33 of the AIA states that no patent may issue on any human organism. (35 U.S.C. § 101 note.) So even if your daughter Alberta is another Einstein, you can't patent her.

E. Requirement #3: Novelty

Now let's look at the novelty requirement of a patent, which is often misunderstood.

1. Prior Art

Your invention must be novel in order to qualify for a patent. In order for your invention to meet this novelty test it must have some physical or method-step difference over all prior developments that are available to the public anywhere in the world. In the realm of patent law, these prior developments and concepts are collectively referred to as "prior art." Unfortunately, like many things in the law, the determination of what is prior art can be quite complex and involved. There are two main considerations: what qualifies as "art," and when art is "prior" to your patent application.

> ### Reduction to Practice
>
> The process of building and testing an invention is called a "reduction to practice," a term that had great importance under the previous First-to-Invent patent system. The filing of a patent application, while not an actual reduction to practice, was termed a "constructive" reduction to practice because the law interpreted it in the same way it did an actual reduction to practice. The filing of a valid Provisional Patent Application (PPA) also qualified as a constructive reduction to practice.

a. What Is Prior Art?

According to the patent laws, the term "prior art" means generally "the state of the art"; that is, all the knowledge existing or publicly available before the date of your earliest patent application. This includes any knowledge that was made publicly available prior to the filing date, unless such knowledge came from the inventor and was not disclosed over a year before the filing date. Prior art also includes a U.S. patent application of another inventor, that is based on an earlier foreign or domestic application and is entitled to the earlier application's filing (priority) date; the earlier application's filing date is the prior-art date. Finally, prior art includes prior use and on-sale activities of the invention, even if done in another country.

b. Date of Your Invention Under FITF

Under the First-Inventor-To-File (FITF) system, anything publicly known before your filing date is prior art. The exception: any disclosure that came from you or was derived from you, the inventor, and was not made over a year before the filing date is not considered prior art to you but it is prior art to anyone else. Thus under FITF, the "date of invention" is the actual filing date of a PPA or an RPA. An inventor will not be able to rely on any date earlier than the filing date of their PPA or RPA, unless the application is based on an earlier domestic or foreign application and is entitled to the filing date (priority) of such an earlier application. An inventor can rely on an earlier domestic application (parent application) for an earlier filing date if the present application is a continuation, continuation-in- part, or divisional application. An inventor can rely on an earlier foreign application for an earlier filing date if the present application is based on the foreign application filed in a "Paris Treaty" jurisdiction (discussed in Chapter 12) and claims the benefit of ("priority") of the foreign application.

c. Specifics of Prior Art

Now that we've broadly defined prior art, let's take a closer look at what it typically consists of, per 35 U.S.C. Section 102(a). The law distinguishes between two types of art: public knowledge, and PTO knowledge. The distinction is important, because each type of art becomes "prior art" at a different time, and can be excluded as prior art under different exceptions found in 35 U.S.C. Section 102(b). These exceptions prevent you from being penalized for your own, earlier work.

The first type of art includes patents issued anywhere in the world, printed publications, public use, sales, and any other knowledge "otherwise available to the public." These documents and acts become "prior art" as of the date they are publicly known. However, there are exceptions for disclosures you personally (or a joint inventor) make one year or less before you file your PPA or RPA (the one-year "grace period"), and for publications by others within that time frame that are based on what you earlier disclosed.

The second type of art overlaps with the first, and includes patents issued by, and PPAs and RPAs filed in, the PTO. The contents of these documents become "prior art" as of the date the PTO first knew about them; that is, when they were "effectively filed" in the PTO. (More on "effective filing" in Chapter 14.) However, they cannot be used against your application until the PTO publishes them. (The PTO does not publish PPAs, but RPAs can claim priority to them to receive an earlier prior art date.) There are similar exceptions preventing these documents from being prior art if their subject matter was obtained from you or a joint inventor, or based on your earlier public disclosure. There is a further exception if you owned the other patent or patent application when you filed your PPA or RPA.

Now that you know about the two types of prior art, let's cover the art that constitutes them in more detail.

i. Prior Printed Publications Anywhere

The "prior printed publications" category is the most important category of prior art and will generally constitute most of the prior art that you'll encounter.

Any printed publication, written by anyone, and from anywhere in the world, in any language, is considered valid prior art as of the day it was published. The term "printed publication" thus includes U.S. and foreign patents, published U.S. patent applications, books, magazines (including trade and professional journals), Russian (or former U.S.S.R.) Inventor's Certificates, and publicly available technical papers and abstracts. Even photocopied theses, provided they were made publicly available by putting them in a college library, will constitute prior art. The PTO has even used old Dick Tracy comic strips showing a wristwatch radio as prior art!

TIP

Computer tip. "Printed publication" includes information on websites; whether that information qualifies as "prior art" depends on whether and when it is "publicly available." This in turn depends on whether an interested person could find the information through reasonable diligence (for example, using search engines, the website's own search facilities, knowledge of the online address (URL), and so on). There's no hard and fast rule, but anything that shows up in search results will likely count as "prior art."

ii. U.S. Patents Filed by Others Prior to Your Application's Filing Date

Most of the prior printed publications that the PTO refers to (cites) when it's processing your application (and that you will encounter in your search) will be patents and pre-grant publications of patent applications, mainly from the United States. Any U.S. patent that has an effective filing date earlier than your effective filing date is considered valid prior art. This is so even if the patent issues after you file your application.

CAUTION

Because of the difference between the two types of art, the PTO can have knowledge of prior art that is not public for some time—18 months from its filing date in most cases, and even longer if the art is part of an RPA that has a nonpublication request (NPR) (see Chapter 10). Unfortunately, this "secret prior art" can spring up without warning and cause significant problems.

> **TIP**
>
> **A common misconception** is that only in-force patents (that is, patents that haven't yet expired) count as prior art. This isn't true. Any earlier patent, even if it was issued 150 years ago and has long since expired, will constitute valid prior art against an invention. Otherwise, patents would have a lesser status than other publications.

iii. Prior Publicly Available Knowledge or Use of the Invention in the United States

Under current law, prior public knowledge is prior art if it occurred before you filed your present application and was not made by the inventor in a patent application or was made by the inventor over a year before the application's filing date. For example, an earlier heat-treating process used openly by a blacksmith in a small town, although never published or widely known, is a prior public use that will defeat your right to a patent on a similar process. It has been held that allowing even one person to use your invention without restriction will constitute public use. With respect to public knowledge, an example would be if you gave a talk at a publicly accessible technical society. Recently, even a showing of a kaleidoscope without restriction at a party with 30 attendees was held to be prior public knowledge. Or as one writer commented, "Throw a party and lose your patent rights!"

For still another example of a public use, suppose that you invented a new type of paint and you use it to paint your building in downtown San Francisco. If the paint did not originate from the inventor and the paint was left on for even one day before the inventor files a patent application on the paint, then the patent application will be invalidated if the painting is discovered. That's because the paint will be considered prior art to the patent application. If the paint did originate from the inventor, the inventor has a year from the date the painting was done to file a valid patent application. Put another way, if an inventor (or someone who obtained details of the invention from the inventor) uses or discloses the invention publicly, then the inventor has up to one year to file a valid patent application on the invention. (But see the Experimental Exception described below.)

This public-use-and-knowledge category of prior art is almost never used by the PTO since they have no way of uncovering it; they search only patents and other publications. Occasionally, however, defendants (infringers) in patent lawsuits happen to uncover a prior public use that they then rely on to invalidate the patent.

> **TIP**
>
> **Experimental exception.** Under court decisions, if the prior public use was for bona fide (good faith) experimental purposes; that is, to develop an incomplete invention, it doesn't count as prior art. Thus suppose, in the "painted San Francisco building" example above, that you painted your building to test the durability of your new paint: each month you photographed it, kept records on its reflectivity, wear resistance, and adhesion, and as a result determined that your paint is superior to others and is therefore ready for patenting. In this case, you must file a patent application before you start any nonexperimental use. We recommend that you avoid public exposure or use of your invention until after filing your application, unless public experimentation is unavoidable.

iv. Your Prior Foreign Patents

Any foreign patent of yours or your legal representatives that issued before your U.S. filing date and that was filed over a year before your U.S. filing date is valid prior art. This category is generally pertinent to non-U.S. residents who start the patenting process in a foreign country. If you're in this class, you must file your U.S. application either within one year after you file in the foreign country or before your foreign patent issues. However, if you want to get the benefit of a foreign filing date for your U.S. application, you should file in the United States within the one year after your foreign filing date. (See Chapter 12.)

v. Prior U.S. Inventor

The patent application of the inventor who files first will be prior art to the later filing inventor and the first-inventor-to-file inventor will get the patent, unless the second inventor to file can prove, in a derivation proceeding, that the first-inventor-to-file inventor derived the invention from the second to file.

Common Assignee or Joint Research Agreement. However, there is an exception: If your invention is novel and the prior inventor and you were obligated to assign your inventions to the same person or organization (35 U.S.C. § 102(b)(2)(C)), or both of you were parties to a joint research agreement and your application is amended to disclose the parties to the agreement (35 U.S.C. § 102(c)), then the prior inventor's work won't be considered prior art. This exception permits companies with independently operating research and development groups working on similar problems to avoid denial of patents based on their own collaborators' work.

vi. Prior Sale or On-Sale Status in the United States

Under Section 102, the law also considers certain actions by humans to be "prior art," even when no paper records exist. These actions involve the "sale" or "on-sale" category. Suppose you (or anyone else) offer to sell, actually sell, or commercially use your invention, or any product embodying your invention, in the United States. Any offer, sale, or commercial use of an invention before the filing date of the application will defeat the application, unless the activity comes from the actual inventor, in which case the inventor has a year from the start of the activity to file a valid application.

> **TIP**
>
> **The type of sale or offer of sale that would bar your patent application must be a commercial offer to sell,** or a sale of actual hardware or a process embodying the invention. Such an offer or sale will defeat a later-filed application (unless it came from the inventor) or will start the one-year period running, even if the invention has not yet been built. This is true so long as it has been drawn or described in reasonable detail. On the other hand, an offer to license, or sell, or an actual sale or license of the invention in concept form or a patent application on the invention (not hardware) to a manufacturer will not defeat a later-filed application.

If someone sells hardware embodying the invention, that will be prior art. However if someone goes to a manufacturer and offers to sell or license the invention in concept form or a patent application on the invention (not hardware), or actually makes a sale or license of the invention in concept form or a patent application on the invention (not hardware), then this is not prior art.

Abandonment

If you "abandon" your invention by finally giving up on it in some way, and this comes to the attention of the PTO or any court charged with ruling on your patent, your application or patent will be rejected or ruled invalid.

> **EXAMPLE:** You make a model of your invention, test it, fail to get it to work, or fail to sell it, and then consciously drop all efforts on it. Later you change your mind and try to patent it. If your abandonment becomes known, you would lose your right to a patent. But if you merely stop work on it for a number of years because of such reasons as health, finances, or lack of a crucial part, but intend to pursue it again when possible, the law would excuse your inaction and hold that you didn't abandon.

---

d. Summary of Prior Art

If these prior-art rules seem complicated and difficult to understand, you're not alone. All you really need to remember is that relevant prior art usually consists of:

- any published writing (including any patent) that was made publicly available anytime before the date you file
- any U.S. patent (RPA) that has a filing or PPA date earlier than your date of filing
- any relevant invention or development (whether described in writing or not) existing before you filed, or
- any public or commercial use, sale, or knowledge of the invention before the date you file, unless the activity came from the actual inventor.

2. Any Physical or Method Step Difference Whatsoever Will Satisfy the Novelty Requirement

Any novel feature, no matter how trivial, will satisfy the novelty requirement. For example, suppose you've "invented" a bicycle that is painted yellow with green polka dots, each of which has a blue triangle in the center. Assume (this is easy to do) that no bicycle has been painted this way before. Your bicycle would thus clearly satisfy the requirement of novelty.

Rarely will an investigation into your invention's patentability (called a "patentability search") reveal any single prior invention or reference that could be considered a dead ringer. Of course, if your search does produce a dead-ringer reference for your invention—that is, an actual device or published description showing all the features of your invention and operating in the same way for the same purpose—obviously your patentability decision can be made immediately: Your invention lacks novelty over the "prior art." Another way of saying this is that your invention has been "anticipated" by a prior invention or conception and is thus definitely unpatentable. The concepts of anticipation and prior art are discussed below in more detail in Requirement #4—nonobviousness.

The law generally recognizes three types of novelty, any one of which will satisfy the novelty requirement of Section 102: (1) physical (hardware or method) difference, (2) new combination, and (3) new use.

a. Physical Differences

This is the most common way to satisfy the novelty requirement. Here your invention has some physical or structural (hardware or method) difference over the prior art. If the invention is a machine, composition, or article, it must be or have one or more parts that have a different shape, value, size, color, or composition than what's already known.

It's often difficult for inventors to distinguish between a physical difference and a new result. When asked, "What's physically different about your invention?" inventors usually reply that theirs is lighter, faster, safer, cheaper to make or use, portable, and so on. However, these factors are new results or advantages, not physical or method step differences, and are primarily relevant to nonobviousness (see Section F), not to novelty. That is, they won't help your invention satisfy the novelty requirement. Again, a new physical feature must be a hardware (including operational) difference—for example, a part with a different shape, a different material, a different size, a different arrangement of the components, and so on.

Even omitting an element can be considered novel. For example, if a machine has always had four gears, and you find that it will work with three, you've satisfied the novelty requirement.

Also, the discovery of a critical area of a given prior-art range will be considered novel. That is, if a prior-art magazine article on dyeing states that a mordant will work at a temperature range of 100–150 degrees centigrade and you discover that it works five times better at 127–130 degrees centigrade, the law still considers this range novel, even though it's technically embraced by the prior art.

A physical difference can also be subtle or less apparent in the hardware sense, so that it's manifested primarily by a different mode of operation. Here are some examples: (a) an electronic amplifying circuit that looks the same, but that operates in a different mode—say Class A rather than Class B; (b) a circuit that is the same physically but is under the control of different software; (c) a pump that looks the same, but that operates at a higher pressure and hence in a different mode; and (d) a chemical reaction that takes place at a substantially different temperature or pressure. All of these will be considered novel, even though they appear the same to the eye.

NOTE

Processes note. If your invention is a new process, you don't need any novel hardware; your physical novelty is basically your new way of manipulating old hardware. Any novel step or steps whatever in this regard will satisfy the physical novelty requirement.

b. New Combinations

Many laypersons believe that if an invention consists entirely of old components, it can't be patented. A moment's thought will show that this couldn't be true since virtually all inventions are made of old components. Thus, the PTO will consider your invention novel even if two or more prior-art references (actual devices or published descriptions) together account for all of your invention's physical characteristics. That is, if your invention is a new combination of two old features, the law will consider it novel. (Note that for two or more old references to be legally combinable to prevent your invention from being patented, the actual hardware or parts of the references don't have to be physically combinable: only the concepts inherent in the parts need be usable together.) For example, suppose you invent a bicycle having a frame made of a new carbon-fiber alloy and the prior art includes a patent from 1870 showing your exact bicycle and a magazine article from *Technology Today* from 2005 showing your exact carbon-fiber alloy: Even though these two references taken together show every feature of your invention, your invention still is considered to be novel under Section 102 of the patent laws since you're the first to "combine" the two old concepts. That is, your bicycle would clearly be considered novel since it has a new physical feature: a frame that is made, for the first time, of a carbon-fiber alloy. For your invention to be considered as lacking novelty and thus subject to rejection under Section 102, all of its physical characteristics must exist in a single prior-art reference. This is often referred to as the "single document rule"; in other words, if two separate documents are necessary to show your invention, it is novel under Section 102. But keep in mind, just because it's novel, useful, and fits within a statutory class, doesn't mean the bicycle is patentable. It still must surpass the tough test of nonobviousness (covered in the following section).

Another type of new combination which inventors frequently overlook is the new arrangement: If you come up with a new arrangement of an old combination of elements, the PTO will consider this a new combination that will satisfy the novelty requirement.

For example suppose you invent an automatic transmission where, for the first time, the torque converter is placed after the gears, rather than before; the PTO will consider that this new arrangement has novelty over the previous arrangement.

> *"Invention consists in avoiding the constructing of useless combinations and in constructing the useful combinations which are in the infinite minority. To invent is to discern, to choose."*
>
> —Henri Poincaré

c. New Use

If you've invented a new use for an old item of hardware, or an old process, the new use will satisfy the novelty requirement, no matter how trivial the newness is. For example, Dorie invents a new vegetable cooker that, after a search, she discovers is exactly like a copper smelter invented by one Jaschik in 1830. Dorie's cooker, even though identical to Jaschik's smelter, will be considered novel, since it's for a different use. (If your invention involves novel physical hardware, technically it can't be a new-use invention.)

If you're the type of person who thinks ahead, you're probably asking yourself, "Why are they bothering with novelty—isn't this requirement inherent in nonobviousness—that is, if the invention is found to be nonobvious won't it also be found to be novel?" Well, you're 100% correct. If an invention is nonobvious, *a fortiori* (by better reason) it must be novel. However, the law makes the determination in two steps (Sections 102 and 103), and most patent professionals have also found it far easier to first determine whether and how an invention satisfies the novelty requirement and then determine if it can be considered nonobvious.

F. Requirement #4: Nonobviousness

We're now entering what's probably the most misunderstood and difficult-to-understand, yet most important, issue in patent law—that is, is your invention nonobvious? Let's start with a "common misconception."

Common Misconception: If your invention is different from the prior art, you're entitled to get a patent on it. **Fact:** Under Section 103 of the patent laws, no matter how different your invention is, you're not entitled to a patent on it unless its difference(s) over the prior art is considered "nonobvious" by the PTO or the courts. Because Section 103 is the heart of all patent laws, we reproduce it below in its entirety:

35 U.S.C. Section 103 Conditions for patentability; nonobvious subject matter.

"A patent for a claimed invention may not be obtained, notwithstanding that the claimed invention is not identically disclosed as set forth in section 102, if the differences between the claimed invention and the prior art are such that the claimed invention as a whole would have been obvious before the effective filing date of the claimed invention to a person having ordinary skill in the art to which the claimed invention pertains. Patentability shall not be negated by the manner in which the invention was made."

Most of the time a patentability search will produce one or more prior-art references that show devices similar to your invention, or that show several, but not all, of the physical features of your invention. That is, you will find that your invention has one or more features or differences that aren't shown in any one prior-art reference. However, even though your invention is physically different from such prior art (that is, it clears Section 102 as Section 103 states), this isn't enough to qualify for a patent. To obtain a patent, the physical (or use) differences must be substantial and significant. The legal term from Section 103 for such a difference is that it must not be "obvious" or, commonly, it must be "unobvious" or "nonobvious." That is, the differences between your invention and the prior art must not be obvious to or anticipated by one with ordinary skill in the "art" or field of the invention. Because this concept is so important, let's examine it in detail.

1. Nonobvious to Whom?

It doesn't tell anyone much to say an invention must be nonobvious. The big question is, nonobvious to whom? Under Section 103, you can't get a patent if a person having ordinary skill in the field of your invention would consider the idea of the invention "obvious" at the time you came up with it.

The law considers "a person having ordinary skill in the art to which said subject matter pertains" to be a mythical worker in the field of the invention who has (1) ordinary skill, but who (2) is totally omniscient about all the prior art in his or her field. This is a pure fantasy, since no such person ever lived, or ever will, but realistically there's no other way to come even close to any objective standard for determining nonobviousness.

Let's take some examples. Assume that your invention has to do with electronics—say an improved flip-flop circuit. A Person Having Ordinary Skill In The Art (PHOSITA) would be an ordinary, average logic-circuit engineer who's intimately familiar with all prior-art logic circuits. If your invention relates to the fields of business or the internet, say a new method of detecting phishing (attempted fraudulent discovery of a password), a PHOSITA would be an internet software engineer of ordinary skill but extraordinary knowledge of everything internet-related. If your invention has to do with chemistry, say a new photochemical process, a PHOSITA, a typical photochemical engineer with total knowledge of all photochemical processes, would be your imaginary skilled artisan. If your invention is mechanical, such as an improved cigarette lighter or belt buckle, the PTO would try to postulate a PHOSITA as a hypothetical cigarette-lighter engineer or belt-buckle designer with ordinary skill and comprehensive knowledge. If your invention is a design, say for a computer case, the PTO would invent a hypothetical computer-case designer of ordinary skill and full knowledge of all existing designs as the PHOSITA.

2. What Does "Obvious" Mean?

Most people have trouble interpreting Section 103 because of the word "obvious." If after reading our explanation you still don't understand it, don't be dismayed. Most patent attorneys, patent examiners, and judges can't agree on the meaning of the term. Many tests for nonobviousness have been used and rejected by the courts over the years. The courts have often referred to "a flash of genius," and this colorful phrase became the title of a 2008 movie about the efforts of Dr. Robert Kearns to obtain compensation and recognition from Ford for manufacturing vehicles with intermittent windshield wipers, which the court held infringed his patent 3,351,836 (1967). Another colorful term that has been used is "a synergistic effect (the whole is greater than the sum of its parts)." One influential court said that nonobviousness is manifested if the invention produces "unusual and surprising results." Foreign countries commonly require an "inventive step." Technically, none of these tests is used any longer. This is because the U.S. Supreme Court, which has final say in such matters, decreed in the famous 1966 case of *Graham v. John Deere* that Section 103 is to be interpreted by taking the following steps:

1. Determine the scope and content of the prior art.
2. Determine the novelty of the invention; that is, the differences between the prior art and the invention.
3. Determine the level of ordinary skill of artisans in the pertinent art.
4. Against this background, determine the obviousness or nonobviousness of the inventive subject matter.
5. While doing so, also consider secondary and objective factors such as commercial success, long-felt but unsolved need, and failure of others.

Unfortunately, while in theory the Supreme Court has the last word, in practice it added nothing to our understanding of the terms "obviousness" and "non-obviousness." In the crucial step (#4), the court merely repeated the very terms (obvious and nonobvious) it was seeking to define. Therefore, most attorneys and patent examiners continue to look for new and unexpected (or unanticipated) results that flow from the novel features when seeking to determine if an invention is obvious.

Despite its failure to define the term "obvious," the Supreme Court did add an important step to the process by which "obviousness" is to be determined. In Step #5, the court made clear that objective circumstances must be considered by the PTO or courts when deciding whether an invention is or isn't

obvious. The court specifically mentioned three such circumstances: commercial success, long-felt but unsolved need, and failure of others to come up with the invention.

So, although your invention might not, strictly speaking, produce "new and unexpected results" from the standpoint of one with "ordinary skill in the art," it still may be considered nonobvious if, for instance, you can show that the invention has enjoyed commercial success. (See Chapter 4, section D for various factors that may be useful to consider here.)

Normally, before you file a patent application you won't be able to consider commercial success as a factor in determining patentability. Any sale by anyone who is not associated with the inventor will invalidate any later filed patent application. Again, in order to prevent theft and avoid problems, it is recommended that you file before you sell. Although you usually can't consider commercial success before you file, you can argue commercial success later to the examiner during the prosecution phase if your invention is commercially successful by then.

Under the reasoning of the *Graham* case, then, to decide whether or not your invention is obvious, you first should ask whether it produces "new and unexpected results" from the standpoint of one skilled in the relevant art. If it does, you've met the test for nonobviousness. However, if there's still some doubt on this question, external circumstances may be used to bolster your position.

The Court shed more light on the issue in its 2007 decision *KSR International Co. v. Teleflex Inc.* Although the Court did not give a clear test, it did give several examples of situations in which "obviousness" was present, including:

- Combining known elements to yield predictable results;
- Substituting one known element for another that operates similarly to obtain a predictable result;
- Applying a known improvement for one device to a similar device to make a similar improvement; and
- Choosing from a finite number of predictable alternatives with a reasonable expectation of success (so-called "obvious to try").

While this list is not comprehensive, it has at least given PTO examiners some direction when rejecting inventions as "obvious," and many rejections citing one or more of these *KSR* "tests" have reached the desk of the author.

In 2024, the PTO issued updated guidance for making a proper determination of obviousness. Their guidance does not have the force of law, but rather tries to aid their Examiners (and the public) to understand when an invention is obvious.

The guidance covers five topics. First, the guidance provides a reminder that the America Invents Act of 2012 changed the relevant time of the invention from "first to invent" (which must be proved, e.g., using witnessed lab notebooks) to "first inventor to file" a patent application (which the PTO can determine independently). Second, the guidance confirms that the five factors from the *Graham* case listed above are still the core of the obviousness test.

The third topic notes that the Federal Circuit (patent) Court of Appeals has implemented the five factors flexibly. In particular, the Person Having Ordinary Skill In The Art (PHOSITA) is not entirely uncreative, but may possess routine or workmanlike creativity, common knowledge, and common sense, and the PTO should consider how the PHOSITA would react to seeing your invention for the first time. Moreover, the prior art is not limited just to the references applied by the Examiner, but includes the understanding of the PHOSITA.

Next, the guidance indicates that Examiners have flexibility in providing a reason to modify prior art used in combinations. That is, there is no formalistic rule or talisman that can be consulted to determine why the PHOSITA might modify a first teaching to work with a second one. Rather, any "motivation" to combine references or modify them to work together may find its source in any place (including common knowledge) available to the PHOSITA, and need not be spelled out in the cited teachings.

However, the guidance is clear that this flexible approach does not negate the court-based requirement for Examiners to articulate their reasoning and provide enough evidence to support any refusal of your invention. The general level of reasoning and evidence required must be enough for you to understand their thinking, and plan next steps accordingly.

The fourth topic indicates that each time the PTO acts, its Examiners must consider all evidence before them. In particular, evidence and arguments presented in favor of nonobviousness should also be considered as to whether they present separate teachings or grounds that would support a refusal for different reasons. (For more information about the process of obtaining a patent and when Examiners can make refusals, see Chapter 13.)

Finally, the guidance notes that, although the process of determining legal obviousness is flexible, the PTO will still identify relevant facts and then articulate sound reasoning based on those facts when evaluating an invention for obviousness. Office personnel are called on to use their legal and technological expertise to determine how best to explain an obviousness rejection.

TIP

If you feel your head spinning, don't worry. It's natural. Because these concepts are so abstract, there's no real way to get a complete and comfortable grasp on them. However, if you take it slowly (and take a few breaks from your reading), you should have a pretty good idea of when an invention is and isn't considered "nonobvious."

3. Examples of Obviousness and Nonobviousness

First, for some examples of nonobvious inventions, consider all of the inventions listed in Chapter 2: the magnetic pistol safety lock, the buried plastic cable locator strip, "Grasscrete," the Wiz-z-zer™ top, the shopping cart, and so on. These all had physically novel features (Section 102) that were considered nonobvious (Section 103) because they produced new, unexpected results—that is, results that weren't suggested or shown in the prior art.

Although generally you must make a significant physical change for your invention to be considered nonobvious, often a very slight change in the shape, slope, size, or material can produce a patentable invention that operates entirely differently and produces totally unexpected results.

EXAMPLE: Consider the original centrifugal vegetable juicer composed of a spinning perforated basket with a vertical sidewall and a nonperforated grater bottom. When vegetables, such as carrots, were pushed into the grater bottom, they were grated into fine pieces and juice that were thrown against the cylindrical, vertical sidewall of the basket. The juice passed through the perforations and was recovered in a container but the pieces clung to the sidewalls, adding weight to the basket and closing the perforations, making the machine impossible to run and operate after a relatively small amount of vegetables were juiced. Someone conceived of making the side of the basket slope outwardly so that while the juice was still centrifugally extracted through the perforated side of the basket, the pulp, instead of adhering to the old vertical side of the basket, was centrifugally forced up the new sloped side of the basket where it would go over the top and be diverted to a separate receptacle. Thus the juicer could be operated continuously without the pulp having to be cleaned out. Obviously, despite the fact that the physical novelty was slight—that is, it involved merely changing the slope of a basket's sidewall—the result was entirely new and unexpected, and therefore was considered non-obvious.

In general such a relatively small physical difference (changing the slope of the wall of a basket in a juicer) will require a relatively great new result (ability to run the juicer continuously) to satisfy the nonobviousness requirement. On the other hand, a relatively large physical difference will need only minor new results for the PTO to consider it nonobvious. That is, in Fig. 5A (The Patentability Mountain) the height of the fourth step can be shortened if the height of the third step is increased.

As indicated, new-use inventions don't involve any physical change at all in the old hardware. However, the new use must be (1) a different use of some known hardware or process, and (2) the different use must produce new, unexpected, or unanticipated results.

EXAMPLE: Again consider the Venetian blind cleaner used as a seed planter, and aspirin used as a growth stimulant, discussed above. In both instances, the new use was very different and provided a totally unexpected result: thus both inventions would be patentable. Also, in another interesting new-use case, the patent court in Washington, D.C., held that removing the core of an ear of corn to speed freezing and thawing was nonobvious over core drilling to speed drying. The court reasoned that one skilled in the art of corn processing could know that core removal speeds drying without realizing that core removal could also be used to speed freezing and thawing. Accordingly, the court held that the *new* result (faster freezing and thawing) was *unexpected* since it wasn't described or suggested in the prior art.

The courts have held that the substitution of a different, but similarly functioning, element for one of the elements in a known combination, although creating a "novel" invention, won't produce a patentable one unless the results are unexpected. For example, consider the substitution, in the 1950s, after transistors had appeared, of a transistor for a vacuum tube in an old amplifier circuit. At first blush this new combination of old elements would seem to the uninitiated to be a patentable substitution, since it provided tremendous new results (decreased power consumption, size, heat, weight, and far greater longevity). However, you'll soon realize that the result, although new, would have been entirely foreseeable and expected since, just as in the carbon-fiber/bicycle case, the power reduction and reduced-weight advantages of transistors would have been already known as soon as a transistor made its appearance. Thus, although substituting them for tubes provided many new results, it didn't provide the old amplifier circuit with any *unexpected* new results. Accordingly, the PTO's Patent Trial and Appeal Board held the new combination to be obvious to a PHOSITA at the time.

A factor that works against inventors is that to most people, many inventions seem obvious once they understand the key ideas. So sometimes we have to convince the patent examiner, a potential licensee, or even a judge, not to use hindsight and to try to view the problem without knowledge of the invention in order to understand why it's actually nonobvious.

If you're still a bit misty about all this, put yourself in the shoes of an electronic engineer who, at the time of the replacement of the vacuum tube with the transistor, was skilled in designing vacuum tube circuits and was currently designing a flip-flop circuit. Along comes this newfangled "transistor" that uses no heater and weighs one-tenth as much as a comparable tube, but which provides the same degree of amplification and control as the tube did. Do you think that it wouldn't be obvious to the engineer to try substituting a transistor for the tube in that flip-flop circuit? Similarly, the PTO would consider obvious the substitution of an integrated circuit for a group of transistors in a known logic circuit, or the use of a known radio mounting bracket to hold a loudspeaker enclosure instead of a radio. Do you think that it wouldn't be obvious to the engineer to try substituting a transistor for the tube in that flip-flop circuit? Similarly, the PTO would consider obvious the substitution of an integrated circuit for a group of transistors in a known logic circuit, or the use of a known radio mounting bracket to hold a loudspeaker enclosure instead of a radio. The Federal Circuit Court of Appeals held in a 2007 decision (*In re Comiskey*) that "the routine substitution of modern electronics to an otherwise unpatentable invention typically creates a prima facie [on its face] case of obviousness."

The PTO will also consider as obvious the mere carrying forward of an old concept, or a change in form and degree, without a new result. For instance, when one inventor provided notches on the inner rim of a steering wheel to provide a better grip, the idea was held to be obvious because of medieval sword handles that had similar notches for the same purpose. And the use of a large pulley for a logging rig was held nonpatentable in view of a small pulley for clotheslines. These situations are known as "obviousness by analogy."

On the other hand, one inventor merely changed the slope of a part in a papermaking (Fourdrinier) machine; as a result the machine's output increased by 25%—a dramatic, new, and unexpected result that was held patentable.

In the recipe field it's usually difficult to come up with an nonobvious invention, since most ingredients and their effects are known.

> **EXAMPLE:** Lou comes up with a way to make mustard-flavored hot dog buns—admix powdered mustard with the flour. Even though Lou's recipe is novel, the PTO will almost certainly hold it to be obvious to a PHOSITA since the result of the new combination was entirely foreseeable and expected.

In sum, the PTO will usually hold that substitution of a different material, shape, color, or size is obvious. But if the substitution provides *unexpected* new results, the law will hold it to be nonobvious.

The courts and the PTO will also usually consider the duplication of a part obvious unless it can see new results. For instance, in an automobile, the substitution of two banks of three cylinders with two carburetors was held obvious over a six-cylinder, single-carburetor engine, since the new arrangement had no unexpected advantages. However, the use of two water turbines to provide cross flow to eliminate axial thrust on bearings was held nonobvious over a single turbine; again, an *unexpected* new result.

Similarly, making devices portable, making parts smaller or larger, faster or slower, effecting a substitution of equivalents (a roller bearing for a ball bearing), making elements adjustable, making parts integral, separable (modular), or in kit form, and other known techniques with their known advantages, will be held obvious unless new, unexpected results can be shown.

Occasionally an inventor will believe that an invention should be considered patentable because it is disposable. As a general rule, that assumption is incorrect. Making products disposable is an old and obvious expedient that has been done with cameras, razors, ballpoint pens, and cigarette lighters. Further, the term "disposable" is too vague to be used in a claim anyway since everything ultimately wears out and thus is disposable. (See Chapter 9 for more information about claims language.) However if you have found a new and nonobvious way to make a product more cheaply so that it can be discarded and a new one purchased at a relatively low expense, then the novel way of making it can be patentable.

EXAMPLE: Elaine discovers a new, cheap paper material that can be used to make soft, wearable underwear more cheaply so that it can be discarded after one day's use and at relatively low expense. Elaine's underwear or other garments made of her new paper material is probably patentable, as is the new paper material per se.

CAUTION

If you create what you believe to be a valuable invention, but it seems simple and obvious to you, don't assume automatically that it's legally obvious. Some very simple inventions, like the vegetable juicer and the Fourdrinier machine, have been granted very valuable patents!

NOTE

Design patent tip. In design cases, the design must have novel features, and the PTO must be able to regard these as nonobvious to a designer of ordinary skill (a PHOSITA). If the design involves the use of known techniques that together don't produce any new and unexpected visual effect, then the PTO will consider it obvious. But if they produce a startling or unique new appearance, then the PTO will hold it to be nonobvious. Since only the ornamental appearance and not the function of a design is relevant, the degree of novelty of the design will be the main determinant of nonobviousness: a high degree of novelty will always be patentable, while a low degree of novelty will encounter rough sledding unless you can set forth reasons why it has a very different appearance or visual effect.

4. Secondary Factors in Determining Nonobviousness

As mentioned, if the new and unexpected results of your invention are marginal, you *may* still be able to get a patent if you can show that your invention possesses one or more secondary factors that establish nonobviousness. The PTO and the courts usually give these secondary factors much less weight than the "new and unexpected results" factor, but they still should be considered, especially in close cases. While the Supreme Court listed only three secondary factors in the *John Deere* case, we have compiled a list of 12 basic and nine combinatory secondary factors that the PTO and the courts actually consider. In the real world, these secondary factors must generally be dealt with only if the PTO makes a preliminary finding of obviousness or if your invention is attacked as being obvious. However, when deciding whether your invention is legally entitled to a patent, you'll have a much better idea of how easy or difficult it will be to obtain if you apply these secondary factors to your invention.

SKIP AHEAD

If you're sure that your invention is nonobvious, feel free to skip directly to Section 7.

Although some of these secondary factors may appear similar, try to consider each independently, since the courts have recognized subtle differences between them. As part of doing this, remember that lawyers like to chop large arguments into little ones so that it will appear that there are a multitude of reasons for their position rather than just one or two. While this approach may seem silly, it's nevertheless a fact (however sad) that the PTO and courts are used to hearing almost exclusively from lawyers (and, in the case of the PTO, from highly specialized patent agents). Accordingly, the general rule is, the more arguments you can use to claim nonobviousness, the better your chances will be of getting a patent.

Now let's look at the secondary factors in detail.

Factor 1. Previous failure of others

If the invention is successful where previous workers in the field were unable to make it work, this will be of great help to your application. For instance, many previous attempts were made to use electrostatic methods for making photocopies, but all failed. Chester Carlson (a patent attorney himself) came along and successfully used an electrostatic process to make copies. This greatly enhanced his case for the patentability of his dry (xerographic) photocopying process.

Factor 2. Solves an unrecognized problem

Here the essence of your invention is probably the recognition of the problem, rather than its solution. Consider the showerhead that automatically shuts off in case of excess water temperature discussed in Chapter 2. As the problem was probably never recognized in the prior art, the solution would therefore probably be patentable.

Factor 3. Solves an insoluble problem

Suppose that for years those skilled in the art had tried and failed to solve a problem and the art and literature were full of unsuccessful "solutions." Along you come and finally find a workable solution, such as a cure for the common cold: you'd probably get a patent.

> **EXAMPLE:** Potato chips used to be sold in relatively expensive, heavy cardboard boxes that manu-facturers thought were necessary to protect against chip breakage. Yet, many chips still broke. Someone thought of packaging the chips in plastic bags that were far cheaper, lighter, and actually reduced the amount of breakage. This invention also satisfies Factor 12.

Factor 4. Commercial success

If your invention has attained commercial success by the time the crucial patentability decision is made, this militates strongly in favor of patentability. Nothing succeeds like success, right?

Factor 5. Crowded art

If your invention is in a crowded field (art)—that is, a field that is mature and that contains many patents, such as electrical connectors or bicycles— a small advance will go farther toward qualifying the invention for a patent than it will in a new, blossoming art.

Factor 6. Omission of element

If you can omit an element in a prior invention without loss of capability, this will count a lot, since parts are expensive, unreliable, heavy, and labor-intensive. A good example is the elimination of the inner tube in tires.

Factor 7. Unsuggested modification

If you can modify a prior invention in a manner not suggested before, such as by increasing the slope in a paper-making machine, or by making the basket slope in a centrifugal juice extractor, this act in itself counts for patentability.

Factor 8. Unappreciated advantage

If your invention provides an advantage that was never before appreciated, it can make a difference. One inventor came up with a gas cap that was impossible to insert in a skewed manner. It was held to be patentable since it provided an advantage that was never appreciated previously.

Factor 9. Solves prior inoperability

If your invention provides an operative result where before only inoperability existed, then it has a good chance for a patent. For instance, suppose you come up with a jet fuel additive that prevents huge fires in case of a plane crash; you've got it made, since all previous fire suppressant additives have been largely unsuccessful.

Factor 10. Successful implementation of ancient idea

Consider the Wright brothers' airplane. For millennia humans had wanted to fly and had tried many schemes unsuccessfully. The successful implementation of such an ancient desire carries great weight when it comes to getting a patent. (See also Factor 1.)

Factor 11. Solution of long-felt need

Suppose you find a way to prevent tailgate-type automobile crashes. Obviously you've solved a powerful need and your solution will be a heavy weight in your favor on the scales of patentability.

Factor 12. Contrary to prior art's teaching

If the prior art expressly teaches that something can't be done or is impractical—for example, humans can't fly without artificial propulsion motors—and you prove this teaching wrong, you've got it made. For example, one inventor realized that packaging potato chips in inexpensive bags (compared to more expensive boxes) actually decreased the amount of breakage. This contrarian discovery militated strongly in favor of nonobviousness.

5. Secondary Factors in Determining Nonobviousness of Combination Inventions

Inventions that combine two or more elements known in the prior art can still be held patentable, provided that the combination can be considered nonobvious— that is, it's a new combination and it produces new and unexpected results. In fact, most patents are granted on such combinations since very few truly new things are ever discovered. So let's examine some of the factors used especially to determine the patentability of "combination inventions" (that is, inventions that have two or more features that are shown in two or more prior-art references).

SKIP AHEAD

The following material is conceptually quite abstract and difficult to understand, even for patent attorneys. We're presenting it in the interest of completeness. However, if you wish, you can safely skip it for now and proceed directly to Section 6. If the PTO or anyone else suggests that two or more prior-art references, taken together, teach that your invention is obvious, come back and read it then.

Factor 13. Synergism (2 + 2 = 5)

If the results achieved by your combination are greater than the sum of the separate results of its parts, this can indicate nonobviousness. Consider the pistol trigger release (Chapter 2) where a magnetic ring must be worn to fire the pistol. The results (increased police safety) are far in excess of what magnets, rings, and pistols could provide separately.

> EXAMPLE: For another example, suppose that a chemist combines, through experimentation, several metals that cooperate in a new way to provide added strength without added density. If this synergistic result wasn't reasonably foreseeable by a metallurgist, the new alloy would almost certainly be patentable.

Generally, if your invention is a chemical mixture, the mixture must do more than the sum of its components. For this reason, food recipes are difficult to patent unless an ingredient does more than its usual function or produces a new and unexpected result. Or, if you come up with a new technique of cooking that produces a new and unexpected result—for example, a cookie that is chewy inside and crisp outside—you've got a good chance of prevailing. Similarly, if you combine various mechanical or electrical components, the courts and the PTO will usually consider the combination patentable if it provides more than the functions of its individual components.

As an example of an unpatentable combination without synergism, consider the combination of a radio, waffle iron, and blender in one housing. While novel and useful, this combination would be considered an aggregation and obvious, since there's no synergism or new cooperation: the combination merely provides the sum of the results of its components and each component works individually and doesn't enhance the working of any other component. On the other hand, the combination of an eraser and a pencil would be patentable (had it not already been invented) because the two elements cooperate to increase overall writing speed, a synergistic effect. The same would hold true for mounting loudspeakers in a plastic insulating picnic box, where new cooperation results: the box holds the food and provides a baffle for the speakers.

Factor 14. Combination unsuggested

If the prior art contains no suggestion, either expressed or implied, that the references should be combined, this militates in favor of patentability. Examiners in the PTO frequently are assigned to pass on patent applications for combination inventions. To find the elements of the combination claimed, they'll make a search, often using a computer, to gather enough references to show the respective elements of the combination. While the examiners frequently use such references in combination to reject the claims of the patent application on nonobvious grounds, the law says clearly that it's not proper to do so unless the references themselves, or the prior art in general rather than an applicant's patent application, suggests the combination or that the results are predictable.

> EXAMPLE: Arthur B. files a patent application on a pastry-molding machine. The examiner cites (or your search reveals) one patent on a foot mold and another on a pastry mold to show the two elements of the invention. It wouldn't be proper to "combine" these disparate references since they're from unconnected fields and thus it wouldn't be obvious to use them together against this invention.

An example of where the law would consider it obvious to combine several references is the case where, as discussed, you make a bicycle out of the lightweight carbon-fiber alloy and, as a result, your bicycle is lighter than ever before. Is your invention "nonobvious"? The answer is "No," because the prior art implicitly suggests the combination by mentioning the problem of the need for lighter bikes and the lightness of the new alloy. Moreover, the result achieved by the combination would be expected from a review of existing bicycles and the new lightweight alloy. In other words, if a skilled bicycle engineer

were to be shown the new, lightweight alloy, it would obviously occur to the engineer to make a bicycle out of it since bicycle engineers are always seeking to make lighter bicycles.

In *KSR v. Teleflex* (2007), the U.S. Supreme Court made it easier for the PTO or the courts to reject claims or hold patents invalid if those patents are based on a combination of references. Prior to this, the cases held that an invention should not be held obvious over several prior-art references unless there is a suggestion, motivation, or teaching that the references can or should be combined. This case held that there only must be some apparent reason in the prior art to justify combining the references. For example, the existence of a problem can make it obvious to try various solutions. The prior art doesn't have to be directed to the precise problem, so long as the references still perform their same functions. If you argue that the combination was not suggested by the prior art, state (if applicable) that the problem solved by your invention is different and the references perform new functions in your combination and the result you achieve was not predictable.

Factor 15. Impossible to combine

This is the situation where prior-art references show the separate elements of the inventive combination, but in a way that makes it seem they would be physically impossible to combine. Stated differently, if you can find a way to do what appears to be physically impossible, then you can get a patent. For example, suppose you've invented the magnetic pistol release. The prior art shows a huge magnetic cannon firing release attached to a personnel shield. Since the step from a cannon to a small handgun is a large one, physical incompatibility might get you a patent—that is, it would be physically impossible to use a huge cannon shield magnet on a small and very differently shaped trigger finger. Note, however, that sometimes by analogy the large can properly be used on the small if a mere change in size is all that's required.

Factor 16. Different combination

Here your combination is A, B, and C, and the prior-art references show a different, albeit possibly confusingly similar combination, say A', B, and C. Since your combination hadn't been previously created, you've got a good case for patentability even though your creation is similar to an existing one. Again the last analogy holds: a personnel shield for a cannon, even though it has a magnetic firing release, is so far different from a finger ring that the prior-art combination must be regarded as different from that of the invention.

Factor 17. Prior-art references would not operate in combination

Here the prior-art references, even if combined, wouldn't operate properly, such as due to some incompatibility. Suppose you've invented a radio receiver comprising a combined tuner-amplifier and a speaker, and the prior art consists of one patent showing a crystal tuner and an advertisement showing a large loudspeaker. The prior-art elements wouldn't operate if combined because the weak crystal tuner wouldn't be able to drive the speaker adequately; thus a combination of the prior-art elements would be inoperative. This would militate strongly in favor of patentability.

Factor 18. References teach away from combining

If the references themselves show or teach that they shouldn't be combined, and you're able to combine them, this militates in favor of patentability. For example, suppose a reference says that the new carbon-fiber alloy should only be used in structural members that aren't subject to sudden shocks, but you were able to make a bike out of the carbon-fiber alloy. If you're able to use it successfully to make a bike frame, which is subject to sudden shocks, you should be able to get a patent.

Factor 19. Awkward, involved combination

Suppose that to make your inventive combination, it takes the structures of three prior-art patents, one of which must be made smaller, another of which must be modified in shape, and the third of which must be made of a different material. These factors can only help you.

Factor 20. References from a different field

If the references show structures that are similar to your invention, but are in a different technical field, this militates in favor of nonobviousness and hence of patentability.

Factor 21. Easier to assemble or manufacture

If the novel feature(s) of your invention make it easier or cheaper to assemble or manufacture, this is an important advantage which can be used to prove nonobviousness.

6. How Does a Patent Examiner Determine "Nonobviousness"?

When patent examiners turn to the question of whether an invention is nonobvious, they first determine the scope and content of the prior art. That is, they make a search and gather all of the patents and other references that they feel are relevant or close to your invention. Then they determine the differences between these materials (including any prior-art references you've provided with your patent application) and your invention, as described in your claims (see Chapter 9), to find any novelty (novel physical features, new combination, or new use) that isn't shown in any reference. If so, your invention satisfies Section 102—that is, it is novel.

Next they see whether your novelty produces any results that would be unexpected or surprising to a person having ordinary skill in the art. If so, they'll find that the invention is nonobvious and allow your patent application. If not (this usually occurs the first time they act on your case), they'll reject your application (sometimes termed a "shotgun" or "shoot-from-the-hip" rejection) and leave it to you to show that your new features do indeed produce new, unexpected results. To do this, you can use as many of the reasons listed above that you feel are relevant. If you can convince the examiner, you'll get your patent.

If a dispute over nonobviousness actually finds its way into court, however, both sides will present the testimony of patent lawyers or technical experts who fit, or most closely fit, the hypothetical job descriptions called for by the particular case. These experts will testify for or against obviousness by arguing that the invention is (or isn't) new and/or that it does (or doesn't) produce unexpected results.

7. Weak Versus Strong Patents

Although this section covers the basic legal requirements for obtaining a patent on an invention, there is, in reality, an additional practical requirement. If the claims in your patent are easy to design around or are so narrow as to virtually preclude you from realizing commercial gain, it's virtually the same as if a patent had been denied you in the first place. The importance of proper claiming cannot be overemphasized. For example, if you claim an improved fan that blows air at 30 miles per hour, and your competitor sells a fan that blows air at 29 or 31 MPH, then their fan will not infringe your patent. For this reason it is vital to understand how to claim your invention, as described in Chapter 9.

8. The Inventor's Status Is Irrelevant

An inventor's status and personal qualifications are totally irrelevant. An invention need merely meet the four legal criteria above. The applicant must qualify as a true inventor of the invention but his, her, or their age, sex, citizenship, country of residence, mental competence, health, physical disabilities, nationality, race, creed, religion, state of incarceration, degree of education, amount or time spent inventing, and so on, are irrelevant. The PTO issued a patent on a glider to a death row inventor (U.S. Patent 6,260,795). Even a dead or insane person can apply (through a legal representative, of course).

Common Misconception: If a person invents something by accident, the law won't consider it to be as good an invention as if a genius had come up with it through years of hard, brilliant work.

Fact: The last sentence of 35 U.S.C. Section 103 reads: "Patentability shall not be negated by the manner in which the invention was made." The mental abilities of the inventor and the manner of making an invention are totally irrelevant to patentability. The invention is looked at in its own right as to whether or not it would be obvious to one skilled in the art; the way it was made or the qualifications or competence of the applicant are never considered by the PTO.

G. The Patentability Flowchart

To get a better grasp of the admittedly slippery concept of nonobviousness and the role it plays in the patent application process, consider Fig. 5C— The Patentability Flowchart. This flowchart is like a computer programmer's flowchart, except that all blocks have been made rectangular to use space more efficiently. In addition to presenting all of the criteria used by the PTO and the courts for determining whether an invention is nonobvious, the chart also incorporates the first three tests (statutory class, usefulness, and novelty) of Fig. 5A. Review this chart and the following description of it well, since it sums up the essence of this crucial chapter. Also, you'll want to use this chart when making your search and when prosecuting your patent application. This chart has been designed to cover and apply to anything you might come up with, so you can and should use it to determine the patentability of any utility invention whatever.

Box A (Statutory Class): (Subject Matter Eligibility): Assuming that you've made an invention, first determine, using the criteria discussed above, whether you can reasonably classify your invention in one of the five statutory classes indicated without being considered a law of nature, natural phenomenon, or

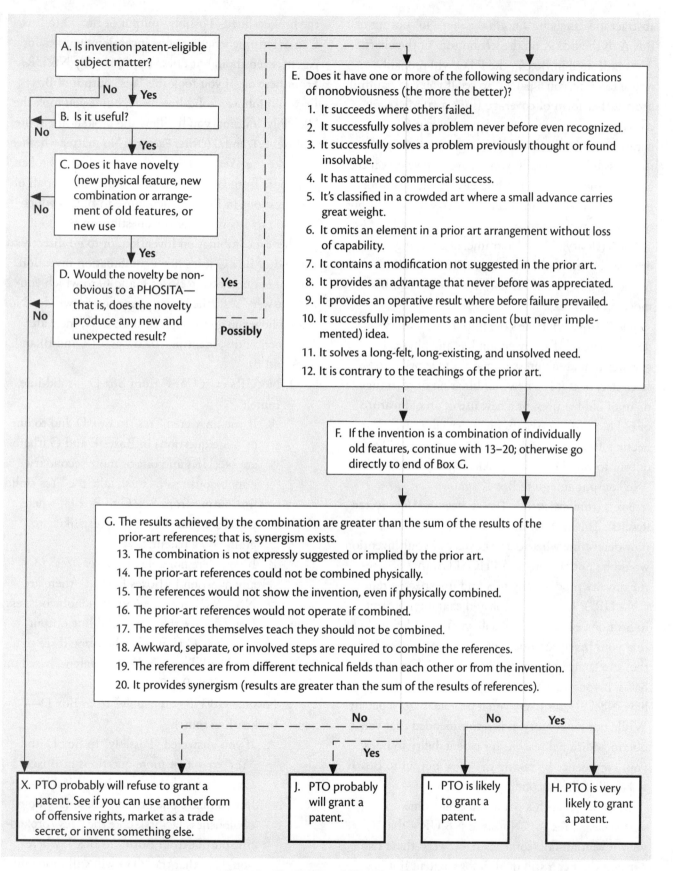

Fig. 5C—The Patentability Flowchart

abstract idea as such. If not, take the "No" output of Box A to the Box X on the left bottom of the chart.

As indicated in Box X, the PTO will probably refuse to grant you a patent, so see if you can gainfully use another form of coverage (such as trade secret, copyright, design patent, trademark, or unfair competition, as discussed in Chapters 1 and 7). If this possibility also fails, you'll have to give up on the creation and invent something else. If the invention can be classified within a statutory class ("Yes" output of Box A), move on to Box B.

Box B (Utility): Now determine, again using the criteria above, whether the invention has utility, including amusement. If not, move to Box X. If so, move on to Box C.

Box C (Novelty): Here's the important novelty determination. If an invention has any physical features that aren't present in any single prior-art reference, or if it is a new combination or rearrangement of old features, or a new use of an old feature or old hardware, no matter how trivial, it will clear Section 102—that is, it has novelty: take the "Yes" output to Box D. If not, it lacks novelty, so take the "No" output and go to Box X again.

Box D (Nonobviousness Due to New and Unexpected Results): This is the heart of the chart. You should now determine whether the novelty of your invention would be nonobvious to a PHOSITA; that is, does the novelty produce any new and unexpected result ("N&UR")? Use the criteria and examples presented in Sections F1 through F4, above. If you definitely feel that your invention does not provide any N&UR, take the "No" output from Box D to Box X. On the other hand, if your answer is a clear "Yes" (you're sure you have N&UR), it's likely you'll be able to get a patent. While not mandatory, it is recommended that you obtain additional reasons for patentability to boost your confidence by taking the "Yes" output to Box E to consider the "secondary" factors.

If, however, at this point you can't come up with a clear "Yes" or "No" as to N&UR—that is, your invention falls somewhere between these two extremes—it can still qualify for a patent if it has one or more secondary factors. In this case, follow

the broken-lined "Possibly" output of Box D to Box E to determine whether your invention qualifies for a patent, even though it doesn't produce any N&UR. From here on, if you took the "Yes" output of Box D, you'll follow a solid-line route, but if you took the "Possibly" output, you'll follow the broken-line route.

Boxes E, F, and G (Other Factors): No matter whether you take the "Yes" = solid line or "Possibly" = broken line route from Box D, you should next answer all of the questions in Box E. Then move to Box F, which tells you to answer all of the questions in Box G if you have a combination invention, or to go directly to the end of Box G if it's not a combination invention. The more questions in Boxes E and G to which you can answer "Yes," the better your chances will be. No matter how you go through Boxes E to G, there are four possibilities, identified below as 1 (A and B) and 2 (A and B).

1. N&URs exist ("Yes" from Box D—solid-line route):
   A. If you answered "Yes" to Box D and to one or more questions in Boxes E and G (there are N&URs and one or more secondary nonobviousness factors), take the "Yes"/solid-line output from Box G to Box H, where you'll see that the PTO is very likely to grant you a patent.
   B. If you were not able to answer "Yes" to any question in Boxes E and F (there are N&URs, but no secondary nonobviousness factors), take the "No"/solid-line output from Box G to Box I, where you'll see that you'll still be likely to get a patent, based on your N&URs (Box D).

2. Possible N&URs ("Possibly" from Box D—broken-line route):
   A. If you answered "Possibly" to Box D and "Yes" to one or more questions in Boxes E and G (you're unsure about N&URs but you have one or more secondary nonobviousness factors), take the "Yes"/broken-line output from Box G to Box J, where you'll see that the PTO will still probably grant you a patent.

B. If you answered "Possibly" to Box D, but were not able to answer "Yes" to any question in Boxes E and G (you're unsure about N&URs and there are no secondary nonobviousness factors), take the "No"/broken-line output from Box G to Box X, where you'll see that you probably won't be able to get a patent. Don't give up though, if you still think you might be able to prove some secondary factors later, such as commercial success after it hits the market.

H. Don't Make Assumptions About the Law

If you encounter an issue you don't know the answer to and can't find the answer in this book, don't act on any assumptions, because you could suffer for acting on an incorrect assumption. True examples:

- LeRoy assumed that—because a regular patent application had to have at least one claim to be entitled to a filing date—his application, which had four independent claims, counted as four patent applications. He then advertised that he had four patents pending that covered his invention.

- Griselda assumed that if a prior patent showed her invention, but didn't claim it, then she was entitled to get claims to this invention allowed in her patent application.

If you can't find the answer to an issue, you look further, ask a patent attorney, call the PTO's Inventors Assistance Center at 800-786-9199, or ask an inventors' organization.

I. Summary

The law has four requirements for getting a patent: (1) the invention must be in a statutory class—a machine, an article, a process, a composition, or a new use of the first four—and not monopolize a fundamental scientific or engineering technique; (2) it must be useful (safe, not illegal, operable, and not a nuclear weapon); (3) it must be novel—that is, it must be different in some way from every single item or prior art (prior art means any publication, public use, or public knowledge before the date you file a patent application or Provisional Patent Application); and (4) the novel features must be nonobvious to one with ordinary skill in the art—that is, it must produce new and unexpected results or have one or more of the secondary factors of nonobviousness.

CHAPTER

6

Search and You May Find

A. Why Make a Patentability Search?	133
1. To Determine Whether You Can Get a Patent	133
2. To Avoid Needless Expenditures and Work	133
3. To Provide Background to Facilitate Preparation of Your Patent Application	133
4. To Know Whether to Describe and Draw Components	133
5. To Provide More Information About Operability and Design	134
6. To Obtain Commercial Information	134
7. To Obtain Possible Express Proof of Nonobviousness	134
8. To Define Around the Prior Art to Facilitate Prosecution	134
9. To Learn Your Invention's Novel Features so as to Expedite Prosecution	135
10. To Facilitate Licensing or Sale of Your Invention	135
11. To Find Out What You've Really Invented	135
12. To Get a Stronger Patent	135
13. To Get Your Patent Application Examined Ahead of Turn	135
14. To Determine If Your Invention Will Infringe Any In-Force Patents	135
B. When Not to Search	135
C. The Two Ways to Make a Patentability Search	136
D. The Quality of a Patent Search Can Vary	136
E. How to Hire a Patent Professional	137
1. Lay Patent Searchers	137
2. Patent Agents	137
3. Patent Attorneys	137
4. Finding Patent Agents and Attorneys	138
F. How to Prepare Your Searcher	139
G. Analyzing the Search Report	139
H. The Scope of Patent Coverage	151
I. Do-It-Yourself (DIY) Computer Searching	153
1. Computer Search Resources	153
2. Searching at PTO Headquarters and Regional Offices	154
3. Patent and Trademark Resource Centers	156
4. Vocabulary Associated With Computer Searches	157

J. Classification Searching 158

    1. Classification Searching 158

    2. Keyword Searching 168

K. How To Computer Search 169

    1. Google Patents 169

    2. PTO Search With EPO Supplement 170

    3. Limitations of the PTO and Other Systems 170

    4. Important Searching Tips 171

L. Summary 172

> **Inventor's Commandment 8**
>
> You should make a thorough patentability search of your invention before deciding whether to file a patent application, and you should not file a patent application unless you believe your invention has—in addition to strong commercial potential—one or more novel features over the prior art which you believe the PTO will consider nonobvious.

A patentability search is a review of the prior art surrounding your invention. You are looking for a preexisting invention, device, or publication that would demonstrate that your invention is not new or that it is obvious to others in the field. (See Chapter 5 for more information on prior art, novelty, and nonobviousness.) In other words, you're looking for evidence that could prevent you from obtaining a patent. In this way, a patentability search is a paradox, because you're looking for something you hope you won't find! The Patent and Trademark Office (PTO) doesn't require a patentability search, but patent practitioners, including the authors of this book, recommend that all inventors make (or have made) such a search prior to deciding whether to file a patent application.

A. Why Make a Patentability Search?

Here are 14 reasons for making a patentability search.

1. To Determine Whether You Can Get a Patent

The main reason for making a patentability search of your invention is to discover if the PTO will be likely to grant you a patent on it. If your search indicates that your invention is likely to qualify for a patent, you can go ahead with your development, marketing, and other work on the invention with far more confidence that your efforts will eventually produce positive results.

On the other hand, if your patentability search indicates that a patent isn't likely to be granted, think carefully about whether to proceed. Most manufacturers won't invest in tooling, producing, and marketing something that their competition can freely copy, and perhaps even sell at a lower cost. (Though there are exceptions as explained in Chapter 7.)

2. To Avoid Needless Expenditures and Work

It makes sense to do a relatively small amount of work—a patentability search—at a modest expenditure in order to gain useful information that may well allow you to avoid wasting considerable time and/or money preparing a patent application.

3. To Provide Background to Facilitate Preparation of Your Patent Application

You'll find it easier to prepare a patent application if you make a patentability search. A search will bring out prior-art references (prior publications including patents and literature) in the field of your invention. After reading these, you're likely to gain valuable background information that will make the task of writing your patent application easier. Patent attorneys almost always routinely review some sample patents from the field of an invention before they begin preparation of a patent application, in order to give them a "feel for the art." While patent attorneys are trained in getting patents and most have technical backgrounds, you are almost certainly more knowledgeable about your particular product or service area than they might be. If you decide you need the help of a patent attorney, your familiarity with the background prior art will help you bring them up to speed quickly, saving you money.

4. To Know Whether to Describe and Draw Components

A patent application must contain a detailed description of your invention, in sufficient detail to enable a person with ordinary skill in the "art" involved to make and use it. If your invention has certain components with which you aren't familiar, you won't have to take the trouble to draw and describe these in detail if you find them already described in prior-art publications, including patents.

Instead, you can simply refer to them by their well-known names. (Names for many such components and processes may be found in the glossaries of Appendix 3.)

5. To Provide More Information About Operability and Design

When you make a search, you will almost always find patents in the field of your invention, possibly on inventions similar to yours. A reading of these patents will give you valuable technical information about your invention, possibly suggesting ways to make it work better and improve its design, or possibly indicating technical approaches that you should avoid because they are already known and therefore not inventive.

6. To Obtain Commercial Information

The patents and other references that you uncover in your search will give you valuable commercial information about developments related to your invention. For instance, suppose you see many patents on inventions that produce the same result as yours, and you know from your familiarity with the field that none of these has attained commercial success. In this event, you might want to reconsider the wisdom of pushing ahead with your own invention because it might suffer the same fate as those others. Or you might conclude that you can do better, because the prior inventions were not marketed effectively or because they did not operate properly due to lack of proper components, proper materials, excessive costs, and so on.

7. To Obtain Possible Express Proof of Nonobviousness

Sometimes a search will uncover references that actually "teach away" from your invention—for example, by suggesting that your approach won't

work. You can cite such a reference to the PTO to help convince the examiner to regard your invention as nonobvious. For instance, suppose you've invented a bicycle frame made of a new carbon-fiber alloy that makes your bike far lighter and stronger than any previously made. Ordinarily, the substitution of a known alternative material (here a carbon-fiber alloy for steel) would not be patentable, since the substitution would not provide any *unexpected* results or advantages. But suppose during your search you find a prior-art reference (such as an article in *Metallurgic Times*) that states that carbon-fiber should not be used for bicycle frames because it cannot absorb shocks. If you find that such alloys can be used successfully, you can cite this reference to the PTO to show that you've turned a past failure into success. Thus you'll have express, positive proof that your invention provides unexpected results and is nonobvious.

8. To Define Around the Prior Art to Facilitate Prosecution

By familiarizing yourself with the prior art, you'll be able to tailor and define the general thrust, structure, and advantages of your patent application around such art and its deficiencies. This will save you work and arm you with the proper terminology and support that you may need later in the "prosecution" stage (that is, the stage where you actually try to obtain a patent from the PTO).

> **EXAMPLE:** LeRoy invented a sturdy but edible baked scoop for dips, including salsa. His search turned up a patent granted to Minerva on a similarly shaped cereal product which was too fragile for scooping dips. As a result of the knowledge gleaned from his search, LeRoy was able to direct his patent application to the novelty of his scoops by knocking the fragility of Minerva's product and explaining and stressing the strength of his scoops with actual (quantitative) performance figures. This enabled him to distinguish and "sell" his invention over Minerva's product and get a patent.

9. To Learn Your Invention's Novel Features so as to Expedite Prosecution

After making a thorough search of the prior art, you'll be able to find out which of your invention's features are novel, enabling you to recite, stress, and direct your patent application to all of those features and advantages. Also, you can tailor your claims to such novel features so as to preclude an early "final action," expedite the ultimate allowance of your case, and avoid the need to narrow the claims. (Claims and their importance are covered in Chapter 9.)

10. To Facilitate Licensing or Sale of Your Invention

When you attempt to sell or license your invention rights, your potential licensees will want to know if your patent application will be likely to get through the PTO. You can address their concern, at least partially, by showing them your search results, providing some confidence in your invention and possibly speeding up and facilitating negotiations. (Marketing your invention is covered in Chapter 11.)

11. To Find Out What You've Really Invented

Many inventors don't realize or understand exactly what they've invented until they see a search report. Indeed, many inventors get a severe case of "search shock" when their "major advance" turns out to be relatively minor. If this happens, don't give up on your brainchild, since your minor advance may be extremely valuable and vital. On the other hand, occasionally an inventor, believing that the invention is a relatively small advance and that its basic broad idea must have already been invented, is very pleased and surprised to learn from the search results that the invention's a gold mine instead of a nugget!

12. To Get a Stronger Patent

A PTO examiner will usually conduct a better search than you or a professional searcher might. Nevertheless, some examiners, at certain times, may miss a highly relevant reference. If anyone uncovers such a reference later, after you get your patent, and brings this reference to the attention of the PTO or any court, it may cast a cloud over, or even invalidate, your patent. However, if you find such a reference in your search, you can (and must) make a record of it in the PTO's file of your patent application, tailor your claims around it, and avoid any potential harm it may cause you later, making your patent stronger and less vulnerable.

13. To Get Your Patent Application Examined Ahead of Turn

It's not always a wise idea to get your patent application expedited (see Chapter 10). But, if you really need to speed things up, you'll be entitled to get it examined ahead of its usual turn if you've made a preexamination search.

14. To Determine If Your Invention Will Infringe Any In-Force Patents

You may wish to know if your invention—if made, used, sold, offered for sale, or imported—will infringe any existing patents, especially if you're considering manufacturing the invention. A search and study of the claims of all relevant in-force patents will reveal this.

B. When Not to Search

Despite our inventor's commandment about doing a patent search prior to filing, there are at least two situations where you can "skip the search."

If you are dealing in a very new or arcane field with which you're very familiar, obviously a search is highly unlikely to be profitable. For example, if you're a biotech engineer who reads all the journals and patents to keep abreast of the state of the art, the newness of your field makes it highly unlikely that you will find any early "prior art." Or, if you make semiconductors and have up-to-the-minute knowledge of all known transistor-diffusion processes, and you come up with a breakthrough transistor-diffusion process, a search will probably not produce any reference showing your idea. Before deciding not to search, however, you should be reasonably certain that you or someone else with whom you are in contact knows all there is to know about the field in question, and that you are fairly confident there is no obscure reference that shows your invention.

In addition, if you've made an improvement to an earlier invention that you've already searched, and you feel the search also covered your improvement, there's obviously no need to make a second search.

TIP

Designs. Generally it's not worth searching design inventions, since the cost and time required to make the search is greater than the time and cost to prepare a design patent application. However, if you believe that some of the reasons expressed, above, are relevant to your situation, you should make a search of your design. Also, you must search your design invention if you want to petition to have your design application examined right away on the "Rocket Docket." (See Chapter 10.)

Common Misconception: There's no reason to make a patentability search prior to filing a patent application because the PTO will make one anyway.

Fact: Even though the PTO will make a search, there are many good reasons (see the 14 reasons, above) to make a search before filing.

C. The Two Ways to Make a Patentability Search

Basically, there are two ways to get your search done: have someone do it for you or do it yourself. If you're a conscientious worker with the necessary free time, and you have access to a search facility (or adequate computer search capability), doing the search yourself is the best way to ensure that it is done thoroughly. This will also save you money and enable you to accumulate valuable information.

However, you may have very good reasons for hiring a professional searcher—for example, you live far from any search facility, or you don't have enough time to conduct a thorough search yourself. Also,

there's the procrastination factor: half the time the only way some of us will ever get a job done, even though we're capable of doing it, is to turn it over to a pro. If you choose to hire a searcher, you'll find advice on choosing one below in Sections D through H. Even if you do use a searcher, read through the instructions on do-it-yourself searching in order to understand what you're paying for and to be able to recognize whether the searcher has done a thorough job. We'll cover do-it-yourself (DIY) searches in Sections I through L.

Paper Patents Are No Longer Searchable

In the past, inventors and searchers were able to walk into the PTO and search paper patents, either in the public search room or the examining division. Nowadays, digital has supplanted paper for patent search purposes. This development, for better or worse, means that in all but a few extremely unusual situations, the patentability search will be made using computer searching, whether you hire a professional searcher or do it yourself (or both). However, the PTO has spent substantial time and money computerizing its paper patents and improving its computer search facilities, which benefits everyone.

D. The Quality of a Patent Search Can Vary

Your patentability search can never be perfect because there is no way to search unpublished pending patent applications. (A patent application that is based on a regular patent application (RPA) or provisional patent application (PPA) that was filed before your filing date may be used to deny your application once it becomes publicly available, e.g., after it issues as a patent.)

Other reasons why your search may not be perfect include:

- some prior-art references can be missing from the database you're searching
- very recently issued patents may yet to be entered in the computer's database

- a relevant reference (patent or nonpatent) may be described using terms or keywords that you would not use, or even think of, or
- the technology you are trying to find may have been used publicly before your invention without being published.

All of this means that nothing is guaranteed, and it will be impossible for a search to prove that your invention is patentable. So take any patentability search with a grain of salt, and keep in mind that the amount of confidence you can take away from a search depends on its quality, and as a general rule, quality is proportional to a patent searcher's experience and the amount of time they have to spend on your search. So if you are unsure whether someone else has invented something like your invention, giving a hired searcher a little extra time (and money) to do a thorough job may go a long way toward maximizing the value of the search.

E. How to Hire a Patent Professional

Here are some suggestions for how to find and work with a patent professional. As a general rule, before hiring any searcher, find out about their fees, technical background, on-the-job experience, and usual amount of time spent on a search.

1. Lay Patent Searchers

A lay patent searcher is usually an engineer or other technologist, but not a patent attorney or agent, and typically not licensed to represent inventors before the PTO. Lay searchers do not need to be licensed by any governmental agency, so exercise care in selecting one. If you are considering hiring a lay searcher, in addition to the general questions discussed above, be sure to ask for the names of some clients as references.

Although there are many good lay searchers out there, attorneys and agents typically have a deeper understanding of the concept of nonobviousness, and tend to dig in more places. Also, since searchers aren't patent lawyers or agents, remember that they're not allowed to express opinions on patentability. But on

the plus side, lay searchers charge about half of what most attorneys and agents charge.

Lay searchers, as well as attorney-agent patent searchers, can be located via online search. Others advertise in periodicals, such as the *Journal of the Patent & Trademark Office Society*, a publication for patent professionals edited and published by a private association of patent examiners (online at www.jptos.org), or *Inventor's Digest* (online at www.inventorsdigest.com).

2. Patent Agents

A "patent agent" is an individual with technical training—generally an undergraduate degree in a science, technology, engineering, or mathematics (STEM) field—who is licensed by the PTO to prepare and prosecute patent applications. A patent agent can conduct a patent search and is authorized to express an opinion on patentability, but since the agent isn't an attorney, they cannot represent you in court (to assert your patent or defend you from someone else's patents), cannot obtain trademarks, and cannot advise you on licensing issues or other legal issues.

Although many agents will serve you well, all other things being equal, use an attorney rather than an agent for searching (and patent application work), since most patent attorneys have experience in licensing and litigation that will usually lead them to make wider and stronger searches for possible use in adversarial situations. However, always consider the competence of the individual, how much time they will spend with you, how much they will charge, and how well you get along.

3. Patent Attorneys

A "patent attorney" or "patent lawyer" is an individual with technical training (generally an undergraduate degree in a STEM field) who is licensed to practice both by the PTO and the attorney-licensing authority of at least one state (such as the state bar organization, state supreme court, and so on). A "general" lawyer licensed to practice in one or more states, but not before the PTO, can obtain copyrights and trademarks but is not authorized to prepare patent applications or use the title "patent attorney." An "intellectual property attorney" handles trademarks and copyrights and may or may not be licensed by the PTO to prepare and file patent applications, and you should be sure to ask specifically whether they are licensed by the PTO.

How to Use a Lawyer or Agent

Here are some tips:

- Make sure the practitioner sends you a copy of every document (letter or official paper) that they generate for you or receive on your behalf.
- Save every paper you receive from the practitioner in a file, keeping official papers, bills, and letters separate.
- Make sure you understand everything the practitioner does or proposes to do for you and why the practitioner is taking this course of action. Almost every possible action is explained in this book, but if not, ask the practitioner to explain it to you.
- Find out in advance the cost of every task the practitioner intends to perform for you and make sure the practitioner understands that you need to approve each and every fee in advance. Have the practitioner agree to obtain your advance approval if any fee will be exceeded. You don't want any open billing. Also make sure the practitioner agrees to send you bills with disbursements itemized and kept separate from the practitioner's fees and that the bills state the basis (time or fixed rate) for the practitioner's fees.
- If you can't communicate with the practitioner, feel that the practitioner is not acting competently, ethically, or honestly, or don't understand what the practitioner is doing and are unable to obtain an adequate explanation, find another practitioner and dismiss the old practitioner. You should have obtained and kept a copy of your papers, but even if you haven't, you are entitled to obtain a copy of your file. In most states you are entitled to the copy without charge, even if you owe the attorney money. Legally, the file belongs to you. Also you are entitled to dismiss your attorney at any time (with rare exceptions).

---

4. Finding Patent Agents and Attorneys

All patent agents and attorneys registered to practice before the PTO are listed on the PTO's website at https://oedci.uspto.gov/OEDCI. Pick one or more of these and then call or write to say you want a search made in a particular field.

Finding a good patent professional often involves more than checking a list. The best way is by personal referral. Another way to check an attorney or agent is to look at the patents they've prepared. You can find these online on the PTO site by entering the attorney's name and reading some of the recent patents. If you do find someone who seems good, make an appointment to discuss the broad outlines of your problem.

Ask what undergraduate degree the attorney has; you don't want to use a mechanical engineer to search for a complex computer circuit or a new drug.

Your next question should be, "Will the professional help you help yourself, or will they demand a traditional attorney-client relationship (meaning the attorney does it all and you pay for it)?" Many corporate-employed and retired patent professionals will be delighted to help you with your search, preparation, and/or prosecution of your patent application. Using this approach, you can do much of the work yourself and have the professional provide help where needed at a reasonable cost. On the other hand, attorneys who work for a law firm that serves multiple clients may want a traditional relationship to protect themselves against liability and conflicts of interest.

When it comes to fees, you should always work these out in advance. Some patent professionals charge a flat fee for searches (and also for patent applications and amendments); others charge by the hour. If you plan to do much of the work yourself, you'll want hourly billing. If you do agree to hourly billing, be sure to first obtain an estimate of the maximum number of hours and an agreement that you'll be notified in advance if this estimate will be exceeded. Many patent attorneys are accustomed to corporate clients who use an open-ended billing arrangement—that is, they bill by the hour without providing any limit or flat fee arrangement. With this system, you can quickly find yourself on the financial hook for far more than you may want to spend. Also, be sure it's clear who will pay for other costs associated with prosecuting a patent, such as copies, postage, drafting, filing fees, and so on.

When you visit a patent attorney or agent, remember that they're not an oracle of knowledge. Don't expect to be able to lay a prototype or sketch of your invention on their desk and say, "What do you think of this?" and have them instantly tell you its commercial value and give you an opinion on patentability. First, they usually are not qualified to do a commercial evaluation. Second, they can't give you an opinion on patentability without making and analyzing a search.

How to Find "Discount" Patent Attorneys and Agents

Active patent professionals (attorneys and agents) are either in private practice (a law firm or solo practice) or employed by a corporation or the government.

Most patent professionals in private practice charge about $250 to $800 an hour. But many corporate-employed or semiretired patent professionals also have private clients and charge considerably less than their downtown counterparts. If you want or ever need to consult a local patent professional, you'll save money by using one of these "discount" patent professionals; their services are usually just as good or better than those of the full-priced law firm attorneys. Also, since they have much less overhead (rent, books, assistants), they'll be more generous with their time (except that patent professionals employed by the federal government are not allowed to represent private clients).

Look in the geographical region listing of PTO's attorney directory (oedci.uspto.gov/OEDCI) or search by ZIP code for corporate-employed or retired (but still licensed) patent professionals in your area.

F. How to Prepare Your Searcher

You'll want to use your patent searcher to maximum efficiency. Do this by sending your searcher easily

understandable drawings (they can be informal sketches as long as they are clear) with a clear and complete description of your invention and the drawings. Be sure to disclose all embodiments, variations, and ramifications so that these will be searched. You won't compromise any trade-secret status of your invention (or start the one-year public disclosure clock running) by such a letter since by law it's considered a confidential communication. If you wish any type of particular emphasis applied to any aspect of your search, be sure to inform the searcher of this fact. If your notebook record of your invention or your invention disclosure is clear enough, you can merely send the searcher a copy. Fig. 6A is an example of a proper search request letter from an inventor and Figs. 6B (a, b, c) are copies of the attachments to the search request letter of Fig. 6A.

You don't need to have a patent agent or a patent attorney sign a Keep-Confidential Agreement, because registered (PTO-licensed) patent professionals are strictly bound by the PTO's rules to keep all client communications confidential. However, if you feel insecure, or you are using a layperson to search, you certainly can ask your searcher to sign Form 3-1. In any case, you should always keep a "paper trail" of all disclosures you make to anyone.

G. Analyzing the Search Report

After you send out your search request, the searcher will generally take several weeks to perform the patentability search, obtain copies of the patents and other references that the searcher feels are relevant, and report back. Most search reports have four parts:

1. A description of your invention provided by the searcher to assure you that the searcher has understood your invention and to indicate exactly what has been searched.
2. A list of the patents and other references discovered during the search.
3. A brief discussion of the cited patents and other references, pointing out the relevant parts of each.
4. A list of the classes, subclasses, or keywords searched and the examiners consulted, if any.

140 | PATENT IT YOURSELF

Millie Inventress
1901 JFK Boulevard
Philadelphia, PA 19103

2024 January 22
Samuel Searcher, Esq.
2001 Jefferson Davis Highway
Arlington, VA 22202

Patentability Search: Inventress: Napkin-Shaping Ring

Dear Mr. Searcher:

As we discussed on the phone yesterday, you were highly recommended to me as an excellent searcher by Jacob Potofsky, Esq., who is a general attorney here and a cousin of my friend, Shirley Jaschik. You said that you would be able to make a full patentability search on my above invention, including an examiner consultation and a search in the examiner's files to cover foreign and nonpatent references, for $1,000, including patent copies and postage. I have enclosed this amount as full payment in advance, per your request. You said that you would mail the search report (without an opinion on patentability) and references to me within three weeks from the date you receive this letter.

Enclosed are three sheets of drawings from my notebook (I have properly signed, witnessed, and dated records elsewhere); these sheets clearly illustrate my napkin-shaping ring invention. As you can see from the prior-art Figs. 1 (A and B), previous napkin rings were simple affairs, designed merely to hold a previously rolled or folded napkin in a simple shape. In contrast, the napkin ring of my invention, shown in Fig. 2, and made of metal or plastic, has a heart-shaped outer member 12, an inner leg 14, and two curved-back arms 16. As shown in Fig. 3, it is used by introducing a corner 8 of a cloth napkin 10 between an end 4 of leg 4 and the adjacent portion of outer member 12. When napkin 10 is pulled partially through the ring, as indicated in Fig. 4, it will be forced to assume the shape of the space between arms 16 and outer portion 12, as indicated.

Thus my napkin-shaping-and-holding ring can be used to make a napkin have an attractive, graceful shape when it is laid flat and placed adjacent to a place setting, as indicated in Fig. 5. The extending portion of the napkin can also be folded up and around, as indicated in Fig. 6-A, so that the napkin and its ring can be stood upright.

In addition to the specific shape shown, you should of course search the broader concept of my invention; namely, a ring-shaped outer member with an inwardly extending tongue or leg that can be used to shape napkins pulled partially through the structure. I believe that I have provided you with sufficient information to fully understand the structure and workings of my invention so that you can make a search, but if any further information is needed, please don't hesitate to call me.

I understand that you will, in accordance with the ethics of your profession, keep all details of my invention strictly confidential, except to consult an examiner.

Most sincerely,

Millie Inventress

Millie Inventress (215-776-3960)
Encs.: $1,000 check, 3 sheets of drawings
(My file: Search.ltr)

Fig. 6A—Inventor's Search Request Letter to Patent Searcher

Fig. 6B(a)—Drawing of Invention, Part a

Fig. 6B(b)—Drawing of Invention, Part b

Fig. 6B(c)—Drawing of Invention, Part c

PATENT IT YOURSELF

SAMUEL SEARCHER
Patent Attorney
2001 Jefferson Davis Highway
Arlington, VA 22202
703-521-3210
2024 February 21

Ms. Millie Inventress
1901 JFK Boulevard
Philadelphia, PA 19103

Search Report: Inventress: Napkin-Shaping Ring

Dear Ms. Inventress:

In response to your letter of January 22, I have made a patentability search of your above invention, a napkin-shaping ring comprising an outer portion with an inwardly extending leg and flared-back arms at the end of the leg. I have also searched the broader concept of an annular member with an inward cantilevered leg for shaping a napkin that is drawn therethrough. My bill for $900, the total cost of this search, including the references and postage, is enclosed and is marked "Paid"; I thank you for your check and enclose a refund of $100.

I searched your invention in the following classes and subclasses: A47G 21/16, 47G 23/00, A47G 19/00, and B65B 9/2049. In addition, I consulted Examiner John Hayness in Group Art Unit 353 regarding this invention. Otherwise, I kept your invention strictly confidential. In my search, I thought the following references (all U.S. Patents) were most relevant, and I enclose a copy of each: **Bergmann**, 705,196 (1902); **Gabel**, 1,771,328 (1930); **Hypps**, 3,235,880 (1966); and **Le Sueur**, 3,965,591 (1976).

Bergmann shows a handkerchief holder that comprises a simple coiled ring with wavy portions.

Gabel is most relevant; she shows a curtain folder comprising a folded metal device through which a curtain (already partially folded) is inserted and then pulled through and ironed at the exit end.

Hypps shows a necktie and holding device.

Le Sueur shows a napkin ring with magnetically attachable names.

I could not find any napkin-shaping devices as such and Examiner Hayness was not aware of any either. However, be sure to consider the Gabel patent carefully, as it appears to perform a somewhat similar function, albeit for curtains.

It was my pleasure to serve you. I wish you the best of success with your invention. Please don't hesitate to call if you have any questions.

Most sincerely,

Samuel Searcher

Samuel Searcher
Encs: $100 Check, Bill, and References

Fig. 6C—Patent Searcher's Search Report

CHAPTER 6 | SEARCH AND YOU MAY FIND | **145**

July 22, 1930

L. GABEL

1,771,328

FOLDER

Filed March 16. 1923

Fig. 6D(a)—Drawing of Prior-Art Gabel Patent

Patented July 22, 1930

1,771,328

UNITED STATES PATENT OFFICE

LOUISE GABEL, OF COLUMBUS, NEBRASKA

FOLDER

Application filed March 16, 1928. Serial No. 262,243.

This invention relates to cloth holding devices and more particularly to a device adapted for holding cloth in the form of plaits while ironing and sewing.

An other object of the invention comprehends an enlarged entrance opening in one end of the device within which the cloth may be introduced.

A further object of the invention contemplates tongue members adapted to form creases in the cloth.

An additional object of the invention consists of a portion removed from the discharge end of the device whereby binding action of a sad iron therewith is obviated while pressing the cloth.

With the above and other objects in view, the invention further consists of the following novel features and details of construction, to be hereinafter more fully described, illustrated in the accompanying drawing and pointed out in the appended claim.

In the drawing:—

Figure 1 is a side elevation of the invention while in use and followed by a sad iron.

Figure 2 is a top plan view of Figure 1.

Figure 3 is a top plan view of the invention per se.

Figure 4 is a sectional view taken on line 4—4 of Figure 3.

Figure 5 is a bottom plan view of the invention.

Figure 6 is a front elevation of the invention per se.

Referring to the drawing in detail, wherein like characters of reference denote corresponding parts, the reference character 10 indicates a plate member having a curved outwardly projecting forward end 11 and a concaved inner end 12.

The sides of the plate are bent upon themselves upwardly and inwardly upon the plate to provide horizontally disposed guide members 13.

As illustrated in Figures 1, 3, 4 and 6, the outermost end, namely 11, is flared to provide an enlarged entrance and to accomplish such construction the outermost ends of the guide members 13 are upwardly flared, as indicated at 14 and concaved, as indicated at 15 upon the foremost edges thereof.

Tongues 16, carried by the guide members 13, are extended reversely thereof and disposed in spaced relation to the upper side of the plate member 10. The side edges of the tongues being also spaced from the guide members. The foremost ends of the tongues 16 are rounded, as indicated at 17, and projected forwardly for greater distances than the adjacent ends of the guide members 13.

In the use and operation of the invention, lengths of cloth, such as indicated at 18, of a desired width, are partially folded along the side edges thereof and the strip per se laid upon the upper side of the plate member 10. The folded portions of the strip being adapted to repose upon the upper sides of the tongues 16 and to be projected within the spaces as defined between the tongues and the guide members. Due to the fact that the outermost end of the device is flared, an enlarged entrance is provided by means of which the cloth may be readily introduced and fed. The rounded portions 17 for the tongues also permit ease in the drawing of the cloth through the device or the sliding of the device upon the cloth. As illustrated in Figures 1 and 2 of the drawing, a sad iron, such as indicated at 19, may travel upon the cloth 18 immediately behind the device to press the folded side edges or plaits of the cloth. By the same token, the invention could be used in the formation of different kinds of braids and etc., and to effectively feed the cloth or strip to a sewing machine, in the event the plaits are to be held against displacement from the strip per se.

The concaved portion 12, upon the innermost end of the strip 10, is adapted to prevent binding action of the sad iron 19 therewith when the latter closely pursues the plate member. Such construction will also prevent injury to the strip and plaits.

Although I have shown, described and illustrated my invention as being primarily adapted for use in the manufacture of plaits, it is to be obviously understood that the invention could be effectively employed for

Fig. 6D(b)—Specification of Prior-Art Gabel Patent

United States Patent [19]
Le Sueur

[11] **3,965,591**
[45] **June 29, 1976**

[54] **NAPKIN RING**
[75] Inventor: **Alice E. J. Le Sueur,** Cobble Hill, Canada
[73] Assignee: **The Raymond Lee Organization,** New York, N.Y.; a part interest
[22] Filed: **Nov. 26, 1974**
[21] Appl. No.: **527,216**

[52] **U.S. Cl.** .... **40/21 R**
[51] **Int. Cl.²** **G09F 3/14**
[58] **Field of Search** .... 40/142 A, 63, 21 A, 40/21 B, 10; 63/2; 24/8

[56] **References Cited**
UNITED STATES PATENTS
198,065 12/1877 Annin .... 63/1 X
2,600,505 6/1952 Jones .... 40/142 A
2,653,402 9/1953 Bonagura .... 40/21 A

FOREIGN PATENTS OR APPLICATIONS
1,308,888 10/1962 France 40/142

Primary Examiner—Louis G. Mancene
Assistant Examiner—Wenceslao J. Contreras
Attorney, Agent, or Firm—Howard I. Podell

[57] **ABSTRACT**

An open cylindrical napkin ring fitted with magnetic means for attaching an identifying name or set of initials in a recess on the outside of the ring.

3 Claims, 4 Drawing Figures

Fig. 6D(c)—Abstract Page of Prior-Art Le Sueur Patent

The searcher will enclose copies of the references (usually U.S. patents, but possibly also foreign patents, magazine articles, and so on) cited in the search report and enclose a bill. Most searchers charge separately for the search, the reference copies, and the postage. If you've paid the searcher a retainer, you should be sent a refund unless your retainer was insufficient. In this case, you'll receive a bill for the balance you owe.

EXAMPLES:

- Fig. 6C is an example of a typical, competently done search report sent by Samuel Searcher, Esq., in response to Millie Inventress's letter of Fig. 6A.
- Fig. 6D(a) is a copy of page 1 (the drawing) of the Gabel patent cited in the search report.
- Fig. 6D(b) is a copy of page 2 of Gabel (the first page of Gabel's specification).
- Fig. 6D(c) is a copy of page 1 of the Le Sueur patent cited in the search report.

The PTO has added "Patent Document Kind Codes" to the numbers of patents and their other publications, in accordance with international practice. These Kind Codes allow you to distinguish between different types of patents, and between patents and pregrant application publications. You'll find a list of these codes on the PTO website (www.uspto.gov/patents/search/authority-files/uspto-kind-codes).

You should now read the searcher's report and the references carefully. Then, determine whether your invention is patentable over the references cited in the search report. Let's use Millie's search report as an example of how to do this.

Note from Fig. 6B that the napkin-shaping ring of the invention has an annular (ring-shaped) outer member with an inwardly projecting leg. The leg has flared-back arms at its free end. When a folded napkin is drawn through the ring, tip first, the arms and annular member will shape the napkin between them in an attractive manner, as indicated in Fig. 6B(c).

Of the four previous patents cited, let's assume that only Gabel and Le Sueur are of real relevance. Gabel, a patent from 1930, shows a curtain folder comprising a bent sheet-metal member. A curtain is folded slightly and is drawn through the folder that completes the folding so that the curtain can be ironed when it is drawn out of the folder. Le Sueur, a patent from 1976, shows a napkin ring with a magnetized area for holding the letters of the name of a user.

Now, as part of analyzing this sample search report, we'll use the master flowchart reproduced below, as Fig. 6E. If any part of this chart confuses you, reread the part of Chapter 5 that explains each box in detail.

Okay, now let's work our way through the chart:

Box A: Millie's napkin-shaping ring can be classified within a statutory class as an article (or even a machine, since it shapes napkins).

Box B: It clearly has usefulness, since it provides a way for unskilled hostesses or hosts to give their napkins an attractive, uniform shape.

Box C: We must now ask whether the invention is novel—that is, physically different from any single reference. Clearly it's different from Le Sueur because of its inwardly extending leg 14. Also, it's different from Gabel because, comparing it with Gabel's Fig. 6, it's rounder and it has a complete outer ring with an inwardly extending leg, rather than a folded piece of sheet metal. It's important to compile a list of the differences (novel features) that the invention has over the prior-art references, not the differences of the references over your invention.

Box D: The question we must now ask is, "Do the novel features (the roundness of the ring, the inwardly extending leg, and the flared-back arms) provide any new and unexpected results?" After carefully comparing Gabel with Millie's invention, we can answer with a resounding "Yes!" Note that Gabel states, in her column 2, lines 62 to 66, that the strip of cloth is first partially folded along its side edge and then it is placed in the folder. In contrast, Millie's shaping ring, because of its roundness and leg, can shape a totally unfolded napkin—see Millie's Figs. 3 and 4. This is a distinct advantage, since Millie's shaper does all of the work automatically—the user does not have to specially fold the napkin. While not an earthshaking development or advance, clearly Millie's ring does provide a new result and one that is unexpected, since neither Gabel, Le Sueur, nor any other reference teaches that a napkin ring can be used to shape an unfolded napkin. Thus we take the solid-line "Yes" output of Box D to Box E.

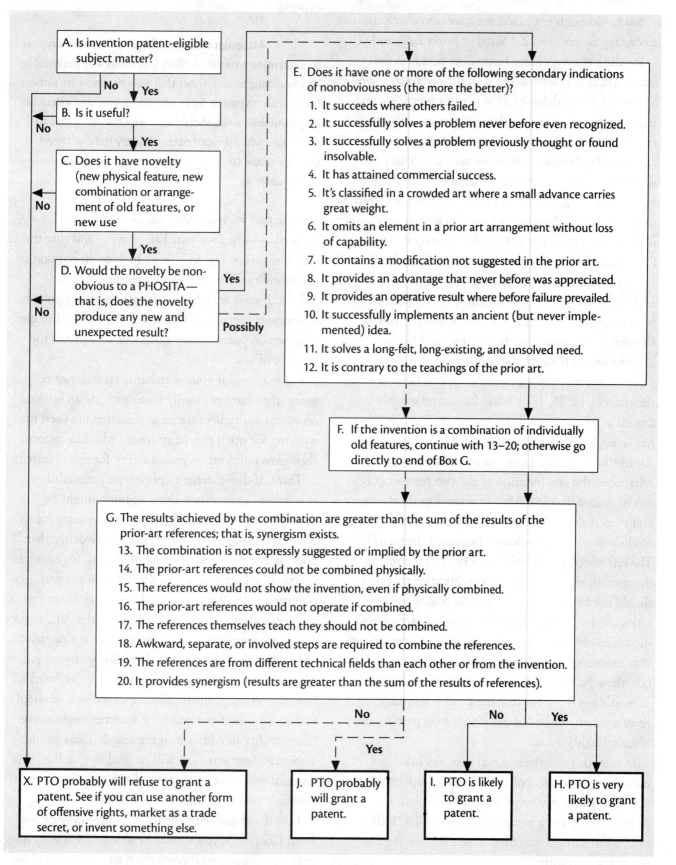

Fig. 6E—Patentability Flowchart

Box E: Although not mandatory, we next check the secondary factors (1 to 22) listed in Boxes E, F, and G.

Reading through these factors, we find first that factor 2 in Box E applies—that is, the invention solves a problem (the inability of most persons to quickly and neatly fold napkins so that they have an attractive shape) that was never before even recognized. Also, we can provide affirmative answers to factors 8 and 11, since the invention provides an advantage that was never before appreciated and it solves a long-felt, but unsolved need—the need of unskilled persons to shape napkins quickly and gracefully (long felt by the more fastidious of those who hate paper napkins, at least).

Boxes F and G: Since two references are present, and each shows some part of Millie's invention, we have to answer "Yes" to Box F and proceed to Box G to consider the possible effect that a combination of these would have on the question of obviousness ("combinatory nonobviousness"). In Box G we see that factors 13, 15, 18, 19, and 21 can reasonably be argued as relevant to Millie's invention. The invention has synergism (factor 21), since the results (automatic napkin folding) are greater than the sum of the references; the combination of the two references is not suggested (factor 13) by the references themselves; and even if the two references were combined, Millie's inward leg would not be shown (factor 15). The references are complete and fully functional in themselves, and hence teach by implication that they should not be combined (factor 18). And it would be awkward, requiring redesign and tooling, to combine the references (factor 19). Thus we can with conviction state that several secondary factors are present, so we take the solid-line "Yes" output of Box G to Box H.

Next, (**Box H**) we see that the PTO is very likely to grant a patent, and our determination on patentability is accordingly positive.

In fact, this exercise is a real case: An examiner initially rejected an application for the napkin-shaping ring as unpatentable over Gabel and Le Sueur. However, he agreed to grant a patent (U.S. Patent 4,420,102) after an argument was filed, forcefully stating the above considerations.

TIP

Although we have analyzed the search report to determine whether Millie's invention was patentable, it's important to remember that a weak patent isn't much better than no patent. So in addition to reaching a decision on patentability, you should also walk the extra mile to determine whether your patent is likely to be of broad enough scope to make it economically worthwhile (see Chapter 4).

Note that we have done our own patentability evaluation—the four-part list, above—and that the search report of Fig. 6C didn't include an opinion on patentability. There are several reasons for this.

First, if your searcher is a layperson (not a patent attorney or agent), the searcher is not licensed to give opinions on patentability since this constitutes the practice of law.

Second, even if your searcher is an attorney or agent, the searcher usually won't provide an opinion on patentability because most searchers are used to working for other patent attorneys who like to form their own opinions on patentability for their clients.

Third, if the searcher's opinion on patentability is negative, a negative written opinion might be damaging to your case if you do get a patent, sue to enforce it, and the opinion is used as evidence that your patent is invalid. This would occur, for example, if your court adversary (the defendant infringer) obtains a copy of the opinion by pretrial discovery (evidence gathering), shows it to the judge, and argues that since your own search came up with a negative result, this militates against the validity of your patent. However, a negative written opinion can be "worked" in court—that is, distinguished, explained, rebutted, and so on—so if you want the searcher's opinion on patentability in addition to the search, most patent attorney/agent searchers will be glad to give it to you without extra charge, or for a slight additional cost of probably not more than $300 to $600.

Fourth, armed with the knowledge you've gained from Chapter 5, you should be able to form your own opinion on patentability by now; the exercise will be insightful to your invention.

Fifth, note that there's no certainty in the law. No one can ever say for certain that you'll be able to get a patent before you get it since no search can cover pending patent applications, and human responses (how your examiner at the PTO will react) are very unpredictable. So take any prediction with a grain of salt.

In any case, don't hesitate to ask any questions about the searcher's practices in advance, and be sure to specify exactly what you want in your search. It's your money and you're entitled to buy or contract for whatever services you desire.

H. The Scope of Patent Coverage

Although you'd probably like things to be simpler, the determination of whether your invention is patentable will rarely be a "yes" or "no" one, unless your invention is a very simple device, process, or composition. Many inventions are complex enough to have some features, or some combination of features, that will be different enough to be patentable. However, your object is not merely to get a patent, but to get *meaningful* patent coverage—that is, offensive rights that are broad enough that competitors can't "design around" your patent easily. Designing around a patent is the act of making a competitive device or process that is equivalent in function to the patented device but that doesn't infringe the patent.

Often you won't be able to get broad coverage because many "modern" inventions are actually old hat—that is, the basic ideas were known many years before and the real inventions are actually just improvements on old ones. Simply put, you'll often find a search will indicate that your invention, while valuable, may be less of an innovation than you thought it was. You'll thus have to determine whether or not your invention is sufficiently innovative to get meaningful patent protection. In other words, your scope of coverage will depend upon how close the references that your search uncovers are to your invention—that is, how many features of your invention are shown by the references, and how they are shown. In the end, your scope of coverage will

actually depend upon the breadth of the claims that you can get the PTO to allow, but this is jumping the gun at this stage—we'll cover this more in Chapter 9.

For an example, let's take a simple invention. As stated, in a simple invention patentability will usually be a black or white determination, and you won't have much of a problem about your scope of coverage. Suppose you've just invented a magnetically operated cat door—that is, you provide a cat with a neck-worn magnet that can operate a release on a cat door. Your search references fail to show any magnetically operated pet release door. Thus, the neck magnet and the magnetic door release are the novel features of your invention. To get a patent, your invention would have to be limited to these specific features, since neither could be changed or eliminated while producing the same result. However, there is no harm in limiting the invention to these features, since it would be difficult for anyone to "design around" them—that is, it would be difficult or impossible for anyone to provide the same result (a cat-operated door release) without using a neck magnet and a magnetic release.

With other inventions, however, your scope of coverage won't be so broad—that is, it won't be as difficult for someone to design around it. For example, suppose you invented the centrifugal vegetable juicer mentioned previously in Chapter 5—that is, a juicer with a sloping side basket permitting the solid pulp to ride up and out so that juicing could continue without having to empty the pulp from the basket.

If the prior art was not "kind" to you—that is, your search uncovered a patent or other publication that showed a juicer with a basket with sloping sides and with a well at the top to catch and hold the pulp—your application would not be allowed if you claimed just the sloping sides (even though it would be superior to the prior art due to the complete elimination of the pulp). To get the patent, you would have to also claim another feature (say, the trough shape). Thus, by having access to the prior art you would know enough to claim your invention less broadly.

Also, suppose you've invented the napkin-shaping ring of Fig. 6B. Suppose further that Gabel did not exist and that your search uncovers only the Le Sueur patent (see Fig. 6D(c)), which shows a plain, circular napkin ring. You'd be entitled to relatively broad coverage, since your novel features are themselves broad: namely, a ring with inner parts that can shape a napkin when it is pulled through the ring.

However, assuming the Gabel patent does exist and your search uncovers it as well as Le Sueur, what are your novel features now? First, your device has a circular ring with a leg extending inwardly from the ring; neither Gabel nor Le Sueur, nor any possible combination of these references, has this combination. Second, your invention has the flaring arms that shape the napkin; these are attached to the end of the inner leg; the references also lack this feature. So, to distinguish over Le Sueur and Gabel, you'll have to rely on far more specific features than you'd have to if only Le Sueur existed. That means your actual invention would be far narrower, since you'll have to limit it to the novel features that distinguish it from Gabel as well as Le Sueur. Unfortunately, this will narrow your scope of coverage, because competitors can design around you more easily than they could if only Le Sueur existed.

As you've probably gathered by now, your scope of coverage will be determined by what novel features you need to use to distinguish your invention over the prior art and still provide new results that are different or unexpected enough to be considered nonobvious. The fewer the novel features you need, the broader your invention or scope of coverage will be. Stated differently, if you need many new features (or very specific features) to define over the prior art and provide new results, it will usually be relatively easy for a competitor to use fewer or alternative features to provide the same results without infringing your patent.

You should make your scope of coverage determination by determining the fewest number or the broadest feature(s) you'll need to distinguish patentability over the prior art. Do this by a repetitive narrowing trial-and-error process: First, see what minimum feature(s) you'll need in order to have some novelty over the prior art—that is, enough to distinguish under Section 102 (Box C of Figs. 5C and 6E)—and then see if these would satisfy Section 103 (Boxes D, E, and G)—that is, would they provide any unexpected new results?

If you feel that your minimum number of features are enough to ascend the novelty slope of the Patentability Mountain (pictured in Chapter 5), but would not be sufficient to climb the big nonobviousness slope—that is, you don't have enough features to provide new and unexpected results—then try narrowing your features or adding more until you feel you'll have enough to make it to the patentability summit.

Common Misconception: If a search shows that your invention is not patentable, you may not manufacture or sell it.

Fact: Even if it's not patentable, you usually still can make and sell the invention because the prior-art reference(s) that prevent you from obtaining a patent probably are either expired patents or don't claim your invention. (For more on how to determine if a prior, in-force patent's claims cover you, see Chapter 15.)

 TIP

This is another one of those aspects of patent law that may have your head spinning. Fortunately, the material covered here under determining the scope of your protection is also discussed in the different context of drafting your claims. (See Chapter 9.)

After you evaluate your search results, you'll have a pretty good idea of the minimum number of novel features that are necessary to sufficiently distinguish your invention over the prior art. If you're in doubt about whether you have enough such features, or if you feel you'd have to limit your invention to specific features to define structure that would be considered nonobvious over the prior art, it probably isn't patentable, or even if patentable, it likely isn't worth filing on, since it would be easy to design around. One possibility, if you can't decide, is to pay for a professional's opinion.

On the other hand, if you've found nothing like your invention in your search report, congratulations! You probably have a very broad invention, since, with the eight million-plus patents that have issued thus far, one or more features of almost all inventions are likely to be shown in the prior art.

I. Do-It-Yourself (DIY) Computer Searching

In addition to (or instead of) hiring someone else to conduct your search for you, as described in the previous sections, you may perform invention searching yourself. All invention searching these days is performed using a computer. It is important to recognize that the computer is only a tool, so bear in mind what computer searching can and cannot do, and have a plan before you sit down at the keyboard.

Searches should be made primarily in patent databases, rather than in general reference or scientific files, because there are about ten times as many devices and processes shown in the patent files as in textbooks, magazines, and so on. That's because commercial practicability is not a requirement for patentability. All PTO examiners make most of their searches in the patent files for these reasons, so you should also. However, if you have access to a good nonpatent database, such as a good technical library in the field of your invention, you can use this as a supplement or alternative to your search of the patent files.

Computer searching is a delicate balance between your precious resources (time and patience) and a level of thoroughness. It is impossible for you to read more than ten million issued patents (and counting) to learn whether someone else has thought of your invention first. It is probably infeasible to read even just the patents that cover your technology (say, bicycles). You need to find and study only the references that are most relevant to your invention, and that by itself can be challenging.

1. Computer Search Resources

There are many computer search resources available to you. Some free databases are published by the PTO and other patent offices around the world, some resources collect databases for free searching, some private companies provide their own paid databases that you can access with their assistance and guidance, and there are nonpatent search tools you can use. Let's discuss each of these in turn.

In the last few years, the PTO has undertaken a great effort to digitize many of its records and make them searchable for free using a computer. The PTO publishes three searchable databases: USPAT, USOCR, and US-PGPUB.

The USPAT database permits searching by patent number, issue date, and current classification (see below) of every U.S. patent issued beginning in 1790 (except for some patents lost in a PTO fire in 1836). The USPAT database also permits searching of the human-verified full text of U.S. patents issued from 1971 to the present, including the abstract, the full description of the invention, the claims, and all bibliographic data from the Bibliographic Retrieval System (BRS), such as the inventor's name, the patent's title, and the assignee's name.

The USOCR database permits full text searching of automated, optical character recognized (OCR) text of U.S. patents issued from 1836 to 1970. Because the text in the USOCR database is unofficial, the database should be used with some caution. It would be ideal for the PTO to go back through its older patents, manually verify their text, and move them to the USPAT database, but it's undoubtedly a question of resources.

The US-PGPUB database permits full text searching of human-verified, published U.S. pre-grant regular patent applications (RPAs) from April 2001 to the present.

The PTO's newest search tool, Patent Public Search (PPS), can be found at www.uspto.gov/patents/search/patent-public-search and at PTO facilities.

Note that the PTO does not provide searching of non-U.S. patents and abstracts. But other searchable databases exist in addition to those published by the PTO. To that end, the European Patent Office (EPO) provides Quick and Advanced search capabilities in three languages (English, German, and French) online (worldwide.espacenet.com), but for patentability searches only the Quick search in English is necessary. To make a Quick search, type the appropriate keyword combinations in the keyword box with a suitable connector—for example, bicycle AND plastic OR wood. The dates of the databases vary; see the site for more information.

Other no-cost online search resources include:

- Google Patents (patents.google.com) has collected patents and published patent applications from 105 patent offices (including all of the PTO data, plus PCT publications and European patents) and permits searching by classification, keyword, inventor, and assignee.
- Free Patents Online (www.freepatentsonline.com), has the same coverage for U.S. patent documents and excellent search-limiting capabilities.

Outside of free resources, here are five fee-based organizations that offer computer searching of patent records. Several of the "for fee" databases also provide foreign patent information.

- Derwent Innovation (www.derwentinnovation.com), from Clarivate Analytics, is a commercial database of patents from more than 50 patent-issuing authorities. The PTO uses this tool.
- LexisNexis Total Patent One (www.lexisnexisip.com/solutions/patent-search is a commercial patent database offering extensive prior-art searching, plus patent optimization tools.
- Questel (www.questel.com) provides a collection of intellectual property databases, as well as consulting and legal services.
- InnovationQ+™ (https://ip.com/innovation-power-suite/innovation-q-patent-search-software) is a service that uses AI searching and includes many databases.
- Washpat (www.washpat.com) uses proprietary search tools and delivers search results in about a week.

While patent databases such as those listed above are the best places to make preexamination searches of inventions, additional prior art can sometimes be found by making a search of non-patent literature (NPL). NPL includes periodicals, textbooks, websites (current and obsolete), published doctoral theses, product manuals, advertisements, and so on.

Remember that any publication dated earlier than your date of invention can be valid prior art against your invention. There are many excellent places to search for NPL. Here are a few:

- **General Search Engines:** Online search engines, including Google (www.google.com) and Bing (www.bing.com) can be searched via keyword: you enter keyword combinations in the search box (for example, "bicycle" and "carbon fiber alloy") and examine the NPL that the engine returns. If you get too many references, add or narrow your keywords. If you don't get enough references, use more inclusive terms to broaden your search.
- **Specialized Search Engines:** A scientific search engine such as Google Scholar (scholar.google.com) will filter out nonscientific sites to speed searching. Google Patents (patents.google.com) provides a checkbox to include Google Scholar results, allowing you to combine a patent search with an NPL search using a single interface.
- **Specialized Libraries:** Don't forget to search the library of any organization or publisher you might have access to. These include technical organizations (for example, the Institute of Electrical and Electronics Engineers, IEEE), standards bodies (such as ASTM), journal publishers (such as Elsevier), or other digital libraries (such as JSTOR). You can also search the free journal preprint archive at arXiv.org.
- **General References:** Lastly, don't forget about Wikipedia (www.wikipedia.org), a free online encyclopedia that provides a great introduction and summary of practically any subject under the sun. It's a great place to start and get a sense of the overall landscape before you drill down using one or more search engines.

2. Searching at PTO Headquarters and Regional Offices

Now that you get the general idea of what data are available, how do you go about making a computer search? The best computer searches are made in person at the PTO Public Search Facility (PSF) in Alexandria, Virginia, or at one of the many Patent and Trademark Resources Centers (PTRCs) scattered across the country. The PSF and PTRCs are the best way to search because they have staff available to answer your questions and help guide your use of their tools. Please note that the staff cannot give you legal advice, help you search your invention, or evaluate patentability. This section discusses searching at the PTO specifically, while the next section discusses searching at PTRCs.

Here are a few things to know about the Patent and Trademark Office (PTO): The PTO is technically part of the Department of Commerce (headquartered in Washington) but operates in an almost autonomous fashion. The PTO employs about 8,000 examiners, all of whom have technical undergraduate degrees in fields like electrical engineering, chemistry, or physics. Many examiners are also attorneys. The PTO also has about half as many clerical, supervisory, and support personnel. The Commissioner for Patents is appointed by the president, and most of the higher officials of the PTO must be approved by Congress. The average pay for a patent examiner was about $130,000 a year in 2020.

The PTO began issuing patents in July 1790, but in 1836 lost all of these early patents in a fire. Some of those 10,000 patents, which were not numbered, have been recovered and are now known as the "X" patents. After the fire, the PTO started numbering patents (Patent 1 issued in July 1836). As of May 2022, the PTO had issued more than 11,343,000 utility patents, up from 10,575,000 at this book's last printing.

The PTO's Public Search Facility (PSF) is located in the Madison East Building, 600 Dulany St., Alexandria, VA 22314, tel. 571-272-3275. Hours are Monday to Friday 8 a.m. to 5 p.m. If you go to the PTO, get there early, as you will need a smartcard ID badge to enter the PSF. Badges are obtained from the Security Service Center in room 1C51 on the lobby level. You must present a valid photo ID to be issued an access badge.

Once you have your badge, go through the security access checkpoint to the public search room to use the PPS systems. If you need help with your search or with the PPS system, you can ask any of the search assistants in the search room. Often, a user at an adjacent terminal or a search assistant can help a new user with the basics to get started.

For help with the search itself (not the search system) you can also ask an examiner in the actual examining division for your art area. For example, if you've invented a bicycle, you might ask a "bicycle examiner" for assistance. You won't be endangering the security of your invention if you ask any of these people about your search and give them all the details of your invention. They see dozens of new inventions every week, are quite used to helping searchers and others, and would be fired if they ever stole an invention. Also, the PTO's rules forbid employees from filing patent applications. In theory a PTO employee could communicate an invention to a friend or relative who could file, but it's very unlikely to occur because such a relationship could be easily discovered during patent litigation.

The PSF in Alexandria provides the *Patent Office Official Gazette* (OG), Annual Indexes of Inventors, the U.S. Patents Quarterly (USPQ), the Cooperative Patent Classification (CPC) Scheme and Definitions, the Manual of U.S. Classification and its subject matter index (useful for design and plant patents, and utility patents before 2013), and other search aids in various formats. These tools were not mentioned above because they provide only very limited usefulness in aiding with your search.

The PTO also has divided the nation into regions, each with its own regional office to promote and facilitate public outreach. Combined with the examining corps, the outreach offices provide inventors, entrepreneurs, and small businesses with a PTO presence in every U.S. time zone. Each regional office has computer search facilities having the same capabilities as those at the headquarters in Alexandria, including computer workstations and staff available to help you with your searching. You can find a regional office by visiting www.uspto.gov/about-us/uspto-office-locations.

3. Patent and Trademark Resource Centers

A Patent and Trademark Resource Center (PTRC) is part of a nationwide network of public, state, and academic libraries designated by the USPTO to support the public with trademark and patent assistance. Accessing the patent information at a PTRC with the help of a trained specialist, you may be able to determine if someone else has already patented your invention.

According to the PTO, the PTRC Program began in 1871 when federal statute (35 U.S.C. § 12) first provided for the distribution of printed patents to libraries for use by the public. Since 1977 the PTRC network has grown to four times its original size. Currently, about half of the membership is academic (college or university) libraries, with nearly as many public libraries. There are also several state libraries and one special research library.

Each PTRC offers reference publications that outline and provide access to the patent and trademark classification systems, as well as other documents and publications that supplement the basic search tools.

Before You Begin Searching: Anticipation Versus Infringement

Many inventors have asked us, "How can an expired patent block me from patenting my invention?" That is, how can an expired patent be a valid prior-art reference?

If a patent ceased to be prior art when it expired, then anyone could repatent the wheel, the sewing machine, and so on. The misconception that a patent ceases to be a prior-art reference when it expires represents a confusion of *anticipation* with *infringement*. They are entirely separate areas in patent law and should be considered independently. Keep this difference in mind when you are conducting your search.

Anticipation is a situation that occurs when a proposed or new invention is discovered or found anywhere in the "prior art" (prior public use or prior publications, including the specification of any in-force or expired U.S. or foreign patent, any prior book, periodical article, and so on). Since the existence of the prior art proves the invention isn't new, the putative invention is said to be anticipated by the prior art and thus can't be patented. (35 U.S.C. § 102.)

Infringement is a situation that occurs only when the claims of an in-force patent "read on" a product or process. If so, then the product or process *infringes* (violates) the patent and the patent owner may be able to negotiate licensing royalties from the infringer, or successfully sue the infringer for money damages and/or an injunction ordering the infringer to cease infringing. (35 U.S.C. § 271.) (Note that a patent application can't infringe anything.)

If an invention is anticipated by a prior-art reference, that does not necessarily mean that it would infringe the reference, since the reference may be (a) a periodical article or book, which can't be infringed, (b) a foreign patent, which can't be infringed by activity in the United States, or (c) an expired U.S. patent, which can no longer be infringed. Even if an invention is anticipated by an in-force U.S. patent, the invention usually will not infringe the patent. Why? Because the patent's claims usually will not read on the invention, most likely because the patentee was not able to get broad enough claims allowed due to even earlier prior art. The PTO is never concerned with and never takes any action with regard to any infringement; their main concern (and yours) is to find anticipations to prevent the issuance of patents on old inventions.

EXAMPLE: In the early part of the 20th century, J.A. Fleming invented a two-element vacuum tube—the diode—that rectified alternating current. Then Lee De Forest added a third element—a control grid—to the diode, making a triode, which was capable of amplifying signals. Even though triodes infringed the diode patent, the Patent Office granted De Forest a patent since the PTO is not concerned with infringements. Although De Forest was not able to manufacture his triode without infringing Fleming's diode patent, Fleming was not able to make triodes without infringing De Forest's patent. Cross-licensing —in which the parties exchanged rights to their respective patents—solved the problem, enabling each to practice the other's invention.

Although many of these resources may be found online, one advantage to using PTRCs is that, like the PTO's Public Search Facility, they provide technical staff who can assist you in using all materials. However, like the PSF, the staff cannot offer legal advice or help you with your search. And unlike the PSF, you do not have access to nearby patent examiners with whom you might discuss your invention.

All information at a PTRC is available for use by the public free of charge. However, each library may charge for the use of its online systems, photocopying, and related services. Since there are variations in the scope of patent and trademark collections among the PTRCs, and their hours of service vary, contact any PTRC you plan to visit and get details on available collections, services, and hours.

For the location and contact information of your nearest PTRC, go to the PTO website (www.uspto.gov/about-us/uspto-office-locations).

4. Vocabulary Associated With Computer Searches

If you're going to do any patent searching, you should learn these terms now:

- A **File** is the actual name of the patent search database provided by the service. For example, the PPS provides issued U.S. patents in the USPAT and USOCR files, and pre-grant publications in the US-PGPUB file.
- A **Record** is a portion of a file; the term is used to designate a single reference, usually a patent within a database.
- A **Field** or a Search Index is a portion of a record, such as a patent's title, the names of the inventors, its filing date, its patent number, its claims, and so on.
- A **Term** is a group or, in computerese, a "string," of characters within a field—for example, the inventor's surname, one word of the title of a patent, and so on, are terms.
- A **Command** is an instruction or directive to the search system that tells it to perform a function. For example, "Search" might be a command to tell a system to look for some key search words in its database.
- **Keywords** or **Search Terms** are the word combinations that are actually searched. "Bicycle" and "carbon fiber alloy" may be keywords.
- A **Qualifier** is a symbol that is used to limit a search or the information that the search displays for your use. Normally no qualifier would be used in patentability searches, but if you're looking for a patent granted to a certain inventor, you could add a qualifier that limits the search to the field of the patentee's name.
- A **Wild Card Symbol** is an ending that is used in lieu of a word's normal ending in order to broaden a keyword. The wild card cuts off immaterial endings so that only word roots are searched. For example, if we were searching Millie's annular napkin-shaping ring, we would want our search to include the words "annular" and "annulus." Thus, instead of using both keywords and the Connector Symbol "or" (see below), we might search for "annul*" where "*" was a wild card symbol that tells the computer to look for any word with the root "annul" and any ending. Similarly, "?" is a wildcard that can substitute for a single letter, rather than any number of letters like "*" does.

Photo by Randy Rabin, Searcher

Searching at a terminal at the PTO

158 | PATENT IT YOURSELF

- **Connector Words** or **Operators** are those words (such as "or," "and," and "not") that tell the computer to look for certain defined logical combinations of keywords. For instance, if you issued a command telling the computer to search for "annulus or ring and napkin," the computer would recognize that "or" and "and" were connector words and would search for patents with the words "annulus" and "napkin," or "ring" and "napkin," in combination. (Note that when you get to writing your claims (Chapter 9), "or" and "not" are generally forbidden.)

- **Proximity Symbols** or **Proximity Operators** are those that tell the computer to look for specified keywords, provided they are not more than a certain number of terms apart. Thus, if you told the computer to search for "napkin ADJ5 shaping" it would look for any patent that contained the words "napkin" and "shaping" within five words of each other, the symbol "ADJ5" meaning "within five words of," are those that tell the computer to look for specified keywords, provided they are not more than a certain number of terms apart. Thus, if you told the computer to search for "napkin w/5 shaping" it would look for any patent that contained the words "napkin" and "shaping" within five words of each other, the symbol "w/5" meaning "within five words of." If no proximity symbol is used and the words are placed adjacent to each other— such as "napkin shaping"—the computer will pull out only those patents that contain these two words adjacent to each other in the order given. However, if a connector word is used—such as "napkin and shaping"—the computer will pull out any patent with both of these words, no matter where they are in the patent and no matter in what order they appear.

- **Stop Words** are words that are not indexed and not searchable, like "a," "an," and "the." Search for the possibly novel concepts of your invention. Keyword searches can be done for combinations of keywords in the texts—specification, claims, abstract, or title—of prior patents.

J. Classification Searching

So how should you search? There are two types of searches that you can make:

By Classification: You can make a search of all patents in a particular class and subclass (classification search).

By Keyword: You can also search for keyword combinations in all patents (keyword search).

To make a Classification search, you first have to find the appropriate Classes and Subclasses where the concepts of your invention might be found. After you get the appropriate Classes and Subclasses, you have to browse through every patent in each Subclass to search for the possibly novel concepts of your invention. Keyword searches can be done for combinations of keywords in the texts—specification, claims, abstract, or title—of prior patents.

You should do both types of searches (Keyword and Classification) to supplement each other because each has some deficiencies. If you do a Classification search you might use the wrong classification, while if you do a Keyword search you might not search with the same keywords as the patent attorneys who wrote the relevant patents and thus miss them. Also, Keyword searches are only available for U.S. patents going back to 1920, while Classification searches find all U.S. patents going back to the very first patent issued in 1790.

1. Classification Searching

There are seven basic steps to take when conducting a Classification search of patents and pre-grant application publications; these are depicted in Fig. 6F and are summarized below and then explained in detail:

Step 1: Write out the nature and essence of your invention, using as many different terms as you can think of to describe it. The PTO describes this step concisely as, "Brainstorm key words related to the purpose, use, and composition of the invention."

Step 2: Find potentially relevant classification(s) for your invention by searching your keywords in the CPC Schedule and Definitions. You can do this online at uspto.gov/web/patents/classification.

Step 3: Check the relevancy of the classification(s) in the Class Definitions related to your invention, and rank relevant classes and subclasses.

Step 4: Retrieve the U.S. patents from the database for each of the relevant subclasses, then narrow the list to the most potentially relevant patents by initially focusing on each patent's abstract and drawings.

Step 5: Carefully review each remaining patent in-depth to see whether it is actually relevant; that is, does it come close to the hardware, steps, or purpose of your invention? Write down the numbers, dates, and first Inventor of any patents that are relevant, and save or print copies of them for later use.

Step 6: Repeat steps 4 and 5 for U.S. pre-grant application publications. Use the same approach in step 4 to narrow the list of publications, and in step 5 to determine whether each publication actually is relevant to your invention.

Step 7: For each relevant patent and/or publication that you find, check the "References Cited" in the patent to work backward, the "Citing References" to work forward, and check the "Field of Search" to find additional relevant classes and subs.

Step 1: Write Out the Nature and Essence of Your Invention

As with any other classification or indexing system, your success will depend on the degree to which the words and phrases you use to define your invention coincide with the terms used by the classifier or indexer. For this reason, you should first figure out several ways to describe your invention. Start by writing down all the physical features of your invention in a brief, concise format so that you'll know exactly what to look for when searching.

For example, if you're searching a bicycle with a new type of sprocket wheel, write down "bicycle, sprocket wheel," and briefly add the details and as many alternative terms as you can think of, such as "gear," "chain," "drive linkage," and so on. If you're searching an electronic circuit, write down in a series of phrases (or in a very brief sentence) the quintessence of your invention, such as "flip-flop circuit with unijunction transistors" or some other very brief and

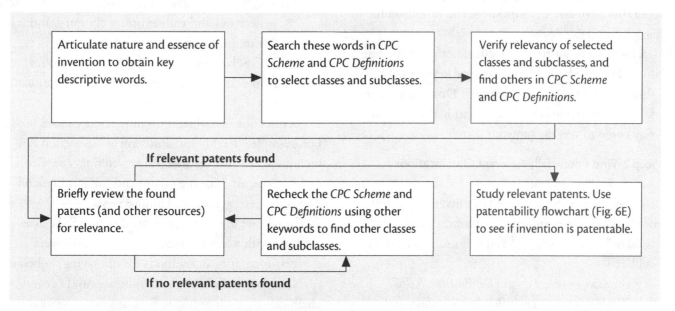

Fig. 6F—Classification Searching Process

concise description. Do the same whether your invention is a mechanical, electronic, chemical, business, internet, or method invention.

No matter what search system you use, be prepared with a well-thought-out group of keywords and all possible synonyms or equivalents. Use a thesaurus or a visual dictionary to get synonyms. Thus, to search for Millie's napkin-shaping ring, in addition to the obvious keywords "ring," "annular," "napkin," and "shaping," think of other terms from the same and analogous fields. In addition to napkin, you could use "cloth."

Or, in addition to "shaping," you could use "folding" or "bending." In addition to "annulus" or "ring," you could try "device," and so on. Also compile a list of all possible Class and Subclass combinations where patents on developments similar to your invention might be classified. To obtain relevant class-subclass combinations, you'll need to use the *CPC Scheme* and its accompanying *Definitions*, discussed just below.

Form 6-1 is a Searcher's Worksheet you can use to facilitate your searching, and Fig. 6G is a completed version of Form 6-1 that you might produce if you had searched Millie Inventress's invention. Note that the invention description part of the worksheet contains a concise description of the invention for easy reference.

Once you've written a concise description of your invention, think of some alternative keywords or phrases to add to your description. Don't hesitate to define your invention in any additional ways that may come to you during your search.

Step 2: Find Potentially Relevant Classifications for Your Invention

To find the places to search your invention you'll need its most relevant search classification (referred to as "class" and "subclass"). You will use two reference publications:

- the *Cooperative Patent Classification (CPC) Scheme*, sometimes called the *Schedule*, and
- the *CPC Definitions*.

These two publications can be accessed online via the PTO website (uspto.gov/web/patents/classification). Let's look at each publication in detail.

Cooperative Patent Classification (CPC) Scheme

The CPC Scheme divides all technology into eight major sections, each given a letter from A through H. These sections are, in order:

A. Human Necessities (agriculture, food and tobacco, domestic articles, and health and amusement)

B. Performing Operations and Transport (separating and mixing, shaping, printing, and transporting)

C. Chemistry and Metallurgy

D. Textiles and Paper

E. Fixed Constructions (roads, railways, bridges, sewers, buildings, locks, safes, windows and doors, and drilling and mining)

F. Mechanical Engineering (engines and pumps, general engineering, lighting, heating, and weapons and blasting)

G. Physics (instruments for measuring, testing, signaling, computing, and music making, and nuclear physics), and

H. Electricity (electrical components, power generation and transmission, circuitry, and communication techniques).

The CPC Scheme also provides a "Y" section for new and emerging technology, and for cross-sectional technology.

Each section is divided into numbered Classes. For example, "health and amusement" in section A includes Class A61 for medical or veterinary service and hygiene; A62 for life saving and firefighting; and A63 for sports, games, and amusements.

The Classes are themselves divided into Subclasses that end with a letter. Thus, Subclass A62B covers devices, apparatus, or methods for life saving; Subclass A62C covers firefighting; and Subclass A62D covers chemicals for extinguishing fires or protecting against harmful chemical agents, and breathing apparatus.

CHAPTER 6 | SEARCH AND YOU MAY FIND | 161

Searcher's Worksheet

Sheet ___1___ of ___1___

Inventor(s): _Millie Inventress_

Invention Description (use keywords and variations): _Napkin folder—Annular member with inner leg, flared-back arms_

Selected Search Classifications

Class/Sub	Description	Checked	Comments
A47G 21/16	Napkin holders	✓	very relevant—the right place
A47G 23/00	misc. tableware	✓	not too good
A47G 19/00	Table service	✓	somewhat relevant
B65B 9/2049	Shaping devices	✓	N.G.

Patents (and Other References) Thought Relevant

Patent # or Title	Name or Country	Date	Class/Sub	Comment
705,196	Bergmann	1902	D06F 55/00	Plain ring
1,771,328	Gabel	1930	D06F 75/30	Curtain shaper
3,235,880	Hypps	1966	A41D 25/08	Fancy ring
3,965,59	LeSueur	1976	A47G 21/16	Ring with magnetic letters

Consulted Examiner
Hayness, John Ext. 353

Searcher: _S. Searcher_   Date: _2024-1-12_

Fig. 6G—Completed Searcher's Worksheet (Form 6-1 in Appendix 7)

Fig. 6H—Sample Page of Classification Search Results

Fig. 61—Sample Page of *CPC Scheme*

164 | PATENT IT YOURSELF

A47G 21/16
Table-cloth or napkin holders

Definition statement

This place covers:

- Napkin rings
- Napkin holders
- Napkin holders with additional functionality (holders for cutlery, condiments, menus, advertisement, etc.)
- Napkin/towel heating/steaming appliances

Fig. 6J—Sample Page of *CPC Definitions*

The Subclasses further divide technology by structure, function, or operation into CPC codes designated by two numbers separated by a forward slash "/." A code ending "/00" represents a particular grouping of inventions, and a code ending "/99" represents miscellaneous inventions not classified elsewhere. Thus, the code A62B 1/00 covers all devices for lowering persons from buildings, and A62B 1/02 covers such devices specifically "making use of rescue cages, bags, or the like." There are about 250,000 CPC codes in total.

Let's search Millie Inventress's napkin-shaping ring. As stated above, the *CPC Scheme* can be accessed at www.uspto.gov/web/patents/classification. Start by entering "napkin" in the "Classification Text Search" box, resulting in Fig. 6H. The third search result is "CPC Scheme – A47G HOUSEHOLD OR TABLE EQUIPMENT" and mentions "napkin holders."

Next, we locate the correct CPC code within this Subclass. Click the link to open the *CPC Scheme* for Subclass A47G. Then search the Scheme page for "napkin holders," resulting in Fig. 6I. (You may need to click the pull-down menu next to "Display" and select "Expand All.") This figure shows that the CPC code "A47G 21/16" covers "Table-cloth or napkin holders." To confirm that this is the appropriate place, click the box labeled "D" on the line with the CPC code to bring up the corresponding definition for that code, resulting in Fig. 6J.

CPC Definitions

The CPC provides definitions for each Class, Subclass, and code. As may be seen from the "Definition statement," the code A47G 21/16 covers napkin rings, napkin holders, napkin holders with additional functionality, and napkin/towel heating/steaming appliances. You may also see pictures illustrating the types of inventions covered, as shown in Fig. 6J.

At the end of each CPC code definition is an "Informative references" section that lists other places that may be of interest for search. For example, the CPC code for table napkins themselves (as opposed to their holders) is A47G 11/001, while the code for towel racks is A47K 10/04. You should consider these

other CPC codes when selecting your search areas, if appropriate.

Be sure to spend enough time searching the *CPC Scheme* and *Definitions* to become confidently familiar with the classification system for your invention. Check all of your potential Subclasses and codes in the *CPC Scheme* and the *Definitions* to be sure you've obtained all the right ones. Usually, two or more codes will be appropriate. For example, if Millie's napkin folder could be considered decorative, Class B44 (decorative arts) should be searched. Note that the cross-references in the napkin holder CPC code won't refer you to "decoration," since this is too far afield—another reason to do a thorough job thinking of keywords in Step 1. It's up to you to consider all aspects of your particular invention when selecting search categories.

Searching analogous classes is usually very beneficial as well. For example, consider an automobile steering wheel that you've improved by adding finger ridges to improve the driver's grip. In addition to searching in the obvious area (automobile steering wheels), consider searching in any other areas where hand grips are found, such as swords, tools, and bike handlebars.

Fortunately, the cross-references in the *CPC Definitions* manual will be of great help here. Note how Sam Searcher, Esq., has completed the "Selected Search Classifications" section of the search worksheet in Fig. 6H with appropriate classes to search for prior art relevant to Millie Inventress's invention.

Step 3: Check the Accuracy of the Relevant Classifications

Check the accuracy of all the classifications you found in Step 2 by reviewing the *CPC Scheme* and *CPC Definitions* for each potential Class, Subclass, and CPC code. Remove any classes and subs that you feel aren't relevant to your invention.

Step 4: Obtain Patents in Relevant Subclasses and Begin to Narrow the List

After obtaining a list of the most relevant classes and subclasses, search through the actual patents in these classes. Online, go to ppubs.uspto.gov/pubwebapp/ and click "Search," in the "Enter query text" box enter the first full class and subclass followed immediately by the text ".cpc." (period-C-P-C-period, without the quotes), and hit "Search." Do this for each relevant class and sub under Issued Patents.

The computer will search according to your class and subclass and present you with a list of patents. As you flip through the patents, you may at first find it very difficult to understand what you're looking at. Don't be discouraged! You'll find it easier to understand newer patents (see Le Sueur—Fig. 6D(c)), because they have an abstract page up front that contains a brief summary of the patent and the most relevant figure or drawing.

You'll find that the older patents (see Gabel—Fig. 6D(a)) have several sheets of unlabeled drawings and a closely printed description, termed a "specification," after the drawings. However, even with older patents, you can get a brief summary of the patent by referring to the abstract, or the summary of the invention, which is usually found in the first or second column of the specification.

Near the end of each patent, you'll find the claims. These are formally worded, legalistic sentence fragments that usually come after and are the object of the heading words "I [or "We"] claim." The claims define the legal scope of offensive rights held by the owner of the patent.

Your goal in this step is to quickly eliminate patents that are clearly irrelevant to your invention. Don't spend a great deal of time (yet) reading each patent thoroughly. Instead, see if you can determine the gist of the patent by reading the abstract, looking at the drawings, or both. If you can immediately see that the patent is not relevant to your invention, skip it and move to the next patent.

Don't think about obviousness as you search, since doing so might overwhelm you and detract from the quality of your investigation. At this stage, try to fish with a large net by merely looking for the physical features of your invention.

As you search, keep a careful record of all patent classes and subclasses you've searched, as Sam Searcher did in Fig. 6G, above. Probably 95% of the references you encounter when you search will not be relevant,

and will be eliminated in this step. If you find potentially relevant patents or other art, make a note of their numbers, dates, names, or other identification for later reference. Although you need only the number to download a patent, note the issue date, first inventor's name, and classification as well, to double-check later in case you write down a wrong number.

If you do find a potentially important, relevant reference, don't stop; simply asterisk it (to remind you of its importance) and continue your search to the end.

When you note a relevant reference, also write down its most relevant features to refresh your memory and save time later.

If you don't find any relevant patents at all, double-check your search classes using the *CPC Definitions* and (if you are at the PTO's public search facility or a PTRC) some help from a patent examiner or assistant in the search room. If you're reasonably sure you're in the right class and still can't find any relevant references, write down the closest ones you can possibly find, even if they're not relevant. This will establish that you made the search, what the closest art is, and how novel your invention is, and you'll have references to cite on your Information Disclosure Statement (discussed in Chapter 13); you should never finish any search without coming up with at least several references. If you do consult examiners, write their names in the comments section of the worksheet.

Step 5: Carefully Review the Relevant Patents and Note Any Relevant Prior Art (Patents and Other Publications) Under Your Classification

By this time, you should have a curated set of potentially relevant patents. Now is the time to determine whether they really are relevant.

After you've made your search and obtained the numbers of all the pertinent references, obtain copies and study them closely, looking for any features that would act as prior art to your invention. Write a brief summary of each relevant patent, even if it has an abstract, to force yourself to really understand it. Then, determine if your invention is patentable over the patents you've found. Follow the steps described earlier in this chapter for analyzing any report of a search done by someone else to determine whether the prior art renders your invention obvious.

Common Misconception: If the claims of a prior patent don't cover your invention, you're free to claim it in your patent application.

Fact: The claims of a patent are there solely to define the monopoly or scope of offensive rights held by the owner of the patent. Patent owners use claims mainly in licensing or in court to determine whether the patent is infringed—that is, whether the hardware that an alleged infringer makes, uses, or sells violates the patent. Thus, when you encounter a relevant patent during a search, you should not fall into the "claims trap," that is, you should not read its claims. You should treat the patent like any other publication (book, magazine article, and so on) to see if the patent's description (the written part other than the claims) or drawings disclose (anticipate) your invention, or any part of it. (According to the patent statutes, the entire written part of a patent or patent application— that is, the description, claims, abstract—is called the "specification." However, some practitioners refer to just the description as the "specification" and consider the claims a separate part.) Because the patent's claims merely repeat what's already in the description and drawings, they won't contain anything new, so you need not even read the patent's claims to understand the full technical disclosure of any patent. The description and drawings will almost always contain more than what is in the claims anyway. So even if a patent's claims don't cover your invention, its description and drawings may still disclose your invention. Since the patent is a prior publication as of its filing date, it can thus anticipate your invention, even if it doesn't claim your invention. (If you were free to claim an invention that a prior patent disclosed but did not claim, that would make patents worth less as prior art than other publications, such as magazine articles!)

Another reason for not reading the claims of searched patents is that they're written in such stilted legalese that they're difficult to understand.

Nevertheless, some searchers do like to read claims of patents to get a quick "handle" on the patent's technical content.

If you do read the claims, keep in mind three considerations:

1. If a prior-art patent shows (that is, describes) but doesn't formally claim your invention, this doesn't mean you're free to claim it.
2. A patent contains much more technical information than what's in its claims; all of this technical information can be used as prior art, just as if the patent were an article in a technical magazine. Thus, you should use the claims only to get a "handle" on the patent; you should not regard them as a summary or synopsis of the patent's disclosure.
3. The scope of coverage you will likely be able to obtain for your invention (see Section H, above) will usually be narrower than the scope of the claims of the closely relevant prior-art patents you uncover.

Common Misconception: If your invention is covered by the claims of a prior patent, you will be liable as an infringer if you file a patent application on the invention.

Fact: Neither a patent application nor its claims can infringe a prior patent. Only the manufacture, use, sale, offer for sale, or importation of an invention in physical form can infringe. And, as previously stated, the PTO has absolutely no concern about patent infringements.

Step 6: Repeat Steps 4 and 5 for Published Applications
Once you have completed the classification search, you should have a handful of the most closely relevant patents. Even if you have not found any patents that would destroy novelty or nonobviousness of your invention, your search is not finished, because prior art may be found in any publication, including pre-grant application publications. Therefore, your next task is to take the classes and subclasses that you identified in step 3, and repeat steps 4 and 5 with the

pre-grant publications. (Some search resources, like the PPS and Google Patents, allow you to look up both patents and pre-grant publications by class and subclass in a single search query, in which case you should make a combined review in steps 4 and 5 and skip this step.)

Searching published applications is very important. Others may have tried to obtain a patent on your invention by filing an application before stalling out and never finishing the process. Since they never obtained a patent, your only clue in such cases may be their published application. Or, someone might be trying to patent your invention at this very moment, but they haven't yet completed the patenting process. Again, you will only know if you search pre-grant application publications (and their application is at least 18 months old and not under a nonpublication request).

Step 7: Obtain Additional Patents and Classifications

After making a computer search and obtaining a group of relevant references, it's possible (and very easy) to use these references to work back and forward and obtain additional, relevant references. How? To work backward, simply look at and/or order each of the "References Cited," which are listed on the abstract page (see Fig. 6D(c) for an example) or at the end of the patent in each computer-selected patent. These references (usually patents) were cited by the PTO during prosecution of the patent and are usually very relevant. You can even look up the "References Cited" in the additional references to go back even earlier, thereby making a "tree" of references. However, the PTO didn't list the "References Cited" before the 1950s.

Another way to work backward, using a hybrid approach, is to find a patent close to your invention using the computer and then find the CPC Class of the patent (it's G09F 3/14 in Fig. 6D(c)) and then search all patents in this class.

To work forward and find more recent patents and pre-grant application publications, look up "Patents which cite this patent" or "Citing references" for any patent that is close to your invention. This may be important if the patent you found hinted at your invention; a later patent that cited the patent you found may have gone the last mile and actually disclosed it.

2. Keyword Searching

Classification searches are often the best kind of searches, because the PTO groups all related inventions together by Class, Subclass, and CPC code, so you can be assured that your search results are highly relevant and that your search thoroughly covers the prior art. However, many inventions are placed into multiple classes and subclasses, so you must be diligent enough to check all of the appropriate classes. And rarely, inventions might not be classified into every possible place they could be, even if they disclose features relevant to those places.

To ensure that you truly have found all inventions that include your keywords, in addition to making a classification search, you can perform a keyword search of your invention. To make a computer Keyword (or Boolean) search, you select a combination of keywords to describe your invention; for example, "bicycle" and "carbon fiber alloy." The computer will look through its database for any patent that contains all of these words. When it finds any patents that contain your keywords in the combination you specified in your search request, it will display these patents, regardless of their classifications.

If the computer reports too much data for you to conveniently examine—say it's found 200 patents with your words in combination—you should first look at one or two of the patents to see if your invention is shown in an earlier patent (that is—your invention has been "knocked out"). If so, your search is over. If not, you'll need to narrow your search. This is easy. Simply add one or more additional keywords, say "frame," or some details of the alloy, and redo the search with these added keywords until you're left with enough patents to manually review conveniently. Also, you can narrow the search by using narrower (more specific) keywords.

On the other hand, if you get too specific, the computer is likely to report no patents, or just one or two. If this occurs, you'll need to broaden your search. This is just as easy. Merely remove one or more keywords, or broaden your present keywords, and redo the search until you get back what you want. For example, you can eliminate "bicycle" or substitute "frame" for "bicycle" to broaden the search. In summary, to broaden your search (pull out more prior art), use fewer keywords, and to narrow your search (pull out less prior art), use more keywords.

Classification searches and keyword searches can complement each other nicely, and it's a good idea to do both. Performing a keyword search likely will turn up many patents and pre-grant publications you have already seen in your classification search. The more of these documents you come across, the more confident you can be that you have searched all of the proper classes and subclasses. On the other hand, a keyword search may turn up patents placed in relevant classes that you did not find during your classification search. You should go back and search these classes as well. Similarly, you may find synonyms during your classification search that become keywords for your keyword search (or further classification searching).

K. How To Computer Search

Free patent searching systems are useful tools for conducting fair-to-good patent searches on inventions using recent technologies and for making free searches for inventions in older technologies. If you are willing to spend the time to do a thorough job, you can make a fairly complete search online. However, if you are unwilling or unable to spend the time, hire a searcher, because it requires diligence and patience to conduct a thorough patent search on the internet.

If we could assign percentage values to the various types of searches: a good examiner's search might be estimated at 90% (that is—it has about a 90% chance of standing up in court), and a good search on the internet at 70%. (Unfortunately, as in business, there's no certainty in the law.) If your invention is in an active, contemporary field, you should reduce the value of the latter type of searches somewhat, due to

the fact that patent applications in this field are more likely to be pending, and would only appear in a search made by an examiner.

1. Google Patents

Google Patents (patents.google.com) provides a complete, accurate, and easy way to make online searches. Simply enter the keywords and all possible variations you can think of and it will search the entire U.S. patent database and return all relevant patents and pre-grant published applications.

Fig. 6K is Google Patents' main page. It is your gateway to search all of the patents and pre-grant applications publications in more than 100 jurisdictions around the world. To search from this page, enter your key search terms, such as "bicycle" and "fiberglass." You'll get a list of patents that have all of your search terms. Click on a patent to get a new page with all of the parts of the patent and a link to download a PDF of the patent. The main search page also links to a help site and to an Advanced Patent Search.

The Google Patents Advanced Search page (Fig. 6L) is where you can refine your search to look for patents with all of your keywords, an exact phrase, only one of a group of words, or omitting a word. Also it can be used to search for patents by number, title, inventor, assignee, or a specific U.S. or international classification. You can restrict the search to U.S. patents or published U.S. patent applications, utility, design patents, and so on, or by a date or issue or filing date range.

The search box will even automatically search for your keywords in the CPC Scheme and suggest classifications for you to look in. For example, if you put "potash" in the SEARCH TERMS box and click "Synonym" next to it, it will suggest Subclass C05F, and if you click that Subclass it will suggest additional Subclasses and CPC codes. With a little patience, you can conduct a full CPC class and subclass search.

All of these helpful features are free. Thank you, Google!

2. PTO Search With EPO Supplement

The PTO's Patent Public Search (PPS) system can be used to make full-text Keyword patentability searches of U.S. patents back to 1836 (although only the text of patents from 1971 forward has been checked by humans), and U.S. patent applications back to April 2001 when they were first published. You can also use it to make Classification searches by patent number or class and subclass of U.S. patents from 1790 to the present. The PTO's URL for searching services is ppubs.uspto.gov/pubwebapp. The PTO's servers have been vastly improved, so that you can easily and quickly download and view the images of any patent back to 1790. Fig. 6M shows the main page of the PTO's search website—note that you can search any of the three databases US-PGPUB, USPAT, and USOCR separately or together, and that there is a "Help" tab that provides online help in addition to the training mentioned above. You can do a rough extension of your U.S. patentability search at the European Patent Office (EPO) (www.epo.org/en). In addition, the EPO also provides a searchable database for some foreign patents.

3. Limitations of the PTO and Other Systems

All previous inventions (prior art) are relevant when determining whether a new invention qualifies for a patent. Therefore, to be effective, a patent search must cover the earliest prior art that might show your invention. The PTO system and other online search resources provide optical character recognition (OCR) text for U.S. patents (which can be inaccurate and introduce misspellings), and verified full-text searching of U.S. patents back only to 1971. Therefore, you can have confidence in your search results on the PTO's site or Google Patents only if you are completely certain that your invention technology— for example an internet invention—wasn't around prior to 1971. For a low-tech invention that requires searching back beyond this date (for instance, a bicycle) these systems will only verifiably provide a fraction of the total

Fig. 6K—Google Patents (Main Page)

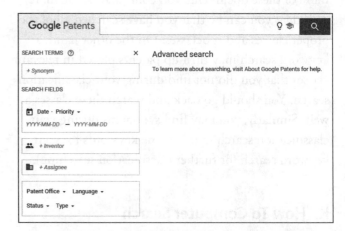

Fig. 6L—Google Patents Advanced Search

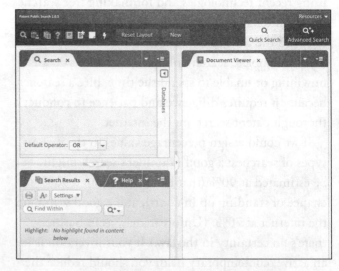

Fig. 6M—PTO Search Site (Main Page)

prior art for that invention. For these inventions, it is absolutely essential to perform a classification search. Luckily, the PTO makes its patent data available to the public, so any online patent search facility that you access should provide the same coverage.

A second limitation is the fact that you must depend on keywords and the PTO's classification system. Traditional patent searching uses just the classification scheme to find relevant prior art.

This scheme is the result of humans grouping like inventions together and does not depend on the whimsy of which search terms you select. The keyword system, on the other hand, requires you to come up with the right words in your search request. However, patents are often written with legal-sounding terms or technical jargon in place of otherwise ordinary terms. For example, a patent for a telephone may be titled "Full Duplex Voice Telecommunication Device." Such a patent may never be found with "telephone" as the search term. Worse yet, early inventors who filed foundational patents may not have used terminology, like "telephone," that later became associated with the technology after its widespread adoption. This limitation is inherent in any computerized searching system based on search terms. The disadvantages of the keyword search system can to some extent be overcome by following the tips described below as well as by using the logic implicit in the Boolean search technique and supplementing your Keyword search with a Classification search.

4. Important Searching Tips

Your searching can be more productive and accurate if you follow these important tips:

1. *Less is more.* The fewer words used to define a search, the broader the results, and vice versa. For example, in 2022, a search done with the three- word term "ergonomic computer mouse" found 78 U.S. patents; a search done with the two-word term "computer mouse" found more

than 28,000 U.S. patents; and a search done with the single term "mouse" found more than 832,000 U.S. patents.

2. *Use alternative terms.* A variety of different terms are often used in patents to describe similar inventions, so search with as many alternative terms as you can think of. For example, a computer mouse is also referred to as a "computer input device" or a "pointing device."

3. *Make good use of the Boolean connectors*, AND, OR, NOT, and XOR ("exclusive or"; that is, A or B but not both) to connect words or terms in a box in any of the search methods, except for Patent Number Search. For example, "ergonomic AND mouse" can be a good search query. When Boolean connectors are used, multiple-word terms must be enclosed in quotes. For example, "ergonomic AND 'pointing device'" will search for all patents that have the word "ergonomic" AND the expression "pointing device." Boolean connectors can also be used to search for inventions with alternative terms simultaneously. For example, "computer mouse OR 'pointing device'" finds all patents with either the word "ergonomic" OR the expression "pointing device."

4. *Use wild cards.* Use the asterisk (*) as a wild card to represent any character or characters. For example, John* finds patents by all inventors with the first or last name starting with John, and ending with any character or characters, including John, Johnny, Johnson, and Johnston. Use the question mark (?) as a wild card to represent any single character. For example, "?am," "ram," "cam," "jam," and so on.

5. *Inventor Names.* Always enter inventor names last-name first; for example, Edison Thomas.

6. *Class and References.* If you find a relevant patent, click on the "Intl. Class" and "U.S. Class" links to display patents for potentially similar inventions, and the "U.S. References" link to view the patents specifically cited as being similar.

L. Summary

There are many reasons to perform a patentability search for your invention: to save needless work and expenditures, to facilitate patent application preparation prosecution, to learn more about your invention, and to facilitate licensing. To possibly avoid making a full search, make a quick preliminary search yourself in stores and catalogs.

If you hire someone to make a search, hire a competent, experienced searcher, preferably a patent agent or attorney, and prepare your searcher with a full description of your invention. In order to analyze a search report, read the cited patents and other references carefully and determine what novel features your invention has and whether these are nonobvious.

All patent searches must now be made on a computer. To search, use the Patent Public Search system, preferably at the PTO in Alexandria, a Regional Office, or a PTRC computer search facility near you where you can get personal help from the staff. If you must, you can resort to using the internet; namely, the free website services of Google, the PTO, and the EPO (or use a fee-based commercial service). Don't forget to search other databases you might know. Computer searches should be made using either keywords by looking for patents with combinations of appropriate keywords, or the CPC system where you can review all the patents in a particular subject-matter class. If you make a computer search, and you have a low-tech invention, a classification search is essential.

CHAPTER

7

What Should I Do Next?

A. Fig. 7A—Invention Decision Chart	174
B. Drop It If You Don't See Commercial Potential (Chart Route 10-12-14-X)	174
C. File an Application and Sell or License It If You See Patentability (Chart Route 14-16-18-20-22-C)	176
1. Offensive Rights for Your Invention	176
2. Respect for Your Invention	176
3. You Have Rights Even If You Sign a Manufacturer's Waiver	176
4. You'll Be Offering More So You'll Get More	176
D. Manufacture and Distribute Your Invention Yourself, Keeping It as a Trade Secret (Chart Route 20-32-D)	177
E. File Patent Application and Manufacture and Distribute Your Invention Yourself (Trade-Secret Protectable Invention) (Chart Route 20-32-34-E)	178
F. File Patent Application and Manufacture and Distribute Invention Yourself (Non-Trade-Secret Protectable Invention) (Chart Route 20-32-34-E)	179
G. Try to Sell Invention to Manufacturer Before Obtaining a "Regular" Patent Application (Chart Route 10-12-14-16-18-B)	179
H. If You Have Commercial Potential Without Patentability, License or Sell Your Invention to a Manufacturer Without Filing (Chart Route 16-24-26-28-30-B)	179
1. Record Conception Properly	180
2. Provide a Clever Trademark	180
3. Provide a Unique Patentable Design	180
4. Provide Distinctive "Trade Dress"	181
5. Provide Copyrightable Labeling	181
6. Consider Trade Secret Protection	181
7. Submit Your Idea to Quirky.com	181
I. Make and Sell Your Invention Yourself Without a Utility Patent Application (Chart Route 16-24-26-28-30-A)	182
J. Summary	182

Inventor's Commandment 9

After making your commercial evaluation and search, consider the following alternatives before proceeding or dropping the invention: File a Provisional Patent Application (PPA), file a Regular Patent Application (RPA), test the market* for up to a year and then consider filing, keep it a trade secret, file a design patent application, use a clever trademark, use copyright coverage, and/or use distinctive "trade dress."

* See caveats on test marketing below.

Now that you have an idea of the patentability and commercial status of your invention, it's time to make a plan for acquiring legal rights. You might think that your next step would be to prepare and file a patent application, but that's not necessarily the case. Review the Invention Decision Chart (Fig. 7A) to simplify and organize the alternatives.

A. Fig. 7A—Invention Decision Chart

The numbers in parentheses in the following discussion refer to the boxes on the chart in Fig. 7A. While there are six final options, some of these can be reached by several routes. Keep in mind that any marketing before filing by anyone other than the inventor or someone who obtained details of the invention from the inventor will defeat any rights to a patent on the invention marketed. And if the inventor, or one who obtained details of the invention from the inventor, publicly discloses the invention, the inventor has one year from the date of disclosure to file a patent application. That's an issue if you, or your company or associates want to test market for up to a year before filing. Beware: if you test market before filing you may lose foreign rights and increase the possibility of theft and an expensive and uncertain derivation proceeding.

B. Drop It If You Don't See Commercial Potential (Chart Route 10-12-14-X)

Assuming that you've invented something (Box 10) and recorded the conception properly (Box 12), you should then proceed to build and test your invention as soon as practicable, or consider filing a Provisional Patent Application (PPA), provided you're aware of all the disadvantages of the PPA. If building and testing would be difficult, you should wait until after you evaluate your invention's commercial potential (Box 14), or patentability (Box 16). But always keep the building and testing as a goal; it will help you to evaluate commercial potential. What's more, as you'll find, a working model can be extremely valuable when you show the invention to a manufacturer.

Your next step is stated in Box 14—investigate your invention's commercial potential using the criteria of Chapter 4. Assuming you decide that your invention has little or no commercial potential, your answer to the commercial question is "No," so you would thus follow the "No" line from Box 14 to the ultimate decision, Box X, which says "Invent something else."

While you may be disappointed at having spent time and effort recording your invention, investigating its commercial potential, building and testing it, or searching it, your time and effort were definitely not wasted. You haven't failed in any way—unless you failed to learn a lesson from your experience. Edison had 3,000 failures, yet he regarded these as positive experiences since he learned at least 3,000 things he didn't know before. Armed with what you learned, you'll have a better chance at success and will encounter smoother sailing with your next invention.

"Our greatest glory is not in never falling, but in getting up every time we do."

—Confucius

CHAPTER 7 | WHAT SHOULD I DO NEXT? | 175

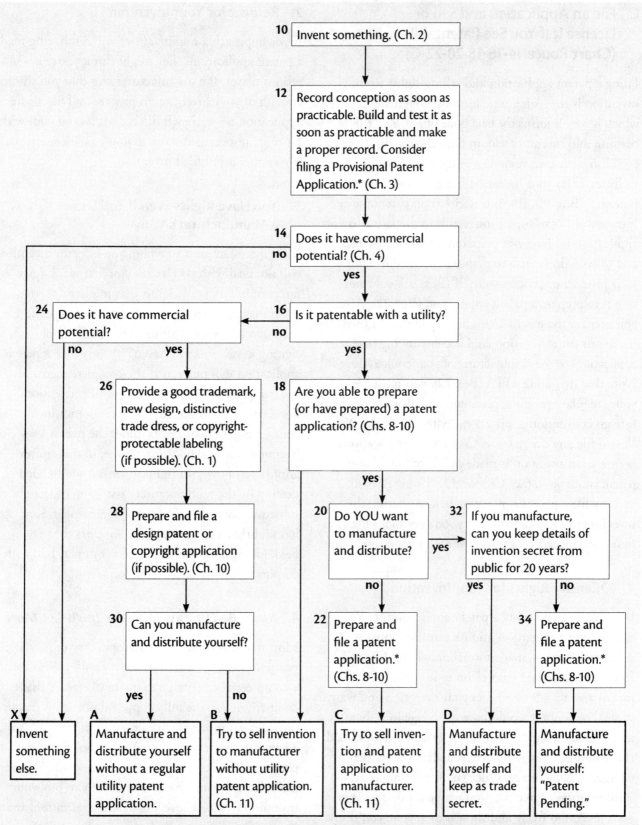

Fig. 7A—Invention Decision Chart

C. File an Application and Sell or License It If You See Patentability (Chart Route 14-16-18-20-22-C)

Filing a patent application and selling rights to the invention is the usual route for most solo inventors, which is why it forms the backbone of Fig. 7A. This is because solo inventors seldom have the capability to establish their own manufacturing and distribution facilities. If (a) your invention has good commercial potential (Box 14), (b) your decision on patentability is favorable (Box 16), (c) you're able to prepare a patent application (or have one prepared for you) (Box 18), and (d) you don't wish to manufacture and distribute your product or process yourself (Box 20), your next step is to prepare a patent application (Box 22). After you prepare the patent application, you should then try to sell your invention (and accompanying patent application) to the manufacturer of your choice (Box C). Note that if you file a PPA (Box 12), you must file your "regular" patent application, and also any desired foreign convention applications, within one year. You should file any desired non-Convention applications before your invention is made public or before any patent issues on it. (See Chapter 12, "Going Abroad.")

Why file a patent application before offering the invention to a manufacturer? A good question, which has four good answers. Let's look at each one individually.

1. Offensive Rights for Your Invention

By preparing and filing a patent application, you've defined your invention and its ramifications in very precise terms, made formal drawings of it, and formally established your claim to it in the PTO. That means anyone who later sees your invention and wants to steal or adopt it would have to engage in elaborate and (usually) illegal forgeries and other activities. And, the would-be thief will have filed after you, which is a serious disadvantage. Once you file the application, most attorneys agree that you may publish details of your invention freely and show it to anyone you think may have an interest in it (unless you've chosen to maintain your invention as a trade secret while your patent application is pending—see below).

2. Respect for Your Invention

If you approach a manufacturer without having filed a patent application, they might think you're not a serious player. If a manufacturer sees that you think enough of your invention to prepare and file a patent application on it, they'll likely treat it (and you) with far more respect and more serious consideration than if you offer an unfiled invention.

3. You Have Rights Even If You Sign a Manufacturer's Waiver

Most manufacturers to whom you offer an invention will not deal with you unless you first waive (give up) certain potential claims that might arise from the transaction (such as your right to charge the manufacturer with stealing your idea). Simply put, signing a waiver if you haven't already filed a patent application will put you at the complete mercy of the company to whom you show your invention. Fortunately, however, such waivers do not involve your giving up your rights under the patent laws. So, having a patent application on file, in this context, affords you powerful rights against underhanded dealing by the manufacturer (assuming the patent subsequently issues). One inventor, Stephen Key, has said that a patent application levels the playing field, giving an inventor the power to play ball with corporate America.

4. You'll Be Offering More So You'll Get More

Most manufacturers want a proprietary or privileged position—that is, a position that entitles them to a commercial advantage in the marketplace that competitors can't readily copy and obtain. A patent provides a very highly privileged position: a 17- to 18-year (approximately) monopoly. So, if you have a patent application that already covers your invention, manufacturers may be far more likely to buy your invention (with its covering patent application) than if you offered them a "naked" invention on which they have to take the time and trouble to file a patent application for you themselves.

> **TIP**
>
> **An exception.** Although, as stated, it's usually best to file your patent application as soon as possible, it may be to your advantage to delay and keep the invention secret or take your chances approaching manufacturers "naked" if your invention is so innovative that it's not likely to be commercialized for many years. Gordon Gould, the inventor of the laser, did this unintentionally when he delayed filing his patent application because he mistakenly believed he needed a working model to file. His mistake worked to his great advantage, since his delay postponed his monopoly period so that it coincided with the laser's commercial period, thereby turning what would have been a worthless patent into pure gold.

Common Misconception: You shouldn't patent your invention, since someone will see your patent, copy your invention, and make it more cheaply.

Fact: Copiers rarely use patents as a basis for their activities. Usually they copy successful products in the marketplace by reverse engineering. They'll be less likely to do this if it is patented (which is one reason that patent number marking is essential—see Chapter 15), and a patent will enable you to sue them to stop their production or importation, or get royalties from them.

D. Manufacture and Distribute Your Invention Yourself, Keeping It as a Trade Secret (Chart Route 20-32-D)

Even though your invention may be commercially valuable and patentable, it isn't always in your best interest to patent it. The alternative, when possible, is to keep an invention a trade secret and manufacture and sell the invention yourself—for example, by direct mail marketing, broadcast or periodical advertising, possibly eventually working your way up to conventional distributors and retailers. A trade secret has numerous advantages and disadvantages. An invention can be maintained as a trade secret right up until the time a patent application is published or a patent actually issues, but after that the trade secret is lost. If you file a nonpublication request (NPR) at the time of filing, and you don't file for a patent outside

the U.S., your application will never be published if it doesn't issue. (Your application will not issue if you can't convince the PTO to grant you a patent, or if you abandon it.) In that case your invention will remain a trade secret as long as you continue to treat it as one, and as long as the invention is not publicly disclosed by others, provided it can't be discovered from the final product (reverse engineered).

You should not consider (and you can't protect) every bit of information as a trade secret. You can only protect secret information that has commercial value because it is not known by others. Write up this important information—the crown jewels. After you write it up, take precautions to keep the information secret. Keep your documentation safe, don't let anyone see it (and don't let anyone witness the actual manufacture of the product) unless they have a "need to know" (for example, an employee) and have signed a nondisclosure (keep-confidential) agreement. Also, keep the trade secret information out of any service or instruction manual that goes with the product. You don't need to file any governmental forms or applications to create trade secret rights.

Remember that you can't maintain trade secret rights on an invention unless it can't be discovered from the final product—even if sophisticated reverse engineering is used. One good example of an invention that was kept as a trade secret is the formula used in the Toni home permanent wave kit. Its inventor, Richard Harris, manufactured and sold the unpatented invention through his own company for many years, making large profits, and thereafter sold his business in 1948 for nearly $20 million.

Although not specifically covered on the chart, there is another possibility in the trade secret category. That is, you may sell your invention to a manufacturer who may choose to keep it as a trade secret, provided you've filed an NPR at the time of filing. This may occur with either unpatentable or patentable inventions (Chart routes 16-24-26-28-30-B or 16-18-20-22-C), but you don't have to worry about this alternative since it's the manufacturer's choice, not yours. If you've filed an NPR, the manufacturer can simply allow the patent application to go abandoned so it won't be published, thereby maintaining the trade secret.

> **CAUTION**
>
> **One disadvantage of keeping a "hardware" (as opposed to a process) invention as a trade secret is that someone else can validly patent the hardware if they invent it independently, and can then sue you for patent infringement,** even if you've been using the trade secret commercially! However, under a "prior user's rights" statute (35 U.S.C. § 273), if someone has a method patent, but you've used the method commercially for over a year before the method patent application was filed, you have a complete defense to any action for patent infringement on the method.

> **TIP**
>
> **You shouldn't refer to your abandoned patent application in any other application that will issue as a patent,** since anyone can gain access to an abandoned application that's referred to in a patent.

E. File Patent Application and Manufacture and Distribute Your Invention Yourself (Trade-Secret Protectable Invention) (Chart Route 20-32-34-E)

Suppose your invention is not discoverable from your final product so that you can keep it secret for a while, but not for the life of a patent (Box 32). Or, suppose, after evaluating the advantages and disadvantages of a trade secret under the criteria above, you don't wish to choose the trade-secret route, preferring instead to patent your invention. You should then prepare and file a patent application (Box 34) and then manu-facture and distribute the invention yourself with the notice "patent pending" affixed to the invention (Box E).

Preparing and filing a patent application is a lot of hassle, but if you have a patentable invention and a commercially viable product and you don't pay for a patent application now (by hiring an attorney or doing it yourself), you will pay for it later. If you have a successful product on the market, competitors will copy it. If you "go naked" by putting it out with no patent rights, you won't be able to stop the copiers and you'll lose far more in market share than what a patent would have cost you.

> **CAUTION**
>
> **Keep it secret.** While the patent application is pending, you should—provided you've filed an NPR—not publish any details of your invention. That way, if the patent application is finally rejected, you can allow it to go abandoned and still maintain your trade secret. Remember, by law, the PTO must keep your patent application secret until it's published (your nonprovisional patent application will be published 18 months after filing unless an NPR was filed), or until it issues (if it was not published). In practice, the PTO is very strict in this regard. Until pending patent applications are published or they issue, outsiders have no access to them, and PTO personnel must keep patent applications in strict confidence. If you've filed a patent application without an NPR and decide to maintain your invention as a trade secret, you can still prevent the normal 18-month publication of the application by abandoning the application before it's published.

> **TIP**
>
> **Effect of "patent pending" notice.** The patent-pending notice on your product does not confer any legal rights, but it is used by most manufacturers who have a patent application on file in order to deter potential competitors from copying their inventions. The notice effectively warns competitors that the manufacturer may get a patent on the product, so that if they do invest the money and effort in tooling to copy the invention, they could be enjoined (legally prevented) from further manufacturing, with a consequent waste of their invest-ment. However, make sure you don't use a patent-pending notice with a product that is not actually covered by a pending application; that's a criminal offense.

F. File Patent Application and Manufacture and Distribute Invention Yourself (Non-Trade-Secret Protectable Invention) (Chart Route 20-32-34-E)

This will be the route followed by most inventors who wish to manufacture their own invention. Assume that the essence of your invention, like most, is discoverable from the final product. You should then prepare and file a patent application (Box 34), and then manufacture and distribute the invention yourself (Box E).

Remember that any patent application will be invalid if the PPA or RPA is filed after marketing done by someone other than the inventor, or someone who obtained details of the invention from the inventor. In summary, test marketing before filing by anyone other than the inventor, or one who obtained details of the invention from the inventor, is now a no-no.

 TIP

Don't give up your day job. While patents can sometimes be very profitable for their inventors, great success stories are few and far between. Do not depend on your invention or any patent to pull you out of poverty or change your lifestyle, because few patents do this. Even if a patent is successful, it usually takes years to bear fruit. Usually, business acumen is more important than a patent to ultimate financial success. Keep your present vocation unless and until you attain success. If your invention does succeed, that's a great win and you should enjoy the success to the fullest. However, in case it does not, you can still continue as before and learn from the experience.

G. Try to Sell Invention to Manufacturer Before Obtaining a "Regular" Patent Application (Chart Route 10-12-14-16-18-B)

This route is especially useful if you've filed a PPA on the invention (Box 12), but it can also be used if you've built and tested the invention and properly recorded your building and testing activities. After filing a PPA or building and testing and recording your efforts (Box 12), see if the invention has commercial potential (Box 14) and if it's patentable (Box 16). If so, try to sell your invention to a manufacturer (Box B) in the hope that the manufacturer will have the patent application prepared for you, either on the basis of your PPA or without the PPA. If you take this route, you should be sure either that your PPA is properly prepared or that you've properly documented conception, building, and testing. Use this route only if you can't prepare (or can't afford to have prepared) a regular patent application because:

- if you've only built and tested the invention without properly recording your activities, you run the risk of an unscrupulous manufacturer stealing your invention by filing a patent application on your invention before you do, and
- if you've filed a PPA, you'll have all of the disadvantages of the PPA. (See Chapter 3 for a discussion of the advantages and disadvantages of filing a PPA.)

H. If You Have Commercial Potential Without Patentability, License or Sell Your Invention to a Manufacturer Without Filing (Chart Route 16-24-26-28-30-B)

If your invention isn't patentable as a utility patent (that is—the decision in Box 16 is negative), don't give up; there's still hope. Many fortunes have been made on products that weren't patentable. For instance, the Apple computer made its designer-promoters, Jobs and Wozniak, multimillionaires, yet lacked any significant inventive concepts and never was awarded a major patent. Ditto for Henry Ford's automobile and George Eastman's Kodak camera.

Thus you should now decide, on the basis of your commercial potential and patentability evaluations, whether your invention nevertheless possesses "significant market novelty" (Box 24). If so, it may in fact be quite profitable if introduced to the market. Put differently, if your patentability search produces close prior art, but not a dead ringer, this indicates that probably no one has tried your specific, particular idea before, although someone has come close enough to preclude you from getting a patent. However, if you feel, looking back on your commercial-potential and patentability evaluations, that it doesn't have significant market novelty—that is, there's little chance of commercial success—then there isn't much hope and you'll have to try again (Box X).

Assuming that your invention does have significant market novelty (Box 24) but does not qualify for a utility patent, there are several ways that you can use to obtain proprietary rights on your invention and make it more attractive to potential manufacturers. Let's take a closer look at these.

1. Record Conception Properly

While recording conception won't provide you with any rights against independent creators, or "reverse engineers," it will establish (a) you as the inventor, and (b) the date of your invention, so you'll be able to prove that you invented it and when you did so. This may be of great help in stopping any invention thieves who copy it illegally before it's out.

2. Provide a Clever Trademark

One good way to make your invention more attractive is to provide a clever trademark for it (Box 26). A trademark is a name or other signifier for a product. A clever trademark can be a very powerful marketing tool—that is, a tool that will greatly enhance the value and salability of your invention and give you added proprietary rights to sell to a manufacturer. Examples of clever, suggestive trademarks are Ivory® for a soap and Hush Puppies® for shoes. Also consider Sunkist® citrus fruit, Red Bull® energy drinks, Roach Motel® roach traps, and Fitbit® activity trackers.

If you think the mark is valuable and that you (or a company that will license the product) will be able to offer a product with the mark within a year or so, then you can file an Intent-to-Use trademark application with the PTO to begin the process of registering the mark.

3. Provide a Unique Patentable Design

If the invention that fails to qualify for a utility patent is a tangible product, the second trick to obtaining proprietary rights is to create a distinctive design (Box 26). Then, perhaps, a design patent can be obtained. By distinctive design, we're referring to a shape or layout that is unique and different from anything you've seen so far. The design, in this case, doesn't mean the function or internal structure of the product, but only its outward, nonfunctional, ornamental, aesthetic shape or layout that makes it distinct visually.

For example, the D-shaped Heavyhands® weights and Dizzy Gillespie's trumpet with its upwardly bent bell section are excellent examples of valuable design inventions. If you've invented a computer, a new case shape can be a design invention. For a bicycle, a new frame shape design would be a design invention. From abacuses to zithers, from airplanes to zippers, almost every humanly made object under the sun can be redesigned or reshaped in a new way so that it can be covered by a design patent and also can be made more attractive to potential buyers.

However, for a design patent to be applicable, the new features must be for aesthetic or ornamental purposes and should not have any significant functional purpose—otherwise the PTO will reject it as nonornamental—that is, only a utility patent will be appropriate. Also, the design must be inseparable from the object and not merely surface ornamentation. In the latter case, copyright is the proper form of coverage. For example, the label design on a jar of juice cannot be protected by a design patent, but a new shape for the jar would qualify for one. If you do come up with a distinctive design, you should, of course, record it in the same manner as you recorded your invention. And as with your invention, you should build a prototype or model as soon as practicable. You should also prepare and file a design-patent application (Box 28) on the ornamental appearance (not workings) of your invention.

A design-patent application consists simply of a drawing and a few forms that you fill out; it's very easy and economical to prepare.

4. Provide Distinctive "Trade Dress"

If you can't come up with a new design (or even if you can), you can enhance the proprietary value of your invention by providing it with a distinctive "trade dress"—distinctive shapes (the Coca-Cola bottle) or packaging (the choice of red colors on the Netflix envelope). Collectively, these types of identifying trade dress features are commonly protected under trademark law. (Note: Functional aspects of trade dress cannot be protected under trademark law.)

5. Provide Copyrightable Labeling

Look closely at some of the packaged products that you see in your home or on display in a store for a copyright notice; for example, "© 2022 S.C. Johnson & Son, Inc." This copyright is intended to cover either the wording on the label or container, the artwork, or both. While relatively easy to design around (that is—come up with a close but noninfringing alternative), unique labeling with a copyright notice nevertheless provides a measure of offensive rights that is well worth the small effort it takes to invoke. Many market researchers have shown that an attractive label can make all the difference in the success of a product. Accordingly, it can pay, if you're marketing a packaged product, to spend some

effort, either on your own or in hiring a designer, to come up with an attractive, unique label, affix a copyright notice—for example, © Smith and Sons—and apply for copyright registration.

6. Consider Trade Secret Protection

A trade secret is any information that has commercial value, that has been maintained in confidence by a business, and that is not known by competitors. An inventor who owns trade secrets is entitled to court relief against those who have stolen the secrets or divulged them in violation of a legal duty—for example, after signing an agreement not to disclose (a nondisclosure agreement or NDA), or the duty of an employee to keep the secrets of his or her employer. Keep your invention secret, at least until you file. Or, if you choose not to file, and your invention is not easy to reverse engineer, consider maintaining trade secrecy as a form of invention protection.

7. Submit Your Idea to Quirky.com

In lieu of submitting your unpatentable but commercially valuable brainchild to conventional manufacturers, one online service, Quirky.com, seeks niche products to evaluate and manufacture even though the product may not be different enough to be patentable. As reported in *Parade* magazine, Quirky, founded by Ben Kaufman, receives ideas from the public, submits them to its members (called "Quirks"), and designs and manufactures the product if (a) the Quirks provide a favorable opinion and (b) Quirky gets enough premanufacturing orders to cover production costs. Quirky isn't concerned with patents and relies on fast production and marketing to head off potential copiers. They charge submitters $10 to submit an idea (to make sure submitters are serious) and they pay royalties on the sales as the product is manufactured and sold.

I. Make and Sell Your Invention Yourself Without a Utility Patent Application (Chart Route 16-24-26-28-30-A)

Here we assume again that you have an unpatentable invention, but hopefully one that you can make and distribute yourself (Box 30). It's generally better to do so (Box A) than to try to sell it to a manufacturer outright (Box B). Even if you have a good trademark, a design patent application, distinctive trade dress, and/or a unique label, the absence of a utility patent application means a manufacturer does not get a privileged position, and so will generally not be as inclined to buy your invention. However, if you decide to manufacture the invention yourself, and you reach the market first, you'll have a significant marketing advantage despite the lack of a utility patent. Also, because you're the manufacturer, you'll make a much larger profit per item than if you received royalties from a manufacturer. Note: If you're not going to, or won't be able to, bring your invention to the market right away and you want to prevent anyone else from patenting it, consider making a "defensive publication" (see Chapter 14) of it to create prior art on it.

J. Summary

After you make your patentability decision and evaluate the commercial potential of your invention, you have a number of possible routes to take.

- If you feel that your invention lacks commercial potential, drop it and move on to something else.
- If you feel that it has commercial potential, but you can't prepare a regular patent application, file a PPA or try to sell it without filing a PPA or an RPA.
- If your invention is patentable, file first and then try to sell it to a manufacturer. (You should file first to secure your rights, especially if you sign a manufacturer's waiver form.)

If your invention isn't patentable, you may be able to file a design patent application, or secure trademark rights, copyright, or trade dress rights before offering it to a manufacturer. You can make and sell the invention yourself with or without a patent application, and you can keep it as a trade secret after putting it on the market if it's the type of invention that can't be reverse engineered. Test marketing before filing a PPA or an RPA by anyone other than the inventor, or one who obtained details of the invention from the inventor, will defeat your patent.

CHAPTER 8

How to Draft the Specification and Initial Drawings

A. Lay Inventors *Can* Do It!	185
B. What's Contained in a Patent Application	185
C. What Happens When Your Application Is Received by the PTO	187
D. Do Preliminary Work Before Preparing Your Patent Application	189
1. Review the Prior Art	189
2. Review Your Disclosure	189
3. Ramifications	189
4. Sources of Supply	190
5. Advantages/Disadvantages	191
E. Flowchart	191
F. Your Written Description Must Comply With the Full Disclosure Rules	191
G. Software, Computer-Related Inventions, and Business Methods	195
H. First Prepare Sketches and Name Parts	197
1. Machine Sketches	198
2. Chemical Composition Sketches	198
3. Computer, Chemical, or Mechanical Process Sketches	201
I. Drafting the Specification	201
1. Drafting Tips	201
2. The Parts of the Specification	203
J. Review Your Specification and Abstract Carefully	215
K. Use of Artificial Intelligence (AI) To Draft the Specification	215
L. Checklist for Your Patent Application Draft	216
M. Specification of Sample Patent Application	216
N. Summary	216

Inventor's Commandment 10

Your patent application should not contain any statements that the courts could possibly use against you to limit the claims of your invention—that is, do not mention any problems with the prior art that are not already known, or that your invention doesn't solve; do not indicate that any embodiment is preferred; do not include any specific advantage unless at least one embodiment has this advantage (even then, indicate only that "one or more aspects" have the advantages); do not include any objects or goals of your invention; make the summary and abstract as broad and nonspecific as possible; do not refer to "the invention" but only to "this embodiment," do not state that any part is essential, and include as many embodiments as possible.

Inventor's Commandment 11

Your patent application specification and drawings must contain a description of your invention in full, clear, concise, and exact terms so that anyone having ordinary skill in the field will be readily able to make and use it. While a statute requires you to disclose the best mode for carrying out the invention, you should disclose all possible modes (embodiments) without indicating any preference, unless the PTO requires you to do so.

Inventor's Commandment 12

You should "sell" your invention to the examiner or anyone else who may read your patent application. State all the disadvantages of the prior art factually (if at all) and the advantages of one or more embodiments (not the invention per se) in a nonlimiting way.

This chapter (and the next two) are the heart of this book: They cover the writing and transmittal of your patent application to the Patent and Trademark Office (PTO). This chapter provides an overview of the patent application drafting process and contains specific instructions on drafting a specification and preliminary drawings. Chapter 9 explains how to draft patent claims (sentence fragments that delineate the precise scope of the patent being sought). Chapter 10 explains how to "final" the application, and the precise steps involved in transmitting it to the PTO. Chapter 10 also covers design patent applications.

Draft the Claims First

Patent attorneys almost always draft the claims before drafting the specification and drawings. Why? Because the specification must show in a figure, and describe in text, every element of every claim. If you draft the claims first, they will provide a good checklist as you draft the specification. How? Your invention disclosure (see Chapter 3) should provide enough information for you to take a first cut at the claims. Drafting the claims and the specification is an iterative process, and you will need to go back and forth between them as you draft. Though you can read chapters 8 and 9 in any order you like—you may find it helpful to draft the claims first.

Have you filed a Provisional Patent Application (PPA)? You may convert the PPA to a regular patent application (RPA) even if the PPA did not include any claims. (35 U.S.C. § 111.) However, converting the PPA to an RPA is not recommended because your patent will expire 20 years from the earlier date of your PPA (rather than the later date of your RPA).

Instead, if you filed a PPA and are ready to file your RPA, file a separate RPA to start the 20-year term from the date of your RPA. To file a separate RPA, follow the instructions in this chapter for preparing an RPA. You should claim the benefit of the PPA in the RPA. If the one-year anniversary of your PPA falls on a weekend or holiday, you can still get the benefit of the PPA—in the United States—by filing the RPA on the next business day. (Other countries are not so generous; see Chapter 12 for more details.) Remember that your PPA will not be read by any

PTO personnel unless you need to rely on its date to predate a reference cited against your claims, or in case you're unfortunate enough to get into a derivation proceeding (an unlikely situation in which the PTO must decide who is entitled to a patent, when two pending patent applications by different applicants claim the same invention).

A. Lay Inventors *Can* Do It!

It's a common myth that a lay inventor won't be able to prepare a patent application, or prepare it properly. Lay inventors can and have done very good jobs, sometimes better than patent attorneys, by following this book. To prepare a proper patent application, you should be mainly concerned with four basic, essential considerations:

1. The specification (description and operation of your invention and drawings) should be detailed enough so that there will be no doubt that one skilled in the art will be able to make and use the invention after reading it.
2. You should not state anything in the application that a court could use to limit your invention.
3. The main claims should be as broad as the prior art permits. (More about this in Chapter 9.)
4. You should "sell" your invention by stressing all of its advantages in a nonlimiting way.

All the other matters are of lesser import and can be fixed if necessary.

B. What's Contained in a Patent Application

A regular patent application that is filed by mail or hand delivery to the PTO consists of the following parts, which are all sent together to the PTO after assembly in the below order. (Certain items that are omitted when filing electronically with the PTO's Patent Center are indicated by the ‡ symbol.) We strongly recommend filing using Patent Center, since the PTO now requires a hefty surcharge when filing by paper.

1. A self-addressed, stamped postcard ‡
2. A check or, if paying by credit card, a completed Form PTO-2038 for the filing fee. ‡

3. A transmittal letter, Form AIA/15 for utility applications, Form AIA/18 for designs, or Form AIA/19 for plants.
4. A Fee Transmittal, Form SB/17.‡
5. An Application Data Sheet (ADS), Form AIA/14, to provide the bibliographic data about the application (inventors' names, addresses, etc.). This document is mandatory if filing by Patent Center, and it is mandatory if filing an RPA that claims the benefit of an earlier patent application, but we also recommended that you file one if you are filing by mail to reduce data-entry errors. You can use a simpler declaration (item 8 below), Form AIA/01, if you include an ADS.
6. A Specification containing the sections listed below.
7. A drawing or drawings of the invention—unless the invention is of a nature where drawings are not needed (this is rare; it is recommended that you include drawings, even if you think you don't need them).
8. A completed Patent Application Declaration (PAD) form, Form AIA/08. (Use the simpler AIA/01 if you include an Application Data Sheet—see Item 10.) The PAD is a statement under penalty of perjury that you're the true inventor and that you acknowledge a duty to keep the PTO informed of all material information and prior art related to your invention.
9. (Optional) A Nonpublication Request (NPR), Form SB/35. Send this if you don't intend to file counterpart applications outside the U.S. and don't want the application to be published 18 months after filing (if it's still pending then), for example, if you want to keep your invention secret if it doesn't issue.
10. (Optional) An Information Disclosure Statement, List of Prior Art Cited by Applicant, Forms SB08a and 08b, and copies of such prior art, other than U.S. patent references. Technically, these aren't part of the patent application, but because they're supposed to be sent to the PTO with or soon after the application, they are included here. These inform the PTO of relevant

186 | PATENT IT YOURSELF

prior art or any circumstances known to you that may potentially affect the novelty or obviousness of your invention.

The specification (item 7 above, and the subject of this chapter), has the following sections in the following order. (Sections having a † might not be applicable; if not, they can be omitted or the phrase "not applicable" should follow the section heading.)

1. Title of the Invention (no more than 500 characters).

2. Cross-Reference to Related Applications.† This is used to refer to and reiterate any claim priority of any PPA or prior related applications that you've filed. As noted, however, it cannot replace references to such applications in an ADS for the purpose of claiming priority.

3. Statement Regarding Federally Sponsored Research or Development.† This is used to indicate that the invention was made under a government contract and that the government has rights in it.

4. Names of Parties to a Joint Research Agreement.† This is used to indicate that the invention may have multiple owners whose earlier work on the subject might not count against the invention as "prior art" (see Chapter 9).

5. Incorporation by Reference Statement.† This is used to identify, for inclusion in the application, a computer program listing, a nucleotide or amino acid sequence listing, or large tabular data attached as one or more data files in an appendix or on a read-only optical disc (i.e., a CD-ROM). If this situation applies to you, you should consult MPEP 608.05 for the particular language that should appear here, and for the types of data accepted by the PTO.

6. Background. This section should state the general field (area) of the invention, any known problems that the invention definitely solves, and discuss the relevant prior art (previous patents and other relevant developments in the same technological areas). Do not include any of your inventive concepts in the Background section, or the PTO will consider them admitted prior art that you are not entitled to protect.

7. Summary. This should briefly describe the invention as claimed.

8. Brief Description of the Drawings. † This is a brief listing of the Drawing figures and may include the subsection below, Reference Numerals. This section must be included if you submit any Drawings, which will almost always be the case.

9. Reference Numerals (optional but desirable). † These are the Drawing numbers that designate the respective parts of your invention, such as "10 motor," "12 shaft," and so on.

10. Detailed Description. This is a narrative description of the structure of the invention's main embodiment, which describes how to make and use "embodiments" of your invention by referring (by number) to the Drawings and Reference Numerals. If you have multiple ramifications, include a separate subsection of the Detailed Description for each. If they are closely related or involve only relatively minor changes to the main embodiment, indicate in the narrative how the main embodiment can be ramified.

11. Conclusion.† Although it need not have a separate heading, this part again summarizes the invention's advantages, the alternative physical forms or uses it can take, and includes a broadening paragraph to remind any judge or jury that it shouldn't be limited to the particular form(s) shown.

12. Claims. These are precise sentence fragments that delineate the exact nature of your invention —see Chapter 9. Begin the listing of claims on a new page with: "What is claimed is:"

13. Abstract. This is a brief (150 words or fewer) summary of the entire technical content of the application.

14. Sequence Listing.† Include this heading only if a nucleotide or amino acid sequence is part of the invention and you provide it on paper.

---

† If this section is not applicable, it can be omitted or the phrase "not applicable" should follow the heading.

37 CFR 1.77 states that the elements of a patent Specification should be arranged in the above order, with the above headings in capital letters, without underlining or bold type. Use this format for the smoothest sailing of your application through the PTO. However, because the headings are rather broad and don't always break your application into enough easily digestible parts, add additional headings as needed, namely: "Advantages," "Reference Numerals," and "Description and Operation" of the various embodiments. Add any further headings you think would be useful, especially if your application is long or technically complex.

Note that the Specification includes the written Description of the invention, the Claims, and the Abstract. This is according to a patent statute (35 U.S.C. § 112) and tradition in the PTO. However, many practitioners and previous editions of this book referred to the Specification as the written Description without including the Claims. To be consistent with the statute and PTO usage, the statutory definition of Specification—that is, the written Description, Claims, and Abstract—is used.

Note also that a printed patent contains additional data, such as references cited, field of search, and so on. You should not include this additional data in your patent application. The PTO will add this data when they print the patent.

A Provisional Patent Application (PPA) must include some, but not all, of the parts just listed for a regular patent application. The parts that must be included for a PPA are:

- items 1–4, and 6 (postcard, payment, cover sheet (Form SB/16), fee transmittal form, and drawings), and
- in the Specification, items 1 (title), 8 (brief description of the drawing figures), and 10 (detailed description).

Note that the PPA uses a different cover sheet instead of a transmittal letter, and has a different fee. Also, if filing the PPA electronically using Patent Center, an ADS (item 5) will be automatically created for you at the time of filing.

C. What Happens When Your Application Is Received by the PTO

Once the PTO receives your application, it will go to the Office of Patent Application Processing (OPAP). They'll scan all of your papers sent by mail or assemble all of your "papers" filed online, assign a filing date and serial number to your application, put this information onto your postcard if you filed by mail, and return it. If you filed online, the PTO's server (computer) will provide you with an instant equivalent of the postcard receipt.

Then, regardless of how you filed, if everything is not complete—for example, you didn't sign the application or pay the proper fee—they'll send you an objections sheet (called a "Notice to of Incomplete Application Parts"), indicating what you must do to complete the application. Once your disclosure is complete, OPAP will send you an official filing receipt and forward your file to the drafting department, where your drawings will be reviewed for formal requirements. If any nondisclosure parts of the application are missing or incomplete—for example, you didn't pay the proper fee, submit a PAD, or submit comprehensible drawings—they'll send you a "Notice to File Missing Parts," indicating what you must do to put the application into a state that can be examined. They may send you a notice stating that your application will not be examined until you file replacement drawings; if so, file corrected drawings in the time allotted. Once you have corrected any deficiencies, your file will be sent to an appropriate examining division.

Within a few months to a few years, your application will be reviewed by an examiner who will usually send you an "Office Action." The Office Action will do one or more of the following:

- allow your application, subject to a final fee payment (this is rare)
- object to one or more informalities of your application
- object to one or more aspects of your specification and/or drawings

Copyright and Patent Issues:
Using or Reproducing Prior Art in Connection With Your Patent Application

It is common for an applicant to reproduce non-patent literature (NPL) when submitting an Information Disclosure Statement (IDS) and occasionally to use text or drawings from a prior-art patent in the patent application. Occasionally there have been disputes as to whether a patent's text or drawings are protected by copyright, or alternatively whether copyrighted NPL can be reproduced to submit prior art with an IDS. With regard to using extracts from patents, it is the position of the PTO that, "Subject to limited exceptions reflected in 37 CFR 1.71(d) & (e) and 1.84(s), the text and drawings of a patent are typically not subject to copyright restrictions." (See: www.uspto.gov/terms-use-uspto-websites.) With regard to copying and submitting NPL with an IDS, in January 2012, the PTO's General Counsel issued the PTO's position on fair use and NPLs and concluded, "We believe that it is fair use for an applicant to make copies of NPL and submit those copies to the PTO during examination in an IDS."

The issue regarding using extracts from patents is somewhat confusing because PTO regulations (37 CFR 1.84(s)) permit copyright notices regarding authorship in patent text or drawings. Even if a patent does not contain a copyright notice, this does not guarantee that the author does not claim copyright in the text or drawings of the patent. The PTO's website also states, "There are also instances where a portion of the text or drawings of a patent may be under copyright. You should consult an attorney regarding these potential trademark and copyright issues." In addition, in a 2003 case, *Rozenblat v. Sandia Corp.*, a federal appeals court acknowledged the copyrightability of an inventor's patent drawings (although ruling against the inventor as to the issue of infringement). Finally, Copyright Office regulations (37 CFR 202.10(a)) do not prohibit registration of patent drawings. As a general rule, the use of technical language or drawings from a prior-art patent for use in a patent application is a fair use and is not a copyright infringement. However, keep in mind the problem with fair use is that there are no distinct boundaries to define it and ultimately, the issue is up to a court. In 2012, a publisher of technical and scientific journals sued a Minnesota law firm for copyright infringement claiming that the law firm made copies of articles from technical journals without permission and submitted them to the PTO. The court found that such copying was permissible under the "fair use" doctrine of copyright law. To address these issues, when the PTO makes files submitted in patent applications available to the public in its Patent Center, NPL documents are listed but are not viewable or downloadable.

- reject some or all of your claims because of imprecise language, or
- reject some or all of your claims because of lack of patentability over the prior art.

To overcome these objections and/or rejections, you'll have to submit an "Amendment" in which you:

- make changes, additions, or deletions in the drawings, specification, or claims, and/or
- convince the examiner that the Office Action was in error.

Your application will be published 18 months from your earliest claimed filing date, unless you filed an NPR (Form SB/35) at the time of filing. If you filed an NPR, the information in your patent application will become publicly available only if a patent eventually issues. If you file the NPR and later decide to foreign file, you must rescind your NPR (use Form SB/36) within 45 days from the day you file your foreign application.

If the examiner eventually decides to allow the application (either as originally presented or as amended), you'll be sent a Notice of Allowance which gives you three months to pay an issue fee, a publication fee if applicable, and fix any remaining drawing errors. Your specification and claims, along with certain other information (your name, address, and a list of all prior art cited by the examiner), will then be sent to the U.S. Government Printing Office. There they'll be printed verbatim as your patent. From filing to issuance, the process usually takes somewhere between 18 months to three years, but sometimes longer.

> **TIP**
>
> **Model of invention.** Usually, you will not be required to furnish or demonstrate a working model of your invention. However, in rare cases, if the examiner questions the operability of your invention, such as if you claim a perpetual motion or energy machine, you may be required to furnish a model to the Examiner. (35 U.S.C. § 114.) Working models also enable the examiner to understand and appreciate the commercial or intrinsic value of your invention.

D. Do Preliminary Work Before Preparing Your Patent Application

If adequate preparations are made beforehand, the actual writing of the application will go far more smoothly and will rarely take more than several partial days. Here are the basic preparatory steps.

1. Review the Prior Art

Assemble all your prior-art references. (Chapter 6 discusses searching for prior art.) Read each of these references carefully, noting the terms used for the parts or steps that are similar to those of your invention. Write down the terms of the more unusual parts and, if necessary, look them up in your prior-art patents, textbooks, magazine articles (see "Glossary of Useful Technical Terms" in Appendix 3), or a visual. In this way you'll be familiar with the term for every art and its precise meaning. Also, note the way the drawings in these prior-art references are arranged and laid out. Pay particular attention to what parts are done in detail and what parts need be shown only very roughly or generally because they are well known or are not essential to the invention.

As a general rule, if you see any prior-art patent whose specification contains words, descriptions, and/or drawing figures that you can use in your application, you can copy what you need. But beware that some patent owners assert copyright claims in their drawings and text, and in nonpatent prior art materials. These assertions are most often based on copying of prior art publications, not on the copying

of patents (see above). Generally, you can copy the ideas in prior art materials if you express those ideas in your own words, instead of simply copying the text and figures.

2. Review Your Disclosure

Review the description (with sketches) of your invention that you prepared in Chapter 3. Be sure you have all of the details of your invention drawn or sketched in understandable form and that the description of your invention is complete. If you haven't done this yet, do it now, referring to Chapter 3 when necessary. With that done, you should use it to make a first draft of your broadest claims.

3. Ramifications

Write down all of the known ramifications (potentially different uses, materials, sizes, and methods of operation) and embodiments (physical forms that the invention can take). That is, record all other materials that will work for each part of your invention, other possible uses your invention can be put to, and other possible modifications of your invention. Think of ways in which its size or shape can be altered, parts (or steps in its manufacture) that can be eliminated, and so on. If your invention is a process or method, other ramifications and embodiments can be different materials that your inventive process modifies, variations of your process (for example, optional steps; steps in a different order), and different environments in which the process can be used.

The more ramifications and embodiments you can think of, the broader your patent claims will be interpreted, and the more you'll be able to block others from obtaining patents either on devices similar to your invention or on improvements to it. Also, you'll have something to fall back on if your main or basic embodiment is "knocked out" by prior art that your search didn't uncover or that surfaced after your search.

For instance, suppose your invention is a delaying device that closes the lid of a potpourri box automatically a few moments after the lid is opened. Another embodiment that could make advantageous use of the delaying device might be in a "roly-poly man" toy to make the man stand up again automatically a few moments after he's tipped over. If you have a process invention, alternative embodiments might be the use of the process for different end purposes.

TIP

Several related inventions. If you have two or more related inventions, such as a car stereo mount and a housing for the same stereo, you may show, describe, and claim both in the same application. The examiner may allow both inventions at once and you'll save fees and effort. However, you're allowed only one invention per filing fee, so the examiner may require you to restrict your application to one invention. If so, you can easily file a divisional application on the other inventions before the original application issues and still get the benefit of your original application's filing date. However, each divisional application will require its own filing, issue, and maintenance fees (a substantial expense). Also, your original application and any divisionals you file will expire 20 years from the filing date of your original application. The advantage of filing a divisional later is that you postpone the second filing fee a year or two, and you'll avoid paying it altogether if you find the invention hasn't panned out and you decide to drop it. The advantage of filing divisionals sooner is that your patent will have more remaining term when it issues. (In any case, don't include several inventions on one application if they're from different inventors or are not related.) See Chapter 14 for more information about divisional applications.

4. Sources of Supply

Suppose your invention contemplates the use of an exotic or uncommon material or component, or involves unusual manufacturing steps. In this case you must obtain the names and addresses of potential suppliers and/or identify textbooks or other references outlining how one should obtain or make such unusual elements or procedures. Describe these unusual dimensions, materials, or components in detail.

For example, with an electrical circuit, you generally don't have to include the technical values

or identifications of components. However, if the operation of the circuit is at all unusual, or if any component values are critical, or if it contains a possibly novel feature, write down their names or identifications. With a chemical invention, write down the source or full identification of how to make any unusual or possibly novel components or reactions. With a mechanical invention, if any unusual or possibly novel parts, assembly steps, or materials are required, be sure you provide a full description and reference as to where to obtain or how to perform them.

EXAMPLE 1: Griselda invents a new photofinishing process that requires the use of a special trademarked developer, Hypoxx, made by the Briskin Co. of Merion, Pennsylvania. If Griselda knows the composition of the developer, she must indicate this in the specification, but if not she can simply refer to the developer as Hypoxx developer from the Briskin Co. of Merion, Pennsylvania. Note, however, that what is described by a trademark can change over time, and the PTO may reject her specification if it believes those changes will affect making or using her invention at a later date.

EXAMPLE 2: Bruce invents a new plumbing fixture that uses a special valve that is positioned where two parts pivot with respect to each other. No such "pivoting valve" exists. In order to fulfill the PTO's disclosure requirement, Bruce must design the pivoting valve and describe and draw it in his patent application.

The reason why you will need the full details of any special aspects of your invention is simple. 35 U.S.C. Section 112(a) mandates that the specification provide a "full, clear, concise, and exact" description of the invention such that anyone skilled in the art can make and use it without too much experimentation. In addition, if any feature is possibly novel, you may have to claim it specifically, so you will want to provide adequate terminology in the specification to support your claim language.

5. Advantages/Disadvantages

List all disadvantages of the relevant prior art that your invention overcomes, referring to the "Positive and Negative Factors Summary" checklist (Form 4-2) in Appendix 7 to make sure your listing is complete. Then list all the advantages of your invention over the prior art.

But make sure you know they are actual advantages over the prior art. If you claim to be the first to solve a problem that someone else has already solved, or if you mischaracterize the prior art, your application will draw additional scrutiny from the PTO. So make sure you do a thorough search of the prior art, as described in Chapter 6, and stick to the facts when describing what others have done.

E. Flowchart

To get you oriented, Fig. 8A below provides a self-explanatory flowchart of the entire application preparation process. Steps A to P, V, and W are covered in this Chapter. Steps Q to U in Chapter 9, and Steps X to Z in Chapter 10.

F. Your Written Description Must Comply With the Full Disclosure Rules

Your goal is to clearly disclose everything you can think of about your invention. If you're in doubt as to whether to include a particular item of information, put it in. The statutory provision that mandates the inclusion of all this information in your patent application (Section 112(a) of the patent laws) reads as follows:

"The specification shall contain a written description of the invention, and of the manner and process of making and using it, in such full, clear, concise, and exact terms as to enable any person skilled in the art to which it pertains, or with which it is most nearly connected, to make and use the same, and shall set forth the best mode contemplated by the inventor or joint inventor of carrying out the invention."

The statute imposes three requirements on a patent specification: (1) it must provide a written description of the invention; that is, it must tell what it is, (2) it

must fully, clearly, concisely, and exactly teach one skilled in the art how to make and use it (in patent parlance, "enable" the invention), and (3) it must set forth the best mode of carrying out the invention. The reason for these requirements is based upon the "exchange theory" of patents. The government grants you a monopoly on your invention for a term of 17 to 20 years in exchange for your disclosing to the public the full details of your invention (written description, how to make and use it, and the best mode of doing so). In this way the public will get the full benefit of your creativity after your patent expires. If you describe the parts of the invention and how it operates, you will satisfy the first two requirements (written description and how to make and use).

However, under current court decisions, it's dangerous to specifically identify a "best mode" since a court may use this to limit your invention to this mode or embodiment. It is no longer possible for a court to invalidate a patent for failure to disclose the best mode. So most practitioners now recommend that, to prevent any court from limiting your invention to one mode, you disclose all of the embodiments "fully, clearly, concisely, and exactly" without stating which one is "best." For example, in the delay device referred to above, its use to close a box lid after a few minutes might be your first embodiment, and the delayed "roly-poly man" might be an alternative embodiment.

Another reason for disclosing as much as you can about your invention is to block others from getting a subsequent improvement patent on your invention. Suppose you invent something and disclose only one embodiment of it, or only one way to do it. If you get a patent that shows only that one embodiment, someone may later see your patent and think of another embodiment or another way to do it that may be better than yours. This person will then be able to file a new patent application on this "improvement invention" and thereby, assuming a patent is issued, obtain a monopoly on the improvement. If this occurs, you won't be able to make, use, or sell the improvement without a license from the person who owns that patent. This is so even though you have a patent on the basic invention.

Fig. 8A—Steps in Preparing a Patent Application Chart

Review
A. Review your invention disclosure and all prior art thoroughly.

Rough Sketches
B. Make rough CAD or penciled sketches of invention in separate, numbered Figs. Show every aspect of invention and ramifications, mainly in perspective views and flowcharts.

Name Parts
C. Pencil a suitable name or names adjacent to every part in the drawings —for example, "lever" and "pivot."

Title*
D. Type a meaningful title that includes some novelty of the invention—for example, "Chair With Water-Filled Seat."

Cross-Reference to Related Applications*
E. Under this heading provide a cross-reference to any parent applications and a claim to priority of any PPA that you've filed.

Federally Sponsored Research*
F. Put in the statement required by your government contract or "nonapplicable."

Sequence Listing or Program*
G. Indicate if the application contains a sequence or computer program listing, or type "nonapplicable."

Background*
H. Indicate field. One sentence is adequate—for example, "This application relates to bicycles, particularly to a derailleur."

Background*—Prior Art
I. Under this heading indicate the problems of the prior art, if any, and describe all prior art.

Summary*
J. Prepare a brief summary of your claimed embodiments by paraphrasing your claims.

Drawings*—Figures
K. Type a "Drawing Figures" section. Use one brief sentence to describe each Fig. without details of the invention.

Drawings*—Reference Numerals
L. While doing this step, list your reference numbers on Form 8-1 and write them at appropriate places on the drawing Figs., using lead lines. Later insert this list after Drawing Figs.

Detailed Description*
M. Type a "Description" section for the first set of figures. Describe overall structure of first embodiment, then structure and function of parts and their interconnections. Number each part (10, 12, and so on).

Operation
N. Write an "Operation" section. Describe in detail the operation, use, and advantages of the structure in these Figs.

Repeat Steps L, M, and N
O. Repeat Steps L, M, and N as necessary for all other sets of figures and embodiments.

Conclusion
P. Type a "Conclusion" section. Repeat advantages, describe less important ramifications, and add broadening paragraph.

Claims* (Chapter 9)
Q. Type first independent claim: type name of invention, then describe essential parts and their interconnections. Then broaden by eliminating as many parts as possible and generalizing remaining parts.

Dependent Claims
R. Type a set of dependent claims. Each must add feature(s) ["The widget of claim 1, further including"] or recite existing features more specifically ["The widget of claim 1 wherein"].

Second Main Claim
S. Type an additional independent claim, phrased differently than the first one; for example, an inventive method to accompany your inventive device.

Second Set of Dependent Claims
T. Type a second set of dependent claims, if possible. These can be similar to the first set of dependent claims.

More Sets of Claims
U. Repeat Steps S and T if possible. Don't exceed three independent or 20 total claims, unless justified.

Sequence Listing*
V. If applicable, type a sequence listing, starting on a separate sheet.

Abstract
W. Type abstract: Describe essence of structure and operation of invention and ramifications. Add reference numbers in parentheses.

Finalize Drawing (Chapter 10)
X. On drawings, remove part names (unless unusual), combine Figs. on same sheet, as possible, and neaten and final.

Finalize Application
Y. Insert claims after "Conclusion" and before Abstract. Start claims and abstract on new pages. Use consecutive numbers. Final specification and claims.

Finalize Check and Formal Papers
Z. Check all reference numbers and part names and proofread carefully. Prepare transmittals. Mail application with check and receipt postcard.

*This word or words should appear as section heading in all capitals without underline or boldface.

"New Matter" Cannot Be Added After Filing

What happens if you don't put enough information in about your invention to enable "one skilled in the art" to make and use it without undue effort? Either your entire application can be rejected under Section 112 on the grounds of "incomplete disclosure," or it may be later invalidated if an infringer challenges it when you try to enforce it. Also, if your patent application is rejected because of incomplete disclosure, usually there is nothing you can do since you aren't allowed to add any "new matter" (additional technical information) to a pending application. (See Chapter 13.) In other words, "You must get it right the first time." While many inventors object to and rail against the "no-new-matter rule" ("Why can't I add improvements to my application?"), the rule has a good purpose. Without it, an applicant could continuously add improvements and modifications, so that you would never know exactly what their invention covers. Imagine looking at a competitor's patent and thinking you are safe, then being sued out of the blue for infringing an improvement they just added!

As mentioned earlier, you must provide enough information in your patent application to enable anyone working in the field of your invention to be able to build and use it, without undue effort. That is, anyone in the field must be able to make a working version of your invention from the information contained in your patent application. To comply with this section, you ordinarily don't have to put in easily inferred dimensions, materials, and values of components, since the skilled artisan is expected to have a working knowledge of these items. However, as described above, dimensions, materials, or components that are critical to the performance of your invention, or that are at all unusual, must be included. If in doubt, include this specific information.

A common error in preparing the specification of a patent application is a failure to include enough detail about the invention, or enough ramifications. If you "sweat the details" like a good professional does, you'll seldom go wrong.

Common Misconception: A patent specification should not include details of the invention since this will limit the invention to those details.

Fact: The scope of the invention is determined by the claims; so including details in the specification will not limit its scope.

It is important that the specification provides enough detail to convince the PTO that the full scope of the claims was actually invented. Although you can leave a reasonable amount of experimentation to others to determine the full scope of the claims, in 2024 the Supreme Court ruled that "if a patent claims an entire class [of embodiments of an invention], the patent's specification must enable a person skilled in the art to make and use the entire class.... The more one claims, the more one must enable."

In that case, *Amgen Inc. v. Sanofi et al.*, the Court held that certain antibodies invented by Amgen were not "enabled" because they were claimed in functional terms (i.e., by their ability to bind to certain molecules) rather than in structural terms (i.e., by amino acid sequence(s)), and that as a result, the specification was required to, but failed to, disclose enough specific examples of antibodies that could provide the claimed function. That is, even though Amgen taught the patent reader how to screen manufactured antibodies to determine whether they would be covered by the claims, it did not demonstrate that its 26 disclosed examples of antibodies were representative of the entire class of potentially millions of antibodies that it claimed it had invented.

To determine whether a specification enables the full scope of the claims without undue experimentation, the PTO and the courts use a non-limiting set of factors (the *Wands* factors) that are listed in MPEP 2164.01(a).

The following Notes provide examples of enabling disclosure in several different areas of technology.

NOTE

Software note. If your invention includes a microprocessor and an application program for it, either in software or in firmware, you should either include a source or object code listing of the program with your patent application, or a flowchart. The flowchart should be detailed enough so that a programmer having no more than ordinary skill would be able to use your chart to write the program and debug it without undue effort or significant creativity—even if the task would take several months. Applicants who file a paper application can now file program listings on a CD-ROM (in duplicate for program listings, see 37 CFR 1.52(e)). When a program has 300 lines or fewer (72 characters per line), you can submit it on drawing sheets or in the specification. (If it has more than 60 lines, put it at the end of the specification.) When it has more than 300 lines, it must be on CD-ROM if you file a paper application. If you file via Patent Center, you can file the program listing in a separate file.

NOTE

Biotechnology note. If your invention requires a biological material that is not widely available, you must make a deposit of your biological material in an approved depository. The Rules define "biological material" as including "material that is capable of self-replication either directly or indirectly. Representative examples include bacteria, fungi including yeast, algae, protozoa, eukaryotic cells, cell lines, hybridomas, plasmids, viruses, plant tissue cells, lichens and seeds." (See 37 CFR 1.801–1.809, and MPEP (*Manual of Patent Examining Procedure*), 608.01(p)(c) and Chapter 2400.) A list of acceptable depositories is included in Section 2405 of the MPEP.

NOTE

Nucleotide and/or amino acid sequence note. If your application contains disclosures of nucleotide and/or amino acid sequences, it must contain, as a separate part of the disclosure, a paper copy disclosing the nucleotide and/or amino acid sequences and associated information using the symbols and format in accordance with the requirements of 37 CFR 1.822 and 1.823. (37 CFR 1.821(c).) A copy of the sequence listing "must also be submitted in computer readable form in accordance with the requirements of Section 1.824," and "a statement that the content of the paper and computer readable copies are the same must be submitted with the computer readable form,"—specifically a statement that "the information recorded in computer readable form is identical to the written sequence listing." (37 CFR 1.821(e) and (f).) (See MPEP 2420 and following for the rules and availability of a program called "PatentIn" (MPEP 2430) for submitting the sequence in electronic form.)

NOTE

Formula note. You can enter formulas in the text the same way you would do if you were writing a college paper or textbook. However, it's best to avoid formulas, Greek letters, and subscripts, if at all possible: The printer may get them wrong, and if your patent ever gets into court, they'll turn off or intimidate a lay judge and jury. For applications that must make extensive use of formulas, you can use an equation editor such as the one provided in Microsoft *Word*.

NOTE

Trademarked chemical note. If your invention uses a trademarked chemical—such as "Ajax developer"— and you don't know its composition, see if any other similar chemicals will work. If so, you can just refer to the chemical by its generic name, with a reference to a suitable manufacturer —for example, "developer, preferably Ajax brand, sold by Ajax Chemical Company, Inverness Park, California." If the trademarked chemical is critical, try your best to find its generic constituents—for example, by contacting the company or doing research. One clever inventor found the composition by calling a Poison Control Center hotline. If you can't find the constituents, you'll have to refer to the chemical by its trademark and manufacturer, but this can limit your invention.

G. Software, Computer-Related Inventions, and Business Methods

Developments in the U.S. law of subject matter eligibility have made it more difficult to get patents on software-implemented inventions. You should understand the standards used by the PTO in examining claims for such inventions, and prepare your claims, text, and figures accordingly.

The main consideration applicable to these inventions is in meeting the full disclosure requirement, including disclosure sufficient to support claims that will pass muster under the U.S. patent law. (35 U.S.C. § 101.)

As noted, a patent application must contain a sufficiently detailed description of the invention so that one having ordinary skill in the art to which it pertains, or to which it is most nearly connected, will be able to make and use the invention without undue effort. In practice, the PTO and courts strictly enforce this requirement when software, computer-related inventions, or business method inventions are involved, since the newness of the field makes most people less comfortable with it. So if you're preparing a patent application on a software or computer-related invention, be absolutely sure that no one will ever be able to challenge it for "incomplete disclosure." That is, make absolutely sure it contains a "full, clear, concise, and exact" description of the invention and how to make and use it.

How should you fulfill this requirement in practice with software inventions? Virtually every software invention uses a computer program of some sort, whether it's in a PROM (programmed read-only memory) or a separate program on a disk that is used with a general-purpose computer. To fulfill the complete disclosure requirement, it is essential that you disclose either a listing of the program or a detailed flowchart of the operations and steps involved with the invention that a programmer can use to create a working version.

If you've already written the program, the easiest way to provide the necessary disclosure is to supply the listing as part of the patent application. (See "Computer Programs Note" in Subsection I2l below, for how to do this.) If you file electronically, the listing must be submitted in ASCII format per 37 CFR 1.52(e). Therefore, unless you can somehow supply the object code in ASCII, you will have to submit the source code.

You should explain in the specification how to implement the listing and any special instructions that may be necessary to implement the invention without undue experimentation. The explanation should detail how to configure the computer to perform the required function and interrelate with any other elements to yield the claimed invention. For instance, you should state what programming language the listing is in (for example, "C++"), how to use it to control the computer or microprocessor, what type of computer or microprocessor to use it with (for instance, "an 11th Gen Intel® Core™ processor"), and what hardware should be connected to the computer, both on the input and output sides as necessary (for instance, "a USB interface" and "a 3D printer").

The program should be free of any serious bugs and should not have too many minor bugs (virtually no program is 100% bug free). In other words, no one should be able to say your listing wouldn't function according to its specifications. (The PTO won't test your program, but if you get a patent and later seek to enforce it during license negotiations or in court, your adversary will!)

All Process Inventions Must Be Hardware Based

In order to have your claims be hardware-based to better withstand challenges, you should describe the hardware (machine or apparatus), and the relationship between the process and that hardware, in the specification. For example, if you have an internet invention that involves transactions between computers, you will have to describe the computer hardware, how the computers are connected to each other physically and functionally, how the computer is instructed to perform the transactions (for example, by software, firmware, or other technique), and how the transactions affect each computer's operation.

196 | PATENT IT YOURSELF

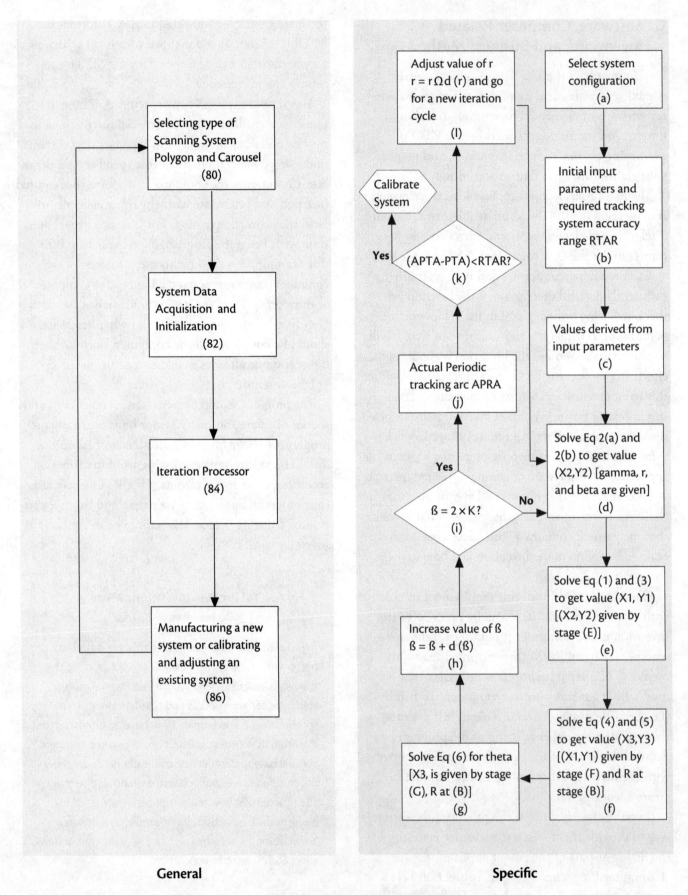

General   **Specific**

Fig. 8B—Software Flowcharts

If you choose to provide only a flowchart, make sure it's complete and detailed enough to enable any reasonably skilled programmer to write a program, using only routine skills. The flowchart will be adequate even if it would take a programmer several months to write the program, so long as only routine skill and not extraordinary effort will be involved. Think of a flowchart like the plans for a building: If the plans are adequate for an ordinary builder to construct the building, they will be adequate, even if it will take the builder several months, or even a year or more. However, if the plans are rough and sketchy, so that the builder has to hire an architect to complete them, or has to use a lot of imagination to fill in gaps, then they're inadequate. Fig. 8B shows adequately detailed flowcharts (from U.S. Patent 5,170,279) in two parts: general and specific. The associated explanation in the specification (not provided here) discusses each block in detail, lists the equations referred to in the blocks, and explains exactly how to implement the flowchart.

You may be able to deter readers of your patent from copying and using your program listing by including a copyright notice in the patent application. Including such a notice will not deter determined pirates from copying your source code, so it's best not to include source code, if at all possible, in favor of detailed flowcharts.

H. First Prepare Sketches and Name Parts

Before you even begin the actual nuts and bolts preparation of your specification, you should make (or have made for you) penciled sketches of your invention. These will form the basis of the drawings you'll eventually send to the PTO along with your patent application. Your sketches will also be the foundation of your application. In other words, you'll build from these as you write your specification and claims.

Always do your sketches prior to drafting the specification, as well as the other parts of the application. You don't have to worry about planning any layout of your figures on the drawing sheets, or the size of the figures—yet. This will be covered in detail in Chapter 10. For now, merely complete a set of sketches showing all of the aspects of your invention without worrying about size or arrangement; these sketch-figures can even be done very large and on separate sheets. Later on they can be reduced and compiled onto the drawing sheets as part of the "finaling" process.

After you've completed your sketches, write down a name for each part adjacent to such part in each sketch, such as "handlebar," "handgrip," "clamp," and "bolt." Write the names of the parts lightly in pencil so that you can change them readily if you think of a better term. Use lead lines to connect each name to its part if the parts are crowded enough to cause confusion. If you have any difficulty naming any part, refer to the Glossary of Useful Technical Terms (Appendix 3), your prior-art patents, or a visual dictionary.

Your drawing should be done in separate, unconnected figures, each one labeled ("Fig. 1," "Fig. 2," and so on, so that all possible different views and embodiments of your invention are shown. If two figures are related, you can refer to them with the same number but with different suffixes or primes; for example, "Fig. 1A," "Fig. 1B." Use as many views as necessary to capture all of the features that you have claimed or will claim. Look at a relevant prior-art patent to get an idea of how it's done. The views should generally be perspective or isometric views, rather than front, side, and top, engineering-type views. If you have trouble illustrating a perspective view, take a photo of a model of your invention from the desired angle and draw the photo—perhaps by enlarging and tracing it. Alternatively you can use a "see and draw" copying device of the type employing a half-silvered mirror in a viewing head on a pedestal; these are available in art supply stores and through gadget mail-order houses. Hidden lines should be shown in broken lines, as shown in Fig. 8C. For complicated machines, exploded views are desirable as shown in Fig. 8D. The drawings must be filed as a separate document from your patent application (whether filing on paper or online). Never include your drawing sheets as part or pages of the written description.

Fig. 8C—Perspective View With Hidden Lines

You can use any reasonable symbols for mechanical, electronic/electrical, and chemical parts; the PTO has no requirements in this area, except that the symbols must not be outrageous. Use conventional symbols, such as those approved by the ANSI (American National Standards Institute), those used in conventional texts, or those used in your prior-art patents. In lieu of graphical symbols, labeled boxes are also acceptable, so long as the part represented by the box is standard or conventional.

If you have an electronic system, a block diagram with each block labeled (for example, "Schmitt Trigger," "flip-flop," "inverter") is fine. If any block represents a nonconventional circuit, however, you must provide a schematic diagram and explain clearly what's in the block or provide a reference to a suitable publication. If any block represents a programmed microprocessor or computer, then remember that you must provide a listing of the program or a software flowchart to provide a complete disclosure.

If possible, one figure of your drawing should be comprehensive enough to show the basic idea of the invention and to be suitable for inclusion in the *Official Gazette* (OG). If the PTO grants your patent, they will publish one figure, the main claim, and the bibliographic details of your patent in the OG. See Chapter 6 for more on the OG. The other figures can be fragmentary or partial views; you don't have to show the same details more than once.

Different colors and different shades of gray can be shown with different types of shading lines, but provide a suitable decoding legend in a separate figure. If your invention is related to a prior-art device, you may want to illustrate the prior-art device in the first figure of drawings so that you can explain it and its drawbacks. This Fig. must be labeled "Prior Art" and described in the Background section.

1. Machine Sketches

If your invention is a machine or an article, your sketches should contain enough views to show every novel feature of the invention in detail. However, you don't have to show every feature that's old and known in the prior art. For example, if you've invented a new type of pedal arrangement for a bicycle, one view can show your pedal arrangement in gross view without detail. Other views can show your pedal arrangement in detail, but you don't have to include any views showing the bicycle itself in detail, since it isn't part of your invention and bicycles are well known. If one figure of your drawing shows a sectional or side view of another figure, it is customary to provide cross-section lines in the latter figure; these lines should bear the number of the former figure. Look at prior-art patents to see how this is done and see the example in Fig. 8E. If your machine is complicated, you should show an exploded view of it, as in Fig. 8D. If you have a moderately healthy budget and complex machine figures, consider hiring a patent figure drafting professional. There is substantial competition in this area, so high-quality figures like Fig. 8E may be obtained for perhaps forty to seventy dollars each.

2. Chemical Composition Sketches

If your invention is a chemical composition, the PTO won't generally require drawings unless the material has a nonhomogeneous composition (internally differentiated through layering, for example), in which case you should show it in cross-section detail. Also, if a step-by-step process is involved, the PTO will require a flowchart, even though the process is fully described in your specification (see the next section). The reason: so examiners, judges, and future searchers will be able to understand your patent more rapidly. Benzene rings and other molecular diagrams can usually be presented in the specification.

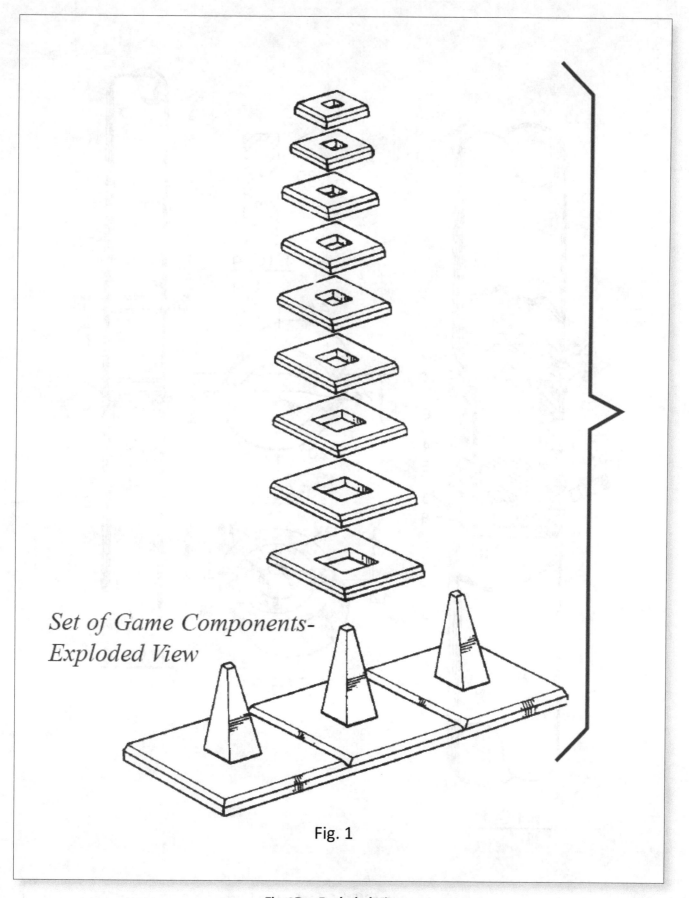

Set of Game Components- Exploded View

Fig. 1

Fig. 8D—Exploded View

Fig. 8E—Views With Cross-Section Lines

3. Computer, Chemical, or Mechanical Process Sketches

If your invention includes a process of the digital, computer, chemical, or mechanical type, you should provide a flowchart (or a program listing for software inventions—see above). This flowchart must show the separate steps involved, each described succinctly in a different block. If your blocks are connected, they should all be labeled as one figure; if disconnected, they should be labeled as separate figures. As before, each figure should be labeled—for example, "Fig. 1," "Fig. 1A," "Fig. 1B," "Fig. 2," and "Fig. 3."

If you desire, you can try providing a short title after each figure, giving a general description of the part of your invention shown in the figure, just as you would do if you were writing a scientific article for an engineering magazine or textbook. However, PTO drafting personnel often object to such titles. If this occurs, you'll have to delete the titles (white out the titles on the originals of your drawing or delete the titles on your computer drawings) and send in replacement figures.

If you believe it will help in understanding your invention, you may (and should) include a drawing of the prior art as one figure of your drawings. This figure must be labeled "prior art" to indicate that it isn't part of your invention.

I. Drafting the Specification

Once you've reduced your invention to sketches, it's time to begin drafting the detailed description portion of your patent application. Review the detailed descriptions of your prior-art patents—or the sample detailed description at the end of this chapter—to find out how they're written. Your detailed description should be written as one continuous document with separate sections, each with a heading, the way this book is written.

1. Drafting Tips

Here are some general rules to keep in mind when drafting your detailed description.

Consider Your Audiences

A patent specification is meant for many different audiences, beginning with you. When you have finished your specification, you should be comfortable that it communicates all of the advantages of your invention. You are also writing for an examiner at the PTO, whose job it is to make sure that your specification complies with the complete disclosure laws. Depending on how you plan to commercialize your patent, you may be writing for potential investors or manufacturers, who need to know how to evaluate your invention for its profit potential. And if you ever need to enforce your offensive rights against an infringer, you are writing for the judge and the jury who will have to read your specification to understand how your invention works, so you can convince them why you should win your case.

Avoid Legalese

You'll be pleased to learn that legalese is not favored by the PTO, since it makes your writing stilted, less clear, and harder to understand. The only legal requirement for the detailed description is that it be a full, clear, concise, and complete description of how to make and use the invention. (The claims, however, should be written with extreme clarity and precision, and to do this you may have to use a few "saids" and "wherebys," as explained in Chapter 9.)

Use Short and Simple Sentences

It's best to write your description in short, simple sentences, with short paragraphs. Each paragraph should generally be shorter than 200–250 words, or one page (double-spaced), and should relate to one part or subpart of your invention. The Cybernetics Institute has found that short sentences communicate best. Your main goal is to include all points of substance of your invention and make your description clear and understandable. There's an especially good legal reason for this: If a disclosure isn't clear, a court will interpret it narrowly. If you get stuck and don't know how to phrase a description of a part or an operation, here's a helpful trick: Simply pretend you're describing your invention aloud to a close friend. Remember what you said (or make an audio recording) and write it down. Then go back and polish the language. If you attack the job in small chunks or in piecemeal fashion, it usually will go much easier.

Write Clearly
Write clearly, not only so you can be understood, but also so that you will not be misunderstood.

Avoid Grammar and Spelling Errors
Although the PTO's examiners aren't very concerned with grammar and spelling errors, you should avoid them in your application and all of your correspondence. You will get more respect from your examiner, potential licensees, or a judge. Proofread or use a spelling and grammar checker. Here are some examples of common grammar errors in redacting patent applications:

Wrong: "lever 202's left end."

Right: "the left end of lever 202."

Wrong: "connected to switch 502 wires."

Right: "connected to the wires 503 leading to switch 502."

Most writing tends to be less formal and even sloppy nowadays thanks to texting, instant messaging, and the like. However a patent application (and any other legal document), should be formal and crystal-clear, because any flaw, error, grammatical mistake, ambiguity, vagueness, or unintelligibility will be attacked or looked upon with disdain by anyone who reads the application, such as an examiner, a potential licensee, a judge, or an adversary.

Use Copious Headings
If you use copious subheadings (such as "Fig. 1—Description of Handlebar Attachment"; "Fig. 2—Front Fork Detail"; and "Fig. 10—Operation of Derailleur" throughout your specification, most people will find it far easier to read. This allows them to take in the information in separate, small, inviting chunks that are easy to digest one at a time. Refer to

the specification at the end of this chapter (Fig. 8G) to see examples of headings in an application.

If you have trouble getting started, don't worry; many writers have blocks from time to time, and lots of inventors initially (and erroneously) lament, "I could never write my own patent application." The words of Lao-Tse might encourage you:

"A journey of a thousand miles begins with a single step."

If you feel that you can't write adequately, give it your best shot and then have someone you trust and who will keep your draft confidential—a writer, college English major, high school English teacher, for example—edit your draft.

> ! CAUTION
>
> **Avoid negative, restrictive, or wishy-washy statements that could be used against you later.** When you write, be especially careful not to include anything that an adversary could later use against you to invalidate or narrow your patent. For example, never say that any novel part of your invention is similar to something that is already known, that the novelty of your invention is solely in a certain part, that something "might" work, that something is always better or necessary or critical, or that something is not done or constructed in a certain way. If your patent is ever involved in litigation, any adversary will use such statements against you in court.

Avoid "Patent Profanity"

Here are some words and phrases that patent attorneys avoid using, or use with caution, to avoid having a judge limit an invention; some call these words "patent profanity." They include: *absolutely, always, beneficial, crucial, critical, desirable, each, eliminate, essential, every, hypothetical, important, invention, key, maximize, minimize, must, necessarily, necessary, never, obviously, only, peculiar, preferred, preferred embodiment, present invention, require(s/d), special, superior, surprisingly, the invention,* and *very important.*

Common Misconception: If you put any specific feature of your invention, such as a preferred size, a preferred material, or a preferred shape, in your specification, the scope of your invention will be limited to this feature, so any device that lacks this specific feature will not infringe.

Fact: The scope of an invention is determined by the claims and not by specifics that are included in the specification. If you do recite any specific feature in a claim, that claim will be limited to this specific feature, but if the specific feature is stated in the specification, it will help provide an adequate disclosure. The patent laws, rules, court decisions, and practitioners actually require and recommend that the specification include as many specifics of the invention as possible, especially in critical areas, so no one will ever be able to validly attack the adequacy of the specification for failure to teach how to make and use the invention. However when stating the specifics of an invention in the specification, it's important to (1) state that these are what you presently contemplate for this embodiment but that other values, dimensions, and so on, can be used, and (2) include as many variations as you can envision. For example, "In some embodiments, the lever has a rectangular cross section 2 mm by 4 mm and is 4 cm long and made of austenitic steel. However, it can have different cross sections, such as oval, triangular, and circular, and different sizes and materials, such as high-carbon steel, titanium, and polycarbonate." Never refer to "the invention"—only to a particular embodiment under discussion. Also never state that any embodiment is preferred; instead just list the embodiments as the first, second, third, and so on.

Make an Outline Before Starting

Prior to starting, in order to guide your path, you may find it helpful first to make an outline, which should be the same as the headings set out below. However, you might want to make the Description and Operation headings more specific and/or break them into several more specific headings each, in accordance with your figures and specific situation. A skeleton patent application is provided in Fig. 8F, which you should copy into a word processor to get you started.

Now let's get to the nitty-gritty of preparing the specification portion of a patent application.

2. The Parts of the Specification

There are some commonsense rules governing the best presentation of each of the separate parts of your specification. Only the sections with a "PPA" superscript, below, are needed to file a Provisional Patent Application, however it is best to file a PPA with as many of the other sections as are appropriate.

a. Title PPA

Have your title reflect the essence of your invention without being too long (500 characters maximum) or so specific that it's narrower than your invention's full scope, including all of its embodiments. For example, if your invention is a foot pedal but the mechanism can be used as a handhold, don't call it "Foot Pedal"; call it "Hand or Foot Pedal" or the like. On the other hand, don't pick a title so broad—such as "Electrical Apparatus"—as to be essentially meaningless. A look at some recently issued patents in your field should give you a good idea of how specific to make your title.

b. Cross-Reference to Related Applications

In this section refer to any PPA that you've filed, to any parent applications (see Chapter 14), or to any technically related application and incorporate it by reference just in case you need to rely on anything in it. For example, if you've filed a PPA, then in the RPA include, "This application claims the benefit of provisional patent application Ser. Nr. xx/xxx,xxx, filed 20xx xxx xx by the present inventor(s), which is incorporated by reference in its entirety." If the application is a continuation-in-part of an earlier application, type, "This application is a CIP of Ser. Nr. xx/xxx,xxx, filed 20xx xxx xx by the present inventor(s), which is incorporated by reference in its entirety." If you want to refer to a technically related case, type, for example, "This application uses the frammis vane disclosed in my patent x,xxx,xxx, granted xxxx xxx xx, which is incorporated by reference in its entirety."

You can omit this part if you don't have any related applications. Also, incorporation by reference may not be accepted by foreign patent offices, so if something is important to your application—that is, it is necessary to describe your invention so that a person of ordinary skill in the art could make and use it—or if it is necessary to support your claims, be sure to put it into the application and don't incorporate it by reference.

c. Federally Sponsored Research

If your invention was made under a government contract, include the required contract clause here. You can omit this part if you don't have any Federally Sponsored Research.

d. Names of Parties to a Joint Research Agreement

Likewise, if you collaborated with a private-sector company to develop your invention under a formal joint research agreement or contract, you may list here the name of the company. If your coinventor(s) were building on previous work that was owned by their company, you may be entitled to have that previous work be excluded from "prior art" that can be used to invalidate a patent.

e. Sequence Listing or Program

If you've included a CD-ROM (if filing on paper) or an ASCII attachment (if filing via Patent Center) to provide a program listing, refer to it here. If your invention uses a biological sequence, refer to it here and state where it can be found. You can omit this part if you don't have any Sequence Listing or Program.

f. Technical Field

Here, describe in general terms the field of technology into which your invention fits. Describe the field at two levels—a broad, general level and a somewhat less general level, but do not drill down to a specific level of technology. Both levels should describe, in a broad sense, some preexisting area of technology. In other words, do not use this section to describe your invention—after all, your invention defines a new part of the technology, so it doesn't fully fit into a narrow preexisting field. For example, if your invention is a new sprocket for a bicycle's gear system, your Technical Field might read: "The present invention relates to bicycles, and more specifically to drive systems for bicycles." It may be helpful to refer to the *CPC Scheme* or *Definitions* (see Chapter 6) for words you might use to describe your field.

g. Background—Discussion of Prior Art

Here, discuss the problem that your invention definitely solves, the way the problem was approached previously (if it was approached at all), and then list all the disadvantages of the old ways of doing it.

 CAUTION

Do not describe your invention in the background section. If you do, it will be interpreted as a confession that your invention is already known in the prior art, and can be used by the PTO to reject your claims, or later used by an infringer to attack your patent. When it comes to writing your Background section, remember the line you've heard so many times when the police arrest someone on television—anything you say can and will be used against you in a court of law—and by the PTO.

Your application will be more interesting if you can write this section as a story describing the history of the field and its sorry state up to the present. For example, you can start as follows: "Originally bicycles were made with a fixed transmission ratio. This made pedaling up hills difficult. This problem has been partially solved by the implementation of derailleur mechanisms, but these had and still have significant problems." Then list the derailleurs that were used in the past and their disadvantages. Again, look at prior-art patents to get an idea of what was done. If you can, tell why prior-art people failed to solve the problem and why a solution is needed. But be sure that every prior-art approach you discuss was definitely known, because by listing approaches in the prior art section you are making a full admission that all of such approaches are old.

Beware of admitting that any problem in the prior art was recognized. If it wasn't recognized and you state otherwise you will deprive yourself of credit for recognizing the problem and enable the examiner or an adversary to cite more prior art against you. If you do want to list a problem that you found, give yourself credit for recognizing it—for example, "I have found that derailleurs often broke down because their linkages were too flimsy." Don't say what the prior art can't do because this can make your invention or the problem that you discovered look obvious.

Cite all prior-art U.S. patents, published patent applications, foreign patent publications, and non-patent literature in a four-part table, in the same format as on the PTO's Information Disclosure Statement (IDS) form, PTO/SB/08a. Then discuss these references later in narrative paragraphs. This makes it easier for the examiner to review your prior art and for you to fill out your IDS later. (See an example in the specification of the sample application, Fig. 8G below.)

While the PTO doesn't want needlessly derogatory remarks about the inventions of others, you should, as much as possible, try to "knock the prior art" here in order to make your invention look as good as possible. Keep your statements factual (for example, "The derailleur in patent 3,456,789 to Prewitt, 1982 May 3, had a limited number of discrete gear ratios") and not opinionated (don't say, "Prewitt's derailleur was an abject failure"). If applicable, tell why prior-art people didn't think of any solution before and why a solution is needed. Do not discuss any detailed structure or operation of any prior art in this section (unless you provide a suitable figure—see next paragraph), since detailed mechanical discussions without the benefit of drawings will be incomprehensible to most people. Occasionally, you may have such a completely unique invention that there's really no prior art directly germane to your invention. If so, just state the general problem or disadvantage your invention solves.

If you've provided a prior-art figure, you can discuss (and knock!) it here. Use reference numerals to refer to the individual parts of the prior-art device.

Alternatively you may discuss (and knock) your prior-art figure in the "Description of Invention" section.

If you are aware of any prior-art publications (including U.S. patents and published patent applications), you must file an Information Disclosure Statement (IDS) listing them, together with copies of any non-U.S. patent publications.

If your invention doesn't solve a specific problem—for example, it's a new game or toy—you won't be able to state any problem that your invention solves. However, you still can discuss the closest prior games or toys and mention some faults or disadvantages of them. Since this is a discussion of the prior art, you should not discuss your invention or any of its advantages here.

h. Advantages

Although it is optional, you may list the advantages of your invention in a narrative form. If you do so, make it appear as part of (or close to) the Detailed Description section. Include this because it helps orient your readers to your subject matter, and helps sell the invention to the examiner or a judge who may rule on your patent. The advantages may also help distinguish your invention from a "judicial exception" that is not patentable.

For example, if your invention does any of the following, explain in narrative form the shortcoming of the prior art and the advantage of your invention: improves another technology or technical field; improves the functioning of a computer; or includes a feature or function that is more than what is well-understood, routine, and conventional in the field. However, it's important not to use language that a court may consider limiting; don't use the words "invention" or "objects," and use weasel words so you don't paint yourself into a corner. First, state that the advantages are for "one or more aspects." Second, list the advantages that are the reverse of the disadvantages listed in the prior-art section, then any additional advantages you know, followed by a catchall sentence. Here's a condensed example incorporating all of the foregoing: "Thus some embodiments provide a computer that is lighter or faster than prior-art computers. Some embodiments

PATENT IT YOURSELF

[Title]

Cross-Reference to Related Applications (if applicable)

[0001] The present application claims priority from _____

Federally Sponsored Research (if applicable)

[0002] _____

Incorporate by Reference CD of Sequence Listing or Program Listing (if applicable)

[0003] _____

Technical Field

[0004] The present invention relates to _____, and more particularly to _____

Background Art

[0005] It is known in the prior art to _____

Summary of the Embodiments

[0006] A first embodiment includes _____

Brief Description of the Drawings

[0007] Fig. 1 schematically illustrates _____;

Detailed Description of Specific Embodiments

[0008] Embodiments provide _____

[0009] Program Code Listing (if applicable and if code more than 60 lines) _____

. . . . page break . . . .

What is claimed is:

1. _____

. . . . page break . . . .

Sequence Listing (if applicable) _____

. . . . page break . . . .

Abstract

Fig. 8F—"Skeleton" Patent Application

provide a computer that is less expensive or more attractive than prior-art computers. These and other benefits of one or more aspects will become apparent from a consideration of the ensuing description and accompanying drawings." Be certain that each advantage that you list is fulfilled by at least one aspect of your invention.

i. Summary

37 CFR 1.73 and 1.77 state that the specification "should" contain a summary of the claimed invention, and Section 1.72 requires an abstract of the entire specification. In practice, some patent attorneys omit the summary, since the abstract, as well as the claims, already provides one. Also if the summary focuses on one embodiment, the courts may limit your invention. However, including a summary is recommended.

Your summary should include a broadly stated overview of your invention, and should also contain text that paraphrases all of your claims. You may want to draft a broad overview paragraph when you begin drafting your specification, but the rest of your summary after you have finalized your claims.

Section 1.73 states that the summary may include the object of the invention. However, you should never refer to any object of the invention, since some courts have used a statement of an object to limit the claims. Instead you can refer to advantages, but always state that they are for one or more aspects and not for "the invention." Also make sure your advantages are not too narrow.

j. Drawings PPA

Here, provide a series of separate paragraphs, each *briefly* describing a respective figure of your drawing—for example, "Fig. 1 is a perspective (or plan, side, exploded, or rear) view of a first embodiment"; or, "Fig. 2 is a view in detail of the portion indicated by the section lines 2—2 in Fig. 1." Do not include any reference numerals, specific parts, or any other details in this section—just a brief overall description of each figure.

k. Drawings—List of Reference Numerals

Although the PTO doesn't require or even recommend a separate list of the reference numerals and the names of their respective parts in an application, it is advisable to include such a list in a separately headed section at the end of Detailed Description, since it would disrupt the flow of the specification if you put it at the beginning. Why? There are three very important reasons for providing the list:

- to help you to keep your reference numerals straight—that is, to avoid using the same number for different parts
- to help you to keep your nomenclature straight— that is, to avoid using different terms for the same part, and
- to provide a very visible and easy-to-find place where examiners, searchers, and others who read your application or patent can go to instantly identify any numbered part on your drawings.

It may be helpful to compile this list in a separate word-processing window or on a separate sheet of lined paper, and then incorporate the list in the text. Also, to keep confusion at a minimum, you use reference numbers with at least three-digits, and that you begin your numbers with the same digit as the figure number in which it first appears. For example, if you have Figs. 1 to 12 of drawings, begin your reference numbers in Fig. 1 at 100 (for example, bicycle 100 having seat 102 and wheels 104 and 106), and in Fig. 12 at 1200 (for example, basket 1200 and bell 1202).

Some inventors use three-digit reference numbers throughout. The first digit represents the figure number, so that the parts of Fig. 1 would be "110," "112," and so on. The parts in Fig. 2 would be "210," "212," and so on. If Fig. 2 has a part that is also in Fig. 1, the reader would instantly know that this part (that is, part 110) was first introduced in Fig. 1. Also this enables any reader of the specification to go directly to the drawing figure where this part is introduced.

Lastly, use even-numbered reference numerals when you write the application (as we've done in the above paragraphs). In this way, if you later have to add another reference number, you can use an odd number and put it between two logically related even numbers. (See the list in the sample specification at the end of the chapter.)

I. Detailed Description PPA

Here you should describe in great detail the static physical structure of the first embodiment of your invention (not how it operates or what its function is). If this embodiment is a process, describe the procedures or machinery involved in it. Begin by first stating what the figure under discussion shows generally— for example, "Fig. 1 shows a perspective view of one version of a widget." Then get specific by describing the main parts and how they're connected. (These main parts can form the basis for your claims, as discussed in Chapter 9.) Then get even more specific: Describe each main part in detail and all of the sub- or component parts in detail. If a detail is worth describing, it is probably worth at least one paragraph of text.

Start with the base, frame, bottom, input, or some other logical starting place of the embodiment. Then work up, out, or forward in a logical manner, numbering and naming the parts in your drawing as you proceed. Use the part names that you previously wrote on your sketches.

To number the parts, write a number near each part and extend a lead line from the reference number to the part to which it refers. Don't circle your reference numerals, since a PTO rule prohibits this. The lead lines should not have arrowheads—for example, a bicycle grip might be designated "22———." You should not use a reference numeral to designate the embodiment of a whole figure; instead just say " … the widget of Fig. 1."

Although you may think that the patent examiner won't need to have parts that are clearly shown in the drawing separately described in detail, all patent attorneys provide such a description. This is part of a repetition technique that is used to familiarize the examiner with the invention and set the stage for the operational description and the claims. When you

mention each part twice, once in the description and again in the operation discussion, the first mention will initially program your reader to relate to the part so that the reader will really understand it the second time around, when it counts. This is the same technique as is used in the lyrics of blues songs, where the first two lines are always restated to enhance communication. Another reason to describe and name each part and each detail is to form a basis for the claims: All terms used in the claims are supposed to be first used in the specification.

Another good technique is to use several different equivalent names for a part the first time you refer to it in order to provide one with which your reader will be familiar—for example, "connected to base 10 is a strut, pylon, or support 12." Then pick one name and use it consistently thereafter.

Before you begin a description of any figure, refer to it by its figure number—for example, "Fig. 1 shows an overall view of the can opener of the first embodiment." Then as you come to each part or element, give it a separate reference number—for example, "The can opener comprises two handle arms 110 and 112 (Fig. 1) that are pivotally attached at a hinge 114." It is essential always to keep your reader apprised of which figure you are discussing.

Also, always try as much as possible to discuss one figure at a time. However, where several figures show different views of an embodiment, you can refer to several figures at once—such as "Figs. 1 and 2 show plan and elevational (front) views of a scissors according to one embodiment. The scissors comprises first and second legs 112 and 114, the second leg being best shown in Fig. 2." However, again don't refer to too many figures at once, and always keep your reader advised as to which figure is under discussion.

Discuss every part shown in your drawings in detail and be sure to use consistent terminology and nomen-clature for the parts in the drawing. For example, if gear 844 is shown in Fig. 8 and also in Fig. 11, label it with the same reference numeral "44" in both figures. However, if the gear is even slightly different in Fig. 11, it must have a different reference numeral, such as,

"844a," "844π," or "844bis." Fill out the Drawing Reference Numerals Worksheet (downloadable Form 8-1, available via this book's online companion page; see Appendix 7 for details) as you write, to keep your numerals and nomenclature consistent. If you use a word processor, refer to each part by a number only and then, consistent part names—such as, you can write "844 is connected to 836" and later change "844" to "widget 844" and "836" to "base 836" throughout your specification.

Lastly, be sure to detail all the interconnections or mountings between parts—for example, "Arm 114 is joined to base 112 by a flange 116."

 TIP

Recall the childhood song that details virtually every bone-to-bone connection in the body in logical order—for example, "The knee bone's connected to the thigh bone, the thigh bone's connected to the hip bone." In a similar manner, your description should also detail every part-to-part interconnection, even if you think the reader would find it obvious from your drawing.

 TIP

Don't be secretive. Suppose your invention uses some special or exotic parts, techniques, or relationships, but you don't want to describe these because such information is valuable and you want to keep it as a trade secret and not give it away to potential copiers and competitors. Unfortunately, you can't be secretive. You must include complete detailed descriptions of these, including dimensions, relationships, materials, and sources of supply, as applicable, in this section in order to comply with the "full disclosure" statute (35 U.S.C. § 112). Putting in such specifics will not limit your invention in any way since the claims will determine its scope. However, failing to include these specifics can render your patent application fatally flawed if they are necessary for one skilled in the art to make and use the invention.

 TIP

Write the prior-art section with care. Anything you say in the PA (Background) section can be used against you. If your invention is an improvement to a prior-art (PA) device, don't describe the PA device in detail in the PA section and then state, in the description of your invention, how your invention improves upon the PA device by describing how you would change the PA device. This will isolate your changes, making it easier for an examiner or future adversary to invalidate your patent by showing a reference with just the changes. Instead describe the PA device generally in your PA section and then, in the description of your invention, describe your whole device in detail and in a manner different from the description of the PA device. This will make it much more difficult for anyone to invalidate your invention. A good rule of thumb is to keep the Background section as short as possible to orient the reader to the problem you have solved—a few paragraphs at most, unless more details are absolutely required.

Including details and dimensions at crucial places can also prove vital later if you have to rely on these in order to support and distinguish your claims over a close prior-art reference cited by the examiner. Thus, it's almost axiomatic in patent practice that you should make your specification as long, specific, and detailed as possible, and your main (independent) claims as short, broad, and general as possible. If you're tempted to skip the details, remember that a few strokes on a keyboard now can save you from losing many thousands of dollars later. Be especially sure to expand your discussion in the areas where you feel that your invention is novel over the prior art.

Despite my admonitions to include full details, you'll be relieved to learn that common sense prevails: you don't need to supply full blueprints or a full list of dimensions, materials, and so on for your invention. The specification need only be detailed enough for a Person Having Ordinary Skill In The Art (PHOSITA) to make and use it, even if some experimentation and design work is required. The standard is that such a

PATENT IT YOURSELF

"skilled artisan" should be given adequate guidance so that there is no need to exercise any inventive facilities to realize the invention. (See MPEP 2164.06 for more on this subject.)

TIP

Selecting and arranging the right words is key to good writing. The following is reprinted with thanks by permission of Leslie A. Gordon, Esq., and the Bar Association of San Francisco:

The key to good writing is "variety, rhythm, and balance," according to my graduate journalism text. In addition to selecting the right words, arranging them optimally can add emphasis and improve readability.

Put the subject, verb, and object close together. The subject is the "doer" of the sentence; the verb is the main action; the object (if any) is the recipient of the action.

1. MEDIOCRE: Lisa, encouraged by her science teacher, applied to MIT. (*Subject and verb are separated.*)
   BETTER: Encouraged by her science teacher, Lisa applied to MIT.

2. MEDIOCRE: My dog walker, because he was sick Monday, could not exercise my bulldog.
   BETTER: Because my dog walker was sick Monday, he could not exercise my bulldog. (*Subject and verb are together.*)

   Put modifying words near what they modify. A modifier is a word or words that explain, describe, or qualify another.

3. UNCLEAR: Concerned about the possibility of salmonella, the cutting boards were washed. (Since cutting boards don't get concerned, this sentence must be rewritten to avoid a dangling modifier.)
   BETTER: Concerned about the possibility of salmonella, the chefs washed the cutting boards.

   Be especially mindful of modifiers like "only" or "always" because placement can significantly change the meaning. For example:

   - Only Ann called Dave a louse.
   - Ann only called Dave a louse.
   - Ann called only Dave a louse.

   Begin and end with punch words. The beginning and end of sentences are more emphatic than the middle. So place words you want to stress—usually the subject, object, or verb—at the front or the back.

4. MEDIOCRE: The defendant died two months later while visiting New York. (Emphasizes location.)
   BETTER: The defendant died while visiting New York two months later. (Emphasizes time.)
   BEST: Two months later, while visiting New York, the defendant died. (Emphasizes the main point.)

   If you're uncertain which words carry the most punch, read your sentences aloud.

Common Misconception: If you put a specific feature of your invention, such as a preferred size, a preferred material, or a preferred shape, in your specification, the scope of your invention will be limited to this feature, so any device that lacks this specific feature will not infringe.

Fact: The scope of an invention is determined mainly by the claims and far less by specifics that are included in the specification. If you do recite any specific feature in a claim, that claim will be limited to this specific feature, but if the specific feature is stated in the specification, it will help provide an adequate disclosure. The specific feature should not be stated in a limiting manner, however. Wrong: "The lever of my invention is made of nylon." Right: "The lever of this embodiment may be made of nylon, but other materials are also suitable." When describing a range, state whether the range includes its endpoints (for example: "The length may be as short as 2 centimeters, but in some embodiments may be longer, up to and including 5 centimeters"). It is to your benefit that the specification include as many specifics of the invention as possible, especially in critical areas, so no one will ever be able to validly attack the adequacy of the specification for failure to teach how to make and use the invention. However, again, when stating the specifics of an invention in the specification, it's important to (1) state that these specifics are what you presently prefer for this embodiment, and (2) include as many variations or ramifications as you can envision—for example, "The embodiment of Fig. 1 may have a rectangular cross section 2 mm by 4 mm and be 4 cm long and made of austenitic steel. However, it can have different cross sections, such as oval, triangular, or circular, and different sizes and materials, such as high-carbon steel, titanium, or polycarbonate."

Use of "A," "The," and "Said"

Although the articles "a" and "the" are two of the most common and elementary words in the American language, many writers often use them improperly.

The articles "a" and "an" are indefinite articles; that is, they do not refer to any definite or already known thing. Example: "I bought a car."

The article "the" and the legal word "said" are definite articles; that is, they refer to a definite or already known thing. Example: "I bought the car that we saw yesterday."

When you first introduce something, your reader is not familiar with it, so always introduce it with an indefinite article. Example: "The device has a handle 110 that is connected to an ax head 112."

When your specification refers again to something that has already been introduced, your reader is familiar with it, so always use a definite article "the." For example, if the parts have already been introduced, say, "The lever 110 and the handle 112 may be made of plastic."

If you are referring to the parts by their number, or if they're plural, you often don't need to use "the." Examples: "Lever 110 and handle 112 may be made of plastic," or "Levers such as this are well known."

In claims the same rules apply, except that you should use "the" to refer to a part that has not been expressly mentioned but is implied and "said" to refer to a part by the exact name by which it has already been recited. For example, if the claim has already recited a tabletop comprising a flat sheet and four elongated legs, say, "... said legs being attached to the underside of said tabletop."

Never use "a" to refer to an already-introduced part. For example, if a lever has been introduced, do not subsequently say, "A lever is connected to the handle."

Never introduce something with "the." For example, if a lever has not been introduced, do not say, "The lever is made of plastic."

Avoid technical language, Greek letters, and subscripts, insofar as possible. If you must use any technical terms, be sure to define them for any lay judge or young examiner who may read your application. Remember, however, that your definition may be used to limit your claims, so craft your definition to support your disclosure, but not too narrowly. One patent litigator has suggested drafting all patent applications for a judge with a degree in political science, English, or government—that is, try to make your description as nontechnical as possible, without eliminating any crucial details. If you do have a technical invention, such as a computer, biotechnical, electronic, chemical, medical, or complex mechanical invention, start your explanation from ground zero, assuming your reader, who may be a new examiner or a judge with a degree in political science, knows nothing about the field. Then explain the field of the invention, the problem you solve, and any technical information your reader will need to understand it. You don't need to write a complete textbook, but you should provide a full guide from ground zero to the level of the invention. For any reasonably complex invention, include a glossary of technical and other terms of the invention and make the definitions as broad as possible. You can put the glossary in its own section after the Drawing Figures section.

Claiming Copyright in a Program, Specification, or Drawing

If you want to put a copyright or mask work notice in the specification or drawings to provide notice that you claim copyright in the program listing, mask work, or other written material in the specification, you may do so since 37 CFR 1.71(d) permits this. Make the notice the first paragraph of your specification; Section 71(e) states that the notice shall read as follows:

A portion of the disclosure of this patent document contains material which is subject to (copyright or mask work) protection. The (copyright or mask work) owner has no objection to the facsimile reproduction by anyone of the patent document or the patent disclosure, as it appears in the Patent and Trademark Office patent file or records, but otherwise reserves all (copyright or mask work) rights whatsoever.

Trademarks

If any material, substance, or component of your invention is a trademarked product, you should refer to it by its generic name, without using the mark—unless the mark is necessary for full identification. For example, if you have a hook-and-loop fastener, you can say, "hook-and-loop fastener 20 holds tab to base 14." It is not necessary to use either of the marks *Velcro* or *Latchlok*, since these fasteners are well known. The same holds true for the trademark *Teflon*—use PTFE instead. However, if the product is not common, you can use its mark, provided you use it properly. This means capitalizing the mark, identifying it as a trademark, using the mark as an adjective with a generic descriptor, and identifying the owner of the mark—such as "Ajax™ developer, manufactured by Goldberger Graphics of San Francisco." If the trademarked product is crucial and you're going to recite it in your claims, and you don't know its composition, see "Trademarked Chemical Note," above. (If you have your own (new) trademark for your invention, you should not use it in your specification.)

NOTE

Computer programs note. If your invention involves a computer program, include a program listing in ASCII format or a detailed flowchart with a detailed explanation as to how to configure the computer to perform the required function and interrelate with any other elements to yield the claimed invention. If the listing is 300 lines or fewer (72 characters per line), it can be submitted as part of the specification, or as part of the drawings. In either case, the listing should be a very black, camera-ready copy. If the printout is to be submitted on drawing sheets, these should be of the proper size, with each sheet including a separate figure number (Fig. 1, Fig. 2, and so on, or Fig. 1-A, Fig. 1-B, and so on). If the printout is to be submitted as part of the specification, it must be on the same size sheets. The printout should be positioned just before the claims if it has more than 60 lines of code.

If your program is longer than 300 lines, and you are filing by Patent Center (strongly recommended), you may submit it as an attachment as an ASCII text file (MPEP 502.05), with the program(s) clearly identified and referenced in the specification. Only one copy is needed.

If your program is longer than 300 lines, and you are filing your application on paper, it must be submitted on two CDs (original and duplicate), as an appendix. It will not be printed with the patent, but will be referred to in the patent. You may use CD-ROMs or CD-Rs with your files in ASCII format. Each CD should be in a hard case in an unsealed, unpadded mailing envelope, accompanied by a transmittal letter. The letter (and a separate paragraph in the specification) must list the machine format (IBM-PC, Macintosh, and so on), the operating system compatibility (MS-DOS, MS-Windows, Macintosh, Unix, Linux, and so on), and a list of files on the CD (including their names, size in bytes, and dates of creation). The discs must be labeled "Copy 1" and "Copy 2" and the letter must state that the discs are identical. The standards for CD-ROMs are contained in 37 CFR 1.96 and 1.52(e), available at all Patent and Trademark Resource Centers (or "PTRCs"), in any law library, and online.

TIP

The terms you need to define, if any, will not come into focus for you until you write the claims. Don't write a glossary to define terms until you have written the claims. Remember that defining terms is a double-edged sword. Definitions may add clarity and precision to your claims, and may make it more difficult for an examiner to construe or interpret your claims with unreasonable breadth. However, definitions may also limit the breadth of your claims in ways difficult to foresee at the drafting stage. Even experienced patent attorneys struggle to know when to define a term, and when to leave it open to interpretation.

m. Operation PPA

After you complete the physical description of your main or preferred embodiment, you should then describe in extensive detail the operation or function of the entire machine or system, followed by the operation or function of individual parts covered in your description. Refer to each part by its name and reference numeral, and be sure to describe the working or function of every part. Your invention may be of such a nature that it may not be possible to include a physical description and an operational description in separate sections. However, you'll find that this mode of description works generally for most inventions, and you should try to adhere to it since it will force you to be complete and comprehensive, and to describe both how to make and how to use your invention as required by the patent law. Your operation section should not introduce any part or use any reference numeral that was not introduced in the description section. Again, always keep your reader apprised as to which figure is under discussion. At the end of or in the Operation section, stress the advantages of your invention—for example, "Thus, since the lever 341 is bent in this embodiment it avoids the jamming that some prior-art couplings experienced." Just say what your invention can do and not what it can't do because this will denigrate your invention and give your adversaries ammunition to attack it.

n. Description and Operation of Alternative Embodiments PPA

If your invention includes several embodiments and ramifications, you should first fully describe the structure of the most preferred or most basic embodiment. (However, never call it a "preferred" or "main" embodiment, even if you view it as such.) Then, describe its operation in a separate section immediately following the structural description. In this way, your reader or examiner will get a full understanding of one embodiment of the invention, including its operation.

Then describe each additional important embodiment—those embodiments that you feel have a good chance of being commercially implemented. Describe these additional embodiments in the same manner, but more briefly, since you only need detail the differences over the first embodiment. Thus, several sets of description/operation sections will result. For example, "Fig. 1—Description of Motor," "Operation of Motor," "Fig. 2—Description of Hand Version," "Operation of Hand Version." You must include a highly detailed description of each and every part of your invention, together with a highly detailed description of the operation of each part and its relation to the other parts.

You should describe, draw, and claim specifically all reasonably important embodiments and ramifications so that you'll have more support for broader claims.

Also, if an infringer is making or selling a ramification, you'll be able to show the judge that you specifically showed that ramification in your application. Infringement is supposed to be determined mainly by the wording of your claims. However, as a practical matter, judges are psychologically influenced in your favor if your specification and drawings show and discuss the very embodiment that is being infringed.

If you are aware of less important embodiments and ramifications, you can describe these in the Ramifications section, discussed below, without drawing or claiming them specifically.

> **TIP**
> **Medical devices and drugs.** If your invention is a medical device or drug, you don't need to supply proof of efficacy if it's obvious that it will work and be safe. For instance, if your invention is a drug that is close or analogous to an existing drug that is already recognized as safe and efficacious, you don't need further proof. But if your invention is a drug that is substantially different from anything on the market, and it's not apparent that the drug will be safe and efficacious, you must be prepared to prove those things. Applications for patents on drugs often are referred to the FDA, which has its own requirements, but in cases where the drug or device isn't radically different, declarations by experts regarding safety and efficacy will usually be accepted by the PTO.

o. Conclusion, Ramifications, and Scope

After you finish your detailed description of the invention's operation, add a "Conclusion" section to sum things up and to remind the judge who sees your patent that the claims control. Here's an example:

"Thus the reader will see that at least one embodiment of the can opener provides a more reliable, lightweight, yet economical device that can be used by persons of almost any age …. [Keep selling it!]"

Some inventors have provided arguments for nonobviousness here, but it's advisable to just state the advantages without discussing nonobviousness.

"While my above description contains many specificities, these should not be construed as limitations on the scope, but rather as an exemplification of one [or

several] embodiment(s) thereof. Many other variations are possible. For example [then continue with brief description of possible variations that aren't important enough to show as ramifications in the drawing].

"Accordingly, the scope of the disclosure should be determined not by the embodiment(s) illustrated, but by the appended claims and their legal equivalents."

In the first paragraph quoted above, the advantages of the invention are restated and summarized to hammer home the great value of your invention. But don't refer to "the invention" here—just the embodiments—and avoid absolute terms; for example, state that you have found that it is "more reliable" rather than that you have found it "completely or highly reliable." In the "for example" portion of the second quoted paragraph, include a brief description of any alternative embodiments you can think of and that you didn't consider important enough to show in the drawing and describe in detail in your description. Put exotic, untested embodiments, as well as minor variations in color, size, and materials in the broadening paragraph. It's very desirable to include as many ramifications as possible in order to get your claims, especially "means" clauses, interpreted as broadly as possible. The courts will interpret a patent in a narrower manner if it describes a single embodiment only. (See Chapter 9 on drafting claims for a discussion of "means" clauses and their relationship to the specification.)

Thus you should go through the entire application and, for each element of the inventive device or method, state in the ramifications paragraph whether that element can be:

- eliminated or duplicated
- changed in size (made smaller or larger)
- made of a different material
- made in a different shape
- made of a different color
- connected or associated with its adjacent elements in a different manner
- given a different mode or function of operation— for example, suction rather than blowing, or
- made integrally or separately (modular or in sections).

It's very important to be as comprehensive as possible when describing ramifications because courts tend to interpret claims narrowly, unless the infringed device is described or mentioned in the specification. Look at the sample specification at the end of this chapter to see how this is done.

That's just about all there is to drafting the specification portion of your application. What's left, you ask? The not-so-small matter of "Claims," that's what. We'll tell you how to write these in the next chapter. As a reminder, it is advisable to draft your claims first, and then draft the remainder of the specification around them. At this stage, your claims should already be drafted, and you can simply insert them at this point in the specification.

p. Sequence Listing PPA

If you provide a sequence listing of a nucleotide or amino acid sequence on paper, you should include this heading and the listing on a separate sheet after your claims and before your abstract. If you have no sequence listing, don't include the sheet or this heading.

q. Abstract

Your abstract should be drafted on a separate sheet, after the claims. However, it will be printed on the first page of your patent and appears right after the sample specification of Fig. 8G, since the claims have been saved for the next chapter. The abstract is relatively easy to do once you've done the specification, and since it's very closely related to the specification, we'll cover it here.

The abstract should be put on a new page with the heading "Abstract." To do the actual abstract, write one paragraph providing a concise summary of the specification in no more than 150 words. Spend enough time writing the abstract to make it concise, complete, clear, and as broad (nonlimiting) as possible. This is because the abstract is usually the part of an application that's read first and most frequently consulted. Look at the abstracts of several of your prior-art patents to get an idea of what's involved. To be concise, your abstract should not include throat-clearing phrases like "This invention relates to," but rather, should get right into it and state—for example, "An improved bicycle pedal mechanism having…," and so on. Also don't limit your abstract to the invention or one embodiment; rather refer to other embodiments and never "the invention." If you think you may file the application in other countries, you should include reference and figure numbers in the abstract (with each one in parentheses) to comply with the international rules. It's also desirable to include some advantages of one or more embodiments in the abstract.

J. Review Your Specification and Abstract Carefully

After you've completed your draft, review it carefully to be sure you've included everything about your invention you can think of. Also, be sure that there is no possible ground for anyone to say that you haven't included enough to teach one skilled in the art how to make and use your invention or that there's anything in the specification that a court can use against you to limit your invention. Also make sure whatever you write is clear and unambiguous because if it's possible to do so, some reader will always interpret anything you write to mean something other than what you intended. You may have to go through two, three, or more drafts to get it right. Be sure to compare your specification with those of other recent patents in the field so that yours is at least as complete as theirs. Allow yourself plenty of time—for example, a few days to do the drawings, a few days to write the introductory parts of your specification, and a few days to do the static description. In this way you won't feel pressured and thus you'll be able to do a better, more readable, more legally adequate job. Because the drafting of an excellent patent application is admittedly a difficult and tiring task, you may be tempted, after finishing the draft, to file it right away and not to check it carefully. It's better to wait a day or two and check it carefully; you'll be grateful that you waited.

> *"Don't do your work in haste. Later on, the public won't ask whether it was completed in three days, but whether it's accurate and complete."*
>
> —Anonymous

CAUTION

Many prior-art patents are not properly described under today's demanding standards, so don't absolutely rely on them. Instead, follow the guidelines of this chapter. After you complete the draft of your specification, show it to a coworker, relative, or friend—someone you can trust to keep your application confidential. Have them double-check that: It clearly teaches how to make and use the invention, it sells your invention and states all of its advantages, it is logical, free of errors (grammatical and technical), it is clearly written, and it doesn't tend to limit your invention.

If You Use an Attorney

If you're able to hire an attorney (or agent) to prepare your patent application, don't blindly accept whatever the attorney gives you to sign, since even the best attorneys make mistakes and omit important things at one time or another. Most attorneys do better work when they have a critical client. Carefully review the attorney's work in detail, making sure the application is well and clearly written, clearly teaches how to make and use the invention, discloses all possible ramifications, isn't limiting, contains broad main claims, and has a spectrum of claims. You're paying the attorney a lot of money, so you deserve a high-quality product. If your attorney won't listen to your suggestions or does less than high-quality work, it might be time to find another one.

K. Use of Artificial Intelligence (AI) To Draft the Specification

For years, computer tools have been ubiquitous in document drafting. Word processing software with features such as spelling and grammar check are commonplace in most industries. More recently, word processing software and other computer tools have begun adopting generative AI features that can develop a written document with much less human involvement. For example, recent tools directed to the IP industry include the ability to draft technical specifications, generate responses to Office actions, write and respond to briefs, and even draft patent claims.

The capabilities of these tools continue to grow, and there is no prohibition against using these computer tools in drafting documents for submission to the PTO. Nor is there a general obligation to disclose to the PTO the use of such tools. However, and especially absent such an obligation, applicants submitting papers to the USPTO should keep in mind the following USPTO policies and duties to the Office when using these computer tools.

1. Any paper submitted to the USPTO must be reviewed by the party or parties presenting the paper. Those parties are responsible for the contents therein. If an AI tool is used in drafting or editing a document, such as a patent specification, you must still review its contents and ensure the paper is in accordance with the certifications being made. Simply relying on the accuracy of an AI tool is not a reasonable inquiry, especially given the potential for generative AI systems to omit, misstate, or even "hallucinate" information.

2. If an AI system assists in the drafting of a patent application and introduces alternative embodiments or ramifications that you did not conceive, you may not be entitled to list yourself as an inventor of those embodiments. If there is a question as to whether there was at least one named inventor who significantly contributed to a claimed invention developed with the assistance of AI, information regarding the interaction with the AI system (e.g., the inputs/outputs of the AI system) could be material to patentability and, if so, should be disclosed to the PTO.

There are additional policies that relate specifically to AI assistance with drafting claims that you should keep in mind. These are discussed in Chapter 9, which deals with claims more generally.

L. Checklist for Your Patent Application Draft

In the following sections are three lists of the most common errors and areas generally needing improvement. The first list (in two parts) covers the preliminary drawings and draft specification. Before you go on to the claims or to the finaling process, check this list carefully and make any needed corrections in your work. The specification checklist includes many grammar and punctuation rules that inventors violate frequently.

M. Specification of Sample Patent Application

The application shown below is reproduced in final form, ready for filing in the PTO. However, your application will be in draft form after completing this chapter.

N. Summary

The specification must describe how to make and use the invention in full, clear, concise, and exact terms. The patent application should also "sell" the embodiments of the invention by stressing their advantages in the Operation and Conclusion sections. But don't include anything that could be used to limit your invention or that could be used against you.

Any layperson who can write a detailed description in conjunction with drawings will be able to write a competent patent application. A patent application should contain certain prescribed headings and additional informative headings.

When your application is received in the PTO it will be processed and put in a file by clerical personnel and later reviewed by drawing reviewers and then an examiner.

Prior to doing your drawings and writing the application you should review your papers and make full preparations. For inventions that use software, the application should have a detailed flowchart or a code listing. Do rough drawings first and provide a name for every part. Then draft the specification according to an outline and without legal terms, using short, simple sentences.

Provide a static description of each embodiment before describing its operation and sell the invention throughout. Follow the checklists for the preliminary drawings and specification draft.

Checklist for Preliminary Drawings

- [ ] Every significant part in the drawings has its own reference numeral.

- [ ] Every unique part has a different reference numeral—that is, the same reference numeral is never used to indicate different parts. (Suffixed numbers (10, 10'; 10A, 10B, and so on) can be used for different parts.)

- [ ] The same reference numeral is always used to indicate the same part when such part is shown in different Figs.; that is, two different numerals are never used to indicate the same part.

- [ ] Arrowheads are not used on any lead line, unless it refers to an entire assembly of elements.

- [ ] The drawings show enough details of your invention to enable it to be fully and readily understood by a lay judge.

- [ ] The reference numerals start with a number higher than your highest Fig. number.

- [ ] Even reference numerals (10, 12, and so on) are used so you can add more numerals in sequence later, if needed.

- [ ] The Fig. details and reference numerals are large enough to be easily read.

- [ ] Separated parts of any figure are joined by projection lines (see Fig. 8D) or a large bracket (unless there is only one figure on the sheet).

- [ ] A descriptive label is placed on or near each component whose function is not apparent. (If the component's function is understandable as shown, you aren't allowed to label it.)

- [ ] The drawings show every part and modification that you intend to include in your claims. (See Chapter 9.)

- [ ] No dimensions are used on drawings (unless essential for the invention).

- [ ] Each figure has a separate number. Suffixed figure numbers (Fig. 1-A, Fig. 1-b; Fig. 1, Fig. 1') are okay.

- [ ] Separate figures are not connected by any line.

- [ ] Exotic or special parts are labeled—for example, "saturated transistor"; "gray water"; "electric conduit."

- [ ] Perspective (isometric) views, rather than engineering (top, side, bottom) views, are used wherever possible.

- [ ] Any figures that show a prior-art device are so labeled.

- [ ] A reference number is not used for an entire figure.

- [ ] A sectional view is indicated by two arrows with crossbars on the main view, numbered with the number of the sectional view. If, within a subsidiary figure, you show an enlarged view of an area of a main figure, draw a circle around the area in the main figure and label the circle with the figure number of the subsidiary figure.

Checklist for Draft of Specification—Writing in General

- ☐ No sentence is over about 13 words (unless really necessary or unless two independent clauses are used).
- ☐ A heading is supplied for approximately every two pages of discussion (if possible).
- ☐ Each discussion relates to and explains only its heading.
- ☐ Adjacent paragraphs are connected by transitions, and no paragraph is longer than about one page, double-spaced.
- ☐ Every sophisticated or technical term is defined clearly.
- ☐ The description is written in simple, nontechnical terms, insofar as possible, so that a lay judge or jury can understand it.
- ☐ All writing is clear, reads smoothly, and is logical.
- ☐ Unisex personal pronouns ("he," "his," "hers," and so on) aren't used exclusively.
- ☐ No sentence is started with a number.
- ☐ Every reference numeral is preceded by a noun ("lever 21").
- ☐ A comma isn't used between subject and verb. (Wrong: "Lever 24, is connected to brace 26.")
- ☐ A comma is used at all natural pauses.
- ☐ Don't omit "Oxford" comma: "He ate bread, ham, and eggs." (Comma indicates the ham and eggs aren't mixed.)
- ☐ All possessives are apostrophized, except "its."
- ☐ Loose, informal writing isn't used.
- ☐ The Specification has been carefully checked for spelling and grammar errors.

- ☐ A descriptive noun ("lever") rather than a general term ("part") is used for every element.
- ☐ A group of words serving as a single adjective is hyphenated—for example, "impact-resistant glass."
- ☐ No sentence fragments are used. (Wrong: "Because the gear is made of nylon.")
- ☐ Writing is proofread carefully.
- ☐ The indefinite article "a" (rather than "the") is used to introduce parts in the specification.
- ☐ Already introduced parts are not referred to with the article "a," but with "the."
- ☐ Every part is referred to by a consistent name throughout. (Multiple alternative names should be used to introduce the part.)
- ☐ Your writing does not contain "flab" phrases such as "It will be noted that." (Flab slows reader's pace and detracts from drama and strength of work.)
- ☐ The writing doesn't change voices (active to passive, or vice versa) in a paragraph, and you use the active voice as much as possible. (*Wrong:* "The second gear is turned by the first gear." *Right:* "The first gear turns the second gear.")
- ☐ The discussion discusses one Fig. at a time, insofar as possible, and doesn't jump from figure to figure too much.
- ☐ Your reader is always kept clearly advised which figure is under discussion.
- ☐ "Fig." (rather than figure) is used throughout to speed reading.

Checklist for Draft of Specification—Specification

- ☐ The title indicates the essence of your invention without being longer than 500 characters.

- ☐ The Background—Prior Art section does not mention your invention.

- ☐ All detailed technical discussions refer to a drawing Fig. (most humans can't comprehend abstract technical discussions).

- ☐ Each prior-art approach you discuss is knocked.

- ☐ When any patent or prior-art reference is referred to, the inventor's or author's name(s), the patent number, or publication and page, and its issue date are included.

- ☐ The Drawing Description section has just one short sentence for each Fig.

- ☐ A List of Reference Numerals section is included.

- ☐ Every reference numeral on the drawings is used in the specification and every reference numeral in the specification is on the drawings.

- ☐ The same reference numeral is not used for two different parts. (Suffixed numerals—10, 10A, 10' for different parts—are okay.)

- ☐ The description and the operation of the invention are discussed in separate sections.

- ☐ Overall or main parts and overall operation are described before describing details of parts and operation.

- ☐ If any part mentioned in the specification isn't shown in the drawings (for example, because it's conventional), state this. (For example, "Output 24 of generator 22 is connected to a conventional storage battery (not shown).")

- ☐ You don't refer to your device as "the invention"; you're specific. (Wrong: "My invention thus ..." Right: "The embodiment of my can opener thus...")

- ☐ Ramifications are discussed after the first embodiment and its operation is explained.

- ☐ A separate "Summary" section is provided (optional) in general terms.

- ☐ Wishy-washy descriptions ("a plastic brace might work here") are eliminated; all descriptions are firm, sure, and positive.

- ☐ The specification doesn't contain any "Patent Profanity" (see Section I.1. above).

- ☐ The dimensions, exemplary materials, relationships, and/or sources of supply are stated for all exotic or critical parts in a nonlimiting manner—for example, "at present I contemplate the use of nylon for the bevel gear, but other materials are suitable."

- ☐ For ease of reading, a shorter term is used when you refer again to a part with a long name. For example, First time: "A liquid-overflow check valve 12." Second time: "Valve 12."

- ☐ Generic terms, rather than trademarks, are used if possible. Each trademark used is identified as such, typed in caps, used with a generic noun, and its owner is indicated.

- ☐ No legal words, such as "said" or "means," are used in the specification or abstract.

- ☐ Metric (or metric followed by British) dimensions are used.

- ☐ All possible novel features of each embodiment are discussed in great detail with dimensions, materials, shapes, interconnections, and so on in a nonlimiting manner, so as to provide language to support any claims that might be directed to this feature.

- ☐ The Description and Operation sections contain enough detail to enable your invention readily to be built, understood, and used. Every part of each embodiment is discussed, its purpose is stated, and the overall operation of the invention is explained.

- ☐ If a best mode is indicated, it is done in a nonlimiting manner. The application does not contain any statements that could be used against you to narrow or invalidate your invention.

- ☐ The Operation section does not introduce any part.

- ☐ A Conclusion section is provided at the end of the specification to repeat the advantages, discuss all possible alternatives (less important embodiments and ramifications), and to indicate that the claims control.

- ☐ The Abstract is broad and nonlimiting, without listing too many advantages.

- ☐ The Abstract has a reference numeral in parentheses "(12)," after each named part, for possible foreign filing.

- ☐ You have had another person check the draft for completeness, accuracy, and clarity.

- ☐ Include a glossary with broad definitions of the terms used in your specification if it's at all complex.

220 | PATENT IT YOURSELF

A2-KoppeLam.SB   your disc and file # (optional)

Note: Dimensions and layout are indicated for typing or printing on letter-size paper (8.5" x 11") so that, if foreign filing is later desired (see Chapter 12), photocopies made directly on A4 paper will have the proper format for foreign filing. If foreign filing is not likely to be desired, legal or letter-size paper with the usual margins (always provide at least a 1" top margin for hole punching), 1.5 or double line spacing, and page numbers at bottom or top can be used.

8-9 cm top margin on p. 1

2.5 cm left margin

Patent Application of

Lou W. Koppe

for

PAPER-LAMINATED PLIABLE CLOSURE FOR FLEXIBLE BAGS

Printout should have minimum 1.5 line spacing (4 lines/inch) but is shown with denser spacing since this example is shown on a reduced scale.

Cross-Reference to Related Applications

This application claims the benefit of provisional patent application Ser. No. 60/123,456, filed 2003 August 9 by the present inventor.

Background—Prior Art

description of and knocking of prior art

The following is a tabulation of some prior art that presently appears relevant:

2.8–3.8 cm right margin on 8.5" x 11" paper

U. S. Patents

Patent Number	Kind Code	Issue Date	Patentee
4292714	B1	1981-08—9	Walker
2981990	B1	1961-05-22	Balderree

U. S. Patent Application Publications

Publication Nr.	Kind Code	Publ. Date	Applicant
200712345678	A1	2007-07-21	Paxton

Foreign Patent Documents

Foreign Doc. Nr.	Cntry Code	Kind Code	Pub. Dt	App or Patentee
883771	GB	B2	1961-12-24	Britt et al.

Non-Patent Literature Documents

Himmelfarb, L. W., *Bread Baker* magazine, "Clips for bread bags come in various colors" (May 2009)

Fig. 8G—Specification of Sample Patent Application

Patent Application of Lou W. Koppe for "Paper-Laminated
Pliable Closure for Flexible Bags" continued
Page 2

continue knocking the prior art

Grocery stores and supermarkets commonly supply consumers with polyethylene bags for holding produce. Such bags are also used by suppliers to provide a resealable container for other items, both edible and inedible.

Originally these bags were sealed by the supplier with staples or by heat. However, consumers objected since these were of a rather permanent nature: the bags could be opened only by tearing, thereby damaging them and rendering them impossible to reseal.

Thereafter, several types of closures were designed to seal plastic bags in such a way as to leave them undamaged after they were opened. Walker discloses a complex clamp which can close the necks of bags without causing damage upon opening; however, these clamps are prohibitively expensive to manufacture. Balderree shows a closure which is of expensive construction, being made of PTFE, and which is not effective unless the bag has a relatively long "neck."

Thus if the bag has been filled almost completely and consequently has a short neck, this closure is useless. Also, being relatively narrow and clumsy, Balderree's closure cannot be easily bent by hand along its longitudinal axis. Finally, his closure does not hold well onto the bag, but has a tendency to snap off.

Although twist closures with a wire core are easy to use and inexpensive to manufacture, do not damage the bag upon being removed, and can be used repeatedly, nevertheless they simply do not possess the neat and uniform appearance of a tab closure, they become tattered and unsightly after repeated use, and they do not offer suitable surfaces for the reception of print or labeling. These ties also require much more manipulation to apply and remove.

Several types of thin, flat closures have been proposed—for example, in U.K. patent 883,771 to Britt et al. (1961) and U.S. patents 3,164,250 (1965), 3,417,912 (1968), 3,822,441 (1974), 4,361,935 (1982), and 4,509,231 (1985), all to Paxton. Although inexpensive to manufacture, capable of use with bags having a short neck, and producible in break-off strips, such closures can be used only once if they are made of frangible plastic since they must be bent or twisted when being removed and consequently will fracture upon removal. Thus, to reseal a bag originally sealed with a frangible closure, one must either close its neck with another closure or else close it in makeshift fashion by folding or tying it. My own patent 4,694,542 (1987) describes a closure which is made of flexible plastic and is therefore capable of repeated use without damage to the bag, but nevertheless all the plastic closures heretofore known suffer from a number of disadvantages:

Fig. 8G—Specification of Sample Patent Application (continued)

Patent Application of Lou W. Koppe for "Paper-Laminated
Pliable Closure for Flexible Bags" continued
Page 3

(a) Their manufacture in color requires the use of a compounding facility for the production of the pigmented plastic. Such a facility, which is needed to compound the primary pigments and which generally constitutes a separate production site, requires the presence of very large storage bins for the pigmented raw granules. Also, it presents great difficulties with regard to the elimination of the airborne powder which results from the mixing of the primary granules.

(b) If one uses an extruder in the production of a pigmented plastic—especially if one uses only a single extruder—a change from one color to a second requires purging the extruder of the granules having the first color by introducing those of the second color. This process inevitably produces, in sizable volume, an intermediate product of an undesired color which must be discarded as scrap, thereby resulting in waste of material and time.

(c) The colors of the closures in present use are rather unsaturated. If greater concentrations of pigment were used in order to make the colors more intense, the plastic would become more brittle and the cost of the final product would increase.

(d) The use of pigmented plastic closures does not lend itself to the production of multicolored designs, and it would be very expensive to produce plastic closures in which the plastic is multicolored—for example, in which the plastic has stripes of several colors, or in which the plastic exhibits multicolored designs.

(e) Closures made solely of plastic generally offer poor surfaces for labeling or printing, and the label or print is often easily smudged.

(f) The printing on a plastic surface is often easily erased, thereby allowing the alteration of prices by dishonest consumers.

(g) The plastic closures in present use are slippery when handled with wet or greasy fingers.

(h) A closure of the type in present use can be very carefully pried off a bag by a dishonest consumer and then attached to another item without giving any evidence of such removal.

Summary

summary paraphrases main claim

In accordance with one embodiment a bag closure comprises a flat body having a notch, a gripping aperture adjacent to the notch and a layer of paper laminated on its side.

Fig. 8G—Specification of Sample Patent Application (continued)

Patent Application of Lou W. Koppe for "Paper-Laminated
Pliable Closure for Flexible Bags" continued
Page 4

Advantages

Accordingly several advantages of one or more aspects are as follows: to provide bag seals that are not permanent and that can be resealed, that do not damage bags, that are relatively inexpensive, that can be used on bags with a relatively short neck, that can be bent without breaking, that are neat and have a uniform appearance, that can be easily manufactured in color with designs, that will accept printing and hold it well against smudging, that do not slip in one's fingers, and that give evidence when removed. Other advantages of one or more aspects will be apparent from a consideration of the drawings and ensuing description.

Drawings—Figures

one short sentence for each figure

In the drawings, closely related figures have the same number but different alphabetic suffixes.

Figs. 1A to 1D show various aspects of a closure supplied with a longitudinal groove and laminated on one side with paper in accordance with one embodiment.

Fig. 2 shows a closure with no longitudinal groove and with a paper lamination on one side only in accordance with another embodiment.

Fig. 3 shows a similar closure with one longitudinal groove in accordance with another embodiment.

Fig. 4 shows a similar closure with a paper lamination on both sides in accordance with another embodiment.

Fig. 5 shows a similar closure with a paper lamination on one side only, the groove having been formed into the paper as well as into the body of the closure in accordance with another embodiment.

Figs. 6A to 6K show end views of closures having various combinations of paper laminations, longitudinal grooves, and through-holes in accordance with other embodiments.

Figs. 7A to 7C show a laminated closure with groove after being bent and after being straightened again.

Figs. 8A to 8C show a laminated closure without a groove after being bent and after being straightened again.

Fig. 8G—Specification of Sample Patent Application (continued)

Patent Application of Lou W. Koppe for "Paper-Laminated
Pliable Closure for Flexible Bags" continued
Page 5

Drawings—Reference Numerals

10	base of closure	12	lead-in notch
14	hole	16	gripping points
18	groove	20	paper lamination
22	tear of paper lamination	24	corner
26	longitudinal through-hole	28	neck-down
30	side of base opposite to bend	32	crease

DETAILED DESCRIPTION—FIGS. 1A AND 1B—FIRST EMBODIMENT

static description of figures

One embodiment of the closure is illustrated in Fig. 1A (top view) and Fig. 1B (end view). The closure has a thin base **10** of uniform cross section consisting of a flexible sheet of material which can be repeatedly bent and straightened out without fracturing. A layer of paper **20** (Fig. 1B) is laminated on one side of base **10**. In one embodiment, the base is a flexible plastic, such as poly-ethylene-tere-phthalate (PET—hyphens here supplied to facilitate pronunciation)—available from Eastman Chemical Co. of Kingsport, TN. However, the base can consist of any other material that can be repeatedly bent without fracturing, such as polyethylene, polypropylene, vinyl, nylon, rubber, leather, various impregnated or laminated fibrous materials, various plasticized materials, cardboard, paper, and so on.

At one end of the closure is a lead-in notch **12** which terminates in gripping points **16** and leads to a hole **14**. Paper layer **20** adheres to base **10** by virtue either of the extrusion of liquid plastic (which will form the body of the closure) directly onto the paper or the application of heat or adhesive upon the entirety of one side of base **10**. The paper-laminated closure is then punched out. Thus the lamination will have the same shape as the side of the base **10** to which it adheres.

The base of the closure is typically 0.8 mm to 1.2 mm in thickness, and has overall dimensions roughly from 20 mm x 20 mm (square shape) to 40 mm x 70 mm (oblong shape). The outer four corners **24** of the closure are typically beveled or rounded to avoid snagging and personal injury. Also, when closure tabs are connected side-to-side in a long roll, these bevels or roundings give the roll a series of notches which act as detents or indices for the positioning and conveying of the tabs in a dispensing machine.

Fig. 8G—Specification of Sample Patent Application (continued)

CHAPTER 8 | HOW TO DRAFT THE SPECIFICATION AND INITIAL DRAWINGS | 225

Patent Application of Lou W. Koppe for "Paper-Laminated
Pliable Closure for Flexible Bags" continued
Page 6

A longitudinal groove **18** is formed on one side of base **10** in Fig. 1. In other embodiments, there may be two longitudinal grooves—one on each side of the base—or there may be no longitudinal groove at all. Groove **18** may be formed by machining, scoring, rolling, or extruding. In the absence of a groove, there may be a longitudinal through-hole **26** (Fig. 6L). This through-hole may be formed by placing, in the extrusion path of the closure, a hollow pin for the outlet of air.

Operation—Figs. 1, 6, 7, 8

operational description of figures

The manner of using the paper-laminated closure to seal a plastic bag is identical to that for closures in present use. Namely, one first twists the neck of a bag (not shown here but shown in Fig. 12 of my above patent) into a narrow, cylindrical configuration. Next, holding the closure so that the plane of its base is generally perpendicular to the axis of the neck and so that lead-in notch **12** is adjacent to the neck, one inserts the twisted neck into the lead-in notch until it is forced past gripping points **16** at the base of the notch and into hole **14**.

To remove the closure, one first bends it along its horizontal axis (Fig. 1C—an end view—and Figs. 7 and 8) so that the closure is still in contact with the neck of the bag and so that gripping points **16** roughly point in parallel directions. Then one pulls the closure up or down and away from the neck in a direction generally opposite to that in which the gripping points now point, thus freeing the closure from the bag without damaging the latter. The presence of one or two grooves **18** or a longitudinal through-hole **26** (Fig. 6L), either of which acts as a hinge, facilitates this process of bending.

The closure can be used to reseal the original bag or to seal another bag many times; one simply bends it flat again prior to reuse.

As shown in Figs. 1C, 7B, and 8B (all end views), when the closure is bent along its longitudinal axis, region **30** of the base will stretch somewhat along the direction perpendicular to the longitudinal axis. (Region 30 is the region which is parallel to this axis and is on the side of the base opposite to the bend.) Therefore, when the closure is flattened again, the base will have elongated in the direction perpendicular to the longitudinal axis. This will cause a necking down **28** (Figs. 1D, 7C, and 8C) of the base, as well as either a telltale tear **22**, or at least a crease **32** (Figs. 7A and 8A) along the axis of bending. Therefore, if the closure is attached to a sales item and has print upon its paper lamination, the fact that the closure has been transferred by a dishonest

Fig. 8G—Specification of Sample Patent Application (continued)

226 | PATENT IT YOURSELF

Patent Application of Lou W. Koppe for "Paper-Laminated
Pliable Closure for Flexible Bags" continued
Page 7

consumer from the first item to another will be made evident by the tear or crease.

Figs. 7A and 8A show bent closures with and without grooves, respectively. Figs. 7C and 8C show the same closures, respectively, after being flattened out, along their longitudinal axes, paper tear **22** being visible.

Figs. 2-5—Additional Embodiments

Additional embodiments are shown in Figs. 2, 3, 4, and 5; in each case the paper lamination is shown partially peeled back. In Fig. 2 the closure has only one lamination and no groove; in Fig. 3 it has only one lamination and only one groove; in Fig. 4 it has two laminations and only one groove; in Fig. 5 it has two laminations and one groove, the latter having been rolled into one lamination as well as into the body of the closure.

Figs. 6A-6B—Alternative Embodiments

There are various possibilities with regard to the relative disposition of the sides which are grooved and the sides which are laminated, as illustrated in Fig. 6, which presents end views along the longitudinal axis. Fig. 6A shows a closure with lamination on one side only and with no groove; Fig. 6B shows a closure with laminations on both sides and with no groove; Fig. 6C shows a closure with only one lamination and only one groove, both being on the same side; Fig. 6D shows a closure with only one lamination and only one groove, both being on the same side and the groove having been rolled into the lamination as well as into the body of the closure; Fig. 6E shows a closure with only one lamination and only one groove, the two being on opposite sides; Fig. 6F shows a closure with two laminations and only one groove; Fig. 6G shows a closure with two laminations and only one groove, the groove having been rolled into one lamination as well as into the body of the closure; Fig. 6H shows a closure with only one lamination and with two grooves; Fig. 6I shows a closure with only one lamination and with two grooves, one of the grooves having been rolled into the lamination as well as into the body of the closure; Fig. 6J shows a closure with two laminations and with two grooves; Fig. 6K shows a closure with two laminations and with two grooves, the grooves having been rolled into the laminations as well as into the body of the closure; and Fig. 6L shows a closure with two laminations and a longitudinal through-hole.

Fig. 8G—Specification of Sample Patent Application (continued)

Patent Application of Lou W. Koppe for "Paper-Laminated
Pliable Closure for Flexible Bags" continued
Page 8

Advantages

From the description above, a number of advantages of some embodiments of my paper-laminated closures become evident:

(a) A few rolls of colored paper will contain thousands of square yards of a variety of colors, will obviate the need for liquid pigments or a pigment-compounding plant, and will permit the manufacturer to produce colored closures with transparent, off-color, or leftover plastic, all of which are cheaper than first quality pigmented plastic.

(b) With the use of rolls of colored paper to laminate the closures, one can change colors by simply changing rolls, thus avoiding the need to purge the extruder used to produce the closures.

(c) The use of paper laminate upon an unpigmented, flexible plastic base can provide a bright color without requiring the introduction of pigment into the base and the consequent sacrifice of pliability.

(d) The presence of a paper lamination will permit the display of multicolored designs.

(e) The paper lamination will provide a superior surface for labeling or printing, either by hand or by machine.

(f) Any erasure or alteration of prices by dishonest consumers on the paper-laminated closure will leave a highly visible and permanent mark.

(g) Although closures made solely of plastic are slippery when handled with wet or greasy fingers, the paper laminate on my closures will provide a nonslip surface.

Figs. 7A and 8A show bent closures with and without grooves, respectively. Figs. 7C and 8C show the same closures, respectively, after being flattened out, along their longitudinal axes, paper tear 22 being visible.

Conclusion, Ramifications, and Scope

repeat advantages— keep selling it! Accordingly, the reader will see that the paper-laminated closures of the various embodiments can be used to seal a plastic bag easily and conveniently, can be removed just as easily and without damage to the bag, and can be used to reseal the bag without requiring a new closure. In addition, when a closure has been used to seal a bag and is later bent and removed from the bag so as not to damage the latter, the paper lamination will tear or crease and thus give visible evidence of tampering,

Fig. 8G—Specification of Sample Patent Application (continued)

228 | PATENT IT YOURSELF

Patent Application of Lou W. Koppe for "Paper-Laminated
Pliable Closure for Flexible Bags" continued
Page 9

without impairing the ability of the closure to reseal the original bag or any other bag. Furthermore, the paper lamination has the additional advantages in that:

additional ramifications

• it permits the production of closures in a variety of colors without requiring the manufacturer to use a separate facility for the compounding of the powdered or liquid pigments needed in the production of colored closures;

• it permits an immediate change in the color of the closure being produced without the need for purging the extruder of old resin;

• it allows the closure to be brightly colored without the need to pigment the base itself and consequently sacrifice the flexibility of the closure; it allows the closure to be multicolored since the paper lamination offers a perfect surface upon which can be printed multicolored designs;

• it provides a closure with a superior surface upon which one can label or print;

• it provides a closure whose labeling cannot be altered or erased without resulting in tell-tale damage to the paper lamination; and

• it provides a closure that will not be slippery when handled with wet or greasy fingers, the paper itself providing a nonslip surface.

broadening paragraph

Although the description above contains many specificities, these should not be construed as limiting the scope of the embodiments but as merely providing illustrations of some of several embodiments. For example, the closure can have other shapes, such as circular, oval, trapezoidal, or triangular; the lead-in notch can have other shapes; the groove can be replaced by a hinge which connects two otherwise unconnected halves; and so on.

Thus the scope of the embodiments should be determined by the appended claims and their legal equivalents, rather than by the examples given.

[CLAIMS FOLLOW, STARTING ON A NEW PAGE, BUT ARE
PRINTED IN THE NEXT CHAPTER]

Fig. 8G—Specification of Sample Patent Application (continued)

Patent Application of Lou W. Koppe for "Paper-Laminated
Pliable Closure for Flexible Bags" continued
Page 13

Abstract: One embodiment of a thin, flat closure for plastic bags and of the type having at one edge a V-shaped notch (**12**) which communicates at its base with a gripping aperture (**14**). The base (**10**) of the closure is made of a flexible material so that it can be repeatedly bent, without fracturing, along an axis aligned with said notch and aperture. In addition, a layer of paper (**20**) is laminated on one or both sides of the closure. The axis of the base may contain one or two grooves (**18**) or a through-hole (**26**), either of which acts as a hinge to facilitate bending. Other embodiments are described and shown.

Fig. 8G—Specification of Sample Patent Application (continued)

see Fig. 10B for permitted drawing sizes

1/3

Fig. 8G—Specification of Sample Patent Application (continued)

FIG.5

FIG.6D   FIG.6G   FIG.6I   FIG.6K

Fig. 8G—Specification of Sample Patent Application (continued)

Fig. 8G—Specification of Sample Patent Application (continued)

CHAPTER

9

Now for the Legalese—The Claims

A.	What Are Claims?	235
B.	The Law Regarding Claims	236
	1. Legal Requirements for Patent Claims	236
	2. Legal Requirements for Patentable Subject Matter	237
	3. Rules of Practice	238
C.	Some Sample Claims	239
	1. Process or Method Claims: Conventional Process, Software Process, Business Method, and Manual Method	240
	2. Machine Claims	242
	3. Article-of-Manufacture Claim	243
	4. Composition-of-Matter Claim	243
	5. New Use Claim	244
D.	Common Misconceptions Regarding Claims	244
E.	One Claim Should Be as Broad as Possible	245
	1. Minimize the Number of Elements	245
	2. Recite Each Element as Broadly as Possible	246
F.	The Effect of Prior Art on Your Claim	247
	1. Novelty	247
	2. Nonobviousness	247
G.	Technical Requirements of Claims	248
	1. Use Proper Antecedents and Be Precise	249
	2. Use Only One Capital, One Period, and No Dashes, Quotes, Parentheses, Trademarks, or Undefined Abbreviations	249
	3. Use Means Clause to Avoid Functionality of Claim	250
	4. Be Complete	251
	5. Keep Language Straightforward and Simple	251
	6. All Elements of Invention Must Logically Interrelate and Interconnect	251
	7. Aggregation	251
	8. Use Only Positive Limitations	251
	9. Use Proper Connective Expressions	252
	10. Avoid Too Many Claims	252
	11. Make Sure Claims Correspond With Disclosure	252

12. Make Sure Claims Are Supported in Drawing	252
13. Avoid the Software-As-Means Trap	253
14. Recite Each Element Affirmatively as Subject of Its Clause	253
15. Include Structural Support in Recitation of Operation	254
16. Recite Each Element Affirmatively, Followed by Its Shape or Function	254
17. Format	254
18. Precede Every Function by an Affirmative Recitation of the Element That Performs That Function	254
19. Make Sure Relative Terms Are Not Ambiguous	254
H. Drafting Your Main (Independent) Claim	255
1. The Preamble	255
2. The Elements	256
3. Interconnections	256
I. Other Techniques in Claim Writing	259
J. Drafting Dependent Claims	261
1. Reasons for Writing Dependent Claims	262
2. The Drafting	263
K. Drafting Additional Sets of Claims	267
L. Checklist for Drafting Claims	268
M. Use of Artificial Intelligence (AI) To Draft Claims	269
N. Summary	270

Inventor's Commandment 13

In your patent application, write at least one main (independent) claim. Make this claim as broad as the prior art permits by (1) reciting as few elements as you can, and (2) using the broadest possible terms for such elements, to make it as difficult as possible for others to avoid infringing your claim.

Inventor's Commandment 14

In your patent application, write (1) one or two alternative independent claims, making these as broad as possible, and distinct from your first independent claim so that you have apparatus, means, and method independent claims, where possible, and (2) follow each independent claim with as many dependent claims as necessary to recite all of the significant additional features of your invention, providing backup for each independent claim and a range of coverage.

Inventor's Commandment 15

Every term used in the claims should have an antecedent basis—that is, a previous reference—in the description, preferably by being defined broadly. Every feature recited in the claims must be shown in the drawings and discussed in the description. The claims must be clearly written and unambiguous. Every term must be clear, and, if a term is recited more than once, it should be preceded by "said" (or "the"), followed by the same term used the first time.

A. What Are Claims?

If you don't yet know what patent claims are, or have never read any, you may be in for a surprise. The word "claim" in the patent context is definitely a term of art.

A patent's claims define the scope of the patent owner's rights. A "claim," in the arcane world of patents, is a very formally worded sentence fragment contained in a patent application or patent. Claims recite and define the structure, or acts, of an invention in very precise, logical, and exact terms. They serve as tools to determine whether an invention is patentable over the prior art and whether a patent is infringed. Just as a deed recites the boundary of a real estate parcel, and a criminal statute defines what acts are punishable by fine or imprisonment, patent claims recite the "metes and bounds" or scope of an invention for the purposes of dealing with the PTO and possible infringers. In other words, claims are the nitty-gritty of patents. While the specification must teach how to make and use the invention, the claims must define its scope.

While claims are literally sentence fragments, they are supposed to be the object of the words "I [or We] claim." In a patent application, claims are interpreted as saying to the examiner, "Here is my definition of my invention. Please search to see whether my invention, as here defined, is novel and nonobvious over the prior art and whether I have defined it clearly." In a patent, claims are interpreted as your own little statutes that say to the public, "The following is a precise description of the elements of this invention; if you make, use, or sell anything that has all of these elements, or all of these elements plus additional elements, or that closely fits this description, you can be legally held liable for the consequences of patent infringement."

Since there are only five statutory classes of inventions, every claim must define something that is classifiable into one of these five classes. That means there are: (1) process or method claims; (2) machine claims; (3) article of manufacture claims; (4) composition of matter claims; and (5) claims reciting a new use of any of the previous four statutory classes. Again, the line between (2) and (3) is blurred. Fortunately, as mentioned in Chapter 5, you don't have to do the classifying unless the PTO decides that your invention doesn't fit within any class at all.

If all of this sounds a bit formidable, we will make it quite clear as we progress, after you see some examples. What's more, when it comes to claims, every layperson who "prosecutes" (handles or controls) a patent application has a safety net: So long as you can convince the patent examiner that you have a patentable invention, the examiner should write at least one claim for you, for free. (MPEP 707.07(j).) We discuss this, along with several aids to claim drafting.

But a word of caution. You must provide at least one claim in your application to obtain a filing date. In addition (and even if you use a patent attorney), familiarity with the information we provide here is essential to securing the strongest and broadest possible patent on your invention. So we urge you to approach this chapter as if there were no safety net. Take this chapter as we present it, in small, easy-to-digest chunks, and you should have no trouble. If you don't understand something the first time, go back again so you'll be further down on the learning curve where you'll see things much more clearly.

Common Misconception: If the devices described in the prior art have disadvantages, and a patent application describes an invention that overcomes such disadvantages, the applicant will automatically be entitled to a patent.

Fact: In addition to describing an invention that is different and superior to the prior art, the application must contain claims that define the invention in a proper way (a) so that it is novel over the prior art, and (b) so that such novelty is also nonobvious over the prior art—that is, it produces new and unexpected results.

B. The Law Regarding Claims

The law (statutes and PTO rules) concerning claims is written in only the most general and vague terms. Let's take a brief look at the statutes and rules.

1. Legal Requirements for Patent Claims

The only pertinent statute comprises the last five paragraphs of our old friend, Section 112 of the patent laws (35 U.S.C. § 112), which states:

a. *IN GENERAL—The specification shall contain a written description of the invention, and of the manner and process of making and using it, in such full, clear, concise, and exact terms as to enable any person skilled in the art to which it pertains, or with which it is most nearly connected, to make and use the same, and shall set forth the best mode contemplated by the inventor or joint inventor of carrying out the invention.*

b. *CONCLUSION—The specification shall conclude with one or more claims particularly pointing out and distinctly claiming the subject matter which the inventor or a joint inventor regards as the invention.*

c. *FORM—A claim may be written in independent or, if the nature of the case admits, in dependent or multiple dependent form.*

d. *REFERENCE IN DEPENDENT FORMS—Subject to subsection (e), a claim in dependent form shall contain a reference to a claim previously set forth and then specify a further limitation of the subject matter claimed. A claim in dependent form shall be construed to incorporate by reference all the limitations of the claim to which it refers.*

e. *REFERENCE IN MULTIPLE DEPENDENT FORM—A claim in multiple dependent form shall contain a reference, in the alternative only, to more than one claim previously set forth and then specify a further limitation of the subject matter claimed. A multiple dependent claim shall not serve as a basis for any other multiple dependent claim. A multiple dependent claim shall be construed to incorporate by reference all the limitations of the particular claim in relation to which it is being considered.*

f. *ELEMENT IN CLAIM FOR A COMBINATION —An element in a claim for a combination may be expressed as a means or step for performing a specified function without the recital of structure, material, or acts in support thereof, and such claim shall be construed to cover the corresponding structure, material, or acts described in the specification and equivalents thereof.*

Paragraph (b) is the one that mandates the use of claims in patents. It also means that the claims must be specific enough to identify an invention described in the specification ("particularly pointing out") and also should be clear, logical, and precise ("distinctly claiming"). This sentence is the most important part of Section 112 and is cited by patent examiners almost daily because of the frequency with which they reject claims for lack of clarity or for some other similar reason.

Paragraphs (c) to (e) define independent and dependent claims (more on this later) and make it clear that a dependent claim incorporates all the limitations of the claim to which it refers. Paragraph (e) refers to multiple dependent claims, but since they require a stiff surcharge and since examiners don't like them, we recommend that you don't use them.

Paragraph (f) was enacted to overrule two famous Supreme Court decisions (*G.E. v. Wabash*, 304 U.S. 371 (1938) and *Halliburton v. Walker*, 329 U.S. 1 (1946)). These decisions held certain claims invalid on technical grounds, specifically for "functionality at the point of novelty" because they expressed the essence of an invention in terms of its novel function, rather than reciting the specific structure that performed the novel function. In other words, they contained a broad expression such as "means for hardening latex" rather than a specific expression like "a sulfur additive." Congress enacted this paragraph to enable patent applicants to continue to claim their inventions more broadly. Under paragraph (f), if a claim uses the word "means" for performing a function, it must be construed to cover the structure, material, or acts described in the specification, and their equivalents. That is, if a claim recites "means for conveying rotational energy from said pedals to said rear wheels" and the specification describes a link chain for performing this function, the "means" claim will be construed by the PTO and the courts to cover the link chain and any equivalents, such as a driveshaft or a gear train.

TIP

Many of the examples in this book are means-plus-function claims (sometimes known simply as "means" claims). Means claims are a good way to capture the embodiments of your invention disclosed in your application, but they are not a panacea. The scope of a means-plus-function claim is limited to the structure actually disclosed in your application for performing the function, and the equivalents of that structure. Consequently, a means claim may not encompass the full range of alternatives to that structure. If you use means claims, you should also include claims that are not means claims. You should write claims using a variety of approaches, including machine claims, method claims, system claims, and means claim.

2. Legal Requirements for Patentable Subject Matter

Most inventions fit comfortably within subject matter that Congress and the courts view as patentable. A new process for mining ore, a new automobile transmission, a new chair with six legs, and a new pharmaceutical compound all easily pass the test. However, not every invention is eligible to be patented, even if it is novel and nonobvious.

If your patent claims are directed to a judicial exception (laws of nature, natural phenomena, and abstract ideas) the PTO will reject them as being ineligible (or "nonstatutory") subject matter under 35 U.S.C. Section 101. The reason is that these are "the basic tools of scientific and technological work" and the courts are concerned about preemption—the "danger that the grant of patents that tie up their use will inhibit future innovation premised upon them." Of course, at some level, nearly every invention and every claim could be viewed to involve one of these judicial exceptions, if one were to think long and hard enough. Fortunately, the *application* of a law of nature, natural phenomenon, or abstract idea to a new and useful end is patentable subject matter.

The key to claiming patentable ("statutory") subject matter is avoiding claims that are "directed to" a judicial exception, and/or including in your claims additional elements that amount to "significantly more" than the judicial exception. In other words, your claims must include an inventive concept beyond the judicial exception. The PTO's approach to examining claims involves a search for such an inventive concept. So, a method for mining ore is not a law of nature, a natural phenomenon (even if the ore itself is natural), or an abstract idea.

The law in this area, and especially for the computer arts where the thing being claimed as inventive often operates invisibly inside a CPU, has been reinvigorated by a series of U.S. Supreme Court decisions, yet important aspects of the law remain ambiguous. For example, the Supreme Court has not defined the terms "directed to"; "significantly more"; or even "abstract idea." Instead, the lower courts are slowly developing a body of case law to distinguish claims that are "directed to" a judicial exception from those that integrate a law of nature, natural phenomenon, or abstract idea into something more, by including elements that transform such claims into significantly more than the judicial exception.

Examples of features that amount to "significantly more" than a judicial exception include (but are not necessarily limited to): improvements to another technology or technical field; improvements to the functioning of a computer itself; applying the judicial exception with, or by use of, a particular machine; effecting a transformation or reduction of a particular article to a different state or thing; adding a specific limitation other than what is well-understood, routine, and conventional in the field, or adding unconventional steps that confine the claim to a particular useful application; or other meaningful limitations beyond generally linking the use of the judicial exception to a particular technological environment.

We provide some examples in this book, but since this area of law is still evolving, we recommend that you learn from the mistakes and successes of others by studying the most recent PTO guidance to examiners on subject matter eligibility. That guidance, which the PTO updates from time to time, appears in the *Manual of Patent Examining Procedure* (MPEP) in section 2106. (The MPEP may be found online at www.uspto.gov/web/offices/pac/mpep.) The guidance includes examples of successful and unsuccessful claims (sections 2106.04(a)(1) and (2), respectively), as well as the materials the PTO uses to train its examiners.

You should study successful claims to understand why they succeed; what features allowed them to avoid a nonstatutory subject matter rejection, and how they were drafted to leverage those features. You should also study unsuccessful claims to understand why they fell into the section 101 quicksand, and how your claims can avoid that fate. However, don't fret if you cannot untangle the web of examples—many patent attorneys can't either! Hopefully, Congress or the courts will provide some clarity in the years to come.

3. Rules of Practice

In addition to Section 112, claims are governed by the PTO's "Rules of Practice" which are codified in Title 37 of the Code of Federal Regulations (37 CFR). 37 CFR 1.75, parts (b), (d)(1), and (e) through (i) add these additional requirements:

(b) *More than one claim may be presented provided they differ substantially from each other and are not unduly multiplied.*

(d)(1) *The claim or claims must conform to the invention as set forth in the remainder of the specification and the terms and phrases used in the claims must find clear support or antecedent basis in the description so that the meaning of the terms in the claims may be ascertainable by reference to the description.*

(e) *Where the nature of the case admits, as in the case of an improvement, any independent claim should contain in the following order: (1) A preamble comprising a general description of all the elements or steps of the claimed combination which are conventional or known, (2) A phrase such as "wherein the improvement comprises," and (3) Those elements, steps, and/or relationships which constitute that portion of the claimed combination which the applicant considers as the new or improved portion.*

(f) *If there are several claims, they shall be numbered consecutively in Arabic numerals.*

(g) *The least restrictive claim should be presented as claim number 1, and all dependent claims should be grouped together with the claim or claims to which they refer to the extent practicable.*

(h) *The claim or claims must commence on a separate physical sheet or electronic page. Any sheet including a claim or portion of a claim may not contain any other parts of the application or other material.*

(i) *Where a claim sets forth a plurality of elements or steps, each element or step of the claim should be separated by a line indentation.*

Paragraph (b) requires that the claims differ substantially from each other and not be too numerous. In practice, minimal differences will suffice. The rule prohibiting numerous claims is more strictly enforced. If more than about 20 claims are presented, there should be some justification, such as a very complex invention or numerous embodiments. One reason for this limitation is that there are substantial charges for each independent claim past three and each claim (independent or dependent) past 20 (see Appendix 4, "Fee Schedule").

Paragraph (d)(1), enforced only sporadically, requires that the terms in the claims should correspond to those used in the specification. It has often been said that the specification should serve as a dictionary for the claims. While U.S. examiners don't often enforce this rule, examiners in other (especially European) countries can be very strict on this point, and most attorneys believe it is very important to follow in view of recent court decisions that tend to narrow the scope of claims.

Paragraph (e) was introduced to require that claims be drafted, insofar as practicable, in the German or "*Jepson*" style (from a famous decision of that name). The *Jepson*-type claim is very easy for examiners to read and understand. It puts the essence of the invention into sharp focus by providing in the first part of the claim an introduction that sets forth the environment of the invention (that is, what is already known), and in the second part, or body of the claim, the essence of the invention (that is, the improvement of the current invention). In practice, this part of

37 CFR 1.75 is rarely enforced. Most patent attorneys recommend that you avoid use of the Jepson-type claim since, by isolating the novel part of the invention, it's easier to invalidate.

Paragraphs (f), (h), and (i) are self-explanatory and paragraph (g) means that the broadest claims should be number 1, all dependent claims should be together and under their independent claim, and the elements or steps of a claim should be listed individually on separate lines (which are sometimes referred to as "subparagraphs," although they're certainly not paragraphs in the traditional sense). More information is provided in Section J of this chapter.

C. Some Sample Claims

As mentioned, claims boil the invention down to its essence. In their broadest sense, they eliminate everything nonessential to the invention. In fact, many inventors first realize what their invention truly is when they write or see a claim to it, especially after the claim has been rejected in the patent prosecution process. Conversely, you won't be able to draft an adequate claim unless you have a clear understanding of your invention. Although not a patent attorney, the great theatrical producer David Belasco showed that he understood the principle behind claims well when he said, "If you can't write your idea on the back of my calling card, you don't have a clear conception of your idea."

And claims are difficult to write just because they are so short. Blaise Pascal once concluded a letter to a friend as follows: "I have made this letter a little longer than usual because I lack the time to make it shorter." Nevertheless, don't get discouraged; if you follow the step-by-step, four-part procedure we give later, you'll find that writing claims is not too much more difficult than writing the specification.

In the following sections, we provide some hypothetical simple claims and some actual ones. Any patent applications containing these hypothetical claims would now be rejected since the "inventions" they define are obviously old and in the public domain. A few of the claims—the "method of putting" and the "new use" claim—are from patents.

1. Process or Method Claims: Conventional Process, Software Process, Business Method, and Manual Method

In this section, you'll see examples of various method claims—one to a conventional process, one to a software-based process, and one to a manual method. We also include an example of a business method claim, although business methods are difficult (if not impossible) to patent under the current state of the law. Note that these claims recite a series of steps (or individual operations), rather than a series of hardware (physical) elements as in an article claim—although claims do bring hardware in via those method steps. Note also that the software and manual method claims are similar in construction, which shows you that these processes are generally claimed the same way as any other process.

Process or "method" claims are facing increased scrutiny by the courts and PTO. If your patent claim is "directed to" a law of nature, a natural phenomenon, or an abstract idea, the PTO will reject it as "nonstatutory" (ineligible) subject matter under 35 U.S.C. Section 101 unless the claim includes "additional elements that amount to significantly more than the judicial exception."

Because the Supreme Court has provided only limited guidance on what it means for a claim to be "directed to" a judicial exception, what constitutes "significantly more," and what constitutes an "abstract idea," courts are tackling these issues by analogizing new cases to prior cases. Some of our examples below are claims that have survived court challenges, or that the PTO has provided as examples of successful claims.

a. Conventional Process

For the conventional process, assume that you just invented sewing and want to claim the process. Here's how you'd do it.

A method for joining two pieces of cloth together at their edges, said method comprising:

   a. providing said two pieces of cloth and positioning them together so that an edge portion of one piece overlaps an adjacent edge portion of the other piece, and

   b. passing a thread repeatedly through and along the length of the overlapping portions in sequentially opposite directions and through sequentially spaced holes in said overlapping adjacent portions, whereby said two pieces of cloth will be attached along said edge portions.

Note that the first part of this claim contains a title, preamble, or genus, which states the purpose of the method but doesn't use the term "sewing," because sewing is the invention and is assumed to be new at the time the claim is drafted. The claim contains two steps, a and b, that state in sequence the acts one would perform in sewing two pieces of cloth. Note that each clause begins with an "—ing" word (gerund). The claim also contains an optional "whereby" clause at the end to point out to the examiner or a judge the advantage of the process. Finally, note that the claim is single-spaced and is formatted in paragraphs with a hanging indent so that the second and subsequent lines are indented. This is the way claims are printed in patents, but when you type them in your patent application you should use the hanging indent with 1.5 line spacing. You can "hang" a paragraph in Microsoft *Word* by placing your cursor in the paragraph and pressing Control-T.

b. Software Process

Computer-implemented inventions, including "software" processes, are very challenging to patent because PTO examiners find them easy to reject as being directed to an "abstract idea." Nevertheless, some computer-implemented inventions have been patented or upheld as patentable.

While this area of the law is still evolving, some patterns are emerging that indicate how courts (and by extension, the PTO) reason when it comes to computer and software inventions. The most common tactic is to first convert the software process into an abstract idea by notionally removing the computer or software entirely from the claim and envisioning the result of the process, then reverse course and argue that the computer is simply an efficient (but wholly conventional) tool to obtain the result. By this logic, then, the claim is not "directed to" the process but rather its result, and thus covers an abstract idea. This "trick" explains the large majority of outcomes, even if the courts don't expressly articulate it as the basis for their analyses, and one early post-*Alice* case (*DDR Holdings*) mentioned its usefulness as follows: "In some instances, patent-ineligible abstract ideas are plainly identifiable and divisible from the generic computer limitations recited by the remainder of the claim."

The first step often isolates a business method produced by the claim, or an algorithm that may be formulated in terms of operating on pure data: collecting, storing, computing, or displaying it. And while it might be obvious that computers require data, a little thought shows that the converse is not true. For example, it is entirely possible to write down a valid extensible markup language (XML) document and then convert it, by hand on paper with ink, to standard generalized markup language (SGML) or some other data format— entirely without a computer (albeit at the expense of great time and effort). Similar computations can be performed with only pencil, paper, and mental effort.

Armed with this logic, the computer-less business method claim becomes "just" a fundamental economic practice, and the computer-less data conversion claim is "just" an algorithm; by themselves, these are unpatentable abstract ideas. The courts and PTO then "reverse course" and argue that the software claim "is directed to" a conventional means (that is, a general purpose computer, or GPC) for applying the abstract idea.

As an example of when this "trick" didn't work to invalidate a claim, the patent appeals court held that the following claim 17 from U.S. Patent 6,151,604 was patentable in the 2016 *Enfish* case:

A data storage and retrieval system for a computer memory, comprising:

    a. means for configuring said memory according to a logical table, said logical table including:

    b. a plurality of logical rows, each said logical row including an object identification number (OID) to identify each said logical row, each said logical row corresponding to a record of information;

    c. a plurality of logical columns intersecting said plurality of logical rows to define a plurality of logical cells, each said logical column including an OID to identify each said logical column; and

    d. means for indexing data stored in said table.

The court indicated that this claim was patentable because it improved an existing technology; namely, computer databases. It found evidence for its conclusion in the specification, which stated "benefits over conventional databases, such as increased flexibility, faster search times, and smaller memory requirements."

The court reasoned that the claim's ability to run on a GPC was not fatal, because the claim was directed to improving the functioning of the GPC itself. This distinguished the claim from other claims using a GPC merely as a means to an end; that is, to implement "well-known business practices" or compute math formulas. Or using the framework above, when the court tried to remove the computer from the claim, no abstract idea remained for it to consider.

In addition, the court reasoned that the claim's lack of explicit physical structure also was not fatal, because having such a requirement would risk resurrecting a bright-line "machine-or-transformation test" that the Supreme Court expressly prohibited in the 2010 *Bilski* case. The "means" for configuring and for indexing could very well be pure software, and the *Enfish* court stated: "Much of the advancement made in computer technology consists of improvements to software that, by their very nature, may not be defined by particular physical features but rather by logical structures and processes. We do not see in *Bilski* or *Alice* an exclusion to patenting this large field of technological progress."

c. Business Method

The claim below would almost certainly be rejected as drawn to a judicial exception (nonstatutory subject matter) under the *Alice* decision (see Section G13, below) since it is directed to an abstract idea—the age-old concept of assessing creditworthiness, and its steps are well-understood, routine and conventional. However, we provide it here to illustrate a true business method claim in case *Alice* is legislatively overruled or broadened.

For the business method, assume that you've just invented a procedure for checking the "creditworthiness" of a customer. Now you want to write a claim to this as a business method. Here's how you might write a suitable claim for a credit-checking process.

A method of passing on the creditworthiness of a customer comprising:
  a. providing a form for said customer to complete, said form having spaces in which said customer must indicate a plurality of credit accounts and a plurality of credit references,
  b. investigating each of said credit accounts and credit references and compiling a score from 1 to 100, for each account and reference, with 1 indicating a minimal credit rating and 100 indicating a maximal or excellent credit rating,
  c. averaging all of said scores to compile an overall average,
  d. rejecting said customer if said overall average is below a predetermined value and accepting said customer if said overall average is above said predetermined value.

d. Manual Methods

A golfer invented a new way of putting that emphasizes the golfer's dominant hand and claimed this as a manual process (U.S. Patent 5,616,089). Here's how he did it.

A method of gripping a putter comprising the steps:
  a. gripping a putter grip with a dominant hand;
  b. placing a non-dominant hand over an interior wrist portion of the dominant hand behind a thumb of the dominant hand;
  c. resting a middle finger of the non-dominant hand on the styloid process of the dominant hand;
  d. pressing a ring finger and a little finger of the non-dominant hand against the back of the dominant hand;
  e. pressing the palm of the non-dominant hand against a forward surface of the putter grip as the non-dominant hand squeezes the dominant hand.

A cat owner invented a new way of exercising a cat using a laser. Some have opined that this invention is ridiculous and obvious, but the examiner didn't think so (U.S. Patent 5,443,036). Here's the main claim.

A method of inducing aerobic exercise in an unrestrained cat, comprising:
  a. directing an intense coherent beam of invisible light produced by a hand-held laser apparatus to produce a bright, highly focused pattern of light at the intersection of the beam and an opaque surface, said pattern being of visual interest to a cat; and
  b. selectively redirecting said beam out of said cat's immediate reach to induce said cat to run and chase said beam and pattern of light around an exercise area.

2. Machine Claims

Here are examples of two machine claims, one to a conventional machine and one to a software-based machine. Note that both claims recite a series of hardware elements, rather than a series of steps as in the process claims. Note also that both claims are similar in construction, indicating again that a software machine is generally claimed the same way as any other machine.

a. Conventional Machine

For the conventional machine, assume now that you've just invented the automobile. Here's how to claim it.

A self-propelled vehicle, comprising:
  a. a body carriage having rotatable wheels mounted thereunder for enabling said body carriage to roll along a surface,
  b. an engine mounted in said carriage for producing rotational energy, and
  c. means for controllably coupling rotational energy from said engine to at least one of said wheels, whereby said carriage will be self-propelled along said surface.

This claim again contains a title in the first part. The second part or body contains three elements, the carriage, the engine, and the transmission. These elements are defined as connected or interrelated by the statement that the engine is mounted in the carriage and the transmission (defined broadly as "means for controllably coupling …") couples the engine to at least one wheel of the carriage. Again, the "whereby" clause recites the advantage of the hardware elements of the preamble and clauses a, b, and c.

b. Software Machine

As mentioned, courts use a "trick" to determine software patentability; namely, removing the computer from the claim to find the abstract idea, then adding back the computer as a conventional, non-inventive implementation. However, even when the "trick" produces an abstract idea, it can still fail during "course reversal" if the claimed implementation is nonconventional. This was the case for claim 1 of U.S. Patent 5,987,606:

A content filtering system for filtering content retrieved from an internet computer network by individual controlled access network accounts, said filtering system comprising:
  a. a local client computer generating network access requests for said individual controlled access network accounts;
  b. at least one filtering scheme;
  c. a plurality of sets of logical filtering elements; and
  d. a remote ISP server coupled to said client computer and said internet computer network, said ISP server associating each said network account to at least one filtering scheme and at least one set of filtering elements, said ISP server further receiving said network access requests from said client computer and executing said associated filtering scheme utilizing said associated set of logical filtering elements.

This system claim, at issue in the 2016 *BASCOM* case, was ruled patentable because, even though it was directed to the abstract idea of "filtering content," and even though it recited generic computer, network, and internet components, the "ordered combination" of these elements was nonconventional and provided an improved process for filtering content itself. The components were not merely invoked as a means to an end; rather, their mutual relationships were unusually altered, with advantageous results.

3. Article-of-Manufacture Claim

You've done it again! Here's a claim to the pencil you've just invented.

A hand-held writing instrument comprising:
  a. elongated core-element means that will leave a marking line if moved across paper or other similar surface, and
  b. an elongated holder surrounding and encasing said elongated core-element means, one portion of said holder being removable from an end thereof to expose an end of said core-element means so as to enable said core-element means to be exposed for writing, whereby said holder protects said core-element means from breakage and provides an enlarged means for holding said core-element means conveniently.

This claim, like the machine claim, contains a preamble and a body with two elements: (a) the "lead" and (b) the wood. As before, the elements of the body are associated; here the wood ("elongated holder") is said to surround and encase the lead ("elongated core"). The "whereby" clause at the end of the claim states the purpose and advantage of the lead and its holder.

4. Composition-of-Matter Claim

Now, great inventor that you are, you've come up with concrete. Here's your claim.

A rigid building and paving material comprising a mixture of sand and stones, and a hardened cement binder filling interstices between and adhering to sand and stones, whereby a hardened, rigid, and strong matrix for building and paving will be provided.

This claim, although not in subparagraph form, still contains a preamble and a body containing a recitation of the elements of the composition (sand, stones, and cement binder), plus an association of the elements (sand and stones are mixed and binder fills volume between and adheres to sand and stones). Again, the whereby clause drives home the advantages of the components.

The height of claim brevity was reached (and will never be exceeded) in two composition-of-matter patents in 1964 when the PTO issued patents 3,156,523 and 3,161,462 to the late Dr. Glenn T. Seaborg, on two new elements, americium and curium. The claim for U.S. Patent 3,156,523 (americium) read simply,

 1. *Element 95.*

The claim for U.S. Patent 3,161,462 (curium) similarly read,

 2. *Element 96.*

5. New Use Claim

Someone discovered that pigs put on weight faster if aspirin is added to their diet. Here's how to claim it.

A method for stimulating the growth of swine comprising feeding such swine aspirin in an amount of at least 500 milligrams per day.

This claim recites the newly discovered use of aspirin and the purpose of the new use in a manner that defines over and avoids the known, old use of aspirin (analgesic). Note that it is a method claim (as all new-use claims must be). This is because aspirin per se is old and thus must be claimed more narrowly, as a new use.

Now that you've read a few claims, I suggest you try writing a practice claim or two of your own to become more familiar with the process. Try a simple article or machine with which you are very familiar, such as a table, chair or pen. Write the preamble and then the body. To write the body, first list the elements or parts of the article or machine, and then associate or interconnect them. Don't worry too much about grammar or style, but try to make the claim clear and understandable.

D. Common Misconceptions Regarding Claims

Inventors' misconceptions about claims are more widespread than in any other area of the patent law, except possibly for the misconception regarding the "Post Office Patent" explained in Chapter 3. Consider some of the following.

Common Misconception: The more claims that the PTO (Patent and Trademark Office) allows in your patent application, the broader your scope of coverage.

Fact: The scope of your monopoly is determined by the wording of your claims, not their number. One broad claim can be far more powerful than 50 narrow claims.

Common Misconception: If you want to get broad coverage on a specific feature of your invention, you should recite that specific feature in your claims.

Fact: If you recite a specific feature of your invention in a claim, that claim will be limited to that feature as recited, and variations may not be covered—for example, if you have a two-inch nylon gear in your apparatus and you recite it as such in a claim, the claim may not cover an apparatus that uses a one-inch gear, or a steel gear. The best way to cover all possible variations of your gear is to recite it simply as a "gear," or better yet, "rotary transmission means," then have separate claims to recite more specific features such as material or dimensions.

Common Misconception: To cover a specific feature of your invention per se, you need merely recite it in a dependent claim.

Fact: As stated in the statute quoted in Section B, above (35 U.S.C. § 112(d)), a dependent claim is construed (and reads) as if it incorporated all of the limitations of the claim to which it refers. Thus if your independent claim (#1) recites a telephone having a connecting cord and your dependent claim reads, "The telephone of Claim 1 wherein said connecting cord is coiled," the dependent claim doesn't monopolize the coiled cord per se, but rather the coiled cord in *combination with the telephone.* More on this later in Section J, below.

Common Misconception: If a claim doesn't recite a specific feature of your invention, then this feature is necessarily not covered. For example, if your invention includes a two-inch nylon gear and you fail to recite it specifically in a claim, then anyone who makes your invention with this gear can't infringe your patent.

Fact: The fact that a feature isn't recited doesn't mean that it isn't covered. An absurd example will make this clear. Suppose your invention is a bicycle and you show and describe it with a front wheel having 60 spokes. You don't mention the spokes at all in a claim; you simply recite a "front wheel." Any bike that has all of the limitations of the claim will infringe it. Thus a bike that has any "front wheel" will infringe, whether it has zero or 600 spokes.

As we explain from time to time, to infringe a claim, an accused apparatus must have at least all of the elements of the claim; if it has more elements than recited in the claim, it still infringes, but if it has fewer, then it doesn't infringe. Claim limitations are thus interpreted using Boolean logic, similar to computer search terms (as explained in Chapter 6, Section K).

Common Misconception: The more features of your invention you recite in a claim, the broader that claim will be. (Stated differently, the longer a claim is, the broader it is.)

Fact: As will be apparent from the previous misconceptions, the less you recite in a claim—that is, *the fewer the elements you recite—the broader the claim will be.* This seeming paradox exists because an accused infringing device must have all the elements of a claim to infringe. Thus, the fewer the elements specified in a claim, the fewer the elements an accused infringing device needs to have to infringe. Put differently, infringement is generally easier to prove if a claim is made shorter or has fewer elements. "To claim more, you should recite less" is a Boolean concept that is difficult for most inventors to absorb, but that you should learn well if you want to secure the broadest possible coverage. (Again, see "Keyword Searching" in Chapter 6, Section J, for further clarification of this point.)

E. One Claim Should Be as Broad as Possible

There are two ways to make a claim broader: (1) *minimize* the number of elements; and (2) *maximize* the scope of these elements. Let's see how this works.

1. Minimize the Number of Elements

Take our automobile claim, above, which recites three elements, a, b, and c—that is, the wheeled carriage, the engine, and the transmission. If an accused machine contains just these three elements, it will, of course, infringe.

If the accused machine has these three plus a fourth, such as a radio, which we'll label d, it will still infringe.

But if our accused machine contains only elements a and b (the carriage and engine), but lacks a transmission, then it won't infringe, since it simply doesn't contain all of the claimed elements, a, b, and c.

If a claim contains many, many elements, say a to m, only devices with all 13 elements, a through m, will infringe. If the maker of the device eliminates just one of the 13 elements, say g, the device will *not* infringe. Thus, it's relatively easy to avoid infringing a claim with many elements.

If a claim contains only two elements, a and b, any device with these two elements will infringe, no matter how many other elements the device has. The only way to have the device avoid infringement is to eliminate either element a or element b, presumably a relatively difficult task.

Thus, *the fewer the elements in a claim, the harder the claim will be to avoid*—that is, the broader it will be and the more devices it will cover. Therefore, when drafting a main or independent claim to your invention, it will behoove you to put in as few elements of your invention as possible. (You do have to include sufficient elements so that the claim recites an operative, complete assemblage that is novel and nonobvious over the prior art. More on this in Sections F and G, below.)

2. Recite Each Element as Broadly as Possible

With regard to the second way of broadening a claim; that is, reciting existing elements more broadly, consider a few examples. Suppose an invention involves a chair. The chair can be drafted broadly as "a seat" or narrowly as a "four-legged maple chair with a vinyl-covered padded seat and a curved plywood back." Obviously, a three-legged plastic stool would be "a seat," and it would infringe the broadly recited element, but would miss the narrowly recited maple chair by a country mile. In electronics, "controllable electron valve" is broader than "vacuum tube" or "transistor." In machinery, "rotational energy connecting element" is broader than "helically cut gear" or "V-belt."

Another way to broaden your claim is to try to anticipate what an infringer or a competitor might do to attack your patent; then cover this in the claims by eliminating it or broadening it. For example, suppose you invented a furnace that uses a blower to force air into the combustion chamber and your claim recites, "a blower for forcing air from outside said furnace into said combustion chamber." But you realize that a competitor may use a blower to draw air from the combustion chamber and thereby cause the combustion chamber to draw outside air in. Since your claim would not cover this variation, you should broaden the limitation in question to, "a blower for causing outside air to enter said combustion chamber" and also amend the specification (for example, in the ramifications section) to state that the blower may alternatively be arranged to draw air from the combustion chamber and thereby cause the combustion chamber to draw outside air in. (Imagine what might have happened if you did not have this realization! This sort of trap is why drafting broad claims can be tricky, and a good reason to carefully consider all ramifications of your invention, as described in Chapter 2.)

One way of reciting elements broadly is to take advantage of Section 112(f) by reciting an element, wherever possible, as "means" plus a specific function. In this way, any device or means that performs the function and is the equivalent of the supporting structure in the specification would infringe. For example, "means for conveying rotational energy" is broader than a drive belt and covers gears, pulleys, and drive shafts if these are the equivalent of a belt, which they will be determined to be if you've mentioned them in the specification. "Amplifying means" is broader than and covers such items as transistor amplifiers, tube amplifiers, and masers.

If you do use the word "means" in a claim, Section 112(f) requires that the claim recite a "combination"— that is, two or more elements or parts. Claims that recite a single element are not supposed to use the word "means" to describe the single element, since this is considered too broad—for example, "17. Means for providing a continuously variable speed/power drive for a bicycle" would be an example of a prohibited "single means" claim. However, you can effectively obtain practically the same breadth of coverage by adding an immaterial second element to the claim to make it a combination claim. Thus, "17. In combination, a bicycle having a pedal mechanism and means for providing a continuously variable speed/power drive for coupling rotational energy from said pedal mechanism to a wheel of said bicycle" would satisfy Section 112(f).

Courts have recently been construing "means" clauses narrowly, so you should also include claims with "structural" (nonmeans) clauses; these clauses can be expanded under the "doctrine of equivalents" (Chapter 15, Section J).

To sum up, while you should write your specification as specifically and with as much detail as possible (Chapter 8), you should make the substance of your main claims as general (broad) as possible by (1) eliminating as many elements as is feasible and (2) describing (reciting) the remaining elements as broadly as possible. In other words, make your specification specific and long and your main claims general and short.

An augmented quote from the French aviator and poet Antoine de Saint-Exupéry (1900–1944) will remind you of the two ways to broaden a claim:

"Perfection is achieved, not when there is nothing more to add, but when there is nothing left to take away [and nothing left to broaden]."

F. The Effect of Prior Art on Your Claim

Now that you've learned how to make your claim as broad as possible, it's time for the bad news. What is "possible" has generally much less breadth than you'd like. This is because each claim must define an invention that is patentable over the prior art. Remember the issues of novelty and nonobviousness covered in Chapter 5? Well, they (especially non-obviousness) are an ever-present factor always to be considered in claim drafting.

1. Novelty

A claim must define an invention that is novel over the prior art. It must recite something that no single reference in the prior art shows—that is, it must contain something new or novel. Your claim must recite novel hardware (or a novel process step) in a positive, structurally supported, unequivocal manner. For example, reciting "a wheel for providing lateral stabilization" won't adequately define over a prior-art wheel that doesn't provide lateral stabilization, since the function isn't supported by novel structure. The remedy: Recite the novel structure that does provide the stabilization—such as a guide for the wheel, or a "means" for providing stabilization.

Just as a claim can be made broader by eliminating elements and reciting the existing elements more broadly, it can be made narrower in order to define novel structure (1) by adding elements, or (2) by reciting the existing elements more narrowly.

For an example of adding elements, suppose a prior-art reference shows a machine having three elements—A, B, and C, and your claim recites these three elements A, B, and C. Your claim would be said to lack novelty over the prior art and would be rejected or held invalid under Section 102. But if you added a fourth element, D, to the claim, it would clear the prior art and would recite a novel invention (but not necessarily a patentable one, because of the nonobviousness requirement). (If the prior art were an in-force patent that *claimed* elements A, B, and C, and your *device* had elements A, B, C, and D, it *would* infringe for reasons given in Section E1,

above. However, the PTO is never concerned with infringements, so you don't need to worry about this issue in a patent application.)

For an example of reciting existing elements more narrowly, suppose the prior art shows a machine having the same three elements—A, B, and C. You could also clear this prior art and claim a novel invention by reciting in your claim elements A, B, and C′, where C′ would be the prior-art element C with any change that isn't shown in the prior art. For example, if the prior art shows element C as a steam engine, and you recite a gasoline engine (C′), you've obviated any question of lack of novelty (though probably not obviousness).

In sum, although you'd like to be able to eliminate as many elements as possible and recite all of your elements as broadly as possible, you will usually have to settle for less because there will always be prior art there to make you toe the line of novelty.

2. Nonobviousness

Under Section 103 the claims must define an invention that in addition to being novel, must also be nonobvious to one having ordinary skill in the art. When you have to narrow a claim to define over the prior art, you must do so by adding one or more elements or by reciting existing elements differently or more narrowly, and you must be sure that the added or narrowed elements define a structure or step that is sufficiently different from the prior art to be considered nonobvious. Of course, your amendment must also be supported by the text and figures of your application, which is why many patent attorneys recommend drafting your claims first.

For the last bit of bad news, note that if the wording of a claim has several possible interpretations, the examiner is entitled to use any one of them, including the one least favorable to you, in determining whether the claim clears the prior art. Moreover, examiners have a limited amount of time in which to work, so they may perform keyword searches and find wording in other patents and applications that, while identical to yours, is from an entirely different field. Use of such other references in a rejection is usually a simple matter to correct, but it's better to know up front that the problem exists, so you can take steps to avoid it entirely.

You should try to write your main claim(s) as broadly as possible while keeping in mind the prior art that you've uncovered. In case of doubt, you should err on the side of too much breadth, since you can always narrow your claims later if your examiner thinks they're too broad. Conversely, if your examiner allows your narrow claims on your first office action (rare), you'll find it very difficult to broaden them later without filing a continuing application (discussed in Chapter 14).

G. Technical Requirements of Claims

In addition to defining adequately over the prior art, each claim must also be worded in a clear, concise, precise, and rational way. If the wording of a claim is poor, the examiner will make a "technical" (non–prior-art) rejection under Section 112(b). It is this technical aspect of drafting claims that most often serves as a stumbling block to the layperson. To put it candidly, claims, like laws, are not written to be easily understood; they should be written so they cannot be misunderstood. Yet claim drafting really won't be that hard if you:

- study the sample claims listed later in this chapter, plus those of a few patents, to get the basic idea
- use the four-step method (preamble-element-interconnections-broaden) set out in Section H, below, and
- are conversant with the appropriate terminology associated with your invention's elements.

Remember also that you needn't write perfect claims when you file the application. Why? Because if you have a patentable invention, the examiner should draft at least one claim for you. A provision of the *Manual of Patent Examining Procedure*, Section 707.07(j), states:

When, during the examination of a pro se [no attorney] application it becomes apparent to the examiner that there is patentable subject matter disclosed in the application, the examiner should draft one or more claims for the applicant and indicate in his or her action that such claims would be allowed if incorporated in the application by amendment.

This practice will expedite prosecution and offer a service to individual inventors not represented by a registered patent attorney or agent. Although this practice may be desirable and is permissible in any case deemed appropriate by the examiner, it will be expected to be applied in all cases where it is apparent that the applicant is unfamiliar with the proper preparation and prosecution of patent applications.

You do have to at least give it a try, since you must file at least one claim with your application to get a filing date. But, as indicated, this claim need not be well written or narrow enough for patent coverage. Instead, during the ensuing prosecution stage, you can ask the examiner to write claims for you pursuant to this section if you feel yours aren't adequate. The examiner is bound to do so if your invention is patentable.

If you do choose this option, be sure the examiner's claims are broad enough, since it isn't in the examiner's own interest to write broad claims for you. As with any other claim, ask yourself if any elements of the examiner's claim can be eliminated or recited more broadly and still distinguish adequately over the prior art. If so, amend it as suggested in Chapter 13.

Also remember that many patent attorneys and agents will be willing to review your specification and drawings or draft your claims at their regular hourly rates. But use this as a last alternative, since most patent attorneys in private practice charge $200 to $500 per hour, or more. If possible, you should choose a company-employed patent attorney or a retired patent attorney who works at home, since such attorneys' rates will usually be one-half to one-third of those charged by their downtown counterparts.

Let's look at some of the basic rules covering the drafting of claims.

1. Use Proper Antecedents and Be Precise

Your claims must be precise, logical, and determinate. One of the most common reasons for claim rejections is the improper use of articles, such as "a," "the," and "said." Generally, the first time you recite an element, use the indefinite article "a," just as you would if you were speaking to someone who is not familiar with your device—for example, "I just bought a car." If you refer to the same element again using exactly the same words to describe it, use the extremely definite article "said"—for example, "… said car has a burglar alarm." "Said" actually means, in patent law, "the following part, which in this claim (or its parent claim) is previously recited in exactly the following word(s):" If you refer to an aspect of an element by using different, but implicitly clear words, use the definite article "the" just as you would do in ordinary speech—for example, "The auto was expensive." Here's an example showing how "a," "said," and "the" are properly used in a claim to a table.

*An article of furniture for holding objects for a sitting human, **said** article comprising:*

    *a. **a** sheet of rigid material having sufficient size to accommodate use by a human being for writing and working,*

    *b. **a** plurality of elongated support members of equal length,*

    *c. **said** support members being joined perpendicularly to **the** undersurface of **said** sheet of rigid material at spaced locations so as to be able to support **said** sheet of rigid material in **a** horizontal orientation.*

Note that the first time any element is mentioned, the article "a" is used, but when it's referred to again by its original designation, "said" is used. When another aspect of it is referred to with a different (but clear) designation—that is, the undersurface of the table—"the" is used.

In addition to being precise in the use of articles, you should avoid ambiguous or missing references. For example, if "said elongated lever" is used in a claim and no "elongated lever" has previously been recited in these exact words, a *non sequitur* has occurred and the PTO will reject the claim under Section 112(b) for indefiniteness due to a "missing antecedent." The solution is to recite the elongated lever earlier in the claim or to change "said elongated lever" to "an elongated lever." Or, if the same element is positively recited twice, such as "a lever" … "a lever," the claim is unclear. The solution is to change the second "a lever" to "said lever." On the other hand, if the two levers are actually different, call them by different names; for example, "a first lever" and "a second lever." You may then refer to "said first lever" and "said second lever," but now "said lever" really is ambiguous and unclear.

In a dependent claim, the antecedent can be provided in the dependent claim itself, the referent claim from which the dependent claim depends (whether independent or dependent), or any lower-numbered referent claim which the first referent claim depends from. Thus, if claim 3 is dependent on claim 2, which is in turn dependent on claim 1, an antecedent for "said lever" in claim 3 can be provided in either claims 1 or 2.

Vagueness and indefiniteness can also occur if you use abbreviations before defining and/or spelling them out—such as "d.c." (say "direct current" or "direct current (d.c.)"); relative terms without any reference—such as "large" (say "larger than…" or "large enough to support three adults"); or vague, casual language, such as "strong," "suitable," "standard," or "sufficient."

2. Use Only One Capital, One Period, and No Dashes, Quotes, Parentheses, Trademarks, or Undefined Abbreviations

Amateurs violate this rule often. While it may be hard for you to accept, and while it may seem silly, the rules are that the only capital letter in a claim should be the first letter of the first word, the claim should contain a period only at its end, and there should be no dashes, quotes, or parentheses, trademarks, or undefined abbreviations. You may use capitals, periods, and parentheses for the lettered subparagraphs of a claim, for instance, "A." or "(A)"; also, hyphens ("hand-held") are okay, but dashes ("—" or "--") are not. The PTO will allow a second capital in a dependent claim when the word "Claim" is capitalized.

3. Use Means Clause to Avoid Functionality of Claim

The technical error of "functionality" occurs when elements of the claim are recited in terms of their advantage, function, or result rather than in terms of their structure. The remedy is to recite the elements of the claim as "means" or a "device" for performing the function or achieving the result (provided the means or device is adequately shown and described in the remainder of the application).

For example, here are some typical improper functional claims actually written by a layperson.

7. *An additive for paints that makes the paint dry faster.*

8. *A belt buckle that does not tend to snag as much.*

Both of these claims would be rejected under Section 112(b) because they don't particularly point out and distinctly claim the invention since they recite what the invention does rather than what it is.

The remedy: Use "means" or "device" clauses and also recite the general composition or structure of the additive or buckle. But remember that the claim must be to a combination; a single "means" claim won't pass muster. Thus, even if Claim 7 were written as follows, it would still violate Section 112(f).

7. *Additive means for paints for making them dry faster.*

Here's how the above two claims can be properly rewritten to pass muster under Section 112.

7A. *paint composition comprising:*
    a. *a paint compound comprising an oil-based paint vehicle and a suspended pigment in said vehicle, and*
    b. *additive means admixed with said vehicle for decreasing the drying time of said paint compound and*
    b'. *a volatile solvent admixed [etc.].*

8A. *belt buckle comprising:*
    a. *a catch comprising two interlocking rigid parts that can be attached to opposite ends of a belt, and*
    b. *anti-snag means for preventing said interlocking parts from snagging on cloth when placed adjacent to said interlocking parts and*
    b'. *a shield for preventing [etc.].*

A moment's reflection will show you that claiming your invention in terms of its unique structure, rather than its results, effects, or functions, makes logical sense. This is because a monopoly, to be precise and to have reasonable limits, must be defined in terms of its structure, rather than the result such structure produces. In other words, if you recited "a belt buckle that doesn't snag" you would be claiming a result only, so that any belt buckle that fulfilled this result would infringe, regardless of its structure. This "functional" type of claim would accordingly be considered unreasonably broad or directed to an abstract idea, and therefore would have to be narrowed and made more explicit by the addition of some additional structure or a means clause in order to make it more commensurate with the invention.

However, there's a downside to using "means-plus-function" clauses: Under the pertinent statute (35 U.S.C. § 112(f)) and court decisions, a means-plus-function clause is supposed to be interpreted according to the corresponding structure or material described in the specification and the equivalents of such structure or material. Thus, a means-plus-function clause is not supposed to be interpreted literally to cover every possible means that fulfills the function of the means, but only according to the corresponding structure or material in the specification and its equivalents. So, in addition to a means-plus-function claim, it's best to include one or more independent nonmeans claims which are as broad as possible without using means-plus-function language.

Of course, while both of the above claims (as we revised them) would pass Section 112, they would not be novel or patentable under Sections 102 or 103, since they recite nothing new according to our present state of knowledge.

> ### Means Must Be Supported
>
> Court decisions have emphasized the importance that every means and even every nonmeans component in the claims, whether for software or hardware inventions, is clearly described and identifiable in the specification. If any component isn't clearly identifiable, we would add a sentence at the appropriate part of the specification, such as follows:
>
> "Thus units xxx and yyy constitute a means for ...."
> If the means is part of a software program, identify the part or object of the listing and state that it constitutes a means for ....

4. Be Complete

Each claim must stand on its own—that is, it must recite enough elements to make a working, complete device in accordance with its recognized status in its art. For example, you can recite a lightbulb per se (without reciting the entire lamp) since lightbulbs are a well-known item of commerce. But a claim to just the glass envelope of a lightbulb would probably be rejected as incomplete, since it won't do anything on its own and isn't a recognized item of commerce. The remedy for failing to include enough elements is simply to add the needed elements. Examiners and attorneys frequently disagree as to whether a claim is incomplete, the examiner wanting the claim narrowed by the addition of elements and the attorney wanting it to remain broad; that is, not to add any more elements.

5. Keep Language Straightforward and Simple

Properly drafted claims use a minimum number of words to delineate the essence of the invention. Excess wordiness of a claim, termed "prolixity" by the PTO, is a frequent error committed by beginners. The remedy is to reword the claim in more compact language. One technique for reducing your word count is to limit your claim to one clause for each necessary part that has a Reference Numeral in your drawings.

6. All Elements of Invention Must Logically Interrelate and Interconnect

Each of the elements in a claim must be logically related and connected to the other elements. When the elements of an invention don't appear to cooperate and to be connected in a logical or functional sense, the PTO will reject the claim. Think of a do-it-yourself kit that comes with all the parts, but no assembly instructions. This is a more substantive type of rejection, since it's often directed at the underlying invention rather than simply the way the claim is drafted. For example, if you claim the combination of a waffle iron and tape recorder, these elements don't cooperate and hence your claim would be rejected as failing to point out and distinctly claim the invention.

Wrong: A foot pedal device, comprising: an elongated element, a spring, and a hinge. [Elements aren't connected together.]

Right: A foot pedal device, comprising: an elongated element, a spring, and a hinge having a pair of leaves, said elongated element being connected to one of said leaves, said spring being mounted on said hinge so that it urges said leaves to be folded adjacent to each other. [Elements are connected together.]

7. Aggregation

Claims drafted to a combination of elements that don't cooperate toward a common end, such as a washing machine and a telephone, can be rejected on the ground of aggregation. But the elements do not have to function simultaneously to cooperate: A typewriter is a good example of elements (keys) that don't function simultaneously but do cooperate.

8. Use Only Positive Limitations

Positive limitations recite what your invention is ("a box"). Negative limitations recite what your invention is not ("a box not used for shipping"). Negative limitations cannot be used when they make the claim unclear or awkward. However, because many examiners still wince when they see negative limitations in claims, it's best to avoid them entirely, by reciting what the invention is, rather than what it isn't. For instance, instead of saying, "said engine connected to said wheels without any transmission," say "said engine connected directly to said wheels." You are permitted to recite holes, recesses, and so on in a recited structure; see "Voids" in the Glossary of Useful Technical Terms in Appendix 3 for a list of "hole-y" words.

Markush Group Claims

Another, sophisticated way to write a claim for an invention with two or more elements is to recite the disjunctive elements by using a *Markush* group. A *Markush* group (from a decision with that name) is a series of related elements joined by "and," which follows these magic words: "*Selected from the group consisting of.*" Thus, a tube or a transistor could be recited in one claim as follows: "Said amplifying circuit containing a device *selected from the group consisting of* tubes and transistors."

---

9. Use Proper Connective Expressions

Be careful when using "and" and "or." As an example of how esoteric claim interpretation can be, in the 2008 case *Ortho-McNeil*, the patent appeals court interpreted the word "and" to mean "or" in a drug case including a claim with a complex chemical formula, because treating "and" as meaning "both" in one claim made some other claims meaningless. Try to separate occurrences of "and" from "or." One way is to limit the use of "and" to necessary structure, and use "or" for optional structure or variations on the main theme. If possible, consider claiming alternative structures or functions using a common name or label in one claim, and reciting the alternatives in a dependent claim. So, for example, claim 1 might say "a magnetic fastener" and claim 2 might say "wherein the magnetic material of the fastener includes iron or steel."

10. Avoid Too Many Claims

If you've put in too many similar claims, even though you've paid for them, you'll have to eliminate some to make the examiner's job easier. If you ever have more than 20 claims, the invention should be complex enough or have enough ramifications to justify them and the claims should differ substantially. This point counterbalances the previous point, which tends to produce more claims.

11. Make Sure Claims Correspond With Disclosure

First, the literal terms or words of the claim must be present somewhere in the specification. For this reason, all patent attorneys we know write the claims first, and then write the specification. If some claim terms are not in the specification, the remedy is to revise the specification by adding the exact terms used in your claims, or to revise the claims by replacing those terms that aren't literally in the specification with terms that are in the specification. This requirement is especially important in view of patent court decisions that have narrowly interpreted terms not defined or described in the specification. As stated, it's useful to provide a glossary in the specification that broadly defines all important terms. Second, any operation, structure, or result recited in a claim must be clearly and completely described in the specification.

12. Make Sure Claims Are Supported in Drawing

Under 37 CFR 1.83, the drawings must show every feature recited in the claims. If they don't, revise either the drawing or the claims. A broad recitation in a claim, such as "fuel atomizing means," can be supported by specific hardware, such as a carburetor, in the drawings. But remember that you can't add any new matter to an application once it's on file. So be sure to include all possibly relevant details of your invention in your drawings and spec. before you file. For example, if an examiner rejects a claim that recites "fuel atomizing means" for lack of support in the drawings, you can overcome this rejection by adding a box labeled "fuel atomizing means" to the drawings because this phrase was present in the application as originally filed (hopefully, not just in the claims but also in the rest of the specification). However, you can't add a carburetor unless your specification mentions a carburetor, since this would be prohibited new matter.

13. Avoid the Software-As-Means Trap

If your invention uses computers, software, or the internet, then your claims must do more than broadly recite an algorithm or other abstract idea. The claims must be directed to an application of the abstract idea to a new and useful end, and include additional elements that amount to significantly more than an abstract idea.

To prevent your claims from being rejected as being "directed to" an abstract idea, don your patent examiner's hat and apply the "trick" discussed above. Try claiming your invention without any software, computers, networks, or even physical hardware. Can you do it? If it's completely impossible (for example, because your invention changes the way a computer program accesses its memory), then you're in luck: your invention is "necessarily rooted in computer technology in order to overcome a problem specifically arising in the realm of computer[s]" (*DDR Holdings*), and should be patentable.

However, if it's at all possible to practice your invention without a computer—no matter how inefficiently—then you may have an abstract idea on your hands. In this case, your goal is to avoid the trap of using software or a computer merely as a means to implement that idea.

You may claim an improvement to the underlying idea itself; for example, the Supreme Court held in *Diamond v. Diehr* that a rubber molding process was improved by using a computer to calculate when to open the mold. Or, you may claim unconventional or unusual hardware, and tie your invention to the specific operation of that hardware that distinguishes it from a general purpose computer. Or, you may

claim an unconventional "ordered combination" of conventional elements—a collection of relationships between these elements that is unusual and provides "something more" than just a straightforward implementation of the idea.

If you find the state of the law difficult to understand, you're not alone! Most attorneys and legal scholars are befuddled too. Perhaps Congress will cut the Gordian knot and clarify the law someday.

Being in a Statutory Class Is Not Enough

Even though a claim recites statutory subject matter, it still must pass the other tests to be patentable. That is, claims still have to particularly point out and distinctly claim the invention, be supported by the specification, and define novel and nonobvious subject matter. Also, all "means-plus-function" language still must have clear supporting structure in the specification.

---

14. Recite Each Element Affirmatively as Subject of Its Clause

For maximum clarity, the elements of your invention should be affirmatively and directly recited; don't bring them in by inference or incidentally—for example, say "A transmission comprising: (a) a gear, and (b) a shaft, said gear being mounted on said shaft" [etc.], and not "A transmission whose gear is mounted on its shaft." In other words, each significant element of the claim should be recited for the first time (introduced) in a positive, affirmative manner, preferably with the word "a," so it's the subject of its own clause, and not with wording that makes it part of the object or assumes that the reader already knows that it's there. This rule is especially important for do-it-yourselfers to follow in order to write clear and understandable claims. An object referred to indirectly may be interpreted as a "workpiece" or object on which the invention acts, rather than as an integral part of the invention itself, and examiners need only reject items that form part of the invention itself.

15. Include Structural Support in Recitation of Operation

Assume a claim recites "a lever connected to move said pendulum back and forth at the same rate as said lights flash." The movement of the pendulum at this special rate is too much for the lever to do all by itself. In other words, there's not enough structural support for the operation recited. The remedy? Recite either (a) enough structure to do the job or (b) use a "means" clause. Here are examples of both methods.

> a. *a photoresponsive electromechanical circuit terminating in a lever that is connected to said pendulum and is arranged to move said pendulum at the same rate as said lights flash.*
>
> b. *means, including a lever connected to said pendulum, for moving said pendulum at the same rate as said lights flash.*

16. Recite Each Element Affirmatively, Followed by Its Shape or Function

Do not follow any element with the function of any other element.

Right:

> *a container for holding said beans*

Right:

> *a container having a cylindrical shape*

Wrong:

> *a container which receives said beans individually at a speed of 40 cm/second or greater.*

Right:

> *a container having a cylindrical shape, means for shooting said beans individually at a speed of 40 cm/second or greater into said container.*

17. Format

As stated in 37 CFR 1.75(i), quoted above, if the claim has several elements or steps, each should be in a separate paragraph with the first line of the paragraph hanging out to the left for maximum clarity, as is done in printed patents and in the claims in Section C above.

18. Precede Every Function by an Affirmative Recitation of the Element That Performs That Function

Don't recite any function without preceding the function with an affirmative recitation of the element that performs the function. Avoid the passive voice unless it is irrelevant to your invention what means accomplishes the function.

Wrong:

> *said beans being shot individually at a speed of 40 cm/second or greater into said container.*

Right:

> *means for shooting said beans individually at a speed of 40 cm/second or greater into said container.*
>
> or
>
> *a gun for shooting said beans individually at a speed of 40 cm/second or greater into said container.*

19. Make Sure Relative Terms Are Not Ambiguous

Generally, the PTO will hold that a claim with a relative term, such as "small," "large," or "close," is indefinite—that is, it fails to particularly point out and distinctly claim the invention under Section 112(b). However if the relative term is such that it would normally be understood by a Person Having Ordinary Skill In The Art (PHOSITA), the Patent Court has held that the PTO should accept it. In the *Power One* case, a claim that stated that a regulator was "near" a load was held to be unambiguous to a PHOSITA because the description stated that the regulator was to be placed close enough to the load so that the system will operate properly and thus no specific distance was needed.

H. Drafting Your Main (Independent) Claim

There are two basic types of claims: "independent" and "dependent." "Independent claims" are those that don't refer to any preceding claim; they stand alone. Examples of independent claims are all of those given in the preceding sections of this chapter. Note that these claims don't refer back to any preceding claim and each defines a complete, operative invention by itself.

"Dependent claims," which will be covered in the next section, refer back to a preceding or "parent" claim (this preceding claim can either be independent or dependent). A dependent claim recites narrower subject matter than its preceding claim in either of the two standard ways—that is, either by adding an additional element(s) or defining one or more elements of the preceding claim more narrowly.

The reasons for providing dependent claims will be covered in the next section also; the main point to remember here is that your independent claims are the important ones, since they're the basic and broadest definitions of your invention. If a dependent claim is infringed, its independent or parent claim(s) must also be infringed. If an independent claim is infringed, however, that's enough to win the case.

To draft an independent claim, the easiest and most direct way to do it is to follow these four basic steps:

1. Write a preamble giving the name or title of the invention, or the problem which it solves.
2. List the elements or steps of the claim.
3. Interconnect the elements or steps.
4. Broaden the claim as much as possible but not so much that it reads on (describes) anything already known; that is, "in the prior art."

The claim can be structured so that the elements of the claim appear together, followed by the interconnections. Or, each element can appear in conjunction with its interconnection(s) to adjacent elements. Most patent attorneys use the latter method—see Claims 2, 3, and 4 in Section C, above, for examples—but you may find it easier to recite the interconnections separately. An exception is process claims, where you'll find it easier to directly associate each step with its predecessor.

Start by writing your first claim without regard to breadth—that is, just get a preamble written, set down the elements of the invention, and interconnect them, paying no attention to how broadly you can recite the invention. In other words, just define your invention as you believe necessary to "get it all down" in a complete manner.

Then, see how many elements (or steps) you can eliminate and how many remaining elements you can broaden so that the result maintains sufficient structure and yet does not tread on the prior art. Remember that the broadest way of defining any element is by using "means-plus-a-function" language. Don't forget to refer to your prior-art patents for examples. And when you are finished, try to make the claim even broader by thinking of ways that an infringer might change your invention while still using your inventive concepts and see if you can broaden the claim to cover these changes, while still defining an invention that is patentable over the prior art.

To provide a real example that everyone can understand, let's assume you've just invented a table. Since you've already written your specification, you have a name for each part of your invention, so that chore is already behind you. If you believe your part names leave something to be desired, you can get additional part names from your prior-art search patents, the Glossary of Useful Technical Terms in Appendix 3, or any visual dictionary (see Appendix 2, "Resources: Government Publications, Patent Websites, and Books of Use and Interest"), or in a thesaurus (in a book or computer). All that remains now is to provide a title or preamble. List the parts, interconnect them, and then broaden your claims.

1. The Preamble

To write the preamble, you can name the statutory class of the claim (recommended in view of recent court decisions) or pick a name or title for the whole unit or the problem that it solves, remembering that you can't use the word "table" since it hasn't been invented until now. To have the preamble recite just a statutory class, it should simply read, "A machine, comprising"; "An article, comprising"; "A method, comprising"; "A composition, comprising"; or "A new use, comprising," followed by a colon (":"). To have the preamble recite a title for the whole unit, you can say, "An article of furniture, comprising" or "A work station device, comprising," followed by a colon (":"). To have the claim recite a function, you can recite, "A support for holding objects to be handled by a sitting human." We've used "an article of furniture" in the sample claim since it would be hard to construe this too narrowly.

2. The Elements

Next, to list the parts of the table, we'll start with the largest, most visible part, the top, and then add the smaller, less apparent parts, the legs. Since the table's just been invented, we'll assume that the words "top" and "legs" are still unknown, but even if they were known, it's not wise to use "top" anyway, since it's a notoriously vague homonym (it can mean anything from a hat to a bottle cap to a toy). To define the top, then, we need a more meaningful term or phrase. Let's suppose we've made a model of our invention and have used a large sheet of chipboard for the top. All we need to do at this stage is to say so; thus our first and most basic element becomes "(a) a large sheet of chipboard."

Suppose our model table has four legs and we've made them of six-cm diameter circular oak dowels, each 65 cm long. Then our legs would be recited simply as "(b) four oak dowels, each having a circular cross section 6 cm in diameter and each 65 cm long." Our elements are now all recited—wasn't that easy?

3. Interconnections

Lastly, we have to interconnect the legs to the top, also an easy task. Suppose our legs are joined at the underside of the top using four metal flanges, attached at the four corners of the top with each having a cylindrical portion with female threads, and with the top sections of the legs having mating male threads that are screwed into the respective flanges so that the legs extend at right angles to the top. Merely recite the flanges positively and add an interconnection clause as follows.

> c. *four flanges, each having means for attachment to one side of said sheet of chipboard and each having a cylindrical portion with female threads, and*
>
> d. *said four flanges being attached to one side of said sheet of chipboard at four respective corners thereof and said four oak dowels having male threads on a top section thereof and being screwed into the cylindrical portions of said respective flangesso that said dowels extend from said sheet of chipboard at right angles.*

Eureka! It's done. You've written a complete independent claim.

Here's how it looks.

> 11. *An article of furniture, comprising:*
>   a. *a large sheet of chipboard,*
>   b. *four oak dowels, each having a circular cross section 6 cm in diameter and each 65 cm long, and*
>   c. *four flanges, each having means for attachment to one side of said sheet of chipboard and each having a cylindrical portion with female threads, and*
>   d. *said four flanges [etc.].*

Note, always recite the elements and their interconnections in lettered subparagraphs. Also, we format paragraphs with a hanging indent style, just as the claims are printed in patents.

Is there anything wrong with this claim? Yes! As you probably will have realized by now, this claim is far too narrow—that is, it has many elements and each of these is recited too specifically. In fact it even recites specific dimensions, which you don't generally even need in the specification. Thus the claim as written would be easy to avoid infringing: All that an infringer would have to do is to use plywood instead of chipboard, use four pine dowels instead of oak, and so on. Let's broaden it, then.

Beware of Divided Infringement

Sometimes the most natural way to write a method claim produces a claim that is difficult to enforce. For example, drafting a method claim by simply listing the steps in order, without considering who performs those steps, may lead to "divided" infringement.

Direct infringement of a method claim requires that a single actor perform all of the claim's steps. Ideally, you should craft your claims to focus the action on a single actor. A claim that divides the steps among two or more actors is more difficult and expensive to enforce, and may render your patent less valuable.

The case of *Akamai v. Limelight* involved a patented content delivery service by which a service provider improves delivery of a customer's webpage to a client web browser by maintaining some of the webpage content on a network of "ghost" servers. When the client requests the customer's webpage, the webpage directs the client to retrieve the content from one of the ghost servers, rather than from the customer's webpage server. However, the customer must "tag," on its webpage, the portions of the webpage content to be delivered in this way, so that webpage can redirect requests for that content to a ghost server. Claim 34 is paraphrased below, along with an indication of which actor performs each step:

- **distributing** a set of page content across a network of ghost servers (performed by the content delivery service)
- **tagging**, on a customer's webpage, page content to be delivered by the ghost servers (performed by the customer), and
- **sending**, to a client in response to a request for the tagged content, an IP address of the ghost server from which the client may retrieve the content (performed by the customer via the customer's webpage).

Akamai accused Limelight of infringing the patent by providing such a content delivery service. The problem, as Akamai found out, is that no single actor performs all of the steps, since Limelight performs the "distributing" step, but Limelight's customers perform the remaining steps. This left Akamai with a very difficult case of "divided infringement."

The claim might have been improved by focusing the action on the customer. For example, remove the "distributing" step and rework the claim so that all steps are performed by the customer:

34. *A content delivery method, comprising:*
    a. *tagging, on a customer's webpage, page content to be delivered by a ghost server;*
    b. *sending, to a ghost server having an IP address, the set of page content that has been tagged;*
    c. *receiving, at the customer's webpage, a request from a client for the page content;*
    d. *sending, to the client in response to the request for the page content, the IP address of the ghost server from which the client may retrieve the page content.*

Better yet, focus the claim entirely on the service provider, since it may be more efficient to sue the service provider than its customers:

34. *A content delivery method, comprising:*
    e. *receiving, from a customer, a set of page content that has been tagged on a customer webpage;*
    f. *storing the set of page content on a ghost server, the ghost server having an IP address;*
    g. *providing, to the customer webpage, the IP address of the ghost server; and after the customer webpage provides the IP address to a client web browser;*
    h. *delivering, from the ghost server to the client web browser, the set of page content in response to a request sent to the IP address from the client web browser.*

Even better, include both such claims in your patent application, to cover the actions of the content service provider, as well as the actions of its customer.

Note: In 2015, the Court of Appeals for the Federal Circuit held that a claim can be infringed by an entity (i) if the entity directs or controls the actions of other actors, (ii) where the entity and one or more other actors form a joint enterprise, or (iii) if the entity "conditions participation in an activity or receipt of a benefit upon performance of a step or steps of a patented method and establishes the manner or timing of that performance."

Remember, you broaden a claim by (1) eliminating elements where possible, and (2) reciting the remaining elements as broadly as possible.

Going through the claim to eliminate elements, we see that the top can't be eliminated since it's an essential part. However, we don't need to recite four legs—we can eliminate one of these since three legs will support the top. But better yet, we can even use the word "plurality" since this covers two or more legs. (The term "plurality" means more than one). Used here, it is an example of how you'll sometimes need to search for a word or phrase that most broadly describes a particular element. Even though two may not be sufficient to support a top, the PTO will usually not object to this word in this context. We could even go further and eliminate the recitation of legs entirely by reciting "support means," but this would include solid supports, such as in a chest or bureau, which would not be suitable for table-type uses. Lastly, we can eliminate the flanges, since these aren't essential to the invention and since there are many other possible ways of attaching legs to a tabletop.

Next, let's go through the claim to see which elements can be recited more broadly. First, the top. Obviously "a large sheet of chipboard" is a very narrow recitation since plywood, solid wood, metal, and plastic tops would avoid infringement. A broad recitation would be "a large sheet of rigid material," but, as stated above, the word "large" is frowned upon by the PTO as too vague to satisfy Section 112. So let's make the top's size more specific. Since we're interested in providing a working surface for humans, let's merely specify that the top is "a sheet of rigid material of sufficient size to accommodate use by a human being for writing and working."

Next, the legs. Obviously, the recitation of four circular oak dowels with specific dimensions is very limiting. Let's eliminate the material, shape, and dimensions and recite the legs as merely "a plurality of elongated support members of substantially equal length." This covers square, round, triangular, and oval legs, regardless of their length or material.

Lastly, instead of the flanges (that we've eliminated as unnecessary) to join the legs to the top, let's use "means" (to make it as broad as possible) as follows:

"means for joining said elongated support members at right angles to the underside of said top at spaced locations so as to be able to support said top horizontally."

The result would look like this.

11. An article of furniture, comprising:

   a. a sheet of rigid material of sufficient size to accommodate use by a human being for writing and working

   b. a plurality of elongated support members of equal length, and

   c. means for joining said elongated support members at right angles to the underside of said sheet at spaced locations so as to be able to support said sheet horizontally.

Obviously, Claim 11 is now far broader than our first effort. Your first independent claim should be as broad as possible, but of course, you can't make it so broad that it lacks novelty or nonobviousness. Thus, when you eliminate as many elements as possible, and when you broaden the remaining elements in the manner just described, keep in mind that you must leave enough structure or acts to define your invention in a novel manner over the prior art so that the novelty is nonobvious.

Put differently, writing claims is like walking on a fence: You can't sway too far on the side of specificity or you'll fall onto the side of worthlessness and you can't sway too far onto the side of breadth or you'll fall onto the prior art. To obtain the broadest possible coverage, you should not draft your main claim primarily to cover your invention; rather draft it as broadly as possible with at least some thought of clearing the prior art, then go back and make sure that it at least covers your invention.

Some patent attorneys compare the writing of their first claim to passing through a wall of fire. However, we have found that if we follow the above four steps—(1) write a preamble, (2) recite the elements, (3) interconnect them, and (4) broaden the claims—the going is relatively painless. In case of doubt, err on the side of breadth at this stage, since you can always narrow your claims later, but you may not be able to make them broader if the application's allowed on the first Office Action.

I. Other Techniques in Claim Writing

Now that you understand the basics, here are some other tricks you may want to use when writing your claims. Obviously, not all apply all of the time, but you will probably find that at least several can be used to improve your claim writing.

- **Antecedents.** Provide a proper antecedent in the beginning of your claim for every term you use in the latter part of the claim. For example, in Claim 11 in the preceding part, the clause "the underside of said sheet" near the end of the claim has no clear antecedent in the beginning of the claim and thus might be rejected by some examiners. The claim would be better if clause a were amended by adding, "said sheet having an underside" to provide unequivocal support for the underside phase later. Conversely, if you recite an element and recite the same element again, you must use the article "said" (some attorneys use "the" to reduce the amount of legalese) before the second occurrence. If you want to recite two similar elements in different parts of the claim, you should use the article "a" or "an" to introduce both elements, but you must use different adjectives to clearly differentiate the levers—for example, "a *prying lever* connected to…; and a *force-transmitting* lever positioned on…."

- **"Whereby" clause.** At the end of your claim, we recommend adding a "whereby" clause to specify the advantage or use of the invention to hammer home to the examiner, or anyone else who reads your claim, the value of your invention. Thus in Claim 11, above, you should add at the end of this claim, "whereby a human is enabled to work, eat, and write in a seated position." "Whereby" clauses don't help to define over the prior art, but they do force the examiner to consider the advantages (35 U.S.C. § 103 nonobviousness features) of your invention and thus help to get the claims allowed. However, don't make the whereby clause too narrow or a court may construe it against you.

- **Reference numbers.** You may put the drawing's reference numerals in your claims after the appropriate elements. Although this is required in some foreign jurisdictions, practitioners in the United States seldom do it unless the elements of the claim aren't clear. Including reference numbers in your draft claims, but removing them before filing the application, is a good way to test whether your drawings show all of the claim elements.

- **Recesses.** If your invention has an opening, hole, or recess in its structure, you may, as stated, recite the hole directly as such, even though it isn't tangible. For example, the recitation "said member having a hole near its upper end" is permissible. (See "Glossary of Useful Technical Terms" in Appendix 3 for a list of recesses.)

- **_Jepson_ claims.** With regard to the rarely enforced 37 CFR 1.75(e) (quoted in Section B2, above) requiring the use of the *Jepson* style (a preamble containing old elements and body of claims containing improvements of your invention), most patent attorneys recommend that claims not be cast in this style unless the examiner requests it or unless the examiner is having trouble understanding exactly what your inventive contribution is. The reason for this is that a *Jepson* claim isolates and hence minimizes your improvement, making it easier to invalidate. If you do claim in the *Jepson* format, draft your preamble so that it includes all the elements or steps and their interconnections that are already known from the prior art; then add a "cleavage" clause such as "the improvement comprising" or "characterized in that"; and then recite the elements of your invention and their interconnections.

- **Predetermined and Given.** Examiners prefer the words "predetermined" and "given" to describe quantities that must be known to implement an invention but are otherwise unspecified. We recommend you use them whenever possible to indicate that something has a size, thickness, length, quality, and so on, without limiting the claim to any specific dimension or quality. For example, "said member having a predetermined cross-sectional shape" and "said valve arranged to open when a predetermined gas pressure is developed."

- **Consisting versus comprising.** A claim that recites a group of elements can be made "open" or "closed." An open claim (the normal case) will cover more elements than it recites, whereas a closed claim is limited to and will cover only the elements it specifically recites. To make a claim open, use "includes" or "comprising"—for example, "said machine *comprising* A, B, and C." In this case, a machine with four elements A, B, C, and D will infringe. To make a claim closed (rarely done), use "consist" or "having only"—for example, "Said machine *consisting* of A, B, and C."

In this case, a machine with elements A, B, C, and D will not infringe, since, in patent law, the word "consist" is interpreted to mean "having only the following elements."

- **A plurality of.** Also, whenever you recite several units of anything, preface your recitation with "a plurality of"—such as, "a plurality of holes in said hose." If you require a minimum number of units to make your invention operable, you may recite, using Claim 11 above as an example, language like "a plurality of at least three elongated support members."

Patent Attorney Words

If you get stuck and don't know how to phrase something, usually one of the "patent attorney words" below will help.

a (used to introduce a part)

about (used to fudge a specific quantity)

at least (used to hammer home that more elements can be used)

contiguous (used to indicate elements are touching)

device for (interpreted like "means for")

disposed (used to indicate a part is positioned in a particular place)

further comprising (used in dependent claims to add additional parts)

further including (used in dependent claims to add additional parts)

heretofore (used to refer back to something previously recited)

indicium (used to recite something that a human can recognize, such as a mark or a sound)

means for (used to claim something broadly, in terms of its function, rather than specific hardware)

member (used to recite a mechanical part when no other word is available)

multitude (used to recite a large, indefinite number)

perimeter (perimetric, perimetrical, permetrically—refers to a border around something)

pivotally (used to indicate that a part is rotatably mounted)

plurality (used to introduce more than one of an element)

predetermined (used to state that a part has a specific parameter)

providing (used to recite a part in a method claim)

releasably (indicates something can be released from a position)

respectively (used to relate several parts to several other parts in an individual manner)

said (used to refer to a previously recited part by exactly the same word)

sandwiching (used to indicate that one part is between two other parts)

selected from the group consisting of (used in a *Markush* claim to create an artificial group)

slidably (used to indicate that two parts slide with respect to each other)

so that (used to restrict a part to a defined function)

substantially (used to fudge a specific recitation)

such that (used to restrict a part to a defined function)

surrounding (used to indicate that a part is surrounded)

the (used to refer to a previously recited part by a slightly different word)

thereby (used to specify a result or connection between an element and what it does)

thereof (used as a pronoun to avoid repeating a part name)

urging (used to indicate that force is exacted upon a part)

whereby (used to introduce a function or result at the end of a claim)

wherein (used in a dependent claim to recite an element (part) more specifically)

(For names of components, see "Glossary of Useful Technical Terms" in Appendix 3.)

- **Less Is more.** Remember that, because of the Boolean "less is more" rule in interpreting claims, it's not necessary to recite a specific feature in your main claim in order to cover that feature in combination with the other elements of your invention. For example, once we drafted a claim for a client where one embodiment of her invention had a fingerlike support. Not seeing the finger in the main claim, she asked me, "Did you claim the finger?" We then explained to her that since the main claim didn't recite the finger, the main claim was broad enough to cover her invention with or without the finger.

- **Is it sketchable?** After drafting your claim, you or a friend should be able to make enough sense out of it to sketch your invention. If this isn't possible, the claim is unclear and needs to be reworked. (The Science Olympiad has a team challenge called "Write It Do It" that operates in a similar manner.)

- **Special terms.** You can use any technical or descriptive terms that you feel are reasonably necessary to define or describe your invention—the claim does not have to be limited to any special "legalese." One patent attorney we know had a devil of a time defining (to the satisfaction of the examiner) a convex transistor structure with a nubbin on top until he simply called it "mammary-shaped."

- **Method claim.** If possible, provide a method claim to cover your invention; you usually can do this if there's any dynamic operation involved in the invention. Most machines and electrical circuits can be claimed in terms of a method. Method claims are usually broader than apparatus claims, since they're not limited to any specific hardware.

- **Gerunds in method claims.** Each substantive clause of a method claim must usually start with an "—ing" or gerund word, such as "attaching," "heating," or "abrading." If you want to recite some hardware in a method claim, use "providing"—such as, "providing a central processor." (Don't say "comprising the steps of" in a method claim since claims that recite "step" may tend to be interpreted less broadly.)

- **Label means.** If you do recite any "means," it's desirable to label the means with a nonfunctional adjective in order to provide a mnemonic aid in case you need to refer to the means later. For example, "first means," "second means," and so on. Also, the "means" must be followed by or be modified by a function or some structure. For example, "first means for printing" (means-plus-function); "second means comprising a doctor blade" (means-plus-structure) (means-plus-function); "second means comprising a doctor blade" (means-plus-structure).

- **Padding.** Lastly, many patent attorneys recommend that a claim not be too short. A claim that is short will be viewed adversely (as possibly overly broad) by many examiners, regardless of how much substance it contains. Thus, many patent attorneys like to "pad" short claims by adding "whereby" clauses, providing long preambles, adding long functional descriptions to their means clauses, and so on. The trick here, of course, is to pad the claim while avoiding a charge of undue prolixity under Section 112(b), and without adding unnecessary limitations.

You'll find that a well-written claim is like a well-written poem. Each has a beautiful symmetry, order, and logic.

J. Drafting Dependent Claims

In Section H, we pointed out that there are two basic types of claims—independent claims (these stand on their own) and dependent claims (these incorporate an entire preceding claim, which can be an independent or dependent claim). A dependent claim is simply a shorthand way of writing a narrower claim—that is, a claim that includes all the elements of a preceding claim, and/or recites one or more additional elements or recites one or more elements of the preceding claim more specifically—without having to duplicate all of the language of the preceding claim.

1. Reasons for Writing Dependent Claims

If an independent claim is broader, you may wonder why you need dependent (narrower) claims—especially since the independent claim must be infringed if its dependent claim is infringed. Below are eight good answers to that question:

1. **Backup.** Dependent claims are by definition always narrower than the claims on which they depend. You may accordingly be wondering, "If my broad independent claim covers my invention, why do I need any more claims of narrower scope?" True, if all goes well, your broad claim will be all you'll need. However, suppose you sue an infringer who finds an appropriate prior-art reference that neither you nor the PTO examiner found and that adversely affects the validity of ("knocks out") your broad claim. If you've written a narrower claim you can then disclaim the broad claim and fall back on the narrower claim. If the narrower claim is patentable over the prior art, your patent will still prevail. Thus the dependent claims are insurance in case of broad claim invalidity. Each claim, whether independent or dependent, is interpreted independently for examination and infringement purposes. If the claim is dependent, it's interpreted as if it included all the wording of its parent (incorporated) claim or claims, even if the incorporated claim is held invalid. Dependent claims are crucial in order to recite all of the significant subsidiary elements of your invention. A feature that doesn't seem significant now can prove to be crucial later. One inventor we know (Morrie) submitted a large set of dependent claims to recite every less-important feature of his invention that he could think of, including one that recited that a certain flap was bendable. He got a patent and was involved in a licensing negotiation where the infringer found an earlier patent that showed his complete invention, except for the bendable flap. While the earlier patent invalidated most of Morrie's claims, fortunately he was able to rely on the still-valid dependent claims that recited the bendable flap to conclude a licensing deal, albeit at a lower rate than he originally wanted.

2. **Reification and differentiation of broad claims.** Dependent claims are useful to explain, reify (make real), and differentiate (broaden) some of the broad, abstract terms in your independent claims. For instance, if you recite in a claim "additive means," many judges may not be able to understand what the "additive means" actually covers, but if you add several dependent claims that state, respectively, that the additive means is benzene and toluene, they'll get a very good idea of what types of substances the "additive means" embraces. If your main claim recites a new parlor game, adding a dependent claim that recites that the game is simulated on a computer will make it clear that the main claim covers more than computer simulations; that is, it covers board versions too. (Don't forget to show the computer version in your drawings and discuss it in your specification.) This independent-claim broadening function of dependent claims is called "differentiation" and is most effective if you recite just one element in the dependent claim.

3. **Provide spectrum of coverage.** Narrower claims can be used to provide a range, spectrum, or menu of proposed coverage from very broad to very narrow so that your examiner can, by allowing some narrower claims and rejecting the broader ones, indicate the scope of coverage the examiner's willing to allow.

4. **Prevent premature final action.** Providing dependent claims of varying scope and approaches forces the examiner to make a wider search of your invention on the first examination. This will prevent the examiner from citing new prior art against your application on the second Office Action, which usually will be made "final." Thus, you should include every possibly novel feature (or novel combination of features) of your invention in your dependent claims.

5. **Provide broader base for infringement damages.** By providing dependent claims that add more elements, you define your invention (in these claims) as a more comprehensive structure, thereby providing a broader base upon which a judge can calculate infringement damages.

6. **Provide a specific, descriptive recitation.** This reason is slightly different than Item 2 above. If the recitation in the independent claim is broad and abstract, such as, "urging means for ...," we strongly recommend that you provide dependent claims with a descriptive, definite recitation (for example, "wherein said urging means is a coil spring") to hit the nail on the head, or provide a specific hardware recitation so a judge won't have to use his or her imagination.

7. **Preserve the right to rely upon doctrine of equivalents.** Traditionally patent owners have been able to rely on the "Doctrine of Equivalents" (DoE) to effectively expand a claim beyond its literal wording if it didn't cover an infringing device. However, the U.S. Supreme Court in *Festo v. Shoketsu* held that a patentee who amended (narrowed) a claim in order to obtain a patent could not rely on the DoE to recover scope that was given up. To preserve your right to rely on the DoE, draft as many dependent claims as possible to cover all aspects of your invention. In this way you'll have some claims that won't have to be amended (narrowed) if the PTO cites relevant prior art against these claims, and thus you'll preserve your right to use the DoE to expand these claims if necessary.

8. **Litigators prefer them.** Litigators prefer narrower and more specific claims (provided they cover the infringing device) because they provide a broader base for infringement damages and are more difficult to invalidate since they read on less prior art. Furthermore, it's easier for a litigator to prove infringement since the claim is less abstract and recited the specific structure that is infringed. And it can be very persuasive to say that the defendant infringed 20 claims instead of just one! Rather than carry on an expensive fight against every claim, some infringers may choose to just settle instead.

2. The Drafting

For the reasons above, when you're satisfied with your first, basic, and broadest independent claim, you should write as many dependent claims as you can think of, keeping in mind that the PTO charges extra if the total number of claims exceeds 20. Each dependent claim should begin by referring to your basic claim, or a previous dependent claim, using its exact title.

EXAMPLE:

Independent claim:

> 1. *A cellular telephone having a hinged body and a coiled antenna.*

Improper dependent claim:

> 2. *The hinged body of claim 1 wherein said hinge has five knuckles.* [The preamble or beginning of the claim does not correspond with claim 1 and there's no antecedent for "said hinge."]

Proper dependent claim:

> 2. *The cellular telephone of claim 1 wherein said hinged body includes a hinge with five knuckles.*

If the dependent claim recites one or more elements of the independent claim more narrowly, it should use the word "wherein"—for example, "The bicycle of Claim 1 wherein"—and then continue by reciting one or more elements of the independent claim.

Note that a dependent claim does not narrow the scope of any previous claim from which it depends; it merely provides an alternative, narrower recitation in a shorthand manner.

If the dependent claim recites additional elements, it should use the words, "further including" or "further comprising"—for example, "The bicycle of Claim 1, further including ..."—then continue by reciting the additional feature(s) of your invention. The additional features can be those you eliminated in broadening your basic claims and all other subsidiary features, including all combinations and permutations of such features of your invention you can think of. The features recited more narrowly or the additional elements recited by the dependent claims can be specific parameters (such as materials and temperatures) or other specifics of your invention (such as specific shapes, additional elements, or specific modes of operation). Refer to your prior art patents for guidance on how to draft these.

Note that a dependent claim must either recite the elements of its parent claim more specifically, or recite additional elements. It may not change any element to a different type or kind. Thus if the parent claim is an apparatus claim, each of its dependent claims must recite additional structure or recite some previously recited structure more specifically. For example, if your parent claim recites "1. A house made of red bricks," its dependent claim can say "2. The house of Claim 1 wherein said bricks are made of clay" (recites bricks more specifically) or "2. The house of Claim 1, further including a layer of paint over said bricks" (recites additional structure). The dependent claim can't say "2. The house of Claim 1 wherein said bricks are yellow." A method claim may not be made dependent upon an apparatus claim and vice versa, but most examiners will allow an apparatus claim that is dependent upon a method claim.

If the parent claim is a method claim, each of its dependent claims must recite an additional step, or recite a previously recited step (or structure in such a step) more specifically. For example, suppose your parent, independent claim recites:

> 1. A method of heating comprising irradiating a foodstuff in a chamber with microwaves.

You can provide a dependent claim that recites one element of claim 1 (the microwaves) more specifically as follows:

> 2. The method of Claim 1 wherein said microwaves have a frequency of 2250 megahertz.

Alternatively (or in addition), you can provide a dependent claim that recites an additional step as follows:

> 2A. The method of Claim 1, further including freezing said foodstuff after it is irradiated.

Or as another alternative (or in addition), you can combine both dependent claims to provide a narrower dependent claim as follows:

> 2B. The method of claim 1 wherein said microwaves have a frequency of 2250 megahertz and further including freezing said foodstuff after it is irradiated.

You can see that many variations and permutations are possible. Although we used letter suffixes to distinguish the above claims, you must use numbers for each set of your claims (an independent and its dependents). An independent apparatus claim (means or structural) requires that you recite a part or a series of parts. In a claim that is dependent upon an apparatus claim you must recite an additional part or modify a previously recited part. In an independent method claim you must recite a step or a series of steps. In a claim that is dependent upon a method claim you must recite an additional step or modify a previously recited step or part.

Here are some dependent claims for Claim 11 (set out in Section H, above). Note that each dependent claim either recites an additional element or recites an already recited element more specifically.

> 11. An article of furniture (etc.).
> > 12. The article of furniture of Claim 11 wherein said sheet of rigid material is made of wood.
> > > 13. The article of furniture of Claim 12 wherein said sheet of rigid material of wood is made of chipboard.
> > > > 14. The article of furniture of Claim 13 wherein said sheet of chipboard has a rectangular shape.
> > 15. The article of furniture of Claim 11 wherein said means for joining comprises a set of flanges, each of which joins a respective one of said support members to the underside of said sheet of rigid material.
> > 16. The article of furniture of Claim 15 wherein each of said flanges is made of iron and includes a cylinder with female threads and wherein one end of each of said elongated members has male threads and is threadedly mated with the female threads of a respective one of said flanges.
> > 17. The article of furniture of Claim 11, further including a layer of a rigid plastic laminate bonded to a top side of said sheet of rigid material.

Note that a dependent claim may be dependent upon the parent claim or another dependent claim. We advise making almost all dependent claims directly dependent upon an independent claim (rather than another dependent claim) since this will make the dependent claims broader: a dependent claim that depends from another dependent claim incorporates the other dependent claim and the independent claim from which the other dependent claim depends. A dependent claim should be numbered as closely as possible to the number of its parent claim (independent or dependent). Note also how we've made a physical indication of claim dependency by indenting (nesting) each dependent claim under its parent claim(s) as shown above. This is optional, but makes things clearer for you and the examiner. Also, you should always skip a line between claims (we didn't do it here in order to conserve space).

A dependent claim will be read and interpreted by examiners and judges as if it incorporated all the limitations of its parent claim(s). Thus suppose your independent and dependent claims read, respectively, as follows:

18. *A rifle having an upwardly curved barrel.*
   19. *The rifle of Claim 18 wherein said barrel is made of austenitic steel.*

The dependent claim (19) will be examined independently, but with Claim 18 incorporated, so that it effectively reads as follows:

19. *A rifle having an upwardly curved barrel, said barrel being made of austenitic steel.*

Multiple Dependent Claims

A dependent claim may be made directly dependent upon several previous claims. This is called "multiple dependent claiming" ("MDC") and is common in Europe. Example: "3. The widget of claims 1 or 2 wherein ..." However we recommend that you do not use MDC since the PTO's examiners dislike the practice, there's a stiff surcharge for the privilege, and for fee purposes each MDC counts as the number of claims to which it refers.

 TIP

Use only significant limitations. You can make your dependent claims as specific as you want, even to reciting the dimensions of the tabletop, its color, and so on. However, extremely specific limitations like this, while possibly defining an invention that is novel over the prior art (Section 102), do not recite nonobvious subject matter (Section 103), so they'll be of little use to fall back on if you lose your independent claim. Thus, you should mainly try to use *significant* limitations in your dependent claims—that is, limitations that an infringer might use if he or she made your invention.

You should draft dependent claims to cover all possible permutations of the subsidiary features of your invention. For example, suppose you've invented a telephone and some of the dependent features are that it has (a) a musical ringer, (b) a coiled cord, and (c) a stand. You can provide three dependent claims with features a, b, and c, respectively. Then write four more dependent claims with features a and b; a and c; b and c; and a, b, and c, if you think these combinations are feasible.

Although most of your dependent claims should have just a single element (to obtain maximum claim differentiation), you should try to draft at least one dependent claim with as many parts as possible so as to provide as broad a base as possible for maximizing infringement damages. Also try, insofar as possible, to draft at least one claim to cover parts of the invention whose infringement would be publicly verifiable, rather than a nonverifiable factory process or machine. (If you cannot determine who is infringing, it will be very difficult to stop them!)

As with independent claims, you should not make your dependent claims purely "functional"—that is, each dependent claim should contain enough physical structure to support its operational or functional language. Here are some examples.

Wrong:

17. *The bicycle of Claim 16 wherein said derailleur operates with continuously variable speed-to-power ratios.* [This claim has no structure to support its operational limitation.]

Right:

> 17. *The bicycle of Claim 16 wherein said derailleur contains means for causing it to operate with continuously variable speed-to-power ratios.* [The "means" limitation is a recitation of structure that supports the operational limitation.]

Right:

> 17. *The bicycle of Claim 16 wherein said derailleur contains a cone-shaped pulley and a belt pusher for causing it to operate with continuously variable speed-to-power ratios.* [The pulley and pusher constitute structure that supports the operational limitation.]

If your independent claim recites a means plus a function, your dependent claim should modify the means and not the function. For example, assume an independent Claim 20 recites, "variable means for causing said transmission to have a continuously variable gear ratio." Here are the right and wrong ways to further limit this "means" in a dependent claim.

Wrong:

> 21. *The transmission of Claim 20 wherein said continuously variable gear ratio ranges from 5 to 10.*

Right:

> 21. *The transmission of Claim 20 wherein said variable means is arranged to provide ratios from 5 to 10.*

Common Misconception: If a dependent claim recites a specific feature of your invention, say a two-inch nylon gear, your invention will be limited to this gear, so that if any copy of the invention uses a one-inch gear, or a steel gear, it won't infringe on your patent.

Fact: Although the copy won't infringe the dependent claim, it will infringe the independent claim so long as it isn't limited to this specific feature. And as long as even one claim of a patent is infringed, the patent is infringed and you can recover as much damages (money) as if 50 claims were infringed.

Common Misconception: If a dependent claim recites a feature or element of the invention, it will protect this feature per se.

Fact: A dependent claim must be read to include all of the features of its referent claim (preceding or independent claim to which it refers). Thus it will not cover the feature it recites per se, but rather will cover that feature in combination with all of the elements of its referent claim.

Common Misconception: The limitations in a dependent claim will narrow its independent claim.

Fact: The independent claim is interpreted independently of its dependent claims and the latter never narrow the former although they can make the independent claim broader by claim differentiation.

If you still don't get the principle of broad and narrow claims, here are three simple claims that illustrate the point:

> 1. *A house that has a sloping roof with a gable.*
> 2. *The house of Claim 1 wherein said gable has a dormer.*
> 3. *The house of Claim 2 wherein said dormer has eight panes of glass.*

Claim 1 is very broad: It will cover any house that has a sloping roof with a gable. Thus it may cover, say, 30 million houses in the United States. Claim 2 is of narrower scope because it incorporates all of Claim 1 and has additional verbiage (houses with sloping roofs that have a gable with a dormer), making it longer than Claim 1. Thus it will cover fewer houses; say, ten million in the United States. Claim 3 is still longer and is far narrower than Claim 2 since it is limited to houses with sloping roofs that have a gable with a dormer with eight panes of glass. Thus it will cover fewer houses still, say one million houses in the United States.

Note that we made the number of the independent claim (#1) bold and we indented the dependent claims to indicate the dependency so that each dependent claim is nested under its referent claim. This is optional but desirable since it makes the claims clearer. As indicated above in Section G1, if you're working on a computer, use its "multiple windows" function (if available) to keep your independent claim displayed while you write your dependent claims.

Claims of Different Scope

The concept of claims of different scope (independent and dependent) is confusing to most inventors. Here's another way of explaining it, if you still don't understand.

An *independent claim* (IC) is one that *doesn't* refer back to any previous claim. For example, "*1. A telephone comprising (a) a base, (b) a handset, and (c) a rotary dial,*" is an example of an IC.

To write another independent claim like Claim 1 (C1), but that is narrower than C1 by reciting a base of black plastic, simply repeat all of Claim 1 and add that the base is black plastic. For example, "*2. A telephone comprising (a) a base of black plastic, (b) a handset, and (c) a rotary dial,*" is an example of a second IC that is narrower than C1.

However, there's an easier, shorter, and cheaper way to avoid repeating all of C1 each time: Simply write a claim that refers to the IC 1 so as to incorporate all of it by reference, and then state one or more additional elements, and/or recite one or more elements of the incorporated claim more specifically. Such a shorthand claim is called a "dependent claim" ("DC"). A DC is thus one that refers back to and incorporates all of a preceding claim and adds or modifies one or more limitations to recite the invention more narrowly. For example, "*2′. The telephone of Claim 1 wherein said base is made of black plastic,*" is a dependent claim that has the same scope as C2. C2′ will be interpreted as if it included *all* of the subject matter of C1, *together with the additional subject matter in C2′.*

It follows that to infringe a DC, a device must have all of the elements of the DC, *plus all of the elements of the incorporated claim.*

Thus, adding a DC to recite a specific feature of your invention won't broaden or narrow your coverage; it will just provide another, yet more precise, missile. The eight reasons for including DCs are in Section J.

Also note that a DC can refer back to a preceding claim, and the preceding claim can in turn refer back to a further preceding claim. To infringe such a *third-level DC*, the device must have all of the elements of *all three claims* in the chain.

K. Drafting Additional Sets of Claims

After you've written your first independent claim (IC) and all the dependent claims you can reasonably think of (all numbered sequentially), consider writing another set of claims (an IC and a set of dependent claims) if you can think of a substantially different way to claim your invention. See the prior-art patents and the sample set of claims at the end of this chapter (Fig. 9A) for examples of different independent claims on the same invention. Your second set of dependent claims can be similar to your first set; copy-and-paste functionality will be of great aid here. Writing more sets of claims will not always give your invention broader coverage, but will provide alternative weapons to use against an infringer. That is, writing a second set of claims is like going into battle with a sword as well as a gun. Also, writing more sets of claims will give your examiner additional perspectives on your invention. That is, your chances of getting your examiner to bite on patentability will be increased if you present many flavors to choose from.

In the example above (Claim 11), you might start the second IC with the legs instead of the top and you might try to define the top and legs differently—for example, instead of "elongated members," you might call the legs "independent support means." Instead of calling the top a "sheet of rigid material," you might call it a "planar member having paralleled, opposed major faces."

Here are still other ways to write a different IC: (1) Rewrite one of the dependent claims from your first set in independent form; (2) wait a few days and write an IC again, with independent thought; (3) write the IC by reciting the elements of the first IC in reverse or inverse order; and (4) if your first IC has any "means" clauses, make your next IC a structure (apparatus) claim (no means clauses), or vice versa; (5) if your invention uses any unique supplies, blanks, or starting elements, or accessories, it is wise to provide claims to these also. For example, if you've invented a unique paper cup that is made from a unique starting blank, provide independent claims to both the cup and the blank.

Another valuable way to write a different IC is to provide a method (process) claim if your first IC is an apparatus claim, or vice versa; you're allowed to have both method and apparatus claims in the same case if they relate to the same invention. You should always include an independent method claim if possible, since a method claim is usually not limited to specific hardware and thus affords broader coverage. Every step of each independent method claim must be an action step, for instance, "providing…." or "heating…." If your invention is a product and the process of making it is novel, or if it uses an intermediate construction in the process, you should claim the process and the intermediate construction.

Another valuable way to write a different IC occurs if your invention involves software: add a claim to cover any manufacture or machine that might contain your software. This can include a computer memory, a hard drive, a CD-ROM, a DVD, or any other medium. Such a claim gives you offensive rights against those who would distribute your software without permission, and you probably would rather assert your rights against an illegal distributor with deep pockets than against your own software users.

A software medium claim might begin as follows:

> *A tangible, nontransitory, computer-readable medium in which is nontransitorily stored computer program code that, when executed by a computer processor, causes performance of a method for …, the method comprising: …*

This phrasing offers the advantage that you can simply copy your method claims, both independent and dependent, after this preamble, and you will only have to renumber the dependent claims and change their preambles to read "The medium of claim X" rather than "The method of claim X." (The "tangible" and "nontransitory" limitations ensure that the claim does not run afoul of any judicial exceptions to patentable subject matter, such as transitory electrical signals, which are unpatentable.)

Note that each independent claim must stand by itself: It may not refer to, incorporate, be based in any way on, or use referents from any previous claim. Even if claim 1 recites "a first lever" you may not recite, in a second independent claim, say claim 10, "a second lever" unless a first lever has already been recited earlier in claim 10. Similarly even if claim 1 recites "a wheel," claim 10 may not recite "said wheel" unless "a wheel" has been recited earlier in claim 10. The basic filing fee entitles you to up to three ICs and 20 total claims. We generally try to use up this allotment by writing three ICs and three sets of five to seven dependent claims each. However, if we feel that we can write a fourth, substantially different IC and the cost can be borne by my client, we will add it, plus more dependent claims. The PTO now charges a substantial additional fee for each IC past three, and for each claim (independent or dependent) past 20. (See "Independent claims in excess of three" and "Claims in excess of 20" in the fee schedule in Appendix 4—this fee is charged for each such claim.)

On the other hand, for relatively simple inventions, we may not be able to think of any substantially different ways to write an IC, so we may submit only one, plus a few dependent claims. We advise you generally not to submit more than the number of claims permitted for your basic filing fee—that is, three ICs and 20 total claims—unless the complexity of your invention justifies it, or you have some other good reason. Don't make your case like one published application (U.S. Pub. 20030100451): It has 7,215 claims!

L. Checklist for Drafting Claims

Below is the second part of the application checklist that we started in Chapter 8.

M. Use of Artificial Intelligence (AI) To Draft Claims

Artificial Intelligence (AI) agents having large language models (LLMs) may be used to draft patent applications. The use of AI to draft the specification is discussed in Chapter 8, section K. As described in this section, AI also may be used to draft claims—at least, in part. There are significant restrictions on the use of AI to draft patent claims that you should understand before asking an AI to help.

The most significant issue is one of public disclosure. Any public disclosure of your invention will prevent you from obtaining a patent abroad, and will begin a one-year grace period in the U.S. to file a PPA or RPA. Existing LLMs are initially trained on publicly available texts, like novels and other literature, but some continue to train even after they are released. Therefore, any prompt you enter into a publicly available LLM should be treated as a public disclosure, since the LLM might use words you have entered when responding to another person's prompt. For this reason, some of our clients have expressly forbidden the use of public LLM systems to draft any portion of their patent applications. This issue can be addressed by the use of an "in-house," privately-hosted AI system that is cut off from communicating with the internet or for which training is disabled (or both).

As noted, any paper submitted to the USPTO must be reviewed by the party or parties presenting the paper. Those parties are responsible for the contents therein. If an AI tool is used in drafting or editing patent claims, you must still review its work and ensure the paper is in accordance with the certifications being made. Simply relying on the accuracy of an AI tool is not a reasonable inquiry, especially given the potential for generative AI systems to omit, misstate, or even "hallucinate" information.

The Federal Circuit Court of Appeals has consistently stated that "only a natural person can be an inventor, so AI cannot be." However, the court explained that it was not confronted with "the question of whether inventions made by human beings with the *assistance* of AI are eligible for patent protection."

In 2024, the PTO clarified in a memo that "In the context of AI-assisted inventions, natural person(s) who create an invention using an AI system, or any other advanced system, must contribute significantly to the invention." The PTO went on to state that "While inventorship may be correctable in certain situations, a new inventor cannot be named if no natural person made a significant contribution to an AI-assisted invention." Thus, you cannot ask a machine to invent for you, then take credit for the invention.

Moreover, "Merely recognizing a problem or having a general goal or research plan to pursue does not rise to the level of conception." That is, a person who only presents a problem to an AI system may not be a proper inventor of an invention identified from the output of the AI system. However, a significant contribution could be shown by the way the person constructs the prompt in view of a specific problem to elicit a particular solution from the AI system.

You should carefully determine that the appropriate inventors are listed on the patent application. It is particularly important to review applications prepared with the assistance of AI, before filing, to see that information is not incorrectly or incompletely characterized.

Because the law in this area is still evolving, we recommend that your fully formulate your invention in your mind before asking a (privately-hosted!) AI to draft an independent claim to it, then review the claim it drafts in accordance with the techniques described in this chapter to ensure it describes what you asked for. In this way, should the question of your inventorship ever arise, you can justify that your "significant contribution" (i.e., the substance of the claim) came before the AI system was involved. Once you have edited the AI output to form your independent claim, you should be able to draft dependent claims on your own (see sections J and K above).

Fully conceptualizing your invention before involving the AI is important for another reason. According to the PTO, "A person who merely recognizes and appreciates the output of an AI system as an invention, particularly when the properties and utility of the output are apparent to those of ordinary skill, is not necessarily an inventor." That is, if the AI output includes ideas that you didn't think of and that anyone would recognize as inventive, then you aren't the inventor of those ideas.

The use of an AI tool to draft the specification or claims can be "material to patentability" (i.e., on its face, might justify denying a patent) which requires disclosure to the PTO. For example, material information could include evidence that a named inventor did not significantly contribute to the invention because the person's purported contributions were made by an AI system. This could occur where an AI system assists in the drafting of the patent application and introduces alternative embodiments that the inventor(s) did not conceive and the applicant seeks to patent.

As you may appreciate, the law surrounding the use of AI in patent drafting is complex and restrictive. Until and unless Congress, the PTO, or the courts intervene to simplify the laws, we recommend proceeding with caution when using AI in patent drafting.

N. Summary

Claims define the invention in logical and precise terms. They are sentence fragments beginning with the words "I claim" and are provided at the end of a patent application.

The patent statute and rules regarding claims require that they (a) be clear and unambiguous, (b) be independent or dependent, (c) must use terms from the specification, and (d) should be phrased in a two-part form (prior art plus improvement). Claims can also have elements expressed in "means-plus-function" form.

Every claim should be classifiable into one of the five statutory classes of invention: machine, article, composition, process (method), or new use. Software or business claims are usually process claims, but can be machine claims. The number of claims is not as important as their breadth and the specific features of the invention need not be recited in a claim to be covered.

For a device to infringe a claim, it must meet all of the elements of the claim. Claims can be made broader by eliminating elements or broadening existing elements, but each claim should define a novel and nonobvious invention over the prior art. When an element is first introduced in a claim, the article "a" should be used, but when the element is referred to again the article "the" or "said" should be used.

A "means clause" in a claim covers the hardware in the specification and its equivalents. A patent application should have means, nonmeans (apparatus), and method independent claims, if possible.

Each independent claim should be followed by a set of dependent claims. Each dependent claim must recite additional element(s) or recite the existing elements more narrowly (specifically). Claims must be logical, complete, unambiguous, and every element in every claim must be shown in the drawings. All method claims must (1) be tied in a substantial way to a particular machine or apparatus, or (2) recite the transformation of an article into a different state or thing.

CHAPTER 9 | NOW FOR THE LEGALESE—THE CLAIMS | 271

Checklist for Draft Claims

☐ Grammatical articles are used properly in the claims: "a" or "an" to introduce any singular part, "the" to refer to a part a second time when using a different (but clearly implied) term as before, and "said" only to refer to a part using the IDENTICAL term as before.

☐ Two articles together, such as "the said," aren't used.

☐ Every part and feature in every claim is shown in the drawings and discussed in the specification.

☐ No claim uses any disjunctive ("or") expression (except to recite two equivalent parts or a disjunctive function of a machine).

☐ No claim uses any naked functional clause; all claims contain a structural recitation or "means" to support every functional recitation.

☐ A memory aid is recited adjacent to each "means," for example, "first means"; also, each "means" is followed by "for ..." plus some function or structure.

☐ For each unique "means" followed by a function in the claims, the specification describes some hardware or an element which implements or provides the function for such means, using the same words as used in the claim to describe the function.

☐ "Consisting" isn't used in any claim (except if you want to say "having only").

☐ No claim uses any abbreviation, dash, parentheses, or quote.

☐ No term is used for the first time in any claim.

☐ The subparagraph form is used in long claims for ease of reading.

☐ Each claim has just one capital letter (two if "claim" is capitalized in a dependent claim) and one period (except lettered paragraphs), and no parentheses (except lettered paragraphs, quotes, or abbreviations).

☐ All significant parts are affirmatively recited in the claims as the subject and not the object of a clause.

☐ The main (independent) claim is made as broad as possible by reciting minimum number of elements and by generalizing existing elements (without reading on prior art).

☐ No vague, loose, or casual language is used in any claim.

☐ Space between adjacent claims is greater than space between adjacent lines of a claim.

☐ No dependent claim recites an additional function unless "means" or structure is specified to support such structure.

☐ All parts recited in claims are connected.

☐ All claims recite enough parts to provide a complete assemblage.

☐ You haven't submitted more than 20 total or more than three independent claims unless the case is very complex or extra claims are justified.

☐ No independent claim refers to any other claim and all dependent claims refer to a previous claim in line 1 or line 2.

☐ You've filed enough dependent claims to cover all features and permutations and you've filed second and third sets of claims (with differently phrased independent claims) if possible.

☐ You've included an independent method claim and a set of dependent method claims, if possible.

☐ Every dependent claim starts with either:
"The _____ of Claim x wherein ..." (to provide a separate recitation of an element(s) of the parent claim in a narrower fashion), or,
"The _____ of Claim x further including ..." (to provide a separate recitation of the element(s) of the parent claim, plus a recitation of one or more element(s)).

☐ No dependent claim is used to substitute a different part for any part recited in the parent claim. Each dependent claim recites an element(s) of the parent claim in a narrower fashion, and/or recites one or more element(s), in addition to those recited in the parent claim.

☐ No dependent claim recites a method limitation if its parent claim is an apparatus claim.

☐ In order to comply with the *Bilski* decision, all process claims recite a process centered on hardware—that is, the process either (1) is tied in a substantial way to a particular machine or apparatus, or (2) transforms an article into a different state or thing.

☐ The same element isn't recited more than once in any claim unless the second and later recitations use "said" before the element.

☐ You've included a set of claims (one independent and several dependent) with means-plus-function clauses and a set without means-plus-function clauses.

☐ Each independent claim has a set of several dependent claims to provide backup.

☐ Every possible novel or significant feature of the invention is recited in the claims to (hopefully) provide some claims that will not have to be canceled or narrowed.

☐ At least one dependent claim has as many elements or parts of the inventive apparatus as possible, providing a larger base for infringement claims and greater damages.

☐ Method limitations and apparatus limitations aren't used together in any single claim or in any *Markush* group.

272 | PATENT IT YOURSELF

start claims on new page

Printout should have minimum 1.5 line spacing (4 lines/inch) but is shown with denser spacing since this example is shown on a reduced scale.

Patent Application of Lou W. Koppe for "Paper-Laminated
Pliable Closure for Flexible Bags" continued
Page 10

first independent claim

CLAIMS: I claim:

Number of each independent claim is bold

1. In a bag closure of the type comprising a flat body of material having a lead-in notch on one edge thereof and a gripping aperture adjacent to and communicating with said notch, the improvement wherein said bag closure has a layer of paper laminated on one of its sides.

Skip a line between claims— omitted here to conserve space.

2. The bag closure of claim 1 wherein said body of material is composed of polyethyleneterephthalate.

3. The bag closure of claim 1 wherein said body is elongated and has a longitudinal groove which is on said one side of said body and extends the full length of said one side, from said gripping aperture to the opposite edge.

optional indent for dependent claims

4. The bag closure of claim 3 wherein said groove is formed into and along the full length of said lamination.

5. The bag closure of claim 1 wherein said body is elongated and has a longitudinal groove which is on the side of said body opposite to said one side thereof and extends the full length of said one side, from said gripping aperture to the opposite edge.

6. The bag closure of claim 1 wherein said body is elongated and has two longitudinal grooves which are on opposite sides of said body and extend the full lengths of said sides, from said gripping aperture to the opposite edge.

7. The bag closure of claim 6 wherein the groove on said one side of said body is formed into and along the full length of said lamination.

8. The bag closure of claim 1 wherein said body has a paper lamination on both of said sides.

9. The bag closure of claim 8 wherein a groove is on one side of said body and extends the full length of said one side, from said gripping aperture to the opposite edge.

10. The bag closure of claim 8 wherein two grooves, on opposite sides of said body, extend the full lengths of said sides, from said gripping aperture to the opposite edge.

Fig. 9A—Claims of Sample Patent Application

Patent Application of Lou W. Koppe for "Paper-Laminated
Pliable Closure for Flexible Bags" continued
Page 11

11. The bag closure of claim 10 wherein said grooves are rolled into and along the full lengths of said laminations, respectively.

12. The bag closure of claim 1 wherein said paper lamination is colored.

13. The bag closure of claim 1 wherein said body is elongated and has a longitudinal through-hole.

14. A bag closure of the type comprising a flat body of material having a lead-in notch on one edge thereof, a gripping aperture adjacent to and communicating with said notch, characterized in that one of its sides has a layer of paper laminated thereon.

15. The bag closure of claim 14 wherein said body of material is composed of polyethyleneterephthalate.

16. The bag closure of claim 14 wherein said body is elongated and has a longitudinal groove on said one side of said body and which extends the full length of said one side, from said gripping aperture to the opposite edge.

17. The bag closure of claim 14 wherein said body is elongated and has a longitudinal groove which is on the side of said body opposite to said one side thereof and extends the full length of said one side, from said gripping aperture to the opposite edge.

18. The bag closure of claim 14 wherein said body is elongated and has two longitudinal grooves which are on opposite sides of said body and extend the full lengths of said sides, from said gripping aperture to the opposite edge.

19. The bag closure of claim 14 wherein said body has a paper lamination on both of said sides.

20. The bag closure of claim 19 wherein a groove is on one side of said body and extends the full length of said one side, from said gripping aperture to the opposite edge.

21. The bag closure of claim 19 wherein two grooves, on opposite sides of said body, extend the full lengths of said sides, from said gripping aperture to the opposite edge.

Fig. 9A—Claims of Sample Patent Application (continued)

Patent Application of Lou W. Koppe for "Paper-Laminated
Pliable Closure for Flexible Bags" continued
Page 12

22. The bag closure of claim 14 wherein said paper lamination is colored.

23. The bag closure of claim 14 wherein said body is elongated and has a longitudinal through-hole.

24. A method of closing a plastic bag, comprising:

   (a) providing a bag closure of the type comprising a flat body of material having a lead-in notch on one edge thereof, a gripping aperture adjacent to and communicating with said notch, and a layer of paper laminated on one of its sides,

   (b) providing a plastic bag and inserting contents into said plastic bag,

   (c) twisting said plastic bag so that it forms a neck portion to hold said contents from falling out of said plastic bag,

   (d) inserting said bag closure onto said neck portion of said plastic bag so that said neck portion of said plastic bag passes said lead-in notch and into said gripping aperture,

   whereby said bag closure can be easily marked to identify and/or price said contents in said plastic bag.

25. The method of claim 24 wherein said flat body of material is composed of polyethyleneterephthalate.

26. The method of claim 24 wherein said layer of paper is colored.

Fig. 9A—Claims of Sample Patent Application (continued)

CHAPTER

10

Finalizing and Filing Your Application

A. The Drawings	277
1. General Considerations	277
2. PTO Rules for Drawings	277
3. Doing Your Own Drawings	279
4. Making Drawings Manually	284
5. Drawing With a Computer	284
6. Photography	289
7. Consider Using a Professional Patent Draftsperson	289
B. Finalizing Your Specification for Paper Filing	289
1. Conduct a Prefiling Review	289
2. Typing and Filing Application on U.S. Letter-Size Paper	290
3. Typing and Filing Application on A4 Paper	290
4. Name All True Inventors and Only True Inventors	291
5. The Essential and Optional Parts of Your Application	291
6. Completing the Patent Application Declaration	292
7. Complete the Transmittal Letter and Fee Transmittal, Payment, and Postcard	298
8. Maintain an Orderly File	307
9. Assembly and Mailing of Your Application—Final Checklist	307
10. Using Priority Mail Express to Get an Instant Filing Date	307
11. Receipt That Application Was Received in PTO	309
C. Finalizing Your Specification for Patent Center Filing	309
D. File the Information Disclosure Statement Within Three Months	314
E. Assignments	320
F. Petitions to Make Special—Getting Your Application Examined Faster	322
1. Simple PTMS Filings Based on Health, Age, Environment, Energy, or Terrorism	322
2. The Accelerated Examination Program	324
3. Patent Prosecution Highway—Expedited Examination of Applications Filed From Abroad	326
4. Request for Prioritized Examination	326
G. Filing a Design Patent Application	328
H. Summary	330

Inventor's Commandment 16

Before signing any document, whether in the patent field or elsewhere, read it carefully and be sure you understand and fully agree to its terms. After signing, obtain and save an identical copy of what you signed.

Inventor's Commandment 17

Avoid Fraud on the PTO: In addition to making a full disclosure of your invention in your patent application, promptly tell the PTO, in an Information Disclosure Statement, about any pertinent "prior art" or other material facts concerning your invention of which you are aware or of which you become aware.

Inventor's Commandment 18

You can and should web-file all papers to the PTO to avoid loss in the mail. When you web-file, be sure all blanks on all forms are completed, all forms and documents are signed, a Credit Card Payment Form is completed or included, if needed, all pages are present, and the document is timely sent. If you do mail any papers, follow the admonitions for web-filing (you may mail a check or a credit card payment form) and always include a receipt postcard addressed to you with all of the paper(s) listed on the back of the card.

Inventor's Commandment 19

Orderly File: Prepare and maintain file folders for (1) Official Papers and (2) Correspondence. Include a copy of every paper you send to or receive from the PTO in the Official Papers file. Include a copy of every relevant paper you send to or receive from anyone other than the PTO in the Correspondence file. Write the date received on every incoming paper, and date and make sure your name, signature, address, and phone number is on every outgoing paper.

Now that you've drafted your patent application, it's time to put it in final form. Since the PTO places great emphasis on thoroughness, this chapter is, accordingly, filled with many picky details. In the event you want to rebel and simply pass over those requirements that are inconvenient, remember that the PTO has many rules with which you must comply. In addition, your patent examiner has discretion to approve or reject your application. An application that fully meets the requirements and standards of the PTO will have much smoother sailing than one that doesn't. If you fail to comply with certain rules—for example, you forget to enclose a check—the PTO will impose substantial monetary penalties.

Fortunately, while you must pay attention to detail, meeting the PTO's requirements and standards is relatively easy if you've followed our suggestions in the previous chapters. Because you've reviewed a number of patents in the same field as your own (Chapter 6), you'll be familiar with the standards for writing the specification and claims. Because you've prepared preliminary drawings in basic conformance with the rules for final drawings (Chapter 8), putting them in final form will not involve great difficulty. Because you've analyzed all relevant prior art known to you and can distinguish it from your invention (Chapter 9), you are in a good position to follow through with your application to a successful completion.

Electronic Filing Note: The PTO has an electronic filing system called Patent Center that enables electronic patent application filing. The PTO charges a $350 filing fee for utility regular patent application (RPA) filings by a "small entity" unless the filing is made using Patent Center. It may take you several extra hours to learn and use the Patent Center system. You must prepare the application as if you were going to file by mail (except that you can eliminate a few forms), convert all papers (except the specification) into PDF files, and fill out various forms online. However, it may be worth your time to become a registered eFiler with the PTO, which will require additional steps. Since you already have to do a lot of learning to file a patent application, the extra time to learn and use Patent Center may discourage you, but the lower cost and numerous advantages of electronic filing make it well worth using.

A. The Drawings

1. General Considerations

When you file your application, the PTO's Office of Patent Application Processing ("OPAP") will review your drawings to determine whether they are "readable and reproducible for publication purposes." If your drawings are not acceptable, the OPAP will send you a Notice specifying the deficiencies and setting a deadline by which you must submit replacement drawings. If the OPAP accepts your drawings, your Examiner may still raise objections in an Office Action, and require that you submit replacement drawings as part of your response to the Office Action. You cannot put off responding to the requirement for replacement figures.

You should be able to avoid these pitfalls by preparing your drawings correctly in the first instance.

Drawings can be filed in either:

- the U.S. letter size (8½" × 11"), or
- the A4 international size (210 mm × 297 mm or 8¼" × 11¹¹/₁₆").

If you want to file abroad, you'll have to prepare formal drawings on A4 size paper approximately 11 months after filing.

As far as the choice of the U.S. or international sizes is concerned, if you have ink drawings and have any serious thoughts about filing abroad, it's better to use the international (A4) size, since you can make good photocopies, file these for your U.S. application, and later use the originals (or another good set of copies) for the international application. (We discuss foreign filing in Chapter 12.) If you do make paper drawings in the U.S. size and later decide to foreign file, you can still make A4 copies by using a scanner, photocopier, or a patent drawing service (about $20 to $50 a sheet).

If color is an absolutely essential part of the invention, color photos or color drawings may also be used. However, be aware that color drawings are not acceptable when filing an "international application" under the Patent Cooperation Treaty, or PCT. (More on the PCT in Chapter 12.) File three sets of color photos or drawings in one of the two permitted sizes with:

1. a petition explaining why color is necessary; use the format of the petition of Fig. 10U ("Petition to Make Special"; Form 10-9, downloadable via this book's online companion page; see Appendix 7 for details) but change the title. For example, write "Petition Explaining Why Color Is Necessary" and change the body of the form to provide an explanation

2. the petition fee, and

3. a statement in the specification as the first paragraph of the brief description of the drawings reading as follows: "The patent or application contains at least one drawing executed in color. Copies of the patent or patent application publication with color drawing(s) will be provided by the Office upon request and payment of necessary fee."

If filing by Patent Center, only one set of color photos or drawings is required. However, the set must be uploaded as file type "Drawings – other than black and white line drawings" with document code "DRW. NONBW."

Black and white photos can no longer be used for patent drawings, unless necessary to illustrate the invention; for example, to show a photomicrograph of a composite material. File one set of black and white photos in one of the two permitted sizes on double-weight photographic paper or mounted on Bristol board. You must also file a petition explaining why black and white photos are necessary. No fee is needed.

All photos must be of sufficient quality that all details can be reproduced in the printed patent and the photos must illustrate all features of the invention, just as ink or CAD drawings must do.

2. PTO Rules for Drawings

The PTO has a number of rules for preparing drawings, which are recorded in 37 CFR 1.84. After arriving at the PTO, whether with your application or after allowance, your drawings are inspected by the PTO's drawing inspectors. If they find that any of your drawings

UNITED STATES PATENT AND TRADEMARK OFFICE

UNITED STATES DEPARTMENT OF COMMERCE
United States Patent and Trademark Office
Address: COMMISSIONER FOR PATENTS
P.O. Box 1450
Alexandria, Virginia 22313-1450
www.uspto.gov

APPLICATION NUMBER	FILING OR 371(C) DATE	FIRST NAMED APPLICANT	ATTY. DOCKET NO./TITLE
09/123,456	02/29/2024	Ann Inventor	7890/1001

CONFIRMATION NO. 2714

FORMALITIES LETTER

Ann Inventor
128 Innovation Road
Washington, MA 09999

Date Mailed:
03/19/2024

NOTICE TO FILE CORRECTED APPLICATION PAPERS

Filing Date Granted

An application number and filing date have been accorded to this application. The application is informal since it does not comply with the regulations for the reason(s) indicated below. Applicant is given TWO MONTHS from the date of this Notice within which to correct the informalities indicated below. Extensions of time may be obtained by filing a petition accompanied by the extension fee under the provisions of 37 CFR 1.136(a).

The required item(s) identified below must be timely submitted to avoid abandonment:

- Replacement drawings in compliance with 37 CFR 1.84 and 37 CFR 1.121(d) are required. The drawings submitted are not acceptable because:
  - Numbers, letters, and reference characters on the drawings must measure at least 0.32 cm (1/8 inch) in height. See Figure(s) all.

Applicant is cautioned that correction of the above items may cause the specification and drawings page count to exceed 100 pages. If the specification and drawings exceed 100 pages, applicant will need to submit the required application size fee.

Fig. 10A—Draftsperson's Drawing Objection Sheet

are informal or in violation of any of the above rules, they will fill out and insert a drawing objection sheet in your file. A copy of this (shown in Fig. 10A) will be sent to you before or with your first Office Action or after allowance. The OPAP will require corrected drawings if: the lines are too light to be adequately reproduced; the drawings contain illegible text, excessive text, or text not in English; the drawings are missing a lead line between a reference number and the feature indicated by that reference number; the pages are not on the correct size of paper or have incorrect margins, have more than one figure and are not distinguished with proper labeling; a photograph is included where another figure would suffice; or color drawings or photographs are included without the required petition.

Other frequently encountered defects are:
- Lines are pale.
- Paper is poor.
- Numerals are poor.
- Lines are rough, blurred, or matrixy (appearing in zig-zag).
- Drawing includes visible copier marks.
- Shade lines are required.
- Figures must be numbered.
- Heading space is required.
- Figures must not be connected.
- Crisscross or double line-hatching is objectionable.
- Arrowheads are used on lead lines for individual parts.
- Parts in section must be hatched.
- Solid black is objectionable (in design patent applications).
- Figure legends are placed incorrectly (for example, inside figure or vertically when drawing is horizontal).
- Drawing has mounted photographs.
- Drawing contains extraneous matter.
- Paper is undersized or oversized.
- Margins are too small.
- Lettering is too small.
- The sheets contain wrinkles, tears, or folds.
- Both sides of the sheet are used.
- Sheets contain broken lines to illustrate regular parts of the invention.
- Sheets contain alterations, interlineations, or overwritings.
- Sheets contain unclear representations.
- Sheets contain figures on separate sheets that can't be assembled without concealing parts.
- Sheets contain reference numerals that aren't mentioned in the specification.
- Sheets contain the same reference numeral to designate different parts.
- Figures aren't separately numbered.

3. Doing Your Own Drawings

Many inventors choose to prepare their own patent applications instead of hiring a patent attorney or agent to do it for them. However, these same inventors frequently conclude that preparing the drawings is beyond their ability, and turn the job over to a professional draftsperson. This can be costly. The typical draftsperson charges $75 to $150 per sheet of original patent drawings (each sheet may contain several figures or separate drawings). Since most patent applications have between two to ten sheets of drawings, an inventor can sometimes pay up to $1,500 for drawings.

Fortunately, as with the application itself, you can take a self-help approach to patent drawings. To be sure, you'll need to follow some PTO rules, and a certain learning curve is involved, but the result will not only save you a lot of money over many patent applications:
- You will be able to better prepare promotional brochures for marketing your invention to prospective manufacturers or customers.
- You will be able to render your invention more accurately than a hired professional might, because you know your invention best. By doing your own drawings, you don't have to spend time familiarizing someone else with your invention, or sending the drawings back and forth for corrections.
- You will have the satisfaction of properly completing the entire patent application by yourself—an impressive accomplishment for an inventor.

There are two methods for making patent drawings: pen and ruler, and computer-aided drafting (CAD). (You cannot use photos unless necessary to illustrate an invention that involves fine details.)

You can file your application with either informal or formal drawings. If you are submitting "informal" drawings, the copies need not be perfectly clean and neat, but if you choose the formal route, the copies must be very clean and neat, and all lines must be sharp and black. You don't have to notify the PTO which type of drawing you're filing; they'll notify you if the drawings are inadequate. (The typed specification sheets must have different margins—see below.)

Even if you file informal drawings, you must include everything necessary in your drawings, since you won't be able to add any "new matter" (any new technical information that is not present in your original sketches) after you file. Be sure to study the drawings of the patents uncovered in your patentability search to get an idea of what's customarily done for your type of invention, and to better understand the PTO rules.

U.S. Letter Size
(8.5" × 11" or 216mm × 279mm)

Notes:

Metric-to-inch conversion numbers are not exact but are copied from Rule 84(f) & (g). In case of doubt, always use a wider margin (smaller sight).

Margin lines should not be used but are shown as broken lines to indicate the margin and "sight" sizes. Visible crosshairs (targets) should be put in either pair of opposite corners and should be about 1.5 cm (0.5") long. (The crosshairs are shown on these two sheets in the lower left and upper right corners.)

A4 Size
(8¼" × 11¹¹⁄₁₆" or 210mm × 297mm)

Layout for Landscape Orientation
(Not Preferred)

Fig. 10B—The Two Permitted Drawing Sizes

Summary of PTO Drawing Rules

The PTO's rules for drawings are found in 37 CFR 1.81–1.85.

1. **Need for drawings.** One or more drawings must be filed whenever necessary to understand the invention.

2. **Flowcharts.** Flowcharts should also be included whenever useful for an understanding of the invention.

3. **Must show features claimed.** The drawings must show every feature recited in the claims.

4. **Conventional features.** Conventional features that are not essential for an understanding of the invention, but are mentioned in the description and claims, can be shown by a graphical drawing symbol or a labeled rectangular box. For example, a motor can be shown by an encircled "M," and a CPU in a computer can be shown by a rectangle labeled "CPU."

5. **Improvements.** When your invention consists of an improvement in an old machine, the drawing should show the improved portion disconnected from the old structure with only so much of the old structure as is necessary to show how your improvement fits in. For example, if you've invented a new taillight for a bicycle, show the bicycle itself without the new taillight (without detail) in one figure labeled as "prior art." Then show just the portion of the bike where the taillight is mounted in detail in another figure, together with details of the mounting hardware.

6. **Paper.** The filed drawings (xerographic copies if filing in paper) should be on paper that is flexible, strong, white, smooth, nonshiny, and durable. Ordinary 20-pound bond is acceptable but a heavier weight paper is more desirable. You should do the originals on Mylar film, vellum, or hard, rather than soft, Bristol board; this is available in most good art supply stores. Strathmore Paper Co. makes excellent patent drawing boards in both U.S. and A4 sizes, but it may be more economical to buy larger sheets of hard Bristol board and cut them to the proper size. If you're using CAD but not filing by Patent Center, do the originals on regular bond paper and, since additional originals are so easy to make, send the originals to the PTO. (Keep your digital copy and a backup of your drawing file!) If filing by Patent Center and you've made the drawings on paper, scan the drawings to PDF. If you've made computer drawings, convert the files to PDF directly and file the PDFs online, via Patent Center.

7. **Lines.** The main requirement for all drawings is that all lines must be crisp and perfectly black. For paper copies, a good photocopy on good quality bond paper is usually used and the lines should be crisp and sharp. A good xerographic copy from a dark-penciled original will be accepted. Jagged slant lines from a dot matrix printer or bitmapped drawing program are forbidden for formal drawings. For Patent Center filers, the same sharp, black lines are required on PDF versions.
   Lines the PTO recognizes on drawings.
   normal lines. Use a solid thin line (_____) to show regular parts and a thick solid line (▬▬▬) to show a shadowed edge—see Rule 14—or hatching a cross-section.
   Hidden lines. This is a dashed line (– – – –) to show a part behind another part—see Fig. 8C.
   Projection lines. This is composed of alternating long dashes and dots (— • — • —) and is used to connect exploded parts—see Fig. 8D.
   Phantom lines. Similar to a projection line, but that uses two dots instead of one (— • • — • •); this is used to show an alternate position of a movable part, or on an adjacent structure that is not part of the invention.

8. **White pigment.** Some use of white pigment (for example, White Out™, Liquid Paper™) to cover lines is acceptable, provided all lines are sharp and black.

9. **Uniform size.** All drawing sheets in an application must be exactly sized in the same U.S. letter or A4 size. Fig. 10B shows these two sizes.

10. **Invisible margins.** The margins must not contain any lines or writing; all writing and lines must be in the remaining "sight" (drawing area) on the sheet. Margin border lines are forbidden, but crosshairs (about 1 cm long) should be drawn over two diagonally opposite margin corners.

11. **No holes.** The drawing sheets should not contain any holes.

12. **Instrument work.** All lines must be made with drafting tools or a CAD computer program. Copies made by a laser printer must be very dense, sharp, uniformly thick, and black. Fine or crowded lines must be avoided. Solid black areas are not permitted. Freehand work must be avoided unless unavoidable.

Summary of PTO Drawing Rules (continued)

13. **Hatching.** Parts in section must be filled with slanted parallel lines (hatching) that are spaced apart sufficiently so that they can be distinguished without difficulty.

14. **Shading.** Objects can be shaded with surface and edge shadings so that the light appears to come from the upper left at a 45-degree angle. Thus the shade sides of all objects (the right and bottom) should be done with heavier lines. Surface shading should be open. On perspective views, the closest edges should be made heavier. Edge and surface shading is mandatory in design patent applications, and optional in utility patents.

15. **Scale.** The scale should be large enough to show the mechanism without crowding when the drawing is reduced to two-thirds of its original size for reproduction. Detailed parts should be shown on a larger scale, and spread out over two or more sheets if necessary, to accomplish this, but the number of sheets should not be more than necessary.

16. **Figures.** The different views should be consecutively numbered figures; for example, "Fig. 1A," "Fig. 1B," and "Fig. 2." Each figure should be separate and unconnected with any other figure. If possible, you should number the figures consecutively on consecutive sheets. However, if you want to arrange the figures in nonconsecutive order to use space efficiently, that's okay, albeit less desirable.

17. **Reference numerals and lead lines.** Numbers must be plain, legible, carefully formed, and not encircled. They should be at least ⅛" high (12-point font should suffice). When parts are complex, they should not be placed so close that comprehension suffers. They should not cross or mingle with other lines. When grouped around a part, they should be placed around the part and connected by lead lines to the elements to which they refer. They should not be placed on hatched or shaded surfaces unless absolutely necessary; if then, they should be underlined and placed in a blank space in the hatching or shading. (Numerals are preferred to letters.) Arrowheads should not be used on lead lines, but if a numeral refers to an entire assembly or group of connected elements, its lead line can have an arrowhead, or it can be underlined to distinguish it from the lead lines of numerals that refer to a single part.

18. **No duplication of reference numerals.** The same part in different figures must always be designated by the same reference numeral. Conversely, the same reference numeral must never be used to designate different parts. Numbers with primes and letter suffixes are considered different numbers.

19. **Graphic symbols.** These can be used for conventional parts, but must be defined in the specification. For instance, if you use an encircled "M" for a motor, the specification should say, for example, "A motor, represented in Fig. 2 by an encircled 'M.'" Conventional symbols, such as those approved by the IEEE, ASA, and so on, or from any standards or symbols book, can be used. Arrows should be used to show direction of movement, where necessary.

20. **Descriptive matter.** The rules state that descriptive matter on the drawings is not permitted. We vehemently oppose this rule, since the use of descriptive matter on drawings makes them far more meaningful, and since textbooks, magazine articles, and so on, all use drawings with ample descriptive matter. Just put the figure number and nothing else under each figure—for example, "Fig. 1," and not "Fig. 1 —Apparatus in Ready State." If a drawing depicts prior art, the figure number should include the words "prior art" in parentheses [that is, "Fig. 1 (prior art)"].

    The Rules permit legends to be used within rectangular boxes, on flowcharts, piping (plumbing) lines, or wherever else additional clarity is highly desirable. If used, the descriptive matter lettering should be as large as, or larger than, the reference numerals.

21. **Views.** The drawings should have as many views (figures) as are necessary to show the invention. The views may be plan, sectional, exploded, elevational, or perspective; detailed larger-scale views of specific elements should be employed. Engineering views (such as front, side, bottom, or back) should not normally be used if perspective views can adequately illustrate the invention. If exploded views are used, the separated parts of the same figure must be embraced by a bracket. (See Fig. 8D.)

    A large machine or schematic or flowchart can be extended over several sheets, but the views should be arranged to be easily understandable and so that the

Summary of PTO Drawing Rules (continued)

sheets can be assembled adjacent to each other to show the entire machine. Never place one figure within another unless the view is the only one on the sheet.

22. **Sectional and enlarged views.** The plane upon which a sectional view is taken should be illustrated in the general view by a broken line, the ends of which should be designated by numerals corresponding to the figure number of the sectional view with arrows indicating the direction in which the sectional view is taken. For example, suppose your Fig. 1 shows a left-side front view of your carburetor and Fig. 2 shows a cross-sectional front of the back half of the carburetor on a plane vertically bisecting the carburetor into front and back halves. In this case, Fig. 1 should contain a broken vertical line spaced halfway from left to right with arrows pointing to the right at the top and bottom of this line; the arrows should each be labeled "2" to indicate the section is shown in Fig. 2. To show an area of a main figure in an enlarged view, encircle the area in the main figure and indicate the circled area with the number of the figure of the enlarged view—that is, if your main figure is Fig. 1 and the enlarged view is to be Fig. 1A, designate the circled area of Fig. 1 with a lead line numbered "1A."

23. **Moving parts.** To show two positions of a movable part, show its main position in full lines and its secondary position in phantom lines, provided this can be done clearly. If not, use a separate view for the secondary position.

24. **Modifications.** Show modifications in separate figures, not in broken lines.

25. **No construction lines.** Construction lines, center lines, and projection lines connecting separate figures are forbidden.

26. **Position of sheet.** All views (figures) on a sheet must have the same orientation, preferably so that they can be read with the sheet upright (that is, in portrait orientation with its short side at the top) so the examiner won't have to turn the sheets or the file to read the drawing. However, if views longer than the width of the sheet are necessary for the clearest illustration of the invention, the views may be drawn with the sheet in the landscape orientation, with the top margin on the right-hand side. The orientation of any lettering on a sheet must conform with the orientation of the sheet, except that the sheet number and number of sheets separated by a slash (1/2) must always be at the top. (See Fig. 10B.)

27. **OG figure.** One figure should be a comprehensive view of the invention for inclusion in the *Official Gazette*, a weekly publication of the PTO that shows the main claim and drawing figure of every patent issued that week.

28. **No extraneous matter.** No extraneous matter—that is, matter that is not part of the claimed invention or its supporting or related structures—is permitted on the drawings. However, you can (and should) place additional matter, such as a hand on a special pistol grip, if necessary to show use or an advantage of the invention. Also, you should put the sheet number and total number of sheets ("1/4," "2/4," and so on) below the top margin, in centered numerals that are larger than the regular reference numerals. If the center space is occupied, the sheet number should be placed to the right.

29. **No wrinkled sheets.** If you're filing by mail, the sheets should be sent to the PTO with adequate protection so that they will arrive without wrinkles or tears. You should send the sheets flat, between two pieces of corrugated cardboard within a large envelope, but they can also be rolled and sent in a mailing tube, provided they don't wrinkle. Never fold patent drawing sheets or typed sheets of the specification.

30. **Phantom lines.** Parts that are hidden, but that you want to show; for example, the inside of a computer, should be shown in phantom lines—that is, broken lines. Reference numeral lead lines that refer to phantom parts should also be broken, in accordance with standard drafting practice. Broken lines must never be used to designate a part of the actual invention, unless to illustrate a phantom part or a moved position of a part.

31. **Identification on back.** So that the PTO can identify and utilize the drawings in case they get separated from the file, you should include the title of the invention, and the first inventor's name and telephone number on the back of each sheet, at least 1 cm down from the top. Use a label or sticker if necessary to prevent this information from showing through to the front.

Make your drawings as comprehensive and meaningful as possible, almost to the point that most people can fully understand the invention by looking at the drawings alone. Most people can understand an invention far more readily from drawings because they are a lower level of abstraction than text.

For example, in electronic schematics, try to arrange the parts so that:

- the signal progresses from left to right
- the input sources and output loads are clearly indicated
- transistor states are indicated (that is, NNC = normally nonconductive; NC = normally conductive)
- signal waveforms are shown, and
- circuits are labeled by function (for example, "Schmitt Trigger").

In chemical and computer cases, we suggest you use a flowchart, if possible. In mechanical cases, we suggest you use exploded views, perspective views from several directions, and simplified perspective "action" views, showing the apparatus in operation and clearly illustrating its function. In other words, do the drawings so completely that they "speak" to their reader.

4. Making Drawings Manually

The oldest way of making patent drawings is manually, with pen, ruler, and other instruments. Pen and ruler allow little room for mistakes, because, except for very small marks, it is very difficult to correct misplaced ink lines. Few professional patent draftspersons still make drawings this way.

The necessary tools include pencils for preliminary sketches, ink drafting pens (also known as "technical pens") for drawing ink lines, straight rules for drawing straight lines, triangles for drawing angled lines, templates for drawing certain standard shapes, French curves for drawing curves, an optional drafting table, and Mylar (best) or Vellum film or Bristol board. Pen and ruler may be used to make patent drawings in the following ways:

a. Drawing From Scratch

You can draw an object by visualizing in detail what it should look like, carefully sketching that image on the film or board with a pencil, correcting it until it looks about right, and finally, inking over the pencil lines. The sketch of a telephone is illustrated in Fig. 10C. You must have some basic drawing skills to draw from scratch.

b. Tracing

Tracing is much easier than drawing from scratch. An obvious method is to trace a photograph of an object that you wish to draw, as shown in Fig. 10D. You can also trace an actual, three-dimensional object by positioning a transparent drawing sheet on a transparent sheet of glass or acrylic, as shown in Fig. 10E, looking at the object through the glass, tracing the lines of the object on the film, and photocopying the tracing onto a sheet of paper. Tracing requires very little skill other than a steady hand.

c. Drawing to Scale

You can also draw by scaling—that is, measuring and then reducing or enlarging—the dimensions of an actual object to fit on a sheet of paper, and drawing all the lines with the scaled dimensions. For example, if an object has a height of 50 cm and a width of 30 cm, you can reduce those dimensions by 50%, so that you would draw it with a height of 25 cm and a width of 15 cm to fit on the paper, as shown in Fig. 10F. All other dimensions of the object are scaled accordingly for the drawing. Making a drawing that looks right is easier by drawing to scale than by drawing based on only a mental image.

After making your ink drawings on film or Bristol board, make good photocopies on good-quality 20- or 24-pound bond paper for submission to the PTO. Keep the originals in case you have to make changes later.

5. Drawing With a Computer

CAD (computer-aided drafting or design) allows you to produce accurate drawings even if you might have little or no artistic ability. In fact, no traditional drawing skills are needed at all. Furthermore, CAD enables you to correct mistakes as easily as a word processing program lets you edit a document. Even if you discover a mistake after you've printed a drawing, you can easily correct the mistake and print a new copy.

Fig. 10C—Sketching Techniques

Fig. 10D—Tracing a Photo

Fig. 10E—Tracing Large Object on Long Table

Fig. 10F—Drawing to Scale

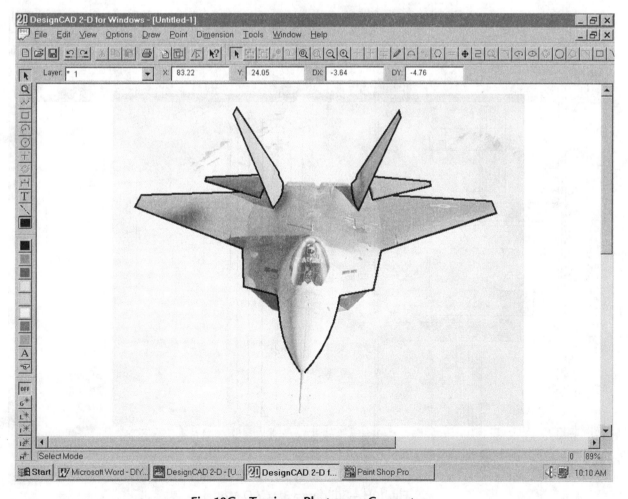

Fig. 10G—Tracing a Photo on a Computer

Some CAD programs are available online at no cost. For example, the Draw utility in the *LibreOffice* suite (www.libreoffice.org) is useful for simple drawings, can export your drawings directly to a PDF document, and even has some 3D capabilities.

a. Tracing

Using a scanner, you can scan a photograph of an object, import the scanned image into a CAD program, and trace it easily, as shown in Fig. 10G, a traced photo of an aircraft (the black outlines are the tracing lines, which may be difficult to see in a black-and-white book). If you have a digital or smartphone camera, you can take a photograph of the object and download or otherwise preserve the image directly onto your device or computer without having to print and scan the photograph. After that, tracing the image is very easy, since you use a mouse or stylus and tablet.

Available photo editing software may also be able to trace a photograph.

b. Drawing From Scratch

A 3D (three-dimensional) CAD program enables you to construct an accurate, 3D representation of your invention within the computer, such as the pipe fitting shown in Fig. 10H. A 3D model is typically built by using and modifying basic geometric building blocks, such as boxes, cylinders, planes, and custom-defined shapes. You may create each part with specific dimensions, or you may simply draw a shape that looks about right. You can easily rotate the finished model to see it from any angle. You can also easily zoom in or out to adjust the viewing distance. Once you are satisfied with the view, you can print it as a line drawing (a drawing of dark lines on a light background).

Fig. 10H—Building a 3D CAD Model

6. Photography

While photographs may no longer be submitted as patent drawings (except in rare cases), they may be converted into acceptable line drawings by tracing them, by scanning them, or by using a digital camera. Their images may be copied directly into and manipulated and cleaned up with a CAD program. Although photography spares you from having any drawing skills, you must have some photographic skills to take clear pictures, including a basic understanding of lighting and exposure. To take an accurate photograph, you will need a high-resolution camera with a selectable aperture, zoom and macro (close-up) lenses, and a tripod.

> ⓘ CAUTION
>
> **Although the PTO has not published anything official, current practice indicates that the PTO may not be rigidly enforcing its drawing rules.** As a result some patents are issuing with sloppy drawings. Still, you should file well-executed drawings and avoid making a negative impression on your examiner or on any judge who may have to rule on your patent.

7. Consider Using a Professional Patent Draftsperson

If you don't feel competent to do your own drawings, you'll want to hire someone to do them for you. You can locate people who specialize in preparing patent drawings by searching the internet. While expensive (about $30 to $50 per hour, or $75 to $150 per sheet), these people should do the job correctly the first time with CAD. Also, you can use a "starving artist" who's proficient in the medium to be used (CAD or India ink), and reads and understands the rules thoroughly.

If you use a professional, take care to avoid inadvertently making a public disclosure of your drawings—have the draftsperson sign a Consultant's Work Agreement—Form 4-3; see Appendix 7. A competent patent draftsperson should understand the public disclosure rule and be willing to sign this Agreement (or a standard one of their own). Under no circumstances should you hire any drafter who will not sign a confidentiality agreement.

You should consider including a copy of your specification under the NDA, to assist the drafter's understanding of your invention. Doing so may speed up the drafting process by reducing back-and-forth communication.

B. Finalizing Your Specification for Paper Filing

Filing by Patent Center requires some learning, but the advantages of online filing are many, including:

- the ability to file from anywhere in the world that has web access, with a substantially cheaper filing fee
- no need to print out the specification and make file copies
- no need to go to the post office to send the application via Priority Mail Express (and pay the Priority Mail Express fee)
- no need to include a receipt postcard
- no need for a fee transmittal form, credit card payment form, or check
- no need to wait several weeks to get a receipt postcard back to learn whether the application was filed okay, and
- no risk of loss in the mail.

Note that if you file your application on paper, the PTO will still convert it to electronic format in its data processing system anyway because they are virtually a no-paper office. In any case, read the following sections on paper filing because these contain certain requirements, and will give you more background and maybe a willingness to tackle electronic filing.

1. Conduct a Prefiling Review

Before putting them in final form, you (and perhaps a trusted acquaintance of yours sworn to secrecy) should reread your specification, claims, and abstract, to make sure your writing is clear, complete, understandable, and free of grammatical and spelling errors. Another alternative is to prepare the application, put it down for the day, and review the application the following day for mistakes. Make sure that the main substantive requirements (as discussed in Chapters 8 and 9) are satisfied.

Try to do a perfect job with your patent application, because doing so will make a better impression on the examiner and anyone else who reads it, such as a judge or potential licensee. Once the application is filed, you are not allowed to add any new matter. Remember that the examiner's job is to seize upon any flaws or faults in the application. The less opportunity you give your examiner to find objections, the smoother the sailing of your application will be in the PTO. And keep in mind the words of Pearl S. Buck: "The secret of joy in work is contained in one word—excellence. To know how to do something well is to enjoy it."

The title should go on the first page. You must start your claims and abstract on new pages, with the abstract on the last sheet, after the claims. Don't submit an application on easily erasable paper, or on paper that has white pigment covering any typewritten lines, since these are not considered permanent, unaltered records. If you're not a good typist, and you don't have a word processing program, one solution is to type your application on easily erasable paper or regular paper, cover the errors with white pigment (or erase them), type in the corrections, and then make bond paper photocopies of your typewritten original for submission to the PTO.

If, after putting your specification in final form, you find you must make a few minor changes (one or two words in a few places), it's okay to do so, provided you make these changes neatly in ink—in handwriting—and date and initial the margin adjacent to each change *before* you sign the Patent Application Declaration.

As with your drawings, you must format your specification, claims, and abstract on either U.S. or A4-size paper. All sheets (whether filing on paper or by Patent Center) must be of the same size, free of holes, and have 2.5 cm (1") top, bottom, right, and left margins. Use 1.5 or double spacing and number the sheets at the top or bottom, in the center, and inside the margin. (All correspondence that you send to the PTO at any time should always be 1.5 or double-spaced; never use single spacing and never type on both sides of a sheet.)

2. Typing and Filing Application on U.S. Letter-Size Paper

If you think you may later want to file corresponding foreign applications, one way to minimize work is to type your application on U.S. letter-size paper with proper margins, so that if photocopied onto A4 size paper it will have the proper A4 margins. To do this print out or type the application on letter-size or computer paper (8.5" × 11"). Use a 1" left margin, 6.2" line width, 1" top margin, and a bottom margin of 0.3," so that the last line is almost at the bottom of the page. Save the original for possible later use in making an A4 version for an international application. Alternatively, since modern word processing programs enable easy reformatting, it's easy to reformat a file for an A4 printout. Use a conventional, sans-serif typeface (such as Arial, Calibri, Helvetica, Lucida Sans, or the like, but not serif typefaces such as Garamond, Palatino, or Times New Roman) in at least 12-point type. You should not justify (line up the right margin of) your typing, since unjustified printing (as in this book) is much easier to follow.

3. Typing and Filing Application on A4 Paper

You can type and file your U.S. application on A4 paper (or in an A4-formatted PDF), following the proper requirements for such matters as margins and line spacing (the abstract page). This format is especially useful if you think you may later want to file corresponding foreign applications. A4 paper can be obtained from your local office supply store. Also, you can cut it yourself or have it cut for you. If you cut it yourself, the sheets should be 210 by 297 mm (8¼" × 11¹¹/₁₆") in size, with top margins 2 to 4 cm, left margins of 2.5 to 4 cm, and bottom and right margins of 2 to 3 cm, with sheets numbered consecutively at the top and typed with 1.5 line spacing—that is, four lines per inch or per 2.5 cm. Keep the originals and file an A4 photocopy. If you later file a PCT application, these measurements must be followed to comply with WIPO (and EPO) requirements.

Alternatively, if you have already prepared your application on U.S.-letter-sized paper, you may photocopy it onto A4 sized paper, and it will have the proper A4 margins.

You don't have to file your drawings and your typewritten papers on the same size sheets; the drawings can be on A4 paper and the typewritten pages on U.S.-size paper, or vice versa. However, all drawing sheets must be the same size, as must all typed sheets. Never use both sides of a sheet, either for drawings or for the specification. A neatly typed specification will certainly make a very favorable impression on your examiner. If you can, make your application with a laser printer with larger heading fonts. As mentioned earlier, if you don't own a laser printer, consider using one at a copy center.

Some inventors have prepared their applications to look like patents, complete with narrow, single-spaced columns and cited references. Don't do this; your application should look like the sample in Chapter 8. When it issues the patent, the PTO will print it in two-column format with a list of references cited, your name, and all other data that normally goes on the abstract page.

The PTO suggests that you number all paragraphs (not including headings) of your application as follows: "[0001]," "[0002]," and so on. (Include the brackets; don't use parentheses.) Since any changes must now be done by replacing entire paragraphs, such numbering will facilitate amendments. Fortunately, this is optional.

4. Name All True Inventors and Only True Inventors

In the application and several of its forms, you're required to name the applicants or inventors. For example, the first page of the application lists the names, and Form 10-1 (Patent Application Declaration) must be signed by the inventors (see Figs. 10I (A and B) discussed below).

While anyone can apply for a patent, the named applicant(s) must be the true inventor(s) of the invention. So, if you discover an invention abroad or that your deceased uncle invented, you aren't allowed to apply to patent it in your name. If you've conceived the invention (as defined by the claims) entirely on your own, there are no coinventors. If you've invented it with someone else, both of you should be named as "joint inventors." But be sure that both of you actually are joint inventors. If somebody other than you played a significant role in conceiving the invention, review Chapter 16 for a more detailed discussion on inventorship.

37 CFR 1.45 states that each joint inventor must have contributed something to at least one claim of the application. However, joint inventors need not have worked together or at the same time, their contributions need not be equal, and each need not have contributed to every claim of the application. Under no circumstances should you name your financier, your boss, or anyone else who was not an actual inventor. If you are not a U.S. citizen or are living outside the U.S., your rights are as good as a U.S. citizen-resident. The PTO will correspond with you in any country. If you're filing from abroad, you may bypass U.S. mail delays by filing from and using a U.S. correspondence address or by filing via Patent Center.

5. The Essential and Optional Parts of Your Application

A basic patent application consists of a set of minimal but necessary parts. (The elements marked with an asterisk are not required when using the Patent Center filing system.) However, for the reasons indicated below, you may wish to file additional or optional parts with your application. The following is a list of the minimal and necessary parts and also the additional and optional parts to get you familiar with them before we discuss them in detail later. The PTO has created many forms to help you provide it with all of the necessary and optional parts of your application. These forms are named below, where appropriate. To ensure that you are working with the correct form for each application part, compare the top right corner of the form with the name of the form given below. (The PTO adds additional letters to the beginning of their forms, so what we call Form AIA/15 they call Form PTO/AIA/15.)

a. Minimal and Necessary Parts

- **Utility Patent Application Transmittal (AIA/15).** This tells the PTO what parts you're sending for your patent application. You should use this form as a checklist to ensure that you have included everything.
- **Fee Transmittal (SB/17).** This makes it easy for the PTO to compute and verify your filing fee.
- **Specification, Including Claims, and Abstract.** These parts are discussed in detail in Chapters 8 and 9.
- **Drawings.** These are required if the invention can be illustrated with a drawing.
- **Patent Application Declaration (AIA/01 if also filing an Application Data Sheet, or AIA/08 if not).** This states who the inventors are, that they've read the application, that they will disclose all material information, and that they understand that they can be charged with perjury if they lie on this form. The PTO no longer requires that the Patent Application Declaration (PAD) be filed simultaneously with the application, but we recommend that you submit the PAD at this stage as long as doing so does not delay the filing of the application.
- **Receipt Postcard.** This is stamped by the PTO and returned to you to let you know when your application was filed and its serial number. (Patent Center provides an instant receipt with an automatically assigned serial number.)
- **Credit Card Payment Form (PTO-2038), Check, or Money Order.** This pays your fees to the PTO.

b. Additional and Optional Parts

- **Request for Claim Drafting by Examiner Under MPEP 707.07(j).** This asks the examiner to draft claims for you if your application contains allowable subject matter. List this in the "Other" box of the Transmittal Letter.
- **Application Data Sheet (AIA/14).** This provides data about the application and the inventors. Whether you file on paper or by Patent Center the PTO can extract your data from this form, thereby obviating errors.

- **CD-ROM or CD-R.** Remember to include this if you are submitting a computer program listing too large for the specification.
- **Assignment and Transmittal.** An assignment transfers ownership of your application to another individual or company. Assignments are discussed in Chapter 16.
- **Information Disclosure Statement (SB/08), and Copies of Any Non-U.S. Patent References.** This form cites any prior art of which you are aware, usually from any search that you made. PTO rules require that you supply a list of such prior art within three months after filing or before the first Office Action.
- **Nonpublication Request (NPR) (SB/35).** This instructs the PTO not to publish your application to preserve your trade secret rights. All applications are normally published 18 months after filing unless they're issued before then. By filing the NPR, you are certifying that the invention disclosed in the application has not been—and will not be—the subject of an application filed in another country, or under a multilateral international agreement, that requires publication of applications 18 months after filing. If you are not sure whether you will file a corresponding application in another country, do not make a nonpublication request. If you do make an NPR, and later change your mind and decide to foreign-file the application, you must file a revocation of the NPR within 45 days after the date you foreign-file. A "Request Not to Publish" check box is included on the Application Data Sheet (ADS).

This book provides access to an online companion page with copies of actual PTO forms. For details on accessing these forms, see Appendix 7. The most up-to-date forms may be obtained directly from the PTO at www.uspto.gov/patents/apply/forms.

6. Completing the Patent Application Declaration

Each patent application must include a patent application declaration (PAD), which is a written statement under oath. Although the PTO no longer requires that the PAD be filed simultaneously with the patent application, you must file the PAD before the PTO issues the patent. We strongly recommend that you file the PAD with the application, but only if it is possible to do so without delaying the filing of the application (since such a delay could be fatal to your claim), or as soon as possible after you have filed the application.

Since the number of pages in the PAD is written into the Patent Application Transmittal, we'll discuss the PAD first. A PAD form is provided as Form 10-1A, and a completed example is provided below in Fig. 10I (A, B, and C).

While completing the PAD is a straightforward process, don't treat it lightly. Read and review it very carefully before you sign. If anyone can prove that you signed the declaration knowing that any of its statements were false, your patent can be held invalid. In fact, we've seen so many inventors sign PADs without reading or keeping a copy that we've provided Inventor's Commandment 16 at the beginning of this chapter to advise you to read, understand, make sure you agree with, and keep a copy of all documents you sign.

You should file a PAD signed by each inventor along with your application, although you can file it later, for a fee. (Fees are reproduced in Appendix 4, but change relatively often. Current fee amounts may be obtained from the PTO's website.)

You can view and complete the PAD on your computer, a typewriter, or with a pen (do it neatly). If you want to use the computer, go to the PTO's forms website listed above, open the editable version of the appropriate form, as described below, and refer to Fig. 10I (A, B and C).

If you can file the PAD with an Application Data Sheet (ADS) when you file your application, use one form AIA/01 for each inventor. Complete the form AIA/01 as follows, as shown in Fig. 10I(A):

Title of Invention: make sure to use the same title here as in your Application Data Sheet;

This declaration is directed to: check the box for "The attached application" (unless you are entering the United States from a PCT international application; more on this in Chapter 12);

Fill in the full name of the inventor on the "Inventor" line, being sure that it is the same here as on the Application Data Sheet; and

Have that inventor sign and date the Declaration. Finally, note the statement in the middle of the PAD. This states that everything on the form is true and that you are liable for perjury, and the patent application and any resulting patent may be held invalid, if you knowingly lie.

In all other cases (for example, if you cannot file the PAD simultaneously with your application), use form AIA/08, and additional sheets for additional inventors on form AIA/10 as necessary. Complete the first page of form AIA/08 as follows, as shown in Fig. 10I(B).

Attorney Docket Number. No entry is needed, but if you prefer you may use any reference characters or names you wish to help you locate your patent application file. The PTO will include this docket number on all correspondence it sends to you.

First Named Inventor. Type the name of the sole inventor or the first inventor if there's more than one. The PTO will put this inventor's name on all correspondence that it sends to you. (This name will hold a prominent place on the patent, if and when it issues.)

Leave the Application Number, Filing Date, Art Unit, and Examiner Name blank, unless the application has already been filed and you have this information. (This will be the case only if you are filing the PAD well after the rest of the application.)

Declaration Submitted With Initial Filing. Check this box, if accurate, otherwise check the other box and fill-in the application number and the date on which the application was filed (even if you don't yet know the Art Unit or Examiner Name).

Title of the Invention. Type the title in this large box. Under "This declaration is directed to," check the box before "The attached application" if you are filing the Declaration at the same time as the application, otherwise check the box for "Declaration Submitted After Initial Filing" and fill in the blanks with the application number and the date on which the application was filed.

294 | PATENT IT YOURSELF

PTO/AIA/01 (06-12)
Approved for use through 11/30/2027. OMB 0651-0032
U.S. Patent and Trademark Office; U.S. DEPARTMENT OF COMMERCE
Under the Paperwork Reduction Act of 1995, no persons are required to respond to a collection of information unless it displays a valid OMB control number.

DECLARATION (37 CFR 1.63) FOR UTILITY OR DESIGN APPLICATION USING AN APPLICATION DATA SHEET (37 CFR 1.76)

Title of Invention	Food Chopper with Convoluted Blade

As the below named inventor, I hereby declare that:

This declaration is directed to:

☑ The attached application, or

☐ United States application or PCT international application number _____

filed on _____ .

The above-identified application was made or authorized to be made by me.

I believe that I am the original inventor or an original joint inventor of a claimed invention in the application.

I hereby acknowledge that any willful false statement made in this declaration is punishable under 18 U.S.C. 1001 by fine or imprisonment of not more than five (5) years, or both.

WARNING:

Petitioner/applicant is cautioned to avoid submitting personal information in documents filed in a patent application that may contribute to identity theft. Personal information such as social security numbers, bank account numbers, or credit card numbers (other than a check or credit card authorization form PTO-2038 submitted for payment purposes) is never required by the USPTO to support a petition or an application. If this type of personal information is included in documents submitted to the USPTO, petitioners/applicants should consider redacting such personal information from the documents before submitting them to the USPTO. Petitioner/applicant is advised that the record of a patent application is available to the public after publication of the application (unless a non-publication request in compliance with 37 CFR 1.213(a) is made in the application) or issuance of a patent. Furthermore, the record from an abandoned application may also be available to the public if the application is referenced in a published application or an issued patent (see 37 CFR 1.14). Checks and credit card authorization forms PTO-2038 submitted for payment purposes are not retained in the application file and therefore are not publicly available.

LEGAL NAME OF INVENTOR

Inventor: _M. Goldberger_   Date (Optional) : _November 11, 2024_

Signature: _Mildred Goldberger_

Note: An application data sheet (PTO/AIA/14 or equivalent), including naming the entire inventive entity, must accompany this form or must have been previously filed. Use an additional PTO/AIA/01 form for each additional inventor.

A Federal agency may not conduct or sponsor, and a person is not required to respond to, nor shall a person be subject to a penalty for failure to comply with an information collection subject to the requirements of the Paperwork Reduction Act of 1995, unless the information collection has a currently valid OMB Control Number. The OMB Control Number for this information collection is 0651-0032. Public burden for this form is estimated to average 1 minute per response, including the time for reviewing instructions, searching existing data sources, gathering and maintaining the data needed, and completing and reviewing the information collection. Send comments regarding this burden estimate or any other aspect of this information collection, including suggestions for reducing this burden to the Chief Administrative Officer, United States Patent and Trademark Office, P.O. Box 1450, Alexandria, VA 22313-1450 or email InformationCollection@uspto.gov. **DO NOT SEND FEES OR COMPLETED FORMS TO THIS ADDRESS.** If filing this completed form by mail, send to: **Commissioner for Patents, P.O. Box 1450, Alexandria, VA 22313-1450.**

Fig. 10I(A)—Completed Declaration for Patent Application Using an Application Data Sheet (Downloadable Form 10-1A; see Appendix 7 for details)

CHAPTER 10 | FINALIZING AND FILING YOUR APPLICATION | 295

Doc Code: Oath
Document Description: Oath or declaration filed

PTO/AIA/08 (11-15)
Approved for use through 11/30/2027. OMB 0651-0032
U.S. Patent and Trademark Office; U.S. DEPARTMENT OF COMMERCE
Under the Paperwork Reduction Act of 1995, no persons are required to respond to a collection of information unless it contains a valid OMB control number.

DECLARATION FOR UTILITY OR DESIGN PATENT APPLICATION (37 CFR 1.63)

Attorney Docket Number	Goldberger-Briskin
First Named Inventor	m. Goldberger
	COMPLETE IF KNOWN
Application Number	
Filing Date	
Art Unit	
Examiner Name	

[✓] Declaration Submitted With Initial Filing   OR   [ ] Declaration Submitted After Initial Filing (surcharge (37 CFR 1.16(f)) required)

(Title of the Invention)

As a below named inventor, I hereby declare that:

This declaration is directed to:

[✓] The attached application,

OR

[ ] United States Application Number or PCT International application number _____

filed on_____.

The above-identified application was made or authorized to be made by me.

I believe I am the original inventor or an original joint inventor of a claimed invention in the application.

I hereby acknowledge that any willful false statement made in this declaration is punishable under 18 U.S.C. 1001 by fine or imprisonment of not more than five (5) years, or both.

Direct all correspondence to: [ ] The address associated with Customer Number: [____]   **OR**   [ ] Correspondence address below

Name		
Address		
City	State	Zip
Country	Telephone	Email

[Page 1 of 2]

A Federal agency may not conduct or sponsor, and a person is not required to respond to, nor shall a person be subject to a penalty for failure to comply with an information collection subject to the requirements of the Paperwork Reduction Act of 1995, unless the information collection has a currently valid OMB Control Number. The OMB Control Number for this information collection is 0651-0032. Public burden for this form is estimated to average 21 minutes per response, including the time for reviewing instructions, searching existing data sources, gathering and maintaining the data needed, and completing and reviewing the information collection. Send comments regarding this burden estimate or any other aspect of this information collection, including suggestions for reducing this burden to the Chief Administrative Officer, United States Patent and Trademark Office, P.O. Box 1450, Alexandria, VA 22313-1450 or email InformationCollection@uspto.gov. **DO NOT SEND FEES OR COMPLETED FORMS TO THIS ADDRESS.** If filing this completed form by mail, send to: **Commissioner for Patents, P.O. Box 1450, Alexandria, VA 22313-1450.**

Fig. 10I(B)—Completed Declaration for Patent Application (Downloadable Form 10-1A(2); see Appendix 7)

296 | PATENT IT YOURSELF

PTO/AIA/08 (11-15)
Approved for use through 11/30/2027. OMB 0651-0032
U.S. Patent and Trademark Office; U.S. DEPARTMENT OF COMMERCE
Under the Paperwork Reduction Act of 1995, no persons are required to respond to a collection of information unless it contains a valid OMB control number.

DECLARATION — Utility or Design Patent Application

WARNING:

Petitioner/applicant is cautioned to avoid submitting personal information in documents filed in a patent application that may contribute to identity theft. Personal information such as social security numbers, bank account numbers, or credit card numbers (other than a check or credit card authorization form PTO-2038 submitted for payment purposes) is never required by the USPTO to support a petition or an application. If this type of personal information is included in documents submitted to the USPTO, petitioners/applicants should consider redacting such personal information from the documents before submitting them to the USPTO. Petitioner/applicant is advised that the record of a patent application is available to the public after publication of the application (unless a non-publication request in compliance with 37 CFR 1.213(a) is made in the application) or issuance of a patent. Furthermore, the record from an abandoned application may also be available to the public if the application is referenced in a published application or an issued patent (see 37 CFR 1.14). Checks and credit card authorization forms PTO-2038 submitted for payment purposes are not retained in the application file and therefore are not publicly available. Petitioner/applicant is advised that documents which form the record of a patent application (such as the PTO/SB/01) are placed into the Privacy Act system of records DEPARTMENT OF COMMERCE, COMMERCE-PAT-7, System name: *Patent Application Files* . Documents not retained in an application file (such as the PTO-2038) are placed into the Privacy Act system of COMMERCE/PAT-TM-10, System name: *Deposit Accounts and Electronic Funds Transfer Profiles.*

LEGAL NAME OF SOLE OR FIRST INVENTOR:

(*E.g.,* Given Name (first and middle if any) and Family Name or Surname)

Mildred Goldberger

Inventor's Signature	Date (Optional)
Mildred Goldberger	11/11/2024

Residence: City	State	Country
Philadelphia	PA	U.S.

Mailing Address

1901 Kennedy Blvd.

City	State	Zip	Country
Philadelphia	PA	10103	U.S.

☐ Additional inventors are being named on the _____ Supplemental sheet(s) PTO/AIA/10 attached hereto

[Page 2 of 2]

Fig. 10I(C)—Completed Declaration for Patent Application (Form 10-1A(2)) (continued)

CHAPTER 10 | FINALIZING AND FILING YOUR APPLICATION | 297

PTO/AIA/10 (06-12)
Approved for use through 11/30/2027. OMB 0651-0032
U.S. Patent and Trademark Office; U.S. DEPARTMENT OF COMMERCE
Under the Paperwork Reduction Act of 1995, no persons are required to respond to a collection of information unless it contains a valid OMB control number.

SUPPLEMENTAL SHEET FOR DECLARATION

ADDITIONAL INVENTOR(S)
Supplemental Sheet (for PTO/AIA/08,09)

Page _____ of _____

Legal Name of Additional Joint Inventor, if any:

(*E.g.*, Given Name (first and middle (if any)) and Family Name or Surname)

Nathan F. Briskin

Inventor's Signature	*Nathan F. Briskin*	Date (Optional)

Residence: City Philadelphia	State PA	Country U.S.

Mailing Address 1919 Chestnut Street

City Philadelphia	State PA	Zip 10103	Country U.S.

Legal Name of Additional Joint Inventor, if any:

(*E.g.*, Given Name (first and middle (if any)) and Family Name or Surname)

Inventor's Signature		Date (Optional)

Residence: City	State	Country

Mailing Address

City	State	Zip	Country

Legal Name of Additional Joint Inventor, if any:

(*E.g.*, Given Name (first and middle (if any)) and Family Name or Surname)

Inventor's Signature		Date (Optional)

Residence: City	State	Country

Mailing Address

City	State	Zip	Country

A Federal agency may not conduct or sponsor, and a person is not required to respond to, nor shall a person be subject to a penalty for failure to comply with an information collection subject to the requirements of the Paperwork Reduction Act of 1995, unless the information collection has a currently valid OMB Control Number. The OMB Control Number for this information collection is 0651-0032. Public burden for this form is estimated to average 21 minutes per response, including the time for reviewing instructions, searching existing data sources, gathering and maintaining the data needed, and completing and reviewing the information collection. Send comments regarding this burden estimate or any other aspect of this information collection, including suggestions for reducing this burden to the Chief Administrative Officer, United States Patent and Trademark Office, P.O. Box 1450, Alexandria, VA 22313-1450 or email InformationCollection@uspto.gov. **DO NOT SEND FEES OR COMPLETED FORMS TO THIS ADDRESS.** If filing this completed form by mail, send to: **Commissioner for Patents, P.O. Box 1450, Alexandria, VA 22313-1450.**

**Fig. 10I(D)—Completed Supplemental Sheet for Declaration
(Downloadable Form 10-1B; see Appendix 7 for details)**

If you have several applications on file at the PTO, you may want to get a Customer Number, which you can use instead of your address. You can apply for a Customer Number using PTO Form SB/125. Then check the appropriate box and fill in your Customer Number.

If you don't have a Customer Number, check the box after "direct all correspondence to" and the box before "Correspondence address below." If a non-inventor (or someone other than the sole or first inventor) is to receive the correspondence, in the next four lines complete the name, address, phone, and fax (if any) of this person. Otherwise, the PTO will use the address of the sole or first inventor listed on the second page of the form, discussed below.

While every joint inventor must sign most papers that are sent to the PTO, the PTO will correspond with one inventor only. Therefore you should list the inventor who is most available (or who has best access to a photocopier or scanner) in the top section of part two of the form.

On the second page of the form (Fig. 10I(C)), complete the given name, family name, city (or county), state, and country of legal residence, and mailing address of the sole or first inventor. Leave the date blank (unless you know the date it will be signed). Non-U.S. citizens have the same rights as U.S. citizens. The PTO will correspond with them no matter where they are and they don't have to be represented by an attorney in the United States.

If there is more than one inventor, check the box at the bottom of this page, then open and complete an additional sheet—Form AIA/10 (see Fig. 10I(D)). Fill out this sheet for each inventor in the same way you filled out the second page of Form AIA/08. You can specify three inventors for each additional sheet.

Use as many additional sheets as necessary. Fill in the number of additional sheets at the bottom of page 2 of the Form AIA/08, then go back and number each additional sheet in its upper right-hand corner.

If you are not the person who wrote the specification and claims, you should carefully read and understand them. Failure to do this can cause you embarrassment and may even result in fines for perjury.

Finally, note the statement in the middle of page 1 of the PAD. This states that everything on the form is true and that you are liable for perjury, and the patent application and any resulting patent may be held invalid, if you knowingly lie. Each inventor should then sign and date the appropriate "Inventor's Signature" spaces on page 2 of the PAD or on the appropriate additional sheet.

CAUTION

The PTO rules are very strict in requiring that you should not sign the PAD until the entire application is completed. If the PTO finds out that you signed it before it was completed, or if you made any changes to the application after you signed the PAD, your application can be stricken or rejected entirely. If you need to make any changes to the application after it's finaled, you can do so neatly in ink, provided you date and initial each change and you do this before you sign the PAD. You can also make changes by amendment(s) after the application is filed (see Chapter 13), provided you don't add new matter to the application.

Claiming the Benefit of a PPA

If you have filed a Provisional Patent Application (PPA) and wish to claim the benefit of its filing date, you should do so in the "CROSS REFERENCE TO RELATED APPLICATIONS" section of your specification—as we have done in the sample specification included in Chapter 8, and must do so in your Application Data Sheet.

7. Complete the Transmittal Letter and Fee Transmittal, Payment, and Postcard

Now it's time to prepare the routine paperwork necessary to actually send your patent application to the PTO. Here's how to do it.

a. Prepare the Transmittal Letter

The transmittal letter (Form 10-2; PTO/AIA/15) is your checklist of all paperwork that should be submitted to the PTO, and should be completed as follows (see Fig. 10J for an example of a completed form):

Attorney Docket No. and **First Inventor:** Complete as you did with the PAD (see above).

Title: Complete as you did with the PAD (see above).

Priority Mail Express Label No.: If you use Priority Mail Express (recommended if paper filing) to mail your application, type or write the Priority Mail Express number from the post office's Priority Mail Express Label here.

Box 1: Check Fee Transmittal and complete this form (Form 10-3) as explained below.

Box 2: Check this Small Entity Box if you qualify for a Small Entity (SE) fee. An individual or individuals qualify for SE fees if they haven't assigned (transferred) or licensed the invention (and they have no obligation to assign or license the invention) to a for-profit company with more than 500 employees.

Box 3: Check this box if you qualify for Micro Entity (ME) status. A micro entity is anyone who is either (1) an independent inventor (a) who has not been named as an inventor in more than four nonassigned patent applications in their lifetime, and (b) whose gross income in the preceding calendar year is less than three times the median U.S. income, and (c) who has no obligation to assign and who has not assigned their application to a non–micro entity, or (2) an employee of a college and who is obligated to assign their invention to the college. You will need to also file a Form SB/15A or 15B, as appropriate. Micro entities qualify for PTO fees that are half of small entity fees; that is, only 20% of the regular fees (an 80% reduction).

Box 4: "Specification" is used here in the statutory sense, meaning the specification (written description), including the claims and abstract. Check this box and type the total pages of all of these parts of your application.

Box 5: Check the Drawing(s) box (unless your application has no drawings) and indicate the total number of drawing sheets.

Box 6: Inventor's Oath or Declaration. Type the number of pages of the declaration you prepared in the previous section. Check Box A, since you're submitting a new application.

Box 7: Application Data Sheet. The PTO's fillable Application Data Sheet form (AIA/14) can be saved to your computer. We provide a downloadable copy of the PTO's AIA/14 Application Data Sheet on this book's online companion page (listed there as Form 3-4); see Appendix 7 for details.

Boxes 8, 9, 11, 12, 14, and 16: Leave these blocks blank unless you're providing a computer program on a CD, a biosequence, a translation, a preliminary amendment, a certified copy based on a foreign filed application, or a continuing application.

Box 10: If you're filing an assignment with the application check this box. (See Chapter 16 for more on assignments.)

Box 13: If you're supplying an Information Disclosure Statement with the application, check this box. Otherwise you must file your IDS within three months. If your IDS cites any foreign or nonpatent references, check the "Copies of citations attached" box. You don't have to send U.S. patent references to the PTO.

Box 15: Check this box and don't forget to complete and include a return receipt postcard.

Box 17: We recommend that you file an NPR (Form 10-7; SB/35) and check this box. (If you file an ADS, you don't need to file a separate NPR if you check the "Request Not to Publish" on page two of the ADS form.) Don't file an NPR if you definitely will be foreign filing, or unless you want an early publication of your application to be able to use against infringers. If you check this box but later decide to foreign-file, be sure to revoke your NPR within 45 days—for that, use Form SB/36. If you don't file an NPR, your application will be published electronically 18 months after filing (if it hasn't issued by then), or sooner if you request it. When your application is published, your application and its history will be open to the public on the PTO's public Patent Application Information Retrieval (PAIR) site, or its successor Patent Center. You may find this undesirable since it will give competitors and potential infringers a peek at your prosecution strategy and arguments before your patent issues. If you check the NPR box and later file abroad and you don't revoke your NPR and notify the PTO of such foreign filing within 45 days (use Form SB/36), your application will be regarded as abandoned unless you pay a stiff fee and declare that delay was unintentional. To fill out the NPR, merely fill in the name of the first inventor, the title, the

300 | PATENT IT YOURSELF

PTO/AIA/15 (10-17)
Approved for use through 11/30/2027. OMB 0651-0032
U.S. Patent and Trademark Office; U.S. DEPARTMENT OF COMMERCE
Under the Paperwork Reduction Act of 1995 no persons are required to respond to a collection of information unless it displays a valid OMB control number.

UTILITY PATENT APPLICATION TRANSMITTAL

(Only for new nonprovisional applications under 37 CFR 1.53(b))

Attorney Docket No.	Goldberger-Briskin
First Named Inventor	M. Goldberger
Title	Food Chopper with Convoluted Blade
Priority Mail Express® Label No.	DP123456789USIUS

APPLICATION ELEMENTS
See MPEP chapter 600 concerning utility patent application contents.

ADDRESS TO:
Commissioner for Patents
P.O. Box 1450
Alexandria, VA 22313-1450

1. ✓ **Fee Transmittal Form**
   (PTO/SB/17 or equivalent)
2. ✓ **Applicant asserts small entity status.**
   See 37 CFR 1.27
3. ✓ **Applicant certifies micro entity status.** See 37 CFR 1.29.
   Applicant must attach form PTO/SB/15A or B or equivalent.
4. ✓ **Specification** [*Total Pages* 12]
   Both the claims and abstract must start on a new page.
   (See MPEP § 608.01(a) for information on the preferred arrangement)
5. ✓ **Drawing(s)** (35 U.S.C. 113) [*Total Sheets* 2]
6. **Inventor's Oath or Declaration** [*Total Pages* _____]
   (including substitute statements under 37 CFR 1.64 and assignments serving as an oath or declaration under 37 CFR 1.63(e))
   a. ✓ Newly executed (original or copy)
   b. ☐ A copy from a prior application (37 CFR 1.63(d))
7. ☐ **Application Data Sheet** * See note below.
   See 37 CFR 1.76 (PTO/AIA/14 or equivalent)
8. **CD-ROM or CD-R**
   in duplicate, large table, or Computer Program (*Appendix*)
   ☐ Landscape Table on CD
9. **Nucleotide and/or Amino Acid Sequence Submission**
   (if applicable, items a. – c. are required)
   a. ☐ Computer Readable Form (CRF)
   b. ☐ Specification Sequence Listing on:
      i. ☐ CD-ROM or CD-R (2 copies); or
      ii. ☐ Paper
   c. ☐ Statements verifying identity of above copies

ACCOMPANYING APPLICATION PAPERS

10. ☐ **Assignment Papers**
    (cover sheet & document(s))
    Name of Assignee _____
    _____
11. ☐ **37 CFR 3.73(c) Statement**   ☐ **Power of Attorney**
    (*when there is an assignee*)
12. ☐ **English Translation Document**
    (*if applicable*)
13. ✓ **Information Disclosure Statement**
    (PTO/SB/08 or PTO-1449)
    ☐ Copies of citations attached
14. ☐ **Preliminary Amendment**
15. ✓ **Return Receipt Postcard**
    (*MPEP § 503*) (*Should be specifically itemized*)
16. ☐ **Certified Copy of Priority Document(s)**
    (*if foreign priority is claimed*)
17. ✓ **Nonpublication Request**
    Under 35 U.S.C. 122(b)(2)(B)(i). Applicant must attach form PTO/SB/35 or equivalent.
18. ☐ **Other:** _____
    _____
    _____

*Note: (1) Benefit claims under 37 CFR 1.78 and foreign priority claims under 1.55 **must** be included in an Application Data Sheet (ADS).
(2) For applications filed under 35 U.S.C. 111, the application must contain an ADS specifying the applicant if the applicant is an assignee, person to whom the inventor is under an obligation to assign, or person who otherwise shows sufficient proprietary interest in the matter. See 37 CFR 1.46(b).

19. CORRESPONDENCE ADDRESS

☐ The address associated with Customer Number: _____   OR ✓ Correspondence address below

Name	Goldberger-Briskin				
Address	1901 Kennedy Blvd				
City	Philadelphia	State	PA	Zip Code	10193
Country		Telephone		Email	

Signature	*Mildred Goldberger*	Date	11/11/2024
Name (Print/Type)	Mildred Goldberger	Registration No. (Attorney/Agent)	

A Federal agency may not conduct or sponsor, and a person is not required to respond to, nor shall a person be subject to a penalty for failure to comply with an information collection subject to the requirements of the Paperwork Reduction Act of 1995, unless the information collection has a currently valid OMB Control Number. The OMB Control Number for this information collection is 0651-0032. Public burden for this form is estimated to average 12 minutes per response, including the time for reviewing instructions, searching existing data sources, gathering and maintaining the data needed, and completing and reviewing the information collection. Send comments regarding this burden estimate or any other aspect of this information collection, including suggestions for reducing this burden to the Chief Administrative Officer, United States Patent and Trademark Office, P.O. Box 1450, Alexandria, VA 22313-1450 or email InformationCollection@uspto.gov. DO NOT SEND FEES OR COMPLETED FORMS TO THIS ADDRESS. **If filing this completed form by mail, send to: Commissioner for Patents, P.O. Box 1450, Alexandria, VA 22313-1450.**

Fig. 10J—Utility Patent Application Transmittal (Downloadable Form 10-2; see Appendix 7)
*Use latest fees—See Appendix 4, "Fee Schedule."

docket number, and the date. The first inventor should sign it and print their name under the signature.

You must file the NPR with the application; if you file it later it will not be considered.

Common Misconception: If the PTO publishes your patent application, this indicates that it believes your invention is patentable.

Fact: If you don't file an NPR at the time of filing the application, the PTO will publish your application 18 months later, regardless of its patentability.

Box 18: Other: If you attach any other documents, check this box.

If you're not sure your claims are entirely proper and would like the examiner to write claims for you if they find allowable subject matter, type "Request Under MPEP 707.07(j)" and file the Request (available on this book's online companion page as Form 10-8; see Appendix 7 for details). We recommend this.

Box 19: If you have a Customer Number, check the first box and enter it. Otherwise, check the box before "Correspondence address below" and complete the next four lines as you did with the PAD (see Section 6, above).

In the next-to-last line type the name of the inventor who is to receive correspondence from the PTO. This inventor should sign and date the bottom lines.

PPA: The form does not contain any box to refer to any PPA that you've filed. (Do not use Box 18 to refer to a PPA.) You must claim the benefit of any PPA that you've filed in the "CROSS REFERENCE TO RELATED APPLICATIONS" section of the specification, as explained in Chapter 8, Section I. Be sure to include the serial number and filing date of your PPA. You must file your regular patent application (RPA) within one year of your PPA's filing date if you want to claim the benefit of your PPA. If the last day of the one-year period falls on a weekend or holiday, you may file your Regular Patent Application (RPA) on the next business day after the weekend or holiday.

However, if you have any desire to seek foreign protection, do not wait for the next business day to file your RPA, as other countries may not recognize the delay as permissible.

The RPA must name at least one inventor who has been named in the PPA. If you file the application without a PPA claim in your specification, you must amend the specification within four months from your RPA's filing date or 16 months from your PPA's filing date.

b. Fill Out Fee Transmittal and Pay by Credit Card or Check

Fill out the Fee Transmittal (Form 10-3 or SB/17) by completing the name of the first (or only) inventor and docket number at the top right. Form 10-3 includes the fees as of this edition. Note, that the PTO usually raises its fees on October 1 of each year, so if you're filing after October 1, check for current fees at the PTO website. The PTO also frequently changes its form SB/17, so you can download the most current version of that, as well. (See Fig. 10K for an example of a completed Fee Transmittal.)

A. Fill out the First Named Inventor and Attorney Docket No. boxes in the upper right corner as before.

B. Check "Applicant asserts small entity status. See 37 CFR 1.27" box if you qualify. You qualify for small entity status if you haven't assigned or licensed (or are not obligated to assign or license) the invention to a for-profit company with more than 500 employees. Check "Applicant certifies micro entity status. See 37 CFR 1.29" if you qualify. Otherwise do not check either of these boxes. (If you have questions about qualifying for either status, see the discussion in Chapter 3 section H(7).)

C. Fill in the "Total Amount of Payment" box. (Do this last, after you calculate the total.)

D. Check the appropriate Check, Credit Card, or Money Order box.

1. Basic Filing, Search, and Examination Fees: Add the Micro Entity fees in the "Utility" line (for a utility application; use the other lines for other types of application) and type the total ($455 in our example in Fig. 10K) in the rightmost column. You must pay all three fees together.

302 | PATENT IT YOURSELF

PTO/SB/17 (01-25)
Approved for use through 11/30/2027. OMB 0651-0032
U.S. Patent and Trademark Office; U.S. DEPARTMENT OF COMMERCE
Under the Paperwork Reduction Act of 1995 no persons are required to respond to a collection of information unless it displays a valid OMB control number.

FEE TRANSMITTAL
(page 1 of 2)

	Complete if known
Application Number	
Filing Date	
First Named Inventor	M. Goldberger
Examiner Name	
Art Unit	
Practitioner Docket No.	

☐ Applicant asserts small entity status. See 37 CFR 1.27.

☑ Applicant certifies micro entity status. See 37 CFR 1.29.
Form PTO/SB/15A or B or equivalent must either be enclosed or have been submitted previously.

TOTAL AMOUNT OF PAYMENT ($) **675**

METHOD OF PAYMENT (check all that apply)

☐ Check ☑ Credit Card ☐ Money Order ☐ None ☐ Other (please identify): _____

☐ Deposit Account Deposit Account Number: _____ Deposit Account Name: _____ For the above-identified deposit account, the Director is hereby authorized to (check all that apply):

☐ Charge fee(s) indicated below ☐ Charge fee(s) indicated below, **except for the filing fee**

☐ Charge any additional fee(s) or underpayment of fee(s) under 37 CFR 1.16 and 1.17 ☐ Credit any overpayment of fee(s)

WARNING: Information on this form may become public. Credit card information should not be included on this form. Provide credit card information and authorization on PTO-2038.

FEE CALCULATION

1. BASIC FILING, SEARCH, AND EXAMINATION FEES (U = undiscounted fee; S = small entity fee; M = micro entity fee)

Application Type	FILING FEES U ($)	S ($)	M ($)	SEARCH FEES U ($)	S ($)	M ($)	EXAMINATION FEES U ($)	S ($)	M ($)	Fees Paid ($)
Utility	350	140*	70	770	308	154	880	352	176	455
Design	300	120	60	300	120	60	700	280	140	
Plant	240	96	48	485	194	97	725	290	145	
Reissue	350	140	70	770	308	154	2,550	1,020	510	
Provisional	325	130	65	0	0	0	0	0	0	

* The $140 small entity filing fee for a utility application is further reduced to $70 for a small entity applicant who files the application via Patent Center.

2. EXCESS CLAIM FEES

Fee Description	Undiscounted Fee ($)	Small Entity Fee ($)	Micro Entity Fee ($)
Each claim over 20 (including Reissues)	200	80	40
Each independent claim over 3 (including Reissues)	600	240	120
Multiple dependent claims	925	370	185

Total Claims		Extra Claims		Fee ($)		Fee Paid ($)
24	-20 or HP =	4	x	25	=	100

HP = highest number of total claims paid for, if greater than 20.

Multiple Dependent Claims
Fee ($) _____ Fee Paid ($) _____

Indep. Claims		Extra Claims		Fee ($)		Fee Paid ($)
4	-3 or HP =	1	x	120	=	120

HP = highest number of independent claims paid for, if greater than 3.

3. APPLICATION SIZE FEE

If the specification and drawings exceed 100 sheets of paper (excluding electronically filed sequence or computer listings under 37 CFR 1.52(e)), the application size fee due is $450 ($180 for small entity) ($90 for micro entity) for each additional 50 sheets or fraction thereof. See 35 U.S.C. 41(a)(1)(G) and 37 CFR 1.16(s).

Total Sheets	Extra Sheets	Number of each additional 50 or fraction thereof	Fee ($)	Fee Paid ($)
_____ - 100 =	_____ / 50 =	_____ (round **up** to a whole number) x	_____ =	_____

A Federal agency may not conduct or sponsor, and a person is not required to respond to, nor shall a person be subject to a penalty for failure to comply with an information collection subject to the requirements of the Paperwork Reduction Act of 1995, unless the information collection has a currently valid OMB Control Number. The OMB Control Number for this information collection is 0651-0032. Public burden for this form is estimated to average 30 minutes per response, including the time for reviewing instructions, searching existing data sources, gathering and maintaining the data needed, and completing and reviewing the information collection. Send comments regarding this burden estimate or any other aspect of this information collection, including suggestions for reducing this burden to the Chief Administrative Officer, United States Patent and Trademark Office, P.O. Box 1450, Alexandria, VA 22313-1450 or email InformationCollection@uspto.gov. **DO NOT SEND FEES OR COMPLETED FORMS TO THIS ADDRESS.** If filing this completed form by mail, send to: **Commissioner for Patents, P.O. Box 1450, Alexandria, VA 22313-1450.**
If you need assistance in completing the form, call 1-800-PTO-9199 and select option 2.

Fig. 10K—Fee Transmittal (Downloadable Form 10-3; see Appendix 7)

CHAPTER 10 | FINALIZING AND FILING YOUR APPLICATION | 303

PTO/SB/17 (01-25)
Approved for use through 11/30/2027. OMB 0651-0032
U.S. Patent and Trademark Office; U.S. DEPARTMENT OF COMMERCE
Under the Paperwork Reduction Act of 1995 no persons are required to respond to a collection of information unless it displays a valid OMB control number

FEE TRANSMITTAL

(page 2 of 2)

4. CONTINUING APPLICATION FEE

If the actual filing date of the application is more than six years after the earliest benefit date, a continuing application fee is due. The earliest benefit date is the earliest filing date for which benefit is claimed under 35 U.S.C. 120, 121, 365(c), or 386(c) and § 1.78(d).

Choose only one of the following:

If the actual filing date is more than six years, and is less than or equal to nine years, after the earliest benefit date, the continuing application fee is $2,700 ($1,080 for small entity or $540 for micro entity). See 37 CFR 1.17(w)(1).

   or

If the actual filing date is more than nine years after the earliest benefit date, the continuing application fee is $4,000 ($1,600 for small entity or $800 for micro entity), less any amount previously paid under 37 CFR 1.17(w)(1). See 37 CFR 1.17(w)(2).

                                                     Fees Paid ($)

                                                     _____

5. OTHER FEE(S)   **Fees Paid ($)**

Non-English specification, $150 fee ($60 for small entity) ($30 for micro entity)   _____

Non-electronic filing fee under 37 CFR 1.16(t) for a utility application, $400 fee ($200 small or micro entity)   _____

Other (e.g., late filing surcharge): _____   _____

SUBMITTED BY

Signature		Registration No. (Attorney/Agent)	Telephone 215-555-0362
Name (Print/Type)	M. Goldberger		Date 11/11/2024

Fig. 10K—Fee Transmittal (Downloadable Form 10-3; see Appendix 7) (page 2)

304 | PATENT IT YOURSELF

2. **Excess Claim Fees:** The Basic Filing Fee entitles you to file up to three independent claims and 20 total claims, assuming that each dependent claim refers back to only one preceding claim (independent or dependent). If you don't have more than 20 total and three independent claims, you can leave this section blank.

   If you're filing more than 20 total claims, three independent, or a multiple dependent claim (not recommended) fill out these blanks. Enter the total number of claims (independent and dependent) in the blank under "Total Claims." Subtract 20 from this figure, enter the difference under "Extra Claims," and type the fee for each extra total claim past 20 (Large, Small, or Micro Entity) from the list in the upper right of this section under "Fee ($)," and type the product under the "Fee Paid ($)." If you have more than three independent claims, enter the total number of independent claims under "Indep. Claims," subtract 3 from this figure, enter the difference under "Extra Claims," type the fee for each extra independent claim over three (Large, Small, or Micro Entity) from the list in upper right part of this section under "Fee ($)," and type the product under the "Fee Paid ($)."

   It's best not to file any Multiple Dependent Claims (MDCs) because the fee is high and examiners don't like them. However, if you do file any MDCs, enter the fee from the right side of this section in the MDC boxes. The fee is also in Appendix 4 and at the PTO's website.

3. **Application Size Fee:** If your specification and drawings exceed 100 pages, fill in the boxes in this section.

   Note that the fees for extra claims and MDCs are very high now.

4. Don't forget to add the nonelectronic filing fee under 37 CFR 1.16(t), under "Other Fee(s)," if you are not filing electronically.

5. **Other Fee(s):** Normally you won't have any additional fees at this stage, so you won't have to enter anything in the Other Fees section. However, if you want to obtain a somewhat speedier processing of your application, file a "Petition to Make Special" (see Section I below). If your petition requires a fee, type "Pet. Special" after "Other Fee" and include the amount in the "Other" box. If you're enclosing an assignment (see Section H below), type "Asgt. Recordal." on the blank line.

Total the amounts in Sections 1 to 4 and enter the sum in the "Total Amount of Payment" box at the top left of the form.

Finally, sign and print the corresponding inventor's name and phone number in the next-to-last line of the form and enter your phone number and sign and type the date on the last line.

The PTO accepts payment by credit card, check, or money order. If you pay by credit card, use the PTO's Credit Card Payment Form (CCPF—Form 10-4 in Appendix 7 or PTO Form 2038) in conjunction with the Fee Transmittal. The PTO will not accept debit cards or check cards that require the use of a personal identification number (PIN) as a method of payment.

Complete the CCPF as in Fig. 10L. Fill in all credit card information, including the amount to be charged to your credit card and your signature. Complete the Credit Card Billing Address. That information is required for verification of your credit card account. Under "Request and Payment Information," complete the "Description of Request and Payment Information" with a short statement of what you are paying for. In the present case, since you're paying a patent filing fee, check "Patent Fee" and write your docket number.

If paying by check or money order, make payment to Commissioner for Patents for the total amount, and attach it to the transmittal letter.

CHAPTER 10 | FINALIZING AND FILING YOUR APPLICATION | 305

PTO-2038 (11-2023)
United States Patent and Trademark Office; U.S. DEPARTMENT OF COMMERCE

Credit Card Payment Form

(Do not submit this form electronically via USPTO's patent electronic filing system)
Please Read Instructions before Completing this Form

Credit Card Information

Credit Card Type: ☑ Visa ☐ MasterCard ☐ American Express ☐ Discover

Credit Card Account #: 2175-3210-1497-3218

Credit Card Expiration Date (mm/yyyy): 05/2027

Name as it Appears on Credit Card: Mildred Goldberger

Payment Amount (US Dollars): $ $675

Cardholder Signature: | Date (mm/dd/yyyy): 11/11/2024

The USPTO accepts a handwritten signature or an s-signature under 37 CFR 1.4(d).
Refund Policy: The USPTO may refund a fee paid by mistake or in excess of that required. A change of purpose after the payment of a fee will not entitle a party to a refund of such fee. The USPTO will not refund amounts of $25.00 or less unless a refund is specifically requested and will not notify the payor of such amounts (37 CFR 1.26). Refund of a fee paid by credit card will be issued as a credit to the credit card account to which the fee was charged.
Maximum Daily Limit: There is a $24,999.99 daily limit per credit card account effective June 1, 2015. There is no daily limit for debit cards.

Credit Card Billing Address

Street Address 1: 1901 Kennedy Blvd.

Street Address 2:

City: Philadelphia

State/Province: PA | Zip/Postal Code: 19103

Country: U.S.

Daytime Phone #: | Fax #: 215-555-0362

Request and Payment Information

Description of Request and Payment Information:

☑ Patent Fee	☐ Patent Maintenance Fee	☐ Trademark Fee	☐ Other Fee
Application No.	Application No.	Application No.	IDON Customer No.
Patent No.	Patent No.	Registration No.	
Attorney Docket No. Goldberger-Briskin		Identify or Describe Mark	

If the cardholder includes a credit card number on any form or document other than the Credit Card Payment Form or submits this form electronically via USPTO patent electronic filing system, the United States Patent and Trademark Office will not be liable in the event that the credit card number becomes public knowledge.

Fig. 10L—PTO's Credit Card Payment Form (Downloadable Form 10-4; see Appendix 7)

CAUTION

Be sure you have enough credit reserve in your credit card account or money in your checking account to cover the charge. If your payment bounces, you'll have to pay a stiff surcharge. (Note that if the PTO makes any fee errors, they are never penalized.)

Unfortunately, the PTO does not discount its fees for the needy, handicapped, or aged, or allow such individuals to postpone their fees. However, the AIA has a Micro Entity fee provision, under which Micro Entities will be able to get an 80% reduction on most fees (see above for the qualifications).

CAUTION

Be sure to make every payment as appropriate for your entity size. The rules for paying discounted fees are different for small entities than they are for micro entities. According to the PTO rules; for small entities, "Once status as a small entity has been established in an application or patent, fees as a small entity may thereafter be paid in that application or patent without regard to a change in status until the issue fee is due or any maintenance fee is due" (37 CFR 1.27(g)(1)). When you pay the issue fee, or any maintenance fee, you must determine whether your eligibility for small entity status has changed, and if so you must notify the PTO and pay the undiscounted fees (37 CFR 1.27(g)(2)). Unfortunately for micro entities, every time you pay a fee to the PTO you must determine whether your eligibility for small micro status has changed ("a fee may be paid in the micro entity amount only if status as a micro entity as defined in paragraph (a) or (d) of this section is appropriate on the date the fee is being paid," (37 CFR 1.29(g)). If you are no longer entitled to micro entity status, you must notify the PTO and pay the fee as a small entity, or pay the full, undiscounted fee, as appropriate.

a. Postcard

As stated in Inventor's Commandment 18 at the beginning of this chapter, you should enclose a self-addressed, postage paid receipt postcard with every paper you mail to the PTO. Those few attorneys who still file by mail use receipt postcards because the PTO receives many thousands of pieces of mail each day and occasionally loses some. It may be months before you receive any reply to a paper you've sent to the PTO, so you'll want to be assured it arrived safely.

Fig. 10M indicates how an application receipt postcard should be completed. Note that the back of the card contains the inventors' names, title of invention, the number of sheets of drawings, the number of pages of specification, claims, and abstract, the Patent Application Declaration (if you are filing it with the application), including the number of pages and date it was signed, the Patent Application Transmittal, the Fee Transmittal, CCPF or the check number and amount, and the NPR. Leave space at the bottom of the back of the card for the PTO to affix its date and Serial Number sticker. Occasionally, receipt postcards get lost because of their size and inconspicuous color. We have had better results by using colored (bright red) postcards.

Patent application of Mildred Goldberger and Nathan Briskin for "Food Chopper With Convolute Blade" consisting of two sheets of drawings, 12 pages of specification, claims, and abstract, Patent Application Declaration (2 pp., signed 2014 November 11), Patent Application Transmittal, Fee Transmittal, Credit Card Payment Form, Nonpublication Request, and Information Disclosure Statement received for filing today:

Fig. 10M—Completed Back of Receipt Postcard to Accompany Patent Application

The PTO will stamp your application postcard receipt with the date your papers arrived and the serial number assigned to your application and mail it back to you as soon as they open your letter (which can take two weeks).

If you're filing from abroad, be sure that your return postcard has sufficient U.S. postage. You can confirm the postcard postage to any nation at the U.S. Postal Service website (www.usps.gov) and you can usually buy U.S. stamps abroad at a philatelic (stamp) store.

8. Maintain an Orderly File

It's good practice to write the date received on every paper you receive connected with your invention and also date every outgoing paper. You should have a two-part folder or jacket for (a) your application, and (b) correspondence to and from the PTO. Keep your prior-art references in a large envelope loose inside the folder. To avoid confusion, we recommend that you keep other nonofficial papers concerning your invention in a separate folder.

9. Assembly and Mailing of Your Application—Final Checklist

Congratulations! You're now ready to mail your patent application to the PTO, unless you want to include an Information Disclosure Statement, an Assignment, and/or a Petition to Make Special. If you do want to include any of these with your application (optional), consult the indicated sections, complete your paperwork, and then come back to this point.

Assemble in the following order—and carefully check—the following items, which are the third part of the checklist we started in Chapter 8; please do this carefully and methodically, as "haste makes waste," especially when applying for a patent.

We suggest that you file a good photocopy of your signed application and keep the original of your application. In this way you can make copies later if the application is lost in the mail, or if you need to send them to manufacturers when you market your invention.

Staple the pages of the specification, claims, abstract, and declarations together. Attach the drawings with a paper clip or other temporary fastener. Only one copy need be filed.

If you mail the application by Priority Mail Express, the papers should be transmitted in a Priority Mail Express envelope. If the application doesn't have more than about eight pages, you should include one or two sheets of cardboard or internal envelopes to protect the drawing from bending.

You may send the application to the PTO by first-class mail, but if it's lost in the mail, you will lose your filing date. We strongly recommend that you use Priority Mail Express (see next section).

10. Using Priority Mail Express to Get an Instant Filing Date

We strongly recommend you send your application to the PTO by Priority Mail Express (PME). This will provide strong protection against loss of your application, secure full legal rights in case it is lost, give you an "instant" filing date (the date you actually mail your application), and will enable you to make absolutely sure your application is on file before the one-year period expires if a PPA was filed or the invention was put on sale, sold, or published. You must use "Priority Mail Express Post Office to Addressee" service and you must indicate that you're using this service by completing the PME section at the top of your transmittal letter (Form 10-2, Fig. 10J). Type the PME number in the box at the top right, fourth line of Form 10-2.

The PTO's Rule 10 (37 CFR 1.10) states, in effect, that mailing any paper to the PTO by PME, with the PME number on the transmittal letter, is the same as physically delivering the paper directly to the PTO. Thus you can consider and call your application "patent pending" as soon as the postal clerk hands you the PME receipt, and your filing date will be the date on this receipt, provided all papers of the application are present and are properly completed. Since postal clerks often don't press hard enough when they date the PME receipt, we recommend you ask the clerk to stamp the receipt also with their rubber date stamp. If you've followed the final checklist above, your application will now be properly on file; that is, patent pending.

> ⓘ **CAUTION**
>
> **You should NOT send your application by fax, registered mail, certified mail, or private courier (for example, Federal Express), and you should NOT use any "Certificate of Mailing."** This is because the PTO does not accept applications by fax due to their uncertain length, and because 37 CFR 10 does not give applicants any advantages if they use the other methods of transmission when filing an application. If you use any of these, your filing date will be the date the application is actually received at the PTO and you'll have no rights if your application is lost.

PATENT IT YOURSELF

Final Checklist for Filing a Patent Application by Mail

☐ Return Receipt Postcard addressed to you with all papers listed on back.*

☐ If you are paying the filing fee by a check or money order, make it out for the correct filing fee (basic fee plus fee for any excess claims).* Make sure you have adequate funds on deposit or available on your credit card.

☐ Transmittal Letter and Fee Transmittal properly completed and signed.*

☐ If you are paying the filing fee using a Credit Card Payment Form, be sure it is made out for the correct filing fee (basic fee plus fee for any excess claims).* Make sure your credit limit is not in jeopardy.

☐ Drawing sheets all present; drawings clear, complete, and understandable. Drawings show every feature in claims. The sheet number and total number of sheets (for example, "1/3") is on the front (below top margin) and your name is on the top back. Originals of drawings (or disk file if CAD used) kept in safe place.

☐ Specification, Claims, and Abstract included; description of invention clear and complete, all reference numbers, dates, spelling, and grammar double-checked, and claims drafted per Chapter 9.

   ☐ Typing is clear and readable and 1.5 or double-spaced; use any normal font, 12-point minimum size.

   ☐ Application is prepared in form for making proper A4 copies later if foreign filing contemplated (optional).

   ☐ Top (above page numbers) and left margin is at least 2.5 cm on all pages.

   ☐ No sentence is longer than about 13 words, paragraphs are not longer than about a half a page, and a heading is supplied about every two pages.

☐ Claims are separated by an extra line.

☐ Claims and abstract start on new pages.

☐ No changes made after application signed.

☐ Patent Application Declaration (PAD) completed, signed, and dated in ink. (The PTO will accept a PAD, or virtually any other document that has a photocopy of your signature.

☐ Parts are assembled in above order and copies are made for your file.

☐ Information Disclosure Statement, Forms 10-5 and 10-6 (A and B) with references attached if you're filing it with your application (see Section G below). Otherwise IDS must be sent within three months.

☐ Petition to Make Special, Form 10-9 and Supporting Declaration (optional to speed application processing; see Section I below).

☐ Assignment and transmittal letter (optional—see Section H below).

☐ Envelope addressed to:
   Mail Stop Patent Application
   P.O. Box 1450
   Alexandria, VA 22313-1450*

☐ If there are joint inventors, all should complete, sign, and date multiple copies of a Joint Owners' Agreement (Form 16-2; Chapter 16, Section D) and each inventor should keep an original. Do not file this with the PTO.

☐ Have another person check your papers for compliance with these rules.

* Not applicable for Patent Center filings.

11. Receipt That Application Was Received in PTO

About two to four weeks after you send your application to the PTO, you'll get your postcard back, with the filing date of your application, and also with an eight digit serial number (for example, "11/123,456") that has been assigned to your application. Within about a week to a month after that (sometimes longer), you should get an official filing receipt back from the PTO indicating that your application has been officially filed. Check the information on the filing receipt carefully and let the OPAP (Office of Patent Application Processing) know if there are any errors. Their telephone number is 571-272-1000 (toll free 800-786-9199, TTY 800-877-8339), and they are open weekdays from 8:30 a.m. to 8:00 p.m.

If for any reason your application is incomplete or deficient, the PTO will not regard it as officially "filed" but rather as "deposited." The PTO will send you a Notice to File Missing Parts or Notice to File Corrected Application Papers letter, as the case may be, stating the deficiency in your application and telling you to promptly remedy it. However, if you follow all the instructions in this chapter, including the checklist on the previous page, carefully, you'll get your filing receipt in due course.

Once you get the filing receipt, your application is officially "patent pending." Unless you want to keep your invention a trade secret in case your patent application is eventually disallowed, you may publish details of your invention or market it to whomever you choose. You will not lose any legal rights in the United States or Paris Convention or Patent Cooperation Treaty countries. If you manufacture anything embodying your invention, you should mark it "patent pending" and keep your application, serial number, and filing date confidential to preserve rights in non-Convention countries and prevent access by potential copiers. As stated, if you mailed your application by Priority Mail Express and you faithfully followed the checklists, you may refer to your invention as "patent pending" as soon as you get the PME receipt.

C. Finalizing Your Specification for Patent Center Filing

The PTO's Electronic Filing System using the internet (Patent Center) enables patent applications, amendments, and other documents to be filed electronically over the internet. It requires some time to master, but its advantages are so great that even if you're filing just one application, it is worth the effort. As stated, its advantages are: You can (1) file an application anytime and from anywhere that has internet access, (2) obtain instant confirmation of receipt of documents by the PTO, (3) send an application to the PTO without having to go to the post office to get a Priority Mail Express receipt, (4) file with confidence because you will get an instant acknowledgment without having to prepare a postcard or wait for a postcard receipt, (5) pay a substantially reduced filing fee with no paper-filing surcharge—see Appendix 4, "Fee Schedule," and (6) file an application without having to prepare an application transmittal, a Fee Transmittal, receipt postcard, or check or Credit Card Payment Form (CCPF).

The PTO now has an optional "e-Office Action" service whereby they will send all correspondence to up to three of your email addresses in lieu of postal mail. To guard against lost emails, they will send a reminder if the email is not opened within a week.

This service can be useful if you're traveling, your mail is unreliable, or you want to get correspondence quickly. If you're a registered eFiler, it is easy to do from within your Patent Center account. Details are at www.uspto.gov/patents-application-process/checking-application-status/e-office-action-program.

If you're ready to file electronically, take the following steps:

- **Prepare the application as usual.** Before you go online, prepare the entire application as instructed in Chapters 8 to 10, except omit the Patent Application Transmittal, Fee Transmittal, Receipt Postcard, and check or CCPF. Sign the Declaration as usual. You may "sign" a downloaded declaration form (AIA/01) by typing an "/s/" signature on the form as follows: "/Sam Smith/." You don't need to print out the form and sign it in ink if you use the /s/ signature format. As of March 2025, you may also use third-party software such as Docu-Sign, Adobe Acrobat Sign, and so on to provide electronic signatures on documents you submit to the PTO, as long as the signer's name is printed or typed immediately below or adjacent to the electronic signature, and is reasonably specific enough to identify the signer.

Become a Registered eFiler (If Time Permits)

If you plan on filing electronically and if you can wait several weeks to file, we recommend you become a registered eFiler. You'll have to deal with red tape, including filling out a form to obtain a customer number, sending a notarized certificate to the PTO, obtaining access codes, and calling the PTO to confirm, but as a registered eFiler you'll be able to track your application's progress and file additional documents or corrections. To register go to www.uspto.gov/patents/apply/applying-online/getting-started-new-users and follow the detailed instructions. If you can't wait several weeks, you can use Patent Center to file an application as an unregistered eFiler and register later.

• **Convert your application to an appropriate data format.** As part of an effort to modernize its application systems, the PTO now allows electronic filers to submit textual portions of applications (that is, the specification, claims, and abstract) in the DOCX format. DOCX is a word processing file format based on open standards, and is supported by many popular word processors including Microsoft *Word*, Google *Docs*, and *LibreOffice*. However, you must still convert your Drawings to PDF documents in your computer (and you may convert your specification, claims, and abstract to PDF if you wish). All PDF documents submitted via Patent Center must have a minimum resolution of 300 DPI and a white background. Put all of the application computer files into a separate Application Holding Folder with a suitable name (for example, "Derailleur RPA Files").

• **Prepare an Application Data Sheet.** You can fill out an ADS either during the online filing process, or you can fill it out in advance (recommended). Find the fillable and savable EFS Application Data Sheet (ADS) (PTO Form AIA/14) by going to www.uspto.gov/patents/apply/forms and downloading the form. This will enable you to fill in the form, save it with the data you filled in, and revise it later if necessary. If you fill in the form online at the time of filing, you won't be able to do this. We also recommend that you download the instructions for Form AIA/14, which provide greater detail. After you've saved Form AIA/14 to your desktop, check "Highlight Required Fields." The program will then automatically fill in the header blanks. Most of the fields are self-explanatory, and/or are explained in the instructions for Form AIA/14, but we draw your attention to the following issues. Leave blank the "Filing by Reference" section, which is only useful in rare circumstances that probably do not apply to you, and in any case do not apply if you submit a complete application as instructed in this book. Check "Request Not to Publish" (recommended, but only if you have decided not to file a corresponding foreign application) but remember to revoke your nonpublication request (NPR) within 45 days of your foreign filing, if you foreign-file later. Then, save the completed form using a suitable name, such as "AppDataSheet.pdf," in your Application Holding Folder with your other application forms. Consider carefully the "Statement under 37 CFR 1.55 or 1.78 for AIA (First Inventor to File) Transition Applications," which rarely applies. Read the text on the form carefully. If your application meets both criteria

(1) and (2), you must check the box; otherwise, leave the box unchecked. Also consider carefully the "Authorization or Opt Out of Authorization to Permit Access." The PTO will not allow others to access your application unless you give them permission, or until your application is published or issues as a patent. If you do not opt out by checking both box A and box B, you grant the PTO permission to allow other patent offices to access your application file. Note that if you do not opt out (that is, if you leave one or both of box A and box B unchecked) your ADS may be somewhat more complicated to sign (more on this in the "Caution" section below). Follow the instructions for the "Applicant Information" section—but note that if the applicant is a juristic entity (for example, a corporation or organization), and you name that juristic entity as an applicant, then the ADS must be signed by a patent practitioner (that is, a registered patent attorney or patent agent; more on this in the "Caution" section below).

> ⚠ CAUTION
>
> **Properly signing your Application Data Sheet requires close attention.** There are three possible scenarios, each with unique requirements. **Scenario 1):** If one or more of the applicants is a juristic entity (for example, a corporation or association), then the ADS *must* be signed by a patent practitioner (that is, a registered patent attorney or patent agent). Otherwise (if no applicant is a juristic entity), there are two other scenarios. **Scenario 2):** If you are submitting the ADS along with your initial filing (most likely), and if you have not checked both box A and box B in the "Opt Out" section, then you are giving permission for the PTO to allow other patent offices access to your application file, in which case the ADS must be signed by (i) all of the applicants; or (ii) a patent practitioner (patent attorney or patent agent) of record; or (iii) an authorized official of an assignee of record (per 37 CFR 3.71); or (iv) a registered attorney or patent agent [see 37 CFR 1.14(c)]. **Scenario 3):** If you have checked both box A and box B in the "Opt Out"

section, and/or you are submitting the ADS sometime after your initial filing (this is rare; for example, you are submitting a revised ADS), then the ADS must be signed by (i) a patent practitioner (that is, a registered patent attorney or patent agent, per 37 CFR 1.32(b) or 37 CFR 1.34); or (ii) an assignee of the application (per 37 CFR 3.71(b)); or (iii) all of the applicants; or (iv) one or more joint inventor-applicants who hold a power of attorney (USPTO form AIA/81, signed by all of the applicants) (see 37 CFR 1.33(b)). If one or more inventors refuse to sign, seek assistance from a registered patent attorney. If you are not sure you are doing this correctly, seek assistance by calling the PTO's Patent Ombudsman's office at 571-272-5555 or 855-559-8589, or the Application Assistance Unit at 571-272-4200 or 888-786-0101.

a. Filing Your Application

Now that you have your documents together, you're ready to file your application. The following instructions are based on the Patent Center process as it existed at the time of this writing. Please understand that the USPTO continues to develop Patent Center, and application screens and menu items might change by the time you file your application.

Here are the steps for filing your application.

- **Sign on.** Go to patentcenter.uspto.gov. If you haven't registered as an eFiler, click on "Patent Center Unregistered eFilers" and fill in your name and email; then click "New application/ proceeding." A series of new dialog boxes will open as you progress, in which you must select the type of application ("Utility" or "Design") and specify a number of other options that are described in this book (for example, for a Utility application, specify "Provisional" if you are filing a provisional application, otherwise select one of the nonprovisional options: "Nonprovisional"; "Accelerated" (not recommended); or "Track 1"), and click "Continue."

  If you have registered, click on "Patent Center Registered eFilers." Then fill in your Digital Certificate and password. You can recover the Digital Certificate by browsing to Program Files/USPTO in your computer and opening the file with your name and a ".epf" suffix; for example, "John Smith.epf." Check the box to confirm that you are not accessing (or permitting access to) technology or software in a manner that would violate or circumvent the Export Administration Regulations, if you are certain that your technology is not export-controlled by those Regulations. Otherwise, consult an export control specialist. Click "Authenticate" and then certify your identity, select "New Application" and the type of application, and click "Continue." If you get stuck at any time, call the PTO's Electronic Business Center at 866-217-9197 or 571-272-4100, or send an email to ebc@uspto.gov.

- **Application data.** On the "Application Data" page in Patent Center, you first will be given an opportunity to manually enter or upload your ADS. In Patent Center, this step is skipped, and you will upload your ADS later. In either case, fill in the title of the invention, a docket number for the application of your choosing (optional, but a suitable docket number can be something like "Krypton Derailleur"), and your name and Customer Number or address. It's best to copy this data electronically from your ADS so that everything will be consistent. (Even if you're not registered you can obtain a Customer Number, which will take a few days but will save you from having to type your address each time.) Click "Continue." If you instead want to create an ADS now, press the button "Web-based ADS" and the form will be replaced with an online version of the ADS form AIA/14 for you to fill out.
- **Upload Documents:** In the "Upload Documents" page, check the "No" button under the Preliminary Amendment question, then click the "Browse files" button and find your Application Holding Folder that contains the DOCX and/or PDF files of your application. Select one of your

application files, such as the Dwgs.pdf file, click open, and you should see it listed. In Patent Center the file will be recognized automatically as a file with "Drawings-only black and white line drawings." Then you will be able to attach more documents to your filing. Repeat the above steps for each of your other application files (that is, Spec.docx and Dec.pdf at least, and Spec.pdf if you are uploading an optional PDF version of the specification).

Patent Center immediately uploads and validates file formats and data, identifies PTO forms and most other document types, and tells you whether you are missing any documents (like your Cover Sheet), or whether any documents have the wrong format. If Patent Center can't automatically detect what file type you uploaded, use the drop-down menu to select "Application Part." When finished with all documents, click "Continue."

- **Calculate fees.** On the "Calculate Fees" page, select your entity size, which will usually be Small Entity or Micro Entity. Check and complete all the applicable boxes on the form, and then click the "Continue" button. If you are filing a lengthy Information Disclosure Statement, you may need to pay an "IDS size fee" (see Section G below), but the "previously paid amount" on this page will be zero.

On the second "Calculate Fees" page, check all of the relevant boxes, which will include at least:

  - box 1011 (basic filing fee-utility)
  - box 1111 (utility patent appl. search fee)
  - box 1311 (patent appl. examination fee)

If you are filing your specification in PDF only (i.e., you are not also filing a DOCX version), you must check box 1054 and pay a hefty filing surcharge. Also, if you are filing an IDS citing more than 50 (i.e., 51+) references, you will need to check the appropriate "IDS size fee": box 1832 (for 51-100 references), 1833 (for 101 to 200 references), or 1834 (for more than 200 references). Then press "Continue."

- **Review and submit application:** This page will list all of your application files, a "Fee-Info.pdf" file, and the filing fee. If everything is okay, click the "Submit" button at the bottom to bring up a "Congratulations!" page with an assigned Application Number, Confirmation Number, and Total Fees due. Click the "YES! I want to pay now" button at the bottom.

- **Review fees and select payment method.** Unless you have a PTO Deposit Account or are set up for EFT, select "Charge Credit Card," then "Start Online Payment Process" to bring up the payment page. Fill out the blanks and click the "Confirm" button at the bottom.

- **Acknowledgment receipt.** If everything is okay you'll get an Acknowledgment Receipt, which is analogous to the receipt postcard that was used for mailed filings. The Acknowledgment Receipt will list the Application (Serial) Number, the Confirmation Number, and the application data and parts that you've filed. Congratulations! You've bypassed the post office, filed an application electronically, and have gotten an instant filing acknowledgment. Select "Print This Page" to print the receipt for your records. In due course you'll get an official filing receipt by mail, as usual.

- **IDS.** As stated in the next section, you must generally file an IDS (Information Disclosure Statement) within three months after filing if you know of any relevant prior art. If you're a registered eFiler you can file an IDS online. Download IDS form SB/08a – Patent Center from the PTO site (uspto.gov/patents/apply/forms). Open the form and fill out the Document Number, Publication Data, Name and Relevant

Information column for each U.S. patent or U.S. published patent application you disclose, and Country Code, Number and Kind Code (if you know it), Publication Data, Name and Relevant Information column for each foreign patent document you disclose. Then save the completed form using a suitable name, such as "IDS.pdf," and file it online in a similar manner as you filed the PDFs of the application. If you're unregistered you'll have to download and fill out the three forms SB/08a, SB/08b, and SB/08c that the above form replaces, then fax or mail all of the forms to the PTO. Remember that you don't have to accompany the IDS with copies of any U.S. patents or published patent applications, but you do have to accompany it with copies of any foreign patents (with an explanation of relevance) and copies of any nonpatent prior art (together referred to as "nonpatent literature" ("NPL")).

- **Assignments.** If you want to file an assignment, you must do this through a separate part of the PTO's website (link below). After you complete your electronic filing and have your Acknowledgment Receipt, or after you receive your official filing receipt by mail, fill in the Serial Number of your application on the assignment, and complete and sign the rest of the assignment. Then convert the signed assignment to PDF and go to assignmentcenter.uspto.gov and follow the instructions.

- **Designs.** To file a design application via Patent Center, prepare it as instructed below, except omit the postcard, Design Application Transmittal, Fee Transmittal, and CCPF or check. Do prepare the drawings, preamble, specification, and claim, and prepare and sign and date the declaration as instructed above and save these documents as PDF files. Then proceed as described above.

D. File the Information Disclosure Statement Within Three Months

The PTO's rules impose on each patent applicant a "duty of candor and good faith" toward the PTO. This means that all inventors (and attorneys) associated with the filing and prosecution of a patent application have a duty to disclose to the PTO information (prior art and any other information such as relevant litigation) of which they are aware. The information must be of the type that might influence the patent examiner in deciding on the patent application; that is, information that is "material to patentability." (This duty is embodied in Inventor's Commandment 17.) To comply with the "prior art" part of Inventor's Commandment 17, all applicants who are aware of any relevant prior art—that is, from a search or personal knowledge— should submit an Information Disclosure Statement (IDS) at the time of filing the application or within the following three months. It's not enough to cite the prior-art references in the Background section of your specification. You must cite them on a SB/08a or SB/08b form and supply copies of non-U.S. patent references to the PTO, along with new Form SB/08c, the "IDS size fee" form.

Even if it weren't required, it's to your advantage to file an IDS and to list as many relevant prior-art references as possible in order to have them considered and noted by the examiner. In this way they will be listed as "References Cited" in the patent. This creates a presumption that the claims of your patent are patentable over these references—that is, you'll have put these references behind you (and behind those who, down the road, might want to challenge the validity of your patent). You may file the IDS with your application but we suggest that you file the IDS immediately afterward; this will prevent overload while preparing your basic application.

The IDS consists of an IDS cover letter (downloadable Form 10-5; see Appendix 7 for details) and the actual IDS (Form SB/08a and SB/08b), on which you list the prior art. A filled-in sample is provided in Figs. 10N, 10O, and 10P. (If you file via Patent Center—discussed in Section C, above—you should first fill out the SB/08a, SB/08b, and SB/08c forms and make PDF copies of any non-U.S. patent references (foreign patents and non-patent literature (NPL)). You will not need a cover letter because the Patent Center form provides its own cover letter.)

The IDS should list all prior-art references known to the inventors (and any assignees) that are relevant to the patentability of the application. These should include all the references you discovered in your patentability search (Chapter 6), plus any other prior art of which you're aware, including even your own papers. In addition, the inventors must include with the IDS a copy of each cited non-U.S. patent reference and a discussion of the relevance of any non-English-language references to the invention. You must cite all references even if you discussed them in the prior-art section of your patent application. (If you haven't made a search or otherwise aren't aware of any prior art, don't file an IDS but make a memorandum that no IDS is required and keep that memo with your application papers.) You should remove all marks and notes from any references that you send to the PTO. If you have compiled a very large number of references, list only those that are truly relevant and don't include any cumulative (duplicative) references.

In January 2025 the PTO instituted an "IDS size fee" to discourage applicants from filing irrelevant references. The first 50 references may be cited in an IDS (or any number of IDS filings) for free. But when filing any IDS that brings the total number of cited references up to 51-100, the PTO will charge a $200 fee. If the total number of references becomes 101-200, the PTO charges a $500 fee (less any amount previously paid). If the total number of cited references ever exceeds 200, the PTO charges an $800 fee (again, less previous payment). At the same time, the PTO required that applicants submit with every IDS a Form SB/08c asserting that the correct size fee is being paid (even if it is zero). For this reason, it is now essential that you keep track of how many references you have cited to the PTO.

In the United States Patent and Trademark Office

Serial Number: 11/123 456

Appn. Filed: 2022 November 11

Applicant(s): M. Goldberger & N. Briskin

Appn. Title: Food chopper with convolute blade

Examiner/GAU: / 3240

Mailed: 2024 December 13, Thursday

At: Philadelphia, PA

Information Disclosure Statement Cover Letter

Commissioner for Patents
P.O. Box 1450
Alexandria, VA 22313-1450

Sir:

Attached is a completed Form PTO/SB/08(A&B) and copies of any non-U.S. patent references cited thereon.

Following are comments on any non-English-language references pursuant to Rule 98:

Rasmussen shows a fruit peeler with a bent guide for controlling the thickness of the fruit as it is being peeled. Gillet shows a knife mounted parallel to a space with knife that can be tilted out or in to adjust the spacing of its edge.

None of the references shows a knife for making a cut of controlled depth wherein a flat-bladed knife with an elongated sharpened edge with an outward protrusion attached to the blade that is spaced back from the edge for limiting the depth of cut that can be made by said edge when it is used to cut in a direction perpendicular to the plane of the blade, as it is recited in independent claims 1 and 17, and hence their dependent claims 2 to 11 and 18 to 20.

To the contrary, all of the references show guides that are mounted generally parallel to the blade for limiting the thickness of the peel that can be cut by the blade when it is used to peel in a direction parallel to its plane.

Also, none of the references show any blade having a substantially right-angle bend parallel to its direction of elongation, as it is recited in independent claim 12 and its dependent claims 13 to 16.

Very respectfully,

Applicant(s): *Mildred Goldberger*

Nathan Briskin

Enc.: PTO/SB/08(A&B)

c/o: M. Goldberger, Applicant Pro Se

1901 Kennedy Blvd.

Philadelphia, PA 19103

Telephone: 215-555-0362

Certificate of Mailing

I certify that this correspondence will be deposited with the United States Postal Service as first-class mail with proper postage affixed in an envelope addressed to: "Commissioner for Patents, P.O. Box 1450, Alexandria, VA 22313-1450" on the date below.

Date: 20 24 Dec 15 _____ *Mildred Goldberger* _____, Applicant

Fig. 10N—Completed IDS Cover Letter (Downloadable Form 10-5; see Appendix 7 for details)

316 | PATENT IT YOURSELF

PTO/SB/08a (07-09)
Approved for use through 11/30/2027. OMB 0651-0031
U.S. Patent and Trademark Office; U.S. DEPARTMENT OF COMMERCE
Under the Paperwork Reduction Act of 1995, no persons are required to respond to a collection of information unless it contains a valid OMB control number.

Substitute for form 1449/PTO

INFORMATION DISCLOSURE STATEMENT BY APPLICANT
(Use as many sheets as necessary)

Complete if Known

Application Number	11/123,456
Filing Date	2024 November 11
First Named Inventor	m. Goldberger
Art Unit	3240
Examiner Name	
Attorney Docket Number	Goldberger-Briskin

Sheet | 1 | of | 2

U. S. PATENT DOCUMENTS

Examiner Initials*	Cite No.[1]	Document Number — Number-Kind Code[2] *(if known)*	Publication Date MM-DD-YYYY	Name of Patentee or Applicant of Cited Document	Pages, Columns, Lines, Where Relevant Passages or Relevant Figures Appear
	A	US- 21,695	10-15-1858	Oot	
	B	US- 602,758	11-11-1898	Landers	p4, ll.21-22
	C	US- 2,083,368	8-9-1937	Gambino	
	D	US- 2,968,867	10-11-1961	Wolff	
		US-			
		US-			
		US-			
		US-			
		US-			
		US-			
		US-			
		US-			
		US-			
		US-			
		US-			
		US-			
		US-			
		US-			

FOREIGN PATENT DOCUMENTS

Examiner Initials*	Cite No.[1]	Foreign Patent Document — Country Code[3]—Number[4]—Kind Code[5] *(if known)*	Publication Date MM-DD-YYYY	Name of Patentee or Applicant of Cited Document	Pages, Columns, Lines, Where Relevant Passages Or Relevant Figures Appear	T[6]
	E	DK-69,640	5-22-1949	Rasmussen	p2, ll. 13-17	
	F	FR-1,029,924	3-23-1953	Gillet		

Examiner Signature		Date Considered	

*EXAMINER: Initial if reference considered, whether or not citation is in conformance with MPEP 609. Draw line through citation if not in conformance and not considered. Include copy of this form with next communication to applicant. [1] Applicant's unique citation designation number (optional). [2] See Kinds Codes of USPTO Patent Documents at www.uspto.gov or MPEP 901.04. [3] Enter Office that issued the document, by the two-letter code (WIPO Standard ST.3). [4] For Japanese patent documents, the indication of the year of the reign of the Emperor must precede the serial number of the patent document. [5] Kind of document by the appropriate symbols as indicated on the document under WIPO Standard ST.16 if possible. [6] Applicant is to place a check mark here if English language Translation is attached.

A Federal agency may not conduct or sponsor, and a person is not required to respond to, nor shall a person be subject to a penalty for failure to comply with an information collection subject to the requirements of the Paperwork Reduction Act of 1995, unless the information collection has a currently valid OMB Control Number. The OMB Control Number for this information collection is 0651-0031. Public burden for this form is estimated to average 2 hours per response, including the time for reviewing instructions, searching existing data sources, gathering and maintaining the data needed, and completing and reviewing the information collection. Send comments regarding this burden estimate or any other aspect of this information collection, including suggestions for reducing this burden to the Chief Administrative Officer, United States Patent and Trademark Office, P.O. Box 1450, Alexandria, VA 22313-1450 or email InformationCollection@uspto.gov. **DO NOT SEND FEES OR COMPLETED FORMS TO THIS ADDRESS.** If filing this completed form by mail, send to: **Commissioner for Patents, P.O. Box 1450, Alexandria, VA 22313-1450.**

If you need assistance in completing the form, call 1-800-PTO-9199 (1-800-786-9199) and select option 2.

Fig. 10O—Information Disclosure Statement (Downloadable Form 10-6A; see Appendix 7 for details)

CHAPTER 10 | FINALIZING AND FILING YOUR APPLICATION | 317

PTO/SB/08b (07-09)
Approved for use through 11/30/2027. OMB 0651-0031
U.S. Patent and Trademark Office; U.S. DEPARTMENT OF COMMERCE
Under the Paperwork Reduction Act of 1995, no persons are required to respond to a collection of information unless it contains a valid OMB control number.

Substitute for form 1449/PTO

INFORMATION DISCLOSURE STATEMENT BY APPLICANT

(Use as many sheets as necessary)

Complete if Known	
Application Number	11/123,456
Filing Date	2024 November 11
First Named Inventor	M. Goldberger
Art Unit	3240
Examiner Name	

Sheet		2	of		2	Attorney Docket Number	Goldberger-Briskin

NON PATENT LITERATURE DOCUMENTS

Examiner Initials*	Cite No.[1]	Include name of the author (in CAPITAL LETTERS), title of the article (when appropriate), title of the item (book, magazine, journal, serial, symposium, catalog, etc.), date, page(s), volume-issue number(s), publisher, city and/or country where published.	T[2]
	G	PHILLIPS, Food Comminuting, Restaurant News, April 1959, Food Press, Willow Grove, PA	

Examiner Signature		Date Considered	

*EXAMINER: Initial if reference considered, whether or not citation is in conformance with MPEP 609. Draw line through citation if not in conformance and not considered. Include copy of this form with next communication to applicant.
1 Applicant's unique citation designation number (optional). 2 Applicant is to place a check mark here if English language Translation is attached.

A Federal agency may not conduct or sponsor, and a person is not required to respond to, nor shall a person be subject to a penalty for failure to comply with an information collection subject to the requirements of the Paperwork Reduction Act of 1995, unless the information collection has a currently valid OMB Control Number. The OMB Control Number for this information collection is 0651-0031. Public burden for this form is estimated to average 2 hours per response, including the time for reviewing instructions, searching existing data sources, gathering and maintaining the data needed, and completing and reviewing the information collection. Send comments regarding this burden estimate or any other aspect of this information collection, including suggestions for reducing this burden to the Chief Administrative Officer, United States Patent and Trademark Office, P.O. Box 1450, Alexandria, VA 22313-1450 or email InformationCollection@uspto.gov. **DO NOT SEND FEES OR COMPLETED FORMS TO THIS ADDRESS. If filing this completed form by mail, send to: Commissioner for Patents, P.O. Box 1450, Alexandria, VA 22313-1450.**

Fig. 10P—Information Disclosure Statement (Downloadable Form 10-6B; see Appendix 7)

318 | PATENT IT YOURSELF

PTO/SB/08C (01-25)
Approved for use through 01/31/2028. OMB 0651-0070
U.S. Patent and Trademark Office; U.S. DEPARTMENT OF COMMERCE
Under the Paperwork Reduction Act of 1995 no persons are required to respond to a collection of information unless it displays a valid OMB control number.

INFORMATION DISCLOSURE STATEMENT SIZE FEE –
WRITTEN ASSERTION UNDER 37 CFR 1.98

Complete if Known

Application or Patent No.:	First Named Inventor:	Art Unit:
11/123,456	M. Goldberger	3240

Filing Date:	Attorney Docket Number:	Examiner:
2024 November 11	Goldberger-Briskin	

Please see 37 CFR 1.17(v) and attached Instructions for completing this form to make the appropriate selection of an assertion under 37 CFR 1.98. For the information disclosure statement (IDS) submitted herewith, the applicant or patent owner certifies the following with respect to the cumulative number of applicant-provided or patent-owner provided items of information submitted to date including those in the accompanying IDS (select only one):

☑ No IDS size fee is required under 37 CFR 1.17(v) at this time.

☐ The IDS is accompanied by the IDS size fee under 37 CFR 1.17(v)(1).

☐ The IDS is accompanied by the IDS size fee under 37 CFR 1.17(v)(2).

☐ The IDS is accompanied by the IDS size fee under 37 CFR 1.17(v)(3).

NOTE: This form must be accompanied by PTO/SB/08a and/or PTO/SB/08b or equivalent.

DEPOSIT ACCOUNT

The Director is authorized to charge the fee indicated above in the amount of $ _____ for the IDS submitted herewith to deposit account _____.

SIGNATURE

This form must be signed in accordance with 37 CFR 1.33. See 37 CFR 1.4(d) for signature requirements and certifications.

If applicant or patent owner is a juristic entity (e.g., an LLC or corporation), this form must be signed by a registered practitioner. See 37 CFR 1.31.

If applicant or patent owner is a person or persons, this form may be signed by either a registered practitioner, or the applicant or patentee. Note that if multiple people together are the applicant or patentee (e.g., there are joint inventors who together are the applicant), then a signature is required from each person who is an applicant or patentee. *Submit multiple forms if more than one signature is required, see below*.*

Signature *M. Goldberger*	Date 2025 March 27
Name (Print/Typed) M. Goldberger	Practitioner Registration Number (if applicable)

☑ * Total of ___1___ forms are submitted.

A Federal agency may not conduct or sponsor, and a person is not required to respond to, nor shall a person be subject to a penalty for failure to comply with an information collection subject to the requirements of the Paperwork Reduction Act of 1995, unless the information collection has a currently valid OMB Control Number. The OMB Control Number for this information collection is 0651-0070. Public burden for this form is estimated to average 2 hours per response, including the time for reviewing instructions, searching existing data sources, gathering and maintaining the data needed, and completing and reviewing the information collection. Send comments regarding this burden estimate or any other aspect of this information collection, including suggestions for reducing this burden to the Office of the Chief Administrative Officer, United States Patent and Trademark Office, P.O. Box 1450, Alexandria, VA 22313-1450 or email InformationCollection@uspto.gov. DO NOT SEND FEES OR COMPLETED FORMS TO THIS ADDRESS. **SEND TO: Commissioner for Patents, P.O. Box 1450, Alexandria, VA 22313-1450.**

Fig. 10Q—Information Disclosure Statement (Downloadable Form 10-6C; see Appendix 7)

If you cite a significant number of irrelevant references, a court may hold that you tried to deceive the PTO by burying the relevant references with a large number of irrelevant references. On the other hand, if you withhold a relevant reference of which you are aware, a court may hold that you tried to deceive the PTO by not satisfying your duty of disclosure. Deciding what to put into an IDS can be tricky indeed!

As a general rule, if you are not sure whether a reference is relevant enough to cite, it's best to cite it, despite the new IDS size fees. The penalty for not citing a relevant reference is severe—your patent can be held invalid. One way to determine whether a reference is relevant enough to cite as prior art in your IDS is to consider not citing it in your IDS and then assume you get a patent.

Further assume that you sue an infringer and they find out through discovery that you knew about the reference. If the infringer then cites the reference to the judge and charges you with fraud on the PTO for not citing it, the reference is relevant if a reasonable judge would be likely to find that you should have cited it to avoid fraud on the PTO.

Note that the PTO's Rule 56 (37 CFR 1.56) states that applicants should examine the following to be sure that they disclose all relevant prior art:

1. Prior art cited in search reports of a foreign patent office in a counterpart application.
2. The closest information over which individuals associated with the filing or prosecution of a patent application believe any pending claim patentably defines, to make sure that any material information contained therein is disclosed to the Office.

The PTO considers that information is material to patentability when it is not cumulative to information already of record or being made of record in the application, and (a) it establishes, by itself or in combination with other information, a *prima facie* (on first sight) case of unpatentability of a claim; or (b) it refutes, or is inconsistent with, a position the applicant takes in (i) opposing an argument of unpatentability relied on by the Office, or (ii) asserting an argument of patentability.

A *prima facie* case of unpatentability is established when the information compels a conclusion that a claim is unpatentable under the preponderance of evidence burden-of-proof standard, giving each term in the claim its broadest reasonable construction consistent with the specification. This is done before any consideration is given to evidence which may be submitted in an attempt to establish a contrary conclusion of patentability.

As mentioned, you can send the IDS with your application instead of taking advantage of the three-month grace period. In this event, the names of the inventors and title of your invention are the only information you need to put at the top of Form 10-5. Don't fill out the Certificate of Mailing at the bottom of the form. However, if you send it after your application is filed, you'll know the serial number, filing date, and group art unit, and can insert them. In that case, you should fill out the Certificate of Mailing at the bottom of the form.

The blanks in Forms 10-5 and 10-6 are self-explanatory. Information about the Art Unit (requested in the upper right-hand corner of Form 10-6) is on your filing receipt. Before each patent number in the Foreign Patent Documents section, you may use a two-letter international country code, as indicated. The most common county codes are FR (France), JP (Japan), CN (China), GB (United Kingdom), CA (Canada), EP (Europe), and DE (Germany). In the right-hand column, headed "Pages, Columns …," you can list any places in the document that you feel are particularly relevant, but this is optional since the pertinent rules (Rules 97 and 98) require that you merely cite the documents.

If you include any non-English-language reference on Form 10-6, Rule 98(a)(3) requires that you also provide a concise explanation of its relevance on a separate paper or in the specification. We recommend that you also state how your invention, as claimed, differs physically from this reference(s). State the relevance of any non-English references, and any discussion as to how your invention differs, on Form 10-5. However, don't write anything that might be used by the PTO to reject your application, for example by saying that one of the references teaches something that you have claimed. It's up to the PTO to identify reasons to reject your application, and you don't need to give them unnecessary help—alerting them to the references is enough, and in fact, it's required. Fig. 10N provides an example.

If you mail in the IDS with the application, note this on the postcard and transmittal letter that you mail with your application and don't fill out the Certificate of Mailing at the bottom of Form 10-5. If you send it in after the application is filed, send it with a separate postcard and fill out the Certificate of Mailing. The acknowledgment receipt you receive will list the IDS. If you file by Patent Center and you're a registered eFiler (or become one later), you can file the IDS via Patent Center after you get your official filing receipt. If you file by Patent Center and you're not a registered eFiler, you will have to mail the IDS and cover sheet with a receipt postcard.

If you haven't made a search and are not aware of any prior art, then you don't have to file an IDS. The PTO won't deny or delay your application if you don't file an IDS. However, if they (or an infringer whom you later sue for patent infringement) discover that you knew of relevant prior art and didn't file an IDS, your patent application or patent can be held invalid for "fraud on the PTO." This is so, even if the examiner discovers the reference you withheld and cites it in a regular Office Action. In one case, a Dallas patent law firm neglected to disclose some relevant prior art to the PTO in its client's patent application. The client got a patent and sued on it, but because of the cloud the nondisclosed art cast on the patent, it had to settle the suit for far less than it would have gotten if the firm had disclosed the prior art to the PTO. The client then sued the firm and a jury awarded the client $72 million in damages for the firm's omission!

Suppose you are aware of information other than prior art that may be material to patentability—for example: relevant litigation, an assertion by another person claiming to be an inventor, or a sale of a product embodying the invention before the filing date (but not before your date of invention). You have a duty to disclose this information also. You can do this with a narrative statement on a form such as Form 10-5. Also, be sure to state why the information does not negate the patentability of your invention.

E. Assignments

As we mentioned, a patent application must be filed in the name or names of the true inventor or inventors of the invention claimed in the patent application. The inventors then become the applicants for the patent, and the law considers that they automatically own equal shares of the invention, the patent application, and any patents that may issue on the application (Chapter 16, Section B). However, inventorship can be different from ownership. Often all or part of the ownership of the invention and the patent application must be transferred to someone else, either an individual or a legal entity, such as a corporation, a partnership, or an individual. To make this transfer, the inventor(s) must "assign" (legally transfer) their interest. The assignment transfers ownership (or part of it) from the inventor(s) to another entity. However, inventorship remains the same after an assignment is made. (Directions and forms for completing the assignment are in Chapter 16, Section E.)

If you have assigned the application to another person or company and you want to send the assignment to the PTO for recording (highly advised), you can either send it in with the patent application or at any time afterward. We prefer to send in assignments later, after we get the postcard receipt back, when we know and can add the serial number and filing date of the application to the assignment. This will make the two documents (the assignment and the application) correspond to each other more directly. In this case, you can add the serial number and filing date to the assignment in the spaces indicated. Then prepare an Assignment "Recordation Form Cover Sheet" (Form 16-4 or PTO Form 1595). In space 1, the conveying parties are the inventor applicants. In space 2, the receiving party is the assignee—the person or organization to whom you're assigning the application. The Internal Address is the mail stop or apartment number if any, in the assignee's building. In space 3, the Conveyance is an assignment and the execution date is the date you signed the assignment. In space 4, the Application Number is the Serial Number of your patent application. We recommend that you also type the filing date. If you don't know these numbers yet, just fill in the execution

United States Patent [19]
Sarriugarte et al.

[11] Patent Number: **Des. 404,074**
[45] Date of Patent: ****Jan. 12, 1999**

[54] **CARD, PLACARD, OR RIGID PICTURE HOLDER**

[76] Inventors: **Jon Sarriugarte; Sina Hanson**, both of 2601 Adeline St., Oakland, Calif. 94607

[**] Term: **14 Years**

[21] Appl. No.: **69,268**

[22] Filed: **Mar. 21, 1997**

[51] LOC (6) Cl. **19-02**
[52] U.S. Cl. **D19/90**; D20/43; D19/86; D6/313
[58] Field of Search D6/313; D11/121; D20/43; D19/65, 75, 78, 86, 87, 90, 91, 95, 99, 100; 211/69.1–69.9, 181.1; 40/606, 659, 642.02; 248/229.26, 175, 475.1, 623; 5/246, 252, 256

[56] **References Cited**

U.S. PATENT DOCUMENTS

D. 26,320	11/1896	Arkin	D19/86
D. 27,364	7/1897	Hill et al.	D20/43
D. 32,692	5/1900	Muth	D20/43
D. 178,356	7/1956	Galef	D19/86
D. 203,185	12/1965	Leaboldi	D19/87
D. 247,265	2/1978	Ledebuhr	D20/43
3,474,555	10/1969	McCaffrey	40/659
3,721,414	3/1973	Yoder	248/175

Primary Examiner—Martie K. Holtje
Attorney, Agent, or Firm—David Pressman

[57] **CLAIM**

The ornamental design for a a card, placard, or rigid picture holder, as shown and described.

DESCRIPTION

FIG. **1** is a front elevational view of a card, placard or rigid picture holder showing our new design, the rear view being substantially a mirror image thereof;
FIG. **2** is a right side elevational view;
FIG. **3** is a left side elevational view;
FIG. **4** is a top plan view; and,
FIG. **5** is a bottom plan view thereof.

1 Claim, 3 Drawing Sheets

Fig. 10R—Sample of Design Patent

(signing) date of your PAD. If you're assigning a patent, fill in the patent number and issue date in space 4B. "Additional numbers attached [ ] Yes [ ] No" should be checked to indicate whether or not you've listed additional cases on an attached sheet. The remaining blocks are self-explanatory. Make sure to include the recordation fee (see Appendix 4, "Fee Schedule").

If you wish to send the assignment in with your patent application, complete the Recordation Form Cover Sheet (Form 16-4), check the "Assignment Papers" (Box 9 on Form 10-2), and on Form 10-3 type "Assignment Recordal" after "Other" in Section 3. Include the fee on this line and in your total at the top of the form.

If an assignment of a patent application has been recorded and it is referred to in the issue fee transmittal form (see Chapter 13), the PTO will print the patent with the assignee's interest indicated. However, even if you fail to indicate the assignment on the issue fee transmittal form, so that the patent doesn't indicate the assignment, the assignment will still be effective if it has been recorded.

If an assignment has been made, and as a result there are two or more owners of the patent application, then the owners should consider signing a Joint Owners' Agreement (Form 16-2). (See the reasons for the JOA in Chapter 16, Section D.)

F. Petitions to Make Special—Getting Your Application Examined Faster

If you need to have your patent issued sooner than the normal course of one to three years, the PTO provides a number of ways that you can get it examined ahead of its normal turn. However unless you have a specific need for the early examination or issuance of a patent—for example, an infringement is occurring and you need a patent to get capital for manufacturing the invention, or the technology is rapidly becoming obsolete, or you're contemplating foreign filing—most patent professionals agree that there is usually little to be gained by advancing examination. We believe that in most cases it is better to allow the patent to issue after a delay of a year or two since this will keep the details of the invention out of the public's eyes until you or your licensee have had time to develop and market it.

But if you still want to have your examination advanced, here are all of the ways:

1. Simple PTMS Filings Based on Health, Age, Environment, Energy, or Terrorism

37 CFR 1.102(c) lists several reasons why you might be able to move your application to the front of the line. If you qualify, file a simple "petition to make special" (PTMS) based on:

- age
- poor health
- your invention enhancing the quality of the environment
- development or conservation of energy resources, or
- countering terrorism.

There is no fee to file a simple PTMS in any of these five categories.

If you file based on age, your age must be 65 or greater. This category is so popular that the PTO has a special form for it and it will be granted automatically by the PTO's server if you file it online. The form is SB/130 and you can fill it out and file it with your application.

The PTO doesn't provide a form for the other four categories but the procedure described below may be used to file a PTMS for the age category as well as any of the other four categories, listed above.

> CAUTION
>
> **These are the only five reasons for which you may use PTMS Form 10-9.** If you choose any other reason, your petition will be dismissed.

If you are filing a PTMS based on any of the five reasons listed above, you may use PTMS Form 10-9 (Fig. 10U, below). You will also need to file a supporting declaration (SD). This can be filed with the application or at any time afterwards. The supporting declaration that accompanies the PTMS should be in the format of Fig. 10T with the introductory paragraph and the last paragraph left intact. The remaining paragraphs must be tailored to your situation and give detailed

CHAPTER 10 | FINALIZING AND FILING YOUR APPLICATION | 323

Design Patent Application—Preamble, Specification, and Claim

Mail Stop Design
Commissioner for Patents
P.O. Box 1450
Alexandria, VA 22313-1450

Sir:

PREAMBLE:

The petitioner(s) whose signature(s) appear on the declaration attached respectfully request that Letters Patent be granted to such petitioner(s) for the new and original design set forth in the following specification. The filing fee* of $_____230_____ , ___3___ sheets of drawings, a patent application declaration, fee transmittal, a credit card payment form or check, and a return receipt postcard are attached.

SPECIFICATION:

The undersigned has (have) invented a new, original, and ornamental design entitled "_____
_____Clothes Hanger_____" of which the following is a specification. Reference is made to the accompanying drawings which form a part hereof, the figures of which are described as follows:

CROSS-REFERENCE TO RELATED APPLICATIONS: None

STATEMENT REGARDING FEDERALLY SPONSORED RESEARCH: None

DRAWING FIGURES:

    Fig. 1 is a front, elevational view of my new clothes hanger
    Fig. 2 is a left-side view of the clothes hanger
    Fig. 3 is a perspective view of the clothes hanger
    Fig. 4 is a rear view of the clothes hanger.

CLAIM: I (We) Claim:
The ornamental design for a _____Clothes hanger_____
_____ , as shown.

Express Mail Label # (EH160200231US) ; Date of Deposit 20 24 Sept 8 _____

Fig. 10S—Completed Design Patent Application (Form 10-10 in Appendix 7)
Use latest fees—see Appendix 4, "Fee Schedule."

facts (MPEP 708.02) in support of the reason for the petition. Here are some suggestions:

If your PTMS is based on age, and you don't use form SB/130, merely state that you're older than 65 and give your birth date. If you file by Patent Center, use form SB/130 and file it with the application or afterwards if you're a registered eFiler; you need not file any supporting PTMS declaration.

If your PTMS is based on poor health, environmental enhancement, conservation of energy, or countering terrorism give detailed facts or reasoning in support of your main reason, as shown in Fig. 10T. Attach photocopies of such documents to your SD if they are relevant and label each document with a sequential exhibit number—for example, Exhibit A, Exhibit B— and explain it in detail in the declaration.

If you mail your PTMS with the application, you should refer to it in your transmittal letter and your postcard receipt. In this case, you won't be able to include the PTO filing data on the PTMS. Don't fill out the Certificate of Mailing at the bottom of the form. If you mail it later, fill out the Certificate of Mailing and add the application filing data to the PTMS, as shown in Fig. 10U. As always, don't forget the postcard receipt. If you file the PTMS via the web, the PTO's server will grant it automatically, but if you file it by mail, you'll receive a letter from the PTO stating that your petition has been granted and the examiner in charge of your application has been instructed to examine it ahead of turn. You should then receive an Office Action (see Chapter 13) several months sooner than normal. Here are more details about the four categories other than age:

- **Health:** Your health must be such that you might not be available to assist in the prosecution of the application if it were to run its normal course.
- **Environment:** The subject matter of the application will materially enhance the quality of the environment.
- **Conservation:** The subject matter of the application will materially contribute to the development or conservation of energy resources.
- **Countering Terrorism:** The subject matter of the application will materially contribute to countering terrorism.

2. The Accelerated Examination Program

If you don't qualify for a simple PTMS, you can file a more complicated PTMS Under the Accelerated Examination Program (AEP). The PTO requires a fee for a Petition under the AEP and it is complicated and difficult to prepare; the PTO estimates that it will take you more than 12 hours to prepare. The Petition may be granted for a limited number of reasons below, some of which duplicate the "free" reasons under the simple PTMS. If any of these three reasons apply in your case, the advantage of going via the AEP route is that you will be able to get the patent in about 12 months, whereas the simple PTMS route will usually take a year or so longer, even with examination ahead of turn. For details, consult the PTO's website at www.uspto.gov/patents/initiatives/accelerated-examination.

If you are filing a simple PTMS based on the condition of your health or age, you can use Form 10-9, below. Otherwise, you must follow the rules in the AEP, described below.

The rules require that you file everything electronically using Patent Center and that you file the AEP Form SB/28 at the same time. You can find Form SB/28 at the EFS website (www.uspto.gov/patents/apply/forms). Again the PTO estimates that Form SB/28 will take 12 hours to complete.

Why does it take so long? Because essentially, you are examining your own application! First, you must make a search, then prepare an Information Disclosure Statement citing the references in the search. You must also identify the limitations of the claims that are disclosed in the references, how the claims are patentable over the references, discuss the utility of the invention, list references that may be disqualified as references because they came from the same organization (see 35 U.S.C. § 103(c)), state where each limitation of the claims finds support in the specification, detail the search that was made, including where it was made, and state the reason for accelerated examination.

The application may not include more than three independent and 20 total claims and must claim one invention only. The fee for the Petition is stated in Rule 17(h) (see Appendix 4, "Fee Schedule"); this fee is in addition to the Patent Center filing fee.

In the United States Patent and Trademark Office

Appn. Number: 11/987,654

Filing Date: 2024 December 3

Applicant(s): Gonzales, David

Examiner: Hayness / GAU 654

Mailed: 2024 December 3

At: San Francisco

Declaration in Support of Accompanying Petition to Make Special

Reason I—Applicant's Health Is Poor

In support of the accompanying Petition to Make Special, applicant declares as follows: *

1. I am the applicant in the above-identified patent application.

2. On August 15, 2024 I had a massive heart attack and was hospitalized in St. Francis Hospital in San Francisco for 6 days.

3. My cardiologist, Dr. Ohad Singh of 909 Hyde St., Suite 2702, San Francisco, advised me during an office visit on September 26, 2024 that I had continuing heart failure and angina and would likely live only about a year from now. Attached is a certificate from Dr. Singh to this effect.

4. By reason of my terminal health condition, I respectfully request that this application be made special so that I may be able to enjoy the benefit of a patent on my invention while I am alive.

5. I further declare that all statements made herein of my own knowledge are true and that all statements made upon information and belief are believed to be true, and further that these statements were made with the knowledge that willful false statements and the like so made are punishable by fine or imprisonment, or both, under Section 1001 of Title 18 of the U.S. Code, and that such willful false statements may jeopardize the validity of the application and any patent issuing therefrom.

Very respectfully,

David Gonzales

David Gonzales

Applicant

1919 Chestnut Street
Philadelphia, PA 19103
215-237-6639

Fig. 10T—Completed Declaration to Accompany PTMS
*This (and all other papers sent to the PTO) should always be typed with 1.5 or double spacing.

However, according to Rule 102(c), no PTMS fee is needed if the invention will enhance the quality of the environment, conserve energy, or counter terrorism. The PTO will endeavor to process your entire application to patent in less than 12 months.

For more information, see the Notice in the *Official Gazette* of July 18, 2006. The PTO has provided samples of Request for Accelerated Examination (Go to www.uspto.gov/patent/initiatives/accelerated-examination and click one of the samples).

If you've already filed your application, it's too late to file a Petition under the AEP, but you can circumvent this restriction by filing a continuation application and filing the Petition in the continuation.

Unless absolutely necessary, we strongly advise you not to file a Petition under the AEP, because it forces you to make very restrictive statements and admissions that could severely cripple any patent that you get if you ever need to use it in licensing or in court.

Also, if your search overlooks relevant prior art, and the examiner also misses it, a court could possibly invalidate your patent for inequitable conduct.

3. Patent Prosecution Highway—Expedited Examination of Applications Filed From Abroad

In addition to the above two basic ways to get your application examined ahead of turn, you can also have your application examined ahead of turn in the USPTO if you first filed your application in a foreign patent office and then filed a U.S. application claiming priority of your earlier-filed foreign application. In order to enter this program in the USPTO, the foreign patent office must have officially allowed at least one claim in the first-filed or foreign application. You may then put your application on the "highway" to a quick first action in the USPTO by filing the correct form.

There are two versions of the Patent Prosecution Highway (PPH). The first includes participants in a multilateral agreement between 29 different patent offices (the "Global PPH"). These patent offices are: Australia, Austria, Brazil, Canada, Chile, China*, Colombia, Denmark, the European Patent Office (EPO)*, Estonia, Finland, Germany, Hungary, Iceland,

Israel, Japan*, Korea*, New Zealand, the Nordic Patent Institute (NPI), Norway, Peru, Poland, Portugal, Singapore, Spain, Sweden, the United Kingdom, the U.S. PTO*, and the Visegrad Patent Institute (VPI). Offices labeled with an asterisk (*) are also members of a separate group of five intellectual property offices (the "IP5") that participate in a separate agreement. If you want to enter the PPH program based on one of these foreign patent offices allowing a claim , you must file a request on Form SB/20GLBL. As with the other forms, we recommend becoming an eFiler and filing this form on Patent Center.

The second version of PPH includes participants in bilateral agreements between the USPTO and other patent offices individually. These other patent offices are: Bahrain, the Czech Republic, France, Malaysia, Mexico, Morocco, Nicaragua, the Philippines, Romania, Saudi Arabia, and Taiwan. If you want to enter this program you must file a request on a SB/20xx form and comply with the other requirements indicated on the form. (The letters "xx" represent the country or jurisdiction code of the foreign country. For example, if you first filed in Mexico, use form SB/20MX.) All forms are available on the PTO site (www.uspto.gov/patents/basics/international-protection/patent-prosecution-highway-pph-fast-track).

In addition to enabling applicants who first file abroad to have their application made special in the PTO, applicants who first file in the USPTO and thereafter file in a foreign patent office listed above can have their application made special in the foreign patent office with a reciprocal procedure under the Patent Prosecution Highway program. To have your application made special in a foreign country your foreign patent agent must file an analogous request in the foreign patent office.

4. Request for Prioritized Examination

Anyone may buy prioritized ("Track 1") examination for a fee ($4,200 for large entities and $1,680 for small entities and $840 for micro entities), plus a $140 "processing fee" (box 1830 if filing on Patent Center) Obviously, the size of this fee limits its use

In the United States Patent and Trademark Office

Serial Number: 11/987,654

Appn. Filed: 2024 December 3

Applicant(s): Gonzales, David

Appn. Title: Wind Generator Using Stratus Rotor, Etc.

Examiner/GAU: Hayness / 654

Mailed: 2024 December 3

At: San Francisco

Petition to Make Special

Commissioner for Patents
P.O. Box 1450
Alexandria, VA 22313-1450

Sir:

Applicant hereby respectfully petitions that the above application be made special under MPEP 708.02 for the following reason(s); attached is a declaration in support thereof:

- ☑ Applicant's Health Is Poor
- ☑ Applicant's Age Is 65 or Greater

Very respectfully,

Applicant(s): David Gonzales

Attachment(s): Fee if indicated and supporting Declaration

Applicant(s): _____

c/o: David Gonzales

119 Walnut St.

San Francisco, CA 94123

Telephone: 415-722-0362

Certificate of Mailing

I certify that this correspondence will be deposited with the United States Postal Service as first class mail with proper postage affixed in an envelope addressed to: "Commissioner for Patents, P.O. Box 1450, Alexandria, VA 22313-1450" on the date below.

Date: 20 24 December 3   David Gonzales   , Applicant

Fig. 10U—Completed Petition to Make Special (Downloadable Form 10-9; see Appendix 7)

to affluent inventors or applicants but it may well be worth it if you have an urgent need for expediting examination. Also, examiners are encouraged to give a Track 1 application more careful consideration in preparing a first Office Action, and to have a telephone interview with the applicant. Although expensive, the Track 1 approach is easier on you than the Accelerated Examination option described above, at least because you do not have to perform an initial search or make potentially damaging statements about your application in the public record. For details, consult www.uspto.gov/patent/initiatives/usptos-prioritized-patent-examination-program.

G. Filing a Design Patent Application

A design patent covers the ornamental or aesthetic appearance, rather than the internal structure, function, composition, or state of an invention. Fig. 10R shows an example of the front (abstract) page of a design patent. You may file both a design patent application and a separate utility patent application on the same device, but of course, they should not cover the same feature of the device. The utility patent application should cover only the structure (or a method) that makes the device or invention function or operate better or differently. The design patent application should cover an entirely separate "invention"—namely, the ornamental (aesthetic) external (nonfunctional) appearance of something; that is, something that makes it look better or different. For example, you can file a utility patent application on a computer program (provided it's associated with some hardware), its circuitry, its keyboard mechanism, or its connector structure, and a design patent application on the aesthetic or ornamental shape of the computer's case.

Design patent applications are very easy to prepare, except for the drawings. If filing by mail, a design patent application consists of:

- A Design Patent Application Transmittal (Downloadable Form 10-11; see Appendix 7; or AIA/18)

- A Fee Transmittal (Downloadable Form 10-3; or SB/17)
- The fee by check, money order, or CCPF (see Appendix 4, "Fee Schedule," or check the PTO website)
- A Drawing or Drawings in black-line format
- A Specification (Downloadable Form 10-10; see Appendix 7) having the following five elements:
  - Preamble (should state the nature and intended use of the design)
  - Cross-Reference to Related Applications† (should state any related applications you have (or will) file)
  - Statement Regarding Federally Sponsored Research† (used when the design was made under a government contract)
  - Drawing Figures (describe each drawing figure briefly), and
  - Claim (state "I claim the ornamental design for (title of your design) as shown.")
- A PAD (Downloadable Form 10-1 or AIA/01 if including an Application Data Sheet; AIA/08 otherwise)
- A receipt postcard, and
- An optional Application Data Sheet (ADS) (Form AIA /14).

† If this section is not applicable, you may eliminate it or add the phrase "Not Applicable."

A design application specification with the five elements, above, is provided as Form 10-10 and a completed version is provided as Fig. 10S.

If you believe that your invention has a unique ornamental appearance that is significantly different from anything heretofore designed, you can file a design patent application on it.

Although it is a questionable practice, some inventors file a design application on the external appearance of a utility invention that is unpatentable in the utility sense, and that has unfinalized or trivial novelty in the design sense. They do this mainly to be able to truthfully and legally state for a few years that the invention is "patent pending."

The first step in completing a design application is to prepare drawings in the same format as for a regular patent application. However, the drawings for the design application should show only the exterior appearance of your invention; no interior parts or workings should be shown and no reference numerals are used. The drawings of a design patent application, whether formal or informal, must be done with good surface and edge shading.

If your invention is a computer-generated symbol (such as an icon like a trash can or a type font), you can file a design patent application on it, but you must show more than just the symbol per se. This is because the pertinent statute (35 U.S.C. § 171) requires that the design be "an article of manufacture" and the PTO does not consider a computer symbol, per se, as an article. The solution? Simply include a computer display (monitor or display panel) in your drawing and show the computer-generated symbol on the display. Both the symbol and the display should be drawn in solid lines.

Usually only one embodiment of a design is permitted. If you have several embodiments or versions of your design, you can include these all in one application. But if the examiner feels they can't all be subsumed under the same inventive concept, you'll be required to restrict the application to one embodiment. In this case, you can file a divisional design application(s) on the other embodiment(s), provided you do so before the original application issues. (See Chapter 14 for divisional applications.)

It's important to remember that drawings of your design application should have enough figures to show all of the details of the external surface of your design. A company we once worked for had an important design patent on a TV set held invalid because the design patent's drawings failed to show the rear side of the TV set.

Once you've made your drawings (in formal or informal form) fill out Form 10-10 as indicated in Fig. 10S. The title of your design can be very simple and need not be specifically directed toward your invention. For example, "Bicycle" is sufficient. Each view of the drawing should be separately indicated. For example, "Fig. 1 is a front perspective view of my bicycle. Fig. 2 is a side view," and so on.

Note that the design application has one claim only, and to write that claim you need merely fill in the blank on Form 10-10 with the title of your design. In the event that you offer more description—for example, you elaborate on figures more than merely stating the type of view—then, at the end of your claim, add the words, "and described."

Fill out the Fee Transmittal (Form 10-3; the amount is on the form, in Appendix 4, and at the PTO's website). Also complete the PAD (Form 10-1). (The SED Statement is on the Fee Transmittal.) No transmittal letter is needed since Form 10-10 inherently provides a transmittal letter.

The design application with the drawings, form, declaration, and receipt postcard, should be sent to the PTO in the same manner as your regular patent application. Be sure to keep an identical copy of your design application, including its drawings.

To file a design application by Patent Center, you need the specification (Form 10-10), drawings, PAD (Form 10-1 or AIA/01), and an Application Data Sheet (ADS)—(Form AIA/14). Fill out the specification (Form 10-10), PAD, and ADS as discussed.

NOTE

Design patent applications. Design patent applications, declarations, drawings, and receipt postcards should be sent to the PTO using the following address:
Commissioner for Patents
P.O. Box 1450
Alexandria, VA 22313-1450

The same address should be used for subsequent mail communications with the PTO regarding your application.

You'll receive your receipt postcard back in a week or two, and you'll receive a filing receipt a month or so thereafter. If you're aware of any prior art, don't forget to file an Information Disclosure Statement (see Section G, above) within three months of your filing date. You must attach copies of any non-U.S. patent references. If the prior art is not in English, the IDS should merely discuss how the appearance of your design differs from such prior art. If the prior art is in English, the IDS need not discuss such prior art.

NOTE

Plant patent applications. We haven't covered plant patent applications, since they're extremely rare and specialized. If you do want to file a plant application, it will be easy to do if you familiarize yourself with this chapter and 37 CFR 1.161 to 1.167.

H. Summary

You may file your application electronically via the PTO's Patent Center, as well as by mail. With the PTO's move toward being fully paperless, they have made the Patent Center user-friendly and less expensive than paper filing.

Use either the U.S. letter or A4 paper size when finalizing the drawings. File formal drawings if possible, since the PTO requires formal drawings before it will examine the application. Ideally, the drawings should almost explain the invention itself, so as to communicate your invention better to the examiner or a judge. Nowadays it is possible to do your own drawings using computer-assisted drawing (CAD) software. One way to make CAD drawings is to use a digital photo and trace the outline. Professional patent drafters are also widely available.

The specification, claims, and abstract can be typed on A4- or U.S. letter-size paper. Strive for perfect work, since that will create fewer obstacles as your application moves through the PTO.

Only the actual and correct inventors should be named in the application. The essential parts of an application filed by mail are the Postcard, Transmittal Letter, Fee Transmittal, Check or Credit Card Payment Form, Drawings, Specification, Claims, and Abstract, and Patent Application Declaration. You may also wish to file a Request for Claim Drafting by the Examiner, a Nonpublication Request, an Assignment and its Cover Sheet, and/or an Information Disclosure Statement (IDS), the AIA/08 form, and copies of the non-U.S. patent references. To file by Patent Center, you need to file only the drawings, specification, declaration, and application data sheet; everything else is handled on the PTO's site.

Take the Declaration seriously. No changes to the Drawings or the Specification should be made after it's signed.

If filing by mail, always include a receipt postcard with the application, which the PTO will return with the Filing Date and Serial Number. It's best to mail your application by Priority Mail Express to get an instant filing date and have protection in case of loss in the mail.

If you are aware of prior art and circumstances relevant to patentability, be sure to file the IDS (with attachments) within three months to advise the PTO of that information. If the application will be owned by anyone other than the inventor(s), prepare and file an assignment. You can petition to make any application special (examined ahead of turn) in a simple manner with no fee if your reason is advanced age, poor health, environmental quality enhancement, energy efficiency, or combating terrorism. If your reason is other than age or health, you must file a far more complex petition at the time of filing (although we advise against it since you have to make potentially damaging admissions). Under the more complex procedure, the PTO will strive to complete its examination within one year. You can also get an application made special, or prioritized on "Track 1," by filing a request for prioritized examination, but each of these options requires a very high fee. You also may be able to move your application ahead by taking advantage of certain pilot programs that the PTO runs from time to time. Usually there's not much advantage in making an application special, unless you have an infringement or you need financing.

How to Market Your Invention

CHAPTER 11

A. Perseverance and Patience Are Essential	333
B. Overview of Alternative Ways to Profit From Your Invention	333
1. Route 1: Using a Contingent-Fee Intermediary	334
2. Route 2: Partial Use of an Intermediary	336
3. Route 3: Finding a Manufacturer and Distributor Yourself	336
4. Route 4: Having Your Invention Manufactured and Distributed for You	336
5. Route 5: You Distribute	336
6. Route 6: You Manufacture	336
7. Route 7: You Manufacture and Distribute	336
C. Be Ready to Demonstrate a Working Model of Your Invention to Potential Customers	337
D. Finding Prospective Manufacturers/Distributors	338
E. "NIH" Syndrome	339
F. The Waiver and Precautions in Signing It	339
G. The Best Way to Present Your Invention to a Manufacturer	341
H. Presenting Your Invention by Correspondence	343
I. Making an Agreement to Sell Your Invention	343
J. Manufacturing and/or Distributing the Invention Yourself	343
1. Financing the Manufacture of Your Invention	344
2. Prepare a Business Plan	344
3. Utilize Government Services	344
4. Publicity	344
5. The Premium Marketing Route	345
6. The Celebrity Endorsement Route	346
K. Summary	346

Inventor's Commandment 20

Try to market your invention as soon as you can after filing your patent application; don't wait until your patent issues. Favor successful companies that are close to you, small in size, and already make and sell items as similar to yours as possible.

Inventor's Commandment 21

If you want your invention to be successful, pursue commercial exploitation with all the energy you can devote to it, and use every avenue available.

Inventor's Commandment 22

Never pay any money to any invention developer that can't prove to you that it has a successful track record—that is, most of its clients have received more income in royalties than they have paid in developer fees.

The Project Team Approach

If you already know how your invention will be marketed, or you work for a corporation that plans to handle this task, you can skip this chapter and continue reading about obtaining patent coverage. Also, if you would rather spend all your time at your workbench and not have to deal with marketing, a good way to go is to put together a team with diverse skills, such as an inventor, a manufacturing expert, a marketing expert, a person to handle the legwork, and a model maker. Chapter 12 deals with obtaining patents in other countries and Chapter 13 with getting the U.S. PTO to grant your patent.

In this chapter we make an important detour from the central task covered by this book—obtaining a valid and effective patent on your invention. The reason for this sudden turn is simple. In the usual course of events, you'll have an interval (18 months to three years) after you file your patent application before you need to either consider foreign filing or reply to an Office Action from the PTO. We strongly recommend that you use this interval to get your invention out on the market.

RESOURCE

For more information on licensing your invention, consult *Profit From Your Idea: How to Make Smart Licensing Deals,* by Richard Stim (Nolo).

"Out on the market?" you ask. Shouldn't you keep your invention, and the fact that you've filed the application, secret? The answer is, "No." In fact, once you file a patent application (including a Provisional Patent Application, or PPA; see Chapter 3) on your invention, you may show it to whomever you think might be interested in buying or licensing it with minimal risk of having someone scoop you on your invention.

This is because it would be very difficult for someone to steal your invention when you're the first to file a patent application on it. Any thief would have to file their patent application after yours, a useless and wasted effort since you would be the first to file, and the PTO would reject the later-filed application based on your earlier filing.

Your next question might be: Why try to sell or license your invention before a patent has been issued? While there are advantages to selling an already-patented invention, generally it's best to try to sell or license your invention as soon as possible after filing your patent application. This is because prospective corporate purchasers of your invention will want time to get a head start on the competition and to have the time the patent is in force coincide with the time the product is actually on the market. Also, you'll be able to offer the manufacturer the right to apply for foreign patents; this right will be lost once your patent issues. The lack of prestige that a pending patent has as compared to an already issued patent can be compensated for by a favorable search report showing that there's no strong prior art—that is, that a patent is likely to issue on your invention.

A. Perseverance and Patience Are Essential

Even if you get a patent, it will be essentially worthless unless it covers a commercially exploited invention. In fact, millions of patents have issued on inventions that were never successfully commercialized. None of these patents ever yielded a nickel to their owners.

To get your invention into commercial production, you'll have to persevere. There's no magic solution to the invention marketing process. As noted toy inventor Paul Brown says, "You almost have to be obsessed with your invention to get it going." Or put another way, Emerson's famous adage about building a better mousetrap might have been better written, "If you build a better mousetrap, you'll still have to beat a path to many doors to get it sold."

Even though you believe you've got the greatest thing since sliced bread, the money won't start flowing in all that quickly in most cases. It takes time to develop, market, and sell a product. Consider the following quote:

"There is no reason anyone would want a computer in their home."

–Ken Olson, President, Digital Equipment Corp., 1977

Chester Carlson, a patent attorney and the inventor of xerography, may have exaggerated somewhat, but he wasn't too far off base when he said:

"The time scale of invention is a long one. Results do not come quickly. Inventive developments have to be measured in decades rather than years. It takes patience to stay with an idea through such a long period.

"In my case, I am sure I would not have done so if it were not for the hope of the eventual reward through the incentives offered by the patent system."

Unfortunately, the marketplace is not rational or linear. An inferior product can be successful and a superior product can be a failure, depending upon how it's promoted.

B. Overview of Alternative Ways to Profit From Your Invention

As you can see from the chart in Fig. 11A, there are seven main ways or routes for the independent inventor to get an invention into the marketplace and profit from it. These choices involve increasing levels

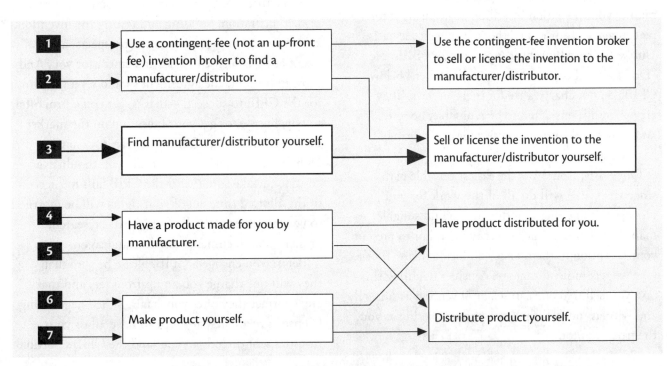

Fig. 11A—Alternative Ways to Profit From Your Invention

1. Route 1: Using a Contingent-Fee Intermediary

Some organizations that market or develop inventions for inventors are legitimate and honest. Many others exist solely to exploit inventors, regardless of the harm caused. There is an easy way to tell the difference. The dishonest ones usually require up-front money before they will lift a finger to develop or promote your invention. The honest ones typically represent you on a contingent fee basis and do not require an up-front fee. In this section, we will discuss dealing with honest contingent-fee invention brokers (CFIBs) and will advise you regarding the up-front-fee types, which we call FBIEs (Fee-Based Inventor Exploiters).

Starting at the top, Route 1 involves getting a contingent-fee invention broker or intermediary to find a suitable manufacturer/distributor for you and then using the broker to represent you in the sale or license of your invention.

Don't confuse a CFIB with fee-based "invention developers," "invention promoters," and the like: A CFIB is a firm that will represent you and try to market your invention by selling or licensing it for a percentage of your rights, the "contingent-fee basis." Unlike fee-based inventor-exploiters (or FBIEs; see "Don't Use a Fee-Based Inventor-Exploiter," below) CFIBs do not charge a fee for their services. They are generally considered to be reputable, honest, and provide a legitimate service for a fair form of compensation.

Obviously, Route 1 is the easiest possible path, since the CFIB will do all of the work for you. However, it's neither that difficult to find suitable manufacturer/distributors if they exist, nor to present your invention to them once you locate them. That's why we recommend that you consider handling this task yourself. No one can sell an invention as sincerely and with as much enthusiasm and conviction as you, the true inventor.

Also, you'll get 100% of the benefits and won't have to share the fruit of your creativity with a salesperson.

Finally, companies will likely respect you and your invention more if you approach them directly, since you're demonstrating the ability and initiative to approach them yourself.

If you do use a CFIB, be on the lookout for two main pitfalls:

1. loss of your invention rights through theft or communication to a thief, and
2. loss of time and hence other opportunities.

The first possibility isn't likely, since you've already got a patent application on file. But the second possibility is very real, and it's why you should verify the efficacy of any CFIB beforehand. Unfortunately, about the only surefire way to do this is by word-of-mouth. Check with a patent attorney, an inventors' organization, or some of the CFIB's clients if your own associates are unable to provide you with a lead.

Once you're satisfied with the CFIB's honesty and references, investigate the contract they offer you to be sure you won't lose time needlessly. The contract should specify that the CFIB will perform substantial services, such as identifying the prospective manufacturers, preparing an invention presentation or demonstration, building and testing the invention, submitting your invention to the prospects, and negotiating a license or sales agreement for you. And most important, the agreement should set a time limit for the CFIB to succeed—that is, get you a firm offer to buy, license, or get your invention on the market in product form. We feel that a year is reasonable; 18 months is about the maximum you should ever consider. Make sure that if the CFIB fails to succeed in the allotted time, all of your rights will be returned to you, together with all of the CFIB's research, presentation documents, models, and so on.

Before you engage a CFIB, please be sure that they will not charge you an up-front fee, and that any contract they offer you is fair. When negotiating license agreements, attempt to have all of your royalties sent directly to you (and the CFIB's portion

Don't Use a Fee-Based Inventor-Exploiter

There are firms we call fee-based inventor-exploiters (FBIEs), and you'd do well to avoid them. Paul Turley of the FTC reported that of 30,000 people who paid such FBIEs a fee, not one ever received any payback. These companies or organizations run ads online, in print, on TV, and elsewhere, stating something like "Inventions and Ideas Wanted!" They will commonly first send you an "inventor's kit" that includes a disclosure form similar to our Form 3-2 and that promises to "evaluate" your invention for free or for a relatively small fee (say $200 to $600). The evaluation is almost always glowingly positive. Then they'll ask for a relatively large fee—$1,000 to $5,000 and up—using very high-pressure sales tactics. They'll promise to do "market research" and try to sell your invention or have it manufactured. They sometimes also take a percentage (for example, 20%) of your invention to make you feel that they are your partner and want success as much as you do.

Generally, FBIEs will do little more than write a brief blurb describing your invention and send it to prospective manufacturers in the appropriate fields. Their efforts are virtually 100% unsuccessful, as reported in the Wall Street Journal and on the news program 20/20. In other words, FBIEs make their money from inventors, not inventions. As a result of federal legislation (35 U.S.C. § 297), FBIEs must now make certain disclosures to prospective customers.

If they don't, they can be sued for false statements or material omission. The invention promoter must disclose to you in writing:

- the total number of inventions evaluated by the FBIE for commercial potential in the past five years, as well as the number of those inventions that received positive evaluations; and the number of those inventions that received negative evaluations
- the total number of customers who have contracted with the FBIE in the past five years, not including customers who have purchased trade show services, research, advertising, or other nonmarketing services from the invention promoter or who have defaulted in their payment to the FBIE

- the total number of customers known by the FBIE to have received a net financial profit as a direct result of the invention promotion services provided by such invention promoter
- the total number of customers known by the FBIE to have received license agreements for their inventions as a direct result of the invention promotion services provided by such invention promoter, and
- the names and addresses of all previous FBIE companies with which the invention promoter or its officers have collectively or individually been affiliated in the previous ten years. This statute also enables defrauded customers to recover damages and sometimes triple damages against an FBIE who violates it.

Despite this strict statute and its penalties, many FBIEs still operate at full steam and still defraud inventors of millions of dollars annually. They do this despite the disclosure requirements detailed above, by telling prospective customers something like, "This means nothing—we're required to show you this. Don't worry about this but look at the bright side: We'll prepare a great color presentation and present your invention to industry and they'll be clamoring for it and you'll make a lot of royalties and will be able to retire, etc."

The PTO does not investigate complaints or participate in legal proceedings against invention promoters. The PTO will accept complaints, forward these complaints to the FBIEs, and make the complaints and responses publicly available on the PTO's Independent Inventor website.

To learn what you will need to file a complaint, visit the PTO website (www.uspto.gov/patent/forms/forms-patent-applications-filed-or-after-september-16-2012) for a complaint form (PTO Form SB/2048A). Complaints should be mailed to the following address:

United States Patent and Trademark Office
Mail Stop 24, P.O. Box 1450
Alexandria, VA 22313-1452

sent to the CFIB). That can head off accounting issues that sometimes result when all the payments must run through the CFIB.

In addition, many universities now have invention marketing departments that exist primarily to market the technology developed in the universities' research labs, but they may also take ideas from outsiders on a contingent-fee basis.

2. Route 2: Partial Use of an Intermediary

Route 2 (a seldom-used path) is the same as Route 1, except that here you use a broker to find prospects, then you take over and do the selling. Contingent-fee brokers typically won't accept this type of arrangement, because they'll want to control the sales negotiations. However, there are many inventor assistance companies that will provide you with product evaluation, illustration, advertising, packaging design, market research, and product testing services for a fee. If you feel that your strong suit is in presenting and selling, and that sales research is for someone else, you can pay a broker or market researcher (either CFIB or fee-based) to research possible purchasers. Then go out and present your invention yourself.

3. Route 3: Finding a Manufacturer and Distributor Yourself

Route 3 is the path we most favor, and the one most independent inventors follow. Here you do your own research and selling. If you succeed, you'll get 100% of the rewards and you'll control the whole process, yet you won't be bothered with manufacturing or distributing.

4. Route 4: Having Your Invention Manufactured and Distributed for You

Route 4 is a viable alternative for some relatively uncomplicated products. Here you have your invention manufactured for you—an overseas manufacturer will usually be cheapest—and then use U.S. distributors to sell the product. Of course, you have the headaches of supervising a manufacturing operation, including such details as quality control and red tape associated with

importing. But, if you succeed, you'll keep much of the manufacturing profit for yourself.

Some words of caution: Make sure the manufacturer is reputable, and have them agree:

- that you are the inventor and that they received the details and information about the invention from you
- not to sell your product to anyone else
- to return any tooling and all files, papers and materials to you if you terminate the relationship
- that they recognize a strict and absolute duty of fidelity and trust to you, and
- that they will not file any patent applications anywhere on the invention.

> CAUTION
> **While a U.S. patent will allow you to prevent knock-offs from being imported,** it will not prevent an overseas manufacturer from selling your invention on the side—unless you also have a patent in their country! (See Chapter 12 for more information on patents in other countries.)

5. Route 5: You Distribute

In Route 5, you handle distribution as well as supervising manufacturing. More profit, but more headaches and work. And the warning about overseas manufacturers in Route 4 also applies if you go this route.

6. Route 6: You Manufacture

In Route 6, you really get into it; you have to do the manufacturing yourself, headaches and all (see Section J), but you'll get a lion's share of the profits, if there are any.

7. Route 7: You Manufacture and Distribute

Last, and most difficult, in Route 7 you do it all yourself—manufacturing and distributing. While you get all of the profits, you'll have all of the headaches. Successful inventor Robert G. Merrick advocates this route in his book, *Stand Alone, Inventor!*

Because we believe that Route 3 makes the most sense for most independent inventors, we devote the bulk of this chapter to finding a manufacturer/distributor to build and market your invention. (If you want to pursue the possibility of manufacturing and distributing your invention, we've included an overview of potential resources, below, to help you do this.)

C. Be Ready to Demonstrate a Working Model of Your Invention to Potential Customers

Assuming that you choose Route 3, the best way to get a manufacturer or others to "buy" your invention is to demonstrate an actual working model. Pictures and diagrams may convey an idea and get a message across, but the working model is the thing that will make believers out of most people and show them that your invention is real and doable.

"Products sell; ideas don't."

–David Kewit, Patent Agent

So, if you haven't made a model before, do your best to make one now, even if it has to be made of cardboard or wood. One essential is to make your model or prototype as simple as possible. Simplicity enhances reliability, decreases cost, decreases weight, and facilitates salability, both to a manufacturer and to the public. If you're somewhat computer-savvy you might consider purchasing and using a 3D printer, if you are willing to learn how to operate it and an extruded plastic model will suffice. Simple but effective 3D printers are now available for hundreds (not thousands) of dollars.

If you're not handy, hopefully you can afford to have a professional model maker or artisan build the model, or you may have a handy friend or relative. Where can you find model makers? Start with your local inventors' organization. If that fails, magazines like Inventors Digest (www.inventorsdigest.com) usually feature ads in every issue from model makers. Another obvious place is online searching under "Model Makers." Also try search terms like "Machine

Shops" and "Plastics—Fabricating, Finishing, and Decorating." One service, eMachineShop (www.emachineshop.com), will supply you with free software you can use to draw your part, then they take over and custom-make it for you.

In addition, your local college or community college might have a design and industry department that may be able to refer you to a model maker. If you live near an industrial plant that employs machinists or model makers, perhaps you can get one of these employees to moonlight and do the job for you—put a notice on the plant's bulletin board, call, or ask around.

If you do use a model maker and you disclose critical information, including dimensions, materials, suppliers, or other data you consider to be proprietary (a trade secret), it is best to have the model maker sign a Consultant's Work Agreement (Form 4-3) before you turn over your drawings or other papers. Follow the instructions in Chapter 4 to fill out this form. I also suggest that you add a confidentiality legend to any drawings or descriptions you turn over to your model maker. Such a legend can be made in rubber-stamp or sticker form or can be typed on the drawings, and should read as follows:

"This drawing or description contains proprietary information of [your name] and is loaned for use only in evaluating or building an invention of [your name] and must be returned upon demand. By acceptance hereof, recipient agrees to all of the above conditions. © [year] [your name]."

After you've made a working model, you should take at least one good photograph of it. The photograph should be of professional quality—if you are not a good photographer, have a professional do it, and order several views if necessary. Then write a descriptive blurb about your invention, stating the title or the trademark, what it is, how it works, its main advantages and selling points, plus your name, address, telephone number, and the legend "Patent Pending." Don't get too bogged down in detail, however. In other words, make your write-up snappy and convincing. You should then make copies (either print or digital depending on your method of communication).

If you can't build a real working model, you can build (or have a designer build) a "virtual prototype" (computer simulation) using computer-assisted-design (CAD) software.

D. Finding Prospective Manufacturers/Distributors

The next step is to compile an initial listing of manufacturers who you believe could profitably manufacture and distribute your invention. You should keep your marketing notes, papers, and correspondence in a separate file from your patent application (legal) file. Your initial list should comprise all the manufacturers who meet the following four criteria:

- they're geographically close to you
- they already manufacture the same or a closely related product
- they're not too large, and
- they're anxious to sell new products.

Nearby or local manufacturers who already work in your field are best. If they manufacture your invention, you can monitor their progress, consult with them frequently, and take any needed action more easily if anything goes wrong. Obviously, it's a big help to deal with a company that has experience with devices similar to yours. They already know how to sell in your field, are aware of competitive pricing policies, can make your invention part of their existing product line—which allows them to keep sales costs low—and presumably want new models related to their existing products in order to keep ahead of the competition. If the manufacturer is not in a closely allied line, both the seller and the product will be on trial, so why start with two strikes against you?

There are several reasons for avoiding giant manufacturers:

1. Smaller manufacturers are more dependent on outside designers. In other words, most don't have a strong prejudice against inventions they did not invent themselves.
2. You can contact the decision makers or the owners of the company directly, or more easily.

3. Decisions are made more rapidly because the bureaucracies are smaller.
4. You are less likely to be required to sign a waiver form.
5. Giant companies have more access to patent lawyers and, hence, a greater tendency to try to "get around" your invention by investigating and trying to invalidate your patent or trying to avoid infringing it. Medium and small companies, on the other hand, will be more interested in your invention's profit potential and its effect in the marketplace.

Obviously, you shouldn't use companies that are so small that they don't have enough money to finance the manufacture of your invention or market it adequately. Companies with sales of about $10 million to $100 million are best (unless you have enormous market potential).

To find companies meeting the above criteria, start by first considering people you know. Which one of them is likely to have contacts in the field of your interest? Put them to work for you and you may be amazed that with a few phone calls or emails you can get just the introduction you need.

If this doesn't work, try looking in your appropriate local stores for manufacturers of closely allied products that are already on the shelves. You'll know for sure that these companies have a successful distribution and sales system or operation.

Research online or at a local library checking resources such as the *Thomas Register* (online at www.thomasnet.com) or the *Dun & Bradstreet Million Dollar Directory*. In addition, check the ads at pertinent trade and hobby websites. Lastly, services that provide stock analysis, such as *Value Line* (www.valueline.com), *Standard & Poor's* (www.spglobal.com/ratings), *D&B Hoovers* (www.dnb.com/products/marketing-sales/dnb-hoovers.html), and *Moody's* (www.moodys.com), supply excellent information about companies. Get the names of the company presidents, vice presidents, directors of engineering, marketing directors, and so on. Find out all you can about each company you select; know its products, sales and corporate history, profitability, and factory location(s).

If your invention is in the gadget category and you believe it would appeal to the affluent, try Hammacher Schlemmer (www.hammacher.com), Sharper Image (www.sharperimage.com), or one of the many other specialty stores that sell gadget exotica. These companies accept a fraction of the thousands of invention ideas they receive each year, and arrange to have the chosen few produced by manufacturers they already work with. Also, trade fairs or shows—such as NY Now (www.nynow.com)—are good places for you to wander around looking for prospective manufacturers. Talk to the people who run the exhibits to get a feel for the companies, whom to contact, and what their attitude toward outside inventions might be.

Some suggestions: If your invention is a new automotive tool or device, Lisle Corp. (www.lislecorp.com) seeks such inventions. Homax Products (www.homaxproducts.com) wants home improvement inventions. The toy store F.A.O. Schwarz (www.faoschwarz.com) looks for toys and gifts, and has "toy auditions" in New York City (usually coinciding with the annual toy fair). If you have an exercise or fitness related invention, consider NordicTrack (www.nordictrack.com).

One company, quirky.com, has a unique approach. You submit a description of your idea to them with a $10 fee, and drawings if you have them. If they like it they will have it made and pay you royalties—about ⅓ of sales. They have a community that assists in evaluations and design. So far they have developed and are selling a wide range of products and have paid their inventors millions in royalties. They do not deal with patents, so you're on your own here. Go to their site and do some research to see if it's right for you.

If you can't find any U.S. companies, try foreign ones. Many U.S. firms have refused to undertake new ventures that foreign firms have jumped at, which can work to your advantage as an inventor.

E. "NIH" Syndrome

Before presenting your invention to any manufacturer, keep two possible impediments in mind:
- the "NIH" (Not Invented Here) syndrome, and
- the common insistence that you give up many of your legal rights by signing a waiver.

Generally, the larger the manufacturer, the greater the chances of encountering one or both of these impediments.

The NIH syndrome is an unwritten attitude that handicaps inventors who submit their ideas to a company, no matter how meritorious such ideas may be. Put simply, many companies have a bias against any outsider ("the enemy") or any outside invention because it was "not invented here." This attitude prevails primarily because of jealousy. The job of the corporate engineering department is to create new and profitable products for their company. If an engineering department were to recommend an outside invention, it would almost be a tacit admission that the department had failed to do its job in solving a problem and coming up with the solution the outside inventor has found.

How can you overcome the NIH syndrome? First, realize that it's more likely to exist in larger companies, or companies with extensive engineering departments. Second, when forced to deal with engineering departments or any department in a company where the NIH syndrome may be present, always remember that the more your invention appears to be a logical extension of ideas already developed within the company, the better your chances of acceptance will be.

F. The Waiver and Precautions in Signing It

Most inventors affected with the paranoia part of "Paranoia/Greed/Laziness Syndrome" (see Chapter 2) are afraid to show their invention to anyone, even after they've filed a patent application. The truth is, however, that most companies are far more afraid of you suing them for taking your invention than they are interested in stealing it. Most companies with access to legal advice will require you to sign their agreement (called a "waiver"), under which you give up a number of important rights that you would otherwise possess under the law. The reason for this waiver is that many companies have been sued by inventors claiming violation of an implied confidentiality agreement, or an implied agreement to pay if all or any part of the invention is used. Even though the company's own inventor may have come up with the invention independently of the outside inventor, many companies have lost these suits or were forced to compromise because of the uncertainties and expenses of litigation.

The waiver itself usually requires you to give up all your rights, except those that you may have under the patent laws. Specifically, the waiver typically asks you to agree that:

1. The company has no obligation to pay you if they use your idea.
2. The company isn't bound to keep your idea in confidence.
3. The company has no obligation to return any paper you submit.
4. The company has no obligation whatever to you, except under the patent laws.

Many companies add many other minor provisions, which are not significant enough to discuss here. The effect of the waiver is that you have no rights whatever against the company if they use your invention, except to sue them for patent infringement if and when you get a patent.

If you send a letter or email mentioning your idea to a company, they'll typically route your correspondence to the patent or legal department, which will send you a form response back stating their policy and asking you to sign the waiver before they agree to review your idea. Once you do so, the patent or legal department will approve your submission for review and send it to the appropriate engineering manager of the company.

It's best to avoid signing any waiver if at all possible: you might not get a patent, the company could use a variation of your idea that might not be covered by any patent you do get, and you would like to have the company keep your submission in confidence. For

this reason, you should, at least initially, concentrate on smaller companies. The smaller the company, the less likely they are to make you sign a waiver. In fact, the best sort of relation you can have with a company to which you submit your ideas is to have them sign an agreement you've drafted yourself. Many small companies actually want to review outside inventions and are willing to sign a proprietary-submission agreement.

If the company is willing, or if you can swing it (say, by touting the commercial potential of your invention, establishing a rapport with the research people, and so on), have the company sign a Proprietary Submission Agreement such as the following:

Proprietary Submission Agreement

X Company agrees to review an invention from [*your name*] for a new and improved [*describe invention*], to keep in confidence such invention and all papers received, to return upon request all papers submitted, and to pay [*your name*] a reasonable sum and royalty to be settled by future negotiation or arbitration if X Company uses or adopts such invention.

If a company won't sign the above agreement, you can make it a bit more palatable by eliminating the last clause regarding the payment of a reasonable fee and royalty. Even with the last clause eliminated, you're in a very good position if you've gotten them to sign. If the company still refuses to sign your agreement, you can add the following clause:

The foregoing shall not obligate X Company with respect to any information which X Company can document (a) was known to it prior to receipt from me, either directly or indirectly, or (b) which is now or hereafter becomes part of the public domain from a source other than X Company.

If you can't get them to sign even this, you're still in a pretty good position legally if you can get them to review your invention without any agreement being signed by either side.

If all else fails and you do have to sign a waiver before the company will look at your invention (that's the usual outcome), it's not all that bad, since you at least have a pending patent application. And most companies are far more afraid of you suing them (for taking your invention) than they are interested in stealing your invention. Now you can understand why we emphasized the need to file your patent application before submitting your invention to any company. If you sign the waiver, your position won't be seriously jeopardized if your patent issues. However, if you're submitting an invention to a company without having first filed a patent application, it's very important that you try to get the company to sign the above Proprietary Submission Agreement or, failing that, try to submit it without signing their waiver.

If you do have to sign a waiver, try to make sure the company is a reputable one, and read the language carefully, or have an attorney do so, to make sure you retain your patent rights and that it's a fair agreement. Also, it's important to insist, by means of a separate letter, that the company make its decision within a given time, say six months, or else return all of your papers to you. This is because many companies, especially large ones, can take many months or years to decide (if you let them), which may interfere with your efforts to market the invention to others.

Note that the above choices provide a continuum of safety when presenting your invention to a company: On one end of the continuum you take a very high risk of theft of your invention if you sign a waiver without filing a patent application, while on the other end, you will be fairly well protected if you have the company sign a Proprietary Submission Agreement like the one above. However, there's no such thing as a completely safe submission, so always be prepared for some risk and minimize it as much as possible.

To the extent you are uncertain about whether signing a waiver is a good idea under the circumstances, a consultation with a patent attorney might be wise. On the other hand, don't let the waiver

prevent you from showing your invention to a reputable manufacturer that promises to give you a decision in a reasonable time. As long as your patent is pending and eventually issues, you'll have reasonably strong rights.

G. The Best Way to Present Your Invention to a Manufacturer

The best and most effective way to sell your invention to a manufacturer is personally to visit the decision maker in the company you elect and demonstrate a working model or prototype of your invention (or present drawings of it if you have no working model). To accomplish this, write a brief, personal, friendly, and sincere letter to the president of the company, saying that you have a very valuable invention you believe would be profitable for the company's business and that you would like to make an appointment when convenient to provide a brief demonstration. You can disclose the general area of your idea, but don't disclose its essence until you can present it properly. Keep the initiative by stating that you will call in a few days. Follow through accordingly. Here's an example:

Mr. Orville Billyer
President, Billyer Saw Co.
[etc.]

Dear Mr. Billyer:

I'm employed as an insurance agent, but in my spare time I like to tinker. While building a gun rack, I thought of and have perfected a new type of saw fence, which I believe can be produced at 60% of the cost of your A-4 model, yet which can be adjusted in substantially less time with greater accuracy. For this reason, I believe that my fence, for which I've applied for a patent, can be a very profitable addition to your line. I'll call you in a few days to arrange a demonstration of my invention for you in your plant.

Most sincerely,

Marjorie Morgenstern

Marjorie Morgenstern

They may ask you to sign their Waiver form (described above) and submit your materials in writing, but try your best (by stressing the advantages of your invention and how much money they'll make) to bypass the Waiver and make an appointment for a personal presentation.

When you come to the demonstration, be prepared! Set up your presentation well in advance. Practice it on friends. Explain the advantages of your invention first: how it works, how it will be profitable for their business, and why it will sell. Make sure your model works. Also, prepare appropriate and attractive written materials and photos for later study by the decision maker.

In your presentation and written material, it's wise to cover the "Three Fs"—Form, Fit, and Function.

Form is the appearance of your invention. Stress how it has (or can have) an attractive, enticing appearance.

Demonstrate how your invention fits with other products, or with the environment in which it is to be used. If your invention is a highly functional device, such as a saw fence, show and tell how it fits onto a table saw. If it's a clock, show (or present attractive pictures showing) how it looks attractive on a desk or coffee table.

Function is what your invention does, how it works, what results it attains. Demonstrate and discuss its function and its advantage here. Mention all of the advantages from your Positive and Negative Factors Evaluation (Form 4-1). In addition, be prepared to discuss such items as cost of manufacture, profit, retail price, competition, possible product liability, and product life. Review all of the positive and negative factors from the list in Chapter 4 to be sure you've covered all possible considerations.

During the verbal part of your presentation, it's wise to use diagrams and charts, but keep your model, written materials, and photos hidden from view. Otherwise, the people you're trying to sell to will be looking at these instead of listening to you. Then, at a dramatic moment, bring out your model and demonstrate how it works. Don't apologize if your model is a crude or unattractive prototype, but radiate enough confidence in yourself and your invention that they will overlook any lack of "cosmetics." If you can't bring or show them your model for any reason, a video, drawing, diagram, or slide presentation that shows the three F's will be a viable, though less desirable way, to show the invention.

If possible, make them think that the invention is basically their idea. You can do this by praising their related product line and then showing how your idea compliments theirs, or by enthusiastically endorsing any reasonable suggestion they make for your idea.

At the end of your verbal presentation, produce your written materials and pictures for study (either then and there or at a later time). If they're interested in the invention, be prepared to state your terms and conditions. (See Chapter 16.) If they're really serious and ask for it, you can show them your patent application without your claims, but only with the understanding that it won't be copied and will be returned to you. You shouldn't offer the claims, prior art from your search, serial number, or filing date, unless you're asked. If you're relying on a Provisional Patent Application for your patent pending status, then you won't have drafted your claims yet, and you also may not have conducted a patentability search.

If you've done your best and still get a rejection, try to turn it into an asset for next time. Talk to the executives about it and learn exactly why they decided not to accept your idea so that in the future you'll be better prepared to answer and overcome the disadvantage that blocked your initial acceptance.

Assuming the company is interested, you shouldn't blindly or automatically accept it as your patron. Rather, you should evaluate the company to which you're demonstrating your invention just as they're evaluating you and your invention. For example, if the company seems to lack energy or vision, don't go with them. Also, you should check out the company's reputation online and with the local Better Business Bureau to see if they have a clean record. After all, you're risking a lot, too, when you sign up with a company. If the company doesn't promote your invention enthusiastically and correctly, it can fail in the market, even if it's the greatest thing to come down the pike in 20 years.

TIP
Don't be afraid of simultaneous submissions. If you're aware of several prospective companies that you feel might be interested, I recommend that you approach all of the companies simultaneously; otherwise, you'll waste too much time. If several companies "bite" concurrently, you'll be in the enviable position of being able to choose your licensee. (Some companies do ask that you not submit your invention to anyone else while they're looking at it; you should honor this request.)

H. Presenting Your Invention by Correspondence

Another way to present your invention is by correspondence—either online or via letters. Because a personal presentation is a thousand times more likely to make a sale, we strongly advise against submitting an invention to a manufacturer in this way if you can avoid it. Try your utmost to arrange a personal demonstration with a working model as described in the previous section. Nevertheless, if you do have to resort to correspondence, don't let your efforts slacken.

Your letter or email should always be addressed to a specific individual. If you receive an expression of interest from the company, you will probably be faced with the waiver question. Our comments in the previous discussion cover how to handle this problem. Before you ship a model, get an advance written commitment from the company that they'll return it within a given time. The key is to present your message as a simple unexpected, credible, concrete, and emotional story.

I. Making an Agreement to Sell Your Invention

If you sell your invention to a manufacturer/distributor, the next step is to sign an agreement of some sort with the manufacturer. This raises a number of questions including, what will be the terms of the agreement, exactly what will you sell them, and for how much? There are many possibilities. These are covered in Chapter 16, which deals with ownership and transfer of patents rights.

J. Manufacturing and/or Distributing the Invention Yourself

For reasons stated earlier, manufacturing and/or distributing a product embodying your invention yourself—unless you already have manufacturing experience, a plant, and/or distribution facilities—is very difficult. Besides, you can spend your time more effectively selling your invention or patent application, rather than dealing with manufacturing and product-marketing problems.

If you do plan to manufacture and/or distribute your invention yourself, we strongly suggest that you learn about the subject thoroughly beforehand so you will know what is involved and which pitfalls to avoid. The best place to obtain literature and reading material is your local SBA (Small Business Administration) office (www.sba.gov), which has resources and aids available to apprise you of the problems and pitfalls. They even have a service that allows you to obtain the advice of an experienced executive free. You should also familiarize yourself with various industrial supply companies that can provide you the tools you need to set up shop. One such company is Grainger (www.grainger.com).

1. Financing the Manufacture of Your Invention

Financing any manufacturing venture of your own is a separate and formidable problem. If you have an untried and unsold product, most banks will not lend you the money to go ahead. However, if you can get orders from various local firms, the bank may lend you the money. A local test-marketing effort on a limited scale may be desirable.

Generally you'll need a money lender who's willing to take a risk. Such a person is usually termed a "venture capitalist" ("VC"). A VC will lend you money in exchange for shares or a portion of your enterprise. *Pratt's Guide to Venture Capital Sources* is the most popular source of VCs, however other resources are available at libraries and online. VCs won't lend you money on the same terms a bank would. Because of the higher risks they take, they demand a much larger return—namely a piece of the action. Also, they'll want to monitor your company and exercise some degree of control, usually by putting their people on your board of directors. While most VCs are companies or partnerships, sometimes wealthy individuals finance inventions, so if you have a rich uncle or know of a suitable patron, include them on your list. A recent development in the VC field is the "Incubator VC." This is a VC that provides several different inventors with offices, labs, and/or a manufacturing area in a special building, called an "innovation center."

2. Prepare a Business Plan

To obtain venture capital to start a business based on your invention, you'll have to prepare a business plan—a presentation that tells all about your invention, the market for it, and how you plan to use the money. Resources for guiding your business plan writing include the SBA (www.sba.gov), Business Plan Pro (www.bplans.com), and Wolters Kluwer's BizFilings (www.wolterskluwer.com/en/solutions/bizfilings).

> ### How to Get Funding From a Venture Capitalist
>
> Ari Zoldan, CEO of Quantum Networks, a venture capital (VC) firm, provided some tips for soliciting VCs in an issue of *Popular Science*. Among his suggestions:
> - Don't send a letter and don't email. Call the CEO and pitch your invention briefly. Be sure to sell both your product and your skills and expertise.
> - Look for a VC that will be actively involved.
> - Review the VC's track record and funding.
> - Don't be intimidated by VCs and never give the VC a majority control of your company.
> - Get the VC to sign a nondisclosure agreement and always bring a business plan and prototype to your meeting.

3. Utilize Government Services

If your invention is or can be used in a product that the federal government might purchase, contact the General Services Administration, Federal Supply Service, (www.gsa.gov). Tell them you're offering a product you feel the government can use. They'll send you appropriate forms and instructions. Also, don't neglect your corresponding state and local purchasing agencies.

If you have an energy-related invention, the Department of Energy may give you a research grant if the National Bureau of Standards gives it a favorable evaluation. Contact the U.S. Department of Energy (www.energy.gov).

4. Publicity

Publicity will sometimes be of great aid to you before you get your invention into production, and is invaluable once it's on the market. Assuming it's not yet on the market and you're either looking for a manufacturer or distributor, or thinking of manufacturing or distributing it yourself, publicity can cut both ways. As stated, many manufacturers like to get a secret head start on their competition and won't be too interested if your invention has already been disseminated to the public.

If you're going to make and sell it yourself, we believe you should wait until you've got the product out before you try to publicize it. Why? The public's memory span is short, so they'll be likely to forget about your product by the time you get it on sale. My advice is to not seek publicity until a product with your invention is almost or actually on the market, unless you've tried unsuccessfully, after substantial efforts, to get it on the market.

Assuming you're ready for publicity, one way to get it (at a price) is to hire a public-relations or marketing research firm to promote your invention for you.

There are many reputable firms that can come up with many creative and valuable ideas for a fee. However, since the cost of public-relations services is very high, I don't recommend it unless you can bear the cost without difficulty.

Many magazines will feature new ideas free if you send them a clear, understandable, professional-quality photo or drawing of your invention, plus a brief, clear, and understandable description of it. They may even write a full-length feature about your invention if they think it's interesting enough.

For advertising of a more transient nature, consider social media. Different social media platforms have different audiences, so the best marketing strategy will be tailored to each platform and your desired level of engagement with your customers.

Facebook is a great choice for selling to people of all ages, but especially to young and middle-aged adults. With a Facebook page, you can show off your product's value while giving the public a chance to contact you with feedback.

If your product's appeal can be easily photographed, especially if you can capture people using it, then Instagram and/or Pinterest should be on your list. Instagram often is used to find new products, but you need to provide a steady stream of photos or short

videos to keep your audience's interest. Pinterest is designed to share images between users, and can be a good way to grow your audience share organically, especially among established and older adults.

If your product is aimed at a younger crowd (younger than 25), and you can show how great it is in short-form videos, then you may want to add TikTok to your marketing strategy. TikTok is a very dynamic platform though, so to stand out from the crowd you need to be on top of trends and create engaging videos that tie into those trends (or even better, start new ones).

Finally, Twitter can be used as a marketing tool, especially to men younger than 30 years old.

Keep in mind that each of these platforms has its own culture and norms, so would do well to spend some time immersed in each before beginning any marketing.

Don't overlook traditional media (radio, TV, newspapers, and magazines) as an excellent source of free publicity, which most experts say is the best kind. Many local radio and TV stations feature talk shows whose hosts are always looking for interesting guests; some stations even have shows in which new inventors can demonstrate or discuss their inventions. One popular syndicated show is *Shark Tank* (abc.com/shows/shark-tank).

One of the best ways to get media publicity (and concomitant interviews) is to dream up or pull a stunt. For example, if you've invented a new bicycle drive mechanism, you might enter and win a local bike race, or sponsor some type of contest (which you can win!).

5. The Premium Marketing Route

If you can't get a manufacturer or distributor to take your invention, try offering it as a premium to accompany a related product that is already on the market. For example, one television magazine show featured a girl, Abbey Mae Fleck, age 8, of St. Paul, Minnesota, who invented a great plastic hanger to suspend bacon in a microwave oven so that the grease dripped away while it cooked. However, none of the manufacturers of plastic microwave accessories would bite (their loss!). So ingenious Abbey approached a bacon company and got them to offer her MAKIN BACON® via a discount coupon on their bacon packages. The result: An instant success! The bacon company's investment was minimal, yet it profited handsomely by providing a way to cook its bacon dryly. And Abbey got her commercial distribution. Abbey's story (makinbacon.com) also shows that creativity has no age limits.

6. The Celebrity Endorsement Route

If a product bears a celebrity's name or endorsement, people will be far more likely to buy it. So, getting a celebrity to endorse it is often a key to instant success. Consider George Foreman's Lean, Mean Fat-Reducing Grilling Machine. Without the champ's endorsement and name it might not have been a fabulous success. Celebrity endorsements are particularly useful if you have a sporting goods invention, such as a golf club. To get a celebrity endorsement, first perfect and get your product ready for market. Prepare suitable sales and promotional materials, with photos, and then approach the celebrity you feel would do your baby justice. While you'll have to share a good portion of your profits, you'll find that your chances of success will be almost assured if you have a good product and can get a famous celebrity to endorse and name it.

K. Summary

After filing a patent application, try to get your invention on the market; don't wait until your patent issues. Since it can take a long time to license an invention, perseverance and patience are essential.

There are seven routes to profit from an invention and they involve using a marketing intermediary, manufacturing and/or marketing your invention yourself, or licensing your invention to a company. Most inventors use the latter.

Don't use a fee-based intermediary (a company that wants up-front money) unless they can demonstrate that many of their clients have made more money than they paid the intermediary.

The best way to sell or license an invention is to demonstrate a working model. Find prospective manufacturers in stores, catalogs, and trade magazines. Larger companies will require that you sign a waiver (giving up all rights except patent rights) before they will look at your invention. You may have better luck with companies that are smaller and geographically close to you. These companies usually communicate in a more direct manner, are typically immune to NIH syndrome, and often don't require a waiver.

If you want to manufacture and/or distribute the invention yourself you may need financing and a business plan, and you should have at least some manufacturing/business knowledge, skills, and experience.

There are many ways to get publicity for your invention including premium marketing and celebrity endorsements.

CHAPTER

12

Going Abroad

A. Don't File Abroad Unless Your Invention Has Very Good Prospects
   in Another Country 348

B. Foreign Filing: The Basics 349

C. The Paris Convention and the One-Year Foreign-Filing Rule 350

D. The World Trade Organization and TRIPS..350

E. European Patent Office/Europäisches Patentamt/Office Européen
   des Brevets (EPO)..350

F. The Patent Cooperation Treaty (PCT) 354

G. Non-Convention Countries...356

H. The Hague Agreement 356

I. The Early Foreign-Filing License or Mandatory Six-Month Delay..............357

J. The Patent Laws of Other Countries Are Different..357

K. Ways to File Abroad..358

   1. Route A: Non-Convention/Convention PCT..359

   2. Route B: Elect Chapter II of PCT If You Want an International Examination....362

   3. Route C: Convention Applications in EPO and Non-EPO Countries.................362

   4. Route D: Convention Applications Only in Individual Countries.........................362

   5. Route E: PPA Filed...363

   6. File the PCT Application First 363

L. Rescind Any Nonpublication Request 363

M. Foreign-Filing Resources 364

N. Summary 365

Inventor's Commandment 23

Foreign Filing: It's not wise to file in any foreign country unless you're confident your invention has very strong commercial potential there (or unless someone else will pay the costs). You can file abroad by filing a Patent Cooperation Treaty (PCT) application or filing directly in Paris Convention (major industrial) countries within one year of your earliest U.S. filing date. Don't file abroad until you receive a foreign-filing license from the PTO or until six months after your U.S. filing date.

A U.S. patent will give you a monopoly in the the United States only. If you think your invention is important enough to be manufactured or sold in large quantities in other countries, and you want to create a monopoly there, you'll have to go through the considerable effort and expense of foreign filing in order to eventually get a patent in each desired foreign country. Otherwise, anyone in a foreign country where you have no patent will be able to make, use, and sell your invention with impunity. On the other hand, if you have a U.S. patent they won't be able to bring what they have made into the the United States without infringing your U.S. patent.

This chapter doesn't give you the full, detailed instructions necessary to file abroad. That would take another book. Instead, our mission is to alert you to the basic procedures for foreign filing, so that you won't lose your opportunity to do so. However, once you decide to foreign-file, you'll probably need some professional guidance from a patent attorney.

The most important points to take away from this chapter are:

- don't foreign-file in any country unless you're confident that your invention has strong commercial potential there
- don't foreign-file until you get a foreign-filing license from the PTO (the filing receipt usually, but not always, includes a foreign-filing license) or until six months has elapsed from your U.S. filing date

- you must file in non–Paris Convention countries before you publish or sell the invention (more on the Convention later in this chapter), and
- you must file a Patent Cooperation Treaty (PCT) application or file in all desired Paris Convention countries within one year of your earliest U.S. filing date (that is, the filing date of your first Provisional Patent Application (PPA) or Regular Patent Application (RPA)).

A. Don't File Abroad Unless Your Invention Has Very Good Prospects in Another Country

Patent prosecution and practice in other countries is relatively complicated and usually very expensive—at least thousands, and often tens of thousands of dollars *per country*. Therefore, you should not file applications abroad unless:

- a significant market for products embodying the invention is very likely to exist (if you anticipate copycats)
- *significant* commercial production of your invention is very likely to occur (if you think your manufacturer might go rogue), or
- you've already located a foreign licensee or there is someone else willing to pay for the foreign filing.

Far too many inventors file abroad because they're in love with their invention and feel it will capture the world. The reality is that almost all inventors who do file abroad never recoup their investment—that is, they usually waste tens of thousands of dollars in fees and hardly ever derive any royalties, let alone enough royalties to cover their costs. That's why, as a general rule, we suggest that you file in another country only if you feel that you're:

- very likely to sell at least $500,000 worth of products embodying your invention there, if you're selling it yourself
- very likely to earn at least $100,000 in royalties from sales of your invention there by others, including a local company or manufacturer, or

- associated with a licensee or sales representative there who contracts to pay you royalties with a substantial advance or guarantee, or who will pay for your foreign filing in that country.

In addition to the high initial cost of foreign filing, you will have to pay substantial expenses to obtain foreign patents and maintenance fees each year to keep them in force.

Note that even if an infringement occurs in a country where you didn't file, it's still not worth paying for foreign filing there, unless the infringement is substantial enough to justify the expense of filing, getting the patent, paying the maintenance fees, on top of the uncertainties of licensing and litigation.

> ### TIP
> **The U.S. provides a huge marketplace that should be a more-than-adequate market from which to make your fortune, especially if it's your first invention.** In comparison, most foreign countries are relatively insignificant. For example, Switzerland, Lebanon, and Israel are each smaller in size than San Bernardino County in California and smaller in population than Los Angeles County; Canada has fewer people than California. In other words, filing in the the United States usually gives you ten to 50 times more bang for your buck than filing abroad, which costs ten to 50 times as much anyway.

B. Foreign Filing: The Basics

Most countries are treaty members of the "Paris Convention," which gives you the full benefit, in a foreign "Convention" country, of your PPA or RPA filing date in your home country (that is, the United States), provided you apply directly in the foreign Convention country within one year (or six months for a design). All jurisdictions that are members of the Paris Convention are indicated in Fig. 12A, where the most popular jurisdictions for foreign filing are indicated in boldface.

Most industrialized countries are also members of the PCT—Patent Cooperation Treaty—that

enables applicants to file a relatively economical PCT application in the patent office of their home country within one year of their home-country filing date. Jurisdictions that are members of the PCT are indicated in Fig. 12B, with the most popular in boldface. There is considerable overlap between Paris Convention countries and PCT jurisdictions, and the pros and cons of filing in one or the other are discussed below. However, it's worth noting here that the PCT gives applicants up to a 30-month delay and enables them to have a search, and optimally an examination, performed before making an expensive filing abroad.

Also, most countries in Europe have joined the European Patent Convention, which has created a single patent office— the European Patent Office (EPO)—to grant European patents that are good in all member countries provided they're registered and translated in each country (and you pay annuities or maintenance fees in each country). EPO countries are indicated in Fig. 12C, and form a single "jurisdiction" for purposes of filing PCT applications. Similarly, most African countries are members of one of two African patent organizations, the African Intellectual Property Organization (OAPI—for French-speaking countries) or the African Regional Industrial Property Organization (ARIPO—for English-speaking countries), while the Eurasian Patent Organization (EAPO) comprises the former Soviet republics.

(We have omitted separate listings for these latter Organizations because they are infrequently used by U.S. inventors, but they may be easily found online if you are interested.)

Next, many countries also are treaty members of the "Hague Agreement," which gives you the full benefit, in a foreign "Agreement" country, of your design application filing date in the United States, provided you file a relatively economical Hague application within six months. That is, the Hague Agreement is for design patents what the PCT is for utility patents. Jurisdictions that are members of the Hague Agreement are indicated in Fig. 12D. Note that what the United States calls a "design patent" is described in most foreign countries as an "industrial design."

Finally, be aware that U.S. patent applications are published 18 months after the earliest claimed filing date, unless the applicant files a nonpublication request (NPR) at the time of filing, stating that the application will not be filed abroad. If you do file an NPR and then file abroad, you must revoke the NPR and notify the PTO of the foreign filing within 45 days (use PTO Form SB/36).

C. The Paris Convention and the One-Year Foreign-Filing Rule

The most important thing to know about foreign filing is the "Paris Convention" or simply "the Convention." (The official title is "International Convention for the Protection of Industrial Property.") The majority of industrialized nations of the world are parties to this international treaty, which was entered into in Paris in 1883 and has been revised many times since. Generally, the Paris Convention governs almost all reciprocal patent filing rights. Like most of these international treaties, the Paris Convention is administered by the World Intellectual Property Organization, or WIPO (www.wipo.int) in Geneva, Switzerland.

For the purpose of this chapter, there's one thing you need to know about the all-important Paris Convention: If you file a patent application (regular or PPA) in any one member jurisdiction of the Paris Convention (such as the U.S.), you can file a corresponding application in any other member jurisdiction (such as the U.K., Japan, the EPO, and Australia), within one year of your earliest filing date. Your application in each foreign jurisdiction will be entitled to the filing date of your U.S. application (regular or PPA) for purposes of predating disclosures by others that would otherwise rob your invention of novelty. ("Jurisdiction" refers to any country or group of countries that have joined under a treaty; that is, the EPO, PCT, AIPO, ARIPO, and EAPO, as listed above.)

You have to claim "priority" to your original application. "Priority" means that a later application is entitled to the benefit of the filing date of an earlier application. If you fail to file any foreign applications under the Convention within the one-year period, you can still file after the one-year period in Convention jurisdictions, provided you haven't sold, published, or patented your invention yet. However, any such late application won't get the benefit of your original U.S. filing date, so any relevant prior art that has been published in the meantime can be applied against (used to reject) your foreign applications. Put differently, once you miss the one-year deadline, your foreign application won't be entitled to the filing date of your original application. Rather, it becomes a non-Convention application, even in Convention countries. Also, once your U.S. application issues, it's too late to foreign-file anywhere (unless you file within the one-year period)—that is, if you file a Convention application.

D. The World Trade Organization and TRIPS

Eight non-Convention countries (Fiji, Hong Kong, Macao, Maldives, Myanmar (Burma), Solomon Islands, Taiwan (Republic of China), and Vanuatu) are members of the World Trade Organization (WTO). Each WTO member is bound by the April 1994 treaty concerning Trade-Related Aspects of Intellectual Property Rights (TRIPS). Article 2 of TRIPS requires WTO members to comply with the patent provisions of the Paris Convention, including those granting the one-year right of priority. Therefore you can claim priority to your original application in these non-Convention countries as if they were Convention members.

E. European Patent Office/ Europäisches Patentamt/Office Européen des Brevets (EPO)

The European Patent Office, or EPO (www.epo.org) is a separate and vast trilingual patent office with its headquarters in Munich, and offices in The Hague, Berlin, Vienna, Brussels, and Haar. (There is a separate website for searching the European Patent Office (www.espacenet.com).)

Members of Paris Convention

Afghanistan	Comoros	Holy See	Monaco	Senegal
Albania	Congo	Honduras	Mongolia	Serbia
Algeria	Costa Rica	Hungary	Montenegro	Seychelles
Andorra	Côte d'Ivoire	Iceland	Morocco	Sierra Leone
Angola	Croatia	India	Mozambique	Singapore
Antigua and Barbuda	Cuba	Indonesia	Namibia	Slovakia
Argentina	Cyprus	Iran (Islamic Rep.)	Nepal	Slovenia
Armenia	Czech Rep.	Iraq	Netherlands	South Africa
Australia	Dem. People's Rep. of Korea	Ireland	New Zealand	Spain
Austria		Israel	Nicaragua	Sri Lanka
Azerbaijan	Dem. Rep. of Congo	Italy	Niger	Sudan
Bahamas	Denmark	Jamaica	Nigeria	Suriname
Bahrain	Djibouti	Japan	North Macedonia	Sweden
Bangladesh	Dominica	Jordan	Norway	Switzerland
Barbados	Dominican Rep.	Kazakhstan	Oman	Syrian Arab Rep.
Belarus	Ecuador	Kenya	Pakistan	Tajikistan
Belgium	Egypt	Kiribati	Panama	Thailand
Belize	El Salvador	Kuwait	Papua New Guinea	Togo
Benin	Equatorial Guinea	Kyrgyzstan	Paraguay	Tonga
Bhutan	Eswatini (formerly Swaziland)	Lao People's Dem. Rep.	Peru	Trinidad and Tobago
Bolivia		Latvia	Philippines	Tunisia
Bosnia and Herzegovina	Estonia	Lebanon	Poland	Turkey
Botswana	Fiji	Lesotho	Portugal	Turkmenistan
Brazil	Finland	Liberia	Qatar	Uganda
Brunei Darusallam	France	Libya	Republic of Korea	Ukraine
Bulgaria	Gabon	Liechtenstein	Republic of Moldova	United Arab Emirates
Burkina Faso	The Gambia	Lithuania	Romania	United Kingdom
Burundi	Georgia	Luxembourg	Russian Federation	United Rep. of Tanzania
Cambodia	Germany	Madagascar	Rwanda	United States
Cameroon	Ghana	Malawi	Saint Kitts and Nevis	Uruguay
Canada	Greece	Malaysia	Saint Lucia	Uzbekistan
Cape Verde	Grenada	Mali	St. Vincent & Grenadines	Venezuela
Central African Rep.	Guatemala	Malta		Vietnam
Chad	Guinea	Mauritania	Samoa	Yemen
Chile	Guinea-Bissau	Mauritius	San Marino	Zambia
China	Guyana	Mexico	Sao Tome and Principe	Zimbabwe
Colombia	Haiti		Saudi Arabia	

Fig. 12A—Membership in the Paris Convention

Members of Patent Cooperation Treaty

Albania	Côte d'Ivoire	Iceland	Montenegro	Senegal
Algeria	Croatia	India	Morocco	Serbia
Angola	Cuba	Indonesia	Mozambique	Seychelles
Antigua and Barbuda	Cyprus	Iran (Islamic Rep.)	Namibia	Sierra Leone
Armenia	Czech Rep.	Iraq	Netherlands	Singapore
Australia	Dem. People's Rep. of Korea	Ireland	New Zealand	Slovakia
Austria		Israel	Nicaragua	Slovenia
Azerbaijan	Denmark	Italy	Niger	South Africa
Bahrain	Djibouti	Jamaica	Nigeria	Spain
Barbados	Dominica	Japan	North Macedonia	Sri Lanka
Belarus	Dominican Rep.	Jordan	Norway	Sudan
Belgium	Ecuador	Kazakhstan	Oman	Sweden
Belize	Egypt	Kenya	Panama	Switzerland
Benin	El Salvador	Kuwait	Papua New Guinea	Syrian Arab Rep.
Bosnia and Herzegovina	Equatorial Guinea	Kyrgyzstan	Peru	Tajikistan
Botswana	Estonia	Lao People's Dem. Rep.	Philippines	Thailand
Brazil	Eswatini (formerly Swaziland)	Latvia	Poland	Togo
Brunei Darusallam		Lesotho	Portugal	Trinidad and Tobago
Bulgaria	Finland	Liberia	Qatar	Tunisia
Burkina Faso	**France**	Libya	Republic of Korea	Turkey
Cambodia	Gabon	Liechtenstein	Republic of Moldova	Turkmenistan
Cameroon	The Gambia	Lithuania	Romania	Uganda
Canada	Georgia	Luxembourg	Russian Federation	Ukraine
Cape Verde	**Germany**	Madagascar	Rwanda	United Arab Emirates
Central African Rep.	Ghana	Malawi	Saint Kitts and Nevis	United Kingdom
Chad	Greece	Malaysia	Saint Lucia	United Rep. of Tanzania
Chile	Grenada	Mali	St. Vincent & the Grenadines	United States
China	Guatemala	Malta		Uzbekistan
Colombia	Guinea	Mauritania	Samoa	Vietnam
Comoros	Guinea-Bissau	Mexico	San Marino	Zambia
Congo	Honduras	Monaco	Sao Tome and Principe	Zimbabwe
Costa Rica	Hungary	Mongolia	Saudi Arabia	

Fig. 12B—Membership in Patent Cooperation Treaty

Member States of the European Patent Organization

Albania	Finland	Latvia	North Macedonia	Slovakia
Austria	France	Liechtenstein	Norway	Slovenia
Belgium	Germany	Lithuania	Poland	Spain
Bulgaria	Greece	Luxembourg	Portugal	Sweden
Croatia	Hungary	Malta	Romania	Switzerland
Cyprus	Iceland	Monaco	San Marino	Turkey
Czech Republic	Ireland	Netherlands	Serbia	United Kingdom
Denmark	Italy			

Fig. 12C—Membership in European Patent Organization

Hague Agreement Parties				
African Intellectual Property Organization (OAPI)	China	Hungary	Morocco	Senegal
	Côte d'Ivoire	Jamaica	Namibia	Serbia
	Croatia	Iceland	Niger	Singapore
Albania	Democratic People's Rep. of Korea	Israel	North Macedonia	Slovenia
Armenia		Italy	Norway	Spain
Azerbaijan	Denmark	Japan	Oman	Suriname
Belarus	Egypt	Kyrgyzstan	Poland	Switzerland
Belgium	Estonia	Latvia	Portugal	Syrian Arab Rep.
Belize	European Union (EU)	Liechtenstein	Republic of Korea	Tajikistan
Benin	Finland	Lithuania	Republic of Moldova	Tunisia
Bosnia and Herzegovina	France	Luxembourg	Romania	Turkey
	Gabon	Mali	Russian Federation	Turkmenistan
Botswana	Georgia	Mauritius	Rwanda	Ukraine
Brazil	Germany	Mexico	Saint Kitts and Nevis	United Kingdom
Brunei Darussalam	Ghana	Monaco	Samoa	United States
Bulgaria	Greece	Mongolia	San Marino	Uzbekistan
Cambodia	Holy See	Montenegro	Sao Tome and Principe	Vietnam
Canada				

Fig. 12D—Hague Agreement Countries

The EPO grew out of the earlier formation of the European Union (EU, formerly EEC), and the economic integration that resulted. Member nations of the EEC are also members of a treaty known as the "European Patent Convention" ("EPC"). Under the EPC you can make one patent filing in the EPO. If this filing matures into a European patent, it will, when separately registered in whatever individual member countries you select, cover your invention in these selected countries. And since the EPC is, in turn, considered the same as a single country (a jurisdiction) under the Paris Convention and the PCT, your effective EPO filing date will be the same as your original U.S. filing date, so long as you comply with the one-year foreign-filing rule. In other words, filing in the EPO allows you to kill many birds with one stone.

Once your application is on file, the EPO subjects it to a rigorous examination, including an opposition publication 18 months after filing. (See Chapter 13.) Even though you'll have to work through a European agent, patent prosecution before the EPO is generally smoother than in the PTO, because the examiners are better trained (all speak and write English, French, and German either fluently or conversationally) and because they actually take the initiative and suggest how to write your claims to get them allowed. If your application is allowed, you'll be granted a European patent that lasts for 20 years from your filing date (provided you pay maintenance fees in the member countries you've selected). Your patent will be valid automatically in each member country of the EPC that you've designated in your application, provided that you register the patent in and file translations in each country and appoint an agent there (called "validating the patent" in that country).

> CAUTION
>
> **Filing in the EPO is extremely expensive for U.S. residents,** who have to pay a substantial annuity to the EPO each year an application is on file there until it issues. Thereafter, U.S. residents must pay substantial fees to register and translate the Europatent and pay annuities in each member country in which the Europatent is registered. That's why you should not file for a Europatent unless you're very confident your invention will be commercially successful there (or unless someone else, such as a European licensee, is paying the freight).

Europe recently established a Unitary Patent system. Unitary Patents make it possible to get patent protection in up to 18 European Member States by submitting a single request to the EPO. They will build on European patents granted by the EPO under the rules of the European Patent Convention, so nothing will change in the pre-grant phase, and the same high standards of quality search and examination will apply. After a European patent is granted, the patent proprietor will be able to request unitary effect, which means getting a Unitary Patent that provides uniform patent protection in Europe and is enforceable in the Unified Patent Court (UPC).

The UP system provides several advantages over a Europatent, primarily a lower overall cost to maintain offensive rights in all European countries at once. This cost equals the sum of annuities charged by the four most "validated" member states back in 2015 (roughly 35,500 Euros spread over 20 years), which is far less than the sum of what each country would charge individually today. However, if you plan to sell your invention only in the major European countries, validating a Europatent in just those countries may be more cost effective. Also, the procedures for invalidating a Unitary Patent are centralized in the UPC, meaning that if a competitor knocks out your patent in the UPC then it is invalid all over Europe. By contrast, if you have a Europatent in several countries and a competitor knocks you out in Germany, you only lose your offensive rights in Germany and not those other countries.

The 18 states currently participating in the Unitary Patent system are: Austria, Belgium, Bulgaria, Denmark, Estonia, Finland, France, Germany, Italy, Latvia, Lithuania, Luxembourg, Malta, Netherlands, Portugal, Romania, Slovenia, and Sweden. Seven more states that have signed on, but have not yet begun to operate under the system, are: Cyprus, Czechia, Greece, Hungary, Ireland, and Slovakia. Three EU member states are not signed up: Croatia, and notably Poland and Spain. The United Kingdom is not a participant either.

F. The Patent Cooperation Treaty (PCT)

The PCT is another important treaty to which most industrial countries are a party. An entire chapter of the MPEP (chapter 1800) is devoted to it. Under the Patent Cooperation Treaty (PCT), which was entered into in 1978, U.S. residents can file in the United States and then make a single international filing in the USPTO within the one-year period. This can cover all of the PCT jurisdictions, including the European Patent Office (EPO). Eventually, you must file separate or "national" applications in each PCT jurisdiction (including the EPO) where you desire coverage. These separate filings, which must be translated for non-English-speaking jurisdictions, must be made for most countries within 30 months after your U.S. filing date.

If you file a PCT application, the USPTO (or another country's patent office, if you so choose), acting under the PCT, will make a patentability search of your invention and will give you an indication of its patentability. This patent office is called the International Searching Authority. If you want an actual examination of your invention to see what claims are allowable or rejected and to prosecute the application and revise claims, elect Chapter II of the PCT by 19 months after your U.S. filing date. Except for the single international filing, the PCT affords you a 30-month extension in which to file in most PCT countries or the EPO.

Also, you can file your first application under the PCT and then file in any PCT jurisdiction (including the U.S.) within 30 months from your PCT filing date. You should take this route if you've filed a PPA and you've decided to foreign-file by one year after your PPA filing date. Further, if you file with the PCT first instead of a PPA, you can file in any other country within one year from your PCT filing date under either the Paris Convention or TRIPS (or both, in the majority of cases). As stated, after you file your PCT application, you'll receive an "international search report" from the International Searching Authority citing any pertinent references against your application.

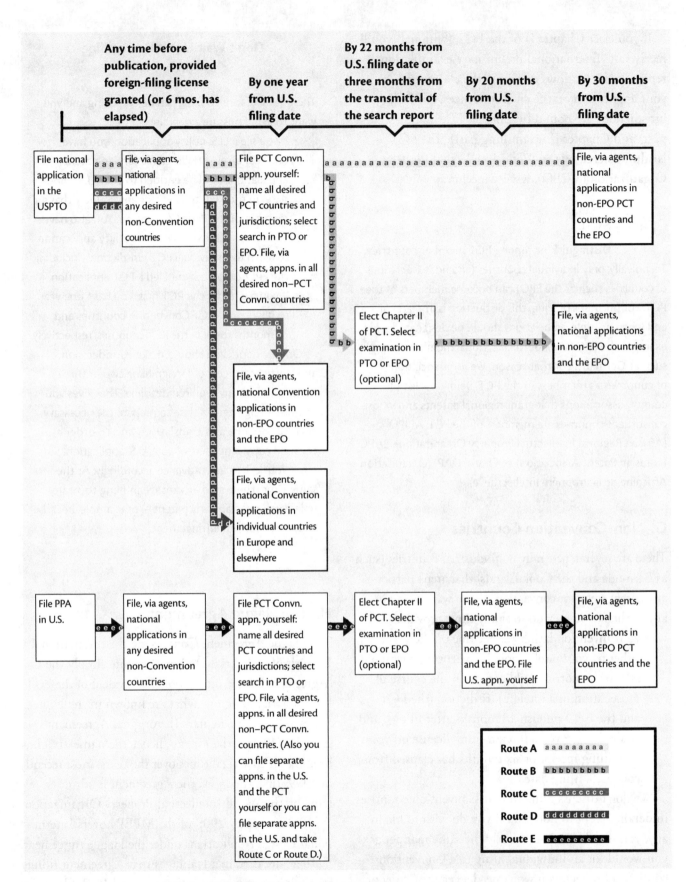

Fig. 12E—Foreign-Filing Routes (After Filing Basic U.S. Application)

If you elect Chapter II of the PCT (optional) you'll receive an "international preliminary examination report," which allows or rejects the claims of your application on the cited references. All PCT jurisdictions are bound by Chapter I (searching part) and Chapter II (examining part). The PCT is administered by the World Intellectual Property Organization (WIPO), www.wipo.int.

NOTE
Distinguishing among PCT member countries. Technically, only individual countries (and not associations of countries such as the EPO) can become members of the PCT. For purposes of filing, this distinction is immaterial and when possible, associations should be designated—for example, the EPO, and not the individual member country such as Germany. For that reason, we list associations of countries as members of the PCT. Below is a list of country associations that grant regional patents and whose constituent countries are members of the PCT: ARIPO (African Regional Intellectual Property Organization), EAPO (Eurasian Patent Association), EPO, and OAPI (Organisation Africaine de la Propriété Intellectuelle).

G. Non-Convention Countries

There are several, generally nonindustrial countries (such as Bermuda and the Cook Islands) that aren't parties to any patent treaty or convention. If you want to file in any of them, you may do so at any time, provided:

- your invention hasn't yet become publicly known, either by your publication, by patenting, by public sale, or by normal publication, in the course of prosecution in a foreign jurisdiction (the PCT and the EPO publish 18 months after filing), and
- you've been given a foreign-filing license on your U.S. filing receipt or six months has elapsed from your U.S. filing date.

We don't discuss filing in non-Convention countries in detail, except to note that if you do wish to file in any, you should do so in exactly the same manner as you would for an individual filing in a Convention country. However, you won't need a certified copy of your U.S. application since you won't be able to obtain priority (the benefit of your U.S. filing date).

Don't Wait Until the Deadline to Foreign-File

The timing of foreign filing can be confusing and you want to avoid missing a deadline.

- If you file a U.S. utility application, you have one year after you file, to file foreign patent applications (and be entitled to your U.S. filing date) in the PCT, the EPO, or any country that's a member of the Paris Convention. You also have 30 months after you file a U.S. utility application to file in the individual PCT jurisdictions, including the EPO, provided you filed a PCT application.
- If you file under the PCT first, you have one year to file in non–PCT Convention countries and 30 months to file in the PCT countries, respectively.

On one hand, you should make your decision and start the process of foreign filing two or three months before any required deadline. That gives you and the foreign agents time to prepare the necessary correspondence and translations and to order a certified copy, if needed, of your U.S. application. So mark your calendar in advance accordingly. At the same time, there's no advantage in filing too early, unless you need an early patent—for example, because you have a foreign infringement.

H. The Hague Agreement

The Hague Agreement Concerning the International Deposit of Industrial Designs, or more simply the "Agreement," is the international equivalent of the PCT for industrial designs—what are known in the United States as "design patents." The original Agreement was signed in 1925 at the Hague (hence the name), but has been modified several times over the years, most recently in 1999. Like the PCT, the Agreement is administered by the World Intellectual Property Organization (WIPO). Chapter 2900 of the MPEP covers International Design Applications under the Hague Agreement.

There are certain advantages that Agreement filings for designs enjoy over Convention and PCT filings for utility inventions. While examination is mandatory under the Agreement, if the examination is favorable then the design is recorded in an International Register and becomes enforceable in all member countries, unless the country files a refusal with WIPO. (The United States does not grant automatic enforceability upon recordation, but requires that a design patent be separately granted.) By contrast, thorough examination of PCT applications is optional unless expressly requested by the applicant, and the international search and examination reports are not binding on member jurisdictions, who are free to issue refusals for their own reasons. Similarly, renewal or maintenance fees are centrally administered, and are extendable in five-year increments up to the maximum term of 15 years, unlike utility patents whose fees must be paid to each country after issue. However, remember that unlike the Convention and the PCT, applications filed under the Hague Agreement are entitled to only six months of priority, not twelve. If you want to file overseas under the Agreement, do not wait a year to do so, or you will have already sacrificed your right to obtain coverage.

I. The Early Foreign-Filing License or Mandatory Six-Month Delay

Normally, the official filing receipt you get after filing your U.S. application gives you express permission from the PTO to file abroad. This permission will usually be printed on your filing receipt, as follows: "If required, Foreign Filing License Granted (DATE)." However, if your filing receipt fails to include a foreign-filing license (only inventions with possible military applications won't include the license), you aren't allowed to foreign-file on your invention until six months following your U.S. filing date.

The reason for this is to give the U.S. government a chance to review your application for possible classification on national security grounds. You probably won't be affected by any of this, as most applications get the foreign-filing license immediately and, in any case, there is usually no good reason to file before six months after your U.S. filing. If

your situation is different, however, and your filing receipt doesn't include a license, you will probably need to see a patent lawyer. If your invention does have military applications, not only will you fail to get a foreign-filing license on your filing receipt, but after you receive the receipt, you may receive a Secrecy Order from the PTO. This will order you to keep your invention secret until it's declassified, which often takes 12 years. (The government kept Dr. William Friedman's application, filed in 1933 on a cryptographic system, secret until August 1, 2000, when it issued as patent 6,097,812—67 years later! Dr. Friedman is regarded as the father of American cryptography.) Your patent can't issue while it's under a secrecy order, but the government may compensate you if they use your invention in the meantime. You can foreign-file an application that is under a secrecy order, but it's complicated; see a patent lawyer who has experience in this area.

In the very rare situation that you weren't automatically granted a foreign filing license in your filing receipt, and you don't believe that your invention has military applications so that you should have gotten a foreign filing license, and you have a pressing need to file abroad so that you can't wait the six months for automatic grant of a license, it's possible to petition the PTO for expedited handling under 37 CFR 5.12 and 5.14. It's also possible that a telephone call to the PTO's Inventor Assistance Center at 800-786-9199 will clear up the issue. However, if the need is truly that pressing, you should almost certainly speak with a patent lawyer.

J. The Patent Laws of Other Countries Are Different

Despite the Paris Convention and other treaties covering patent applications, and except for Canada, whose patent laws and practice are practically identical to ours, almost all countries have some differences from the the United States in their substantive patent laws and practices that can result in "gotcha" moments that you will want to avoid. These differences have been reduced under TRIPS, but some that still exist are as follows:

- In the United States, once an application is examined and allowed, the patent issues without any further proceedings. However, most foreign countries have an opposition proceeding under which the application is published and anyone who believes the invention isn't patentable can cite additional prior art to the patent office in order to block the patent.

- Many countries with relatively smaller economies (for example, Belgium, Brazil, and Portugal) don't conduct novelty examinations on applications that are filed there directly (that is, not through the EPO), but instead simply issue a patent on every application filed and leave it up to the courts (in the event of an infringement) to determine whether the invention was novel and nonobvious.

- Some jurisdictions (the EPO, France, Germany, Italy, Australia, the Netherlands) require the payment of annual maintenance fees while the application is pending. But if you file in these countries (except Australia) through the EPO, no individual country fees are due until the European patent issues and is registered in each country. However, substantial annual EPO fees plus European agent fees are due until the Europatent issues.

- Any disclosure of your invention before filing will be fatal to the application, unless the disclosure was made by the inventor or another who obtained the subject matter from the inventor or a joint inventor.

- Some countries such as Italy don't grant patents on drugs and some don't grant patents on computer programs or business methods.

- In Japan, the filing and translation fees are very high. Then, examination must be separately requested within seven years, requiring another stiff fee. After examination is requested, it takes about three years before the Japanese Patent Office, which is understaffed, gets around to it. Getting the application allowed is very difficult. However, it will be given more respect than in the United States. That is, competitors will be far less likely to infringe or challenge it. Nevertheless, Japanese courts tend to interpret patents narrowly.

- The U.S., United Kingdom, and Japan use "peripheral claiming": each word in a claim shrinks a notional fence that surrounds and defines the legal right. So, fewer words mean broader U.S. claims. However some countries, especially in Europe, use "central claiming": each word in a claim more accurately pinpoints the center of the legal right and the fence is as large as the nature of the inventive contribution permits, so more words actually may mean broader claims. Therefore, you may want to use different claims in the U.K. and Japan than in other jurisdictions. In particular, you may want to put two sets of claims in your PCT application to cover both cases.

K. Ways to File Abroad

Until several years ago, there was only one way to foreign-file; namely, to file a separate application in each country in which you wished to file. As this was a cumbersome and expensive process, many of the countries got together to simplify things. Now there are five basic approaches to filing abroad in Convention countries. You may end up using different approaches for different countries, or the same approach for all. The chart above, Fig. 12E, summarizes these alternatives. The lettered routes in the explanation below are keyed to the paths in the chart (see the legend at the bottom right of the chart). In essence, the routes are:

Route A: This is the most common. File a Regular Patent Application (RPA) in the United States. Then file in non-Convention countries before publication or sale. Then, within one year of your RPA, file a PCT application to cover the PCT countries and jurisdictions (including the EPO).

Select the USPTO or EPO for the search (there are other countries whose patent offices are allowed to do the search, and many of them are less expensive than the PTO and EPO, but they often produce prior art in languages other than English). Then, by 30 months from your U.S. filing date, file national applications (you'll have to hire foreign patent agents and spend big bucks) in the EPO and non-EPO PCT countries.

Route B: This is the same as Route A, except that within 19 months from your U.S. filing date, or three months from the transmittal of the search report, you have the option to elect Chapter II of the PCT to get the application examined, either in the PTO or EPO. Finally, file in the EPO and non-EPO countries within 30 months from your U.S. filing date.

Route C: This is the same as Route A, except that instead of filing under the PCT, you file Convention applications in the EPO and non-EPO countries within 12 months from your U.S. filing date.

Route D: This is the same as Route C, except that you file directly in the individual EPO countries (rather than the EPO). Caution: this route is not available for France, which requires that an application go through the EPO, as described in Route A.

Route E: If you've filed a Provisional Patent Application (PPA), and by the time almost one year elapses from your PPA's filing date you decide to file in the United States and abroad, you can do so in three basic ways: (1) File a PCT application yourself, naming the United States and all other desired PCT countries. File in non–PCT Convention countries using foreign patent agents. By 22 months from your PPA filing date or three months from the transmittal of the search report, you may elect Chapter II of the PCT and select examination in the PTO or EPO. By 30 months from your PPA filing date, file, via agents, national applications in the EPO and non–EPO countries and file yourself in the United States, claiming priority of your PCT application. (2) File separate applications in the United States and PCT countries yourself. Continue as in Route A for your PCT application. (3) File separate applications in the United States and either (a) use agents to file in non-EPO countries and the EPO (Route C), or (b) use agents to file national Convention applications in individual countries in Europe and elsewhere (Route D).

Let's discuss each of these alternatives in more detail.

1. Route A: Non-Convention/Convention PCT

Route A is the most popular way to go. Not surprisingly, it's also the cheapest way to go in the short run, since you won't have to file national applications (with foreign patent agents and the huge expense they entail—indicated by boxes with bold lines on the chart) until 30 months from your U.S. filing date. Under Route A, you file in the United States first and then go abroad through the PCT, to the extent possible. Here's how it works for U.S. inventors:

- First file in the United States in the usual manner. Next, file directly in any non-Convention countries you desire, before your application or invention is published, but after you get your foreign-filing license or six months has elapsed from your U.S. filing date.

- Then, before one year from your U.S. filing date, file a PCT request form and a separate "international application" under the PCT with the USPTO within 12 months from your filing date. The application designates the PCT member countries or jurisdictions (such as the EPO) in which you desire coverage.

- The request and application are forwarded to the "International Searching Authority" (a branch of the PTO or foreign patent office if you've elected to have your search made there) where an "international search report" is prepared. If you select the PTO, the examination will generally be done by the same examiner who handles your U.S. application. Other competent searching authorities include the EPO, Korea, Australia, Russian Federation, Israel, Japan, and Singapore.

- Copies of the search report and application are then forwarded to the countries designated in the application. Cite any new references to the PTO on your basic U.S. case through another Information Disclosure Statement.

- Within 30 months from your U.S. filing date, you must hire agents and prosecute the application in the individual countries. You must also provide a translation (except in the EPO) and must pay any fees that are required. While separate prosecution is required in each country, it's commonly made easier by the fact that the PCT member countries generally rely on the international search and examination. It is no longer necessary to elect Chapter II to obtain the 30-month delay, except for certain individual country filings.

a. How to Prepare a PCT (International) Application

To prepare an international application under the PCT, first prepare your original U.S. application and drawings in the A4 international format. The main differences between the PCT and U.S. national formats (both of which are acceptable for U.S. applications) are the paper and drawing size and margins. (These differences are detailed in Chapter 10.)

The World Intellectual Property Organization has software ("PCT-SAFE") that enables you to pay somewhat reduced fees and automates the process of completing the PCT filing forms. You can download PCT-SAFE from the WIPO's website (www.wipo.int/pct-safe/en/download/download_client.html).

You can file a PCT application on Patent Center or by mail. We strongly recommend using Patent Center since the paper size restrictions will be looser and you won't have to fuss with making file copies and using Priority Mail Express. If you want to file by mail, obtain and complete a multipage "Request" (Form PCT/RO/101) including the Fee Calculation Sheet and the Transmittal Letter (Form PTO 1390) from the PTO's website (www.uspto.gov). The form can also be obtained from Mail Stop PCT, Commissioner for Patents, P.O. Box 1450, Alexandria, VA 22313-1450, Phone 571-272-4300 or Fax 571-273-0419. Ask for the latest fees when you call, or you can find these in the latest *Official Gazette* on the PTO's website. Complete the forms (full instructions and examples are attached), **requesting the PTO to prepare a certified copy of your** U.S. application for use with your PCT application, and attach a copy of your application in PCT (A4) format (with drawings) and a credit card payment form or check (payable to "Commissioner for Patents") for the international application filing fees as computed on the Fee Calculation Sheet—the last page of the Request form. To file a PCT application by Patent Center, first prepare a PDF copy of your application and drawings in A4 size. Then complete the "Request" (Form PCT/RO/101) including the Fee Calculation Sheet and Transmittal Letter (Form PTO 1390) from the PTO's website (www.uspto.gov). Full instructions are on the forms.

Then file the forms (all must be in PDF format) on Patent Center (https://patentcenter.uspto.gov). You will be able to pay the fees by credit card as part of the process. Call the PTO's PCT Help Desk at 571-272-4300 if you have any questions.

b. PCT Fees

The PCT fees frequently vary due to exchange rate fluctuations. They're composed of several parts:

- Transmittal Fee
- Search Fee: (a) if you haven't already filed in the United States (that is, you filed your first application in the PCT, rather than the United States—very rare), (b) if you've already filed in the United States (the usual case), and (c) if you want to use the EPO as your searching authority (recommended), and
- International Filing Fee.

You should designate the EPO as your searching authority if you intend to seek a patent there since they generally do a more effective search than the USPTO and you'll save money and time in the EPO later. But be warned: Sometimes the EPO search is so effective that you might have to abandon both your U.S. and EPO applications. If any foreign patent office cites a new reference against your application, be sure to cite it in your U.S. application by filing it with a supplemental IDS and PTO-1449. (See Chapter 10.)

c. How to File PCT and Non-PCT Applications

To file a paper PCT application by mail, mail the Transmittal Letter, Request (including the Fee Calculation Sheet), a copy of your application and drawings (both on A4 size), and CCPF or check, and a receipt postcard to: Mail Stop PCT, Commissioner for Patents, P.O. Box 1450, Alexandria, VA 22313-1450, which, as mentioned, is a designated receiving office for the International Bureau. Like Convention applications, the international (PCT) application should be filed within one year of your U.S. filing date, also known as the "priority date."

We advise filing the PCT application at least a month before the anniversary of your U.S. filing date, so you'll have time to correct any serious deficiencies. But you can mail the PCT application as late as the last day of the one-year period from your U.S. filing date if you use Priority Mail Express and complete the PME on page 1 of the Transmittal Letter. (Never use a plain Certificate of Mailing for any PCT correspondence.)

Prepare a copy of your application and drawings and convert them to PDF. Then, file online at the PTO's Patent Center site (in the same manner as instructed for your U.S. application in Chapter 10). You will get an instant acknowledgment and PCT Serial Number.

To file any non-PCT applications, use a foreign patent agent in each country you select to prepare an appropriate application. The easiest way to do this is to send the agent a copy of your U.S. application and ask what else is needed. The requirements vary from country to country, but special drawings in each country's format will always be needed and you'll likely need to pay for someone to translate your application into the official language of that country (which will inevitably cost a few thousand dollars). You can have your foreign agent prepare these documents, or you can have them prepared yourself at lesser cost by the same companies that make drawings and translations for U.S. applications.

Also, the agent will send you a power of attorney form that you'll have to sign. Further, you'll generally need a certified copy of your U.S. application; this can be obtained from the PTO for a fee. (See Appendix 4, "Fee Schedule.") The cost for filing a foreign application in each individual country is about $1,000 to $5,000, depending on the country and the length of your application (not including translation costs).

If you wish to correspond directly with the foreign patent agents yourself, you'll first have to get the name of a patent agent in each country.

d. What Happens to Your International Application?

You'll receive a (PCT) filing receipt and separate serial number for your international application, and the application will eventually be transmitted for filing to the countries (including the EPO) you've designated on your request form. If you make any minor errors in your PCT application, the PCT Department of the USPTO will give you a month to correct them.

e. Search Report

When you receive your PCT search report (either from the PTO or EPO and usually after several months), it will include a written opinion on patentability. You can comment on it and amend your claims if necessary, but no extended prosecution or negotiation is permitted. If you enter Chapter II of the PCT (optional), you will receive a more formal examination of your application, but it will be similar to the written opinion on patentability of Chapter I. The WIPO will publish your PCT application 18 months from your priority date. Your priority date is the date you filed a PPA or an RPA if you didn't file a PPA.

CAUTION

If the search report cites any new references, be sure to cite these to the PTO by way of a supplemental IDS (see Chapters 10 and 13).

f. National Stage

Within 30 months from your U.S. filing date, whether or not you elect Chapter II, if filing in Europe you must hire an agent there (get one in London if you are seeking one who is fluent in English, or in Munich if you're seeking an agent close to the EPO offices) and file an EPO application based on your PCT application. Also, you must have an agent in each non-EPO PCT country (such as Japan or Australia) in which you wish to file, and get national applications on file in these countries. Expect to pay fairly stiff filing fees and a substantial maintenance fee each year the EPO application is pending.

As mentioned, each of the separate countries and the EPO will rely to a great extent on the international examination they'll receive from the International

Bureau. (In most cases this will be the EPO search or an adoption of the U.S. search.) One advantage of the PCT approach is you'll save much of what used to be the agonizing, extremely expensive job of separately and fully prosecuting an application in each country in which you elected to file.

> **CAUTION**
>
> **You will not receive a reminder to enter the national stage by 30 months from your priority (U.S. filing) date.** You are solely responsible for meeting the deadline. We suggest setting your own calendar reminders in the weeks leading up to the 30-month deadline.

2. Route B: Elect Chapter II of PCT If You Want an International Examination

Route B is the same as Route A, except that instead you elect Chapter II of the PCT before filing your national applications. You have, as indicated, 22 months from your U.S. filing date or three months from the transmittal of the search report, to do this.

Get the form (PCT/IPEA/401) from the PTO's site or the PCT department of the PTO, and learn the latest fees for Chapter II. If you select the EPO to do the examination, you must file the papers with the EPO in Munich and pay the fee in Euros. You'll get an examination report where claims will actually be allowed or rejected. You can amend your application once and even interview your examiner.

You file your EPO and non-EPO applications in the same way you did under Route A—that is, you elect agents, send them copies of all of your papers, and tell them you want to file national applications in their countries based upon your U.S. and PCT applications. Route B will cost more than Route A since you incur the expense of Chapter II of the PCT.

3. Route C: Convention Applications in EPO and Non-EPO Countries

Under Route C, you bypass the PCT entirely and file (through agents) national Convention applications in the EPO and non-EPO countries within 12 months of your U.S. filing date. This is the cheapest way to go in the long run if you wish to file in several European countries. However, you lose the advantage of the extra 18 months that a PCT filing provides. An EPO filing, while expensive, is generally considered cheaper than separate filings if:

1. Two or more non-English-speaking countries are involved (for example, it's cheaper to file in the EPO than to file separate applications in Italy and Germany), or
2. The U.K. and more than one non-English-speaking country are involved. Conversely, it's cheaper to file separate applications in the U.K. and Germany, for instance, than to go through the EPO.

As mentioned, to file a Convention application in the EPO you'll have to go through a European patent agent, unless you have an address in one of the EPO countries, in which case you can do it yourself. Correspondence with the EPO must be in English if your application is based on your U.S. case.

Including the agent's fee, expect to spend a sizable amount getting your application on file and examined in about six countries. (See Appendix 4, "Fee Schedule.") Additional large fees will be incurred for prosecution (getting your application approved once it's filed) and issuance. Then you'll have to arrange to get translations and individual agents for the respective countries you designate. For more information, read the *European Patent Guide: How to Get a European Patent* on the EPO website (www.epo.org).

4. Route D: Convention Applications Only in Individual Countries

Here you bypass both the PCT and the EPO. It's not a wise idea to bypass the EPO unless you want to file in just two countries in Europe—in which case it's usually cheaper to make individual filings rather than go through the EPO. This is the simplest way to go, chart-wise, although it can get very complex and involve a lot of parallel correspondence and paperwork, since you'll have to make simultaneous prosecutions in each country. Filing is accomplished by sending a certified copy of your U.S. application to a patent agent in each country and instructing the agent to file a Convention application based upon your U.S. application. The agent will tell you what else is needed.

5. Route E: PPA Filed

If you've filed a PPA (see Chapter 3), your choices and procedures are the same as Routes A to D, except that at each stage there's another national country in which you can file: the United States. If you've filed a PPA, we recommend you file in the United States, separately, by one year after you file your PPA, because it's simpler and somewhat cheaper. However, if you want to delay your U.S. filing, you can name the United States in your PCT application when you file your PCT application within one year after your PPA's filing date. You can then file your U.S. national application by 30 months after your PPA date, deferring RPA filing costs by 18 months. Your U.S. application should be identical to a "regular" U.S. application, except that you should add the following sentence to the PAD (Form 10-1A) to get the benefit of your PCT filing date: "I hereby claim foreign priority benefits under 35 U.S.C. 119 of PCT patent application, Ser. No. _____, Filed 20___; which in turn claims priority of provisional patent application Ser. Nr. _____filed _____."

6. File the PCT Application First

Although not listed on the chart because it's not a very popular method, if you haven't filed a PPA you can file a PCT application first (before you file any other application for your invention) and then file in the United States and PCT countries (including the EPO) through the PCT. File in the non-PCT countries through the Convention or TRIPS. You can use this method to postpone the examination of your U.S. application until 30 months after your PCT filing date.

If you haven't filed a PPA and you know for certain, before you file anywhere, that you'll want to file in the United States and at least one foreign PCT country, then you can save some fees and effort by filing the PCT application first, before you file in the United States. Then, within one year of your PCT filing date, you should file Convention or TRIPS applications, based upon your PCT application, in any non-PCT country.

Within 30 months of your PCT filing date, file separately (claiming priority of your PCT application) in each country or jurisdiction you've designated in your PCT application, including the United States and the EPO. Then order (from the PTO) a certified copy of your PCT application and file this within a few months after your U.S. filing date.

Whether you're filing in a PCT or non-PCT jurisdiction based upon a PCT filing, your foreign patent agents will tell you what you'll need to file PCT-based applications in their countries; allow at least two months before the 20- or 30-month deadline to give them (and you) time to prepare the applications and translations, if necessary.

Patent Prosecution Highway—Expedited Examination of Applications Filed Abroad

Your application is examined ahead of turn in almost all major foreign patent offices if you first filed your application in the United States and then filed a foreign application claiming priority of your earlier-filed U.S. application. In order to enter this program in the foreign patent office, the USPTO must have officially allowed at least one claim in the first-filed U.S. application. If you want to enter this program you must have your foreign agent file a request in the foreign patent office.

L. Rescind Any Nonpublication Request

When you filed your U.S. application, you had the opportunity to file a nonpublication request (NPR) (see Form 10-7). If you filed an NPR, you must file a rescission of this Request with the PTO within

45 days after filing your foreign application. You must file the rescission regardless of whether you are filing directly in a foreign country or using a PCT application. If you do not file the rescission, the PTO will cancel your U.S. application.

Beware of Scams

Scammers have invaded the world of the PCT and foreign patent filings. Once your application is published, you may get offers from scammers seeking to lighten your wallet. For example, after filing a PCT application for a client and revoking the nonpublication request that my client had originally filed, the PTO published his application about 18 months after filing. He soon got a letter from a "Patent Registry" in Washington, D.C., offering to register his patent in their private "American Patent and Trademark Register"—an apparently worthless endeavor—for a mere $2,489.46! WIPO "names and shames" these scammers at www.wipo.int/pct/en/warning/pct_warning.html.

To make the rescission, complete and file Form SB/36, available on the PTO's website. If you don't have internet access, you can use Form 13-1, but title it "Request to Rescind Previous nonpublication request." Remove the sentence stating "In response to Office Letter ..." and substitute the following statement: "Applicant has foreign filed the above application on or about [date] and therefore hereby rescinds the previously filed Nonpublication Request under 35 U.S.C. § 122(b)." Remember to complete or include a Certificate of Mailing at the end of the rescission as in Form 13-2. (If you forget to rescind the NPR within 45 days of your foreign filing your application is technically abandoned but you may revive it by a petition under Rule 136(6), accompanied by a substantial fee.)

After notification, the PTO will schedule publication of your application 18 months after your U.S. filing date (or as soon as possible after the 18-month period).

M. Foreign-Filing Resources

There are a number of resources to assist you in foreign filing your patent application. Let's look at them separately.

- **U.S. Patent Practitioners.** Most U.S. patent attorneys and agents have experience in foreign filing and will handle the PCT filing and national stage filings for you for a fee, in addition to the filing fees.

- **Foreign Patent Agents.** You'll almost certainly need to find a foreign patent agent who's familiar with patent prosecution in the countries where you desire protection. (In most countries, patent professionals are called "agents" rather than "attorneys.") Your best bet is to find one through a U.S. patent attorney, as most are associated with one or more patent agents in other major countries. If you don't know a U.S. patent attorney, do an online search using terms like "patent agent [name of country]" or look in the telephone directory of the city where the patent office of the foreign country is located. Foreign consulates also often have a list of patent agents. *Martindale-Hubbell* (www.martindale.com), also lists some foreign patent agents in each country. Finally, you can hire a British firm of patent agents to do all your foreign filing. The main reason for selecting British agents is that they speak English and they're familiar with non-U.S. filing. This would be especially appropriate if you're filing with the EPO (although most German agents in Munich, though perhaps not as fluent in English, have the compensating advantage of their physical proximity to the EPO). Whichever way you find your foreign patent agent, be careful, since many foreign agents are bound by a minimum fee schedule, which is sometimes exorbitant. Also, keep in mind that some foreign patent agents— like their U.S. counterparts—are incompetent or inclined to overcharge.

- **Written Materials.** Read *Patents Throughout the World*, by Henry Teegarden (published by Clark Boardman Callaghan, a Thomson Reuters brand). This book is revised annually, so be sure you have the most recent version. For more information on how to utilize the PCT, "The PCT Applicant's Guide," "Basic Facts," and other instructive materials and forms are available online at www.wipo.int and from the PCT Department of the USPTO.

N. Summary

A U.S. patent provides a monopoly in the United States only, so it is necessary to file for corresponding foreign patents in any other countries in which you want offensive rights. Foreign filing is very expensive and few inventors who foreign-file ever recoup their investment, so an inventor should foreign-file the application in a country only if the invention has extremely strong commercial potential there, or if someone else is footing the bill.

Various treaties and conventions govern foreign filing. The Paris Convention grants anyone who files a basic application in any member country the benefit of the basic filing date in any other country where a corresponding application is filed within one year. TRIPS provides the same benefit from World Trade Organization (WTO) countries. The Patent Cooperation Treaty (PCT) allows inventors to delay the decision of what countries to enter, and the associated costs, by 18-30 months through the filing of a separate application.

The European Patent Office enables one to file a single patent application and get a European patent that is valid in any European country, provided the Europatent is registered in and translated for each country.

The Hague Agreement is the international equivalent of the PCT for industrial designs in about 75 countries, and requires that an international design application be filed within six months of a U.S. design filing.

An inventor who files a U.S. utility application must wait six months before foreign filing, unless the PTO grants a foreign filing license, which it usually grants on the filing receipt. The laws of other countries are different from the United States in certain respects—for example, some countries have no interferences, no one-year grace period, and no patents on drugs. Some countries have maintenance fees during pendency, hold opposition proceedings, and companies can apply for patents in the name of the company or an assignee.

There are several routes for filing abroad, but most inventors file in the United States first, then file a PCT application within a year, and then file national-stage applications within 30 months of the U.S. filing date. An inventor can file a PCT application in the USPTO by completing the PCT forms and filing an A4 copy of the application with the appropriate fees. You can file a PCT application on paper or via Patent Center.

If an inventor files a U.S. application with a non-publication request, the inventor must revoke this within 45 days after any foreign filing. It is necessary to hire a foreign patent agent in any jurisdiction where a national-stage application (in an individual country or in a regional office like the EPO) is to be filed.

CHAPTER

13

Getting the PTO to Deliver

A.	**What Happens After Your Patent Application Is Filed**	370
	1. Receipt Postcard	370
	2. Official Filing Receipt	370
	3. Patent Pending Status	371
	4. Try Signing in As an eFiler	372
	5. Send in Your Information Disclosure Statement (IDS)	373
	6. First Office Action	375
	7. Response to First Office Action	376
	8. Second/Final Office Action	376
	9. Notice of Allowance	376
	10. Issue Fee and Issue Notification	376
	11. Receipt of Official Patent Deed	376
B.	**General Considerations During Patent Prosecution**	376
	1. The PTO Can Write Claims for You	376
	2. Consultation With a Patent Professional Might Be Wise	377
	3. Intervals Are Approximate	377
	4. You'll Be Able to Correct Technical Errors	377
	5. Dates Are Crucial	377
	6. Situations Not Covered	378
	7. Standards of Patentability Vary Widely	379
	8. Don't Take Rejection Personally	379
	9. Dealing With the PTO Can Feel Frustrating and Unfair	379
	10. PTO Reference Books	380
	11. Never Make Negative or Limiting Statements on the Record	380
	12. Remember Your Continuing Duty to Disclose Material Information	380
	13. The PTO Can Request Search Information and Literature	381
	14. Be Available to Answer Office Actions	381
	15. Consider Foreign Filing	382
	16. You Can Call and Visit Your Examiner	382
	17. Working or Commercial Model	383
	18. No New Matter Can Be Added to Your Application	383
	19. Official Dates Are When the PTO Receives Your Submission	383
	20. Know Who Has the Ball	383

21. Reread Appropriate Chapters	383
22. Respond to Each and Every Point in the Office Action	383
23. Form Paragraphs	384
24. Preliminary and Supplemental Voluntary Amendments	384
25. Double Patenting Obviousness Rejections	384
26. Eighteen-Month Publication	384
27. *Festo* Considerations	384
28. Rejection Versus Objection	385
29. When Submitting Arguments, Rely on Statutes, Rules, and the MPEP, Rather Than Case Law	385
30. Don't Wait Until the Last Minute	385
31. Patents and Published Patent Applications Are Prior Art as of Their Filing Date as Well as Their Publication Date	385
32. Patent Examiners Are Overwhelmed	386
33. Beware of "Whack-a-Mole" Rejections	386
34. Limitations on Number of Claims	386
35. The PTO Has Been Very Difficult on Applicants	386
36. Avoid Fraud on the PTO	387
37. Keep Your Remarks as Short as Possible	387
38. Enablement	387
39. Patent Ombuds Office	387

C. A Sample Office Action 388

D. What to Do When You Receive an Office Action (OA) 394

1. Record Due Date on Your Calendar and OA, and Mount OA in Your File	394
2. Check the References and Review Your Application	394
3. Read and Analyze Each Cited Reference, Except Patent Claims	395
4. Make a Comparison Chart	395
5. Follow the Flowchart	395
6. Compare Your Broadest Claim With the Cited References for Novelty	397
7. Analyze Novel Features for Nonobviousness	397
8. If References Are Cited in Combination Against Your Broadest Claim	400
9. Does the Combination Disclose Subject Matter of Your Broadest Claim?	400
10. If Your Claims Are Rejected Under 35 U.S.C. Section 112	400
11. If Your Claims Are Rejected Under 35 U.S.C. Section 101	400
12. What to Do If You Disagree With the Examiner	404
13. Making Amendments Without Narrowing Scope of Claim	404
14. Amending Your Claim When You Agree With the Examiner	404
15. Plan an Outline of Your Response	415

CHAPTER 13 | GETTING THE PTO TO DELIVER | **369**

E. Format for Amending the Specification and Claims 415

    1. Changes to Specification 416

    2. Amendments to Claims 416

F. Drafting the Remarks 417

    1. General Rules for Drafting Remarks 417

    2. How to Draft Your Remarks 420

G. Drawing Amendments 425

H. Typing and Filing the Amendment 426

I. If Your Application Is Allowable 428

J. If Your First Amendment Doesn't Result in Allowance 429

    1. Comply With Examiner's Requirements 430

    2. Convince the Examiner 430

    3. Amendment After Final Rejection 431

    4. Appeal and Pre-Appeal Request for Review 431

    5. File a Continuation Application or Request Continued Examination 433

    6. Petitions to the Commissioner for Nonsubstantive Matters 434

    7. Abandon Your Application 434

K. Derivation Proceedings 434

L. Defensive Publication 435

M. If Your Application Claims More Than One Invention 435

N. The Public May Cite Additional Prior Art Against Your Published Patent Application 436

O. NASA Declarations 436

P. Design Patent Application Prosecution 437

Q. What to Do If You Miss or Want to Extend a PTO Deadline 437

    1. Buy an Extension Before the Six-Month Period Ends (37 CFR 1.136(a)) 437

    2. Petition to Revive If Delay Was Unintentional (37 CFR 1.137(b)) 438

    3. Request Extraordinary Relief 438

R. Summary 439

Inventor's Commandment 24

Never admit or state anything negative or limiting about your invention on the record (in writing), since anything negative you admit will be used against you later by an adversary or construed against you in a judicial proceeding.

Inventor's Commandment 25

Your application will go abandoned if you don't file a timely response to any PTO communication. Whenever you have a patent application pending, you must be available to receive Office Actions (letters) from the PTO and you must respond to every OA within the time allotted or within the time period of any extension you buy (when possible).

Inventor's Commandment 26

You cannot add any "new matter" (technical information not in the application as filed) to any patent application. If you want to add any new matter you must file a continuation-in-part application as explained in Chapter 14.

Inventor's Commandment 27

In answering an Office Action from the PTO, you must respond to each and every point (objection or rejection) in the OA, either by suitable argument or by complying as required.

Inventor's Commandment 28

When drafting an amendment in response to the first Office Action, do your very best job. Include a complete response, all available arguments for patentability, and the narrowest and most comprehensive claims possible, since the next OA will almost certainly be made final, foreclosing any future substantive changes unless you pay another filing or continued examination fee.

You can file a lawsuit against anyone for anything. Whether you can prove your case and win is, of course, a very different matter.

Similarly, anyone can file a patent application on anything. But getting the Patent and Trademark Office (PTO) to issue you a patent is, again, a very different matter.

This chapter tells you how to get the PTO to deliver, assuming your invention meets the standards of patentability in Chapter 5. This material is sure to seem confusing the first time you read it. A little familiarity with the process, however, should do a world of good when it comes to your understanding.

A. What Happens After Your Patent Application Is Filed

It will be helpful to review exactly what will occur after your patent application is filed.

1. Receipt Postcard

If you filed by mail, you'll receive your receipt postcard back in about two to four weeks. If you filed electronically, you'll receive your filing acknowledgment immediately. The postcard or acknowledgment will have an eight-digit number—for example, "U.S. Patent & TM Office, 22 August 2012; 12/123,456." The date is the "deposit" date (date of receipt), and the number is the serial number (sometimes called "application number") of your application. Your electronic acknowledgment will also contain another four-digit number, called a "confirmation number," which you will need to file amendments via Patent Center if you're a registered eFiler. Keep your serial number and filing date confidential unless a prospective manufacturer has shown serious interest and asks for this information—for example, because you're about to enter into a license or sale agreement.

2. Official Filing Receipt

About one to three months later you should receive an official filing receipt by mail. This is a sheet containing the following:

- the name(s) of the inventor(s)
- the title of your patent application
- the examining group (art unit) to which your application has been assigned
- the filing date and serial number of your application and the confirmation number
- the number of claims (total and independent)
- the filing fee you paid
- your name and address
- the words "Small Entity" if you filed as a small entity, and
- the words "Foreign Filing License Granted [date]" if the invention hasn't been militarily classified (most won't be).

Check all of this information carefully; it's what's entered into the PTO's data-processing system. If the filing receipt has any errors, indicate the error on the filing receipt and send a copy or fax it to the Office of Patent Application Processing (OPAP) whose numbers will be on the filing receipt. Request a new filing receipt.

Assuming you've done everything properly, your patent application is technically pending once you receive your Priority Mail Express receipt from the Post Office clerk, or when you get an electronic acknowledgment.

However, the actual filing receipt makes it official and shows that it's actually recorded in the PTO.

If You Receive a Foreign Filing License

The words "Foreign Filing License Granted," along with a date, on your filing receipt mean that you can foreign file at any time, rather than waiting six months. However, you still should wait until approximately nine months have passed before considering filing abroad in Convention countries. There is a slim chance you will receive an Office Action during that time, and if you do, you'll be better informed about patentability and have a chance to accumulate additional commercial information on your invention. You should file abroad in non-Convention countries before you sell or publish details of the invention.

You may continue to label your invention and any descriptive literature "Patent Pending," or "Patent Applied For." They have the same meaning. Note that it's a criminal offense to use the words "patent applied for" or "patent pending" in any advertising when there's no active, applicable Regular or Provisional Patent Application on file.

If for any reason, your application hasn't been filed properly (for example, your check bounced, or you didn't pay enough for the filing fee), you won't get the filing receipt. Instead, the PTO will send you a deficiency notice telling you what's needed and what surcharge (fine) you'll have to pay to fix the error. Once you comply with the deficiency notice (they usually give you two months), you'll get your filing receipt a few weeks later.

3. Patent Pending Status

The patent pending period begins when your Regular Patent Application or Provisional Patent Application is filed and lasts until the RPA issues as a patent or the PPA expires after 12 months. During the patent pending period, your rights depend upon whether you have filed a nonpublication request (NPR). If you have not filed an NPR, the PTO will publish your regular patent application 18 months after the filing date. Once it is published, you obtain "provisional rights" that allow you to obtain royalties from an infringer for activities that occurred from the date the infringer gets actual notice of the published application, if your patent issues with claims that are substantially identical to the claims in the published application (35 U.S.C. § 154(d)). (You can provide actual notice to the infringer by sending a copy of the published application by certified mail, return receipt requested.) You must wait until after the patent issues to request (and sue if necessary for) these "patent pending" royalties. If the patent does not issue, you cannot obtain any royalties.

If, at the time of filing your application, you filed an NPR, your application will not be published prior to issuance and no provisional remedies will accrue during the patent pending period. In other words, if it is not published prior to issuance, anyone can freely make, use, sell, and offer your invention for sale during the entire pendency period.

In general, a potential infringer won't copy a device that they know is patent pending. This is because the infringer would have to take the chance that a patent will later be issued and you'll use your patent to enforce your monopoly—that is, stop any further production and marketing. In this case, the money the infringer would have to spend on expensive tooling, product development and marketing will have been wasted. (If you're willing to license the infringer under your patent, the infringer's tooling outlay will be worthwhile, but few infringers will be willing to take this chance.) Another reason for marking a device "patent pending" is to show that you have given notice to potential infringers, which gives a court discretion to assess treble damages and attorneys' fees (after your patent issues) if the court finds that the infringement was willful.

After your application is filed, you may publish articles on your invention without loss of any legal rights in the United States or foreign Paris Convention countries, but you'll lose rights in non-Convention countries. However, it's not desirable to reveal details of your invention to potential competitors at this early stage, especially since your application may not become a patent.

4. Try Signing in As an eFiler

If you registered as an eFiler and submitted your patent application online through Patent Center, you can use your eFiler account to electronically file all additional paperwork that may be required to usher your application through the PTO to the finish line and get your patent. Right after you initially file your application is the best time to test the PTO website to ensure that you can sign in. If you cannot, you will have given yourself the maximum amount of time to correct any technical issues with the sign-in process.

To sign in, direct your web browser to patentcenter. uspto.gov. In the upper right corner of the screen, click the yellow "Sign In" link. Enter your registered eFiler email address and password, then enter your six-digit

multifactor authentication (MFA) code to complete your sign-in to your uspto.gov account. Beginning May 1, 2025, the only acceptable MFA methods are (1) an email to your eFiler email address, (2) Okta Verify, available as an app, (3) an authenticator app such as Google Authenticator, Authy, Duo Security, Microsoft Authenticator, Okta Verify and others, or (4) a Fast Identity Online (FIDO) hardware security key. You should have chosen and set up one of these options when you first enrolled in the eFiler program. If you need any assistance with signing in, contact the PTO Inventors Assistance Center by calling 800-786-9199 (toll free) or 800-977-8339 (TTY/TDD) between 8:30 am and 8:00 pm Eastern time on weekdays, or emailing usptoinfo@uspto.gov for after-hours support.

Once you are signed in, you will see an agency-wide dark gray navigation bar at the top of the screen that allows you to access menus for Patents, Trademarks, Fees and payment, "Contact Us," and "MyUSPTO" (a configurable intellectual property portfolio dashboard), and your account profile. Below that is a blue navigation bar for Patent Center specifically, with a Home button and menus for:

- New submissions (i.e., new PPA or RPA filings)
- Existing submissions (i.e., to add paperwork to a previously-filed PPA or RPA for which you have the serial number)
- Petitions (e.g., to make your RPA "special"—see Chapter 10, section F)
- Post grant (to request reexamination, reissue, or supplemental examination—see Chapter 15, section L)
- Workbench (for viewing submissions that were started but not filed, applications in your portfolio, PTO correspondence, and your transaction receipts), and
- Manage (for managing correspondence addresses and customer numbers).

There is also a Search button that will allow you to search for patents and applications in the PTO database by application number, attorney docket, patent number, PCT number, publication number, or international design registration number.

5. Send in Your Information Disclosure Statement (IDS)

If you haven't done so already, after receiving your official filing receipt send in your Information Disclosure Statement as discussed in Chapter 10. If you filed your application by mail send in the IDS by filling out a Transmittal Form (PTO Form SB/21, Form 10-05 in Appendix 7). Accompany it with the PTO Forms SB/08a, SB/08b, and SB/08c (Forms 10-6A, 10-6B, and 10-6C in Appendix 7) as necessary, and copies of any non-U.S. patent references you listed on the form.

If you filed electronically, and you're a registered eFiler, you won't need a transmittal form. Instead get the electronic SB/08 Patent Center form by going to www.uspto.gov/patents/apply/forms. Follow the instructions below, with the understanding that Patent Center screens and menu options may have changed since the writing of this book.

You will need to make a PDF copy of any non-U.S. patent references and non-patent publications like journal articles and websites (collectively known as Non-Patent Literature or "NPL"), and file all of these using the PTO's Patent Center.

To file the IDS electronically, which we strongly recommend, make sure you have your electronic acknowledgement receipt or filing receipt handy, along with digital copies of the documents to submit, and a count of the total number of references you will have cited in the application after the IDS is filed. First, sign in to Patent Center as described above. Then select "Existing submissions," and "Add Documents / Responses / Pay Fees" from the blue navigation bar. On the next page, enter your application number and confirmation number from the filing receipt and select "Continue." Next, upload your Form SB/08 (IDS.pdf) using the "drag-and-drop" area of the page, or press the "Browse files" button to bring up a file browsing dialog box. Patent Center should automatically recognize the document type as "Information Disclosure Statement (IDS) Form (SB08)." (If not, click the three vertical dots next to the word "Preview" to the right of the file name and select "Edit document description.")

Repeat the process for each foreign patent and NPL reference that you need to upload. Patent Center will not recognize these files, so when the empty document description box appears, click the pull-down arrow on the right, then select the "IDS/References" submenu, then "Non Patent Literature." The document description will then update. When you are finished uploading, click "Continue."

In January 2025 the PTO instituted progressive IDS size fees for applications citing more than 50, more than 100, and more than 200 references in total. The size fees are $200, $500, and $800 respectively (less any previously-paid IDS size fees). On the first Calculate Fees page, enter any previously-paid IDS size fee. On the second Calculate Fees page, if this IDS filing will bring you over one of the three thresholds in this paragraph, check the appropriate box (2832 for more than 50 items, 2833 for more than 100 items, and 2834 for more than 200 items). Click "Continue."

Review your submission one last time to ensure that you have uploaded all of the documents you intended to, and that the fees look correct. If not, you can jump to the correct part of the filing workflow using the navigation links at the top of the screen. If everything looks good, click "Submit." You will be taken to an acknowledgement page that indicates your IDS has been received.

There are three time periods in which you can file an IDS:

1. After your application has been filed, but before the later of three months and a first office action (see section C below).
2. After a first office action, but before prosecution has been closed by a final office action or notice of allowance (see sections I and J below).
3. After prosecution has been closed.

The longer you wait to file, the more burdensome the requirements become. If you file in period 1, i.e., before your application is examined, you can make any number of IDS filings without an IDS timing fee. If you file in period 2, i.e., after examination has begun, you can file the IDS with either a timing fee OR a statement indicating that you first learned about all of the references within the previous three months. If you file in period 3, i.e., after examination has ended, you can still file the IDS if you provide both the timing fee AND the statement.

There are two kinds of statements specified in the law and provided in the Form SB/08. Make the first statement if you learned about the references from a foreign patent office in a counterpart foreign application (e.g., as an International Search Report, or the references cited in an ISR, or as an action from a national patent office, or any references it cites—see Chapter 12). Make the second statement if you learned about the references some other way, AND you can also certify that no individual involved in the patent application process knew about any of the references more than three months prior.

If you are filing electronically, simply check each box next to the timing statement that applies. If you learned about the references both from a foreign office and otherwise, you may check both boxes. (When the PTO was considering adding these statements to the SB/08 form rather than having them submitted in a separate paper, I asked them about this issue since the two statements seem to be mutually exclusive. They indicated that the IDS will be processed normally even if both boxes are checked.)

If you are filing by paper and you need to include a statement, save a space on your cover sheet to write "I certify:" followed by the correct timing statement(s) copied verbatim from the SB/08. Do not omit any words or add any additional words. And regardless of whether you are filing by paper or electronically, do not make a timing certification that is false, as you may be subject to a charge of perjury. If you need to file the IDS during period 2 and you cannot make the timing certification, you will be required to pay a "late IDS" fee (see Appendix 4, Fee Schedule) as your only option. If you need to file the IDS during period 3, i.e., after examination has concluded, and you cannot make the timing certification, you will need to reopen examination by filing a continuation application or a Request for Continued Examination, "RCE" (see Chapter 14, sections B and C) before the Examiner is allowed to consider this new information. However,

once examination has been reopened through either of these two methods, you are once again in period 1 and may file the IDS without either a fee or a statement.

To facilitate "compact prosecution" and bring the process to a conclusion as quickly as possible, the PTO has instituted a program called the Quick Path Information Disclosure Statement (QPIDS). If you need to file an IDS after receiving a notice of allowance (so you are in period 3), you may file the IDS with the issue fee through Patent Center (not by paper) along with a Form SB/09, which requests treatment of the IDS under QPIDS. By doing so, you are making the following certifications:

1. You have paid the issue fee.
2. You agree to one or both of the IDS timing statements described above (using the checkboxes in the form).
3. You are submitting an IDS size fee written assertion (even if no size fee is due).
4. If an IDS size fee is due, you authorize the PTO to charge the indicated amount to your deposit account.
5. You authorize the PTO to charge your deposit account for the required late IDS fee.
6. You are submitting a "conditional" (a) ePetition to Withdraw from Issue, and (b) petition fee.
7. You are submitting a "conditional" (a) RCE and (b) RCE fee.
8. In the event the examiner determines that any item of information contained in the IDS requires reopening examination, the Petition and RCE will be processed; otherwise, these will not be processed and the payments returned to you.
9. The application is not being otherwise amended; any amendment will result in the RCE being processed automatically.

If you send an IDS and later discover any additional references—for example, in the course of foreign prosecution—you must bring these to the attention of the PTO through a supplemental IDS. (Don't send an IDS for any references the examiner cites in your U.S. case; these will automatically be listed, along with those which you cited, on the patent.)

If you haven't done so already, after receiving your official filing receipt send in your Information Disclosure Statement as discussed in Chapter 10. If you filed your application by mail send in the IDS by filling out a Transmittal Form (PTO Form SB/21, Form 10-05 in Appendix 7). Accompany it with forms SB/08a, SB/08b, and SB/08c (Forms 10-6A, 10-6B, and 10-6C in Appendix 7), as necessary, and copies of any non-U.S. patent references you listed on the form.

If you filed electronically, and you're a registered eFiler, you won't need a transmittal form. Instead get the electronic SB08a Patent Center form by going to www.uspto.gov/patent/forms/forms-patent-applications-filed-or-after-september-16-2012. Open the SB08a Patent Center form, fill the blanks, and save the form as a PDF file, (for example, "IDS.pdf") as you did with the Data Sheet when you filed, and make a PDF of any non-U.S. patent references (known as "non-patent literature" or "NPL"), and file all of these using the PTO's electronic business site. Remember that the PTO wants the IDS to be filed within three months of the application's filing date. Don't forget to fill in all the blanks that identify your application.

If you don't file the IDS within three months of your filing date, or before your first Office Action, or within three months after entry into the "national" stage for references cited in foreign applications (whichever comes last), the PTO will still consider it. However, you must file it before a final action or a notice of allowance is sent, and (1) pay a "Late IDS Fee" (see Appendix 4, "Fee Schedule"), or (2) include a certificate as follows.

"(A) Each item of information contained in this Information Disclosure Statement (IDS) was cited in a communication from a foreign patent office in a counterpart foreign patent application not more than three months prior to the filing of such IDS, or (B) no item of information contained in this IDS was cited in a communication from a foreign patent office in a counterpart foreign patent application, or, to my knowledge after making reasonable inquiry, was known to any individual designated in 37 CFR 1.56(c)

(inventor, attorney, assignee, and so on) more than three months prior to the filing of such IDS."

You can even file the IDS after a final action or notice of allowance is sent, but before you pay the issue fee. However, you must include the above certificate, a petition requesting consideration of the IDS, and a petition fee (see Appendix 4, "Fee Schedule").

If you send an IDS and later discover any additional references—for example, in the course of foreign prosecution—you must bring these to the attention of the PTO through a supplemental IDS. (Don't send an IDS for any references the examiner cites in your U.S. case; these will automatically be listed, along with those which you cited, on the patent.)

6. First Office Action

About twelve months to three years after the filing date (patent prosecution is mostly a waiting game) you'll receive a communication from the PTO known as a "first Office Action" ("first OA"), sometimes called an "official letter." It consists of forms and a letter from the examiner in charge of your application, describing what is wrong with your application and why it cannot yet be allowed. (Rarely will an application be allowed in the first OA.) Specifically, the OA may:

- reject claims
- list defects in the specification and/or drawings
- cite and enclose copies of prior art that the examiner believes shows your invention is either:
  - not novel, or
  - obvious, and/or
- raise various other objections.

The PTO sends foreign patents and non-patent literature with the first OA in which they were cited. You must download the patent references from the internet, and Google Patents is often a good source. The PTO has a batch downloading procedure in Patent Center, but you must be a registered eFiler to use it. You can also download the patents from the free patent copy supply sites listed in Chapter 6.

To find out approximately when you'll receive the first OA from the PTO go to the PTO's patent dashboard page (www.uspto.gov/dashboard/patents), then select "First Office Action pendency." Also, you can call the clerk of the examining group where your application has been assigned. The name of this group will be typed on your filing receipt. PTO phone numbers are listed on the PTO website, are in Appendix 5, and are published irregularly in the *Official Gazette* (OG). Each issue of the OG also gives date status information for patent applications in each examining group.

We suggest that you write three date entries (as shown below) on every paper you receive from the PTO:

Received ____[*date*]_____

Start preparing response by ____[*date*]____

Response due by___[*date*]_____

7. Response to First Office Action

Every OA itself will specify a deadline, usually three months (extendable, for a fee, up to six months from the date of the OA) after the OA was mailed, by which you must file a response. Your response must take whatever action is necessary to overcome the objections and rejections listed in the OA. The response you file is technically called an "amendment" if it contains any changes, or a "response" if it contains no changes. The entire process of correspondence (Office Actions and amendments) to and from the PTO is known as "prosecuting" your patent application, although no one is "prosecuted" in the usual sense.

8. Second/Final Office Action

About 12 months after you file your first amendment or response, you'll receive a second OA from the PTO; this will usually be designated a "final" OA by the PTO. A final OA is supposed to end the prosecution stage before the examiner. However, as we'll see later, this is far from true. In other words, a "final action" is rarely final. Again, you have three months to reply, but you must reply to a final OA in a way that takes definitive action on the application, as we will see.

9. Notice of Allowance

After the first OA, if you are fortunate enough to submit an amendment or whatever is necessary to get your application in condition for allowance, you'll be sent a Notice of Allowance, indicating that all of your claims are allowed and that an issue fee is due within three months (this term is not extendable). Sometimes you'll get a "Notice of Allowability" before or with the formal allowance; this merely states that your claims are all allowed, the Notice of Allowance will be sent, and whether formal drawings are due.

10. Issue Fee and Issue Notification

Four to six weeks after you pay the issue fee and file formal drawings (if you didn't do so before), you'll receive an Issue Notification from the PTO, indicating the forthcoming issue date and number of your patent. Be sure to file any desired divisional application or continuation application by the day before the patent issues.

11. Receipt of Official Patent Deed

The PTO no longer issues printed patents as a matter of routine, but they may be ordered for a nominal fee. The electronic patent grant is the official statutory patent grant.

B. General Considerations During Patent Prosecution

Patent application prosecution is generally more difficult than the preparation of the initial application. Assuming that you're going to handle the prosecution phase on your own, we recommend that you keep the following general considerations in mind.

1. The PTO Can Write Claims for You

You can ask the PTO examiner to write one or more claims for you if the application contains allowable subject matter (MPEP 707.07(j)). Then you can either accept this claim or amend it if you think you can get the examiner to accept it.

You should generally have several sets of varied claims (one independent and several dependent per set) to fully cover your invention.

2. Consultation With a Patent Professional Might Be Wise

You might wish to consult with a patent expert at this point to amend your claims and argument (which is usually what's required). We particularly recommend seeking the assistance of a registered patent attorney if you run into an issue that's over your head—for example, the PTO rejects a claim for being directed to nonstatutory subject matter, or you're unable to think of a convincing way around a claim rejection.

The cost of hiring legal representation can be a barrier for some inventors when applying to protect their intellectual property. To address that barrier, the PTO helped create (and coordinates) the Patent Pro Bono Program (PPBP), which connects inventors with registered patent agents and attorneys who will contribute their time for free. To participate in the PPBP, inventors and small businesses must meet certain financial thresholds and other conditions. The eligibility criteria vary for each regional program, but in general, there are three basic requirements: income below three times the federal poverty level guidelines, knowledge of the patent system (filing an application is enough), and the ability to describe the features of your invention and how it works. To find out more, go to the PTO website (www.uspto.gov) and type "pro bono" in the upper-right search box.

3. Intervals Are Approximate

Except for official periods, such as the three-month period for response to an OA or to pay the issue fee, the dates and times we've given in this chapter are only approximate and are gleaned from recent experience. They can vary quite widely, depending on conditions in the PTO at the time you file your patent application. Be patient—the law considers the first 14 months after your application filing date to be a reasonable period in which to hear from the PTO. If you don't receive any communication from the PTO

by then, you should check the PTO patent dashboard for the status of the cases in your group; you can download data for all Technology Centers as a spreadsheet, and look up your TC or Group Art Unit based on the numbered unit on your Filing Receipt. For example, Group Art Unit 2112 (computer error detection/correction and fault detection/recovery) is in Technology Center 2100 (Computer Architecture and Software). Also, if it's over four months after you file an amendment, you should make a call, or send a letter, to the examiner or examining group to determine the status of your case. (If you are willing to submit a lot of paperwork, install software, and so forth, you can access Patent Center, which enables you to see a docket sheet and all of the papers for your patent application on the PTO's website. To get on Patent Center, see the instructions in Chapter 10.)

4. You'll Be Able to Correct Technical Errors

Don't worry too much about minor technical errors (except for dates—see next consideration) when dealing with the PTO. If you make one, you'll be given an opportunity to correct it. The PTO has so many rules and regulations that even patent attorneys who deal with them all the time can't remember them all. Also, the PTO is flexible in giving do-it-yourself (pro se) applicants opportunities to correct nondate errors that don't affect the substance of the application.

5. Dates Are Crucial

Every OA that you receive from the PTO will specify an interval by which you must respond. If you fail to reply in the time the PTO allots you, the penalty is draconian: Your application will go abandoned (you will lose all your rights), although it can be revived at a stiff price. (See below.) Write the due date for response to every OA promptly on the OA and on your calendar and heed it carefully. If you're not the type who can faithfully keep track of deadlines, hire a methodical friend to bug you. You can even turn the whole job of prosecution over to a patent attorney. If you miss a crucial date, you'll find that the PTO is a cruel and unforgiving bureaucracy.

6. Situations Not Covered

If you find yourself in a situation not covered in this book, and you can't find the answer by looking in the *Rules of Practice* or *Manual of Patent Examining Procedure*, then call the PTO, consult an attorney or agent, or use common sense judgment and do the logical thing in response to the situation.

Newly Discovered Reference: For example, suppose that after you've filed your patent application you find a prior-art reference that is very close to what you thought your invention to be. You must bring this to the attention of the PTO by way of another (supplemental) IDS and Form SB/08, and you probably should submit an amendment substituting narrower claims that avoid the reference. Remember that you have a continuing duty to disclose all material information about your invention to the PTO.

Embodiment Changes: If you discover that an embodiment of your invention doesn't work, delete it from your application. If you discover a new embodiment of your invention that supersedes the presently described embodiments, file a continuation-in-part application. (See Chapter 14.)

Entity Size Change: If you license or assign your application to a large entity (or such a license is terminated or your application is reassigned back to you), you should send a letter to the PTO asking that your small-entity status be canceled (or send in a letter to establish small-entity status, as the case may be).

Change of Address: If you change your address, you should send a change of address form (use Form AIA/122 on the PTO's site) or an appropriate letter (caption as in downloadable Form 13-1, "Amendment," (see Appendix 7 for details) but change the heading to read "Change of Applicant's Address") to the PTO.

PTO Mistakes: If the examiner cites a prior-art reference against your application that is later than your filing date, the examiner has made an error (this happens occasionally). Call or write to bring it to the examiner's attention so that a new Office Action can be issued. If the PTO fails to send you a copy of a non-U.S. patent reference that it has cited against you, send an appropriate paper (captioned as in Form 13-1,

"Amendment") headed "Request for Copy of Missing Reference" to the PTO. If a part of the OA doesn't make sense, or a part seems to have been omitted, send an immediate "Request for Clarification of Office Action."

Finally, as a wise person said, "Don't be afraid to ask dumb questions: They're easier to handle than dumb mistakes."

Bureaucratic Static: The examiner may object to something in your application if it's unusual or irregular, even if it's otherwise proper and harmless. Examiners, like many a bureaucrat, tend to rigidly enforce a "standard" administrative procedure. The remedy is to explain to the examiner that what you have done is proper and to respectfully challenge the examiner to provide a specific reason for the objection and a suggestion for correction. The next paragraph shows how we responded to an examiner who objected when we typed "stateless" in the citizenship blank of the declaration form, even though the applicant was stateless; the examiner did not repeat the objection again.

*"**The Objection to the Declaration:** The Office Action objected to the Declaration since it listed the citizenship of the applicant as 'stateless.' The Examiner required a new declaration. Applicant does not understand this objection, the legal basis therefor, or what remedial action the Examiner would like on any new declaration. Applicant's citizenship is indeed 'stateless.' In the past, applicant's representative has filed other patent applications for various stateless individuals. He always listed their citizenship as 'stateless' and all of these cases went on to patent without ever before encountering any objection. Therefore applicant respectfully submits that the 'stateless' entry is proper.*

"Applicant is willing to file a new declaration if the Examiner still desires, but he doesn't know what the Examiner would like applicant to enter in the Citizenship blank in lieu of 'stateless.' If the Examiner continues the objection, applicant respectfully requests that the Examiner explain what specifically he objects to about the 'stateless' entry, the legal basis for the objection, and exactly what replacement entry Examiner

would like in any new declaration. Thereupon applicant will be pleased and eager to comply. Note that applicant cannot enter any specific country in the Citizenship blank since he is not a citizen of any country."

7. Standards of Patentability Vary Widely

What actually happens when your application is examined will vary, depending upon the personality, whims, training, and current emotions of the examiner assigned to handle it (who is human, after all). Most examiners adhere to the basic standards of patentability outlined here and are competent, knowledgeable, and occasionally helpful when it comes to telling you what to do to put the case in condition for allowance.

The solution to the problem with an unreasonably tough or inexperienced examiner is to, first, be persistent. Go to the PTO (or hire a patent attorney to go) to interview your examiner. If necessary, appeal.

Appealing is a powerful weapon against a tough examiner. Examiners don't like to write answers to appeal briefs since these take a lot of time. Also, they usually must have an appeal conference with two other examiners, and it looks bad on their record if they get reversed.

On the other hand, if your examiner is "too easy," your allowed application might not stand up in court (should this ever become necessary). Accordingly, if you believe that your examiner is not rigorous enough (for instance, all your claims are allowed in the first Office Action), make especially sure yourself that at least some of your claims are clearly patentable. That is, they should define a novel enough invention to withstand a court challenge. (See Chapter 15.)

It may help to know that examiners themselves have to contend with two opposing forces. On the one hand, they're expected to dispose of a certain number of cases per biweekly period. That is, they have a quota of applications that they need to either allow, or have the applicant give up. On the other hand, they're subject to a quality review program to make sure they're not too lenient.

Note that even if you have a great invention that is clearly patentable, but you haven't claimed it properly, most U.S. PTO examiners, unlike their counterparts in the European Patent Offices, won't volunteer help or constructive suggestions, or otherwise try to assist you. They'll simply reject your claims or make a requirement and leave it to you to figure out how to do what's necessary to remedy the situation. It's up to you to claim and fight for what's rightfully yours. Never automatically accept any examiner's rejection. Remember, if any subject matter may be patentable, you can ask the examiner to draft a claim for you.

8. Don't Take Rejection Personally

If the examiner rejects your claims, don't take it as a condemnation of you personally. The examiner doesn't know you. They're merely rejecting your claims, not you as an applicant. In other words, a rejection of your claims just means one examiner, at one point, feels that your claims are not different enough from the prior art or clear enough to be allowed. You still are a good and worthwhile person and your innovation may still be patentable with revised claims, or if you successfully argue over the rejection.

9. Dealing With the PTO Can Feel Frustrating and Unfair

Dealing with the PTO, as with any other government agency, can sometimes be a very difficult, time-consuming, and frustrating experience. We could spend a whole chapter listing the PTO-generated errors and mistakes we've encountered recently, but one example will suffice. We once filed an application for an inventor whose last name was "Loe." The filing receipt came back with the name "Lee." After several letters and calls with no response, a "corrected" filing receipt arrived with the name spelled "Leo." After a few more calls and much frustration, a correct filing receipt finally arrived. Put succinctly, dealing with the PTO is not like dealing with an efficient and competitive private company. All we can tell you is to be philosophical, scrupulously check your correspondence with the PTO to make sure they get it right, and persist in correcting errors when they occur.

As far as the unfairness goes, that can stem from the fact that there's no reciprocity when you're dealing with the PTO. For example, while you have to reply to an OA when the PTO tells you to, they can reply to you whenever they get around to it. Your patent term will be extended to give you a minimum of 17 years of coverage provided the delay wasn't your responsibility. While you are supposed to make your claims and specification clear, grammatically correct, and free of spelling errors, you'll often find that the correspondence you receive from the PTO doesn't meet these standards. While you have to pay a stiff fine if you forget to sign your check or make some other inadvertent error, the PTO remains liability-free, no matter how negligent they are. There's nothing you can do about this inherent unfairness except, again, to be philosophical and convince yourself to accept the rules of the game before you play.

One inventor was so frustrated that he sued his examiner and the PTO for negligence. The judge said, "This is the sad tale of an inventor frustrated by the bureaucratic mindset and Byzantine workings of the PTO." While he won in trial court, the appellate court reversed, holding that examiners cannot usually be held liable for any alleged harm resulting from their actions.

10. PTO Reference Books

During patent prosecution, you may need to refer to the MPEP, the PTO's Rules of Practice, and/or the patent statutes. All can be viewed on or obtained from the PTO's website and the latter two can be obtained from regional government bookstores in paperbound forms or through a web search. The PTO's patent rules are given the prefix number "1" to distinguish them from trademark rules "2" and copyright rules "3." For example, Patent Rule 111, referred to later in this chapter, is officially identified as Title 37 of the Code of Federal Regulations, Section 1.111, or in legal citation form, 37 CFR 1.111. The *Manual of Patent Examining Procedure* (MPEP), which is often referred to as the "examiner's bible," covers almost any situation you can encounter in patent prosecution

and contains the patent rules and statutes. It's a large, loose-leaf volume with about four megabytes of text, but you can view and print any part (or all of it) from the PTO's website (www.uspto.gov/web/offices/pac/mpep). A complete copy of the MPEP is available on the PTO's site and it contains the PTO's Rules of Practice (37 CFR) and all of the Patent Statutes (35 U.S.C.). While the PTO has been getting better about keeping the MPEP up to date, it's always wise to search for any update notices about your subject of interest in the search box on the PTO's home page.

11. Never Make Negative or Limiting Statements on the Record

When dealing with the PTO, always remember this "Miranda" warning: anything you say can and will be used against you in a court of law (should you ever have to enforce your patent). Never say or write anything that diminishes your invention, never admit that any prior-art reference shows (includes) any feature of your invention, and never state anything that a court could use to limit your invention. For example, here are some improper statements that could be used against you:

- "While applicant's device is not as good as Smith's …"
- "It is true that Jones shows applicant's gear ratio …"
- "Applicant's device is designed for use with an electronic control."

Admittedly, this advice may be very difficult to follow in some situations, but it's important to comply with it. Why? The PTO puts all correspondence into your official file (called your "file wrapper"), and if litigation arises regarding your patent, your adversary will use any negative admission or limiting statement against you.

12. Remember Your Continuing Duty to Disclose Material Information

You have a duty to disclose all material information known to you, such as relevant prior art, that bears on the patentability of your invention. This duty is normally fulfilled when you send in your IDS as discussed above.

However, if you discover any additional information later, you must send in a supplemental IDS. Of course, if you find a prior-art reference that you feel is so close that you believe your invention is not patentable, you should abandon your application.

13. The PTO Can Request Search Information and Literature

In connection with your continuing duty to disclose, discussed above, the PTO can require, under 37 CFR 1.105, that any applicant supply any search information and literature that:

- the applicant knows of
- the applicant used to draft the application, or
- the examiner can use to examine the application properly.

This may include a form paragraph or letter in your application requesting this. If you receive such a Request, comply with it, but don't include any information that you already included with your IDS (because the PTO will already be aware of it).

14. Be Available to Answer Office Actions

As mentioned, you'll normally be required to respond to a PTO Office Action within three months. If an OA is sent while you're away or unavailable and you fail to reply to it, your application will, as stated above, be considered abandoned, although you ordinarily can respond within six months if you request an extension of time and pay a fee that increases with each months' delay. We've provided Inventor's Commandment 25, at the beginning of this chapter, to give you ample

---

Fax and Internet Filing Available

The PTO prefers that responses, including amendments, petitions, appeals, and elections, be filed via Patent Center if you're a registered eFiler, since otherwise they have to scan and upload paper responses. If you're a registered eFiler, go to the PTO's Electronic Business site and eFile the papers in PDF format as you did with the original application.

If you're not a registered eFiler, you should file responses by fax. (Do not file applications, fees, or drawings by fax.) Faxed papers should include, "I certify I have transmitted this paper by fax to the Patent and Trademark Office at [#] on [date]." The PTO will consider the paper as having been filed on the date of transmission or the next business day if you fax it on a nonbusiness day. Keep your signed original and your machine's record of successful transmission. The PTO's fax machines will now automatically fax back a "fax received" receipt. (The PTO's main fax numbers are in Appendix 5, "Mail, Telephone, Fax, and Email Communications With the PTO.") If you don't have a fax machine, there are methods to fax via computer—using either fax software that is included with your computer's operating system or using an online fax service (that can also provide you with a telephone

number to receive faxes). To fax a signed document, you will need to scan or convert it to PDF.

As a last alternative, you still can mail your responses; be sure to always include a receipt postcard.

Email communications may be used for minor matters, such as status requests, minor corrections in a paper, and notification that a communication has been sent, but not major papers, such as amendments and patent applications. However, since email is not a secure form of communication and the PTO is obligated to preserve all patent applications in secret, PTO employees are not allowed to send email containing any sensitive information unless you specifically authorize this. If you are willing to receive email from the PTO containing sensitive information about your application, you must file the following statement in your application: "Recognizing that internet communications are not secure, I hereby authorize the PTO to communicate with me concerning any subject matter of this application by electronic mail. I understand that a copy of these communications will be made of record in the application file." This statement is available as a checkbox on the AIR form. Similarly, you should print out and put in your file a copy of all email communications you receive from the PTO.

warning. If you will be unavailable for an extended period while your application is pending, you should empower a patent attorney to handle it for you or arrange to have your mail forwarded by a reliable friend or relative. You can ask to have correspondence from the PTO sent to anyone you choose, but the PTO generally won't allow you to appoint a layperson to represent you, and you (or your patent attorney) must sign every paper that is sent to the PTO.

15. Consider Foreign Filing

About eight to ten months after you file your patent application, you should consider whether you want to file for coverage in other countries. Foreign filing is extremely expensive, time-consuming, and arduous, so do it only if you have a very important, innovative invention or a foreign licensee who will pay the bill. There are international conventions or agreements among most countries that entitle you to the benefit of your U.S. filing date on any foreign applications you file within one year after you file your U.S. regular or provisional application. See Chapter 12 for more information about foreign filing.

16. You Can Call and Visit Your Examiner

If you have any questions about your application, or any reference that is cited against it, you are permitted to call, and/or make an appointment with and visit, the examiner in charge of your application. The PTO permits in-person interviews, telephone interviews, and (as of February 2022) video interviews using Microsoft Teams®. Your examiner's telephone number will be listed on official letters that you receive from the PTO. (If the first action hasn't been sent yet and you're a registered eFiler you can go to Patent Center and view the docket sheet for your application to obtain the name of your examiner.) However, usually only one, or at most two, applicant-initiated interviews are permitted. So save this privilege for when you really need it. If you have an interview, you must summarize its substance in the next amendment, even if the examiner sends a summary of the interview to you.

An interview is often a very valuable way to get a difficult case allowed, since communication is greatly enhanced when you and the examiner can discuss your differences and reach an understanding through the give and take and multiple feedback loops an interview permits. Also, it's harder to say "no" directly to a person face-to-face, or on a video conference. Lastly, an interview provides an excellent opportunity to bring in and demonstrate a working prototype or sample of the invention to the examiner; this is usually an excellent persuader.

However, we recommend that you try to avoid calling or interviewing any examiner on Fridays, since, like most of us, they're likely to be less attentive then. An excellent guide for negotiating with examiners is presented by Examining Group Director A.L. Smith at page 168 of the February 1990 *Journal of the Patent and Trademark Office Society*.

We cannot overstate the value of an interview. One pro se applicant that we know (Alex) had a very difficult time getting his case allowed. On our suggestion he traveled to the PTO to have an interview with his examiner. To his dismay Alex found from discussing the case that the examiner had likely never read his application and definitely did not understand the invention. Fortunately, he was able to explain the invention on the spot and, with some claim adjustments, managed to get the case allowed. Some websites have statistical data on examiners, indicating types of rejections; average number of OAs sent per case; average time between filing and issuance; the percentage of cases allowed, abandoned, and appealed; the percentage of cases allowed after appeal; and so on. The PTO provides some of these data (aggregated) for free in its Data Visualization Center (www.uspto.gov/dashboards/patents).

Sometimes your examiner will call you, offering to allow the application if some changes are made in it. If the changes are minor you can agree to them on the spot. But if the changes touch on the substance of the claims, we suggest you tell the examiner you would like to study them for a day or two before calling back. Study the proposed changes carefully. If they would unduly narrow the claims, try to formulate and suggest some less restrictive changes that are still allowable.

17. Working or Commercial Model

If you have a working or commercial model of your invention, it's usually desirable to show or send this (or literature on it) to your examiner. This may make the examiner a believer in your invention, its operability, its advantages, and its commercial success. If your invention is out on the market and has had commercial success, you should submit a Declaration Under 37 CFR 1.132 with exhibits attesting to such success and explaining why such success is a result of the novel features of your invention. The Supreme Court has specifically stated that the PTO must consider such commercial success when deciding on patentability (see MPEP 1504.03).

18. No New Matter Can Be Added to Your Application

Once your application is filed, 35 U.S.C. Section 132 prohibits you from adding any "new matter" to it. (New matter consists of any technical information—including dimensions, materials, parts, values, arrangements, connections, and methods—that was not present in your application as originally filed.) This prohibition makes sense since. After all, if patent applicants were permitted to add continuing improvements and changes to their applications, the date of invention, and what was invented when, would be too difficult to determine.

If you do want to add any new developments to your application, consider a special type of supplementary application (termed a "continuation-in-part application" or "CIP," covered in Chapter 14). If your improvement is really significant, you should seek an independent, subsequent patent application.

New matter should be distinguished from prior art that may be discovered after an application has been filed. You are obligated to inform the PTO about any newly discovered, relevant prior art. Such prior art doesn't form part of your specification, nor does it affect the nature of your invention. Rather, it provides the PTO with more information by which to judge your invention for patentability. Also note that if you submit new claims that are broader, narrower, or different, the PTO does not consider them new matter, unless the new claims contain new information that was not originally present in the application.

19. Official Dates Are When the PTO Receives Your Submission

Every paper that you send to or receive from the PTO has an official date. This is the date on which it was mailed from or received by the PTO. You should put your actual date of mailing on anything you send to the PTO, but the date of the PTO's "Received" stamp on your paper will be the "official" date of the paper. If you send in your application by Priority Mail Express with PME Certification (see Chapter 10), the PTO will stamp it as of the date you express mailed it, even though they receive it one to three days later. This is because, under 37 CFR 1.10, they consider your local post office their agent to receive your correspondence, provided you use PME.

20. Know Who Has the Ball

To use an analogy drawn from the game of football, during patent prosecution the "ball" (burden of action) will always be either on your side or the PTO's. If you just sent in your case, the ball will be with the PTO until they return your postcard, send you an official filing receipt, and send you a first Office Action. The ball doesn't go back to your side until that first OA. Once they send the first OA, you have the ball and must usually act within three months. Once you file an amendment, the PTO has the ball again, and so on.

21. Reread Appropriate Chapters

When you respond to an OA, you should go back and reread the chapter that covers the issue you need to address. For example, if a claim is rejected for prolixity (a wordy word for "wordiness"), reread Chapter 9.

22. Respond to Each and Every Point in the Office Action

A typical OA will contain several criticisms (termed "objections" and/or "rejections"), such as drawing objections, specification objections, claim rejections for indefiniteness, and claim rejections based upon prior art. You must respond to each and every criticism in your next amendment or your amendment will be considered nonresponsive, in which case you'll usually be given two weeks to complete the amendment. Suitable responses can be an argument against the criticism or some action to eliminate the criticism— for example, by canceling claims, amending the specification, supplying new drawings, or substituting different claims and arguing that the substituted claims are patentable over the prior art cited.

23. Form Paragraphs

Your actual Office Action, unlike the sample below, will usually include several form paragraphs that quote statutes or rules. Examiners love to use form paragraphs like these, soif you receive an Office Action with numerous form paragraphs that quote basic statutes and rules, don't assume you've been singled out or that your application is substandard: All attorneys get OAs with these form paragraphs as well. Also, the form paragraphs that the examiner chose may sometimes be inapplicable or only partially applicable. If so, courteously point this out in your response.

24. Preliminary and Supplemental Voluntary Amendments

In addition to the "regular" amendments discussed in this chapter (sent in response to an OA), you can also file a voluntary Preliminary Amendment before your first OA to correct any errors in the specification or claims, or narrow or broaden the claims. Also, you may file a Supplemental Amendment (after you file a regular amendment, but before the next OA) to correct any errors or omissions in your Amendment. However, under 37 CFR 1.111(a)(2) you don't have the right to file a Supplemental Amendment unless it is clearly limited to (a) canceling claims, (b) adopting an examiner's suggestions, (c) placing the application in condition for allowance, (d) replying to an Office requirement made after the first reply was filed, (e) correcting informalities, such as typographical errors, or (f) simplifying issues for appeal. The best way to avoid the need for a Supplemental Amendment is to do the first amendment well in advance of the due date, wait a day or two, and then review it again and polish and correct it as necessary. Also remember the rule against adding any new matter to your patent

application. Finally, you aren't allowed to amend your application after allowance or after a final action, unless the examiner authorizes it.

The patent term for any invention will be extended in the event of certain delays caused by the PTO in the course of the patent prosecution process. Every patent is guaranteed an in-force period of at least 17 years provided you did not delay unduly on your side.

25. Double Patenting Obviousness Rejections

If the PTO rejects a claim of your application under Section 103 for obvious-type double patenting on an earlier patent or application that you own, and it is not early enough to be prior art against your application, you can disqualify the earlier patent as prior art. You should submit a terminal disclaimer (37 CFR 1.321(c), with a fee and a declaration stating that the patent is owned by you and has the same inventor (37 CFR 1.131).

26. Eighteen-Month Publication

If you haven't filed a nonpublication request, your application will be published on the PTO's website 18 months after filing (if it's still pending) and anyone can view and download and print out a copy of your application and prosecution history. Anyone will then be able to cite prior art against your application if they think your claims are not patentable. (37 CFR 1.290.) We advise you of this so that you will be aware of the fact that, even if the PTO allows your application, they can change their mind and still reject it if someone cites better prior art than your examiner found. Publication by the PTO after 18 months does not confer patent rights enforceable in court, and does not mean that the application has been allowed.

27. *Festo* Considerations

You should have drafted a full spectrum of claims (from broad to specific) that cover every aspect of your invention and all possible permutations. The reason for this is the Supreme Court's decision in *Festo v. Shoketsu*, which holds essentially that the Doctrine of Equivalents (DoE) can be used to broaden any claim that was amended during prosecution provided

(a) the equivalent was unforeseeable at the time the application was filed, or (b) the equivalent is not related to the way the claim is amended. However, if the claim was amended to overcome prior art, or if the court cannot determine the reason for the amendment, the DoE cannot be used. By submitting a full spectrum of claims, at least some of them will stand a good chance of being allowed in the prosecution stage without amendment, thereby preserving your full DoE rights for those claims. During the prosecution stage, you should try, if at all possible, not to amend any claims, or to amend as few as possible. If you have to amend any claims, state the reason for the amendment.

28. Rejection Versus Objection

Office actions may contain (either or both of) two types of disapproval or criticism of various parts of your application. It's useful to know the difference so that you can use these terms correctly in writing your amendment, and if you have to appeal.

A *rejection* is made by an examiner in response to a substantive claim deficiency, such as a lack of patentability of a claim over a prior-art reference or indefiniteness in the claim. An *objection* is made to a nonclaim defect, such as an unclear drawing or a misspelling in the specification, or to a non-substantive claim matter, such as a dependent claim that is allowable in substance, but contains a typo or is dependent upon a rejected independent claim. You have to fix or successfully argue over both types of disapproval (rejection or objection) to get the application allowed; the only practical difference is that a rejection that can't be overcome must be appealed, while an objection that can't be overcome must be petitioned (unless it's associated with a rejection).

29. When Submitting Arguments, Rely on Statutes, Rules, and the MPEP, Rather Than Case Law

When drafting the remarks portion of an amendment, it's helpful to cite authority for any rule of law or requirement that you rely upon. We've tried to provide most of the rules and main arguments in this chapter,

but there are many more that we don't have room to include. If you need to find an authority for your position, look in the MPEP, which is available online at the PTO's site (www.uspto.gov/web/offices/pac/mpep). The MPEP has a full online index and its Chapter 2100 on patentability is very helpful. If and when you do cite any authority, keep in mind that examiners consider the patent statutes (35 U.S.C.), the *Rules of Practice* (37 CFR), and the MPEP to be the most meaningful authorities. Examiners are strictly bound to follow these authorities. There are thousands of patent cases available also, but examiners find these far less persuasive and less useful. (One reason is that it's difficult and time-consuming for an examiner to look up and analyze a case.) In fact, when we were employed as examiners, our supervisors told us never to cite a case since the attorney for the applicant could always rebut us by citing a *different* case with a contrary holding!

30. Don't Wait Until the Last Minute

We find that most inventors who receive an Office Action tend to wait until near the end of the three-month period, or even later, to draft their response. This procrastination is usually based on fear of tackling a new task. However we strongly advise you grit your teeth and do the job as soon as possible so that you won't be rushed, you can ramp up to the nuances and intricacies of the process, and you'll have time to review and polish your work.

31. Patents and Published Patent Applications Are Prior Art as of Their Filing Date as Well as Their Publication Date

As discussed in Chapter 5, patents and published patent applications, unlike other publications, are effective as of their filing date, in addition to their publication date. So if the examiner rejects your claims on a patent or application, you may have to consider both dates when formulating your response. Check the date of all prior art cited against your application, since examiners sometimes make mistakes—for example, after the PTO published an application of Nokia's, an examiner mistakenly cited the published patent application against itself!

Any U.S. patent or U.S. application is prior art as of its filing date. Such patent or application can be used in a rejection against any patent application that was filed after such filing date; there is no longer any way to overcome the earlier-filed patent or application unless the inventor in the patent application can prove, in a derivation proceeding, that the inventor on the patent or application derived it from such inventor.

Teachings in patent applications that are referred to by the PTO are prior art as of their date of first disclosure to the PTO. If the patent or application claims priority (the benefit of the filing date) of an earlier-filed foreign application or PPA, some or all of the patent or application is prior art as of its priority date—that is, the filing date of the foreign application or PPA. However, it may be worth obtaining a copy of the foreign application or PPA to ensure that the cited teaching is actually present there.

We had a situation where the PTO cited a teaching in a regular patent application (RPA) filed after our application, that claimed priority to a PPA filed before our application. The PTO claimed that we were knocked out because the PPA was filed first. We looked at the PPA, and the cited teaching was entirely missing! When we pointed this out to the examiner, the rejection was withdrawn.

If a pending patent application of another person claims the same invention as your application, the pending application of the other person, being prior art as of its filing date, can be used to reject your application under 35 U.S.C. Section 102 (lack of novelty) and thereby prevent your application from issuing.

32. Patent Examiners Are Overwhelmed

You may have to wait a long time before you receive a first Office Action. You can obtain an estimate of when your application will receive a first office action by using the PTO's First Office Action Estimator (www.uspto.gov/dashboard/patents).

33. Beware of "Whack-a-Mole" Rejections

Examiners can make subsequent rejections on a different ground from a previously rebutted rejection, even though the subsequent rejection could have been made earlier. Some patent attorneys have termed this practice "Whack-a-Mole Rejecting." (It's also called "piecemeal prosecution," and is condemned in the MPEP.) There is no good solution except to be aware that it may occur, take it philosophically if you run into it, and patiently respond to each new rejection in the usual manner. If it becomes excessive, it is possible to complain to the examiner's supervisor, but frankly supervisors usually support the examiner in these situations.

34. Limitations on Number of Claims

The basic filing fee entitles an applicant to submit three independent and 20 total claims. If an application is filed with or amended to have more than three independent claims or more than 20 total claims, the PTO requires a large fee for each extra independent claim and a medium fee for each extra total claim. However if you file more than the basic "3/20" allotment of claims, be sure that they differ significantly because examiners don't like to examine a lot of claims, even if you pay for them. The examiner can reject excessive claims (that is, those that do not differ substantially) as unduly multiplied.

35. The PTO Has Been Very Difficult on Applicants

Make sure your claims are in optimal condition and that they define your invention's novelty over the references, taken individually or in any combination. If necessary, file a continuation to revise your claims after a final action. Don't hesitate to appeal if necessary. If you appeal, be sure to try a "Pre-Appeal Request for Review" (see Section J4 below). Always keep your composure and don't attack your examiner personally since they're merely following instructions or doing the best that they can under the circumstances.

Remember to always use the two-part 102 (novelty)/103 (nonobviousness) approach whenever you argue patentability (see Inventor's Commandment 7 in Chapter 5).

36. Avoid Fraud on the PTO

Be honest and forthright and don't make any statements meant to deceive, mislead, or "snow" the examiner. A court can hold your patent invalid if it ever discovers that any statement that you made to the PTO amounted to "fraud on the PTO" and you intended to deceive the PTO. Note that deception includes withholding prior art references that you know might be used against you, and courts have a long history of making already-issued patents legally unenforceable in such cases. When dealing with the PTO, it's in your best interest to tell the truth, the whole truth, and nothing but the truth.

37. Keep Your Remarks as Short as Possible

Examiners tend to be put off by (and might not read) overly long responses. So keep your remarks as short as possible, while including all necessary arguments. Longer arguments tend to be less persuasive than shorter arguments, can be more prone to error, and might even be easier to poke holes in.

38. Enablement

Remember our old friend, 35 U.S.C. Section 112(a), which reads as follows:

> *The specification shall contain a written description of the invention, and of the manner and process of making and using it, in such full, clear, concise, and exact terms as to enable any person skilled in the art to which it pertains, or with which it is most nearly connected, to make and use the same, and shall set forth the best mode contemplated by the inventor or joint inventor of carrying out the invention.*

This statute contains at least three requirements: (1) The specification must have a written description of the invention, (2) It must enable a PHOSITA (person having ordinary skill in the art) to make and use it, and (3) It must set forth the best mode contemplated by the inventor. While requirements 1 and 2 appear similar, the courts have held that they are distinct.

Part 1 requires that the specification describe (identify) the invention but not necessarily to any degree of detail—that is, it requires a writing showing that the inventor had conceptualized the claimed invention.

Part 2 specifies the detail: it must be sufficient for a PHOSITA to make and use it. In practice the courts have held that Part 2 means that any specific embodiments claimed must be disclosed in the description. So, when one inventor's description described a needle holder with a pressure jacket, his claims to a needle holder with the pressure jacket complied with Part 2. However when he broadened his claims to recite a needle holder alone, the courts held that they were invalid because the description did not describe this. To avoid violating Part 2, you must be sure that every embodiment covered by your claims (originally and as amended) is described in the specification and shown in the drawings. While 35 U.S.C. Section 112(a) still requires that you set forth the best mode, objections on this ground are rare, and a failure to do so will not be grounds for invalidating the patent. Nevertheless, you should do your best to comply.

39. Patent Ombuds Office

The PTO has implemented a Patent Ombuds Office under which you may be able to resolve breakdowns in the normal patent prosecution process (for example, your examiner is being extremely unreasonable) with the aid of a Technology Center Ombudsman (TCO). This program is not intended to resolve normal issues, such as good-faith differences of opinion on issues of patentability, but only applies when you have a question about a specific application in prosecution and have not been able to find the right person to assist you or when you have not been able to obtain assistance from your examiner or the Supervising Patent Examiner (SPE). To invoke the aid of a TCO, go to www.uspto.gov/learning-and-resources/support-centers/patents-ombuds-office to see if it is applicable to your situation. If so, complete and file the form in the notice. The TCO will contact you by phone to obtain the details, and will work to resolve the problem.

C. A Sample Office Action

Fig. 13A, below, shows a sample OA in an imaginary patent application filed June 14, 2015. A study of this example will enable you to deal with your first OA far more effectively. It has been purposely written to include the common objections and rejections; an actual OA is usually not this complicated and quotes applicable statutes.

First let's look at Fig. 13A/1 (page 1 of the OA).

At the top of the OA, the examiner's name and examining section (Art Unit 2540) are given. Art Unit 2540 is part of Technology Center 2500. Before that, in the large brackets, are the serial number and applicant's name(s).

The next paragraph indicates that the period for response will expire in three months and that failure to respond will cause the application to be abandoned. If the last date of the period falls on a Saturday, Sunday, or holiday, the period for response expires on the next business day. Be sure to calculate the period for response from the date the OA was mailed, not the date you received it. These dates are found on the OA cover sheet.

Under that Status section, box 1 is checked "Responsive to communication(s) filed on 6/14/97," because this OA responds to the original application filing (that is, it's a first OA). Also, box 2b is checked because this is the first OA; had it been a final OA, box 2a, "This action is FINAL," would have been checked.

Under "Disposition of Claims," the examiner has checked various boxes to indicate what action he has taken with the application. He has rejected all seven claims pending. Under "Application Papers," he has acknowledged the drawings filed on 6/14/15, but objected to them as being unsuitable for printing.

Under "Attachments," the checked box indicates that one attachment, a "Notice of References Cited," is part of the OA. A typical page 2 of the OA is shown in Fig. 13A/2, below, a Notice of References Cited is shown in Fig. 13A/3, below, and the drawing notice is shown in Fig. 13A/4.

Now it's time to look at Figs. 13A/2 and 13A/3 (pages 2 and 3 of the OA).

On page 2 of the Office Action, the examiner gives his specific reasons for rejecting or objecting to the claims.

The first paragraph of page 2 of the OA objects to the drawings because they fail to show certain features recited in the claims. Remember (Chapter 10) that the drawings must show every feature recited in the claims. In the past, the PTO would allow informal drawings to be filed, which could be formalized once patentable claims were identified. However, the PTO now publishes applications 18 months after an application is filed, so drawings must be print-ready in advance, and objections to the drawings must be addressed immediately.

The second paragraph objects to the specification as inadequate. The specification must teach, in full, clear, and exact detail, how one skilled in the art would make and use the invention. This is a serious and potentially fatal flaw, since it is not permissible to add new matter to supply the missing description.

In the third paragraph, the examiner rejects all of the claims under Section 112, since they are based on an inadequate specification for reasons stated in the second paragraph.

The fourth paragraph rejects Claims 1 to 6 on the Ohman reference (see Fig. 13A/3—page 3 of the OA), under Section 102 of the patent statute. This means that the examiner feels that these claims contain no novelty over Ohman. The requirement that the claims contain novel physical features was discussed in Chapters 5 and 9.

In the fifth paragraph of the OA, the examiner has rejected Claim 7 under Section 112 since a "said" clause in Claim 7 has no proper antecedent in parent, independent Claim 1 from which Claim 7 depends. Remember (Chapter 9) that every "said" clause must contain an identical antecedent earlier in the claim or in a parent claim. Many examiners, especially young ones, lean heavily on any Section 112 defects.

CHAPTER 13 | GETTING THE PTO TO DELIVER | 389

Office Action Summary	Application No. 12/345,678	Applicant(s) INVENTOR, ANN et al.		
	Examiner JOHN S. HEYMAN	Art Unit 2540	AIA (First Inventor to File) Status Yes	

-- The MAILING DATE of this communication appears on the cover sheet with the correspondence address --

Period for Reply

A SHORTENED STATUTORY PERIOD FOR REPLY IS SET TO EXPIRE __3__ MONTHS FROM THE MAILING DATE OF THIS COMMUNICATION.

- Extensions of time may be available under the provisions of 37 CFR 1.136(a). In no event, however, may a reply be timely filed after SIX (6) MONTHS from the mailing date of this communication.
- If NO period for reply is specified above, the maximum statutory period will apply and will expire SIX (6) MONTHS from the mailing date of this communication.
- Failure to reply within the set or extended period for reply will, by statute, cause the application to become ABANDONED (35 U.S.C. § 133). Any reply received by the Office later than three months after the mailing date of this communication, even if timely filed, may reduce any earned patent term adjustment. See 37 CFR 1.704(b).

Status

1)☒ Responsive to communication(s) filed on 6/14/2015.

☐ A declaration(s)/affidavit(s) under **37 CFR 1.130(b)** was/were filed on _____.

2a)☐ This action is **FINAL**.   2b)☒ This action is non-final.

3)☐ An election was made by the applicant in response to a restriction requirement set forth during the interview on _____; the restriction requirement and election have been incorporated into this action.

4)☐ Since this application is in condition for allowance except for formal matters, prosecution as to the merits is closed in accordance with the practice under *Ex parte Quayle*, 1935 C.D. 11, 453 O.G. 213.

Disposition of Claims*

5)☒ Claim(s) __1-7__ is/are pending in the application.

    5a) Of the above claim(s) _____ is/are withdrawn from consideration.

6)☐ Claim(s) _____ is/are allowed.

7)☒ Claim(s) __1-7__ is/are rejected.

8)☐ Claim(s) _____ is/are objected to.

9)☐ Claim(s) _____ are subject to restriction and/or election requirement.

* If any claims have been determined <u>allowable</u>, you may be eligible to benefit from the **Patent Prosecution Highway** program at a participating intellectual property office for the corresponding application. For more information, please see http://www.uspto.gov/patents/init_events/pph/index.jsp or send an inquiry to PPHfeedback@uspto.gov.

Application Papers

10)☐ The specification is objected to by the Examiner.

11)☒ The drawing(s) filed on 6/14/15 is/are: a)☐ accepted or b)☒ objected to by the Examiner.

    Applicant may not request that any objection to the drawing(s) be held in abeyance. See 37 CFR 1.85(a).

    Replacement drawing sheet(s) including the correction is required if the drawing(s) is objected to. See 37 CFR 1.121(d).

Priority under 35 U.S.C. § 119

12)☐ Acknowledgment is made of a claim for foreign priority under 35 U.S.C. § 119(a)-(d) or (f).

Certified copies:

    a)☐ All   b)☐ Some**   c)☐ None of the:

      1.☐ Certified copies of the priority documents have been received.

      2.☐ Certified copies of the priority documents have been received in Application No. _____.

      3.☐ Copies of the certified copies of the priority documents have been received in this National Stage application from the International Bureau (PCT Rule 17.2(a)).

** See the attached detailed Office action for a list of the certified copies not received.

Attachment(s)

1)☒ Notice of References Cited (PTO-892)

2)☐ Information Disclosure Statement(s) (PTO/SB/08a and/or PTO/SB/08b) Paper No(s)/Mail Date _____.

3)☐ Interview Summary (PTO-413) Paper No(s)/Mail Date. _____.

4)☐ Other: _____.

U.S. Patent and Trademark Office
PTOL-326 (Rev. 11-13)   **Office Action Summary**   Part of Paper No./Mail Date

Fig. 13A/1—Sample Office Action

Application/Control Number: 12/345,678 -2-

Art Unit: 2540

1. The drawing is objected to under 37 CFR 1.83(a) in that all the features recited in the claims are not shown. See Claims 1 and 2 regarding the "electronic counter means" and "first and second solid state counters."

2. The specification is objected to under 37 CFR 1.71(b) as inadequate. In particular, there is insufficient information regarding the "counter," "counter memory," and how the counter controls the illumination of the lights. Applicant is required to amplify the disclosure in this regard without the introduction of new matter, 608.04 MPEP.

3. Claims 1-7 are rejected under 35 U.S.C. § 112(a), as based on an insufficient disclosure. See above.

4. Insofar as adequate, Claims 1-6 are rejected under 35 U.S.C. § 102(b) as fully anticipated by Ohman. Ohman shows an electronic cribbage board counter that fully meets these claims. See Fig. 1. The microprocessor 300 shown in Fig. 3 inherently includes the counter means of Claims 1 and 2.

5. Claim 7 is rejected under 35 U.S.C. § 112(b). The term "said LCD readout" lacks proper antecedent basis in parent independent claim 1 as claim 1 recites only an "LCD monitor."

6. Claim 7 is rejected under 35 U.S.C. § 103 as unpatentable over Ohman in view of Morin. Ohman shows an electronic cribbage board counter, as stated. Morin shows an LCD tally monitor. It would be obvious to substitute Morin's LCD tally monitor for Ohman's mechanical readout, since the substitution of LCD readouts for mechanical readouts is an expedient well known to those skilled in the art. See column 13, lines 34-41 of Morin, which indicate that in lieu of the LCD readout shown, other types of readouts may be used.

7. No claim is allowed.

8. The remaining art cited shows other electronic board games containing the claimed structure. Note Morin, which shows the details of a computer as containing first and second counter means.

9. Any inquiry concerning this communication should be directed to Examiner Heyman at telephone number 703-557-4777, Fax number 703-872-9314.

October 14, 2024

/John S. Heyman/

Examiner

Group Art Unit 2540

Fig. 13A/2—Sample Office Action

CHAPTER 13 | GETTING THE PTO TO DELIVER | 391

FORM PTO-892	U.S. DEPARTMENT OF COMMERCE PATENT AND TRADEMARK OFFICE	SERIAL NO. 12/345,678	GROUP ART UNIT 2540	ATTACHMENT TO PAPER NUMBER 3
NOTICE OF REFERENCES CITED		APPLICANT(S) LeRoy Inventor		

U.S. PATENT DOCUMENTS

*		DOCUMENT NO.	DATE	NAME	CLASS	SUBCLASS	FILING DATE IF APPROPRIATE
	A	4 3 6 8 5 1 6	1/1983	Morin	377	5	
	B						
	C						
	D						
	E						
	F						
	G						
	H						
	I						
	J						
	K						

FOREIGN PATENT DOCUMENTS

		DOCUMENT NO.	DATE	COUNTRY	NAME	CLASS	SUB-CLASS	PERTINENT SHTS. DWGS	PP. SPEC.
	L	8 1 0 1 7 6 6	6/1981	International P.U.B. (ACT)	Ohman	273	148R	5	21
	M	1 1 9 5 0 0 1	10/1985	Canada	Mah	273	148R	3	14
	N	2 1 7 3 4 0 6	10/1986	Gr. Britain	Armstrong	273	148R	3	6
	O								
	P								
	Q								

OTHER PRIOR ART (Including Author, Title, Date, Pertinent Pages, Etc.)

R	
S	
T	
U	

EXAMINER J.S. Heyman	DATE 4/1/20xx	

*A Copy of this reference is not being furnished with this office action.
(See Manual of patent Examining Procedure, section 707.05(a).)

Fig. 13A/3—Notice of References Cited

APPLICATION NUMBER	FILING OR 371(C) DATE	FIRST NAMED APPLICANT	ATTY. DOCKET NO./TITLE
09/123,456	02/29/2024	Ann Inventor	7890/1001

CONFIRMATION NO. 2714
FORMALITIES LETTER

Ann Inventor
128 Innovation Road
Washington, MA 09999

Date Mailed:
10/14/2024

NOTICE TO FILE CORRECTED APPLICATION PAPERS

Filing Date Granted

An application number and filing date have been accorded to this application. The application is informal since it does not comply with the regulations for the reason(s) indicated below. Applicant is given TWO MONTHS from the date of this Notice within which to correct the informalities indicated below. Extensions of time may be obtained by filing a petition accompanied by the extension fee under the provisions of 37 CFR 1.136(a).

The required item(s) identified below must be timely submitted to avoid abandonment:

- Replacement drawings in compliance with 37 CFR 1.84 and 37 CFR 1.121(d) are required. The drawings submitted are not acceptable because:
  - Numbers, letters, and reference characters on the drawings must measure at least 0.32 cm (1/8 inch) in height. See Figure(s) all.

Applicant is cautioned that correction of the above items may cause the specification and drawings page count to exceed 100 pages. If the specification and drawings exceed 100 pages, applicant will need to submit the required application size fee.

Fig. 13A/4—Draftsperson's Drawing Objection Sheet

In the sixth paragraph of page 2 of the OA (Fig. 13A/2), the examiner has rejected Claim 7, under our old and troublesome friend Section 103, as unpatentable over two references. Note that the examiner states what each reference shows and why it would be obvious to combine the teachings of these references. Also note that by using two references, or by relying on Section 103, the examiner has tacitly admitted that this claim has satisfied the novelty (Section 102) requirement.

The examiner next states in paragraph 7 that no claim is allowed.

In the eighth paragraph, he refers to certain other prior art, which he cites but does not apply, to provide background and to put on the record in case he wants to use it later.

The examiner has electronically signed the Office Action at the bottom and lists his telephone number and fax above his official name stamp.

Next, we turn to Fig. 13A/3 (the Notice of References Cited). It lists one U.S. and three foreign patents. All of the foreign references will be attached to the OA, except any checked in the column marked with the asterisk (*), which were furnished in a prior Office Action, a prior related application, or were furnished by you in your Information Disclosure Statement. The "Document Number" column generally lists patent numbers.

Because the PTO no longer includes copies of U.S. patent documents with OAs, you will have to download them from the internet.

The date column indicates the date the patent issued, or the document was published. If this date is later than your filing date, the reference is not a good reference against your application, unless it is a U.S. patent filed before your application. In the latter instance, the examiner is supposed to indicate the filing date of the patent reference in the last column.

Finally, if the OA objects to the drawings (see Fig. 13A/4), be sure to file replacement figures with your response to the OA. In many cases, the OPAP will deliver a Notice To File Corrected Application Papers immediately, before sending the application to an examiner.

If you've sent in your IDS and PTO-1449, the OA will also include a copy of your PTO-1449, and a list of your references will be included under "References Cited" in the printed patent.

When the PTO cites patents as prior-art references, some inventors react in various illogical ways, as indicated by the following Common Misconceptions:

Common Misconception: The PTO can't cite foreign or non-English patents or other publications against a U.S. patent application.

Fact: Any publication, including a patent from anywhere in the world, in any language, is valid prior art against your patent application, provided it was published before your filing date. If the publication is a U.S. patent or published U.S. patent application, its filing date, or the filing date of any U.S. or foreign application from which it claims priority, is treated the same as a publication date.

Common Misconception: An in-force foreign patent that shows or claims your invention will prevent you from making, using, or selling the invention in the United States.

Fact: A patent of any country is enforceable only within the geographical area of that country and has no enforceability elsewhere. So, for example, a French patent is enforceable only in France and has no enforceability or effect in the United States. However, it is a good prior-art reference in the United States and will prevent you from obtaining a patent.

Common Misconception: If an examiner cites an in-force U.S. patent as a prior-art reference against your application, this means that your invention, if manufactured, sold, or used, would infringe this patent.

Fact: The only way you can tell if your invention would infringe any patent is to compare the cited patent's claims against your invention. Most cited in-force patents would not be infringed by your invention, since their claims are directed to a different invention. Again, examiners hardly ever read claims of patents they cite and the PTO is never concerned with infringements.

Common Misconception: If an examiner cites a very old prior-art reference against your application, it is not as good a reference as an in-force patent or a very recent reference.

Fact: The age of a reference is totally irrelevant, so long as its date is earlier than your filing date or your earliest provable date of invention. (See Chapter 5.)

D. What to Do When You Receive an Office Action (OA)

When you receive an OA, don't panic, don't be intimidated, and don't take it personally. It's common for some examiners to reject all claims, even if the rejections are not valid. This type of rejection is termed a "shotgun" or "shoot-from-the-hip" rejection. Examiners sometimes resort to tactics like this because of the pressure of the job, or to force you to state more clearly the essence of your invention and its true distinguishing features. You'll find that even if your examiner rejects all of your claims, if you approach your OA in a calm, rational, and methodical manner, as outlined below, you shouldn't have too much difficulty in ultimately getting your patent if your invention meets the legal tests for patentability.

1. Record Due Date on Your Calendar and OA, and Mount OA in Your File

After you get your Office Action, write the date you received the OA and the due date of your response right on it, and enter it on your analog or digital calendar (or both) so you don't forget it. You should actually enter the date three times on your calendar: once on the date it's actually due, once two weeks before it's due, and once one month before it's due. If the due date falls on a weekend or holiday, your due date is the next business day.

If the PTO Suggests You Get an Attorney

Some examiners insert a form paragraph in an OA, suggesting that you hire a patent attorney, regardless of how well the application is prepared, if there is no attorney of record. This has been done even in cases where attorneys prepared applications, but where they did not appear as the attorney of record. You can safely ignore this form paragraph, unless you feel uncomfortable without an attorney.

---

2. Check the References and Review Your Application

Your OA will usually cite prior-art references. Some will be applied against your claims and some will be cited as background as a matter of interest. In either case, the PTO does not send copies of any cited U.S. patent and published patent application references with OAs. They do send copies of cited foreign patents and nonpatent references. If you receive an OA that cites U.S. patent references, you must obtain copies of the cited references yourself. You have several ways to do this: (1) Download them from the PTO's website, (2) Download complete patents for free from one of the free patent sites, (3) download complete U.S. patents cited against your patent application from Patent Center.

After you obtain copies of the cited references, check all of them carefully to make sure you've received all the correct references listed in the Notice of References Cited. If there's any discrepancy, or if any seem irrelevant, call or write the examiner at once. This call will not count as an interview. (You are usually limited to two interviews.)

If you sent in an IDS and Form SB/08, the examiner will send, with your first OA, a copy of your SB/08, with the blank adjacent to each reference initialed to show that the examiner has considered it.

If you don't get the SB/08 back with every reference initialed, check with your examiner. Otherwise, the references you cited on your SB/08 won't be listed on your patent when it's printed, and you won't get deserved credit for the PTO having reviewed those references.

Next, read the OA carefully and make a detailed written summary of it so that you'll have it impressed in your mind. After that, reread your application, noting all grammatical and other errors in the specification, claims, and drawings that you would like to correct or improve. Remember, however, that you can't add any "new matter" to your application.

3. Read and Analyze Each Cited Reference, Except Patent Claims

Next, read every applied prior-art reference (except the claims of patent references) completely and carefully. (You don't have to read the nonapplied references carefully, but you should review them to be sure none is more relevant than an applied reference.) Make sure you take enough time to understand each reference completely, including all of the structure involved and how it works. Write a brief summary of each reference, preferably on the reference itself, even if it has an adequate abstract, in order to familiarize yourself with it in your own words.

CAUTION

Don't fall into a claims trap. Don't read the claims of any patent cited as a reference. Why not? Because the patent probably has not been cited for what it claims, but rather for what it shows about the prior art. The claims generally only repeat parts of the specification and are not directly relevant to the patent prosecution process, since they are only used to determine whether infringement exists. If you think of cited patents as magazine articles, you'll avoid this "claims trap" that most laypersons fall into.

4. Make a Comparison Chart

You'll find it helpful to make a comparison chart showing every feature of your invention across the top of the chart and listing the references down the left-hand side of the chart, as in Fig. 13B:

Features of My Invention

References	Pivot arm	Bracket at end of arm	Bracket has screw tightener
A	X	X	
B	X		X

Fig. 13B—Comparison Chart

Be sure to break up your invention so that all possible features of it, even those not already claimed, are covered and listed across the top of the chart. Remember that a feature can be the combination of two known separate features or a new use of an old device. Then indicate, by checking the appropriate boxes, those features of your invention that are not shown by each reference. This chart, if done correctly and completely, will be of tremendous aid in drafting your response to the first OA.

5. Follow the Flowchart

Fig. 13C provides a comprehensive, self-explanatory flowchart for dealing with all prior-art (35 U.S.C. § 102 and 103) rejections. Fig. 13D provides a list of all possible arguments we've found against obviousness rejections. For each claim (or set of claims) rejected, follow the chart and list carefully.

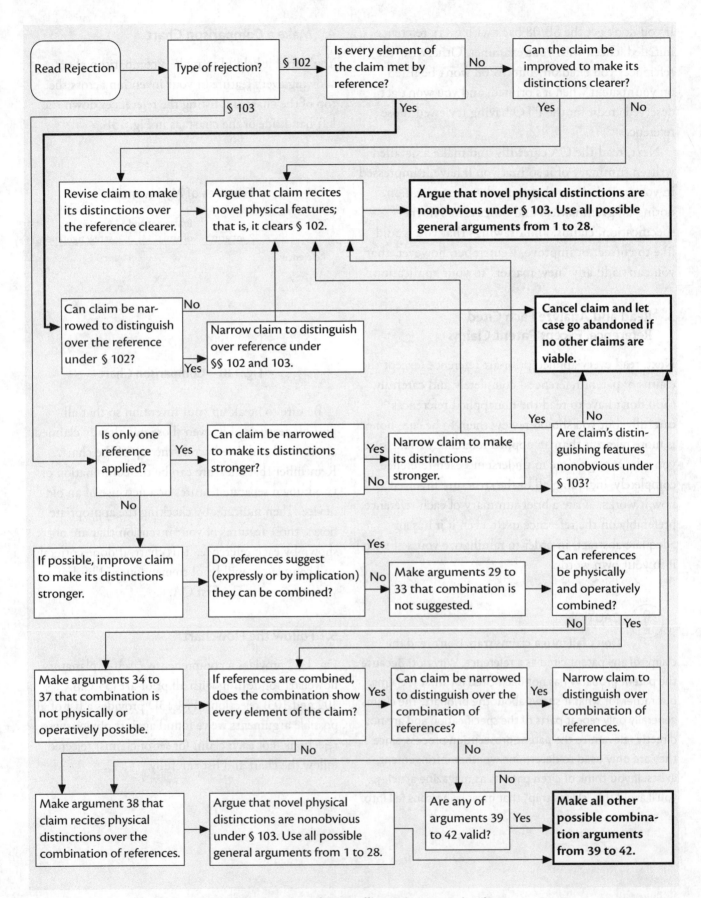

Fig. 13C—Flowchart for Handling Prior-Art Rejections

6. Compare Your Broadest Claim With the Cited References for Novelty

If the examiner applies any prior-art references under 35 U.S.C. Section 102, you'll need to deal with the novelty question. However, if the reference is said to apply under 35 U.S.C. Section 103 (obviousness), the examiner is tacitly admitting that your claimed structure is novel. Therefore, you won't have to go through the full analysis in this section. Instead, review the section briefly, and then concentrate on Section 7.

First, reread your broadest claim to see which features it recites. Remember, only positively recited physical structure or acts (steps in a method claim) count. Then consider whether these features distinguish your invention from each reference cited against this claim. Don't pay any attention to the advantages of your invention, your statements of function, or your "whereby" clauses. Only focus on the novel features (physical, structural, or method steps), including those that are in the form of a means clause followed by a function.

> **EXAMPLE:** "A lever having a threaded end with a counterbalance thereon" is a proper physical recitation that can distinguish your invention from the prior art. The phrase "means for counterbalancing" is a means clause followed by a function and is equivalent to a physical recitation. But "said lever counterbalancing said arm" is a mere statement of result or function and can't be used to distinguish the prior art.

If only one reference has been cited against your broadest claim, consider whether your claim distinguishes over this reference under 35 U.S.C. Section 102 (that is—whether your claimed structure is novel; see Chapter 5, Section E). In other words, are there any features recited in the claim that are not shown in the reference being cited against it? If not, the claim is "fully met" or anticipated by this reference and will have to be narrowed or canceled.

Remember that the examiner is entitled to interpret any claim in any reasonable way against you. That

is, if your claims, or any word in one of your claims, has two reasonable interpretations, the examiner is entitled to take the one least favorable to you when determining if your claim has novel physical structure or method steps. For example, suppose your invention uses a clamp that is halfway between two ends of a rod and a reference shows a clamp near one end of a rod. If your claim recites that the clamp is "intermediate" the ends of the rod, this won't distinguish over the reference since "intermediate" means "between" as well as "in the middle." The remedy? Recite that your claim is "substantially in the middle" of the rod in order to distinguish as novel over the reference (but not necessarily as nonobvious).

Suppose the physical features of your claim are all shown in a prior-art reference, but the features are used for a different purpose than yours. For example, you claim "a depression in a wall plate for holding a clock" and the prior art shows a large oil drip pan under a milling machine; this pan literally constitutes "a plate with a depression." Thus your claim literally "reads on" the prior art, but your claimed elements are directed to a different purpose than the elements of the prior-art reference. Unfortunately, the rejection is valid: You'll have to narrow the claim, or consider claiming your structure as a "new use" invention.

Sometimes, even though a claim recites a limitation that is novel, the examiner will overlook the limitation. In order to force the examiner to consider the limitation, it will help to rewrite the limitation in a stronger, separate, more prominent clause in its own paragraph—that is, change "a series of beads" to two paragraphs reading "a plurality of beads, said plurality of beads being connected in series to form a chain of said plurality of beads."

7. Analyze Novel Features for Nonobviousness

If the claim recites (or has been amended to recite) novel features, consider whether these are nonobvious over the reference cited against it. Many possible reasons for arguing nonobviousness are listed in Fig. 13D (Part I). When you use any reasons from this chart, you should not merely copy the reason, as we've seen some inventors do. Rather, you must state

Part I—General Arguments Against Obviousness

Below are arguments you may be able to make in response to a charge that your invention is obvious. You can use these statements in your response, but you will have to provide specific evidence for each argument. For example, if you are responding that the invention achieves unexpected results, you will have to list those unexpected results. For arguments 16 through 20, you may also need—in addition to a detailed explanation—a suitable declaration (Rule 132) with attached exhibits. In addition, some arguments contain references to the MPEP. Check these sections before responding to make sure they have not been amended and that they are still relevant.

1. **Unexpected results.** The results achieved by the invention are new, unexpected, superior, disproportionate, unsuggested, unusual, critical, and/or surprising.

2. **Assumed unworkability.** Up to now those skilled in the art thought or were skeptical that the techniques used in the invention were unworkable or presented an insuperable barrier.

3. **Assumed insolubility.** Up to now those skilled in the art thought or found the problem solved by the invention to be insoluble—that is, the invention converts failure into success. The failures of prior-art workers indicate that a solution was not obvious.

4. **Commercial success.** The invention has attained commercial success. (Prove this by a declaration with supporting documents showing that the commercial success of your invention is due to its novel features that you are claiming.)

5. **Unrecognized problem.** The problem solved by the invention was never before even recognized, much less solved. The recognition and solution of an unrecognized problem militates in favor of patentability.

6. **Crowded art.** The invention is classified in a crowded art; therefore, a small step forward should be regarded as significant.

7. **Omission of element.** An element of a prior-art device has been omitted or a prior-art version has been made simpler without loss of capability.

8. **Unsuggested modification.** The prior art lacks any suggestion that the reference should be modified in a manner required to meet the claims.

9. **Unappreciated advantage.** Up to now those skilled in the art never appreciated the advantage of the invention, although it is inherent.

10. **Inoperative references.** The prior-art references that were relied upon are inoperative.

11. **Poor references.** The prior-art references are vague, foreign, conflicting, or very old, and, therefore, are weak and should be construed narrowly.

12. **Ancient suggestion.** Although the invention may possibly have been suggested by the prior art, the suggestion is many years old, was never implemented, and produced greatly inferior results.

13. **Lack of implementation.** If the invention was in fact obvious, because of its advantages, those skilled in the art surely would have implemented it by now. That is—the fact that those skilled in the art have not implemented the invention, despite its great advantages, indicates that it is not obvious.

14. **Misunderstood reference.** The reference does not teach what the examiner relies upon it as supposedly teaching.

15. **Solution of long-felt and unsolved need.** The invention solves a long-felt, long-existing, but unsolved need.

16. **Commercial acquiescence.** The invention has been licensed, especially to a competitor.

17. **Professional recognition.** The invention has been given an award or recognized in a professional publication.

18. **Purchase offers.** Others, especially accused infringers, have tried to purchase or take a license under the invention.

19. **Copying by others.** Others have chosen to copy and implement the invention, rather than using the techniques of the prior art.

20. **Competitive recognition.** The invention has been copied by an infringer; moreover, the infringer has made laudatory statements about it, or has admitted it is nonobvious.

21. **Contrarian invention.** The invention is contrary to the teachings of the prior art—that is, the invention goes against the grain of what the prior art teaches.

22. **Strained interpretation.** The examiner has made a strained interpretation of the reference that could be made only by hindsight.

Fig. 13D—Arguments Against Obviousness Rejections (Part I)

Part I—General Arguments Against Obviousness (continued)

23. **Paper patent.** The reference is a "paper patent"—that is, it was never implemented or commercialized and therefore should be construed narrowly. (Don't use if reference completely anticipates your invention.)

24. **New principle of operation.** The invention utilizes a new principle of operation. Applicant has blazed a trail, rather than followed one.

25. **Inability of competitors.** Competitors were unable to copy the invention until they were able to learn its details through a publication or reverse engineering a commercial model; this indicates nonobviousness.

26. **Nonanalogous art.** The reference is from so different a field that it would not have commended itself to an inventor's attention when considering the invention as a whole. (MPEP 2141.01.)

27. **No convincing reasoning.** The examiner has not presented a convincing line of reasoning as to why the claimed subject matter as a whole, including its differences over the prior art, would have been obvious.

28. **Reference is nonanalogous art or isn't pertinent to the problem applicant has solved.** If a cited reference is nonanalogous or is directed to a different problem, this weighs against its use in a rejection.

Part II—Arguments Also Used When Combination of References Applied

29. **Unsuggested combination.** The prior-art references do not contain any suggestion (express or implied) that they be combined, or that they be combined in the manner suggested. In 2007 the U.S. Supreme Court held that that an invention should not be held obvious over several prior-art references unless there is a suggestion, motivation, or teaching that the references can or should be combined. (MPEP 2143.)

30. **References are individually complete.** Each reference is complete and functional in itself, so there would be no reason to use parts from or add or substitute parts to any reference.

31. **References take different approaches.** The references take mutually exclusive paths and reach different solutions to a similar problem. Since they teach away from each other, it would not be logical to combine them.

32. **References teach away.** The references themselves teach away (expressly or by implication) from the suggested combination.

33. **Reference is from different field.** One reference is from a very different technical field than that of the invention—that is, it's "nonanalogous art." (MPEP 707.07(f).)

34. **Impossible to combine.** Those skilled in the art would find it physically impossible to combine the references in the manner suggested.

35. **Inoperative combination.** If they could be combined, the references would produce an inoperative combination, or render the reference being modified unsuitable for its intended purpose.

36. **Modifications necessary.** It would be necessary to make modifications, not taught in the prior art, in order to combine the references in the manner suggested.

37. **Mutually exclusive paths.** The references can't be legally combined because they take mutually exclusive paths to reach different solutions to a problem, and, therefore, by implication each teaches away from combining itself with the other.

38. **Claimed features lacking.** Even if combined, the references would not meet the claims.

39. **Synergism.** The whole (that is—the result achieved by the invention) is greater than the sum of its parts (that is—the respective results of the individual references).

40. **Multiplicity of steps required.** The combination suggested requires a series of separate, awkward combinative steps that are too involved to be considered obvious.

41. **Multiplicity of references.** The fact that a large number of references (over three) must be combined to meet the invention is evidence of nonobviousness.

42. **Intended function destroyed.** The references are not legally combinable since doing so will destroy the intended function(s) of at least one of the references.

Fig. 13D—Arguments Against Obviousness Rejections (Part II)

facts in support of each reason you use. For example, if you select Reason 1 (Unexpected Results) after stating that your novel claimed structure produces new and unexpected results, you must go farther and state precisely what they are—such as that it does a job faster or more reliably.

If you consider the features of your invention obvious, you'll have to narrow the claim, either by adding more features from your specification or from narrower (dependent) claims (refer to Fig. 13C, above) or by reciting the existing features more narrowly.

8. If References Are Cited in Combination Against Your Broadest Claim

If two or more references have been cited in combination against your broadest claim, refer to Fig. 13D (Part II) to see whether the examiner has a point.

TIP

You should especially consider reasons 29 to 33—that is, ask yourself whether it is proper to combine these references in the manner that the examiner has done. Also note that when you use any of the reasons of Fig. 13D, you should not merely state the applicable reason, but also supporting facts that pertain to your invention.

9. Does the Combination Disclose Subject Matter of Your Broadest Claim?

Assuming that the references are combined (whether or not they can be), ask yourself if the combination discloses the subject matter of your claim (Reason 37). If not, are the distinctions in your claim nonobvious (Reasons 1–28 and 39–41)? Also ask yourself whether there are any other errors in the examiner's logic or reasoning.

10. If Your Claims Are Rejected Under 35 U.S.C. Section 112

If your claim has been rejected under 35 U.S.C. Section 112—a very common occurrence, even for patent attorneys—the examiner feels that the language of your claim is not clear or proper. For

example, a very common rejection is for failure to supply an antecedent for a "said xxxx" phrase. This is easy to fix. Either positively recite the missing antecedent earlier in the claim or in a referent claim which the claim depends from, or rewrite the phrase to eliminate the "said." If you accept an examiner's rejection that the claim has vague or unclear language, you'll have to substitute a more specific recitation. Try not to limit your invention too much. For example, if you recite that a sheet is "flexible" and the examiner objects to this word as too vague, try substituting a recitation such as, "flexible enough so that it can be repeatedly folded and opened without tearing." You may benefit by calling the examiner to seek suggestions or approval for new proposed language. If the examiner makes any other type of Section 112 rejection, try to work out alternative language that will obviate this rejection. Alternatively, you can ask the examiner to write clear claims for you.

11. If Your Claims Are Rejected Under 35 U.S.C. Section 101

If your claim has been rejected under section 101 for being directed to a "judicial exception" (a law of nature, natural phenomenon, or an abstract idea), begin by reviewing the rejection to determine whether the examiner has faithfully followed the required process, and note any shortcomings in the analysis.

To reject a claim under 35 U.S.C. Section 101, the examiner must conclude either that the claim does not fall within one of the four statutory categories of patentable subject matter (process, machine, manufacture, or composition of matter), or that it does fall into a judicial exception (laws of nature, natural phenomena, abstract ideas). The examiner is not allowed to simply jump to such a conclusion. Rather, the examiner must support the rejection by performing a thorough analysis to establish a *prima facie* (at first sight) case that the claim fails to define patentable subject matter under Section 101, and then by clearly explaining the rejection in writing.

To establish a *prima facie* rejection based on a judicial exception, the examiner's analysis must follow a two-step process (known as the "Alice/Mayo test," which was applied to method claims in the *Alice v. CLS Bank* case in 2014) described by the U.S. Supreme Court. In Step 1, the examiner determines whether the subject matter is "directed to" one of the statutory classes. The PTO rarely rejects a claim for falling outside of the four statutory categories of patentable subject matter. The *Manual of Patent Examining Procedure* (MPEP) lists the following examples of claims rejected for this reason: "transitory forms of signal transmission (for example, a propagating electrical or electromagnetic signal per se); human per se; a legal contractual agreement between two parties; a computer program per se; a company; a mere arrangement of printed matter; and data per se." Because we are confident that you will be able to avoid such rejections by thoughtful claim drafting, or to amend your claims to overcome such objections without much difficulty, we focus on the judicial exceptions.

Step 2 has two parts, called "Step 2A" and "Step 2B." In Step 2A, the examiner first determines whether the claim is "directed to" a judicial exception, and if so, then in Step 2B she determines whether the elements of the claim transform the claim into something significantly more than the judicial exception itself. This second step has been called "the search for an inventive concept."

In step 2A, the examiner must distinguish claims that are "directed to" a judicial exception from those that merely involve a law of nature, natural phenomenon, or abstract idea. The PTO instructs examiners to proceed cautiously, because the Supreme Court has cautioned that "all inventions at some level embody, use, reflect, rest upon, or apply laws of nature, natural phenomenon, or abstract ideas." The PTO's guidance confirms that "an invention is not considered to be ineligible for patent simply because it involves a judicial exception."

Examiners typically will not identify a claimed concept as an abstract idea unless it is similar to at least one concept that the courts have identified as an abstract idea, such as "fundamental economic practices," "certain methods of organizing human activities," "an idea of itself," and "mathematical

relationships/formulas." Concepts that are not abstract ideas include:

- a method isolating malicious code from email messages, because that invention is "inextricably tied to computer technology and distinct from the types of concepts found by the courts to be abstract"; and
- a system that implements a method of manipulating webpages to convince a shopper that he or she remains on a host website when viewing information from a merchant's website, because the invention does not merely recite a process "known from the pre-internet world" with instructions to apply the known process using the internet, but instead claims a solution that is "necessarily rooted in computer technology in order to overcome a problem specifically arising the realm of computer networks."

In practice, because it is easy to identify an abstract idea within a method claim, examiners find it easy to conclude that a claim is "directed to" an abstract idea. Note that the examiner's standard here is low: the examiner must only conclude that it is more likely than not that your claim is "directed to" a judicial exception. As discussed below, in making rejections of this type, examiners often rely heavily on examples drawn from post-*Alice* court cases by arguing that your claims are like one of the examples.

If you receive such a rejection, we recommend reviewing the discussion in Chapter 5, and assessing the PTO's rejection of your claim accordingly. For example, does the alleged abstract idea fall within one of the four categories listed above ("fundamental economic practices," "certain methods of organizing human activities," "an idea of itself," and "mathematical relationships/formulas")? Is the claim directed to something that is "inextricably tied to computer technology and distinct from the types of concepts found by the courts to be abstract," or "necessarily rooted in computer technology in order to overcome a problem specifically arising the realm of computer networks?" Conversely, is it possible to perform the processes of the claim to achieve its intended result using an arbitrary mechanism, however inefficiently?

If you agree that the Office Action's analysis meets its low (and subjective) standard, then move on to step 2B of the analysis. Otherwise, develop an argument as to how and why the analysis fails—and then move on to step 2B of the test for good measure. For example, you may argue that your claims are analogous to claims that are allowable under the most recent PTO guidance, and/or that your claims are different from the kinds of claims that are not allowable under the most recent PTO guidance. Amend the claims if doing so makes your argument stronger.

In step 2B of the analysis, the examiner must study the claim again and determine whether the claim's elements limit the claim to an application of the abstract idea to a new and useful end. This has been called the "search for an inventive concept," and it requires that the claim do more than recite an abstract idea alongside a general instruction to "apply it." Since such an instruction implies a conventional application, you may think of step 2B as a hunt for unconventionality. For example, if you have invented a new way of converting a number expressed in one format into a different format, that method will be deemed an abstract idea, and your claim will be rejected if it is directed to that method, even if the claim requires that the method be performed via computer because a conventional computer is designed to perform arbitrary computations, including format conversions.

Step 2B of the Alice/Mayo test requires the examiner to consider the elements of your claim both individually and as an "ordered combination," to assess whether the claim amounts to significantly more than the exception itself. In practice, when considering the claim elements individually, it is often easy for the examiner to conclude that the elements fail to amount to significantly more than the exception itself by observing that each of the elements is well-understood, routine, and conventional in the field (in other words, none of the elements, considered individually, introduces an "inventive concept").

You should confirm that the Office Action includes some reasoning for a conclusion, rather than simply jumping to one. However, the examiner may be

correct; after all, most inventions involve the use of previously known elements, even when those elements are arranged to describe a novel invention. If you agree that each of the elements is well-understood, routine, and conventional, and their combination as you have described it is either known or would produce a predictably conventional result, then arguing with the examiner on this point is unlikely to be fruitful. Otherwise, be prepared to argue why at least one of the elements is not well-understood, routine, and conventional in the field, or why the particular combination yields unknown or unconventional functions or results.

To assist you in this regard, the 2018 appeals court case *Berkheimer v. HP Inc.* clarified that the determination of whether claim elements represent "well-understood, routine, conventional activity" must be based on evidence. The PTO subsequently issued guidance stating that an examiner must support the step 2B analysis with one or more of the following types of evidence:

- a citation to an express statement in the specification or by the applicant during prosecution that demonstrates the well-understood, routine, conventional nature of the claim elements
- a citation to one or more prior court decisions listed in MPEP 2106.05(d)(II) that demonstrate this nature
- a citation to a publication (for example, a book, manual, or article) that demonstrates this nature, and/or
- a statement that the examiner is taking "official notice" of this nature.

If the OA argues that your claims are conventional, but fails to provide any of the above types of evidence to support that argument, or fails to state specifically which claim elements it finds conventional, then the examiner's argument is insufficient and you should argue as much in your response.

Examples of features that amount to "significantly more" than a judicial exception include (but are not necessarily limited to): improvements to another technology or technical field; improvements to the functioning of the computer itself; applying the judicial exception with, or by use of, a particular machine; effecting a transformation or reduction of a particular article to a different state or thing; specific limitations other than what is well-understood, routine, and conventional in the field, or adding unconventional steps that confine the claim to a particular useful application; and other meaningful limitations beyond generally linking the use of the judicial exception to a particular technological environment.

In responding to rejections of this type, try to find one or more examples in the guidance that are determined to be patent-eligible, and show the examiner why those examples should apply to your situation.

Here are a few examples drawn from that guidance, in which claims were found to be "significantly more" than a judicial exception:

- A method for processing a digital image in a computer, which involves executing a mathematical operation (the claim is thus "directed to" an abstract idea, so the analysis continues to step 2B of the Alice/Mayo test). When considered individually, some elements of the claim require using a computer processor to manipulate the image data into a "halftoned" image. The PTO guidance concludes that these steps "tie the mathematical operation to the processor's ability to process digital images"; and "add meaningful limitation to the abstract idea ... more ... than mere computer implementation." When considered in an "ordered combination," the claim steps "improve the functioning of the computer itself" because the process "allows the computer to use less memory than required" in the prior art, "results in faster computation without sacrificing the quality of the resulting image," and "produces an improved digital image."
- A method for calculating an absolute position of a GPS receiver and an absolute time of reception of satellite signals, which involves executing algorithms on a mobile GPS processor, and a number of other related steps (the claim is thus

"directed to" an abstract idea—mathematical operations—so the analysis continues to step 2B of the Alice/Mayo test). When "taking all the additional claim elements individually, and in combination, the claim as a whole amounts to significantly more than the mathematical operations by themselves." In the PTO's analysis of a corresponding system claim (a system for implementing the method), the PTO concluded that the "claim is not directed to performing mathematic operation on a computer alone" because "the elements impose meaningful limits in that the mathematical operation are applied to improve an existing technology (global positioning) by improving the signal-acquisition sensitivity of the receiver...."

Based on your study of step 2B of the Office Action's analysis, develop arguments as to how and why your claims amount to substantially more than an abstract idea. For example, you may argue that your claims are analogous to those that are allowable under the most recent PTO guidance, and/or that your claims are different from the kinds of claims that are not allowable under the most recent PTO guidance. You may also argue that your claims amount to more than a judicial exception, according to the list above. Amend the claims if doing so makes your argument stronger.

Before you file your response to the Office Action, we advise that you have a telephone call or video conference interview with the examiner (or even meet with the examiner in person) to discuss the rejections, and options for responding. Throughout this process, bear in mind that the PTO examiner is not your adversary. Most examiners are just trying to do their jobs to comply with the patent laws and rules, and are suffering with the same vague standards that plague inventors and patent attorneys. At the same time, you must hold the examiner to those standards as best you can, but remember to always be professional and courteous.

In the interview, politely remind the examiner that you are working *pro se* (that is without the assistance of a patent attorney), and ask the examiner to walk you through any part of the rejections that you don't understand, or with which you don't agree. You can politely press the examiner on any weak points of the Office Action's analysis by asking the examiner to elaborate on the reasons for each such point (or at least the weakest points), but your effectiveness will depend on your understanding of the law (for example, the Mayo test) and your ability to express similarities and distinctions between your claims and the examples in the most recent PTO guidelines.

Don't expect to change the examiner's mind during the interview, or get them to admit a fatal flaw in the Office Action analysis—examiners are human, too, and don't like to be told (or to admit that) they are wrong. Also, remember that as a pro se applicant, you can ask the examiner to suggest ways to amend your claims in order to overcome the rejection. In any case, an examiner interview will allow you to test the rejection and your own analysis, and better understand the examiner's point of view, and in that way strengthen your response strategy.

Finally, we suggest that you seek assistance from a patent attorney with experience in your area of technology, and with experience addressing subject matter eligibility issues for patent applications in your area of technology. Even skilled professionals are struggling with these issues, and you might benefit from an attorney's experience and insight.

12. What to Do If You Disagree With the Examiner

If you believe your broadest claim is patentable over the prior art and that there is a serious flaw in the examiner's logic, it is theoretically permissible to "stand pat"—that is, leave the claim as it is and argue its patentability in your response. It can be desirable to do this to emphasize the rightness of your position if the examiner is very wrong. If you do file a reply to an OA without changing the specification or claims, your reply is technically not an "amendment," so call it a "response."

In most situations, it is advisable not to stand pat, because it's difficult psychologically for the examiner to back down. In other words, it's easier to get the examiner to change directions slightly than get them to make an about face. So, to save the examiner's ego, it may be best to try to make some amendment to the claim, even if it's insignificant.

"Treat all persons you deal with as if they had a sign around their neck reading, 'Make Me Feel Important.'"

—*Mary Kay Ash*

13. Making Amendments Without Narrowing Scope of Claim

It's usually possible to make amendments to a claim that don't narrow its scope. For example, you can recite that a member, which of necessity must be elongated, *is* elongated. By doing this, you have amended the claim without narrowing your scope of coverage. Also, in the electronic field, you can state that a circuit is energized by a direct-current source. For almost any claim you can add a "whereby" clause to the claim stating the function of the mechanism of the claim, and you can add a longer preamble stating in more detail (but not in narrower language) the environment of your invention. The important thing is to add some words to the claim(s), even if you already believe they distinguish over the prior art under 35 U.S.C. Sections 102 and 103, in order to show that you're meeting the examiner partway.

14. Amending Your Claim When You Agree With the Examiner

If you believe your broadest claim isn't patentable as written, and you agree with all or part of the examiner's rejection, you'll have to narrow the claim by adding physical or structural limitations, or by narrowing the limitations already present, in the manner outlined in Chapter 9, or by canceling the broadest claim(s) and making a dependent claim the new independent claim.

Provide 1" top margin (omitted here) to allow for mounting hole punching.

In The United States Patent and Trademark Office

Applicant: R. Wood
Appl Ser No: 07/910,721   Art Unit: 2872
Filed: 3/20/2024   Examiner: Yon J. Couso
Title: Pathway Lamp with Adjustable Illumination Pattern   Date: July 4, 2025

Confirmation No: 1961

Mail Stop AMENDMENT
Commissioner for Patents
P.O. Box 1450
Alexandria, VA 22313-1450

AMENDMENT A

Dear Sir:

In response to the Office Action of March 22, 2025, please amend the above-identified application as follows:

Amendments to the Description begin on page 2 of this paper.

Amendments to the Claims are reflected in the listing of claims which begins on page 3 of this paper.

Amendments to the Drawings begin on page 5 of this paper and include both an attached replacement sheet and an annotated sheet showing changes.

Remarks begin on page 6 of this paper.

An Appendix including amended drawing figures is attached following page 8 of this paper.

Fig. 13E/1—Sample "Regular" Amendment

Appn. Number 07/910,721   (Wood)   GAU 3303   Amnt. A contd.   2 of 8

Amendments to the Description:

Please replace the second paragraph on page of the application as filed with the following new paragraph:

The lamp housing 200 also contains a rotatable reflector 208, as schematically illustrated in Fig. 2A and Fig. 2B. The rotatable reflector 208 includes a concave reflecting surface 209 that reflects light from the light source 204 so that the reflected light 206 exits the lamp housing 200 <u>through</u> the translucent bell 203. The reflected light 206 exits the translucent bell 203 in a direction substantially perpendicular to the post axis 110. The rotatable reflector 208 is movably coupled to the lamp housing 200 by bearing 221 so as to be controllably rotatable around the post axis 110.

Fig. 13E/2—Sample "Regular" Amendment (continued)

Appn. Number 07/910,721 (Wood) GAU 3303 Amnt. A contd. 3 of 8

Amendments to the Claims:

This listing of claims will replace all prior versions, and listings, of claims in the application:

Listing of Claims:

1. (currently amended) A pathway light with adjustable illumination pattern for illuminating the ground near a pathway, comprising:
    a post having a first end and a second end, and defining a post axis extending through the first end and the second end;
    a spike coupled to the first end of the post, the spike configured to engage the ground and support the post in a vertical position relative to the ground;
    a lamp housing coupled to the second end of the post, the lamp housing comprising a translucent bell;
    a light source disposed within the lamp housing; and
    a concave reflector movably disposed within the housing between the light source and the translucent bell, the concave reflector configured to controllably rotate around the post axis so as to controllably reflect light from the light source through the translucent bell.

2. (original) A pathway light according to claim 1, wherein the translucent bell comprises a transparent glass hemisphere.

3. (original) A pathway light according to claim 1, wherein the translucent bell comprises a diffusive plastic hemisphere.

4. (original) A pathway light according to claim 1, wherein the light source is a halogen lamp.

5. (original) A pathway light according to claim 1, wherein the light source is an incandescent lamp.

6. (original) A pathway light according to claim 1, wherein the light source is an LED light, and the pathway light further comprises a rechargeable battery, and solar cell electrically coupled to the battery and disposed to capture sunlight to recharge the battery.

7. (original) A pathway light according to claim 1, wherein the post comprises a hollow tube.

8. (original) A pathway light according to claim 7, wherein the post comprises an aluminum tube.

Fig. 13E/3—Sample "Regular" Amendment (continued)

Appn. Number 07/910,721   (Wood)   GAU 3303   Amnt. A contd.   4 of 8

9. (original) A pathway light according to claim 7, wherein the post comprises a plastic tube.

10. (canceled)

11. (original) A pathway light according to 7, further comprising a battery compartment configured to hold batteries for powering the light source.

12. (new) A pathway light according to claim 7, further comprising electrical wires extending through the tube from the first end to the lamp housing and electrically coupled to the light source.

Fig. 13E/4—Sample "Regular" Amendment (continued)

| Appn. Number 07/910,721 | (Wood) | GAU 3303 | Amnt. A contd. | 5 of 8 |

Amendments to the Drawings:

- The attached sheet of drawings includes changes to Fig. 1, Fig. 2A and Fig. 2B.
- The attached sheet, which includes Fig. 1, Fig. 2A and Fig. 2B, replaces the original sheet including Fig. 1, Fig. 2A and Fig. 2B.

Attachments: One Replacement Sheet

Fig. 13E/5—Sample "Regular" Amendment (continued)

| Appn. Number 07/910,721 | (Wood) | GAU 3303 | Amnt. A contd. | 6 of 8 |

REMARKS

Claims 1-11 were pending. Claim 1 has been amended. Claim 10 has been canceled. New claim 12 has been added. Therefore, claims 1-9, 11 and 12 are pending. The Applicants respectfully requests reconsideration of the claims in view of the above amendments and the following remarks.

The office action of March 22, 2018 (herein, the "Office Action") objected to the figures, and rejected the claims under 35 U.S.C. Section 103 as obvious over U.S. patent 6,874,905 to Beadle (herein "Beadle") in view of U.S. patent 2,569,069 to Maxwell (herein "Maxwell"). The Applicant provides the following response.

I. Amendments to the Specification

The Applicant has amended the second paragraph on page 4 of the application as filed to correct a typographical error.

II. Amendments to the Drawings

The Office Action objected to Fig. 1, Fig. 2A and Fig. 2B for being too light. In response, the Applicant has darkened the lines of the figures.

III. Response to Rejection Under 35 U.S.C. Section 112

The Office Action rejected claim 1 under 35 U.S.C. Section 112(a) as failing to point out and distinctly claim the subject matter that the Applicant regards as the invention. In particular, the Office Action alleges that the claim must include some structure for supporting the pathway lamp relative to the ground. In response, the Applicant has amended claim 1 to include the spike, as originally included in claim 10. The Applicant has therefore canceled claim 10.

IV. Beadle in View of Maxwell Does Not Render the Claims Obvious Under 35 U.S.C. Section 103

The Office Action rejected independent claim 1 over Beadle in view of Maxwell. However, the Office Action fails to establish a prima facie case of obviousness under 35 U.S.C. Section 103 as explained below.

A. The Office Action Fails to Establish a Prima Facie Case of Obviousness Because Beadle May Not Be Modified By Maxwell as Alleged in the Office Action

Claim 1 requires, among other things, "a concave reflector movably disposed within the housing between the light source and the translucent bell, the concave reflector configured to controllably rotate around the post axis . . ."

The Office Action cited Beadle and Maxwell, and concluded that claim 1 was obvious over Beadle in view of Maxwell.

As set forth in section 2143.01 of the *Manual of Patent Examining Procedure* (MPEP), a "proposed modification cannot render the prior art unsatisfactory for its intended purpose"

Fig. 13E/6—Sample "Regular" Amendment (continued)

| Appn. Number 07/910,721 | (Wood) | GAU 3303 | Amnt. A contd. | 7 of 8 |

("If proposed modification would render the prior art invention being modified unsatisfactory for its intended purpose, then there is no suggestion or motivation to make the proposed modification.").

The proposed modification of Beadle by Maxwell would render Beadle unsatisfactory for its intended purpose, with the result that there is no motivation to modify Beadle with Maxwell.

In short, the purpose of the invention in Beadle is to produce a "uniform dispersion of light" (Beadle, column 5, line 36-42). In contrast, the purpose of the reflector 10 in Maxwell is to reflect light emitted by a lamp bulb, while the reflector is supported so that the reflector does not move during use (Maxwell, column 1, lines 1-16). The reflector in Maxwell prevents light from scattering in a uniform direction, since some of the light from the lamp bulb is reflected by the reflector.

As such, while Beadle teaches the production of a uniform dispersion of light, Maxwell teaches the nonuniform dispersion of light. Therefore, modifying Beadle with the reflector of Maxwell, as proposed by the Office Action, would render Beadle unsatisfactory for its intended purpose.

Consequently, there is no motivation to modify Beadle in view of Maxwell, and for at least this reason, the Office Action has failed to establish a prima facie case of obviousness for claim 1 over Beadle in view of Maxwell under 35 U.S.C. Section 103. Therefore, claim 2 and all claims that depend from claim 1 are also not rendered obvious over Beadle in view of Maxwell under 35 U.S.C. Section 103.

B. Beadle in View of Maxwell Fails to Teach All of the Elements of Claim 1

Claim 1 requires, among other things, "a concave reflector movably disposed within the housing between the light source and the translucent bell, the concave reflector configured to controllably rotate around the post axis . . . ."

Neither Beadle nor Maxwell teaches such a rotatable reflector, and therefore Beadle in view of Maxwell fails to teach all of the elements of claim 1.

Beadle does not teach a reflector at all. Maxwell teaches a reflector, but does not teach a reflector that is movable around an axis with respect to a lamp housing. Rather, Maxwell's reflector is a fixed part of the lamp.

Consequently, the combination of Beadle and Maxwell as proposed by the Office Action fails to teach all of the elements of claim 1.

For at least this reason, the Office Action has failed to establish a prima facie case of obviousness for claim 1 over Beadle in view of Maxwell under 35 U.S.C. Section 103. Therefore, claim 1 and all claims that depend from claim 1 are also not rendered obvious over Beadle in view of Maxwell under 35 U.S.C. Section 103.

For all of the foregoing reasons, the applicant submits that all pending claims are in condition for allowance. The applicant respectfully requests early allowance of the application.

Fig. 13E/7—Sample "Regular" Amendment (continued)

Appn. Number 07/910,721   (Wood)   GAU 3303   Amnt. A contd.   8 of 8

V. New Claim 12

The Applicant has added a new claim 12, directed to electrical wires extending through the tube from the first end to the lamp housing and electrically coupled to the light source. This claim is supported at least by Fig. 4 and the text at page 7 of the application as filed.

Conditional Request for Constructive Assistance

Applicants have amended the specification and claims of this application so that they are proper, definite, and define novel structure which is also nonobvious. If, for any reason this application is not believed to be in full condition for allowance, applicants respectfully request the constructive assistance and suggestions of the Examiner pursuant to MPEP 707.07(j) in order that the undersigned can place this application in allowable condition as soon as possible and without the need for further proceedings.

The Applicants petition for a one (1) month extension of time. In the event that a further extension is needed, this conditional petition of extension is hereby submitted.

Date: July 4, 2025

Respectfully submitted,

Richard Wood

Richard Wood, Inventor

Fig. 13E/8—Sample "Regular" Amendment (continued)

Fig. 13E/9—Sample "Regular" Amendment

Here are some suggestions on how to approach the amendment of your claims:

1. Look for the physical feature(s) in Fig. 13B that constitute the essence of why your invention can be distinguished from the prior art. Then try to put this essence into your claim. Note that you should amend the main claim so as to distinguish physical novelty over the references. The physical distinctions should also be significant enough to define structure that is nonobvious. Merely reciting a single descriptive word will usually not be enough. For example, "Manifold" might not distinguish over a single pipe (even though it should), but reciting "a pipe with an inlet and a plurality of outlets" will be explicit enough to do the trick. In addition to putting the reasons as to why the physical distinctions are nonobvious in your remarks or in a "whereby" clause at the end of the claim, you can also put them in the body of the claim right after the novel physical distinction. That is, "said bolt having a triangular cross-section [novel feature] so that only wrenches with triangular openings will fit it to increase security [reason for nonobviousness]."

2. "Whereby" clauses can state the advantages of the invention in a relatively informal manner, without as much concern for antecedents and other qualifiers. Keep in mind that the examiner doesn't have to give a "whereby" clause any weight in defining your invention over the prior art.

3. Don't make your main claim narrower than necessary. Often you can find the limitation you are looking for in one or more dependent claims.

4. Show your invention and the cited references to friends or associates; often they can readily spot the distinguishing essence of your invention. (Remember to use the Nondisclosure Agreement (Form 3-1) if you are maintaining the invention as a trade secret in the patent prosecution phase.)

5. After you've narrowed your main independent claim so that it distinguishes over the prior art cited by the patent examiner, and you feel the distinguishing features are nonobvious, do the same for all your other independent claims.

6. If you've changed any independent claims, change your dependent claims so that they properly correspond in language and numbering with your main claim. If you incorporate a limitation from a dependent claim into your main claim, cancel the dependent claim, since the dependent claim will no longer be able to add anything to narrow the independent claim. You may also think of other, narrower dependent claims to replace those that you've canceled; refer to the comparison chart to be sure you've claimed every feature.

7. Write the narrowest possible claims you're willing to accept, since it will be difficult to amend again if your amended claims are rejected next time around.

Changing Claim Language or Invention

If you have to amend your claims to define over the prior art, you should, of course, try to keep them as broad as possible and worded appropriately to cover your invention in its latest and most likely commercial embodiment. If you change the design of your invention from what's shown and described in your application, this will not prejudice you so long as your claims are still broad enough to cover the new design. Judges recognize that designs frequently change as inventions mature. If your design changes substantially, consider filing a "continuation-in-part" or a new application.

---

8. Be sure all of the less-important specific features of your invention are recited in your amended dependent claims.

9. Try to distinguish by adding quantitative or relative (rather than qualitative) recitations to your claims, since these carry far more weight. For example, say "a rod at least one meter long" or "a rod that is longer than said post" not "a rod of great length" (or "strength"). Adding qualitative or relative words to your claim can also subject you to a rejection under 35 U.S.C. Section 112(b).

15. Plan an Outline of Your Response

Indicate in pencil on a copy of your application, or on separate sheets, the amendments you intend to make to your specification, your claims, your drawing, and your remarks. The "remarks" section of your amendment (as shown in Fig. 13E, above) should consist of:

1. a positive statement indicating that you have amended the application to place it in condition for allowance
2. a brief summary of all your amendments
3. a discussion of any technical (35 U.S.C. § 112) rejections, indicating that the new claims overcome them or how you overcame them
4. a review of the first prior-art rejection made by the examiner, containing
    4a. review of the rejection
    4b. review of your invention, emphasizing its novelty
    4c. review of the reference(s) cited by the examiner
    4d. summary of how you changed the independent claims of this rejection, quoting your changes, and a request for reconsideration of the examiner's position
    4e. statement as to how your independent claims under this rejection recite novel subject matter over the reference under 35 U.S.C. Section 102 if one reference was cited (be sure to quote the novel limitations from the claim)
    4f. statement of why the references can't legally be combined, if more than one reference was cited
    4g. statement that even if the references were to be combined, the claims would still recite novel subject matter over the combination, if more than one reference was cited (be sure to quote the novel limitations from the claim)
    4h. statement that the novel features of the claim are nonobvious, using all possible arguments from Fig. 13D (be sure to elaborate on each argument and not merely state the argument from the chart)
    4i. discussion of dependent claims under this rejection, indicating that they incorporate all of the features of their referent (independent) claims and add additional limitations and thus are a fortiori (by stronger reason) patentable
    4j. discussion of any independent claims that are independently patentable
5. repeat steps 4a through 4h for each additional prior-art rejection, but don't repeat any text, just refer to it above
6. any request for aid you may wish to make under MPEP 707.07(j) requesting the examiner to write claims, and
7. a conclusion restating your main arguments briefly.

(See below, for specifics on drafting your remarks. At this point, read Fig. 13E.)

E. Format for Amending the Specification and Claims

Form 13-1 ("Amendment"), downloadable via instructions in Appendix 7, provides the initial part of your amendment. Copy the text from this form into a new file in your word processing program.

Fill in the serial number, filing date, your name, title of your application, and the examiner's name and examining unit or group art unit. The date on which you actually mail the amendment goes after "date," and the date of the office letter goes at the space indicated in the first paragraph. Put an appropriate letter (A, B, and so on) after "Amendment" or "Response" to indicate which response it is (your first, second, and so on). Then immediately after the "In response to ..." sentence, list the sections of your application (Drawings, Specification, and/or Claims, and Remarks) and their page numbers in the manner indicated below. (You should refer to yourself and the examiner in the third person as we have done in the sample amendment and never format your amendment in the form of a personal letter to the examiner, as we have seen some inventors do. That

416 | PATENT IT YOURSELF

is, do not say anything like, "Dear Examiner: I have revised my claims and I hope you will now find them allowable.")

1. Changes to Specification

If you're going to make any changes to the specification, provide the heading "SPECIFICATION:" on a new page after the sentence printed on Form 13-1. Then indicate the specific paragraphs (or sections) in your application that you want to replace and provide replacement paragraphs marked to indicate deletions by ~~strikethroughs~~ and additions by <u>underlining</u>. If you are deleting five characters or fewer, indicate the deletion by double brackets (for example, "[[claim]]") instead of strikethroughs. If you are deleting a short item, such as a number or punctuation mark, it's better to delete and replace extra portions of the text for clarity (for example, "[[lever 4 and bracket 5]] <u>lever 6 and bracket 5</u>"). See the second page of the sample amendment below. (You may refer to paragraphs to be replaced by number; for example, "Paragraph [0005]," if you numbered the paragraphs when you filed the application.)

When your amendment is received, the clerk of the examining group will make each change on the official copy of your application in the manner you direct, so make sure there's no ambiguity in your amendments.

Be sure that your amendments to the specification don't contain any "new matter."

If you want to make a large number of amendments to the specification, it's better to submit an entirely retyped specification, called a "substitute specification." To file a substitute specification you must submit an entirely new specification with the changes made in clean copy form, plus a comparison specification with each change highlighted so the examiner can verify that you haven't added any new matter. Many word processing programs will compare the original and revised specifications and generate a suitable comparison specification easily.

Also, you must certify that the substitute specification doesn't contain any new matter (see MPEP 608.01(q) for instructions).

2. Amendments to Claims

If you want to amend your claims, start on a new page with the following heading and text:

CLAIMS: Please amend the claims according to the status designations in the following list, which contains all claims that were ever in the application, with the text of all active claims.

The number and status of each claim that is now or was ever in the application must be indicated by providing one of the seven parenthetical expressions, below, after the claim number. (We've indicated the meaning of each parenthetical expression.)

A. (ORIGINAL) The claim has the same number and content as originally filed.

B. (CURRENTLY AMENDED) The claim has the same number as originally or later filed, but is marked up to make amendments (<u>additions</u> and ~~deletions~~) to it.

C. (PREVIOUSLY PRESENTED) The claim was previously amended in marked-up form. It is now typed in clean copy form with the same number as before.

D. (CANCELED) The claim has been or is currently being canceled. Its text is not typed here.

E. (WITHDRAWN) The claim is directed to a nonelected invention, so it is no longer active but since it is still pending it must be typed. (It may be submitted in a divisional application.)

F. (NEW) The claim is new and is typed with a new number.

G. (NOT ENTERED) The claim was previously submitted but the examiner refused to enter it.

You must list all claims in numerical order, regardless of what action you're taking with them; you may not group all deleted claims together unless they're consecutive. (See the example below.)

For canceled and not entered claims, you should provide only the number and status, but not the claim's text. You should provide the number, status, and claim text for every active (currently under examination) claim. (Your word processing program's "Copy" function allows rapid entry.)

You must present the text of all active claims in clean copy form, except for claims that are being currently amended; use the CURRENTLY AMENDED format for the latter.

Which format should you use to amend claims—CURRENTLY AMENDED or NEW?

I recommend that you use the CURRENTLY AMENDED (marked-up) format if you are making minor changes only to the claim, and/or if you want to point out to the examiner just how you're amending the claim. Use ~~strikethroughs~~ to show deletions and <u>underlining</u> to show additions—the same as for specification amendments. As with specification amendments, if you are deleting five characters or fewer, indicate the deletion by double brackets (for example, "[[lever]]") instead of strikethroughs. If you are deleting a short item, such as a number or punctuation mark, it's better to delete and replace extra portions of the text for clarity (for example, "[lever 4 and bracket 5] <u>lever 6 and bracket 5</u>").

If you are making any major changes to the claim or prefer to present it in clean copy form, as we usually do and as is done in all foreign countries, we recommend that you use the NEW format: Type the status expression (CANCELED) after the number of the old claim or claims that you're replacing and retype the claim with a new number (use the next highest number) followed by the status expression (NEW), followed in turn by the text of the claim in clean copy form. Include all the changes that you care to make.

Don't forget to re-present all other active claims (those that you're not currently amending) in clean copy form with their statuses indicated. If you cancel a claim that has dependent claims, be sure to change the dependency of the dependent claims so that they don't refer to the canceled claim.

Here's an example of a claim listing for an amendment.

CLAIMS: Please amend the claims according to the status designations in the following list, which contains all claims that were ever in the application, with the text of all active claims.

1–5 (CANCELED)
6. (ORIGINAL) A bucket made of nylon.
7. (WITHDRAWN) A bucket with a carrying strap.

8. (PREVIOUSLY PRESENTED) A bucket with a handle.
9. (CANCELED)
10. (CURRENTLY AMENDED) A bucket with a <u>blue</u> green handle and a round and oval bottom.
11. (WITHDRAWN) A bucket with a bottom hole.
12. (CANCELED)
13. (NEW) A bucket with sides and a bottom that are both made of plastic.

F. Drafting the Remarks

Next, add the "remarks" portion of your amendment, starting on a new page. The general rules for drafting remarks stated below may seem strange, but they're the customary practice, and deviating from them could make the examiner uncomfortable and more likely to take a negative attitude toward your invention.

1. General Rules for Drafting Remarks

Rule 1: Never admit that any prior art anticipates or renders any part of your invention obvious. Similarly, never diminish your invention or any part of it. Also, never state that your invention is limited in any way—that is, don't state anything that an adversary could use against you in a legal dispute.

Rule 2: Never get personal with the examiner. Your response is formally directed to the Director of the Patent Office, not to the examiner personally. If you must refer to the examiner, always use the third person. For example, never state "You rejected…"; instead, state "The Examiner [note the capitalization] has rejected…." Better yet, state "The Office Action rejects…" or "Claim 1 was rejected…." Never, never address the examiner by name (do list the examiner's name in the caption), and never make your amendment a "Dear [Examiner's Name]" letter. (See the sample amendment of Fig. 13E, above, for how it's done.)

Rule 3: If there's an error in the OA, refer to the error in the OA, and don't state that the examiner made the error. Even if you find the examiner made a blatant error, just deal with it in a very formal way, keep emotions and personalities out of your response, and don't invalidate the examiner. It's okay to respectfully challenge an examiner who you feel is wrong. For example, "If this rejection is repeated, applicant respectfully requests that the examiner explain where, in the references themselves, or in the art, there is a suggestion that they be combined."

Rule 4: When referring to yourself, always refer to yourself in the third person as "Applicant" and never as "I."

Rule 5: Stick to the issues in your remarks. Stay on point and don't discuss personalities or irrelevant issues. Never antagonize the examiner, no matter how much you'd like to. It's improper, and, if you turn the examiner against you, it can considerably narrow the scope of claims that are ultimately allowed.

Rule 6: Use only the legally relevant, logical arguments that are listed in Fig. 13D. Don't use arguments that, although plausible, aren't legally relevant or logical. Among these "don'ts" are stating: (1) stating that your invention is superior to a prior patented device (§ 103) without first stating that your claims recite novel hardware (or method steps) over the prior patent (§ 102); (2) that a cited patent shouldn't have been granted or has less novelty than yours (the PTO isn't bound to repeat its past mistakes); (3) that you have a Ph.D. and spent a lot of ingenuity to come up with the invention (the qualifications of the inventor and the amount of time it took to come up with an invention are irrelevant); (4) that you put your heart and soul and years of effort into the invention (again irrelevant); (5) that the apparatus of the reference as shown in its drawings or claims is different from yours (only the differences of your claims over the reference's specification and drawings are relevant). Also, some inventors have actually telephoned the patentee-inventor of a cited patent. This is a futile exercise, since there's nothing a patentee can do to help you; a patent speaks for itself. As a further example, if the examiner says pages 11 and 12 of your specification don't provide a clear description of the invention, tell why these pages do the job; don't simply explain how it works without reference to these pages.

Rule 7: Whenever you write any new claims or make any additions to a present claim, you must tell why the claim was amended and how the amendments distinguish over the prior art the examiner has cited under 35 U.S.C. Sections 102 and 103. Follow Inventor's Commandment 7 from Chapter 5, repeated below, and 37 CFR 1.111(b) and (c):

Inventor's Commandment 7

To evaluate or argue the patentability of any invention, use a two-step process. First determine what novel features (§ 102) the invention has over the closest prior-art reference(s). Novelty can be a new physical (hardware) feature, a new combination or rearrangement of two separate old features, or a new use of an old feature. Second, determine if the novelty produces any new and unexpected results or otherwise indicates nonobviousness (§ 103).

---

37 CFR 1.111(b) In order to be entitled to reconsideration or further examination, the applicant or patent owner must reply to the Office Action. The reply by the applicant or patent owner must be reduced to a writing which distinctly and specifically points out the supposed errors in the examiner's action and must reply to every ground of objection and rejection in the prior Office Action. The reply must present arguments pointing out the specific distinctions believed to render the claims, including any newly presented claims, patentable over any applied references. If the reply is with respect to an application, a request may be made that objections or requirements as to form not necessary to further consideration of the claims be held in abeyance until allowable subject matter is indicated. The applicant's or patent owner's reply must appear throughout to be a bona fide attempt to advance the application or the reexamination proceeding to final action. A general allegation that the claims define a patentable invention without specifically pointing out how the language of the claims patentably distinguishes them from the references does not comply with the requirements of this section.

37 CFR 1.111(c) In amending in reply to a rejection of claims in an application or patent under reexamination, the applicant or patent owner must clearly point out the patentable novelty which he or she thinks the claims present in view of the state of the art disclosed by the references cited or the objections made. The applicant or patent owner must also show how the amendments avoid such references or objections.

Rule 8: If you do disagree and think the OA was wrong, you must state exactly why you disagree. If you agree that a claim is obvious over the prior art, don't admit this in your response; simply cancel the claim and don't give any reason for it, or if you must comment, state merely that it has been canceled in view of the coverage afforded by the remaining claims. However, if you amend any claim be sure to state why you are amending it to preserve your rights to use the Doctrine of Equivalents later.

Rule 9: Make a careful, complete, and convincing presentation, but don't agonize about words or minutiae. The reality is that many examiners skim through your remarks very rapidly, or don't read them at all. This is because they're generally working under a quota system, which means they have to dispose of (finally reject or allow) a certain number of cases in each fiscal quarter. That means the examiners are under time pressure, and reading remarks takes time. It's important to cover all the substantive points in the Office Action and to deal with every objection and rejection. If you do make an error, as stated, the PTO will almost always give you an opportunity to correct it, rather than forcing you to abandon your application.

Two good ways to make sure your examiner reads and (hopefully) understands your points and reasons are to liberally sprinkle your amendment with boldfaced "arguing" headings that themselves tell your whole story (as is done in the sample amendment of Fig. 13E), and to keep your paragraphs short and inviting. For example, some arguing headings might be, "Briskin Does Not Show Any Elongated Lever," "Claim 1 Clearly Defines Over Warner Under Section 102," "Ihara Could Not Be Operatively

Combined With Harolde," and "Applicant's Rasterizer Produces New and Unexpected Results Over Hearsh."

Rule 10: If possible, thank or praise the examiner if you can find a reason to do so with sincerity—for example, "Applicant thanks the Examiner for the clear and understandable Office Action." Examiners get criticized so often that they'll welcome any genuine, deserved praise.

Rule 11: Don't emphasize your beliefs; they're considered irrelevant. For example, don't say "Applicant *believes* this invention is patentable." Rather say, "Since the claims define novel structure that produces new and unexpected results as described above, Applicant *submits* that such claims are clearly patentable."

Rule 12: Although it's okay to state *briefly* why your invention is superior to that of the reference(s), the main thrust of your position should be a two-part legal argument that tells (a) how your invention, as claimed, differs from the reference(s), and (b) why these differences are important. Again, see Inventor's Commandment 7 above.

TIP

You may wonder whether it makes sense to put much effort into your remarks even though the chances are great they won't be carefully read. Our opinion is that it does make sense, because you never know. Think of your effort as a kind of insurance against being the one in five (or whatever) whose remarks are in fact subjected to close scrutiny.

Although it's difficult, we recommend you do the best job possible in your first response (which you might call Response A), since it will probably be the last chance you get to amend your claims in this application. This advice is so important and goes unheeded so often, we've made it Inventor's Commandment 28, at the beginning of this chapter. After you draft your response, we suggest that you wait a few days and come back and review it again, pretending that you're the examiner. This will probably give you important insights and enable you to improve it further.

2. How to Draft Your Remarks

Your remarks should first provide a brief positive summary of what you've done to the specification and claims. For example, you can start off with a summary such as: "Applicant has amended the specification and claims to put this application in full and clear condition for allowance. She has amended the specification editorially and to correct those errors noted by the Examiner. Also she has rewritten claims 1 to 5 as new Claims 13 to 18 to more particularly define the invention in a patentable manner over the cited prior art." Then briefly summarize what each claim recites, as is done in Fig. 13E, above. If the drawing has been objected to, you must submit a corrected drawing, because objections to drawings will not normally be held in abeyance. If you want to make a voluntary amendment to the drawing, refer to the drawing amendment explanation on page one of the amendment, include a drawing amendment on a separate drawing amendment page, and attached replacement sheets and a red-marked sheet indicating the changes, if necessary. Then include a separate section for each rejection in the amendment.

a. Restate First Rejection

After providing a positive heading for the first rejection of the OA (for example, "The New Claims Overcome the Rejection on Jones and Smith"), restate this rejection. For example, "The Office Action rejected Claims 1 to 5 as unpatentable over Jones in view of Smith." This hopefully saves the examiner, the time it would take to reread the OA.

b. Review Each Reference Relied on in the Rejection

One or two sentences for each is sufficient. For example: "Reference A (Smith patent 1,234,567) shows a ... [and so forth]."

c. Specifically Describe Any Claim Changes and Argue Section 102 and Then Section 103

Discuss specifically how and why the claim in question has been amended and how it recites structure that physically distinguishes over each reference under Section 102. The flowchart of Fig. 13C gives the specifics as to how to do that. For example, "Claim 1, now rewritten as new Claim 5, recites...." "This language distinguishes over Smith and Jones under Section 102 because Smith does not show [etc.] and Jones does not show [etc]."

If the examiner rejected a claim on one or more references individually under Section 102, the examiner is stating that the claim doesn't recite any novel feature(s) over any of these references. If the examiner rejected a claim on one reference under Section 103, the examiner is stating that the claim recites a novel feature(s) over the reference but the examiner doesn't consider the novel feature(s) significant enough to be patentable. If the examiner rejected a claim on a combination of two or more references under Section 103, the examiner is stating neither reference shows all of the features of the claim but the combination of references does. To argue against such a combination, state—if accurate—that (1) the references can't be legally combined because (a) there is no reason in the references themselves or in the art to combine them, and that (b) the combination would not be operable, and (2) even if they were to be combined the claim would recite novel features over the combination and these are nonobvious. Don't state that the novel features of the claims define over the combination under Section 102 since Section 102 only applies to a rejection on a single reference.

Then, once you've established the novelty of your claim(s), show why the novel features are nonobvious and patentable—for example, "These distinctions are submitted to be of patentable merit under Section 103 because [discuss new results that flow from your novel structure, giving as many reasons as you can from Fig. 13D, Part I, and your completed Form 4-2]."

Even if an independent claim was rejected under Section 102 (lack of novelty) over a single reference, you should consider whether the examiner might consider the claim to be obvious over the same art under Section 103, and if so, address that as well as Section 102, as follows: (1) rebut the Section 102 rejection by showing that the claim contains novelty over the single reference, and (2) cover Section 103 (obviousness) by describing how the novel feature(s) are also nonobvious (produce new and unexpected results) over the single reference.

Even if you show that that the independent claim is novel and nonobvious over the single reference, be aware that the independent claim may also be unpatentable over a combination of the single (main) reference with any pertinent secondary references. This is because, even though the independent claim is novel and nonobvious over a single reference, it might be obvious to combine the main reference with a pertinent secondary reference. So review all of the other cited references to be sure that no valid combination of the main reference and a pertinent secondary reference shows all the features of the independent claim. If you do find a pertinent secondary reference, you should also argue patentability over the combination of references (if warranted) to head off any future rejection on such combination. You may want to add a new dependent claim, to bolster your chances of getting a claim allowed over the secondary reference.

Once you argue the patentability of the independent claim over the single reference and any combination of the single reference with any pertinent secondary reference(s), you don't need to argue the patentability of any claims that are dependent on this independent claim because they are narrower than the independent claim and thus are *a fortiori* (by stronger reason) patentable. You only need to state that dependent claims y-z are dependent upon claim x and thus incorporate all the limitations of claim x and include further limitations and thus are *a fortiori* patentable. However, if any dependent claim contains a significant additional limitation, you can state that it is independently patentable and state the reasons.

You should discuss how your invention, as claimed, distinguishes over—that is, has novel physical features not shown in—the reference, not how the reference differs from your invention, and not, at this stage, why your invention is better than the reference. Remember that under 35 U.S.C. Section 112(f), a means plus a function is considered a physical recitation.

Use a 102/103 Approach

You must use a 102/103 approach even if your claim was rejected on Section 102 alone. This 102/103 approach is useful if you don't understand the examiner's reasoning. That is, rather than trying to figure out what the examiner was trying to say, or questioning the examiner, just present a detailed, cogent 102/103 argument. This will usually win the day, or at worst, reframe the issues in your favor.

The following jingle may help you remember this important rule:

> *"Never argue what's not in your claim*
> *You'll miss the mark and may lose the game."*

Also, be logical in your arguments. For example, if you're claiming B and a reference shows A and B, don't argue that A is no good. Also, don't argue that a reference should be taken lightly—that is, it's a "paper patent," because its invention was never put into commercial use—unless you're absolutely sure of your facts and the reference isn't a dead ringer for your invention.

d. Refute Any Improper Combination of References

If a combination of several references has been cited against your claim, first state why the combination cannot properly be made and then discuss your distinctions under 35 U.S.C. Section 103. MPEP 2142 and 2143 require that, in order for two references to be combined in a rejection, the examiner must establish a prima facie (at first sight) case for obviousness. Below are relevant excerpts from MPEP 2142:

> *The legal concept of prima facie obviousness is a procedural tool of examination which applies broadly to all arts. It allocates who has the burden of going forward with production of evidence in each step of the examination process.*

To reach a proper determination under 35 U.S.C. Section 103, the examiner must step backward in time and into the shoes worn by the hypothetical "person of ordinary skill in the art" when the invention was unknown and just before it was made. In view of all factual information, the examiner must then make a determination whether the claimed invention "as a whole" would have been obvious at that time to that person. Knowledge of the applicant's disclosure must be put aside in reaching this determination, yet kept in mind in order to determine the "differences," conduct the search, and evaluate the "subject matter as a whole" of the invention. The tendency to resort to "hindsight" based upon the applicant's disclosure is often difficult to avoid due to the very nature of the examination process. However, impermissible hindsight must be avoided and the legal conclusion must be reached on the basis of the facts gleaned from the prior art.

The key to supporting any rejection under 35 U.S.C. 103 is the clear articulation of the reason(s) why the claimed invention would have been obvious. The Supreme Court in KSR International Co. v. Teleflex Inc., *550 U.S. 39, 82USPQ2d 1385, 1396 (2007) noted that the analysis supporting a rejection under 35 U.S.C. 103 should be made explicit. The Federal Circuit has stated that 'rejections on obviousness cannot be sustained with mere conclusory statements; instead, there must be some articulated reasoning with some rational underpinning to support the legal conclusion of obviousness.'*

If you feel that the examiner has not set forth a prima facie case, make your case tactfully. For example, *"Applicant submits that the rejection of claim 1 on Jones and Smith does not set forth a prima facie case of obviousness, as required by MPEP 2142. This section requires that there must be a clear articulation of the reason(s) why the claimed invention would have been obvious. Applicant submits that the rejection does not meet this requirement because the rejection gives a mere conclusory statement that the combination would be obvious. Note that neither Smith nor Jones suggests such a combination, and one skilled in the art would*

have no reason to make such a combination. That is, the fact that Smith shows a specific lever does not suggest that his lever can be used with Jones's pedal mechanism, especially since Jones shows his own workable lever. Further the references are from a different field than that of applicant's invention [explain why] *and/or they are not directed to solving the same problem as applicant's invention solves* [explain why].

Moreover, applicant submits that the rejection is improper because the combination could not be made physically since the lever of the Smith type would not fit in or work with Jones's pedal mechanism because.... Also the references are not combinable because their intended function would be destroyed if one attempted to combine them [explain why].

Finally, applicant submits that the rejection is improper because, even if the combination could be legally made, the combination does not show [here quote novel language of claim]. *Applicant submits that these distinctions are patentable under Section 103 because* [discuss new results and give as many reasons as you can from Fig. 13D and Form 4-2]."

If the references themselves don't suggest that they should be combined (Reasons 29–33 in Fig. 13D), and there is no reason in the art to combine them, you can use the arguments in MPEP 2142 and 2143. In our experience most rejections do not articulate any clear reasons to support a combination rejection and these MPEP sections provide powerful arguments.

e. Note Secondary Factors of Nonobviousness

If your invention has achieved any commercial success or has won any praise, this is relevant, and you should mention it here. If possible, submit copies of advertisements for your invention, copies of industry or trade praise, sales figures, a commercially sold sample, and so on. These things reify the invention (that is, make it a "fait accompli") and impress most examiners. If you are submitting any evidence of commercial success, do it with a declaration with attached exhibits stating how the invention has achieved commercial success and how such success is related to the novel features of the invention. (See the next section for the format (not the substance) of such a declaration.)

Checklist for Sending In a Regular Amendment

Before you mail your amendment, please check the following list carefully to be sure that the amendment is complete and properly done.

- ☐ You have responded to each point in the OA.

- ☐ You have responded to any needed drawing objection.

- ☐ You have re-proofed the specification and have made any needed corrections.

- ☐ You have amended the prior-art portion of the specification to account for any significant new prior art (optional).

- ☐ You have not included any new matter in any amendments to the specification.

- ☐ You have checked all new claims against the checklist in Chapter 9.

- ☐ All claims recite structure that is physically different from every cited reference (Section 102).

- ☐ You have presented the amendment in the prescribed format: (a) a list of contents is on page 1, (b) the Specification and Drawing Amendments (if any) start on respective new pages, (c) the Claim Amendments (if any) start on a new page, (d) the Remarks start on a new page, (e) the specification is amended by replacing whole paragraphs with words to be deleted struck through and words to be added underlined, (f) all claims that were ever in the application are listed in numerical order, (g) the number of every claim is followed by one of the seven required parenthetical expressions (Original, Currently Amended, Previously Presented, Canceled, Withdrawn, New, and Not Entered), (h) for Canceled and Withdrawn claims, only the claim number without the text is provided, and (i) for claims in the Currently Amended format, words to be deleted are struck through and words to be added are underlined.

- ☐ The physically different structure in every claim is sufficiently different to produce new and unexpected results or otherwise be considered nonobvious (Section 103).

- ☐ The application includes several very narrow dependent claims with a variety of phraseologies so that you won't have to present them for the first time if the next action is made final.

- ☐ The wording in the remarks is clear, grammatically correct, and understandable.

- ☐ The remarks are written in short paragraphs with ample "arguing" headings.

- ☐ Every embodiment covered in your claims (originally and as amended) is described in the specification and shown in the drawings.

- ☐ The patentability of all new claims is argued with respect to the references, using a two-part approach: (a) The claim has physical distinctions over the references under Section 102; (b) The claimed physical distinctions produce new and unexpected results or are otherwise nonobvious under Section 103.

- ☐ You have included all possible arguments for nonobviousness (Fig. 13D).

- ☐ A request for claim-drafting assistance under MPEP 707.07(j) has been made, if desirable.

- ☐ The amendment is 1.5- or double-line-spaced with an ample top margin for punching mounting holes.

- ☐ The last page of the amendment includes your name, address, and phone number.

- ☐ If the amendment will cause the case to have more than 20 total or more than three independent claims, the proper additional fee is included (if not previously paid).

- ☐ The amendment is signed and dated (no pencil) by all applicants.

- ☐ An identical file copy of the amendment has been made if you are mailing the amendment.

- ☐ The amendment is being transmitted on time or includes a properly completed Petition to Extend with the proper fee included.

- ☐ A Certificate of Faxing or Mailing is typed in the amendment unless it's being filed electronically.

- ☐ All pages are complete and present.

- ☐ A receipt postcard is attached to the amendment, if you are mailing it.

- ☐ If mailing, the envelope is properly stamped and addressed to "Mail Stop Non-Fee Amendments, Commissioner for Patents, P.O. Box 1450, Alexandria, VA 22313-1450." If you are sending any money with your amendment, omit "Non-Fee Amendments." If you're faxing the amendment, make sure you feed your pages carefully.

f. Draft Any Needed Declaration Under 37 CFR 132 to Refute Technical Points Raised by Examiner

If you want to challenge any technical points raised by the examiner, such as proving that your invention works in a superior manner to a reference, that two references can't be combined, or that a cited reference works in a far inferior way to yours, you or an expert in the field should do the necessary research and make the necessary tests (including building and testing a model of the cited reference) and then submit a "Declaration Under Rule 132." The Declaration should have a caption as in Form 13-1 and an appropriate heading, such as "Rule 132 Declaration Regarding Inferior Performance of Elias Patent." The body of the Declaration should start,

> *Jane Inventor declares as follows:*
>
> *I am the inventor [or I am a mechanical engineer (state education, experience, and awards)] in the above patent application.*

Then, in numbered paragraphs, detail your technical facts and/or reasons, including tests you made, but state facts, not conclusions or arguments. Whenever you make any legal declaration or affidavit (as opposed to a brief or remarks), heed the words of the immortal Joe Friday, of television's *Dragnet* fame: "Just the facts, ma'am." You can attach and refer to "exhibits"—that is, documents in support of your arguments.

Then conclude with a "declaration paragraph," as in the last paragraph of Form 10-1 (that states "I hereby declare...") and sign and date the declaration.

Similarly, if you want to mention any additional factors relating to your invention, such as commercial success or copying by an infringer, which are relevant to patentability, you can submit a similar Rule 132 declaration. You can attach relevant "Exhibits," such as a prototype, a commercial sample, advertising, or sales reports. As stated, working models usually make believers out of negative examiners.

g. Request Reconsideration

Request reconsideration of the rejection(s) and allowance of the claim: "Therefore applicant submits that Claim 5 is allowable over the cited references and solicits reconsideration and allowance."

If you have dependent claims that were rejected, treat these in the same manner. Since a dependent claim incorporates all the limitations of the parent claim, you can state that the dependent claim is patentable for the same reasons given with respect to the parent claim, and then state that it is even more patentable because it adds additional limitations, which you should discuss briefly. If a dependent claim is independently patentable—that is, its added limitations are independently patentable—state this and explain why.

h. Respond to Rejections Under 35 U.S.C. Section 112 for Lack of Clarity or Conciseness

If a technical rejection has been made (under Section 112), discuss how you've amended your claim and why your new claim is clear and understandable. Often an examiner will reject, for indefiniteness, a claim that you feel is clear and unambiguous. Even if we disagree with the examiner we always try to fix the claim in a way that will overcome the examiner's rejection because this is always easier than arguing with the examiner and risking the uncertainty of another rejection. If you can't figure out how to fix the claim you can call the examiner and ask for a suggestion. Sometimes a claim may seem perfectly clear and not amenable to any improvement. In this case you can point out to the examiner that the Court of Appeals for the Federal Circuit has stated that the definiteness requirement of Section 112 "is satisfied if a person skilled in the field of the invention would reasonably understand the claim when read in the context of the specification."

i. Request Claim-Drafting Assistance From PTO

Once again, we emphasize that if you feel you have patentable subject matter in your application but have difficulty in writing new claims, you can request that the examiner write new claims for you pursuant to MPEP 707.07(j). Your remarks are the place to do this. For example, state, "Therefore Applicant submits that patentable subject matter is clearly present. If the Examiner agrees but does not feel that the present claims are technically adequate, applicant respectfully requests that the examiner write acceptable claims pursuant to MPEP 707.07(j)." If the examiner writes any claims for you, don't rest on them unless you're sure that the broadest one is as broad as the prior art permits, or at least broad enough to prevent competitors from copying your product, using the criteria above and in Chapter 5. Remember, if you are dissatisfied with the examiner's claims, you can once again submit your own claims, or submit the examiner's claims with whatever amendments you choose, or interview the examiner to discuss the matter. You should request claim drafting assistance when you file, or after the first OA, not after a final OA.

j. Repeat the Above for Any Other Rejections in the Office Action

After you've covered and hopefully decimated the first rejection as discussed in Subsections a to i, above, it's time to do the same for each additional rejection—that is, provide a separate heading for the rejection, review the rejection, review the reference(s), review your new claims, discuss why they are novel under Section 102, then why the novel features are patentable under Section 103, and request reconsideration and allowance.

k. Discuss Nonapplied References

If any references of interest have been cited but not applied against any claim, read these to be sure they are less relevant than the applied references. If they are less relevant, state that you've reviewed them but that they don't show your invention or render it obvious. If any reference is more relevant or you think it might be used against you later, be sure your claims define your invention in a patentable manner over it and lightly explain the differences between that art and your claims.

l. Acknowledge Allowed or Allowable Claims

Often the examiner will allow some claims, or indicate that certain claims would be allowed if amended in a certain way or rewritten in independent form. You should acknowledge this statement and if necessary, tell how you handled it—for example,

"Applicant acknowledges the allowance of Claims 1 to 7 with appreciation," or "Applicant has rewritten Claim 13 (indicated to contain allowable subject matter) in independent form as new Claim 26."

m. Conclusion

Last, provide a conclusion that should repeat and summarize—for example, *"For all the reasons given above, applicant respectfully submits that the errors in the specification are corrected, the claims comply with Section 112, the claims define over the prior art under Section 102* [briefly repeat why], *and the claimed distinctions are of patentable merit under Section 103 because of the new results provided* [repeat them briefly again]. *Accordingly, applicant submits that this application is now in full condition for allowance, which action applicant respectfully solicits."* Then add the closing, "Very respectfully," followed by your signature, typed name, your address, and telephone number on the left-hand side. If you have a coinventor(s), all of you must sign the amendment.

n. Do Your Very Best Job

It's important to do your very best job in your first amendment, since it's the only full opportunity you'll get to answer the examiner's position. We suggest that after writing the amendment, you have a friend or coinventor read it or you come back to it after a few days and read it from the viewpoint of your examiner. Make sure your amendment in response to the first OA is complete, carefully crafted, and includes all arguments and the narrowest claims possible, since the next OA will be final.

G. Drawing Amendments

If your Office Action includes any objections to the drawing(s), you must correct these in your response. The replacement sheet should include a notation in the top margin reading, "Replacement Sheet, Appl. No. __/." Fill in your application number and be sure that the replacement sheet includes the correct sheet number below the top margin—that is, "1/2" for sheet 1 of 2 total drawing sheets. A replacement sheet must include all of the figures that were on the sheet that it is replacing. In other words, if you are replacing a sheet that originally included Fig. 1 and Fig. 2, the replacement sheet must also include Fig. 1 and Fig. 2, even if only one of those figures is being amended.

A common drawing objection, made under 37 CFR 1. 83(a), is that the drawing doesn't show every feature recited in the claims. For example, suppose your original claim was directed to a hose having an atomizer head and your drawing shows only a hose with a sprinkler head. How can you add an atomizer head to the drawing to remedy this objection without showing details of the atomizer, which would violate the rule against adding new matter to your application? Easy: just add a legend or label adjacent to the end of the plain hose reading, "Can be atomizer." This will not add any new matter since it's no more specific than the claim, which already recites an atomizer.

To deal with any drawing objections by the examiner or the OPAP, first include or check the listing paragraph on page 1 (contents page) of your amendment as follows:

"DRAWINGS: A statement explaining the drawing amendments made by this amendment begins on page *[state page]* of this amendment; or text to that effect."

Then, on the appropriate DRAWINGS page of the amendment, state that you have attached a replacement sheet with the drawing objections corrected. Although not necessary, we prefer to refer briefly to the corrected sheets at the beginning of the Remarks. To make the corrections correct your Bristol board or Mylar film originals, or make new CAD originals, and file new, good xerographic (or CAD output) copies. All lines must be crisp, black, and sharp, and all objections on the drawing objection sheet must be corrected.

List the sheets as an enclosure at the end of the amendment and attach new (corrected) sheets to the amendment for substitution for your original drawings. (If filing by mail, attach the new drawing sheets with a paper clip—do not staple them.) In the top margin of each replacement sheet, write "Replacement Sheet" and add your name, Serial Number, and Examination Group.

If *you* find any errors in your drawings, you should voluntarily make any necessary (nonrequired) amendments or corrections. The PTO used to require advance approval, but now you may go right ahead and file replacement sheets. If the examiner or the PTO's drawing checkers disapprove of the changes they will notify you.

Make the changes and attach new, good copies of the changes sheets. List the sheets as an enclosure at the end of the amendment and attach red-marked sheets and new (corrected) sheets to the amendment for substitution for your original drawings.

If you want to send any replacement drawing sheets separately from an amendment, or with your issue fee transmittal form, use Form 13-1. Check the box on this form if you are also including a copy of any sheets marked in red to indicate any changes.

Remember that the PTO prohibits the addition of any new matter to the drawings. However, you may correct obvious errors, such as a reversed diode, a missing reference numeral, or a missing line. We recommend that you keep a file copy of every version of every drawing sheet in case you ever have to refer to any sheet before changes.

H. Typing and Filing the Amendment

The amendment should be typed with 1.5- or double-line-spacing on letter-size or A4 paper with 1-inch top and 1-inch left, right, and bottom margins. The PTO prefers that you file the amendment by Patent Center (so it won't have to scan it into its computers). Less preferred is that you fax the amendment, and last, you may mail the amendment. In the last two cases—fax and mail—don't forget to keep an identical copy of your amendment in your file. If you mail the amendment, be sure to attach a receipt postcard addressed to you (postage paid) with a full identification of the amendment on the back. The PTO won't return any paper you send them, although they will make a copy of any paper or record for the per-sheet photocopy charge in the Fee Schedule. If you mail it, don't forget the postcard. The signatures of all inventors must be on the copy you send to the PTO.

If you file the amendment by Patent Center, the online forms will provide a transmittal for the amendment.

However, if you file the amendment on paper (by fax or by mail) no transmittal letter is needed. If your amendment increases the number of claims above what you originally paid for when you filed the application, you have to pay for the extra claims. It's helpful (but not necessary) to attach a completed Form SB/06 to calculate the extra fee.

Documents With Copies of Signatures Now Okay

The PTO now accepts documents that contain a copy of any required signature, provided you retain a copy of the document with an original signature, in case it's ever needed. (Original signatures are required only on (a) documents involving the registration of an attorney or agent and (b) certified copies.)

If you intend to mail or fax your amendment, after your signature, add a "Certificate of Facsimile Transmission" (preferable) or a "Certificate of Mailing" as required by 37 CFR 1.8 (don't use Priority Mail Express as it isn't necessary and the cost is high) as follows.

Certificate of Facsimile Transmission

I certify that on the date below I will fax this communication, and attachments if any, to Group _____ of the Patent and Trademark Office at the following number: 571-273-8300.

Date: _____

Inventor's Signature: _____

Certificate of Mailing

I hereby certify that this correspondence, and attachments, if any, will be deposited with the U.S. Postal Service by First-Class Mail, postage prepaid, in an envelope addressed to Mail Stop "Non-Fee Amendments, Commissioner for Patents," P.O. Box 1450, Alexandria, VA 22313-1450" on the date below.

Date: _____

Inventor's Signature: _____

While all inventors must sign the amendment, only one inventor need sign this certification. If you include this certificate, you can fax or mail your amendment even at 23:59 on the last day of your response period. Even if you're mailing the amendment two months ahead of time you should use the Certificate anyway, since if the amendment is lost in the mail, causing your application technically to go abandoned, you can get it revived easily by filing a declaration stating the full facts and enclosing a photocopy of the amendment with the Certificate of Mailing—see 37 CFR 1.8(b). If you use mail, don't forget to attach a postcard to your amendment reading as in Fig. 13F. If you fax the amendment, and your fax machine is programmed to transmit your fax number, the PTO will send an immediate faxback receipt.

Amendment A (5 pages) plus amended and red-marked copies of sheet 2/4 of drawings in Application of John A. Novel, Ser. Nr. 999,999, filed 20xx January 9, received today:

Fig. 13F—Back of Receipt Postcard for Amendment

> ### Draft Amendments May Be Faxed or Emailed for Discussion
>
> Applicants may now send a proposed amendment for discussion to "sound out" and negotiate with the examiner. Mark the amendment "DRAFT" or "PROPOSED AMENDMENT," do not sign it, and fax it or email it to the examiner. Then call the examiner in a few days to discuss the amendment by phone or visit the examiner personally. You still must file a regular, signed amendment by the due date to avoid abandonment.

Make sure your amendment won't cause the total number of claims of your application to exceed 20, or the number of independent claims to exceed three (unless you've paid for excess claims when you filed the application). Otherwise, you'll have to pay an additional claims fee (expensive and usually not advisable, since three independent and 20 total claims should be more than adequate).

I. If Your Application Is Allowable

Hopefully, your first amendment will do the trick and the examiner will decide to allow the case. If so, you'll often be sent a Notice of Allowability and/or a formal Notice of Allowance (N/A), the latter accompanied by an issue fee transmittal form. You have a statutory period of three months to pay the issue fee; the three-month period is not extendable and the forms are self-explanatory. You can fax or electronically transmit the issue fee transmittal form, but if you mail it, be sure to include a receipt postcard. You can also place an advance order for printed copies of your patent (a space is provided on the issue fee transmittal form); the minimum order is ten. However, printed copies aren't necessary as you can download copies from the PTO or any of the many free websites that provide patent copies to the public. Also, be sure to fill in the Certificate of Mailing or Faxing on the Issue Fee Transmittal, unless you file this electronically as an eFiler. If your application was published 18 months after filing you will also have to pay the PTO patent publication fee, although in 2014 the PTO reduced the publication fee to $0. The fee is included on your issue fee transmittal form. The PTO no longer sends a "Notice of Patent Term Adjustment" with your N/A, but now sends it with the notice of the issue date.

Usually the patent term will not be extended, but if the PTO delayed in responding to an amendment or you had to appeal, you will get a commensurate adjustment.

When you receive your N/A, review the application and drawings once again very carefully to make sure everything is correct, logical, grammatical, and so on. If you want to make any amendments at this time, you can still do so, provided they don't affect the substance of the application. Generally, only grammatical changes are permitted after the N/A. The format of the amendment should be similar to that of Fig. 13E, except that the first sentence should read, "Pursuant to 37 CFR 1.312, applicant respectfully requests that the above application be amended as follows:"

Then make any amendments to your specification and claims in the previously used format. Under "Remarks," discuss the amendments, stating that they are not matters of substance and noting that they will require very little consideration by the examiner.

If you've amended your claims in any substantial way during prosecution, after the Notice of Allowance is received you should also file a Supplemental Declaration (downloadable Form 13-3; see Appendix 7) to indicate that you've invented the subject matter of the claims as amended and that you know of no prior art that would anticipate these claims. Sometimes when a case is allowed the examiner will include a "Reasons for Allowance" section. Review this carefully to be sure the reasons aren't too narrow, since this may adversely affect the scope of your patent. If the reasons are too narrow, submit a rebuttal statement to neutralize the examiner's statement.

Prior to sending in the issue fee, go through the checklist shown below.

Checklist for Paying an Issue Fee

- [ ] You made all needed drawing corrections and enclosed any needed formal drawings.

- [ ] You have made any needed specification or claim amendments (37 CFR 1.312).

- [ ] You have properly completed and signed the issue fee transmittal form.

- [ ] You have filed a completed Supplemental Declaration if you have made any significant claim changes during prosecution.

- [ ] If transmitting by mail, you have enclosed a check or a completed credit card Form PTO-2038 for the issue fee. If transmitting by fax, you used Form PTO-2038.

- [ ] If you are mailing the issue fee, you have attached a receipt postcard, properly stamped and addressed.

- [ ] If transmitting by mail you have completed a certificate of mailing or faxing on the Notice of Allowance.

- [ ] You are transmitting the issue fee papers by the due date (no extensions allowed).

- [ ] If you are mailing the papers you have made a file copy of all issue fee transmittal papers.

Once your issue fee is received, your application goes to the Government Printing Office and no further changes are permitted. However, until the patent issues, you are still under an obligation to disclose any prior art of which you are aware that may be material to patentability of your invention. If you discover additional prior art after payment of the issue fee, you are required to disclose it. Ordinarily, you will be required to file a Request for Continued Examination (RCE) to file an IDS at this late stage. However, the PTO has implemented a program called "Quick Path Information Disclosure Statement" or "QPIDS," that permits you to submit an IDS after payment of the issue fee, with a statement authorizing payment of the fee normally associated with an RCE. If the examiner determines that no item of information in the IDS necessitates reopening prosecution, the USPTO will issue a corrected notice of allowability, and the additional references will be printed on the face of the patent. If the examiner does decide that the new references prevent the claims from being granted, the RCE fee will be charged and you will receive a new OA with rejections based on the newly submitted prior art. If this situation applies to you, more information and the required form SB/09 can be found on the PTO website (uspto.gov/patents/initiatives/quick-path-information-disclosure-statement-qpids).

Four to six weeks after the issue fee is paid, you may receive an Issue Notification Form, which will indicate the number of your patent and the date it will issue, usually a week or so after you receive the receipt.

J. If Your First Amendment Doesn't Result in Allowance

If your first amendment doesn't place the application in condition for allowance, the examiner will usually make the next OA final. However, if the second OA cites any new references, it won't be made final unless the examiner had to dig out the new references to meet some new limitations in your amended claims. If your second OA isn't made final, you should respond to it in the same manner as you responded to the first OA. However, if the second OA is made final—and it usually will be— note the provisions of 37 CFR 1.113 and 1.116, which govern what happens after a final action is sent:

37 CFR 1.113—Final Rejection or Action

(a) On the second or any subsequent examination or consideration by the examiner the rejection or other action may be made final, whereupon applicant's ... reply is limited to appeal in the case of rejection of any claim (§ 41.31 of this title), or to amendment as specified in § 1.114 or § 1.116. Petition may be taken to the Director in the case of objections or requirements not involved in the rejection of any claim (§ 1.181). Reply to a final rejection or action must comply with § 1.114 or paragraph (c) of this section. ...

(b) In making such final rejection, the examiner shall repeat or state all grounds of rejection then considered applicable to the claims in the application, clearly stating the reasons in support thereof.

(c) Reply to a final rejection or action must include cancellation of, or appeal from the rejection of, each rejected claim. If any claim stands allowed, the reply to a final rejection or action must comply with any requirements or objections as to form.

37 CFR 1.116—Amendments After Final Action

(b) After a final … action … in an application …

(1) An amendment may be made canceling claims or complying with any requirement of form expressly set forth in a previous Office Action;

(2) An amendment presenting rejected claims in better form for consideration on appeal may be admitted; or

(3) An amendment touching the merits of the application or patent under reexamination may be admitted upon a showing of good and sufficient reasons why the amendment is necessary and was not earlier presented.

(c) The admission of, or refusal to admit, any amendment after a final … action, … will not operate to relieve the application or reexamination proceeding from its condition as subject to appeal or to save the application from abandonment….

These rules mean, in effect, that "final" isn't final after all. It's just that the rules shift a bit. If you want to continue prosecuting your patent application after a final OA, you must take one of the following actions:

1. Narrow, cancel, or fix the claims *as specified by the examiner.*
2. Negotiate with and convince the examiner to change position.
3. Try a further amendment narrowing the claims. Such a further amendment should not raise any new issues.
4. Appeal to the Patent Trial and Appeal Board (PTAB), together with an optional Pre-Appeal Request for Review.
5. File a continuation application or an RCE (Request for Continued Examination) (see Chapter 14).
6. Petition the PTO Director.
7. Abandon the application.

Let's examine these options in more detail.

1. Comply With Examiner's Requirements

If the examiner indicates that the case will be allowed if you amend the claims in a certain way—for example, if you cancel certain claims or add certain limitations to the claim—and you agree with the examiner's position, submit a complying amendment similar to the previously discussed amendment. However, instead of stating, "Please amend the above application as follows:" (Form 13-1), state "Applicant requests that the above application be amended as follows:" This is because the clerk won't enter any amendments after a final OA unless the examiner authorizes it.

Generally, no other amendments after a final OA are permitted unless you can show very good reasons why they weren't presented earlier. If your amendment changes the claims in the manner required by the examiner to get them allowed, this will clearly entitle it to entry. You should file your complying amendment as soon as possible, since you have to get the case in full condition for allowance within the three-month period, plus any extensions you've bought. If you file an after-final amendment near the end of the three-month period and the examiner agrees that it places the application in condition for allowance, but the period has expired, you'll have to buy an appropriate extension (Form 13-4): A case can't be allowed when it's technically abandoned. If you file an amendment or argument and it doesn't convince the examiner to allow your case, the examiner will send you an "advisory action," telling you why, and the three-month period will continue to run.

2. Convince the Examiner

You can try to convince the examiner to change position, either by written argument, by phone, or in person. Phone and personal interviews are especially effective because of the multiple feedback loops and give-and-take they provide in a short period. Also, it's more difficult to say no when facing someone, as any salesperson will tell you. Try to come to some agreement to get the case allowed. This is often an excellent, effective choice, especially if you have a friendly examiner and you're willing to compromise. Do this as soon as possible so you'll have time to appeal or file a continuation application, if necessary.

3. Amendment After Final Rejection

You can try a further amendment, narrowing your claims, or submitting other claims, provided you raise no new issues. If the examiner agrees that the amendment narrows or changes the claims sufficiently to place the case in condition for allowance, the examiner will authorize its entry and allow the case. Otherwise, the examiner will send you an "advisory action," reiterating the examiner's former position, and you'll still have the opportunity to exercise the other choices. Even if the examiner doesn't want to enter the amendment because it raises new issues, the advisory action will state whether the amendment will be entered for purposes of appeal. The examiner will enter it for appeal if it places the case in better condition for appeal and neither raises any new issues nor requires further search or consideration.

Provide your amendment after final rejection as soon as possible. eFiling is preferable. Fax or/and mail can also be used. One reason for the rush: it may save you some money. Ordinarily, you will have three months to respond to the final OA. If you respond later, you will have to buy an extension. However, if you fle a response within two months of the final OA, then the extension period starts the *later* of the three-month date and the date the examiner sends the advisory action. (MPEP 710.02(e)(I).) The PTO will try to reply to after-final amendments within 45 days, so try to file your response within one month of the final OA to save some of the original three months in case the examiner quickly turns around an advisory action. (In all cases you must respond within six months of the final OA, even if your initial quick turnaround lets you buy a shorter extension.)

If you file by mail, do the following with a red marker on paper or faxed filings: (1) mark the upper right of page 1 of your amendment "RESPONSE UNDER 37 CFR 1.116—EXPEDITED PROCEDURE—EXAMINING GROUP NUMBER [insert number]," (2) address the envelope and the amendment "Box AF, Commr. of Pats... [etc.]," and (3) write "BOX AF" in the lower left of the envelope.

If you do file an amendment after a final OA, you should head it "Amendment Under Rule 116," and request (not direct) that the case be amended as follows to place it in condition for allowance. Also comply with the checklist above.

4. Appeal and Pre-Appeal Request for Review

If you don't see any further way to improve the claims, and if you believe the examiner's position is wrong, you can appeal a final or secondary rejection (not objection) to the PTAB (Patent Trial and Appeal Board), a tribunal of senior examiners (administrative law judges) in the PTO. If the issues are clear, prior to the appeal you can request an appeal conference of senior examiners in your examining division to review the case, hopefully to avoid filing a full brief and sending the case up to the Board.

To appeal, you must file a Notice of Appeal stating that you appeal to the PTAB from the examiner's final action. Filing an appeal is free, but there is a fee for forwarding the appeal to the Board, triggered when the examiner files a response to your brief. If you also want an appeal conference (strongly recommended) the Notice of Appeal should be accompanied with a "Pre-Appeal Brief Request for Review" (Form AIA/33—no extra fee), plus a "succinct, concise, and focused set of arguments" (no more than five pages at 1.5-line spacing) in support of your position. A copy of a Form AIA/33 is downloadable on this book's online companion page (as Form 13-5); see Appendix 7 for details. When providing the five pages of argument, you can condense your last amendment. You do not have to include the claims. The Notice of Appeal, Pre-Appeal Request for Review, and Focused Set of Arguments may be mailed, but the PTO prefers that you eFile them. The PTO prefers that you use this process only where there are clear errors in fact or law and not where the issues are in gray areas, such as interpretations of the prior art or claim scope. A panel of three examiners, including a supervisor and the examiner of record, will review your arguments and issue a decision to either (1) continue the appeal because they agree with the examiner of record, (2) reopen prosecution and propose changes that will place the application in condition for allowance or advise that a further communication from the examiner will follow, (3) allow the application, or (4) dismiss your request because it fails to comply with the submission requirements. If the panel's decision is alternative 1 or alternative 4, you must file the usual brief and fee within one month from the decision or within two months from the date you filed the Notice of Appeal, whichever is longer.

If you made a pre-appeal request for review and the decision was negative, or if you didn't request an appeal conference, file an appeal brief in triplicate if by mail, or a single copy if by fax or electronically, describing your invention and claims in issue and arguing the patentability of your claims. This brief is due within two months after you file your Notice of Appeal (or as stated above if you requested an appeal conference) and must be in a specific format specified by the Rules. Enclose an Appeal Brief fee.

You can request an oral hearing and enclose a further hearing fee (see Appendix 4, "Fee Schedule"). If you want an oral hearing, you'll have to travel to the PTO in Alexandria, Virginia, or ask for a telephone/video conference hearing. As always, include a Certificate of Mailing and postcard or Certificate of Faxing with all correspondence that is mailed or faxed.

For information on how to comply with the appeal procedure and write the brief, see Part 41 of the PTO *Rules of Practice* (37 CFR 41).

After you file an appeal brief, the examiner must file a responsive brief (termed an "Examiner's Answer") to maintain the rejection, and at that point, you will have to pay an appeal fee. To do this, the examiner (and usually two other examiners) must take another

good, hard look at your case. Sometimes this review will change the examiner's mind. More commonly, the examiner will maintain the rejection and file an Examiner's Answer. You may then file a reply brief to respond to the Examiner's Answer. You should then file a reply brief within two months of the Examiner's Answer to respond to the Answer.

If you do have a hearing, you will be allowed 20 minutes for oral argument. Sometimes the examiner attends; if so, 15 minutes will be allowed for the examiner's presentation.

If the Board disagrees with the examiner, it will issue a written decision, generally sending the case back with instructions. If it agrees with the examiner, its decision will state why it believes your invention to be unpatentable. The Board upholds the examiner in about 65% of appeals.

If the Board upholds the examiner and you still believe your invention is patentable, you can take a further appeal within 60 days of the date of the PTAB's decision to the Court of Appeals for the Federal Circuit (CAFC) or file a civil lawsuit against the Director of the PTO in the U.S. District Court for the Eastern District of Virginia. The CAFC is located in Washington, but sometimes sits in local areas. The Virginia District Court is in Alexandria, near the PTO. If the CAFC upholds the PTO, you can ask the U.S. Supreme Court to hear your case, although the Supreme Court rarely hears patent appeals.

Under TRIPS, patents expire 20 years from the filing date of the patent application, but the PTO will extend this term up to five years if delay occurs due to an appeal to the PTAB, the CAFC, or because of an interference. (35 U.S.C. § 154.)

Appeal briefs aren't easy to write, so we suggest consulting a professional if you want to appeal. Inventors that meet certain financial thresholds and other criteria may be eligible for free legal assistance when appearing before the Patent Trial and Appeal Board (PTAB). The PTAB Pro Bono Program matches volunteer patent professionals with financially under-resourced inventors to provide free legal assistance in preparing *ex parte* (one-sided) appeals to the PTAB.

The PTAB Pro Bono Program is administered by the PTAB Bar Association. If you need help appealing your case, and you believe you may qualify on the basis of income (and in particular, the patent application must be certified as having "micro entity status"), then consider visiting the PTAB Bar Association's website for this program (ptabbar.org/ptab_pro_bono.php).

Appealing to Extend Your Patent's Term

If you want to obtain the maximum term possible for your patent, and three years have elapsed since the filing date of your application (or the filing date of any parent applications if it's a divisional or continuation—see Chapter 14), we recommend that you appeal after the second Office Action if the case is still under rejection, even if your second Action is not a final Action. Why? As stated, your patent will expire 20 years from your first filing date, regardless of when your patent issues. However, the PTO must extend this 20-year term (for up to five more years) from the date you file an appeal until the date of a final decision on appeal, except that if any portion of the appeal period occurs within three years of your filing date, this will not be counted in extending the expiration date (Rule 701).

This all means that any time you take to negotiate with the examiner or file another amendment will shorten your patent's term. However, if three years have elapsed after your first filing date, you can avoid this shortening and actually extend your patent's term by filing an appeal and doing any negotiation or filing any amendments while your appeal is pending. If you can't get the examiner to allow the case, just follow through with the appeal by filing a brief and fee within two months after the date you file the notice of appeal. If you do get the examiner to allow the case while it's on appeal, just file a notice withdrawing the appeal; your patent's term will be extended for the time your appeal was active.

---

5. File a Continuation Application or Request Continued Examination

If you have received a final action and you want to have your claims (or new claims) reviewed further in another new round with the examiner, you can file a new "continuation application" or request continued examination in the same application.

Filing a continuation application is a relatively simple procedure involving writing new claims, paying a new filing fee, and sending in a special form requesting that a continuation application examination be prepared. (See Chapter 14 for how to do this.) As explained in Chapter 14, if you file a "regular" continuation application with a new copy of the specification, drawings, and formal papers (37 CFR 1.53(b)), you'll receive a new serial number and filing date for the purpose of your patent's duration, but you'll be entitled to the benefit of the filing date of your original application for the purpose of determining the relevancy of prior art. Your application will be examined all over again with the new claims.

An easier approach is to file a Request for Continued Examination (RCE) under 37 CFR 1.114 (preferable). By filing an RCE you won't have to file a new copy of the specification or drawings and you won't receive a new serial number or filing date. You simply file an RCE form, pay an RCE fee (this is slightly less than a new filing fee), and submit another amendment including an RCE. (See Chapter 14 and Form SB/30.)

If you're filing a continuation, you must actually get it on file before the end of the three-month period or any extensions you buy. You should not use a Certificate of Mailing (CM) with a continuation since, according to the PTO's Rules, a CM isn't effective when an application is being filed; you must actually get it physically on file before the other case is abandoned. The best way to do this is to use Priority Mail Express with a Priority Mail Express certificate or an electronic transmission if you're a registered eFiler. However, if you file an RCE, you can fax this or use a CM (which is included on the RCE form).

6. Petitions to the Commissioner for Nonsubstantive Matters

If the examiner has issued a ruling on a matter other than the patentability of your claims—for example, has refused to enter an amendment or has required the case to be restricted to one of several inventions—you have another option. Although you can't appeal from this type of decision, you can petition the Commissioner of Patents and Trademarks to overrule the examiner.

The Commissioner of Patents has power to overrule almost anyone in the PTO or any objection made by an examiner. (The PTAB has jurisdiction over rejections and objections if they're associated with a rejection. See 37 CFR 1.181–183.) So, if the examiner has made an objection that you think is wrong or if you think something unfair or illegal occurred with respect to your case, you can petition the Commissioner to overrule a subordinate. For example, if the PTO's application branch (OPAP) has made a ruling regarding your patent application, such as that it's not entitled to the filing date you think you're entitled to (but not a rejection of your claims), you can petition the Commissioner to overrule this ruling.

If you petition the Commissioner for any reason, you must do so promptly after the decision or event giving rise to the petition, and you must make your argument as strong and as complete as possible. Generally, most petitions must be accompanied by a verified showing and fee. A verified showing is a statement signed by you and either notarized or containing a declaration such as that in the paragraph of Form 10-1 (that starts "I hereby declare ...."). (The petition fee is indicated in Appendix 4, "Fee Schedule.")

7. Abandon Your Application

You must take any action in response to a final OA within the three-month period for response or any time extensions you buy (see below); otherwise the application will go abandoned. That is, you must either appeal, file a continuation application, or get the examiner to allow your application within the period for response. However, if you're going to file an amendment or an argument, do it as soon as possible, preferably within one month, so the examiner's reply will reach you in time for you to take any further needed action within the three-month period.

If all claims of your application are rejected in the final OA, and you agree with the examiner and can't find anything else patentable in your application, you'll have to allow the application to become abandoned, but don't give up without a fight or without thoroughly considering all factors involved.

If you do decide to allow your application to go abandoned, it will go abandoned automatically if you don't file a timely reply to the final action, since the ball's in your court. You'll be sent a Notice of Abandonment advising you that the case has gone abandoned because you failed to reply to an outstanding Office Action.

If you do abandon the application, that doesn't mean that you've abandoned the invention. If your invention has a unique shape and it hasn't been made available to the public, offered for sale, or sold more than a year ago, consider filing a design patent application on it. Even if a utility or design patent isn't available, it may still be commercially viable; consider trade secret or trademark protection.

K. Derivation Proceedings

If two patent applications claim the same invention, the later-filed (or "junior") application can be rejected as unpatentable over the earlier-filed (or "senior") application and the inventor in the junior application has no recourse, unless they can prove (in a derivation proceeding) that the senior applicant derived the invention from the junior applicant. If a patent claims the same invention as a pending application, and the pending application was filed before the patent, then the claims of the patent can be canceled, unless it is proven that the applicant in the patent application derived the invention from the patentee.

> ## Monitoring Patent Applications
>
> If you really want to do a thorough job of patent prosecution, find the class and subclass of your patent application (you can find this by calling the clerk of the examining division to which your application is assigned) and then monitor the *Official Gazette* in that class/subclass for all patents that issue and all patent applications that are published while your application's pending. If you find a patent that is relevant prior art to your invention, you should cite it via a supplemental IDS.

If you find the patent, and its filing date is earlier than that of your application, you will have to abandon your application, unless you can prove that the patentee derived the invention from you, or unless you can change your claims to focus on a different aspect of your invention. If the patent has a later filing date than yours, it will not be prior art to your application, so you don't have to worry about it.

If you find a patent that is relevant prior art to your invention, but doesn't claim your invention, cite it via a supplemental IDS, unless your filing date is earlier than that of the patent.

L. Defensive Publication

If you want to abandon your application, but want to prevent anyone else who files after you abandon it from ever getting a valid patent on it, you can have your invention published privately, either by using a service or by yourself. (See Chapter 14 for details.)

M. If Your Application Claims More Than One Invention

Often patent applications claim several embodiments of an invention, and the PTO will regard these embodiments as separate inventions. The PTO will thus require you to "restrict" the application to just one of the inventions. The theory is that your filing fee entitles you to have only one invention examined.

Also, if two of your claims are directed to one invention, but the examiner feels that the two claims are directed to subject matter that is classified in two separate technology classes or subclasses, the examiner can require you to restrict the application—that is, to elect one set of claims for prosecution.

Another situation in which restriction may be required occurs when your application contains both method and apparatus claims. Even when both sets of claims are directed to the same invention, examiners often consider them two separate inventions and require you to elect either the method or the apparatus claims.

Generally speaking, it's very difficult to successfully "traverse" (argue against) a PTO-imposed restriction. Fortunately, it's possible to file a second application (called a "divisional application"—see Chapter 14) if you think pursuing the nonelected claims is worth the cost (new filing fee) and if present indications are that your divisional application will comprise allowable subject matter. You can file the divisional application any time until your first (parent) application issues, and your divisional application will be entitled to the filing date of your parent application. However, you should file any divisional application(s) as soon as possible since, under TRIPS, any patent that issues on the divisional application will expire 20 years from the filing date of the original application in the chain.

One way to overcome a requirement for restriction is to add or include a "linking" claim—a claim that includes features of both inventions. If a linking claim is found allowable, the examiner will drop the restriction requirement. A linking claim is one that includes features of both inventions. For example, product and process claims can be linked by a claim to the product made by the process. While details of linking claims are found in MPEP 809.03, we recommend that you seek professional help in this area.

Another, related situation occurs when you claim several embodiments or "species" of one invention. In the first OA, the examiner may require you to elect claims to one species for purpose of examination; this is to facilitate the search. If you don't get any generic claim allowed—that is, a claim that covers all of your different species—you'll be allowed to claim only the elected species; you can file divisional applications on the nonelected species. (In this case, the PTO will consider each species to be a separate invention.) If you do get a generic claim allowed, you'll be allowed to claim a reasonable number of different species of the invention (37 CFR 1.146).

If your application contains claims to more than one invention, you may preempt the examiner by filing a Suggested Requirement for Restriction and an election of the claims that you wish to be examined (37 CFR 1.142).

N. The Public May Cite Additional Prior Art Against Your Published Patent Application

Most other countries have a practice under which they permit the public to see pending and allowed applications before they issue in order to give the public a chance to cite prior art or otherwise object to the allowance of the application. This practice has now been implemented in the United States by the 18-month publication system. This means, among other things, that if you allow your application to be published after 18 months from filing, you give up the confidentiality of your invention. Copies of any published application can be obtained by any member of the public who wants to download or order them; anyone can then cite prior art against your application upon payment of a fee. The public may cite prior art against your application before the earlier of (1) a notice of allowance, or (2) the later of (a) six months after publication or (b) the first rejection of any claim of the application. The citation must state the relevance of the prior art and pay a fee.

Although there are disadvantages to publication of your application (the cost, the delay, the possibility of more examination, the possibility of fatally damaging prior art being cited against your application, and the loss of any trade secret rights in the application which you could otherwise maintain if the application is not allowed), an application that is published and survives the process will be a stronger patent. Also, a published patent application can be used to recover damages from infringers for infringing activity during the pendency of your application (although such recovery will not occur until after the patent issues).

How to Cite Prior Art Against a Pending Application of Another

If you know of any prior adverse information against a published patent application of another and you want to bring this to the attention of the examiner to prevent the application from issuing, you can cite the art against such application. Use the caption of Form 13-1, filling in as much information as possible, and head the paper "Citation of Prior Art." List and enclose, but do not explain the relevance of the prior art. Be sure to cite the application's Serial Number and the name of the applicant. Under the AIA, you must file the citation before the earlier of (1) a notice of allowance, or (2) the later of (a) six months after publication or (b) the first rejection of any claim of the application. You must send a copy of your citation to the applicant in the published application and pay a Prior-Art Citation Fee (see Appendix 4).

O. NASA Declarations

If your invention relates to aerospace, the PTO may send you a form letter (PTOL-224) with your filing receipt or after your application is allowed. The letter will state that because your invention relates to aerospace, you'll have to file a declaration stating the "full facts" regarding the making of your invention. This is to be sure NASA has no rights in it. If you don't file the declaration, you won't get a Notice of Allowance. Fortunately, the PTO now includes a declaration form for you to fill out. Check the appropriate blanks, indicating that you made the invention on your own time, and with your own facilities and materials, and not in performance of any NASA contract, if this is the case.

P. Design Patent Application Prosecution

Design patent application prosecution is much simpler than regular patent application prosecution, and, armed with the instructions of this chapter, you'll be in good shape. Design patent application prosecution will never require anything but the most elementary changes to the specification and claim; the examiner will tell you exactly what to do.

To be patentable, the *appearance* of your design, as a whole, must be nonobvious to a designer of ordinary skill over the references (usually earlier design patents) that the examiner cites. If your design has significant differences over the cited prior art, it should be patentable. If not, you'll have to narrow your claim, which can be very difficult in a design application. A claim can be narrowed only by including more limitations, and because you cannot add "new matter" (that is, brand new lines in the drawing figures) this means you will have to convert existing unclaimed (dashed) lines into claimed (solid) lines. Unless your figures already included such dashed lines upon initial filing—for example, to show portions of your article of manufacture that do not form part of the design— such an amendment will be impossible and you will have to abandon the application.

If the examiner rejects your design as obvious over one or more references, use the 102-then-103 attack explained earlier in this chapter—that is, point out the differences in your design and then argue their importance and significance, albeit from a purely aesthetic viewpoint. To reject a design claim on two or more references, one must look basically like the claimed design.

If your design case is allowed, you must pay an issue fee (see Appendix 4, "Fee Schedule"), which makes the design patent effective for a term of 15 years from its date of issue. There are no maintenance fees for a design patent. You can convert a design application to a utility application, or vice versa, by filing a continuing application under 35 U.S.C. Section 120. However a design patent application may not claim priority of a PPA.

Q. What to Do If You Miss or Want to Extend a PTO Deadline

If you miss any PTO deadline—for example, the three-month period to reply to an OA—your application technically becomes abandoned, but you have the right to buy an extension. If your application goes abandoned, or if you want more time to reply to an OA, it can be "revived" or extended in either of the following ways:

- buy an extension
- file a Petition to Revive if delay was unintentional, or
- request extraordinary relief.

Let's look at these avenues.

1. Buy an Extension Before the Six-Month Period Ends (37 CFR 1.136(a))

Most substantive OAs give you three months from their mailing date to reply. Most nonsubstantive OAs (for example, a requirement for restriction to one of two inventions) allow only one month. If you don't reply within your designated period, you can send in your reply at any time up to the end of the sixth month (from the date of the OA) by buying an extension of up to five months (if it won't carry you over six months) at the prices indicated in the Fee Schedule. To buy an extension in this manner, eFile, fax, or mail your reply (amendment) by the last day of the extension month, together with a "Petition for Extension of Time under 37 CFR 1.136(a)" (AIA/22 or download Form 13-4; see Appendix 7), completed as necessary, and a check or credit card charge. It is not necessary to apply in advance. If you fax or mail, make sure you include a Certificate of Faxing or Mailing on your amendment. You should calculate your total number of months from the date of the OA; don't add your extension months to your original due date. For example, assume your OA was mailed May 12, 2014 and provided a three-month period to reply. Your original period expired August 12, 2014. You buy a two-month extension. Now, your total period for reply is five months from May 12—that is, you have until October 12, 2014—not two months from August 12. Mail your response, petition for extension, and petition fee (which can be quite expensive) by midnight on October 12. It does not have to go out or be postmarked by October 12. Remember that by statute you can't extend any response period beyond six months. Also, you can't buy an extension to send in your issue fee; the three-month statutory period from the Notice of Allowance is not extendable.

2. Petition to Revive If Delay Was Unintentional (37 CFR 1.137(b))

If you failed to send in your amendment or issue fee within the three-month period and your delay was "unintentional"—such as, you merely dropped the ball, or misinterpreted the time to reply to the OA—you can still petition to revive the application, albeit at a much higher cost. (Again, this petition can be used for any delay beyond the three-month period but most applicants use it for delays beyond the six-month period because the petition for delays up to six months can be obtained at a cheaper cost using the Extension petition of Form AIA/22 above.) You should file two papers:

- your reply
- a petition to revive (use Form SB/66) with the fee; and
- if you foreign-filed your application but failed to notify the PTO within 45 days, use Form SB/64a to revive the application; the fee is high.

The PTO requires applicants to provide "additional information" (beyond just the petition) to explain a claim of unintentional delay when:

- a petition to revive an abandoned application is filed more than two years after the date the application became abandoned
- a petition to accept a delayed maintenance fee payment (see Chapter 15, section H) is filed more than two years after the date the patent expired for nonpayment, and/or
- a petition to accept a delayed priority or benefit claim (see Chapter 14) is filed more than two years after the date the priority or benefit claim was due.

Previously, the PTO allowed you (or your patent attorney) to simply sign a sworn statement that the entire delay was unintentional, and they took you at your word. Apparently, the PTO is becoming less trusting in the above situations, and you will need to explain the surrounding facts and circumstances to assure the PTO that the delay was "unintentional."

3. Request Extraordinary Relief

In an extraordinary situation, when justice requires, any requirement of the patent regulations that does not come from Congress may be suspended or waived by the Director, or on petition of the interested party. (37 CFR 1.183.) Extraordinary situations are, as you might expect, unusual. However, extreme weather events such as hurricanes, tornados, and wildfires are routinely viewed by the PTO as "extraordinary situations" that fall within the intent of this catch-all provision.

Thus, for example, patent applicants and reexamination parties affected by the recent wildfires in California may request that the PTO restart the time period for reply set in an Office Action or other Office communication. All that is required is a correspondence address in the affected areas, and a communication that is outstanding as of a particular date (in this case, January 7, 2025) and requires a response by a deadline that has not yet expired. Upon the applicant's request, the PTO may restart the time period for reply by either withdrawing and reissuing the Office communication or sending a notice stating that the time period for reply to the Office communication is being restarted. If the response period has expired, the PTO will waive the fee for a petition to revive.

The PTO makes declarations that relief of this sort is available to all of its customers (including patent and trademark applicants, owners, and others) in the *Official Gazette* (patentsgazette.uspto.gov) and on its Patent Related Notices page (uspto.gov/patents/laws/patent-related-notices). Instructions for taking advantage of this kind of relief are given in the text of each declaration.

R. Summary

After your application is filed, you will receive an online acknowledgment or receipt postcard in a few weeks and an official filing receipt soon after that, usually with a foreign-filing license that permits you to file abroad before six months has elapsed.

Check the information in the filing receipt carefully and apply for any needed corrections. Your application is now "patent pending" and you can release details if necessary without undue risk. Be sure to file an IDS within three months.

When you receive a first Office Action check it carefully and be sure to respond in the time allotted or any extensions you buy. After you respond you'll receive a second and usually final Office Action or a notice of allowance.

If you didn't file an NPR when you filed the application your application will be published on the PTO's website 18 months after filing and the public can cite new prior art against your application. If the case is allowed you'll have to pay an issue fee and then will receive the patent deed.

During prosecution you can ask the examiner to write claims for you if the invention is patentable. Note that standards of patentability vary widely and the PTO can be unfair, so you should argue against and appeal any rejection you feel is improper.

It's important to avoid making any negative statements on the record, comply with your continuing duty to disclose material information about the invention, avoid amending your claims unless necessary, and consider foreign filing within one year of your filing date. It's often useful to call or visit your examiner. You are not allowed to add any new matter to your application, but you must respond to every point in any Office Action.

To respond to an Office Action first review your application, then the cited references, and then decide what is novel and nonobvious about your invention and consider amending the claims to define over the prior art if necessary. When drafting your remarks in the amendment, go through the flowchart and use possible arguments for patentability. Be sure to separate your arguments into novelty and nonobvious parts and distinguish between physical novelty and new results.

Your amendment should argue the patentability of your claims. It should not argue the patentability of the inventive idea generally, nor the drawings, or specification.

The PTO requires a specific format for an amendment, with each section starting on a new page and a listing of every claim that was ever in the application. Follow the specific rules for drafting remarks.

The PTO prefers that you eFile the amendment if possible. Otherwise fax your amendment rather than mail it, unless it includes new drawing sheets. If you receive a final action your only options are to appeal, amend the claims as required, interview the examiner to come to an agreement, try a further amendment without raising new issues, file a full or RCE continuation application, or abandon the application. You can petition the Commissioner for nonsubstantive matters.

Design patent application prosecution is similar to utility prosecution, except that the design must be nonobvious in the aesthetic sense. If you miss a PTO deadline, you can buy an extension, petition to revive the application if the delay was unintentional, or ask the PTO to restart the clock in the event of a natural disaster.

CHAPTER

14

Your Application Can Have Children

A. Available Supplemental Cases	442
B. Continuation Application	444
C. Request for Continued Examination (RCE)	446
D. Divisional Applications	448
E. Continuation-In-Part and Independent Applications	450
F. Reissue Applications	453
G. Defensive Publications	453
H. Substitute Applications	454
I. Double Patenting and Terminal Disclaimers	454
J. Summary	455

Inventor's Commandment 29

Get familiarity with supplemental applications (continuations, RCEs, divisions, continuations-in-part, reissues, and substitutes) if you have a patent application pending, and be aware of the double-patenting trap and the shortening of your monopoly period before filing any such extension application.

A. Available Supplemental Cases

The patent laws and PTO rules allow you to do much more than either get a patent or abandon your patent application. Perhaps a patent application can best be understood by comparing it to a family tree, as shown in Fig. 14A, which shows all of the different extensions you may file.

The root of the family tree is a "Basic Application" or BA, which is always a Regular Patent Application (RPA) and never a Provisional Patent Application (PPA). The Basic Application is like a parent, and just as a parent has children, the parent application can be used to produce offshoots. Depending upon the situation, the parent application is called by many names (for example, "parent," "prior," "basic," or "original" application), while the offshoot applications are referred to as "daughter," "continuation," "divisional," "reissue," "independent," or "substitute" applications.

Note that some extensions come from the bottom point of the Basic Application (BA) or the basic patent. These are "sequential" supplements or extensions, since they replace the BA or its patent.

Other supplements come from the sides of the BA; these are "parallel" supplements or extensions since they can exist alongside the BA or its patent.

The various extensions, starting from the upper left and proceeding down, then the middle and down, and so on, are:

- **Division or divisional application:** Suppose your examiner held that your BA covered two or more inventions, and required you to "restrict" it to one of these inventions by making an "election." To cover the other, "nonelected" invention you'll have to file a separate application on it. You do this by filing a divisional application. Your divisional application gets the benefit of the filing date of your BA, but also expires 20 years from your BA's filing date. Your divisional patent can be in addition to your original patent.

- **Continuation application:** Suppose your examiner sends you a Notice of Allowance (NOA) and you want to try a new and different set of claims, or the examiner sends you a final Office Action (OA), and you want to get another round with the examiner on the same claims, or to try a new and different set of claims. You can do this by filing a new application that "continues" your original application. The continuation application gets the benefit of the filing date of your original application but also expires 20 years from your BA's filing date. A continuation patent can be in addition to your original patent, but its claims must have a different scope or you will receive a "double patenting" rejection.

- **Request for Continued Examination (RCE):** Moving down the middle column of the chart, you will see the RCE box. An RCE enables you to purchase another round with the examiner in the same application. Note from the chart that the RCE is like a detour or second chance on the path to a patent.

- **Reissue:** If you've received an original patent, but you want to revise the claims of the patent or correct significant errors in the specification (for a valid reason), you can file a reissue application. As indicated, your reissue patent takes the place of your original patent.

- **Continuation-In-Part (CIP):** Moving up to the top of the right column, if you've improved or changed your basic invention in some material way during the pendency of your application, and you want to obtain specific claims to the improvement, you can file a continuation-in-part (CIP) application. As indicated, your CIP patent can coexist with your original patent, or your CIP application can replace your BA.

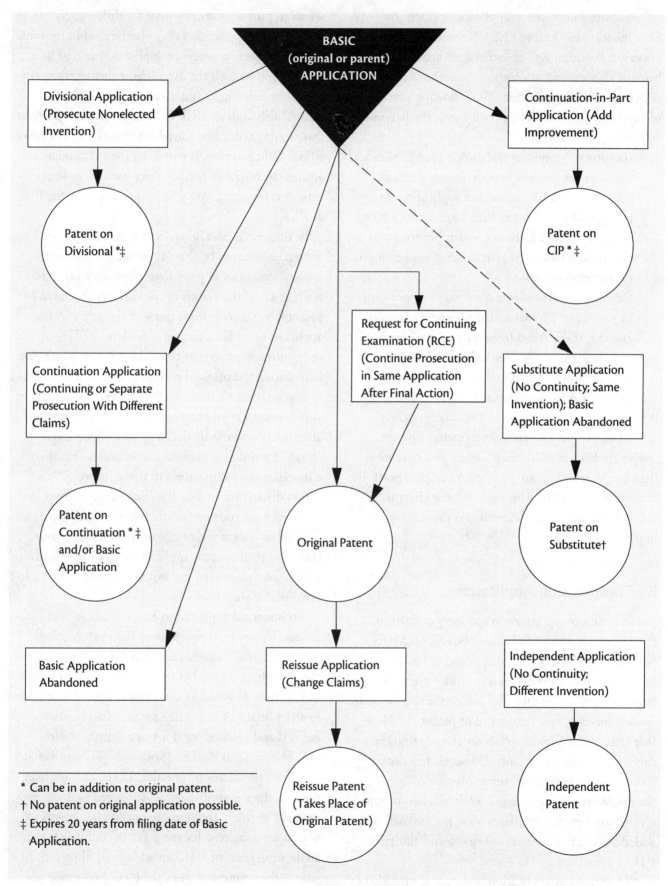

Fig. 14A—Available Supplement Cases

The above four types of applications (Division, Continuation (including RCE), Reissue, and CIP) are called "continuing" or "extension" applications because they extend or continue from (have continuity with) the parent application. The following two types of supplements have no continuity with the parent or original application.

- **Substitute:** Suppose you abandon your application and later refile a new application on the same invention. The new substitute application, as indicated by the broken line, has no copendency or continuity with the original application. Of course, any patent on your original application is no longer possible.
- **Independent:** If you've made a major improvement in your basic invention that uses new concepts and can really stand by itself, you can file an independent application, which is entirely separate from your BA, although you may refer to your BA in the independent.

Before you decide to file a continuation or other extension, give serious thought to seeing a patent lawyer for help with strategy—when you have more than one patent, you are building a complex portfolio of interrelated rights. Also note that the chart is abbreviated, so do rely primarily on the text, rather than the chart.

B. Continuation Application

A continuation application is concisely defined in the *Manual of Patent Examining Procedure* (MPEP), Section 201.07, as "a second application for the same [or similar] invention claimed in a prior nonprovisional [regular] application and filed before the original prior application becomes abandoned or patented." Note that both the original application and continuation can issue as separate patents. However they cannot claim the same invention since this would violate the double-patenting rule that prohibits two patents on the same invention. That's why "[or similar]" was added after "same" above, to expand and clarify the PTO's definition.

A continuation application is almost always filed in response to a Notice of Allowance, when an applicant wants to pursue another patent for different claims. A continuation application may also be filed in response to a final rejection when an applicant wants to have another round with the examiner, either to try again to get the existing claims allowed, or to try new claims, although an RCE is usually a better option in this circumstance (see the next section). In the case of a final Office Action, if you don't file a continuation within the response period (three months unless extended for a fee), you give up your right to file it at all.

In the case of an allowed application, if you don't file a continuation by the day before the allowed application issues to patent, you give up your right to file it at all. If the claims of the continuation aren't patentably different from those of the original, the applicant must file a terminal disclaimer (TD) in the continuation so that the second patent won't run longer than the original patent.

If you think it's inconsistent for the PTO to allow you to continue prosecuting claims to an invention after it has supposedly declared an Office Action "final," a word of explanation is in order. "Final" has a special, unusual meaning in this context. A "final" action doesn't mean that the examiner has given the final word on your invention, but merely that they've decided to cut off your right to freely change your claims in your current application. In other words, you've gotten as many go-arounds as they're going to give you for your filing fee.

An historical explanation might make it even clearer. Up to the early 1960s, patent prosecution proceeded at a leisurely pace. The PTO (then just the Patent Office) allowed examiners to send four or five OAs before they had to issue a final action. Examiners issued a final OA only after an issue had been clearly defined and reached, or if it was a fourth or fifth OA. However, in the late 1960s the PTO instituted a "compact prosecution" practice. Under this practice the examiner is almost always supposed to make the second OA final. The purpose of this change was to obtain more income for the PTO (a continuation application gets the PTO an additional filing fee), to reduce the amount of work the PTO performed, and to shorten the backlog of pending applications.

You must file a continuing application like a regular application. The procedure is governed by 35 U.S.C. Section 120 and 37 CFR 1.53(b).

A continuation application must cover the same or a similar invention as the parent or Basic Application (BA). The BA can either be abandoned or can issue after a continuation is filed. The continuation application is entitled to the benefit of the filing date of the parent or prior application for purposes of overcoming prior art.

You can also file a continuation of a continuation. In fact, it's theoretically possible to file an unlimited sequence of continuation applications. The PTO has attempted, but so far failed, to implement rules to limit the number of continuations. However, each continuation in the chain will expire no later than 20 years from your earliest BA filing date, so you cannot play this game forever. Also, each successive patent will have a shorter enforceable term, so at some point the costs to obtain another continuation will outweigh the economic benefits.

Also, if an issue has been reached in a parent application, the examiner can, and often will, make the first OA final in a continuation application or will make the next OA final after a continuation is filed. In other words, a continuation application will be quickly rejected unless you truly come up with a different slant on or definition of your invention that was not previously considered by the PTO.

If you want to delete any inventors when you file a continuation, you may do so by including a simple request on a separate form. All inventors named in the prior application should sign the form.

As with a regular application, you'll receive your email acknowledgment or postcard back with the filing date of (and a new serial number for) your continuation. After that, you'll receive a filing receipt and the first Office Action in due course.

Filing a continuation application is very similar to filing a regular, original application. You must prepare the continuation like an original application—that is, provide a complete new copy of the specification and claims, and drawings. You should amend the specification at the beginning (under "CROSS-REFERENCE TO RELATED APPLICATIONS") with the following sentence:

"This is a continuation of application Ser. Nr. _____/_____ filed, with title "_____" and naming _____ as inventor(s) [or now Patent Nr. [fill in later], granted [fill in later], the entire content of which is hereby incorporated herein by reference in its entirety."

If your continuation application claims priority through a chain of previous applications (for example, BA, continuations, divisions, continuations-in-part), include an appropriate reference to each of those applications, such as:

"The present application is a continuation application of U.S. application serial no. _____/_____ filed, with title "_____" and naming _____ as inventor(s), which is a divisional application of U.S. application serial no._____/_____ filed with title "_____" and naming _____ as inventor(s). All of the foregoing applications are hereby incorporated herein by reference in their entirety."

The PTO is very strict when it comes to the language used in this sentence. For complete details, refer to MPEP 211.02, which describes how to made the required references in the Application Data Sheet (ADS), also described below, and how to draft sentences that refer to prior PPAs and RPAs.

Rewrite the claims as you want them and number them starting with "1." Prepare and sign a new patent application declaration (PAD—Form 10-1A), or simply refile the declaration(s) from the parent application, and an Application Data Sheet (PTO form AIA/14). If you are going to file by mail, fill out a Utility Patent Application Transmittal (Form 10-2) and a Fee Transmittal (Form 10-3) as before. Don't forget the return postcard. You must get the continuation application on file while the parent case is pending, so if mailing it, make sure you allow enough mailing time, or you can use Priority Mail Express with Form 10-2. (Don't use a Certificate of Mailing.) If you want to file the continuation electronically, which we strongly recommend, especially if you are already a registered eFiler, go to the PTO's electronic filing website and fill out the forms and a new ADS (application data sheet) on your computer and file the specification, claims, drawings, declaration, and ADS in PDF format as before. In the ADS, in the "Domestic Benefit/ National Stage Information," under "Prior Application Status" select "Pending"; for "Continuity Type" select "Continuation of"; and fill in the Prior Application's Ser. Nr. and Filing date. Your continuation will receive a new serial number and filing date, but it will be entitled to the filing date of the parent case.

You also have to file an IDS again. If you're filing by mail, prepare the cover letter (Form 10-5) and the actual IDS Forms (10-6) (use a photocopy of the IDS in your parent case but change the Serial Number and the filing Date), but you don't have to send in copies of the references again if your IDS cover letter refers to the IDS in the prior case. Just type the following on Form 10-5:—"Pursuant to 37 CFR 1.98(d), the references listed on attached Forms SB/08 (A and B) are not enclosed because these were supplied in the parent case, Ser. Nr.____/_____." If you're filing electronically follow the instructions in Chapter 13 for filing an IDS online. You may file the IDS when you file or up to three months later. Of course, you should file a supplemental IDS any time you learn of more prior art to disclose, but generally, the sooner you file the IDS, the better.

> **TIP**
>
> **Changing examiners.** If you feel that the examiner in your parent case was unduly tough, it may be possible to get a different examiner in your continuation case by claiming your invention differently. The examining division to which a patent application is assigned is determined by the class and subclass to which the application is assigned. The class and subclass is in turn determined by the subject matter of the narrowest (longest or most specific) claim in the case.
>
> **EXAMPLE:** Suppose you've invented a new gear for a bicycle and the narrowest claim of your parent case recites the fine details of the gear per se. Your case will be assigned to an examining division in the "gear" arts. If your "gear" examiner is a hardnose, you'll probably be able to get it into bicycles, a different examining division, by adding the bicycle to your narrowest claim. You can do this by providing a "bicycle" preamble for the claim or by actually reciting other parts of the bike in the body of the claim. If your narrowest claim is directed to a bike, your whole case will be classified in the bike division, and you'll have a different examiner.

Obviously, this maneuver can't be done in every instance. You should do some research on the PTO's Examining Division art assignments (see the "Patent Examining Corps" page of any recent *Official Gazette*) to make sure your end run around a particular examiner will work. Lastly, in an effort to get a new examiner, it also helps to change the title of your invention to one that is commensurate with your revised narrowest claim. For example, change "Gear with Anti-Backlash Pawl" to "— Bicycle Pedal Drive Gear—."

SEE AN EXPERT

Changing examiners is one of several situations where a consultation with a patent attorney or agent may be called for, due to the nature of claims drafting.

C. Request for Continued Examination (RCE)

Two OAs are often not enough to adequately define the invention, resolve an issue with the examiner, and complete the prosecution in a proper manner. Therefore, continuation applications and RCEs are often filed after a "final" OA. Because an RCE is much simpler to prepare and costs less to file, it is recommended that you file the RCE instead of a continuation application.

Note that Congress has given the PTO authority to set its own fees to recoup costs, and the PTO has taken to setting the fee for the second and subsequent RCEs in an application higher than for the first RCE. The reasoning is that one application fee and one RCE fee typically buys enough examiner time for four OAs, and applications that require more than that typically are complex enough to justify the added expense. At present, the fee for filing a continuation application (with at most 3 independent and 20 total claims) is greater than that of a first RCE, but less than that of a second RCE. If you are four OAs in and still having trouble with the examiner, you may wish to file a continuation application rather than another RCE. (You may also wish to consult a patent attorney to make sure you're making the best use of your time and money.)

Requesting a Continued Examination (RCE) of an existing application has the same effect as filing a continuation application, but without going through the paperwork of filing a new application. The applicant simply sends in a form, pays an RCE fee, and continues prosecuting the same application.

Prosecution continues as if the application were newly filed, but in its present condition with any amendments to the specification, claims, or drawing. In other words, filing an RCE is a way of buying your way out of a final action so you can continue prosecution for one or two more go-arounds, as in the old days before compact prosecution.

In order to file an RCE, prosecution in the application must be "closed"—that is, the last OA must have been a final action, a notice of allowance, or some other action closing prosecution. Also, the application must be a regular utility application (not a PPA or design application). When a patent issues on an RCE, the heading of the patent will not indicate that it's based on the RCE.

When you file an RCE, the PTO uses your same file jacket, papers, Serial Number, and filing Date. The procedure is covered by 37 CFR 1.114 and the RCE Transmittal Form (Form 14-1/PTO Form SB/30).

To file an RCE:

- If filing by mail, complete Form 14-1.
- Prepare an amendment containing the new claims you desire to prosecute or check the appropriate block on Form 14-1 if you want to have your Amendment under 37 CFR 1.116 entered.
- Prepare an amendment containing the new claims you desire to prosecute or check the appropriate block on Form 14-1 if you want to have your Amendment under Rule 116 entered.
- If you file by mail, attach a receipt postcard.

You must send your RCE before the period for response to the final rejection expires or before any time extensions you've bought expire. (For an explanation of purchasing extensions of time, see Chapter 13.) As is the case with an amendment, you can eFile, fax, or mail your RCE request on or before the last day of the period for response if you complete the Certificate of Mailing section at the bottom of Form 14-1. Because you're not filing a new application, you don't have to use Priority Mail Express, but do mail the RCE with a Certificate of Mailing or Faxing before the period expires. Fax the papers to the PTO's central fax number or mail them to Mail Stop RCE, P.O. Box 1450, Alexandria, VA 22313-1450.

If you're a registered eFiler, you can file the RCE electronically at the PTO's Electronic Business site. Convert the completed RCE Transmittal Form (Form 14-1/PTO Form SB/30), and amendment to PDF and file them as if filing an amendment. Pay the RCE fee on the PTO's site by credit card. You don't have to file a new IDS (unless you have become aware of previously undisclosed prior art) or ADS when you file an RCE.

For the Amendment, complete Form 13-1 exactly as you would do with a regular amendment. Then proceed as usual: Cancel the old claims and insert the new claims in the normal amendment manner, numbered in sequence after the highest numbered claim of the prior application. Under "Remarks," you should state, "The above new claims are submitted to be patentable over the art of record for the following reasons." Then give your reasons and arguments in the same manner as you would for a regular amendment.

Be sure to include all the claims you desire in the amendment, since the next OA after the RCE is filed may be made final if the examiner doesn't cite any new prior art. If you mailed your RCE, you'll receive your postcard back with the filing date of your RCE but no new serial numbers. After that, you'll receive the next Office Action.

Note that Divisional and CIP applications, discussed below, must be filed like regular applications under 37 CFR 1.53(b). They cannot be filed via an RCE.

448 | PATENT IT YOURSELF

(!) CAUTION

20-year term. If you file an RCE or continuation application (or a continuation of a continuation) and get a patent on your RCE application or continuation, the patent will expire 20 years after the filing date of your first, original, or parent application. So it's a good idea to file any RCE application or continuation as soon as possible and to prosecute it diligently if you don't want your monopoly to be shorter than the former 17-year term. Since any continuing application (continuation, division, or CIP) will expire 20 years from the filing date of its parent case, before filing any continuing application, consider whether you'll really need to rely upon the parent case's filing date. If you're certain that no adverse prior art has issued since the parent's filing date, you can have any new case expire 20 years from its filing date (rather than from the filing date of the original case) if your new case doesn't claim priority of your original case; that is, if you file it as a regular patent application, rather than as an extension.

D. Divisional Applications

A divisional application or "division" is "a later application for a distinct or independent invention, carved out of a pending application and disclosing and claiming only subject matter disclosed in the earlier or parent application" (MPEP 201.06). File a divisional application when (1) the PTO decides that two separate or distinct inventions have been claimed in the parent application (not permitted, since your filing fee entitles you to get only one invention examined), (2) you've agreed to restrict the parent application to the set of claims to one of the inventions, and (3) you want to get a patent on the other, nonelected invention. You don't have to file a divisional application on the other invention, and should do so only if you think it's patentable and important enough to justify the expense of a separate application and patent acquisition (including later maintenance fees). Divisional applications are so named because they cover subject matter that is "divided out" of the parent case.

A divisional application is entitled to the filing date of the parent case for purposes of overcoming prior art. The parent application of a divisional application can either issue as a patent or become abandoned if you feel the parent is not patentable over the prior art. The divisional must be filed as a complete, new application under 37 CFR 1.53(b), and, like the continuation application, it will receive its own serial number and filing date for PTO administrative purposes. A patent issuing on a divisional application will show the serial number and filing date of the divisional as well as that of the parent application; that means the parent's filing date will be the divisional's effective filing date. But remember that the divisional application must be filed while the parent is pending.

Also note that you can file a division of a continuation application, and a continuation of a divisional application. (Definitely consult an expert if you get into these murky waters.)

Whether or not you're abandoning the parent case you'll have to proceed under 37 CFR 1.53(b). To file by mail, send in a complete copy of the divisional application, including a Utility Patent Application Transmittal (Form 10-2), Fee Transmittal (Form 10-3), filing fee, drawings, specification, claims, and abstract, PAD (Form 10-1A), postcard, and optionally an ADS. Optionally, you may also file a Preliminary Amendment. Everything should be the same as if you were filing a completely new application, with the following exceptions:

a. The claims of the divisional application should be directed solely to the invention that you are dividing out of the parent case. So replace the original claims that you filed with the parent case with claims just to the divisional invention. The divisional claims may be some of the claims that you originally included when you filed the parent case, or you may draft new claims in light of the prior art that was cited in the parent case.

b. Add the following sentence to the specification under "CROSS-REFERENCE TO RELATED APPLICATIONS":

"This is a division of application Ser. Nr. _____/_____, filed 20 _____, with title "_____" and naming _____ as inventor(s) [or now patent Nr. [fill in later], granted [fill in later] the entire content of which is hereby incorporated herein by reference."]

If your divisional application claims priority through a chain of previous applications (for example, BA, continuations, divisions, continuations-in-part), include an appropriate reference to each of those applications, such as:

"The present application is a divisional application of U.S. application serial no. _____ /_____, filed, with title "_____" and naming _____ as inventor(s), which is a continuation application of U.S. application serial no. _____ /_____, filed with title "_____ and naming _____ as inventor(s). All of the foregoing applications are hereby incorporated herein by reference in their entirety."

The PTO is very strict when it comes to the language used in this sentence. For complete details, refer to MPEP 211.02, which describes how to make the required references in the Application Data Sheet (ADS), also described below, and how to draft sentences that refer to prior PPAs and RPAs.

Also, be sure to amend the specification to make any editorial changes you desire, or which you've made in the parent case, but be careful not to add any new matter.

c. Complete the Utility Patent Application Transmittal (Form 10-2). Fill out box 18 to refer to the parent case and to indicate you're filing a divisional.

d. You also have to file an IDS transmittal letter (Form 10-5) and the actual IDS Forms (10-6) (use a photocopy of the IDS in your parent case but change the Serial Number and the Filing Date). Do this when you file or up to three months later. You don't have to file any references again if your IDS cover letter refers to the IDS in the prior case. Just type the following on Form 10-5: "Pursuant to 37 CFR 1.98(d), the references listed on attached Forms SB/08 (A and B) are not enclosed since these were supplied in the parent case, Ser. Nr. _____ /_____.""

To supply drawings for a parallel divisional case (the parent case will be issuing), you have at least four choices:

1. If you are a registered eFiler, or if the PTO has published your application, you can download a PDF of the formal drawings from Patent Center and print them out.
2. If you've made formal Mylar film or Bristol board originals of your drawings, you can file very good xerographic copies of these for your divisional's formal drawings.
3. You can file rough xerographic copies as informal drawings and file formal drawings later.
4. If you've made CAD drawings, print out new copies.

If you want to delete any inventors when you file a division, or if you are required to because not all inventors contributed to conceptualizing at least one claim in the division, you may do so by including a simple request on a separate form. All inventors named on the prior application should sign.

If you want to file the divisional electronically, prepare your specification, (including new claims directed just to the divisional invention), drawings, and signed declaration, fill out an ADS online, convert them all to PDF, and file from the PTO's Electronic Business site using similar procedures as used when filing a regular application. In the ADS, in the "Domestic Benefit/National Stage Information" portion, under "Prior Application's Status" select "Pending"; for "Continuity Type" select "Division of"; and fill in the Prior Application's Ser. Nr. and Filing date.

! CAUTION

20-year term warning. The 20-year term warning for continuation and RCE applications in Section C also applies to divisional applications.

CAUTION

Double patent warning. You're not permitted to obtain two patents on the same invention. Doing so is called "double patenting," ("DP"), a situation in which both patents may be held invalid. However, if in your parent case the examiner required you to restrict the application to one of several inventions, there's a special statute (35 U.S.C. § 121) that helps you. This statute states that if you file your divisional(s) on the nonelected invention(s) after a requirement for restriction, you can do so with total immunity from DP. However, if the examiner didn't require you to restrict, and you're filing your divisional "voluntarily," you must be sure that it's to a clearly different invention than that claimed in the parent case. Otherwise, both patents can be held invalid for DP.

Consult with a patent attorney in the event you (or the PTO) decide that a divisional application is indicated.

E. Continuation-In-Part and Independent Applications

As defined in MPEP 201.08, "a continuation-in-part" (CIP) is an application filed during the lifetime of an earlier application by the same applicant, repeating some substantial portion or all of the earlier application and adding matter not disclosed in the earlier application. CIP applications are not common; they're used whenever you wish to cover an improvement of your basic invention; for example, if you've discovered a new material or a better design. (Remember, you can't add these to a pending application because of the proscription on "new matter" discussed in Chapter 13 and mandated by 37 CFR 1.121(f).)

Generally, a CIP is filed to obtain protection of an improvement, which may be done in parallel with obtaining protection of the base invention. That means, if you want the parent application to issue, you must be sure that the claims of the CIP application are patentably different—that is, they define subject matter which is nonobvious over that of the parent application. Otherwise the CIP and parent application patent can both be held invalid

for double patenting, unless you file a terminal disclaimer.

The advantage of a CIP application over a separate application is that the CIP is entitled to the filing date of the parent application for all subject matter common to both applications. However, if any claims of the CIP cover subject matter unique to the CIP, such claims are entitled to the filing date of the CIP only.

If your "improvement" of your Basic Application is different enough to be nonobvious over the basic invention, you can file an entirely separate, independent application, rather than a CIP. However, it's usually better to use a CIP application, since the common subject matter gets the filing date of the parent application.

EXAMPLE 1: Suppose you've invented a bicycle gear with a new shape. You've claimed this shape in a patent application, which we'll call the parent application. After you file the parent application, your research shows you that the gear works much more quietly if it's made of a certain vanadium alloy (VA). The VA isn't patentable over the invention of the parent case and your parent case's claims cover the gear no matter what material it's made of. However, since the VA works much better, you'd like to add a few dependent claims specifically to cover a gear made of the VA. In this way, if there's an infringer who copies your gear made of the VA, you can show the judge that the infringer is infringing your specific as well as your broad claims. Also, you will have specific claims to VA to fall back on if your broad claims are held invalid. You can't add the VA to the specification or the claims of the parent case, since it would be forbidden "new matter." The solution: File a CIP, describing the VA in the specification, keep all of the original claims, and add a few dependent claims that recite that the gear is made of VA. You may need to file a terminal disclaimer in the CIP, since the VA isn't patentable over the invention of the parent case. For purposes of clearing the prior art, your broad claims to the gear shape per se will get the benefit of the parent case's filing date. However, the claims to the gear made of the VA will be entitled only to the later filing date of the CIP.

EXAMPLE 2: On the other hand, suppose your gear shape works well, but you've come up with a related, but nonobvious different shape that works better. That is, the new shape is patentable over the invention of the parent case. You should file a CIP with claims to the new shape and continue to prosecute the parent case to a patent. The CIP's claims generally will be entitled to only the CIP's filing date. However, their CIP status will entitle you to refer back to the parent's filing date to show when you came up with the underlying concept common to the parent and CIP gears. This will be useful in case the CIP is ever involved in litigation.

EXAMPLE 3: Lastly, suppose your gear shape works well, but you come up with an unrelated, and nonobvious different shape that works better. You should file a new, independent application, not related to the "parent," with claims to the new gear shape. The two applications would be entirely separate.

You can file a CIP of a continuation or divisional application or vice versa in either case. It's also theoretically possible to file an unlimited number of successive CIP applications to cover successive improvements. There have been rare cases where inventors have filed chains of CIPs with as many as eight or more applications, each of which issued into a patent.

When filing a CIP, you should amend the specification at the beginning (under "CROSS-REFERENCE TO RELATED APPLICATIONS") with the following sentence:

"This is a continuation-in-part of application Ser. Nr._____ /_____ , filed, with title "_____" and naming _____ as inventor(s) the entire content of which is hereby incorporated herein by reference."

If your CIP claims priority through a chain of previous applications (for example, BA, continuations, divisions, continuations-in-part), include an appropriate reference to each of those applications, such as:

"The present application is a continuation-in-part of U.S. application Ser. Nr. _____/_____, filed, with title "_____" and naming _____ as inventor(s) which is a continuation application of U.S. application Ser. Nr._____/_____, filed, with title "_____" and naming _____ as inventor(s). All of the foregoing applications are hereby incorporated herein by reference in their entirety."

The PTO is very strict when it comes to the language used in this sentence. For complete details, refer to MPEP 211.02, which describes how to make the required references in the Application Data Sheet (ADS), also described below, and how to draft sentences that refer to prior PPAs and RPAs.

If you are abandoning the parent case, you may claim whatever you want in the CIP, provided that the specification supports the claims. Only those claims that are supported by the specification of the parent case will be entitled to the filing date of the parent case. If the claims of the CIP are patentably different from those of the parent case, and the parent case issues, you don't need to file a terminal disclaimer. If the claims of the CIP are not patentably different from those of the parent case, you must file a terminal disclaimer to avoid double patenting.

If you're filing the CIP by mail, you must use the same procedure (37 CFR 1.53(b)) as outlined above for filing a divisional when the parent case will issue, except substitute or check "continuation-in-part" for "divisional" in the transmittal letter (Form 10-2) and specification. Don't forget the filing fee and postcard.

If you're filing the CIP electronically, use the same procedure as above for filing a continuation or divisional electronically. Also use the checklist in Chapter 10. The new subject matter in the CIP and any claims directed to it will be entitled to the CIP's filing date, not the filing date of the parent case.

As with continuation and divisional applications, you also have to file an IDS cover letter (Form 10-5) and the actual IDS Forms (10-6) (use a photocopy of the IDS in your parent case but change the Serial Number and the Filing Date). File the IDS when you file the CIP or up to three months later. However, you don't have to send in copies of the references again if your IDS cover letter refers to the IDS in the prior case. Just type the following on Form 10-5:

> *"Pursuant to 37 CFR 1.98(d), the references listed on attached Forms SB/08 (A and B) are not enclosed since these were supplied in the parent case, Ser. Nr. _____ /_____."*

Remember that the inventors for an application are determined by the claims, and a CIP may have claims with a different scope than the parent application. If you want to add or delete any inventors when you file a CIP, you may do so by including a simple request on a separate form. All inventors named on the prior applications should sign.

If you're filing an independent application (rather than a CIP), do it in the usual manner (see Chapter 10). If you want to abandon any parent case, you can do so in a separate letter or by not responding to an Office Action.

> ! **CAUTION**
> **20-year term warning.** The 20-year term warning for continuation and RCE applications in Section C also applies to CIP applications.

If You Want to Broaden the Claims by Reissue

If you wish to broaden the claims of your patent through a reissue application, you must do so within two years from the date the original patent issued. Moreover, anyone who manufactures anything between the issue dates of the original patent and the reissue patent that infringes the broadened but not the original claims is entitled to "intervening rights." These preclude a valid suit against this person for infringement of the reissue patent's broadened claims. (35 U.S.C. § 251, 252.)

EXAMPLE: Suppose you invent a new gear shape and get a patent, but unfortunately you included an unnecessary limitation in your independent claims as filed; namely, they all recite that the gear is made of carbon steel. If you discover your error within a two-year period after your patent's issue date, you can file an application to reissue the patent with broader claims—that is, claims that specify only the gear's shape and not its material. Your patent will be reissued with the broader claims. However, suppose that an infringer (Peg) made gears with your inventive shape, but out of aluminum, between the date of your original and reissue patents. Peg's aluminum gears would not infringe the claims of your original patent, but they would infringe the broader claims of the reissue. Nevertheless, Peg can continue to make her aluminum gears with impunity since she has "intervening rights" by virtue of her manufacture of the aluminum gears in the interim.

Note that a reissue can't be filed to "recapture" subject matter you deliberately gave up in the original case. In the example above, suppose that in your original case you simply recited "a gear" in the claims, but during prosecution you added that the gear was made of nylon to define over the prior art. Since this was a deliberate, conscious act, you aren't permitted to eliminate the "nylon" limitation (and thus "recapture" your broader claims) in a reissue.

F. Reissue Applications

As stated in MPEP 201.05, "A reissue application is an application for a patent to take the place of an unexpired patent that is defective as a result of an error in the patent which was made without deceptive intention." Sections 1400 to 1401.12 of the MPEP discuss reissue applications extensively. Suppose you've received a patent and believe that the claims are not broad enough, that they're too broad (you've discovered a new reference), or that there are some significant errors in the specification. To remedy this, you can file an application to get your original patent reissued during its term. The reissue patent will take the place of your original patent and expire the same time as the original patent would have expired.

Note that reissues to claim broader scope must be filed within the first two years of the grant of the original patent. (35 U.S.C. § 251(d).) The PTO is very strict about this requirement, and usually treats any reissue claim with language deleted as being broader than the original, patented claim.

To file a reissue application you must:
- Reproduce the entire specification of the original application (a copy of the printed patent pasted one column per page is acceptable), putting brackets around matter to be canceled and underlining matter to be added. When the reissue patent issues, it will include the brackets and underlining.
- Supply a request for a title report on the original patent and offer to surrender the original patent deed.
- Provide a declaration stating you believe the original patent to be wholly or partially inoperative or invalid and referring to and discussing at least one error in the patent. (See 37 CFR 1.171–179.)

Reissue patents are relatively rare and are identified by the letters "RE" followed by a five-digit number; for example, "Patent RE 26,420."

Although the procedure has been somewhat simplified recently, it is still relatively complicated, so consult a patent lawyer if you are interested in filing a reissue.

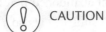 CAUTION

Reissue warning. If you file a reissue, the reissue retains the priority date of the original application, but all of the claims of your original patent will be examined and can be rejected. Thus you should consider whether you want to take this chance before filing a reissue.

G. Defensive Publications

If you want to (or must) abandon your application, you will not be able to obtain offensive rights in your invention. However, you can prevent anyone else from getting a patent on your invention as well, by publishing details of your invention. Doing so creates a prior art reference showing your invention with an effective date as of the date you publish. You can either hire a service to publish the details for you or you can create your own publication. One service that does this for inventions of a general nature is the Technical Disclosure Commons (tdcommons.org). If your invention is in the field of physics, mathematics, computer science, quantitative biology, quantitative finance, statistics, electrical engineering, systems science, or economics, you can publish your invention to arXiv (arxiv.org). You can also publish the details of your invention on your own website or go to a fee-based publisher (vanity press) to have a book about your invention published. If you create your own website, it will be a good defense if any later-filed patents are asserted against you. However, if you use a service, the patent examiners are more likely to search it and use it to reject any such later-filed patents. While the effective date of publication will be later than your filing date, the cost is low and the later date won't make any difference unless someone has filed on the same invention before you published it.

H. Substitute Applications

The term "substitute" is defined in MPEP 201.09 as "any application which is in essence the duplicate of an application by the same applicant abandoned before the filing of the later application." A substitute (also called a "refile") can be filed for the same purpose that you can file a continuation, division, or CIP. That is, you can file a substitute to continue prosecution that you didn't complete, to cover a different invention, or to cover an improvement invention.

A substitute application doesn't get the benefit of the filing date of the earlier case. This is because it wasn't filed while the earlier case was pending. Thus any prior art that issues after the filing date of the earlier case and before the filing date of the substitute case can be used against the substitute case. Suppose, however, that you somehow abandon your application (not your invention) and you can't successfully petition the Commissioner of Patents to revive the application. You still may be able to cover your invention by filing a substitute application, assuming significant prior art hasn't been published in the meantime.

There are no special forms or procedures for filing a substitute application; just file it like you would a regular patent application. If your substitute application issues into a patent, the patent will expire 20 years from the filing date of the substitute, rather than 20 years from the filing date of the earlier application.

I. Double Patenting and Terminal Disclaimers

Double patenting (DP) is a situation that exists when one person or entity obtains two patents on the same invention, or on two inventions that are not patentably distinct. It's very important to avoid DP, since both patents can be held invalid by a court. Also, if the PTO sees that you have two applications pending that aren't patentably distinct, it will reject them on the grounds of potential DP. Thus, you must always be aware of the DP trap whenever you file a second case on any invention.

There are two types of DP: statutory DP and non-statutory (or "obviousness-type") DP.

In statutory DP, claims in the two patents cover the exact same subject matter. This situation is prohibited by 35 U.S.C. Section 101, which says that "Whoever discovers any new and useful [invention] … may obtain a patent therefore …." This means that an inventor may obtain only one patent for an invention, not two patents. Statutory-type double patenting is absolutely prohibited and cannot be overcome by a terminal disclaimer. To overcome a potential statutory DP, you must either amend or cancel one of the duplicate claims in a pending application.

In obviousness-type DP, an inventor obtains two patents on respective inventions that are not identical, but that are also not different enough to be considered nonobvious over each other. This situation is prohibited by judicial decisions, because a second patent could historically extend the inventor's monopoly beyond the expiration date of the first patent. However, obviousness-type DP can be overcome by filing a terminal disclaimer (TD) in the later application so that any patent issuing on it will not extend beyond the expiration date of the first patent. It is important to ensure that both patents will continue to be owned by the same entity. (37 CFR 1.130(b) and 1.321(b).) Also, obviousness-type DP can be avoided if your examiner has required restriction. As explained in Section D, above, under "Double Patent Warning," a special statute (35 U.S.C. § 121) states that you have total immunity from DP if you file a divisional after the examiner required restriction.

Under a TD, you agree to give up the terminal (end) period of your second patent so that both patents will expire on the same date, and will continue to be commonly owned, thereby eliminating the harm to the public interest of double patenting (that is, extension of monopoly beyond normal term or prohibiting a second patent that is not patentably different from issuing to a different entity). If you feel brave enough to venture into this area alone, TD forms and the filing fees are available on the PTO's website.

J. Summary

A patent applicant can file a number of possible supplements from an original, parent, or base patent application. If the base application has two or more inventions and is restricted to only one of these inventions, a *divisional application* may be filed to cover the other invention. If you've gotten a final action in the base application and want to submit new claims and continue prosecution, you may file a *continuation application* or a *request for a continued examination* (RCE). If you develop an improvement on the invention of the base application and want to claim it specifically and still keep the filing date of the base application for the base invention, you may file a *continuation-in-part application* (CIP). The divisional, continuation, RCE, and CIP all get the benefit of the filing date of the base application, but also expire 20 years from the base application.

If you come up with a substantially different improvement or new invention, it's best to file an *independent application.*

If you get a patent and discover an error in it, such as claims that are too narrow, you can file a *reissue application* to have the patent reissued. The reissue patent takes the place of the original patent and expires when the original patent would have expired. You cannot use a reissue patent to claim (recapture) subject matter that you voluntarily gave up in the original case; any reissue with broader claims must be filed within two years from the original patent and is subject to the intervening rights statute.

If you can't get or don't want to get a patent on an invention, but want to prevent someone else from getting a patent on it, you can defensively publish your application privately by using a service or by creating your own paper or web-based publication.

If you abandon your application and want to file on it again, you will have to file a *substitute application*; such an application has no connection to the base application. No one may legally receive two patents for the same invention since this would constitute statutory *double patenting.* Also no one may legally receive two patents for two inventions that are not patentably different since this would constitute *obviousness-type double patenting.* However *obviousness-type double patenting* can be avoided by filing a terminal disclaimer so that the two patents will expire at the same time.

CHAPTER

15

After Your Patent Issues: Use, Maintenance, and Infringement

A. Issue Notification..459

B. Press Release and Marketing..459

C. Check Your Patent for Errors..459

    1. If the Errors Aren't Significant...459

    2. Certificate of Correction..460

D. Patent Number Marking...460

E. Advertising Your Patent for Sale...461

F. What Rights Does Your Patent Give You?..462

    1. Enforceable Monopoly Against Manufacture, Use, Sale, Offer for Sale, Importing, Etc...462

    2. Property Rights..463

    3. Medical Procedure Exemption..463

G. Be Wary of Offers to Provide Information About Your Patent................464

H. Maintenance Fees..466

I. Legal Options If You Discover an Infringement of Your Patent..............467

J. What to Do About Patent Infringement...468

K. Product Clearance (Can I Legally Copy or Make That?).............................474

    1. Common Misconceptions...474

    2. Find Out If There's an Applicable Patent and Whether You Will Infringe It......475

    3. What to Do If an In-Force Patent Is Applicable...476

    4. If No In-Force Patent Is Applicable...477

L. How to Cite Prior Art and Other Information in Patent Applications and Patents..477

    1. File a Passive Citation Against Your Own Patent Application................478

    2. Request Supplemental Examination of Your Patent...............................478

    3. File a Passive Citation Against Any Patent Application 478

    4. File for a Post-Grant Review of Patent..478

    5. File a Passive Citation Against a Patent 478

    6. Request *Ex Parte* Reexamination of a Patent..478

    7. Request *Inter Partes* Review of a Patent...479

458 | PATENT IT YOURSELF

M. Injunctions 479

N. Jury Trials 479

O. Arbitration 479

P. Court Appeals 480

Q. How Patent Rights Can Be Forfeited 480

R. Tax Deductions and Income 481

S. Patent Litigation Financing 481

T. Summary 481

> **Inventor's Commandment 30**
>
> Once your patent issues, check it for printing errors, consider patent marking if you manufacture a product covered by the patent, and pay three maintenance fees (3.0 to 3.5, 7.0 to 7.5, and 11.0 to 11.5 years after issue) to keep your patent in force. You should also monitor all products in the field of your patent to discover any possible infringements.

A. Issue Notification

Three to six weeks after you pay the issue fee, you'll usually receive an Issue Notification indicating the number and issue date of your patent. On the issue date, which will usually be on a Tuesday about two weeks after you receive the Issue Notification, the patent will be granted, published, and mailed to you. Allowing for the Post Office to do its job, several days later you'll receive your patent deed (also called "letters patent"). This consists of a copy of your patent on stiff paper, a fancy jacket with a seal, and ribbon. You'll also receive (separately) the printed copies of your patent if you ordered them when you paid your issue fee. The *Official Gazette—Patents*, which is usually published electronically on the Tuesday of grant, will list the highlights of your patent. (The PTO publishes patent applications in which nonpublication requests have not been filed online every Thursday.) Be sure to file any continuation or divisional applications *before* the day the patent issues, or you will lose the ability to do so.

B. Press Release and Marketing

When you learn the number and date of your patent, you may wish to prepare a press release about it. See any book on advertising to learn how to prepare a press release; it should cover the six facets of reporting: *who* received the patent (and *who* do you contact for more information)?; *what* is the invention?; *where* is the patent owner located?; *why* is there a need for this invention?; *when* will the product or service be available?; and *how* does the invention work? Make your headline and text simple and short yet interesting and catchy—for example, "Midgeville Inventor Gets Patent on Jam-Free Bike Mechanism." Be conversational; don't use jargon or technical language. Type on only one side of the paper, double spaced, and include your name, address, phone number, and "For Immediate Release" at the top. Type "###" at the end to signal the end of the press release. Send it to your local papers and trade magazines (each with a copy of your patent) on the day you get the patent.

Also consider using social media to market your patent. If you have set up a company to manufacture, distribute, or license your invention, you can publish the press release directly on its social media outlets or website.

C. Check Your Patent for Errors

After you receive your patent, proofread it carefully, preferably aloud with a friend or coworker. Carefully examine the information in the heading of the patent—serial number, filing date, title, your name, and so on—to make sure all is correct. Then read the patent word for word and compare it with the application in your file as amended during the prosecution phase. If you find errors, you have several possible courses of action.

1. If the Errors Aren't Significant

If the errors aren't significant; that is, if the meaning you intended is still obvious and clear, you should make the error of record in the PTO's file of your patent. To do this, simply write a "make-of-record" letter to be put in the file of your patent, listing the errors you found. This letter should be captioned similarly to Form 15-1 ("Request for Certificate of Correction") with the patent number, issue date, and patentee(s) name(s). Change the heading to read "Make-of-Record Letter for Errors in Printed Patent." Then list all the errors in the patent. File the letter by mail, fax, or online if you're a registered eFiler.

2. Certificate of Correction

If any of the errors you discover are significant—that is, if the meaning is unclear because of a wrong reference numeral, missing or transposed words, failure to include a significant amendment, any errors in the claims, and so on—you may obtain a Certificate of Correction without charge to you. If the errors are the fault of the printer, the PTO will issue the Certificate of Correction free. If the errors are your fault—that is, they appear in your file as well as in the printed patent—you still can get a Certificate of Correction. However, the error must be of a clerical or minor nature and must have occurred in good faith. Examples are a wrong reference numeral or an omitted line or word. (The fee for a Certificate of Correction to fix your error is listed in Appendix 4, "Fee Schedule.") To obtain a Certificate of Correction (printer's fault or yours), do the following:

Step 1: Fill out Forms 15-1 ("Request for Certificate of Correction") and SB/44 (or Form 15-2 "Certificate of Correction"). In Form 15-1 (the request letter), insert the patent number, issue date, patentee(s), Ser. Nr., filing date, and the date you mailed the form. Check paragraph 2 if the error is the fault of the PTO; check paragraph 3 and insert the amount from the Fee Schedule if the error is your fault.

In either case (whether you checked paragraph 2 or 3), in paragraph 4 list the places in the application file where the errors occurred and explain who was at fault; for example:

"4. Specifically, on p. 4, line 12, of the specification, applicant erroneously typed '42' instead of '24' and neither applicant nor the examiner detected this error during prosecution."

or

"4. Specifically, on p. 4, line 12, of the specification, the reference numeral '24' has been erroneously printed by the GPO in the patent as '42' instead of '24.'"

Step 2: Go to the PTO Forms webpage and save the fillable version of SB/44 to your computer (or download Form 15-2; see Appendix 7 for details). Fill in the patent number, issue date, and inventor(s). In the body of the form, describe each correction in a sentence beginning with the word "Column" or "Col." and use semicolons to separate corrections if there are more than one in a column. Indicate the necessary corrections to the actual printed patent by (a) putting quotes around existing words to be changed, deleted, or followed by words to be added, and (b) sandwiching words to be inserted with dashes. For example:

"Col. 3, line 54, change 'the diode' to — varistor 23—."

"Col. 4, line 21, after 'a' insert —red—"

"Col. 5, line 58, delete 'the former.'

Put your return address and the patent number on the bottom of the form.

Step 3: If you're a registered eFiler you can file the Request and the Certificate by Patent Center, but if not, send one copy of completed Form 15-1 and two copies of completed Form 15-2 to Commissioner for Patents, Office of Data Management, ATTN: Certificate of Correction Branch, P.O. Box 1450, Alexandria, VA 22313-1450, with a receipt postcard, and a check for the correct amount if the error was your fault. Certificates of Correction are issued solely in electronic form, appearing as the last page of your electronic patent. They are viewable on the PTO's Patent Center website (patentcenter. uspto.gov).

D. Patent Number Marking

If you already have sales blurbs promoting your invention, change them to indicate that your invention is "patented" rather than "patent pending." If you or a licensee of yours are manufacturing a product embodying the invention, consider marking your product with the patent number.

A section of the patent laws (35 U.S.C. § 287) states that products embodying a patented invention may be marked with the legend "Pat." or "Patent," followed by the patent number. In addition, patent law allows patentees to simply mark the product with a reference to a website and list any applicable patent numbers on the site; that is, "Patented—see www.JonesWidgets.com for patent numbers." If you make or sell properly marked products embodying your invention, you can recover damages from any infringers you sue from the date you began marking, whether they see your notice or not. If you make or sell products but don't mark them with your patent number, or mark them "Patented" without the number, your rights are reduced and you can recover damages only from the date you notify the infringer of infringement, or from the date you file suit against the infringer, whichever is earlier.

Do the actual marking on the product itself, on its package, or by means of a label affixed to the product.

Suppose you don't manufacture any product embodying the invention, or your invention relates to a process that's not associated with a product, so it can't be marked. In these situations you can recover damages from an infringer for the entire period of infringement.

The disadvantage of patent marking is that any sophisticated person who wants to copy your product can easily see the number of your patent, download the patent, read its claims, and attempt to design around the claims of your patent. If you don't mark your product, the potential infringer can probably still get this same information, but only through more expense and effort. In other words, by not marking you may depend in part on human inertia to prevent your invention from being copied. That's why some companies favor not marking their patented products, or simply marking them "Patented" without including the number. They rely on their own familiarity with

the field to enable them to quickly spot and promptly notify any infringer of the existence of the patent.

In the past anyone who falsely marked a product could be sued by a private party and ordered to pay substantial damages, even if the private party was not injured by the false marking. Now, under the AIA, only the government can sue for false marking that doesn't result in harm, although private parties can still sue to recover compensatory damages; that is, damages that the private party incurred due to the false marking. (35 U.S.C. § 292.) In any case, to avoid the possibility of lawsuits from the government or a private party, be sure you don't mark any products with incorrect, inapplicable, or expired patent numbers. Of course, if your patent expires or is found invalid or unenforceable, be sure to omit that patent number from any patent marking.

E. Advertising Your Patent for Sale

If you haven't licensed or sold your invention by the time your patent issues, you can advertise the availability of your patent (that is, your right to exclude others from the market) for license or sale online or in one or more of several publications, such as:

- *Official Gazette for Patents*, Commissioner for Patents, P.O. Box 1450, Alexandria, VA 22313-1450
- *Wall Street Journal*, *U.S.A. Today*, local newspapers in large cities, and so on.

Contact the publications for listing information and fees.

The internet provides many opportunities for advertising your invention and many sites provide methods for listing inventions for sale or license including Patent Auction (www.patentauction.com). Intellectual Ventures (www.intellectualventures.com) buys patents from inventors. Keep in mind that the number of patentees who make successful contacts by advertising their patents is relatively low. Your chances of a successful nibble will be far greater if you use the targeted, individual approach described in Chapter 11.

F. What Rights Does Your Patent Give You?

Now that you've actually obtained a patent, you'll undoubtedly want to know exactly what rights you receive under it.

1. Enforceable Monopoly Against Manufacture, Use, Sale, Offer for Sale, Importing, Etc.

The grant of a patent gives you, or any person or entity to whom you "assigned" (legally transferred) your patent or patent application, a monopoly on the invention defined by the claims of the patent. The monopoly begins with the patent's date of issuance and expires 20 years (plus any extension granted by the PTO), from the date you filed your application. If the patent was issued on an application that is a divisional, continuation, or continuation-in-part (see Chapter 14), the 20 years starts from the filing date of the first application in the priority chain.

The PTO will extend any term if you encountered a delay due to PTO lag, FDA processing of a new drug or medical device application, an appeal, an interference, or a secrecy order. (35 U.S.C. § 154 and 156.)

If the PTO published your patent application prior to issue—usually 18 months after filing (unless you requested earlier publication)—and you actually notified an infringer of your patent application, once your patent issues you can recover from the infringer all damages incurred starting from the actual date of notification. (35 U.S.C. § 154(d).)

Your monopoly gives you the right (35 U.S.C. § 271) to bring a valid suit against anyone who does any of the following during the term of your patent:

1. Makes, uses, offers to sell, sells, or imports the invention defined by the claims of your patent. (There is a DNA exemption that is too complicated to cover here. See 35 U.S.C. § 271(e)(1).) Note also the medical exemption discussed below.
2. Files a new drug application on your invention in the United States.
3. Imports a product made abroad by your patented process (if your U.S. patent covers a process).
4. Induces others to infringe your patent.

5. Offers to sell, sells, or imports a material component of your patented machine or process made especially for use in infringement of your patent and not a staple article of commerce with substantial noninfringing use.
6. Supplies in or from the United States a substantial portion of the components of your patented machine for assembly outside of the United States.

You can use your ownership of the patent to obtain value in any of seven ways:

1. Sell the patent outright.
2. License others to make, use, and/or sell the patented invention in return for royalties under a variety of conditions, subject to the antitrust laws mentioned in the note below.
3. Create a monopoly by preventing anyone else from making, using, or selling the invention. In this case you would manufacture the invention yourself (or have it manufactured for you) and charge more than could have in a competitive situation. Xerox did this in the early days of photocopiers. In other words, a patent will give you the right (within limits) to fix the price of your product! (But you can fix only the price of the patented product, not any accessories—see "Patent and Antitrust," below.)
4. If accused of patent infringement by the owner of another patent, you may be able to assert your patent against the other patent holder and generate a cross-licensing arrangement to avoid paying royalties or having to stop infringing.
5. You can tout your patent in advertising.
6. The patent is a publication (as of its filing date or the filing date of any PPA or foreign patent application from which the patent claims priority) that will prevent others from patenting the same thing.
7. While a patent does not give you any immunity from infringing others' patents, if you are manufacturing anything and another patent holder charges you with infringement, you can sometimes use your patent to (a) show that your

products are separately patentable and not direct copies, and (b) prevent the infringer from using the Doctrine of Equivalents.

Extending the Effectiveness of Your Patent

If you want to continue to make money from your creativity after your patent expires, consider plowing back some of your royalties or proceeds from the sale of the patent for research. In this way you can invent further developments and improvements, and get more and later patents to effectively extend your monopoly beyond its relatively short term. You can even file a new patent application on the improvements when you invent them, but withhold the introduction of products with the improvements until you've milked the market with the basic products. DuPont did this with its *Teflon* and *Teflon II*.

Patent and Antitrust

Occasionally, companies or individuals who own a patent or manufacture a patented invention use their patent to extend their monopoly in ways that violate the antitrust laws. Practices that violate antitrust law include:

- compulsory package licensing (requiring that if a company wants to buy a patent from you, then it must license other, unrelated patents from you)
- product tying arrangements (requiring that anyone who buys your patented salt shaker must fill it with your unpatented salt)
- improper extension of patent term (requiring a licensee pay royalties tied to your patent even after the patent expires),
- compulsory price fixing, and
- other practices that impose undue restraints on free trade all violate the antitrust laws.

Antitrust is very rarely a problem for the independent inventor but can occasionally raise complications for large corporations.

2. Property Rights

The law considers a patent to be personal property (35 U.S.C. § 261) that its owner can sell, give away, or otherwise dispose of. It can even be seized by your judgment creditors, just like your car, a share of stock, or any other item of personal property. Although it's personal property, the actual patent deed you receive from the PTO has no inherent value; so you need not put it in your safe-deposit box or take any steps to preserve it against loss. Your ownership of the patent is recorded in the PTO (just like the deed to your house is recorded by your county's Recorder of Deeds). If you lose the original deed, you can download copies, or the PTO will sell you copies of the printed patent (certified if you desire) and/or certified copies of a title report showing that you're the owner.

Expiration Dates

If you are uncertain as to the expiration date of a patent. Google Patents will tell you the expiration date. Simply enter the patent number into the search bar, ensure that you select the correct patent, and look on the right side of the screen under the "Application XX/XXX,XXX events" section for the current status and expiration date.

---

3. Medical Procedure Exemption

A few years ago, one physician sued another for infringement of a patented ophthalmic surgery technique. This upset the medical establishment, which used its considerable clout to back a federal statute exempting health care providers (for instance, doctors, nurses, and hospitals) from liability for performing medical procedures covered by in-force patents. (35 U.S.C. § 287(c).) In view of this statute, it no longer makes sense to patent medical procedures. However, the statute still allows patent owners to sue health care providers for any activity that infringes a patent on (a) a device, (b) a drug, (c) the use of a drug or device, or (d) a biotechnology process invention.

G. Be Wary of Offers to Provide Information About Your Patent

Soon after being awarded a patent, you may receive an offer by mail, advising that an "article" about you patent was published and offering to send you a copy of the article for a fee. What you'll probably get is a photocopy of a page from the PTO's *Official Gazette*, showing the usual main drawing figure and claim of the patent! Keep in mind that new rackets originate all the time. Another offer very frequently received by patentees, usually about a year or more after their patent issues, comes as a postcard, such as in Fig. 15A. It's an offer with marginal utility to most inventors, and at a very high cost. You can find the same information by searching the USPTO patent database.

A third offer is the "Patent Certificate." This offer is sent to many patentees in an official-looking letter from Washington, marked "U.S. Patent Certificate," "For Official Use Only" (next to the postage stamp), and "Important Patent Information." In reality, it's from a private company that wants to sell you a nicely framed version of your patent. Needless to say, this product has no official value. If you would like to obtain a patent plaque, there are plenty of stores that can make one for you, typically in the $50–$75 range for a basic plaque made of brushed aluminum on a wood frame. (They make excellent wall decorations!)

Fig. 15A—Postcard Offer of Dubious Value

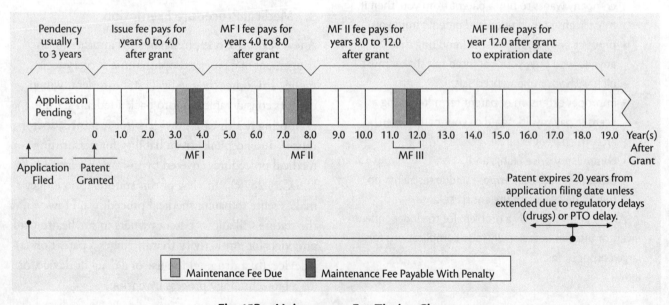

Fig. 15B—Maintenance Fee Timing Chart

Maintenance Fee Reminder

Next fee due: __2018__ / __7__ / __16__
yr   mo   date

(Write year in pencil and change after each payment)

Patent Nr.: __8,032,015__   Issued: __2007/7/16__

Application Serial Nr.: __07/427,862__   Filed: __2005/10/27__

Title: __"Auto mirror with valve"__

Patentee(s) (Inventor[s]/Applicant[s]): __T.R. Jones__

Assignee(s) (if any): __T.R. Ltd.__

Expires __2025/10/27__ (if all three maintenance fees are paid).[1]

☒ Small entity status was filed in application or patent.
(If not, large entity fees[2] must be paid.)

Maintenance Fee Number	Fee Due		Sent Form & Check[4]	Amount	Received Receipt Statement
	From:	To:			
I. Due 3.0 - 3.5 YAI[3]	10 / 7 / 16	11 / 1 / 16	11 / 8 / 16	$ 320	11 / 9 / 15
II. Due 7.0 - 7.5 YAI	14 / 7 / 16	15 / 1 / 16	14 / 8 / 12	$ 1,020	14 / 9 / 14
III. Due 11.0 - 11.5 YAI	18 / 7 / 16	19 / 1 / 16	/ /	$	/ /

Notes: _____

_____

_____

_____

_____

_____

_____

_____

[1] For applications filed after 1995 June 7, expiration is 20 years from filing date of application, or from any earlier domestic nonprovisional (regular) application from which it claims priority, plus any adjustment (extension) granted by the PTO.

[2] Please check all fee amounts before paying, since PTO fees change often.

[3] YAI = Years After Issue date.

[4] Send or make Internet payment at least a month before due date to allow time to take corrective action before entering grace (penalty) period in case PTO does not accept payment.

Fig. 15C—Maintenance Fee Reminder (Form 15-3 in Appendix 7)

A fourth offer, definitely of questionable value, also comes on a postcard that states something like: "Our search of your patent has located X companies that manufacture, market, or sell products in a field allied to your invention." It offers to sell you the names of the X companies for a stiff fee.

A fifth offer is to include you in a compendium of inventors, such as a "Who's Who" of inventors, or an offer to sell you such a volume with your name included. Keep in mind that anyone can publish (or claim to publish!) such a book, but this does not guarantee that anyone else will read it.

Be sure to investigate and think about it carefully (or ask a trusted adviser) before you follow up on any offer.

H. Maintenance Fees

Under the U.S. maintenance fee (MF) system, your patent, when granted, will subsist in force for 20 years from the filing date of its application, provided three maintenance fees are paid.

If you don't pay any MFs, your patent will expire four years from grant. If you pay a first MF between years 3.0 and 3.5 from grant, the PTO will extend the patent to expire eight years from grant. If you pay a second (much higher) MF between years 7.0 and 7.5, the PTO will extend the patent to expire 12 years from grant. And if you pay a third and final (much higher yet) MF between years 11.0 and 11.5, the PTO will extend the patent to expire 20 years (plus any extension the PTO has granted), from filing. This information is presented in Fig. 15B, an MF timing chart. The adjustable arrow indicates that the expiration date varies, depending upon the length of pendency of the application. The online calculator discussed above will calculate your maintenance fees for you.

To help you remember when to pay your MFs, we've provided an MF Reminder Sheet as Form 15-3; a sample is completed in Fig. 15C. Print this sheet and fill it out in ink—except write the year of MF I (three years after issue) in pencil on the top line and leave the last three columns in the table blank. Put the sheet at the end of your current year's calendar. Keep

moving it ahead to the end of each new year's calendar at the end of each year, until the third year after issue when the fee is due. Write that the MF is due on the appropriate date on your calendar for the third year. Fill in the last three columns in the table. When you pay the first fee and receive your receipt statement, change the year at the top of the sheet to the seventh year after issue and repeat the process.

If you forget to pay any fee during its normal six-month payment period, you can pay it in the six-month period grace period following its normal six-month payment period. However, as always, whenever you miss a PTO date you must pay a penalty or surcharge. If you pay a maintenance fee in the grace period, infringers do not acquire "intervening rights"—see below.

If you forgot to pay a maintenance fee in the normal and grace periods, the patent will expire at the end of the grace period. However, an expired patent can be revived on petition if you show, by declaration, that the delay was "unintentional" (Rule 378(c)).

An "unintentional" petition (SB/66 if filing by mail, or Patent Center SB/66 if filing electronically) must merely state that the nonpayment was unintentional. You must accompany the petition by the MF, the MF transmittal letter, and a very high "unintentional" fee (see Appendix 4, "Fee Schedule"). The form is self-explanatory; just be sure to pay the fee for appropriate entity size. If you previously claimed small-entity status, but no longer qualify as a small entity, be sure to check the appropriate box.

Be sure to file the petition and pay the fee as soon as you can. You cannot decide to pay it later, as that would make the intervening period an intentional delay. If you are filing the petition two years after the patent expired or later, the PTO will require you to provide additional information of the facts and circumstances surrounding the delay, to assure itself that the entire delay actually was unintentional.

If any infringement occurred or was prepared for after the patent expired and before it was revived, the infringer has "intervening rights." This means that the infringer can continue any infringing activity performed in the lapse period as if the patent were not revived. (35 U.S.C. § 41(c).)

The easiest way to pay an MF is with a credit card through the PTO's website. Go to the PTO website (www.uspto.gov) and click "Patents," then under "Maintaining a patent" click "Maintenance fees." Next, click "Pay maintenance fees." At this point you must enter the patent number and the application serial number. You can find out how much is currently due by clicking "Retrieve Fees to Pay" or you can view the payment dates by clicking "View Payment windows." After that, click "Pay Using Credit Card" and complete the form by supplying your credit card information. The PTO will present a Maintenance Fee Statement (receipt) on the website showing receipt of payment. Print out the Statement for your records.

If you don't want to pay the fee online, use Form 15-4 ("Maintenance Fee Transmittal Form") or PTO Form SB/45 to pay the maintenance fees.

Complete every blank in the form including the serial number of the application, or the PTO won't accept your fee and the delay may carry you into the grace period, costing you a surcharge. (If you've assigned or licensed your patent to a large entity, check "large entity" on Form 15-4 and pay the large-entity fee.) If the PTO accepts your maintenance fee, they'll send you a Maintenance Fee Statement to this effect.

If you use the Certificate of Mailing at the end of the form, you can send in the fee on the last day of the period. If the last day of the period falls on a Saturday, Sunday, or holiday, it's extended to the next business day. And don't forget a postcard! Of course if, at any time a maintenance fee is due, you feel that your invention's prospects have become nil, you shouldn't pay the fee. In this case, your patent will expire as indicated above.

The PTO won't accept a maintenance fee before its due period and usually sends you an MF reminder only after the due period expires, when you're in the six-month grace (penalty) period. They also usually send you a Notice of Patent Expiration if you don't pay the fee in either the regular or grace periods. The PTO publishes the numbers of lapsed patents in the *Official Gazette* and on its website. If you move, you must notify the PTO of your new address with a separate letter or AIA/123 sent to Mail Stop Post

Issue, Commissioner for Patents, P.O. Box 1450, Alexandria, VA 22313-1450; otherwise the PTO will send your MF receipt to your old address (even if you put your new address on your MF transmittal).

I. Legal Options If You Discover an Infringement of Your Patent

If you find an infringer, you may wish the earth to shake, the skies to thunder, and a mighty lightning bolt to vaporize the miscreant. Failing this, you might wish you could present details of the infringement to the PTO, who will get on a white horse, ride out to the infringer, and strike them down with the sword of justice. In reality, nothing will happen and the infringement will continue unless you affirmatively do something about it. The PTO plays no role in infringement situations. The PTO is in the business of simply issuing patents and doing whatever ancillary functions are necessary. The patent owner must assume the full burden for stopping the infringer and obtaining damages.

Here, viewed broadly, are the steps you can take to get the remuneration you deserve:

- Ask the infringer to stop infringing and pay you compensation for the past infringement (but see the warning below regarding declaratory judgment actions).
- Ask the infringer to pay you compensation for past infringement and royalties for future activity.
- Ask the infringer to buy your patent for a sum that will cover past infringement and the present value of future activity.
- If you're a manufacturer and the infringer has a patent of interest to you, exchange licenses with the infringer.
- Sue the infringer in federal court in the district where the infringer resides or has committed infringement (in the event your above requests are unsuccessful). If you win in court, you will be awarded damages and may also get an injunction, precluding the infringer from using your invention during the remaining term of the patent.

How much can you recover if you successfully sue for infringement? 35 U.S.C. Section 284 states that the court shall award damages adequate to compensate for the infringement, but in no event less than a reasonable royalty for the infringer's activity, plus interest and costs. Sometimes the court will award a patent owner the profits that the infringer made, if it's difficult to determine a reasonable royalty.

In addition to the above "regular" damages, this provision also states that the court may award up to triple ("treble") the damages, and another provision (35 U.S.C. § 285) states that in exceptional cases the court may also award attorneys' fees. In 2016, the Supreme Court ruled that Section 284 enhanced damages are available at the discretion of the trial judge, not for a typical infringement case but "as a 'punitive' or 'vindictive' sanction for egregious infringement behavior. The sort of conduct warranting enhanced damages has been variously described as willful, wanton, malicious, bad-faith, deliberate, consciously wrongful, flagrant, or characteristic of a pirate."

Patent infringement damages and fees sometimes can even exceed the infringer's gross sales. In addition to monetary damages, the court can issue an injunction— an order signed by a federal court ordering the infringer not to infringe any more. If the infringer violates the injunction, they can be subject to contempt-of-court sanctions, including imprisonment and fines.

Unfortunately, and especially in the field of patent enforcement, our legal system is mainly accessible to (and manipulated primarily by) organizations and individuals with deep pockets—those companies that can afford to hire expensive patent litigators and pay the costs of litigation. However, it is often possible for individual inventors to obtain relief by using a contingency-fee litigator or by just implying that they will sue as described below. However, a contingency-fee litigator will not take your case unless (1) you have a fairly strong patent, (2) the infringement is obvious or relatively easy to prove, (3) the damages would be substantial, and (4) the infringer has deep pockets.

Having said all this, it's also fair to add that the patent system would be far more valuable (and equitable) if it provided an effective way for those with shallow pockets to enforce their patents.

J. What to Do About Patent Infringement

Let's now take a closer look at what to do if your patent is infringed.

Claim 1 of Smith Patent x,xxx,xxx	Peel-O-matic Device
1. A device for peeling potatoes, comprising:	The Peel-O-matic device (POMD) is designed to peel potatoes. See description on package (Exhibit A) which states, "Peels all produce faster." A potato is an item of produce.
a handle with a series of finger grips,	The POMD has a handle with a series of finger grips as can be seen in the lower part of the photo on the package (Exhibit A).
a head attached to said handle,	The POMD has a head attached to its handle as shown in Exhibit A.
said head having an elongated blade,	The head includes an elongated blade as also shown in Exhibit A.
said elongated blade having a longitudinal slot,	The elongated blade of the POMD has a longitudinal slot as also shown in Exhibit A.
said longitudinal slot having a pair of elongated, sharpened edges on opposite sides of said slot, said edges facing each other,	The longitudinal slot of the POMD has a pair of elongated, sharpened edges on opposite sides of the slot and these edges face each other as clearly shown in Exhibit A.
whereby said device may be securely held in one's hands by said handle without slipping and may be used to peel potatoes using said sharpened edges of said slot.	The POMD device can be held securely by its handle due to its finger grips and the sharpened edges of its slot may be used to peel potatoes.

Step 1: Obtain Details of the Infringement

If you discover a potential infringement of your patent, obtain as many details and particulars as possible about the infringing device (and about the infringer). To do this, track down service manuals, photographs, actual samples of the infringing device, advertisements, product-catalog sheets, and so on, plus details of the individual or company that is committing the infringement.

Step 2: Compare Your Broadest Claim With the Infringing Device

Many inventors, after being awarded a patent, somehow get the notion that it covers everything in the field, no matter what the claims recite. A patent covers only what the claims recite, plus their equivalents and contributory components (see Steps 3 and 4, below). That means you must compare your patent's claims with the physical nature of the infringing device or process.

To infringe your patent, the device in question must physically have or perform all of the elements contained in the main or broadest claims of your patent. Even if the infringing device has additional elements, it will still infringe. For example, if your claim recites three elements, A, B, and C, and the infringing device has these three elements, it will infringe. If the infringing device has four elements, A, B, C, and D, it will still infringe. But if the infringing device has only two of the three elements, A and B, it *won't* infringe. (See Chapter 9 for more on how to draft broad claims.) Similarly, if the supposed infringing device has three elements A, B, and C′, it won't infringe, provided element C of your claim doesn't "read on" (describe) element C′ of the supposed infringing device. A patent claim is, in effect, a little statute that says, "If each and every one of the following elements is met, infringement occurs. If not all of the elements are met, there is no infringement. If more than all elements claimed are present, infringement still occurs."

To analyze infringement, make a claim chart with two columns. Break the first independent claim into its elements, each one in a respective block in the left column. In each corresponding block in the right column write a brief narrative stating why you feel the corresponding element in the left column is met by the infringing device. Refer to an attached drawing or exhibit. You need do only one independent claim that you believe to be infringed, but if you can do all independent claims, that's best. If the other independent claims differ substantially from Claim 1, you should definitely chart them. A sample claim chart is shown above.

You don't need to do the dependent claims at this time. Remember that each dependent claim incorporates all of the limitations of its referent claim(s) (the claim it refers to and any claim(s) the referent claim(s) refer to). Also, each dependent claim is considered independently of its referent claim(s), after the limitations of the referent claim(s) are incorporated. This is so even if its referent claim(s) is held invalid.

Moreover, even if your patent has 50 claims, you need prove that only one claim is infringed to prove infringement; your damages do not depend upon the number of claims that are infringed. And even if your claims don't literally read on the infringing device, there are still two ways you may be able to bag the infringer: the "doctrine of equivalents" and the "doctrine of contributory infringement."

Step 3: Determine the Extent of the Infringement and the Ability of the Infringer to Pay Damages

In order to convince a contingency-fee litigator to represent you, you must show that (a) your patent is valid, (b) it is infringed, (c) the extent of the infringement is great enough to result in significant damages (money awarded to compensate you for the infringement), and (d) the infringer has enough resources to pay the damages. With regard to (a), since your patent was examined and issued by the PTO, it is presumed valid, but if a litigator wants to make a further validity search or investigation, they'll do it or tell you what to do, so it's not necessary to worry about this now. Your claim chart (Step 2) will show whether it is infringed. To determine the extent of the infringement and the ability of the infringer to pay, you'll have to do some research. Use an online search engine to find out all you can about the infringer and the infringing product. There are services that have

470 | PATENT IT YOURSELF

sales figures for various products and can research them. A business school professor may be able to provide suggestions. You may have to spend several days and travel down many avenues to get enough information to present to the litigator.

Step 4: Apply the Doctrine of Equivalents If Possible

Under the doctrine of equivalents (DoE), even if each element of a patent's claim is not literally met by an element of the device, so long as the element of the device is the "equivalent" of the claimed element, the device can still infringe that element. A device element is equivalent if it performs the same function in the same way to achieve the same result as the claim element, or the role of the device element is substantially the same as that of the claim element.

However, the DoE is severely limited by the "*Festo* rule," named after a 2002 Supreme Court case. Under the *Festo* rule, if the patentee amends a claim in any way during prosecution to make it allowable (this is almost always the case with amendments), the DoE can't be used with that claim unless the patentee can show that the narrowing amendment did not surrender the particular equivalent in question—that is, if the particular infringing equivalent is not related to the way the claim was amended or was not foreseeable at the time. If the patentee fails to make this showing, or if the court can't determine the reason for the amendment, the DoE will not be available.

Even without *Festo*, the DoE did not apply if "file wrapper estoppel" (also known as "prosecution history estoppel") existed—that is, the claim element was amended during prosecution to define over prior art. And the Court of Appeals for the Federal Circuit, which handles patent appeals, said in 2019 that DoE applies "only in exceptional cases" because the public has a right to rely on the language of patent claims.

> **EXAMPLE:** Minerva Murgatroid of San Francisco has a patent on a mechanism for bunching broccoli. Its main claim recites the mechanism, including a recitation that the broccoli is banded with a wire-reinforced paper band. She didn't claim the band more broadly because she didn't think to do so, this being the only type of band that would work at the time she got the patent.

A few years later, LeRoy Phillips of Philadelphia discovers a plastic broccoli band that will work just as well as Minerva's wire-reinforced band. He makes broccoli-banding machines and sells them, with his plastic bands, to Fred Farmer, who uses them to band broccoli on his farm in Fresno. Minerva can sue either LeRoy in Philadelphia or Fred in Fresno. Even though her main claim doesn't literally read on LeRoy's machine—that is, describe all of its physical elements—she can win the infringement suit using the DoE, provided she didn't amend her claims during prosecution so as to invoke the *Festo* doctrine. LeRoy's plastic band is equivalent in structure, function, and result to the wire and paper band, the band material being a relatively minor change that won't get LeRoy or Fred off the hook.

However, suppose during prosecution of her patent application before the PTO, Minerva originally had broad claims to any type of band but then narrowed them to the wire-reinforced paper band to avoid a prior-art reference. In this situation Minerva is subject to the doctrine of file wrapper estoppel and may not use the DoE to rebroaden her claim. Even if Minerva merely amended her claims to make them clearer, under the *Festo* doctrine, she can't use the DoE.

Even though the courts have severely limited the DoE, some patentees can use it in certain circumstances. If one or more elements of claims don't literally read on the infringing device, include something like the following in the right-hand block of your claim chart, adjacent to each element that is not literally met by the infringing device: "This element is not literally met by the Ajax thresher, but the Ajax thresher's crossbeam B meets it under the Doctrine of Equivalents because…."

The Negative Doctrine of Equivalents

There's a rarely used converse of the doctrine of equivalents, the so-called negative (or reverse) doctrine of equivalents. Under this, even if your claims literally read on the infringing device, but the infringing device has a different structure, function, or result than your invention, the device may be held not to infringe. If you have questions about the Doctrine of Equivalents, consult a patent litigator.

Step 5: Consider Whether a Contributory Infringement Has Occurred

If your claims don't read on the infringing device, but the infringing device is a specially made component that's only useful in a machine covered by your patent, the infringer may be liable under the doctrine of contributory infringement.

> EXAMPLE: In the example above, LeRoy makes an entire broccoli-banding machine like Minerva's, except that he doesn't sell or supply any bands. Minerva's claims don't literally read on LeRoy's machine since her claims recite the band. Nevertheless, Minerva can bag LeRoy under the doctrine of contributory infringement, since his broccoli-banding machine is useful only in the mechanism of Minerva's patent claim and since it has no other noninfringing use.

Note that, if a patent holder sues to enforce a method or process claim, a defendant can escape liability if the defendant built and commercially used the invention more than one year before the patent application filing date. (35 U.S.C. § 273.)

Step 6: Find a Patent Attorney

When you first reasonably suspect an infringement, consult with a patent litigator (an attorney who has experience suing patent infringers), since you're getting into waters that are very difficult for the nonlawyer to navigate. Unfortunately, the cost is high, and it's difficult to get a patent litigator to take this type of case on a contingency fee (that is, a case for which you pay them only if you win). This means you'll have to pay the attorney up front (or at least partially up front). It depends on the complexity of your case, but an initial retainer of $20,000 would be typical.

However, if you've got a very strong case and if the infringer is solvent (would be good for the damages if you win), it's possible to find a litigator who will take your case on a contingency-fee basis. If you do get an attorney to work with you, you still may have to pay the out-of-pocket costs through trial; these can run as high as $100,000, so be sure you can afford them.

If, as will usually happen, you can't get a contingency fee arrangement, be prepared for a shock: patent trial attorneys generally charge about $350 to $700 per hour, and a full-blown infringement suit can run to hundreds or even thousands of hours' work, most of it before trial! While in recent years cost-conscious patent owners have tightened belt buckles in court, and challenged issued patents out of court, the American Intellectual Property Law Association (a trade group for patent attorneys) still estimates that the median cost of patent infringement actions through trial (with between $1 million and $10 million at stake) is in the $1.7 million range. Be certain that your damages, if you win, will make this worthwhile. Also, be sure the defendant can pay any judgment you obtain. And don't depend on getting attorneys' fees or triple damages; these are awarded only in "exceptional cases."

Of course, an infringer will usually have the same fee burden, and may be inclined to settle if they think you're serious about suing after your attorney writes a few letters. A substantial number of cases are in fact settled before suit is even brought, and most are settled before trial.

Bear in mind that even if you think you have a good case and that your patent is being willfully infringed, it's impossible to predict anything with certainty when it comes to the law. Unfair outcomes happen, and infringers sometimes prevail. As one cynical lawyer in San Francisco stated, "Whoever puts on the better show wins."

 TIP

The material in the following steps is not intended to help you do your own patent infringement litigation. However, it will give you an overview of what's involved so that you can play an active role in deciding on your course of action and helping your attorney bring its prosecution to a successful conclusion.

Step 7: Write a Letter

In the event an infringement has occurred, the first step is to write a letter:
- Asking the infringer to stop infringing your patent and to pay you royalties for past activity.

- Offering the infringer a license under your patent for future activity and again asking for a settlement for the past infringement.

Remember, any infringer is a potential licensee, so don't make war right away. Beware, however, that your offer of a license may prevent you from ever getting an injunction if a court construes it as evidence that infringement does not cause you irreparable harm.

As is often the case, the letter may go unanswered, or your demands may not be acceded to. If so, you'll have to sue for patent infringement if you want to recover damages or an injunction. Also, if your letter creates a reasonable apprehension that you will sue them, the infringer can sue you in an inconvenient location to have your patent declared invalid under what is known as a "declaratory judgment (DJ) action." To prevent this, don't threaten to sue, but instead simply notify the infringer about your patent. Previously we advised that you could offer the infringer a license, but, under recent anti-patentee decisions, many litigators feel that even this may give the infringer a reasonable apprehension of suit and enable them to file a DJ action against you.

Step 8: Act Promptly

The statute of limitations for patent infringement is six years, which means you cannot recover damages that occurred more than six years back from the date you filed suit. Despite this rather lengthy limitations period, it's important to act rapidly once you become aware of an infringement. Otherwise, the infringer may reasonably argue that it continued to infringe because you appeared not to be concerned. Your inactivity may prevent you from collecting the bulk of the damages you would otherwise be entitled to. This would occur under the legal doctrines known as "estoppel" and "laches," which generally mean that a court won't award you damages if your action (or lack of action in this case) in some way brought those same losses about.

If you're selling a product embodying the invention and you failed to mark it with the patent number, the six-year term of damages can be shortened considerably as a practical matter by application of the patent-marking statute (35 U.S.C. § 287). On the other hand, you can bring suit even after your patent has expired and still go back six years during the time the patent was in force (again, provided that you had some valid reason for delaying your action).

Step 9: Who Should Be Sued?

Obviously, you can sue any manufacturer who makes, uses, sells, imports, or offers for sale any device or practices any process covered by the claims of your patent. You must bring suit against the manufacturer where (1) it has a place of business, and (2) has committed an act of infringement. (If you have a patent that covers a process used abroad to make a device that is imported into the U.S., the importation, sale, offer to sell, and use of the device will be considered to infringe.)

You can also sue the retailer or ultimate purchaser of the invention (including a private individual) as well as the manufacturer. Suits against the retailer or customer are sometimes brought in order to find a court that's favorable, or at least geographically close, to the patent owner. If a suit is brought against the retailer or customer of a patented invention, under the Uniform Commercial Code the manufacturer of the patented invention must step in and defend or reimburse the customer's suit. If your infringer is an out-of-state manufacturer and you can sue its local retailer, it puts a tremendous burden on the manufacturer to defend at a distance.

If the Infringer Has a Government Contract

If the infringer of your patent is a company or individual who's making products embodying your invention under a government contract, you can sue only the government in the Court of Claims in Washington D.C. You can't sue the company and you can't sue in your local jurisdiction. What's more, you can't get an injunction prohibiting the company from manufacturing your invention, since the infringing device may be useful for national defense. In other words, we have compulsory licensing of any patent that covers an invention used by the government. You can, however, recover damages and interest.

Lastly, don't be afraid to take on a big company simply because they have more resources to defend a patent infringement suit than you have to prosecute it. You have the right to a jury trial (see Section N, below), which helps even the playing field.

Note that if you assert patent rights, your opponent may cite prior art including (a) any publication, including a patent, that was published before your filing date, or (b) a U.S. patent that was filed on any date, or claims priority of any earlier application (PPA or foreign) that was filed before your filing date. If this prior art anticipates or renders your invention obvious, it will defeat your right to sue unless you can prove (1) you conceived the invention before the date of the reference and you were diligent in filing your patent application or building and testing the invention, or (2) you built and tested the invention before the date of the reference. The law in this area is complicated and was changed by the AIA, so consult a patent litigator.

Step 10: Consider Stopping Importation of the Infringing Device

If a device covered by your invention is being imported into the United States and the effect of the importation is to harm a domestic industry, you can bring a proceeding before the United States International Trade Commission (USITC, or simply ITC) to have the device stopped at the port of entry by U.S. Customs and Border Protection agents. This proceeding can be brought in addition—or as an alternative—to any other legal action. While it's a complex and expensive process, the exclusion remedy is extremely powerful. The pertinent statute is 19 U.S.C. Section 1337(a), and more information is available at www.usitc.gov.

Patent Trolls and Submarine Patents

You may have heard the terms "patent troll" and "submarine patent." What do these terms mean and how do they affect inventors?

As defined by Wikipedia, "patent troll" is "a pejorative term for a person or company that enforces its patents against one or more alleged infringers in a manner considered unduly aggressive or opportunistic, often with no intention to manufacture or market the patented invention." Less pejorative synonyms are *nonpracticing entity, patent assertion company, nonmanufacturing patentee, patent marketer,* and *patent dealer,* which describe a patent owner who does not manufacture or use the patented invention. Under the U.S. and most other patent systems, patentees are not required to practice their inventions—and most patentees feel that their rights should not be lessened if they don't. Many inventors are more creative than business oriented, and want their creativity fully rewarded even if they don't commercialize their inventions. If you have a patent but don't practice the invention, we suggest you consider yourself no less worthy than a patentee who manufactures the patented invention.

Wikipedia defines the related term "submarine patent" as "a patent first published and granted long after the initial application was filed … . [I]t stays under water … for long periods, then emerges … and surprises the relevant market."

We prefer to call these "delayed-issue" patents. However under present U.S. law, where supplemental cases (divisions, continuations, and CIPs) expire 20 years from the date of the original application, any patent that is significantly delayed by being a supplemental case will have a much shorter in-force period. If you obtain a patent after delay due to one or more supplemental cases, we similarly suggest you consider your patent no less worthy than a patent that issued directly from the first filing.

Remember that each type of patent (from nonpracticing entities and delayed-issue), already covers a significant advance in the art since it issued only after the PTO found that the claims defined an invention that was in a statutory class and a useful, novel, and nonobvious invention.

Design Patent Infringement

Unlike the specificity of utility patent claims, the claim of a design patent is general, so the courts cannot rely on it to determine infringement. Instead, the courts must compare the drawing of the design patent with the accused infringing device. Design patent infringement is determined by the "deceived purchaser" test: The court will hold the design patent infringed if the defendant's accused design could reasonably be viewed as so similar to the patented design that a purchaser familiar with the prior art would be deceived by the similarity between the claimed and accused designs, "inducing him to purchase one supposing it to be the other." As in most evidentiary trials, both sides will call in their "hired guns" (experts) to testify for their side.

If You Discover an Infringement During Pendency

You can recover a reasonable royalty for an infringement that occurs during the pendency of your application, but you must wait until the patent issues to sue for those royalties, and the royalty will only be applicable to infringements that occur after the publication of the application. You must also notify the infringer of the published patent application, and the infringing device or process must be substantially identical to the invention as claimed. (35 U.S.C. § 154(d).) The royalty you receive will be applicable to any infringements that occur after the publication of the application.

If you filed a nonpublication request, and you want to take advantage of this "royalties before issuance" provision, you should rescind the NPR in order to have your application published so that you can rely on the statute. If you discover the infringement well before the normal 18-months-after-filing publication date, you may request that the application be published earlier than 18 months by requesting same and paying the publication fee. (Rule 219 (37 CFR 1.219).)

K. Product Clearance (Can I Legally Copy or Make That?)

This is the other side of the coin: Here we'll assume that, instead of having your own invention, you're interested in copying the invention or product of someone else or making a new product that you feel may be covered by someone else's patent.

1. Common Misconceptions

Before giving you the applicable rules and information, first we want to dispel some widespread misconceptions so you'll start in neutral territory.

Common Misconception: If you make an identical copy of a device or circuit, you can be validly sued for infringement, even if the copied device is not patented.

Fact: You are free to copy any device or circuit, even to the minutest detail, so long as you (1) do not infringe any applicable in-force patent, trademark, or copyright, and (2) don't copy any features that have a "secondary meaning."

Common Misconception: If a product is not marked "Patented" and it does not have a patent number, you are free to copy the product.

Fact: Patented products don't have to be marked as such. (See "Patent Number Marking" in Section D.)

Common Misconception: If a product that you intend to make is shown in the drawing of another's patent, you would be an infringer of that patent if you made the product.

Fact: The claims of a patent essentially determine infringement, but the courts are often allowed to interpret the claims in accordance with the description of the patent.

Common Misconception: What you do in your own home, or for your own personal use, or for charity will not infringe a patent that is otherwise applicable.

Fact: While "home, personal, or charity infringement" may be difficult to detect, these remain legally actionable forms of infringement, opening the door to liability for damages and/or an injunction prohibiting further infringement.

Common Misconception: If you change a patented product a fixed percentage, say 20%, you won't be an infringer.

Fact: The extent to which you can change a patented product and still avoid infringement is not subject to quantitative analysis; it's determined by the breadth of the patent's claims. (See Section J, above.)

2. Find Out If There's an Applicable Patent and Whether You Will Infringe It

Suppose you do want to manufacture a specific product or perform a specific process commercially, and you have some reason to believe it may be covered by an in-force patent or pending application. Under the law, you have a duty of due care to determine whether or not you infringe any in-force patents. How can you fulfill this duty and determine whether you can proceed without infringing any existing or future patent?

Unfortunately, there is no way to be 100% sure, because no search can cover unpublished pending patent applications. However we can give you some pretty specific instructions and guidelines.

If the process or product you wish to duplicate is already manufactured or used, look at the product, the literature accompanying it (including the manufacturer's website), and the packing material, to see if any patent number is given. If you can get the patent number, download it from the PTO website or order the patent from the PTO or a private service. If the patent issued from an application filed before June 8, 1995, it expired on the later of 17 years from issue or 20 years from its filing date. If the patent issued from an application filed on or after June 8, 1995, it expires 20 years from its filing date, or the filing date of any parent cases from which it originated, whichever is

sooner. A patent will expire earlier than its full term if its owner fails to pay the required maintenance fees, so if you are concerned about a patent, check to see if there might have been a fee-based expiration.

If the patent is in force, things usually aren't as bad as they seem. A patent that theoretically covers a product may in reality cover only a minor aspect of the product (such as the housing) that is easy to design around. (But beware: sometimes the claims are narrow because someone else already covered the main function of the product. Check parent patents, the history of claim amendments, and the references cited by the patent as well.) Sometimes the patent doesn't cover the product at all. How can you be sure? The only way is to read its claims carefully, diagramming them and preparing a claim chart, if necessary, to know exactly what they cover. (See Section J, above.) If what you want to manufacture is not covered by the claims, and if you feel there is no other patent on the item you wish to manufacture, you are free to proceed.

If the product or process you wish to manufacture is simply marked "Patented" and carries no number, your task is more difficult. You can write to the company, asking for the number and date of their patent, or whether their patent is in force, but they're not bound to answer, and you'll have tipped your hand by communicating with them.

You can perform a (relatively cheap) search in the PTO or on its website of all of the patents issued to the company in question. But there is no guarantee that this will uncover the manufacturer, since the patent might not be owned by the company in question; the manufacturer may simply be a licensee. The best way to determine applicability of an in-force patent is to make a search in the relevant classes and subclasses of the PTO, have someone make the search for you, or search on the Google or PTO sites. The search should seek any patent on the invention in question. This will involve a greater expenditure of time or money, but at least you will be fairly certain of your position. If, however, there is a patent pending on the product or process, there is no way to obtain any details, even if the manufacturer marks the product "patent pending"; as you can see, not all risks can be eliminated.

If the product or process you wish to manufacture has been known or used in the marketplace for more than 17 years, you can be pretty sure that no in-force patent will be applicable, or that even if one is applicable, it is just about to expire anyway.

If you can't find any U.S. patents and the product or process is relatively new, you shouldn't feel free to copy it because it may be the subject of a pending patent application. It's not possible to search pending U.S. patent applications, since they're kept secret unless published 18 months after filing. You can search published U.S. applications, and you can often find some pending U.S. applications by searching for published corresponding foreign applications, which are all published 18 months after filing. (Also, if the probable owner of a patent application you want to research has been selling the product under a trademark, such as "the Zorch widget," investigate the item in the PTO (trademark applications are not kept secret) to obtain the date of first use of the trademark in the United States. It's likely that the filing date of any patent application is just before the date of first trademark use.

If you find an applicable in-force patent or patent application, and you don't think you can break it, avoid it, or get a license at a reasonable royalty, consider designing around the patent or using older (nonpatented) technology.

3. What to Do If an In-Force Patent Is Applicable

If there is an in-force patent applicable, and you still wish to manufacture the product, you have several alternatives:

- Your first instinct should be to review the claims of the patent and then try to design around them. Often you will find that the claims of a patent have one or more limitations that can be eliminated in your product or process so that you can make the patented invention even cheaper than the patentee. Alternatively, you can design around one of the elements of the patent, make an improved device, and get your own patent on it. Remember, if you don't infringe the independent claims, you won't have to worry about the dependent claims.

- Although we don't advise it, some companies manufacture or use the product or process and hope that the patentee won't catch them. Companies going this route usually follow a good accounting practice, by keeping reasonable royalty reserves (see Chapter 16 for what is a reasonable royalty) in case they're ever caught. Also, they usually analyze the patent, or have a patent attorney do so, to see if there are any good defenses to show that they were not a "willful" infringer, since willful infringers may be subject to triple damages or attorneys' fees in a lawsuit. They must always be aware that the patent owner may discover the infringement, and sue them, and get an injunction prohibiting further manufacturing. Although the idea of manufacturing without a license may seem deceitful, risky, and inadvisable, it's done pretty frequently in the the United States. The infringer simply takes the full-speed-ahead-and-damn-the-torpedoes attitude and hopes to be able to negotiate a favorable settlement or break the patent if caught.

- You can ask the patent owner for a license to manufacture under the in-force patent. However, if you aren't familiar with the patent owner's practices, you take the risk of being refused a license. On top of that, you'll have shown your hand, so that if you do manufacture, the patent owner will be looking out for you and will certainly sue or accuse you of willful infringement in short order.

- You can make an extended validity search to try to "break" (or "invalidate") the patent. Use a professional, experienced searcher to do this, and expect to spend several thousand dollars for a thorough, reliable search. Also, you should obtain a copy of the PTO's file of the patent to see if there are any weaknesses or flaws in the patent that are not apparent from the printed patent itself. The PTO's Public PAIR site makes the files for most recent patents available for free download; otherwise you will have to order it from the PTO (see Appendix 4, "Fee Schedule," for cost) or a private service. Again, the services of an experienced attorney should be employed here, because breaking a patent requires a highly specialized skill set. If the attorney feels that the patent can be invalidated or is not infringed, you can have them write a "green-light letter" to you, explaining in detail why it's highly unlikely you would be liable for infringing the patent. Such a letter can show you are not a willful infringer and help you avoid liability for triple ("treble" in legalese) damages or the patent holder's attorneys' fees if you are sued.

- If you find highly relevant prior art, you can bring it to the patent owner's attention and ask them to disclaim or dedicate the patent to the public, or ask the PTO to review the patent in view of that prior art.

Defending Against Method (Process) Claims

If you are commercially using a method or process that has been patented by someone else and your use preceded the patent's filing date by more than one year, you have an absolute defense against an infringement charge. However, this defense is personal to you and will generally not invalidate the patent. (35 U.S.C. § 273.)

---

4. If No In-Force Patent Is Applicable

Unless there is an in-force patent covering an item, anyone is free to make and manufacture identical copies of it, provided:

- you don't copy the trademark of the product
- the shape of the product itself is not considered a trademark (such as the shape of the world-famous Coca-Cola bottle), and
- you don't copy "secondary meaning" features.

If you buy a product from another in the course of business, your vendor is obligated to indemnify you for any such infringement under the Uniform Commercial Code. However, you can be sued for infringement and be liable for damages. (Hopefully, your vendor will be around to reimburse you.) You can also be subject to an injunction ordering you not to infringe anymore.

One manufacturer's effort to copy a small hardware item by having it manufactured cheaply in Asia backfired. He sent the item overseas with instructions to make several thousand identical copies of the item. Since he didn't give any further instructions, the Asian manufacturer did as instructed, manufacturing and shipping back several thousand copies of the item, including a faithful copy of the embossed trademark of the manufacturer's competitor. The manufacturer then had to spend significant money obliterating the trademark, thereby losing his entire profit in the process.

L. How to Cite Prior Art and Other Information in Patent Applications and Patents

Suppose you're aware of prior art that would affect a patent or patent application, and you want to make the PTO or the public aware. Perhaps you want to get the art in the file of your own patent or application to get it behind you, show your good faith, and put forth your arguments as to why it doesn't invalidate your claims. Or maybe you are manufacturing (or contemplating manufacturing) something based on the invention and you don't want someone to get a patent on it. Or possibly you just want to do it as a public service to prevent an improper patent from issuing or cast a cloud on a patent you know was improperly issued. There are seven ways to cite prior art and other relevant information in order to invalidate or validate patents and patent applications:

- File a passive citation against your own patent application (37 CFR 1.97).
- Request supplemental examination of your patent.
- File a passive citation against any patent application.
- File for a post-grant review of patent.
- File for review of a business method patent.
- File a passive citation against a patent (37 CFR 1.501).
- Request *ex parte* reexamination of a patent.
- Request *inter partes* review of a patent.

Let's examine each of these in more detail.

1. File a Passive Citation Against Your Own Patent Application

As part of your "duty of disclosure" under 37 CFR 1.97 you are required to provide an Information Disclosure Statement (IDS) in which you cite prior art that you are (or become) aware of, against your own application. Once your patent issues, this obligation ends, although it would be considered highly improper and open you up to sanctions if you sue on a patent that you know is invalid.

2. Request Supplemental Examination of Your Patent

Section 12 of the AIA establishes a new procedure, called "supplemental examination," by which a patent owner may request reexamination of the patent in order to have the PTO consider, reconsider, or correct any information relevant to the patent. In addition to prior art, the information can even be inequitable conduct, which the patent holder may correct. If you're aware of any defects in your patent or in your past conduct that may cast a cloud on your patent, request supplemental examination.

3. File a Passive Citation Against Any Patent Application

Under 37 CFR 1.291, a third party (that is, anyone but the patent applicant) can cite prior art against a patent application. The PTO will consider the citation if it includes a fee (see Appendix 4, "Fee Schedule"), an identification of the citation(s), a copy of each citation, and its relevance. Also the relevant portions of non-English citations must be translated. A copy of the citation must be sent to (served upon) the applicant. The citation must be filed before the earlier of (a) a notice of allowance, or (b) the later of six months after the application is published or the date of rejection of any claim in the application. If you are aware of someone else's application and feel it's not patentable, submit a timely citation.

The protest may cite prior art and even raise issues of inequitable conduct, but the rules are complex, and the situation warrants the assistance of a patent attorney.

4. File for a Post-Grant Review of Patent

A post-grant review (PGR) procedure allows anyone to challenge a patent on any invalidity ground for nine months after the patent issues. However the standard is high: The challenge must initially show it's likely that at least one claim of the patent is unpatentable, or that a novel and unsettled legal question is involved. If someone initiates a post-grant or *inter partes* review (see below), they cannot use this as the basis or grounds for the review in a later declaratory judgment or infringement civil action. If you're aware of another's patent that you feel should not have issued, and your evidence meets the criteria, file for a post-grant review within nine months after issuance. If the post-grant review is not successful, you may institute an *inter partes* review—see below.

5. File a Passive Citation Against a Patent

Under 37 CFR 1.501, anyone can cite prior art in the file of a patent. (If the patentee makes the citation, it must include an explanation of the pertinence of the art and how the claims differ from the art.) The person making the citation may make it anonymously and should send copies to the PTO (no fee required) and the patentee, or should file it in duplicate with the PTO.

6. Request *Ex Parte* Reexamination of a Patent

Anyone can cite newly discovered prior art against a patent and have it reexamined at any time during the pendency of the patent. If you're aware of another's patent that you feel should not have issued, your evidence meets the criteria, and you're willing to go through the expense of filing, you may institute an *ex parte* reexamination. As the *ex parte* reexamination procedure is somewhat complicated and the PTO fee is expensive, we suggest you consult an attorney if you want to go this route. Once you file a request for *ex parte* reexamination, that is the end of your participation in the process. The PTO will either deny your request, or grant it and reopen prosecution of the patent with the patent owner.

7. Request *Inter Partes* Review of a Patent

Unlike an *ex parte* reexamination, in which your participation ends after you file the request, an *inter partes* review is like a miniature trial between you and the patent owner, conducted by the PTO's Patent Trial and Appeal Board (PTAB).

The standard for review in an *inter partes* review is the higher standard of the post-grant review (above), and the grounds for overturning the patent are limited to prior art patents and other publications. An *inter partes* review must be initiated after nine months after grant or after termination of post-grant review proceedings. If you're aware of another's patent that you feel should not have issued, your evidence meets the criteria, and you're willing to go through the expense of filing and litigating an adversary proceeding, you may institute an *inter partes* review no sooner than nine months after issuance. Again, the procedure is complicated, the PTO fee is expensive, and attorney fees will be high, so we suggest you consult an attorney if you want to institute an *inter partes* review.

M. Injunctions

Litigation favors wealthy or large corporations, which are far better equipped to defend and maintain patent infringement suits than a single individual. Nevertheless, for the patent owner a successful suit holds the promise of monetary damages for past infringement, and the potential for a court-ordered injunction forbidding the infringer from continuing the infringement.

However, the U.S. Supreme Court has held that even if a court finds that a patent is valid and infringed, the patent owner is not automatically entitled to an injunction against further infringement. Under the Supreme Court's ruling, a trial court shouldn't issue an injunction unless the patent owner shows a balance of equity in its favor—for example, the patent owner is selling products employing the invention and would be damaged by letting the defendant continue to infringe.

An accused infringer of a patent can avoid liability (that is—defend against the infringement action) in three different ways:

- by showing that the claims of the patent aren't infringed (discussed above)
- by showing that the patent is invalid (discussed below), or
- a showing that the claims are too vague and indefinite under 35 U.S.C. Section 112, or

With regard to the second item in the above list, the validity of the patent being sued on can be challenged by:

- prior-art references that the PTO didn't discover or use properly
- proof that the specific machine covered by the patent is inoperable
- a showing that disclosure of the patent is incomplete; that is, it doesn't teach one skilled in the art to make and use the patented invention
- a showing that the claims are too vague and indefinite under Section 112, or
- a showing that the patent was issued to the wrong inventor, or some other fundamental mistake.

N. Jury Trials

Most juries favor individual patent holders, and many have awarded large damages in patent infringement actions, especially where an individual patent holder has sued a large corporation. So, if you sue on a patent, always demand a jury trial: most juries usually award more than a judge will. Be aware, however, that only judges, not juries, have the power to interpret claims; juries have the power to determine whether a particular device or process fits the meaning of those claims.

O. Arbitration

Instead of a lawsuit, if both parties agree, the entire infringement dispute can be submitted to arbitration. An arbitrator, usually a patent attorney or retired judge, will hear from both sides in a relatively informal proceeding. The arbitrator will adjudicate the patent's validity, infringement, and so on. The arbitrator's fee (about $10,000 to $50,000 and up) is far cheaper than the cost of a regular lawsuit complete with depositions, formal interrogatories, and other formal proceedings. The process is also much faster than litigation. The arbitrator must file the award with the PTO. The American Arbitration Association is frequently used and has rules for arbitration of patent disputes, but the parties can use any arbitrator(s) they choose. Note, however, that the results of an arbitration cannot be appealed, unlike the results of a trial.

P. Court Appeals

After trial, either party to a suit may appeal the case to the Court of Appeals for the Federal Circuit (CAFC) if they believe the law was erroneously applied at trial. Both parties will be required to submit written legal briefs, explaining their positions. On appeal, the CAFC will review the law that the judge used, and whether it was applied correctly to the facts of the case, but the CAFC will not disturb the factual conclusions of the judge or jury. A decision from the CAFC could affirm that outcome at trial, or could reverse that outcome, or could send the suit back to the trial court for further proceedings.

If either party believes that the Federal Circuit also decided the case incorrectly based on the law, or that the law itself is flawed, it may appeal the decision to the court of last resort, the Supreme Court of the United States (SCOTUS). Unlike the CAFC, the SCOTUS does not have to hear the appeal, and can deny it without further comment. If it does decide to hear the case, it will require further briefing from the parties, hear oral arguments, and render its decision.

Each court of appeals may leave the decision of the court under it intact, or direct that court to take some further action. Thus, the SCOTUS may direct the CAFC to consider the case again with a different interpretation of the law, or applying a different test

(e.g., for infringement). The CAFC may direct the trial court to alter the amount of an award to the patent owner, or even to retry the entire case. Or, an appeals court may reverse the decision of the lower court outright.

Q. How Patent Rights Can Be Forfeited

Patents and their claims can be, and often are, retroactively declared invalid or unenforceable by the PTO or the courts for various reasons, including:

- relevant prior art that wasn't previously uncovered
- public use or sale of the invention prior to the filing date of the patent application
- misuse of the patent by its owner—for example, by committing antitrust violations, or
- fraud on the PTO committed by the inventor— for example, by failing to reveal relevant facts about the invention and the prior art.

Your airtight infringement action goes down the drain when the PTO or the judge declares your patent invalid or unenforceable. Still, about 50% of patents that get to court are upheld. In addition, the percentage of patents that are treated as valid is higher than the court statistics indicate, since they don't count the many patents that don't get to court because the infringers saw the impossibility of invalidating them or didn't want to spend the $250,000 or more necessary to fight the patent.

In addition to showing that the patent is invalid or not infringed, an accused infringer of a patent can avoid liability by convincing a court that the patent should be declared nonenforceable by showing that the owner of the patent has misused the patent in some way or has engaged in some illegal conduct that makes it inequitable for the owner to enforce the patent. Some examples of conduct that will preclude enforceability of a patent are:

- false marking (marking products with patent numbers that don't cover the product marked)
- illegal licensing practices, such as false threats of infringement

- various antitrust violations, such as package licensing (also known as "tying" arrangements) where the patent owner requires purchasers of the product to also buy its consumable parts (for example, salt for a patented salt shaker)
- extended delay in bringing suit, which works to the prejudice of the accused infringer
- fraud on the PTO, such as withholding a valuable reference or information about your own actions from your Information Disclosure Statement, or failing to disclose the full and truthful information about your invention in your patent application, and
- expiration of the patent due to failure to pay a maintenance fee, or acquisition of intervening rights by a defendant who engaged in activity that would have infringed during a period when a maintenance fee was not paid (see Section H above).

R. Tax Deductions and Income

Unfortunately, most inventors give no thought whatever to taxes, either with regard to the money they spend to get their patents, or to the money they make when they sell or license their patents. We say "unfortunately" because the government may effectively subsidize your patent expenses by allowing you to deduct them. Because of space limitations, we'll provide only the basics. The following information does not constitute tax advice, and you should consult a tax professional or the IRS for the final word:

1. You may be able to legally deduct your patent and invention expenses (that is, the cost of this book, patent searches, drafting and attorney fees, PTO fees, technical research, models, experimentation and testing, depreciable property, and so on) if the IRS considers that your inventing constitutes a trade or business.

2. If you license your invention on a nonexclusive basis, you haven't given away all of your rights, so your royalties are considered ordinary income.

3. If you sell all of your patent rights, or grant a full exclusive license, the IRS considers that you've sold it all; your receipts or royalties, even though received over a long number of years, are considered capital gains.

S. Patent Litigation Financing

Because of the high cost of litigation, cost assistance (at a price) is now available from several companies. Lloyd's of London (www.lloyds.com) and Intellectual Property Insurance Services Corp. (www.ipisc.com) write policies directly. These companies will, in return for an annual premium, reimburse part or all of the cost of patent enforcement litigation, up to the policy limit. You can even begin coverage while your patent application is pending. However, some companies may have a less-than-optimal rating and some may require you to jump through difficult hoops, such as getting an infringement and validity opinion from an independent attorney, before they will reimburse your expenses.

Carefully investigate any company before engaging them. Also, remember that most attorneys will take on contingency-fee litigation only if the damages are substantial, the defendant has a deep pocket, and the patent is strong and clearly infringed.

If you want to sell your patent, Ocean Tomo (www.oceantomo.com) holds auctions of patents and provides other patent fiscal services.

RESOURCE

Nolo.com. Nolo (publisher of this book) maintains a lawyer directory with links to many patent and intellectual property attorneys.

T. Summary

After you pay the issue fee, the PTO will print your patent and send you an Issue Notification and then the deed, within a few months. It may be helpful to prepare a press release or advertise your patent for sale at this time. Check your patent for printing or other errors and obtain a Certificate of Correction if necessary. If the error is yours, the PTO charges a fee for issuing a Certificate. If you or a licensee is manufacturing a product under the patent, consider marking the product with the patent number. If you mark you can recover damages from infringers from the date you started marking, but they will have easy access to your patent number and may be more inclined to break your patent or design around it. A patent is intangible personal property that gives you a monopoly on the invention covered by the claims (so long as maintenance fees are paid), against anyone who makes, uses, sells, imports, or otherwise gains an advantage from the invention. You can profit from a patent by selling or licensing it or using it to exclude others to create a monopoly (with higher prices) for yourself. However patents on medical procedures are no longer enforceable against health care providers. Patentees often get offers for goods or services, but most are of no value.

Be sure to pay the three maintenance fees to keep your patent in force: The first is due 3.0 to 3.5 years after issue, the second at 7.0 to 7.5 years, and the third at 11.0 to 11.5 years. If you neglect to pay any fee in the due period you may pay it in a grace period (next six months) with a surcharge and thereafter if the delay was unintentional (two-year limit). However if you pay it after the grace period any infringer will acquire intervening rights.

If you discover an infringer, the PTO will not help you; you must contact or sue the infringer. First get details of the infringing product, the company that makes it, including the amount of product sales, and the financial resources of the company. Then, compare your

claims to verify infringement (be aware of the doctrine of equivalents and contributory infringement), write a letter, and sue in court or with the ITC if necessary.

To determine if you can make a product it is usually necessary to make a subject-matter search for applicable in-force patents. If an in-force patent is applicable you can design around the patent, ask for a license, or try to break the patent.

There are seven ways to cite prior art and other relevant information in order to invalidate or validate patents and patent applications:

- File a passive citation against your own patent application.
- Request supplemental examination of your patent.
- File a passive citation against any patent application.
- File for a post-grant review of patent.
- File a passive citation against a patent.
- Request *ex parte* reexamination of a patent.
- Request *inter partes* review of a patent.

All patent appeals must go to the Court of Appeals for the Federal Circuit. Juries no longer have the power to interpret patent claims, but they are usually otherwise pro-patentee. Arbitration is an alternative to patent infringement lawsuits. Patent rights can be forfeited in various ways—that is, if relevant prior art or a prior public use or sale is discovered, the patent is misused, or the patentee committed fraud on the PTO by not citing prior art that it knew of.

Patent expenses can be deducted from ordinary income if you're a serious inventor, or otherwise just against royalties. Insurance is available to finance patent litigation and companies and attorneys are available to finance patent infringement litigation on a contingency basis.

CHAPTER

16

Ownership, Assignment, and Licensing of Inventions

A. Inventor, Applicant, Owner	484
B. The Property Nature of Patents	485
C. Who Can Apply for a Patent?	485
D. Joint Owners' Agreement	487
E. Special Issues Faced by the Employed Inventor	487
F. Assignment of Invention and Patent Rights	490
G. Record Your Assignment With the PTO	492
H. Licensing of Inventions—An Overview	492
I. Universal License Agreement	495
J. How Much Should You Get for Your Invention?	499
K. Summary	500

Inventor's Commandment 31

The inventor(s) named in a patent application will be considered the owner(s) of the application and patent, unless they assign their ownership to another person or legal entity. To transfer partial or complete ownership of an application or patent, the inventor-applicant(s) must sign an assignment. To give permission to practice a claimed invention (usually in return for royalties), the inventor-applicants(s) must use a license agreement.

Inventor's Commandment 32

If a patent has several owners, unless an agreement says otherwise the law permits any owner to practice the invention without accounting to any other owners. All joint owners should consider signing a Joint Owners' Agreement requiring cooperation and sharing of any profits from the patent.

In the simplest possible situation, a single inventor invents something, obtains a patent on it, manufactures it, and markets it directly to the public for the full period that the patent remains in force. In most instances, things are not that simple. Two or more people may be involved in the conception of the invention, and many more might play a part in its development and marketing. A business could want to use the invention and be willing to pay large royalties for the privilege. Employees and employers may disagree over who owns a particular invention that was developed at least partially on company time, or with company materials or facilities. It's easy to see how questions of invention ownership and use can become complex.

This chapter outlines some of the ways to deal with these various ownership questions and the agreements often used in the process. However, because the subject of invention ownership, licensing, and transfer is complicated, you'll probably want to retain a lawyer, if only to review your plans and paperwork.

TIP

Licensing resource. For detailed assistance with the licensing process, consult *Profit From Your Idea: How to Make Smart Licensing Deals* by Richard Stim (Nolo). This guide helps to understand the licensing process, determine ownership rights, work with agents effectively, find potential licensees, publicly show inventions without risk, and draft a comprehensive licensing agreement.

A. Inventor, Applicant, Owner

The process of monetizing an idea as a patent involves people playing different roles at different times, each role having distinct duties and privileges. Sometimes, a single person involved with different stages of the process may fill several roles, "wearing many hats" at once, and from this person's perspective the lines between these roles may blur. However, it is important to keep in mind these distinctions, and know which "hat" you are wearing at what times.

"Inventor" is a term reserved for those involved in the creative side of the process. The U.S. patent laws define an inventor as "the individual or, if a joint invention, the individuals collectively who invented or discovered the subject matter of the invention." (35 U.S.C. § 100(f).)

"Applicant" is used for anyone (whether a natural person or a "juristic entity"; that is, a corporate or other state-licensed business) who is applying for a patent for an invention. In many cases, the patent applicant will be the inventor. However, as discussed below in section E, the applicant commonly is an inventor's employer. While the applicant may change over time, the inventor of a particular claimed invention does not.

An "owner" is someone who has the ability to direct how an invention may be exploited. When a patent application is filed it creates new property that is owned initially by the inventor. But like any other property, it may be transferred ("assigned") to others, whether sold or gifted. As a common example, when the applicant is the inventor's employer, the employer may require the inventor to assign her rights in the invention as part of the employment contract. The application may be carved up for sale like plots of land within a subdivision. And once it issues as a patent, the nature of the property changes, with its owner or owners taking on new responsibilities (such as the obligation to pay maintenance fees).

B. The Property Nature of Patents

Think of a patent as a valuable property right, although the "property" is essentially intangible and physical possession doesn't count. The patent property right gives you the right to exclude others from manufacturing, using, selling, and importing your invention. This means that society has given you, in effect, an enforceable legal monopoly on the invention for the in-force period of the patent.

If you do grant a company permission to use your invention, but do not sell the patent outright, the law terms this permission a "license." As with most other intangible economic rights—such as the right to operate a business, the right to withdraw money from a bank account, and the right to vote stock in a corporation—patent rights, or a portion of them, can be sold to others, or licensed for a particular use over a particular period of time.

An invention has virtually no economic value to its inventor unless it is patented, sold, licensed, or used as a trade secret, or it has some other protection under intellectual property laws.

C. Who Can Apply for a Patent?

Until September 2012, only inventor(s) could apply for patents in the United States absent the existence of certain special hardship situations (for example, the inventor refused to file an application for an assignee, or could not be found). The inventor was considered the owner of rights in the invention unless the inventor assigned those rights to someone else. After passage of the America Invents Act (AIA), the inventor's assignee (person or entity to whom the patent is assigned) or someone to whom the inventor is legally bound to assign the invention (for example,

through contract, such as an employment contract) is allowed to file a patent application. However, even though an assignee can file and prosecute a patent application, each inventor must still execute an oath or declaration. Further, the PTO has indicated that it will continue to use the inventor's name for application and patent identification purposes.

What happens to patent ownership if more than one person is involved in a particular invention? If others are involved in the inventing stage, they're considered joint or coinventors. Most often, the challenge is to determine what type of activity constitutes invention. For instance, suppose one person came up with the concept of the invention, while the other merely built and tested it—that is, did not contribute any inventive concepts but merely did what any skilled artisan or model maker could do. In this situation the PTO does not consider the second person to be a coinventor. Similarly, financiers, or others who provided business advice, but not technical input, should not be listed as coinventors.

On the other hand, suppose one person came up with the idea for an invention and a model maker then came up with valuable suggestions and contributions that went beyond the skill of an ordinary model maker or machinist, making the invention work far better. In this situation both people should be named as coinventors on the patent application, provided the model maker's contribution is present in at least one claim.

The PTO and the courts don't recognize degrees of inventorship, so the order in which the inventors are named on a patent application is legally irrelevant,—although the first-named inventor will be more prominent in the printed patent.

If the joint applicants invented different parts of the claimed invention, they should keep accurate records as to what part each invented. That way, if one inventor's part is dropped later during the prosecution, they can change the named inventors. For this purpose downloadable Form 16-1, Joint Applicants—Statement of Respective Contributions, is provided. See Appendix 7 for details.

Completing this form is straightforward: Enter the title of the application or invention, then fill out each inventor's contribution. Have each inventor sign and date in the column adjacent to their contribution. Each inventor should keep a copy of the form (don't file it with the PTO) and refer to it later—for example, if the claims are changed in any way so that one inventor's contribution is no longer claimed, the inventors should remove that inventor from the application. (For more information, see 37 CFR 1.48 and 1.324.) Joint inventors need not have worked together either physically or at the same time, and each need not have made the same type or amount of contribution. To qualify as a coinventor, an inventor need merely have contributed something conceptually to at least one claim of the application, even if it's a dependent claim.

Another problem sometimes arises when two or more persons work on an invention, but not all of them are named in the patent application. Inventorship disputes with the omitted inventor(s) sometimes arise later. For example, a model builder may come back after an application is filed and claim to have been wrongfully excluded as an inventor. One way to avoid such problems is for all inventors to keep a lab notebook—that is, a technical diary, which faithfully records all developments and is frequently signed by the inventor(s) and witnesses. In that way the complaining model builder's argument can be answered by positive proof from the true inventor(s). Using the Consultant's Work Agreement (Form 4-3) will also help eliminate many potential disputes, since it requires the consultant to assign (legally transfer ownership of) all inventions that they make to the inventor who hires the consultant. Absent such documentation or agreement, expensive disputes can arise, with only vague memories to rely upon.

It's important to include in your application all the inventors who are true inventors and to exclude those who aren't inventors. For example, it is a practice in some companies that the Chief Technology Officer (CTO) or other Important Person like a project lead is considered an "inventor" on all inventions under their purview, even if the person is not directly involved in the conceptual development. While this designation might be important internally; for example, for reasons of compensation, it would be wrong to list this person as an inventor on an application submitted to the PTO unless they directly contributed some concept to one or more claims. If it is discovered later that your inventorship is incorrect, and that the mistake resulted from bad faith, your patent can be held invalid, although this rarely happens. (If you do discover that the wrong inventor(s) is (are) named on a patent or patent application, this can be corrected under 37 CFR 1.48 or 1.324.)

Common Misconception: If you came up with a bare concept for a valuable invention and your associate "took your ball and ran with it"—that is, built and tested the invention after hundreds of hours of work leading to final success, then your associate must be named as a coinventor with you.

Fact: As stated above, only the true inventor(s)—that is, the one(s) who came up with at least one inventive concept recited in at least one claim—should be named. An associate who did only what any model maker would have done should not legally be named as coinventor, no matter how much work was involved. On the other hand, if your associate contributed at least one inventive concept that made the invention work better, and that is recited in at least one claim, then the associate should be named as a joint inventor with you.

Changing Inventorship

If you find that the incorrect inventors are named in a patent application or patent—for example, due to a change in the subject matter claimed (that is, cancellation of a claim that recited one inventor's contribution), or discovery of an earlier error—you can correct inventorship by following the procedures under 37 CFR 1.48 (patent applications) or 1.324 (issued patents). At least one original inventor must always be retained; that is, it is not possible to change inventorship so that none of the inventors named in the application as originally filed remain.

D. Joint Owners' Agreement

Problems commonly arise in situations where there are two or more inventors or owners of a patent application or patent. These include questions as to who is entitled to commercially exploit the invention, who is entitled to any financial shares, and what type of accounting must be performed on partnership books. Fortunately, most of these problems can be predicted and ameliorated, if not completely prevented, by the use of a Joint Owners' Agreement (JOA).

The JOA is also desirable because a federal statute (35 U.S.C. § 262) provides that either of the joint owners of a patent may make, use, or sell the patented invention without the consent of and without accounting to (paying) the other joint owner(s).

This statute might seem unfair, since it can work a severe hardship on one joint owner in either of two ways:

1. If one joint owner exploits and derives income from the patent while pushing the other aside, the passive joint owner (PJO) will not be rewarded for any inventive contribution (if the PJO is an inventor) or any capital contribution (if the PJO is an investor—that is, someone who has bought part of the patent).

2. If one joint owner works hard to engineer and develop a market for the patented product, the other joint owner can step in as a competitor without compensating the engineer or marketing pathmaker for the efforts accomplished.

Form 16-2 (Joint Owners' Agreement) prevents these results from occurring and also accomplishes the following:

- Prohibits any joint owner from exploiting the patent without everyone's consent, except that if there is a dissenter, a majority can act if consultation is unsuccessful.
- Provides that in case of an equally divided vote, the parties will select an arbiter, whose decision shall control.
- Provides that disputes are to be resolved by mediation or binding arbitration if mediation fails.
- Provides that the parties shall share profits proportionately, according to their interests in expenditures and income, except that if one party does not agree to an expenditure, the other(s) can advance the amount in question, subject to double reimbursement from any income.
- Provides that if an owner desires to manufacture or sell the patented invention, that owner must pay a reasonable royalty to all other owners, including the manufacturing owner.

Think of this agreement as one solution to an unfair statute. You may ignore, modify, add to, or replace this agreement with any understanding you wish, so long as you're aware of the problems of Section 262, as paraphrased above. As with any contract, you should consider seeking advice from an attorney before signing.

Completing the JOA of Form 16-2 is straightforward. Fill it in after or concurrently with an assignment or a joint patent application. Fill in the names and respective percentages owned by each at the top of the form, identify the patent application (or patent) next, and have each joint owner sign and date the end of the form. As with all agreements, each signer (joint owner) should get and preserve an original signed copy. The JOA should not be filed in the PTO.

CAUTION

If you want to be sure that your joint owners' agreement accurately reflects your needs, consult a patent attorney.

E. Special Issues Faced by the Employed Inventor

Many inventors are employed in industries that are at least somewhat related to the inventing they do on their own time. Such inventors naturally have a strong desire to learn what rights, if any, they have on inventions that they make during their employment, both on their own time and when they are on the job. This complex subject is covered in detail in *Profit From Your Idea: How to Make Smart Licensing Deals*, by Richard Stim (Nolo). We'll just cover the high points here.

Agreement

IN CONSIDERATION of my employment or the continuance of my employment by VARIAN ASSOCIATES, I agree as follows:

For the purpose of this Agreement the term "the Company" shall include VARIAN ASSOCIATES, its subsidiaries and, or its affiliates in which VARIAN ASSOCIATES now or hereafter during the term of this Agreement owns more than twenty percent of the stock eligible to vote for directors and the assignees and licensees of VARIAN ASSOCIATES, its subsidiaries and affiliates.

I agree that all information and know-how, whether or not in writing, of a private, secret or confidential nature concerning the Company's business affairs, including its inventions, products, processes, projects, developments, and plans are and shall be the property of the Company, and I will not disclose the same to unauthorized persons or use the same for any unauthorized purposes without written approval by an officer of the Company, either during or after the term of my employment, until such time as such information has become public knowledge. I also agree to treat all U. S. Government classified information and material in the manner specified by applicable Government regulations.

I agree that all files, letters, memos, reports, sketches, drawings, laboratory notebooks or other written material containing matter of the type set forth in paragraph 2 above which shall come into my custody or possession shall be and are the exclusive property of the Company to be used by me only in the performance of Company duties and that all such records or copies thereof in my custody or possession shall be delivered to the Company upon termination of my employment.

I agree that my obligation not to disclose or to use proprietary or confidential information of the types set forth in paragraphs 2 and 3 above also extends to such types of information of customers of the Company or suppliers to the Company, who may have disclosed or entrusted such information to the Company or me in the course of business.

I hereby assign and agree to assign to the Company or its designee all my right, title and interest in and to all inventions, improvements, discoveries or technical developments, whether or not patentable which I, solely or jointly with others, may conceive or reduce to practice during the term of my employment and which are conceived or first actually reduced to practice (a) in the utilization by the Company of my services in a technical or professional capacity in the areas of research, development, marketing, management, engineering or manufacturing, or (b) pursuant to any project of which I am a participant or member and that is either financed or directed by the Company, or (c) at the Company's expense, in whole or in part. All other inventions, improvements, discoveries or technical developments shall remain my property.

I agree to promptly disclose to and to cooperate with the Company or its designee, both during and after employment, with respect to the procurement of patents for the establishment and maintenance of the Company's or its designee's rights and interests in said inventions, improvements, discoveries or developments, and to sign all papers which the Company may deem necessary or desirable for the purpose of vesting the Company or its designee with such rights, the expense thereof to be borne by the Company.

Since I am to assign to the Company certain inventions which I may conceive or first actually reduce to practice after I enter the employ of the Company, I have listed below all those inventions which I own at this time and which I believe should be brought to the attention of the Company to avoid future misunderstandings as to ownership.

I agree that I will make no claim for pecuniary award or compensation under the provisions of the Atomic Energy Act of 1954, as amended, with respect to any invention or discovery made or conceived by me, solely or jointly with others, in the course of or under any contracts that the Company now has or may have pertaining to work for the Atomic Energy Commission during the term of my employment.

DATE _____ EMPLOYEE _____

DATE _____ WITNESS _____

PRIOR INVENTIONS OWNED BY EMPLOYEE
(PLEASE USE REVERSE SIDE IF MORE SPACE IS REQUIRED)

_____
_____
_____
_____

Fig. 16A—Typical Employment Agreement

Generally, the rights and obligations of employed inventors are covered by the Employment Agreement (EA) they sign with their employer—that is, the EA prevails—unless it conflicts with state law. Above is an example (Fig. 16A) of a typical EA.

If you have *no* EA, it is possible that an employer may own rights to your employee-created invention under the "employed to invent" doctrine. How does this rule apply? If you are employed—even without a written employment agreement—to accomplish a defined task, or are hired or directed to create an invention, your employer will own all rights to the subsequent invention. This doctrine is derived from a Supreme Court ruling that stated, "One employed to make an invention, who succeeds, during his term of service, in accomplishing that task, is bound to assign to his employer any patent obtained." Generally, most companies prefer to use an EA because it is more reliable and easier to enforce than this judicially created obligation.

If you have no EA and are not employed to invent, you'll own all your inventions, subject to the employer's extensive "shop rights" (that is, a right to use the invention solely for the employer's business, without paying the employee) on inventions made using company time, facilities, or materials.

If you *have* an EA, it will almost certainly require that you assign (legally transfer) to your employer all inventions, that are:

1. made during the term of employment (note that Form 16A asks you to list all inventions you owned prior to employment—those are excluded from the agreement)
2. related to the employer's existing or contemplated business
3. made by using the employer's time (that is, the time for which the employee is paid), facilities, or materials, or
4. made as a result of activity within the scope of the employee's duties.

Note that under items 1, 2, and 4, even if an employee makes an invention at home, on the employee's own time, the employer still can be entitled to ownership.

Also, you'll usually be bound to disclose all inventions to the employer (so the employer can determine if they're assignable). Lastly, most EAs will require you to keep your employer's trade secrets confidential during and after your employment. Some states, such as California, have enacted statutes prohibiting the employer from requiring the employee to sign any EA with terms broader than those listed above. For example, under such statutes the employee can't be made to turn over all inventions, no matter where and when made, to the employer. Similarly, the employer is prohibited from providing an EA that states that everything an employee acquires from the employer (except salary) belongs to the employer.

EXAMPLE: Griselda is an engineer employed by Silicon Valley Chips (SVC) to design integrated circuits. Griselda's EA requires her to disclose to SVC all inventions made during the term of her employment at SVC and to assign to SVC all inventions which relate to integrated circuits or SVC's business, or which she makes using SVC's time, facilities, or materials. While employed, Griselda invents a new toilet valve at home in her workshop. The toilet valve is clearly outside the scope of SVC's business and therefore, Griselda owns it totally. However, she should make a signed and dated and witnessed and dated written record of the valve and disclose it to SVC (regardless of whose time it was invented on). Later, Griselda, while still employed but on vacation, is cogitating about an integrated circuit design problem she had last week at work. She comes up with a valuable, less-expensive integrated circuit passivation technique. Since this invention relates to SVC's business, SVC owns it and Griselda must disclose it to SVC and sign any patent application and assignment on it that SVC requests.

If the invention is clearly within the scope of the EA, or is in a gray area, it is wise to first disclose it to the employer. If the employer isn't interested in the invention after reviewing it, the employee can apply for a release, a document under which the employer reassigns or returns the invention to the employee. (The employer may retain a "shop right" under the release—that is, a nontransferable right to use the invention for its own purposes and business only.)

If the invention is in the gray area and the employer wants to exploit the invention, the employee can then try to negotiate some rights, such as a small royalty, or offer to have the matter decided by arbitration. Failing this, a lawsuit may be necessary.

Most EAs also require the invention-assigning employee to keep good records of inventions made and to cooperate in signing patent applications, giving testimony when needed, even after termination of employment. Most companies give the employee a small cash bonus, usually from one hundred to several thousand dollars or more, when the employee signs a company patent application. This bonus is not in payment for the signing (the employee's wages are supposed to cover that) but to encourage employees to invent and turn in invention disclosures on their inventions. Some employers give their inventor-employees a generous cut of the royalties from their invention, and some will even set up a subsidiary entity (partly owned by the employee-inventor) to exploit the invention. Most, however, prefer to reward highly creative employees via the salary route.

F. Assignment of Invention and Patent Rights

In the arcane patent world, to make a transfer of ownership of an intangible thing like an invention or a patent application, you must sign an "assignment"—a legal document that the law will recognize as effective to make the transfer of ownership. An assignment for transferring ownership of an invention and its patent application is available as downloadable Form 16-3 on this book's online companion page. See Appendix 7 for details. (The PTO does not provide an assignment form.) The assignment should be recorded in the PTO to be fully effective.

As indicated, employed inventors ("assignors") usually make full assignments—transfer of 100% of the invention and its patent application—to their employers ("assignees"). They do this because they have agreed, in their EA, to assign all inventions they make within the scope of their employment to their employer. In these cases the assignee is usually a corporation.

A partial assignment (transfer of less than 100%) is usually made where the assignee (the person getting the transferred interest) has financed all or part of the patent application.

The downloadable assignment document (Form 16-3), like the Joint Owners' Agreement, is but one of many possible alternatives. If you use it, you may want to change a number of provisions to fit your situation. Also, a consultation with a patent attorney is advisable if you wish to fully understand how this agreement will affect your rights. For example, where there will be many owners of the patent application, the percentage interest of each should be specifically listed in the last sentence of paragraph 1.

The assignment can also be used to convey title to provisional applications, as well as title or ownership of any reissues or continuing cases (see Chapter 14) of the basic application referred to in part (B) of the assignment, as well as any provisional applications that the basic application claims priority of, and any regular (nonprovisional) applications which claim priority of the basic application, if the basic application is a provisional. A regular patent application can claim priority of a provisional application even if the regular and provisional are not commonly owned, so long as they both have a common inventor and the regular is filed within a year of the provisional. (This is one example where it is important to understand the difference between an inventor and an owner.)

To complete the assignment:

Lines 1-3: Insert the names of the assignors (the inventor patent applicants) on lines 1 and 2 of the first paragraph after "received," and insert their cities and states of residence after "of" on line 3.

Lines 4-6: Do the same for the assignee on line 4.

Line 7: Put the percentage of the patent rights being assigned (normally 100%).

Lines 8-9: Put the title of the invention on line 7.

Lines 10-12: Put the date the patent application was signed (sometimes termed "executed" in the law) on line 11. If the application has already been filed, also put the serial number of the patent application on line 11 and put the filing date on line 12. Put the percentages owned by the assignor and assignee in the penultimate line of this paragraph.

Assignment of Invention and Patent Application

For value received, **Roberta Ann Briskin**,

of **Merion Station, PA**

(hereinafter ASSIGNOR), hereby sells, assigns, transfers, and sets over unto **Rotten Kid Enterprises, Inc.**

of **Marcus Hook, PA**

and her or his successors or assigns (hereinafter ASSIGNEE) **100** % of the following: (A) ASSIGNOR's right, title, and interest in and to the invention entitled " **Poetry Therapy Systems** "

invented by ASSIGNOR; (B) the application for U.S. patent therefor, signed by ASSIGNOR on **2024 January 11**, U.S. Patent and Trademark Office Serial Number **10/123,456**, filed **2024 January 5**; (C) any patent or reissues of any patent that may be granted thereon; and (D) any applications which are provisional patent applications which said application claims priority of, or nonprovisional applications which claim priority of said application, or continuations, continuations-in-part, substitutes, or divisions of said application. ASSIGNOR authorizes ASSIGNEE to enter the date of signature and/or Serial Number and Filing Date in the spaces above. ASSIGNOR also authorizes and requests the Commissioner for Patents to issue any resulting patent(s) as follows: **0** % to ASSIGNOR and **100** % to ASSIGNEE. (The singular shall include the plural and vice versa herein.)

ASSIGNOR hereby further sells, assigns, transfers, and sets over unto ASSIGNEE, the above percentage of ASSIGNOR's entire right, title, and interest in and to said invention in each and every country foreign to the United States; and ASSIGNOR further conveys to ASSIGNEE the above percentage of all priority rights resulting from the above-identified application for U.S. patent. ASSIGNOR agrees to execute all papers, give any required testimony, and perform other lawful acts, at ASSIGNEE's expense, as ASSIGNEE may require to enable ASSIGNEE to perfect ASSIGNEE's interest in any resulting patent of the United States and countries foreign thereto, and to acquire, hold, enforce, convey, and uphold the validity of said patent and reissues and extensions thereof, and ASSIGNEE's interest therein.

In testimony whereof ASSIGNOR has hereunto set its hand and seal on the date below.

Signature **Roberta Ann Briskin**   Date **2024 January 11**

Signature _____   Date _____

Witnessed by:

Signature **Maxwell Spillane**   Date **2024 January 11**

Signature **Michael Barre**   Date **2024 January 11**

Fig. 16B—Completed Assignment Form (Downloadable Form 16-3; see Appendix 7 for details)

Each assignor should sign and date the assignment. If the assignment is to be used abroad, have two witnesses sign and date the bottom two lines to make it recordable abroad. The PTO no longer requires notarization. A completed assignment is shown in Fig. 16B.

G. Record Your Assignment With the PTO

To be fully effective, the assignment must be recorded in the PTO (just as the deed to your house must be recorded with your county clerk). If the assignment is not recorded, and the assignors make a subsequent (fraudulent) assignment to a different assignee, unaware of the first assignment, the second assignee's rights will prevail over those of the first assignee if the second assignee records the assignment first. (Lawyers call this situation a "race arrangement" since the assignee who prevails is the one who wins the race to the PTO.) This means any assignee should record the assignment as soon as possible after it's signed.

The easiest way to record an assignment in the PTO is to do so online. Make a PDF copy of the signed assignment, then go to assignmentcenter.uspto.gov and follow the instructions: Fill out the recordation form online, attach the assignment, and submit the forms for recording. There is no fee for recording an assignment online.

If you don't have internet access, you can record the assignment by mail or fax. First fill out a Recordation Form Cover Sheet (downloadable Form 16-4 available via this book's Appendix 7, or PTO-1595) and note the PTO's recordation fee, which is listed in Appendix 4, "Fee Schedule." Then mail or fax the assignment and cover sheet to the PTO with the recording fee ($54 as of this writing). You can pay the recording fee by a credit card payment form or check. The mail address and the fax number are listed at the bottom of the cover sheet form. The PTO will record the assignment by making a copy of it and the cover sheet, and return the cover sheet and a record sheet listing the assignment data to the person requesting recording.

If an assignment has been signed before the patent application is filed, it is permissible to send the assign-ment in with the application and have it recorded at that time (see Chapter 10). However, you must fill in the date the application was signed (executed) on the assignment and cover sheet. (You won't be able to insert the application serial number or filing date since you don't know those yet.) However, even if the assignment is signed before filing, you may prefer to wait until you can add the filing date and application (serial) number to it before sending it in for recording. This will connect it to the application in an unequivocal way. If you want to file the assignment after you file the application, you can file it online, or you can fax the assignment, the cover sheet, a CCPF or check (mail only) for the fee to Fax: 703-306-5995, or mail to "Mail Stop Assignment, Commissioner for Patents, P.O. Box 1450, Alexandria, VA 22313-1450." If you mail the papers, don't forget the usual receipt postcard.

H. Licensing of Inventions—An Overview

A patent owner can give someone else permission to manufacture and market an invention in exchange for compensation (such as a royalty or flat payment) by creating a "license." It is essential that a license agreement be written and signed by the inventor or owner of the patent or patent application (the licensor) and the manufacturer (the licensee). Here are just a few major considerations and terms that can be written into a license agreement:

1. The proposed licensee can buy an option from you (the licensor) under which you give it the exclusive (or nonexclusive) right to obtain a license under your patent application or patent within a fixed time, say two years. The payment for this option can be merely the company's agreement to research and develop your invention (this is a typical arrangement), or it can involve a cash payment. The general rule is that the more you receive up front, the more seriously the licensee will view and promote your invention.

2. As noted, if you grant the company a license, the license can be exclusive, meaning you agree not to license to anyone else, or nonexclusive, giving you the right to license to others. Exclusive

CHAPTER 16 | OWNERSHIP, ASSIGNMENT, AND LICENSING OF INVENTIONS | 493

Universal License Agreement

1. Parties and Summary of Terms:

Parties: This agreement is between:

Licensor: _Henry Beresofsky_

of _Chernegov, Ukraine_

Licensee: _Chernobyl Reactor Works, Inc._

of _Russian Hill, CA_

Summary: Type of License: ☑ Exclusive ☐ Nonexclusive

Invention Title: _Perpetual Energy Machine_

Patent Application Ser. Nr.: _07/123,456_ , Filing Date: _2024 August 9_

If Exclusive License, minimum number of units to be sold to compute Minimum Annual Royalty (MAR):

_____

MARs start first quarter of _20xx_ .

☑ Option Granted: Premium $ _5,000_ For term of: _18_ months

Patent Royalty Rate _2.00_ % ☑ Know-How Licensed: Know-How Royalty Rate: _3.00_ %

Total Royalty Rate (Patent Royalty Rate plus Know-How Royalty, if applicable): _5.00_ %.

Estimated 1st year's sales (units): _200_ x Estimated Unit Price $ _1,000.00_

x Total Royalty Rate _5.00_ % = Licensing Fee $ _10,000.00_

2. Effective Date: This agreement shall be effective as of the latter of the signature dates below written and shall be referred to as the Agreement of such date.

3. Recitals:

    A. LICENSOR has developed an invention having the above title and warrants that LICENSOR has filed a patent application on such invention in the U.S. Patent and Trademark Office, which patent application is identified by the above title, Serial Number, and Filing Date. LICENSOR warrants that LICENSOR has full and exclusive right to grant this license on this invention and LICENSOR's patent application. If the "Know-How Licensed" box above is checked, LICENSOR has also developed know-how in connection with said invention and warrants that LICENSOR owns and has the right to license said know-how.

    B. LICENSEE desires, if the "Option Granted" box above is checked, to exclusively investigate LICENSOR's above invention for the term indicated. If said "Option Granted" box is not checked, or if said box is checked and LICENSEE investigates LICENSOR's invention for the term indicated and such investigation is favorable, LICENSEE desires to make, use, and sell the products embodying such invention and covered by the claims of LICENSOR's patent application and any patent(s) issuing thereon (hereinafter "Licensed Product").

4. If Option Granted: If the "Option Granted" box above is checked, then (A) the patent license grant of Part 5 below shall not take effect except as defined in this part, and (B) LICENSOR hereby grants LICENSEE, for the option premium stated above, an exclusive option to investigate LICENSOR's invention for the term indicated above, such term to commence from the date of this Agreement. LICENSOR will furnish LICENSEE with all information and know-how (if any) concerning LICENSOR's invention in LICENSOR's possession. LICENSEE will investigate LICENSOR's invention for operability, costing, marketing, etc. LICENSEE shall report the results of its investigation to LICENSOR at any time before the end of the option term. If LICENSEE's determination is favorable, it may thereupon exercise this option and the patent license grant of Part 5 below shall become effective. If LICENSEE's determination is unfavorable, then said option shall not be exercised and no patent license grant shall take effect, all rights hereunder shall revert to LICENSOR, LICENSEE shall deliver to LICENSOR all results of its investigations for LICENSOR's benefit, and LICENSEE shall promptly return to LICENSOR all know-how (papers and things) received from LICENSOR or generated by LICENSEE in its investigations.

Fig. 16C—Completed First Page of Universal License Agreement
(Downloadable Form 16-5; see Appendix 7 for details)

licenses are more common, since manufacturers want to have a monopoly. Nonexclusive licenses are usually used for valuable inventions where several manufacturers want licenses to get into the business. For example, Pilkington Brothers, the great British glass company, granted many nonexclusive licenses under its float glass patents.

3. The license, if granted, can be for the life of the patent, or for a limited term (say five years) with an option to renew for succeeding five-year terms.

4. The license can require the payment of an advance that may be recoverable against royalties, or it may be in addition to royalties. You, of course, want to get as much money at the beginning as possible under the old "bird-in-the-hand" theory.

5. The license can require the payment of minimum annual royalty payments during each year of its existence. This is usually done when an exclusive license is granted.

6. The license rights can be transferred ("assigned") by your licensee to another manufacturer, or any such assignment can be prohibited. From your point of view, it's a good idea to try to get a provision included in the agreement prohibiting assignment without your approval.

There are a few license agreement traps to avoid.

1. Expiration: You cannot demand perpetual royalties for a patented product, because patents expire. The implicit "bargain" struck between the inventor and the government is 17 years (or so) of exclusive rights in the invention, in exchange for the public's ability to make and use the invention afterward. Courts look unfavorably at attempts to extend the lifespan of a patent, because doing so goes against the public's interest in this bargain, and they have the power to rule a patent unenforceable based on its owner's bad behavior. (However, you can require ongoing payment for product support, the continued use of trade secrets and other know-how, and other nonpatent services—if your license agreement clearly separates the value of these services from that of the patent itself.)

2. Illegal tying arrangements: A tying arrangement is one where you sell or lease one product or service only on the condition that the buyer also take a second product or service. For example, if you sell a salt shaker only on the condition that the buyer also comes to you for the salt, that would be a tying arrangement. Tying by itself is not always illegal, but if the first product (the salt shaker) is patented and a license agreement requires purchase of the second service (the salt) based on that patent, that leverage disappears when the patent expires. If the license agreement requires purchase of the second product or service past the patent's expiration, a court may rule that the tying is illegal and you will lose the right to enforce your patent.

3. Sale versus License: Once your product is sold, your right to demand ongoing royalties or condition use of the product is destroyed. This rule prevents you from "double dipping": obtaining payments both from a manufacturer for making your product, and from the wholesaler, retailer, or end purchaser of your product for owning or using it. This rule is akin to the "first sale" doctrine in copyright law, which protects book resellers.

There are hundreds of other, less important, considerations in licensing. Licensing, as you may have gathered by now, is a difficult, complex subject, and one that requires knowledge as well as negotiation skill. Unfortunately, most invention licensing agreements tend to be tailor-made by large corporations to protect their interests. Again, for a detailed discussion about the licensing process, consult *Profit From Your Idea: How to Make Smart Licensing Deals*, by Richard Stim (Nolo).

It's important to realize that even though you can make a great invention, prepare a patent application on it, and sell it to a manufacturer, you might not be able to represent yourself adequately in negotiating a license agreement unless you're familiar with licensing and adept at business. That's why it's often wise to hire a patent lawyer to review any contract that is offered to you.

This will probably cost several hundred dollars or more, but, you'll likely find that the money will be well spent, especially if you have a major deal in the offing.

In fact, most reputable companies would prefer that you be represented by an attorney when you negotiate a license agreement and they may even give you money to pay an attorney. The reason for this is that an agreement between an unrepresented inventor and a much larger company is likely to be interpreted against the company by the courts. If the inventor is represented by an experienced lawyer, the courts will tend to treat the parties equally if a dispute later arises.

What Is Know-How?

Know-how usually refers to a particular kind of technical knowledge that is needed to accomplish some task. For example, your know-how may be necessary to train the licensee's employees how to make or use your invention. Think of know-how as a combination of secret and non-secret information that has value because it is needed to commercialize your invention.

I. Universal License Agreement

If you do feel confident enough to represent yourself, and you're the type of person who can go through a long license agreement with nitpicking skill and then competently negotiate with corporate pros, more power to you. Start your quest by referring to downloadable Form 16-5, Universal License Agreement, available on this book's online companion page (see Appendix 7 for details on accessing this page). This agreement can be used to license your invention exclusively or nonexclusively, and to license know-how. It can also be used to grant a potential licensee an option to evaluate your invention for a given period in return for a payment. As we've said, most companies will either prefer their own license agreement or make one up from scratch, but you can use the Universal License Agreement for purposes of comparison.

The sample shown above (Fig. 16C) is for the first page of an exclusive license with an option grant and a know-how license.

Part 1: Parties and Summary of Terms. The licensor is the party, usually the inventor, who does the licensing, while the licensee is the party who licenses—that is, is given permission to make, use, and sell the invention, patent, know-how, and so on.

The Patent Royalty rate is the percentage rate the licensee pays for use of the patent. This rate is set low (2%) purposely, since a know-how license has been granted at a rate of 3% for an overall (total) royalty of 5%. It's usually to an inventor's advantage to license know-how, as well as patent rights, and to make the know-how rate as high a proportion of the total rate as possible. This is because patents can be held invalid and can only be licensed for a limited term (the duration of the patent application plus the approximately 18-year term of the patent), usually a total of about 19 years; whereas a know-how license can extend indefinitely. In order for know-how to be licensed, the inventor must actually transfer (or be able to transfer) some actual know-how to the licensee.

A licensing fee (advance) is customarily paid to the licensor upon signing the agreement as a reward for past work. In the agreement, the licensing fee is computed as an estimate of the first year's sales by multiplying (a) the Patent Royalty Rate by (b) the Estimated First Year's Sales in Units by (c) the Estimated Unit Price in dollars. Again, it's usually in the inventor's interest to get as large a signing bonus as possible, and not to have this money be set off against later royalty payments.

The "Exclusive" box is checked, indicating that only the licensee will be entitled to make, use, or sell the invention. If the "Nonexclusive" box is checked, the licensor will be able to license others, and the licensee and the licensor will be able to make, use, and sell the invention. The title, serial number, and filing date of the patent application are identified next.

The "Minimum Number of Units to Be Sold to Compute Minimum Annual Royalty" (whether or not they are actually sold) is provided to ensure that the licensor receives an adequate income from the licensee inasmuch as he can't, under an exclusive license, license others to derive more income. This minimum annual royalty has been computed on the basis of a minimum annual number of units to be sold (rather than a fixed dollar amount) to give the licensor the benefit of inflation in unit price. While the manufacturer can cut the price of the licensed product and thereby reduce its royalty payments to you, it's generally not in its interest to do this, since it will be reducing its profits as well. However, if you want to guard against this possibility, you can substitute a fixed dollar amount for the minimum annual royalty.

For the privilege of obtaining an option to exclusively evaluate the invention for the Option Term, an Option Premium (a one-time cash payment) has been paid to the licensor.

The Know-How Royalty Rate is stated and is added to the Patent Royalty Rate to get the total, or Running Royalty Rate.

Part 2: Effective Date. The effective date of the agreement is the date when the last signature is made.

Part 3: Recitals. Here the Recitals provide the background reasons or premises for the agreement to aid in interpreting it. The recitals simply state that the licensor has an invention, a patent application, and possibly know-how, and the licensee desires to evaluate licensor's invention (if an option has been granted) and to make, use, and sell the licensed invention.

Part 4: Option Granted. This covers the parties' rights if an option has been granted. In this case, the regular license grant doesn't take effect yet, but the licensee has the exclusive right to investigate the invention for the option term indicated in Part 1. If the investigation is favorable, the licensee will exercise its option and the patent license grant of Part 5 will take effect. If not, the option will not be exercised and all rights will revert to the licensor and the licensor will get the results of the licensee's investigation of the invention.

Part 5: License Grant. This contains the actual license grant. This comes into play immediately if the invention is licensed or if an option is granted or if the option is granted and exercised. Remember, if an option is granted, the actual license isn't granted until the option is exercised. The license granted (exclusive or nonexclusive) gives the licensee the right to make, use, and sell the licensed product in the United States, and it includes any derivative applications and patents (see Chapter 14). If the "know-how" box of Part 1 has been checked, then know-how is also licensed.

Part 6: Know-How. If know-how is licensed, then the licensor is obligated to communicate all of its know-how to the licensee within one month, plus provide up to 80 hours of consultation to the licensee, with travel and other expenses paid by licensee. The licensor disclaims any guarantee that the know-how is workable. The know-how royalty is to be paid for three years and thereafter for so long as the licensee enjoys a U.S. competitive market share of at least 15%. This means that the licensor can enjoy know-how royalty payments indefinitely, provided its know-how was valuable enough to give the licensee a market share of more than 15% after three years have passed.

Part 7: Royalties. This concerns royalties and is the heart of the agreement.

Subpart A: If a Licensing Fee is paid; it's an advance against future royalties. If the estimated Licensing Fee has been computed inaccurately (Part 1) then an adjustment is made when royalties are paid. (Note: It is permissible to draft an agreement whereby the licensing fee is a one-time payment and not an advance against royalties.)

Subpart B: The running royalty is covered and is paid quarterly, within one month after the end of each quarter, together with a report of the sales made in the quarter.

Subpart C: The minimum annual royalty (MAR) is to be paid if an exclusive license has been granted. The MAR payment is computed using the royalty rate times the minimum number of units of Part 1. Minimum annual royalties start as also stated in Part 1. If the minimum number of units is not sold in any year, the licensee must pay the appropriate makeup difference to the licensor with its payment for the fourth quarter.

Subpart D: If the minimum is not paid by licensee, either due to lack of sufficient sales or licensee's choice, then the license grant will be converted to a nonexclusive one, and the licensor can immediately license others.

Subpart E: If the license is or becomes nonexclusive, then the licensor may not grant more favorable terms to any other licensee.

Subpart F: Patent royalties are not due after the patent expires, or if it is declared invalid, or if no patent is granted.

Subpart G: Late payments earn interest at 10%.

Subpart H: The "Net Factory Sales Price," on which royalties are based, is the factory selling price, less shipping, insurance, taxes, and so on, if billed separately. If the units are imported, then the importer's gross selling price is the basis for royalties. The royalty paid on returns is deductible against future royalties.

Part 8: Records. This requires the licensee to keep full records for at least two years after each payment, so that the licensor can verify the royalty payments.

Part 9: Sublicensees. Here the licensee's sublicensees are bound by all of the terms of the agreement and the licensee must notify the licensor if it grants sublicenses. A licensee will usually grant a sublicense when it has the licensed product made for it by a contracting company.

Part 10: Patent Prosecution. This simply states the parties' responsibilities for patent prosecution.

Subpart A: Requires the licensor to pay for prosecution of the U.S. patent application, together with the patent maintenance fees that are payable after the patent issues. If the licensor intends to abandon the patent application, it must notify the licensee at least two months in advance to give it the opportunity to take over.

Subpart B: The licensor may file for patent coverage abroad, but if it doesn't do so, then the licensee may do so. If licensor wants to license any foreign licensees, it has to give the licensee the opportunity of first refusal.

Subpart C: If the licensee takes over the U.S. patent prosecution, and is successful, then it can reduce its royalties by 25%, and can deduct its patent prosecution expenses. If the licensee elects to file abroad, then the royalty rate on foreign sales is 50% of the U.S. rate, less foreign prosecution expenses.

Part 11: Patent Marking. This requires the licensee to mark products sold with the legend "patent pending" while the patent application is pending and with the patent number (see Chapter 15) after the patent issues.

Part 12: Infringements. This states that if the patent is infringed, the licensor can sue to enforce its patent rights. If it doesn't choose to do so, the licensee may do so. If the licensee sues, it can keep 75% of this recovery, less costs of the suit. (Note that, under current law, the licensor will have to join the lawsuit as a plaintiff because only the patentee/licensor owns the patent right that is enforceable in court.)

Part 13-A: No Validity Guarantee. This clause states that the licensor doesn't guarantee that its patent is valid or that it has any particular scope (breadth).

Part 13-B: Liability. This clause states, in effect, that if someone is injured by the patented product, the licensor is not liable.

Part 14: Term. This clause states that the term or maximum duration of the agreement shall be until the last patent of licensor expires, unless know-how is licensed, in which case Part 6 governs the term.

Part 15: Termination. This clause covers when the parties may terminate the agreement before the term expires. Under Subparts A and B, the licensor may terminate the agreement if the licensee defaults in making royalty payments, or if it ever declares bankruptcy. Subpart C, the anti-shelving clause, is very important. This protects the licensor in case the licensee stops production for 1.5 years, or doesn't start production within 1.5 years from the date the license agreement is signed. In these cases, the licensor can terminate the agreement.

Clauses like this one (and others) are designed to put teeth into the agreement to deter the licensee from defaulting: it is not enough to make a fair agreement; all agreements should also be structured to ensure the other party's performance by giving an incentive for performance, or a penalty for nonperformance.

Part 16: Notices. This clause states how and where notices under the agreement are to be sent.

Part 17: Mediation and Arbitration. This clause provides that if the parties have any dispute, they shall submit the matter to mediation. If mediation can't resolve the dispute, the parties must submit the dispute to binding and final arbitration. In no case will the dispute go to a court for resolution, since

Lump-Sum Payment

If you're offered a single lump-sum payment for all your rights (this is rare), should you take it, and if so, how much should you get? To answer the first question, only you can decide if a relatively large bird in the hand is worth more than a potential (but by no means assured) stream of smaller, but aggregately heavier, birds in the bush over the years. To grapple with the second question, estimate the potential sales of your invention for the life of your patent application (one to three years), plus the term of the patent (approximately 18 years), then apply your royalty to this figure. Be willing to take half of this as a single-payment lump sum for a fully paid-up license.

For example, suppose you expect your widget to be sold for the next 20 years (two years during patent pendency, and 18 years during life of patent), for an average factory price of 50 cents and an average yearly quantity of 150,000 units, and that a patent royalty of 5% is fair. Applying the formula, the substitute lump-sum payment for your royalty would be ½ × 20 years × 50¢ unit price × 150,000 units × 5% rate, or $37,500. If you are offered much less than this, it may be unwise to sell.

Don't make Mary Jacobs's mistake. She invented the bra (out of two hankies and a ribbon) and was able to sell her patent for $15,000 in 1914. Although this was a princely sum then, she practically gave it away since (as you know) her invention soon took hold and her patent eventually was worth $15 *million*!

The disadvantage with the alternative lump-sum calculation is that it's very hard to estimate anything about what will happen in the next 20 years. Will sales go up or down? Will the product become obsolete or even more popular? Will competition or some other factor affect its price? These are just some of the imponderables and unknowables, so, as stated, be extremely careful before selling your rights for a single lump-sum payment.

---

litigation is extremely expensive and works to the detriment of the independent inventor.

Part 18: Transfer of Rights. This clause allows the licensor to assign (legally transfer) its rights to anyone without permission, but the licensee needs the licensor's advance permission to assign the licensee's rights unless it makes an assignment to its successor in business (for example, if it is acquired by another company).

Part 19: Controlling Law. This clause specifies that the laws of the licensor's state shall govern interpretation of the agreement. Normally, state law on the interpretation of contracts doesn't vary much, but since a licensor is usually at an economic disadvantage, we've given the licensor the benefit here. Also, this clause specifies that any lawsuit over the agreement shall be brought in the licensor's county.

Part 20: Good Faith. This states that in case of any mistake in the agreement, it will be fixed in a way that best conforms to the parties' intentions. The clause is designed to save a misdrafted agreement that otherwise might be thrown out.

Part 21: Rectification of Mistakes. This states that in case of any mistake in the agreement, it shall be rectified to conform to the parties' intentions. The clause is designed to save a misdrafted agreement that otherwise might be thrown out.

Part 22: Supersession. This makes it clear the agreement supersedes prior or concurrent oral, or prior written, understandings.

Part 23: Counsel Consulted. This one states that the parties have carefully read the agreement and have consulted, or have been given an opportunity to consult, counsel and that each has received a signed original. This makes a challenge to the agreement more difficult.

Other terms that can be added to the Agreement, if necessary, are Definitions of Terms (use if any unusual terms are present in the Agreement); Other Obligations of Licensee (for example, "Licensor has the right to approve the quality of Licensee's product" or "Licensee will spend certain efforts to commercialize product"); or Improvements (if Licensee or Licensor make improvements, who owns these and is royalty adjusted?).

All that remains is to sign and date the agreement. Each party should get an original, ink-signed copy.

TIP

While the Universal License Agreement incorporates most of the customary terms and covers many common licensing situations, it probably won't be appropriate for your situation without modification. Obviously, if your arrangement won't fit within the terms of this agreement, or if you don't like any of the "fixed" terms, such as the 80 hours of consultation, the 15% market share, or compulsory arbitration, you should propose changes, or hire an expert to help you.

J. How Much Should You Get for Your Invention?

Many inventors seem to believe that patents are almost always licensed at a royalty rate of 5%. The 5% royalty generally means that you get 5% of the money received by the factory for its sales of the item embodying your invention. This is sometimes termed 5% of the "ex-factory" price. This assumption is simply not true. While 5% is often used as a starting point in many license negotiations, very few licenses are granted at this rate. We've seen them run from 0.1% to 15% of the factory price of licensed hardware items (as high as 30% of the retail price for software).

As you've likely guessed, many factors affect the royalty rate. Obviously, the more desirable your invention is to the licensee, the better royalty you'll get, subject to industry norms. Here's a list of some factors that support increasing the royalty rate. Use as many of these as possible in your negotiations:

- the product has a potential for large sales volume
- the product can be offered at a low selling price
- the product will not have much competition
- the product will have a high profit margin
- the product is ingenious and novel
- the product required a lot of development
- the invention substantially pervades the product
- the licensed territory is a large, significant, or important market
- the inventor will furnish considerable services, materials, parts, and/or tooling
- there is no competition between licensee and licensor
- this industry respects patents
- it would be difficult to avoid the patent—that is, the patent is strong
- negotiating the license agreement was difficult—for example, you expended considerable time or attorneys' fees
- the licensee will save money on costs
- the inventor has a strong reputation in the field
- the product will have a long life
- the start-up costs to produce the invention are low
- the inventor has a number of patents or patent applications
- consumers will pay a premium price for the product
- the product can be sold at lower cost than its competition, and
- a higher up-front payment will reduce the rate and vice versa.

Of course, your bargaining skill will transcend all of these considerations. As business negotiating seminar leader C.L. Karrass says: "In business, you don't get what you deserve—you get what you negotiate." Also, the custom of the industry will dominate—for example, toys usually get an exclusive royalty rate of 2.5% to 4%, medical products 6% to 7%, and software inventions up to 10% and sometimes more. An exclusive license will entitle you to about 50% more than a nonexclusive license.

In some industries the royalty rate may be a fixed (or per-unit) amount. For example, a patent owner may grant a license to a television manufacturer for a payment of 50¢ for each patented and manufactured LCD screen, 25¢ for each patented chrominance demodulation circuit used, and so on.

If your licensee doesn't want to pay the rate you ask, a good technique is to accept the lower rate they're willing to pay. However, add a proviso stating that the rate will be increased to the rate you want if "x" number of units are sold.

Instead of a negotiated percentage, some experts advocate getting a royalty equivalent to "one-third of the manufacturer's profit." This means that the company will take its selling price for your invention, say $10, subtract its cost of manufacture, including overhead, say $7, and give you one-third of the difference—that is, $1 = ⅓ of its $3 profit. This type of royalty is often enticing to a manufacturer since the company only contemplates parting with a portion of its profit, not paying a fixed sum per item, whether the particular product turns out to be profitable or not. If your licensee is willing to accept this type of royalty, you can substitute this language in the Universal Agreement. But, if you do so, be sure you include an auditing right (such as Clause 8) to ensure that you can verify its cost of manufacture and profits, to prevent any "fancy" bookkeeping.

K. Summary

When dealing with a patent application or patent, always distinguish between inventorship and ownership. All actual inventors must be named in the patent application, provided each contributed something to at least one claim. Financiers, advisers, model makers, or others that did not contribute any inventive concepts should not be named as inventors, but can be made owners. If the claims of a patent application are changed, inventorship should be reviewed and changed if necessary. Use Form 16-1 to preserve each inventor's contribution.

Under patent law statute, any joint owner of a patent can practice the invention without paying any other inventor. To guarantee that all inventors receive compensation if the invention is commercialized, use the Joint Owners' Agreement—Form 16-2.

An employed inventor's rights are usually governed by an Employment Agreement, which mainly requires the employee to assign to the employer all inventions that are made in the course of the employer's business, use the employer's time, facilities, or materials, or are within the scope of the employee's duties. Employees who are hired to invent have a common law obligation to assign inventions made in the scope of their duties. Other inventions are the property of the employee, but the employment agreement may require the employee to notify the employer about them.

A patent application and a patent are intangible personal property and part or full ownership must be transferred by an assignment, which should be recorded in the PTO to prevent a subsequent, fraudulent assignment.

To collect royalties for use of an invention, an inventor (licensor) should make a licensing agreement with the manufacturer (licensee). The main considerations are the amount of any upfront payment, whether the license is exclusive or nonexclusive, and the royalty rate. It's advantageous to license know-how as well as patent rights. The Universal License Agreement (Form 16-5) covers most situations, but the terms must be negotiated. Factors affecting the royalty rate are the strength of the patent, the amount of design work already done, the anticipated sales volume, the profit margin, the field of the invention, and so on. Never assign a patent or application for a series of payments; always get full payment at the time of assignment.

APPENDIX

1

Abbreviations Used in *Patent It Yourself*

Throughout *Patent It Yourself* we've used many abbreviations to save space and to spare you the tedium of repeatedly reading long phrases like "Manual of Patent Examining Procedure." We've tried to define each abbreviation the first time we've used it and again if we've used it at a location remote from the first usage. However, in case we've failed to define any abbreviation adequately, here's a list of (hopefully) all the abbreviations we've used:

A&ARTP	Attorneys and Agents Registered to Practice
ADS	Application Data Sheet (PTO Form SB/14)
AF	After Final
AIA	America Invents Act; Approved September 16, 2011
AIPO	African Intellectual Property Organization
BA	Basic Application
BBS	Bulletin Board System
BNA	Bureau of National Affairs
BRS	Bibliographic Research Services
CAD	Computer-Aided Drafting
CAFC	Court of Appeals for the Federal Circuit
CASSIS	Classification And Search Support Information System
CCPF	Credit Card Payment Form
CFIB	Contingency-Fee Invention Broker
CFR	Code of Federal Regulations

CIP	Continuation-In-Part
CM	Common Misconception; Certificate of Mailing
CRTP	Constructive Reduction to Practice
D	Design Patent
DJ	Declaratory Judgment
DOE	Department of Energy; Doctrine of Equivalents
DP	Double Patenting
EA	Employment Agreement
EEC	European Economic Community
EFS	Electronic Filing System
EPC	European Patent Convention
EPO	European Patent Office
FBIE	Fee-Based Inventor Exploiter
FDA	Food and Drug Administration
FITF	First Inventor to File
FTI	First to Invent
GATT	General Agreement on Tariffs and Trade
GPC	General-Purpose Computer
GPO	Government Printing Office
IC	Inventors' Commandment
IDS	Information Disclosure Statement

ITC	International Trade Commission
JOA	Joint Owners' Agreement
JPTOS	*Journal of the Patent and Trademark Office Society*
KISS	Keep It Simple, Stupid
MAR	Minimum Annual Royalty
MDC	Multiple Dependent Claim
MF	Maintenance Fee
MPEP	*Manual of Patent Examining Procedure*
N/A	Notice of Allowance
N&UR	New and Unexpected Results
NCC	Non-Convention Country
NDA	Nondisclosure Agreement
NIH	Not Invented Here
NM	New Matter
NPL	Non-Patent Literature
NPR	Nonpublication Request
OA	Office Action
OG	*Official Gazette*
OPAP	Office of Patent Application Processing
P	Problem
PA	Prior Art
PAD	Patent Application Declaration
PCT	Patent Cooperation Treaty
PDF	Portable Document Format
PGL	Paranoia, Greed, Laziness

PHOSITA	Person Having Ordinary Skill In The Art
PME	Priority Mail Express
PPA	Provisional Patent Application
PPS	Patent Public Search
Pre-Ex	Preliminary to Examination
PTAB	Patent Trial and Appeal Board
PTDL	Patent and Trademark Depository Libraries
PTMS	Petition to Make Special
PTO	Patent and Trademark Office (U.S.)
RCE	Request for Continued Examination
RPA	Regular Patent Application
RTP	Reduced to Practice
S	Solution
SBA	Small Business Administration
SD	Supporting Declaration
SE	Small Entity
SED	Small-Entity Declaration
SIR	Statutory Invention Registration
SSM	Statutory Subject Matter
TD	Terminal Disclaimer
TM	Trademark
TN	Trade Name
TS	Trade Secret
UC	Unfair Competition
UCC	Uniform Commercial Code
U.S.C.	United States Code
VA	Vanadium Alloy

APPENDIX

2

Resources: Government Publications, Patent Websites, and Books of Use and Interest

A. Government Publications 504

B. Patent Websites 504

   1. Inventor Resources 504

   2. Patent Law and Intellectual Property Law Websites 504

   3. Patent Searching Online 505

The patent resources listed below may assist you in applying for, prosecuting, and maintaining your patent rights.

A. Government Publications

All of the resources listed below are available on the internet (www.uspto.gov) and many are also available in print and on CD-ROMs, which are updated quarterly and which may be read on the computer in any Patent and Trademark Resource Center. (See the list of libraries in Chapter 6.)

- *Classification Resources.* Contains all subclasses and cross-references arranged alphabetically. Also contains 300 search classes for patents arranged numerically, together with subclasses in each class. www.uspto.gov/web/patents/classification
- *Manual of Patent Examining Procedure* (MPEP). Revisions issued on a rolling basis. Called "the patent examiner's bible," the MPEP provides answers to most questions about patent prosecution. mpep.uspto.gov
- *Patent Laws* (Title 35 of U.S. Code). The federal statutes governing patents. Available as "Appendix L" (for "Laws") in the MPEP.
- *Patent Practitioner Home Page.* Attorneys and agents authorized to practice in patent matters before the United States Patent and Trademark Office (USPTO)
- *Rules of Practice in Patent Cases* (Title 37, Code of Federal Regulations). The PTO's Rules of Practice. Available at the PTO's website as "Appendix R" (for "Rules") in the MPEP.

B. Patent Websites

Below are three groups of patent links. The first group provides sources of information for inventors, the second group includes resources on patent law and intellectual property law, and the third provides patent searching databases. As with all internet links, we cannot guarantee the continued accuracy of any of these sites.

1. Inventor Resources

Intellectual Property Owners Association (IPO) (www.ipo.org). An association that serves owners of patents, trademarks, copyrights, and trade secrets.

InventNet Forum (www.inventnet.com). Provides an online forum and mailing list.

Inventors Digest Online (www.inventorsdigest.com). Publishes online information and a print publication for independent inventors.

Nolo (www.nolo.com). Patent, copyright, trade secret, and trademark resources and products.

United Inventors Association (UIA) (www.uiausa.org). A national inventors' organization.

2. Patent Law and Intellectual Property Law Websites

Copyright Office (www.copyright.gov). The Copyright Office has numerous circulars, kits, and other publications that can help you, including one on searching copyright records.

European Patent Office (EPO) (www.epo.org). Agency that implements the European Patent Convention.

Government Publishing Office (www.gpo.gov). Searchable source for U.S. Code of Federal Regulations, *Congressional Record,* and other Government Publishing Office products.

Legal Information Institute (www.law.cornell.edu). Intellectual property links and downloadable copies of statutes and cases.

Patent and Trademark Office (PTO) (www.uspto.gov).

PCT Applicant's Guide (www.wipo.int). PCT information and software for facilitating completion of the PCT forms.

3. Patent Searching Online

Here are several organizations that offer computer searching of patent records and a description of their services. Several of the "for fee" databases also provide foreign patent information.

U.S. Patent and Trademark Office (www.uspto.gov/patents/search). Free online classification-searchable database of patents and drawings that covers the period from 1790 through 1975, and full-text searchable database from January 1976 to the most recent weekly issue date (usually each Tuesday).

Google Patents (https://patents.google.com) is an excellent free resource that includes U.S. and foreign patents.

European Patent Office (www.epo.org/searching-for-patents.html). Enables searching of text, titles, and abstracts back to the 1920s.

Patent One (www.lexisnexis.com). Commercial database of U.S. patents searchable from 1971 to the present.

This additional free site can be used to search patents and obtain patent copies: www.freepatentsonline.com.

Nolo's Legal Encyclopedia

Nolo's website (www.nolo.com) features an extensive Legal Encyclopedia that includes a section on intellectual property. You'll find answers to frequently asked questions about patents, copyrights, trademarks, and other related topics; as well as sample chapters of Nolo books and a wide range of articles. Under "Legal Issues Explained," click "Patent, Copyright & Trademark."

Nolo Books on Intellectual Property

Nolo, the publisher of this book, also publishes a number of other titles on intellectual property, including:

- *Nolo's Patents for Beginners,* by David Pressman and Glen Secor
- *Patent Pending in 24 Hours,* by Richard Stim
- *Patent, Copyright & Trademark: An Intellectual Property Desk Reference,* by Richard Stim
- *Profit From Your Idea: How to Make Smart Licensing Deals,* by Richard Stim
- *The Copyright Handbook: What Every Writer Needs to Know,* by Stephen Fishman
- *The Public Domain: Find and Use Free Content for Your Website, Book, App, Music, Video, Art, and More,* by Stephen Fishman, and
- *Trademark: Legal Care for Your Brand,* by Glen Secor.

APPENDIX

3

Glossaries

A. Glossary of Useful Technical Terms 508

B. Glossary of Legal Terms 514

Section A contains a glossary of words used to describe parts and functions of inventions. Section B contains a glossary of legal terms and their definitions as used in patent law.

A. Glossary of Useful Technical Terms

This Glossary[1] provides a list of useful words to describe the hardware, parts, and functions of your invention in the specification and claims. The most esoteric of these words are briefly defined. While some definitions are similar, this is due to space limitations; all words have nuances in meanings.

If you're looking for a word to describe a certain part, look through the list for a likely prospect and then check a dictionary for its precise meaning. If you can't find the right word here, look in your search patents, in *What's What* or another visual dictionary, or in a thesaurus. If you can't find an appropriate word, you'll probably be able to get away with "member" or "means-plus-a-function" language. Also, for new fields, you may invent words, preferably using Latin or Greek roots, as Farnsworth did with "television," or by extending the meaning of words from analogous devices (for example, "base" for a part of a transistor). Very technical or specialized fields have their own vocabulary (for example, "catamenial" in medicine, "syzygy" in astronomy); look in appropriate tutorial texts for these. The words are grouped loosely by the following functions:

1. Structure
2. Mounting and Fastening
3. Springs
4. Numbers
5. Placement (Relation)
6. Voids
7. Shape
8. Materials and Properties
9. Optics
10. Fluid
11. Electronics
12. Movement
13. Rotation/Machine, and
14. Biology.

[1] Expanded and used with kind permission and thanks from a list originally prepared by Louis B. Applebaum, Esq., of Newport, Rhode Island.

1. Structure

annulus (ring)
apron
apse (semicircular recess)
arbor (shaft)
arm
bail (arch wire)
band
barrel
bascale (seesaw)
base
batten (support strip)
beam
—cantilever
—simple
belt
bib
billet (ingot or bar)
blade
blower
board
bob (hanging weight)
bodkin (stiletto)
body
bollard (thick post)
boom
boss (projection)
bougie (body-insertion member)
boule (pear-shaped)
branch
breech (back part)
bunker
caisson
canard (front wing)
carriage
case
channel
charger (shallow dish)
chase
chord
cincture (encircling band)
clew (sail part)
column
configuration
container
conveyor

cornice (horiz. top of structure)
cover
crenation (rounded edge)
cupola (projection)
cylinder
dasher (plunger, churn)
derrick
detent
device
dibble (pointed tool)
die
disparate (dissimilar)
diversion
doctor blade (scraper)
dog (holder)
drum
echelon (staggered line)
element
enclosure
felly (rim of spoked wheel)
fence (stop on tool)
fillet (narrow strip)
fin
finger
finial (ornament)
flabellate (fan-shaped)
flange
fluke (triangular part)
flute (groove on shaft)
frame
fret
frit (vitreous substance)
frustrum (cut-off area)
furcate (branch)
futtock (curved ship timber)
gabion (support cylinder)
gaff (hook, spar)
gauge
generatrix (path traced)
gnomon (sundial upright)
graticulate (squares)
grommet
groove
gusset (triangular insert)
handle
head
header (base, support conduit)

homologous
horn
housing
hub
jacket
jaw
jib (crane arm)
knocker (clapper)
lagging (support)
ledger (horizontal support)
leg
lip
list (margin strip)
lobe
magazine
mandrel (tapered axle)
manifold
marge (edge)
marginate (w/margin)
medium
member
mullion (dividing strip)
nacelle (pod)
napiform (turnip-shaped)
neck
obcordate (heart-shaped)
object
outcrop
panel
parietal (wall)
particle
partition
piece
piston
placket (slit in garment)
platform
plug
plunger
pontoon
portion
post
pounce (fine powder)
projection
purlin (horiz. rafter support)
putlog (horiz. support above ledger)
race
raceway
rank (row, series, range)

reticulum (netlike)
rib
riddle (sieve)
riffles (obstructions)
ring
rod
sash (frame)
score (notch, scratch)
screed (guide strip)
scroll
sear (catch)
shell
shoe
shoulder
skeleton
sleeve
sluice (channel)
snare
snorkel
spandrel (area adjacent to an arch)
spar (pole, support)
spline (projection on shaft)
spoke
sponsor (projection)
sprag (spoke stop)
spur
stanchion
station
stay
stem
stent (stretcher)
step
stepped
stile (dividing strip)
stop
strake (band around ship's hull)
strip
strut
stylet
tang (shank, tool)
tare (net weight)
tendril (long, slender curl)
tine
tip
tittle (a tiny bit)
tongue
trace (pivoted rod)

510 | PATENT IT YOURSELF

tracery (scrolling)
track
trave (crossbar)
truss
tuft
turret
tuyere (air pipe)
upright
vang (guy)
volar (palm, sole)
wall
ward (ridge or notch)
warp
woof (weft)
ziggurat (pyramid with
 terraces)

2. Mounting and Fastening

attach
belay
billet (tip of belt)
bolt
bonnet
braze
busing
cable
camber
caster
clamp
cleat (reinforcer)
clevis (U-shaped pin)
colligate (bound together)
connection
corbel (cornice support)
couple
coupling
cribbing (support)
demountably
dentil (block under cornice)
docking
dowel
engage
fay (join tightly)
ferrule (barrel)
ferruminate (attach, solder)
fix
funicular (ropelike)

gib (holding member)
gland (sliding holder)
gunnel/gunwale (vessel's
 upper edge)
guy wire
harp (lampshade support)
hold
holder
hook
imbricate (regular overlap)
joint
—universal
keeper
key
latch
lock
lug
matrix
mount
nail
nut
pin
plinth (base)
pricket (holding spike)
pylon (support)
restraint
ribband (holds ribs)
rivet
scarf (notched joint)
screw
seam
seat
secure
set
sheathed
sliding
snare/loop
solder
spike
spline (projection or
 groove on a shaft)
springably
support
thill (horse joinder stake)
thrust
toe-in
trammel (restraint)
weld

3. Springs

air
bias
—element
coil
compressed
elastic
expanded
helical
—compression
—tension
leaf
press
relaxed
resilient
torsional
urge

4. Numbers

argument
caboodle (collection,
 bunch)
compound
congeries (collection,
 aggregation)
difference
dividend
divisor
equation
formula
index
lemma
minuend
modulo
multiplicand
multiplicity
multiplier
plurality
power
product
quotient
remainder
sheaf
subtrahend
variable

5. Placement (Relation)

adjacent
aft
aligned
angle
apposition (facing)
array
attached
axial
bottom
close
complementary
concentric
contiguous
contracted
course
crest
disposed
distal
divided
edge
engaged
equitant (overlap in two
 ranks)
evert (inside out)
extended
external
face
fiducial (reference)
film
fore
horizontal
imbricate (overlapping series)
incline
integral
intermediate
internal
interposed
juxtaposed
layer
located
lower
mating
meshing
mesial (between)
normal

APPENDIX 3 | GLOSSARIES | 511

oblique
obtuse
offset
open
opposed
overlapping
parallel
perpendicular
pitched
positioned
projecting
prolapsed (out of place)
proximal
proximate
raked (pitched)
reference
removable
resting
rim
row
sandwich
section
slant
spacer
staggered
superimposed
supported
surface
surrounding
symmetrical
tilt
top
ubiety (located in a place)
vernier (9:10 gauge)
vertical

6. Voids

aperture
bore
cavity
chamber
concavity
cutout
dimple
duct
embrasure (slant opening)
engraved

erose (irregular notch)
filister (groove)
foramen (opening)
fossa (depression)
furrow (groove)
gain (notch)
gap
groove
hole
hollow
infold
intaglinated (engraved)
invaginate (enclosed,
   turned in)
lumen (bore of tube)
lunette (crescent opening)
mortise (cutout)
nock (notch on arrow)
notch
opening
orifice
passage
placket (garment slit)
polled (dehorned)
rabbet (groove)
raceway
recess
rifling (spiral groove)
separation
slit
slot
spandrel (triangular gap
   above arch side)
sulcus (groove)
ullage (lost liquid)
via (path)
void
wicket (small door or gate)

7. Shape

acclivity (slope)
acicular (needle-shaped)
agonic (no angle)
annular
anticline (peak)
applanation
arch

arcuate
bandy (bowed out)
barrel
bevel
bifurcated (2 branches)
bight (bend)
botryoidal (like a bunch of
   grapes)
bucket
buckled
catenary (curve of hanging
   cable)
chamfer (beveled)
channel
circular
coin
concave
congruent (same shape)
conical
convex
convoluted (curled in)
corner (inside, outside)
corrugated
crest
crimp
crispate (curled)
cup
cusp (projection)
cylinder
depression
dihedral (two-faced)
direction
disc
dome
draw (depression)
drawing (pulling out)
elliptical
fairing (streamlined)
fin
flange
fold
fork
fossa (groove)
fundus (base)
furcate (branched)
goffer (ridges or pleats)
helical
hook

incurvate (curved in)
infundibuliform (funnel-
   shaped)
invaginate (sheathed,
   folded in)
line
lobe
lozenge (diamond-shaped)
lune (crescent)
mammilated (nipple-shaped)
navicular (boat-shaped)
notch
oblate (flattened)
oblong
ogive (pointed arch)
orb (globe)
oval
parabolic
parallelogram
plane
plicate (pleated)
prolate (cigar-shaped)
rectangular
reticulated (gridlike)
rhomboid (nonequal
   adjacent sides)
rhombus (equal adjacent
   sides)
rick-rock
rill (long narrow valley)
round
salient (standing out)
serrated
setaceous (bristlelike)
sheet
shelf
sinusoidal
skive (shaven)
slab
spall (broken chips)
spherical
spica (overlapping reverse
   spirals)
square
stamped
striated (grooved or
   ridged)
swaged (flattened)

swale (depression)
syncline (V-shaped)
taper terminus (end)
tesselated (tiled)
topology (unchangeable geometry)
tortuous (twisting)
tram (on wheels)
trefoil (three-leaved)
triangular
trihedral (three sided)
trough
tubular
tumescence (detumescence)
turbinate (top/spiral shaped)
twist
upset (distorted)
vermiculate (worm-eaten)
volute (spiral)
wafer
web
wedge
whorl (spiral)
xyresic (razor-sharp)

8. Materials and Properties

adhesive
alluvial (sand or clay deposited by water)
concrete
cork
dappled (spotted)
denier (gauge)
dense
elastic
enlarged
fabric
fiber
flexible
foraminous
frigorific (chilling)
frit (fused glass)
frosting (dull finish)
gloss

haptic (sense of touch)
humectant (moistener)
insulation
intenerate (soften)
liquid
material
metal
nappy (fuzzy or downy)
opaque
passivation (inert coating)
pied (splotched)
placer (glacial deposit)
plastic
porous
prill
refractory
resilient
rigid
rubber
sand
screen
shirred (gathered)
smectic (cleaning)
stratified (layered)
strong
sturdy
translucent
transparent
wood
xerotic (dry)

9. Optics

aniseikonic (unequal sizes)
astigmatic
bezel
bulb
—fluorescent
—incandescent
fresnel
lamp
light
—beam
—ray
opaque
parallax (change in direction)
pellicle

pellucid (clear)
reflection
refraction
schlieren (streaks)
translucent
transmission
transparent
window

10. Fluid

accumulator
afferent (to center)
aspirator
bellows
bibb (valve)
bung (hole or stopper)
cock (valve)
conduit
confluent (flow together)
connector
convection
cylinder
—piston
—rod
dashpot
diaphragm
discharge
dispenser
efferent (away from center)
filter
fitting
flue
gasket
hermetic
hose
hydraulic
medium
navicular (like a boat)
nozzle
obturator (blocker)
outlet
pipe
plunger
poppet (axial valve)
port
—inlet
—outlet

pump
—centrifugal
—gear
—piston
—reservoir
—seal
—siphon
—tank
—vane
sluice (water channel with gate)
sparge (spray)
sprue (vent tube)
spud (short connecting pipe)
suctorial (sucking)
sufflate (inflate)
swash (channel barrier)
trompe (water-pipe blower)
tube
valve
—ball
—check
—control
—gate
—shutoff
wattle (intertwined wall)
weir (dam)
wicket (gate or door)

11. Electronics

adder
amplifier
astable
capacitance
clipping
conductor
contact
control element
demodulator
diode
electrode
electromagnet
filament
flip flop
gate (AND, OR, etc.)
impedance

inductance
insulator
integrated circuit
laser
lead
light emitting diode
line cord
liquid crystal
maser
memory
motor
multiplier
multivibrator
oscillator
pixel (CRT spot)
power supply
raster
read-and-write memory
read-only memory
resistance
sampling
Schmitt trigger
Schottky diode
shift register
socket
solenoid
switch
terminal
thermistor
transformer
transistor
triode
valve
varistor
wire
Zener diode

12. Movement

alternate
articulate (jointed)
avulsion (tear away)
cadent (rhythmic)
cam
compression
cyclic
detent (click)
downward

draft (pull)
drag
drift pin
drill
eccentric
emergent
epicyclic (on circle)
equilibrate (bring into
  equilibrium)
escapement
extensible
extrude
grinding
impact
inclined plane
inertia
interval
lag
lead
lever
linkage
—parallel
longitudinal
machine
meeting
nutate (to and fro)
pressing
propelling
pulverize
sagging
sequacious (regular)
severing
shuttle (to and fro member)
skive (peel)
slidable
snub (stop)
straight line
—motion
terminating
toggle
torque
traction
transverse
traversing
triturate (grind to powder)
trochoid (roll on circle)
urging

vibrating
wedge

13. Rotation/Machine

antifriction
—ball
—needle
—roller
—tapered
arbor (shaft)
bell crank
bobbin (spool)
brake
—band
—disk
—shoe
bushing
cam
chain
clevis (circular holder)
clutch
—centrifugal
—one-way
—sprag (stop)
—toothed
cog (tooth)
comminute (pulverize)
connecting rod
crank arm
drive
—belt
—pulley
—sheave
—toothed
flexible coupling
friction
fulcrum
gear
—bevel
—crown
—internal
—noncircular
—pinion
—right-angle
—spur
—wheel
—worm

gimbal (double pivot)
gin (hoist, pile driver, pump)
gudgeon (axle)
guide
hinge
intermittent
—escapement
—geneva
—pawl
—pendulum
—ratchet
jack
journal
mandrel
orbit
pinion (small wheel)
pintle (axle)
pivot
pulley
radial
radius bar
score (thinned strip)
screw
seal
sheave (pulley)
spindle
sprocket
swash (wobble) plate
tappet (valve cam)
trunnion
variable speed
vertiginous (turning)
ward (ridge or notch)
winch
yoke

14. Biology

anastomosis (connection
  of tubes)
atrium (cavity)
brady (slow)
catamenial (menstrual)
explant (transplant living
  tissue)
fibrillation (twitching)
tachy (rapid)
ventricle (chamber)

B. Glossary of Legal Terms

Abandonment. (1) allowing a pending, active patent application to be removed from the PTO's active files and treated as if the inventor has given up all claims to a patent on the invention. An inventor can expressly abandon an application by letter or allow an application to go abandoned by not timely replying to an office action. (2) treating an invention as if the inventor has lost all interest in exploiting it, usually by not developing it or by not filing a patent application on it for a very long time.

Abstract. A concise, one-paragraph summary of the patent. It details the structure, nature, and purpose of the invention. The abstract is used by the PTO and the public to quickly determine the gist of what is being disclosed.

Actual damages (also known as "compensatory damages"). In a lawsuit, money awarded to one party to cover actual injury or economic loss. Actual damages are intended to put the injured party in the position he was in prior to the injury.

Agent (patent). A person licensed by the PTO to represent others in handling patents and patent applications before the PTO. Patent agents are required to have a technical degree or technical knowledge in a specific field.

Answer. A written response to a complaint (the opening papers in a lawsuit) in which the defendant admits or denies the allegations and may provide a list of defenses.

Assignee. A person or legal entity to which an assignment is made.

Assignment. A document transferring ownership of an invention and/or a patent application or patent.

Assignor. One who makes an assignment.

Attorney (patent). A person licensed by the PTO to represent others in handling patents and patent applications before the PTO and who is also licensed to practice law. Patent attorneys are required to have a technical degree or technical knowledge in a specific field.

Best mode. A term indicating that a patent application should disclose the way the inventor presently prefers to make the invention. The best mode requirement is a safeguard against the desire on the part of some people to obtain patent protection without making a full disclosure as required by the statute.

Cease and desist letter. Correspondence from the owner of a proprietary work that requests the cessation of all infringing activity.

Clear and convincing proof. Evidence that is highly probable and free from serious doubt.

Complaint. Papers filed with a court clerk by the plaintiff to initiate a lawsuit by setting out facts and legal claims (usually called "causes of action").

Compositions of matter. Items such as chemical compositions, conglomerates, aggregates, or other chemically significant substances that are usually supplied in bulk (solid or particulate), liquid, or gaseous form.

Conception. The mental part of inventing, including how an invention is formulated or how a problem is solved.

Confidentiality agreement (also known as a "nondisclosure agreement"). A contract in which one or both parties agree not to disclose certain information.

Continuation application. A new patent application that allows the applicant to re-present an invention and get a second or third bite at the apple. The applicant can file a new application (known as a "continuation") while the original (or "parent") application is still pending. A continuation application consists of the same invention, cross-referenced to the parent application, and a new set of claims. The applicant retains the filing date of the parent application for purposes of determining the relevancy of prior art.

Continuation-In-Part (CIP). Less common than a continuation application, this form of extension application is used when a portion or all of an earlier patent application is continued and new matter (not disclosed in the earlier application) is included. CIP applications are used when an applicant wants to present an improvement but is prevented from adding a pending application to it because of the prohibition against adding "new matter."

Contributory infringement. Occurs when a material component of a patented invention is sold with knowledge that the component is designed for an unauthorized use. This type of infringement cannot occur unless there is a direct infringement. In other words, it is not enough to sell infringing parts; those parts must be used in an infringing invention.

Copyright. The legal right to exclude others, for a limited time, from copying, selling, performing, displaying, or making derivative versions of a work of authorship such as a writing, music, or artwork.

Counterclaim. A legal claim usually asserted by the defendant against an opposing party, usually the plaintiff.

Court of Appeals for the Federal Circuit (CAFC). The federal appeals court that specializes in patent appeals. If the Board of Appeals and Patent Interferences rejects an application appeal, an applicant can further appeal to the CAFC within 60 days of the decision. If the CAFC upholds the PTO, the applicant can request that the U.S. Supreme Court hear the case (although the Supreme Court rarely hears patent appeals).

Date of invention. The earliest of the following dates: (a) the date an inventor filed the patent application (provisional or regular), (b) the date an inventor can prove that the invention was built and tested in the United States or a country that is a member of the North American Free Trade Association (NAFTA) or the World Trade Organization (WTO), or (c) the date an inventor can prove that the invention was conceived in a NAFTA or WTO country, provided the inventor can also prove diligence in building and testing it or filing a patent application on it. Note: Though once a crucial concern for inventors (prior to adoption of the America Invents Act) the date of invention is of little importance under first-inventor-to-file rules (that is, after March 16, 2013).

Declaratory action. A request that the court sort out the rights and legal obligations of the parties in the midst of an actual controversy.

Deed (patent). A document under seal or certificate issued by the PTO containing a printed copy of a patent and granting a patent monopoly to the patentee and the patentee's assignee.

Deposit date. The date the PTO receives a patent application.

Deposition. Oral or written testimony of a party or witness and given under oath.

Derivation hearing. A PTO hearing brought by an applicant against a patent owner claiming to have the same invention and who has an earlier effective filing date. The derivation hearing must be filed within a one-year period beginning on the date of the first publication of a claim in the earlier filed application. The procedure, implemented under the America Invents Act, replaces interference proceedings.

Design patent. Covers the unique, ornamental, or visible shape or design of a nonnatural object.

Divisional application. A patent application used when an applicant wants to protect several inventions claimed in the original application. The official definition is "a later application for a distinct or independent invention, carved out of a pending application and disclosing and claiming only subject matter disclosed in the earlier or parent application" (MPEP 201.06). A divisional application is entitled to the filing date of the parent case for purposes of overcoming prior art. The divisional application must be filed while the parent is pending. A divisional application can be filed as a CPA.

Doctrine of Equivalents (DoE). A form of patent infringement that occurs when an invention performs substantially the same function in substantially the same manner and obtains the same result as the patented invention. A court analyzes each element of the patented invention separately. The DoE must be applied on an element-by-element basis to the claims.

Double patenting. When an applicant has obtained a patent and has filed a second application containing the same invention, the second application will be rejected. If the second application resulted in a patent, that patent will be invalidated. Two applications contain the same invention when the two inventions are literally the same or the second invention is an obvious modification of the first invention.

Embodiment. A physical version of an invention as described in a patent application; a patent application may describe several embodiments of an invention, but is supposed to state the one that the inventor considers the **best mode** as of the filing date; see "ramification."

Enhanced damages (triple or "treble" damages). In exceptional infringement cases, financial damages may be increased, at the discretion of the court, up to triple the award for actual damages.

Examiner's answer. A brief submitted by a patent examiner in response to an applicant's brief in an appeal to the PTO's Board of Appeals and Patent Interferences.

Exclusive jurisdiction. The sole authority of a court to hear a certain type of case.

Exhaustion (see "first sale doctrine").

Ex parte (Latin: "one party only"). Refers to legal proceedings where only one party is present or represented, including normal patent prosecution.

Experimental use doctrine. A rule excusing an inventor from the one-year bar provided that the alleged sale or public use was primarily for the purpose of perfecting or testing the invention.

File wrapper estoppel (or "prosecution history estoppel"). Affirmative defense used in patent infringement litigation that precludes the patent owner from asserting rights that were disclaimed during the patent application process. The term is derived from the fact that the official file in which a patent is contained at the Patent and Trademark Office is known as a "file wrapper." All statements, admissions, correspondence, or documentation relating to the invention are placed in the file wrapper. "Estoppel" means that a party is prevented from acting contrary to a former statement or action when someone else has relied to his detriment on the prior statement or action.

Final Office Action. The examiner's response to the applicant's first amendment. The final Office Action is supposed to end the prosecution stage but a "final action" is rarely final.

First Office Action (sometimes called an "official letter" or "OA"). Response from the patent examiner after the initial examination of the application. It is very rare that an application is allowed in the first Office Action. More often, the examiner rejects some or all of the claims.

First sale doctrine (also known as the "exhaustion doctrine"). Once a patented product (or product resulting from a patented process) is sold, the patent owner's rights are exhausted and the owner has no further rights as to the resale of that particular article.

Generic (genus). An entire group or class, or a group of related items or species.

Grace period. A period in which an action may be taken even though the normal period for taking action has passed.

Indirect infringement. Occurs either when someone is persuaded to make, use, or sell a patented invention without authorization ("inducing infringement"); or when a material component of a patented invention is sold with knowledge that the component is designed for an unauthorized use (contributory ("contributory infringement"). An indirect infringement cannot occur unless there is a direct infringement. In other words, it is not enough to sell infringing parts; those parts must be used in an infringing invention.

Infringement. A product or service is infringing if it is a literal copy of a patented invention or if it performs substantially the same function in substantially the same manner and obtains the same result as the patented invention (see "Doctrine of Equivalents (DoE)").

Injunction. A court order requiring that a party halt a particular activity. In the case of patent infringement, a court can order all infringing activity be halted at the end of a trial (a "permanent injunction") or the patent owner can attempt to halt the infringing activity immediately, rather than wait for a trial (a "preliminary injunction"). A court uses two factors to determine whether to grant a preliminary injunction: (1) Is the plaintiff likely to succeed in the lawsuit? (2) Will the plaintiff suffer irreparable harm if the injunction is not granted? The patent owner may seek relief for a very short injunction known as a "temporary restraining order" or "**TRO**," which usually only lasts a few days or weeks. A temporary restraining order may be granted without notice to the infringer if it appears that immediate damage will result—for example, that evidence will be destroyed.

Intellectual property (IP). The law dealing with works that are produced by mental activity, including ideas, inventions, patents, trademarks, trade secrets, copyrightable material, and unfair competition.

Intellectual property attorney. A person licensed to practice law by one or more states and who specializes in intellectual property. There are two types of IP attorneys: those who are licensed by the PTO (and can handle invention and patent matters before the PTO), and those who are not.

Interference. A costly, complex PTO proceeding that determines who will get a patent when two or more applicants are claiming the same invention. It is basically a method of sorting out priority of inventorship. Occasionally an interference may involve a patent that has been in force for less than one year.

***Inter partes* (Latin: "between parties").** Refers to legal proceedings where all parties to the action are represented.

Interrogatories. Written questions that must be answered under oath.

Invention. Any new article, machine, composition, or process or new use developed by a human.

Jury instructions. Explanations of the legal rules that the jury must use in reaching a verdict.

Lab notebook. A system of documenting an invention that usually includes descriptions of the invention and novel features; procedures used in the building and testing of the invention; drawings, photos, or sketches of the invention; test results and conclusions; discussions of any known prior-art references; and additional documentation such as correspondence and purchase receipts.

Literal infringement. Occurs if a defendant makes, sells, or uses the invention defined in the plaintiff's patent claim. In other words, the infringing product includes each and every component, part, or step in the patented invention. It is a literal infringement because the defendant's device is actually the *same* invention in the patent claim.

Machine. A device or things used for accomplishing a task; usually involves some activity or motion performed by working parts.

Magistrate. An officer of the court, who may exercise some of the authority of a federal district court judge, including the authority to conduct a jury or nonjury trial.

Manufactures (sometimes termed "articles of manufacture"). Items that have been made by human hands or by machines; may have working or moving parts as prime features.

Means-plus-function clause (or "means-for clause"). A provision in a patent claim in which the applicant does not specifically describe the structure of one of the items in the patent and instead describes the function of the item. Term is derived from the fact that the clause usually starts with the word "means."

Micro entity. A patent applicant status that enables qualifying applicants to pay the lowest USPTO fees (approximately one-quarter of regular fees, and one-half of small entity fees).

New matter. Any technical information, including dimensions and materials, that was not present in the patent application as originally filed. An applicant can never add new matter to an application (37 CFR 1.118).

New-use invention. A new and nonobvious process or method for using an old and known invention.

Nonobviousness or unobviousness. A standard of patentability that requires that an invention produce "unusual and surprising results." In 1966, the U.S. Supreme Court established the steps for determining unobviousness in the case of *Graham v. John Deere*, (383 U.S. 1 (1966)).

Notice of Allowance. A document issued when the examiner is convinced that the application meets the requirements of patentability. An issue fee is due within three months.

Objection. A disapproval made by an examiner to a nonsubstantive matter, such as an unclear drawing or dependent claim having a rejected claim.

Objects and advantages. A phrase used to explain "what the invention accomplishes." Usually, the objects are also the invention's advantages, since those aspects are intended to be superior over prior art.

Office Action (OA, also known as "official letter" or "examiner's action"). Correspondence (usually including forms and a letter) from a patent examiner that describes what is wrong with the application and why it cannot be allowed. Generally, an OA will reject claims, list defects in the specifications or drawings, raise objections, or cite and enclose copies of relevant prior art demonstrating a lack of novelty or nonobviousness.

One-year rule. A rule that permits an inventor one year to file a U.S. patent application after she, or a joint inventor, makes the invention public—either through publication, public use, or sale.

Patent. A grant from a government that confers upon an inventor the right to exclude others from making, using, selling, importing, or offering an invention for sale for a fixed period of time.

Patent application. A set of papers that describe an invention and that are suitable for filing in a patent office in order to apply for a patent on the invention.

Patent Application Declaration (PAD). A declaration that identifies the inventor or joint inventors and provides an attestation by the applicant that the inventor understands the contents of the claims and specification and has fully disclosed all material information. The PTO provides a form for the PAD.

Patent Center. A system and website provided by the PTO that enables the filing of most documents required during patent prosecution, including applications, amendments, petitions, cover letters and other transmittals, fee payments, and the like. Patent Center also provides the Patent Public Search facility, as well as allowing eFilers to view private information about their pending applications.

Patent misuse. A defense in patent infringement that prevents a patent owner who has abused patent law from enforcing patent rights. Common examples of misuse are violation of the antitrust laws or unethical business practices.

Patent pending (also known as the "pendency period"). Time between filing a patent application (or PPA) and issuance of the patent. The inventor has no patent rights during this period. However, when and if the patent later issues, the inventor will obtain the right to prevent the continuation of any infringing activity that started during the pendency period. If the application has been published by the PTO during the pendency period and the infringer had notice, the applicant may later seek royalties for these infringements during the pendency period. It's a criminal offense to use the words "patent applied for" or "patent pending" (they mean the same thing) in any advertising if there's no active, applicable regular or provisional patent application on file.

Patent prosecution. The process of shepherding a patent application through the Patent and Trademark Office.

Patent Public Search (PPS). The PTOs web-based patent search system.

Patent Rules of Practice. Administrative regulations located in Volume 37 of the Code of Federal Regulations (37 CFR 1).

Patent Trial and Appeal Board (PTAB). A tribunal of judges at the PTO that hears appeals from final Office Actions and conducts derivation proceedings. Formerly called the Board of Patent Appeals and Interferences.

Pendency period (see "patent pending").

Permanent injunction. A durable injunction issued after a final judgment on the merits of the case; permanently restrains the defendant from engaging in the infringing activity.

Petition to Make Special. An applicant can, under certain circumstances, have an application examined sooner than the normal course of PTO examination (one to three years). This is accomplished by filing a "Petition to Make Special" (PTMS), together with a Supporting Declaration.

Plant patent. Covers plants that can be reproduced through the use of grafts and cuttings (asexual reproduction).

Power of attorney. A document that gives another person legal authority to act on your behalf. If an attorney is preparing an application on behalf of an inventor, a power of attorney should be executed to authorize the patent attorney or agent to act on behalf of the inventor. The power of attorney form may be combined with the PAD.

Prima facie (Latin: "on its face"). At first sight, obvious.

Prior art. The state of knowledge existing or publicly available either before the date of an invention or more than one year prior to the patent application date.

Priority. The benefit of the filing date of an earlier patent application accorded to a later-filed patent application.

Process (sometimes referred to as a "method"). A way of doing or making things that involves more than purely mental manipulations.

Provisional Patent Application (PPA). An interim document that clearly explains how to make and use the invention. The PPA is equivalent to a reduction to practice (see below). If a regular patent application is filed within one year of filing the PPA, the inventor can use the PPA's filing date for the purpose of deciding whether a reference is prior art. In addition to an early filing date, an inventor may claim patent pending status for the one-year period following the filing of the PPA.

Ramification. A version or variation of an invention that is different from a main version or **best mode**.

Reduction to practice. The point at which the inventor can demonstrate that the invention works for its intended purpose. Reduction to practice can be accomplished by building and testing the invention (actual reduction to practice) or by preparing a patent application or provisional patent application that shows how to make and use the invention and that it works (constructive reduction to practice).

Reissue application. An application used to correct errors in a patent. It is usually filed when a patent owner believes the claims are not broad enough, the claims are too broad (the applicant discovered a new reference), or there are significant errors in the specification. In these cases, the applicant seeks to correct the patent by filing an application to get the applicant's original patent reissued at any time during its term. The reissue patent will take the place of the applicant's original patent and expire the same time as the original patent would have expired. If the applicant wants to broaden the claims of the patent through a reissue application, the applicant must do so within two years from the date the original patent issued. There is a risk in filing a reissue application because all of the claims of the original patent will be examined and can be rejected.

Rejection. A disapproval made by an examiner to a substantive matter such as a claim which is deemed obvious over the prior art.

Repair doctrine. Affirmative defense based on the right of an authorized licensor of a patented device to repair and replace unpatented components. It also includes the right to sell materials used to repair or replace a patented invention. The defense does not apply for completely rebuilt inventions, unauthorized inventions, or items that are made or sold without authorization of the patent owner.

Reply. A brief submitted by a patent applicant in response to an examiner's answer.

Request for admission. Request for a party to the lawsuit to admit the truthfulness of a statement.

Request for Continued Examination (RCE). A paper filed when a patent applicant wishes to continue prosecuting an application that has received a final **Office Action**. Filing the RCE with another filing fee effectively removes the final action so that the applicant can submit further amendments—for example, new claims, new arguments, a new declaration, or new references.

Request for production of documents. The way a party to a lawsuit obtains documents or other physical evidence from the other side.

Reverse doctrine of equivalents (or negative doctrine of equivalents). A rarely used affirmative defense to patent infringement in which, even if there is a literal infringement, the court will excuse the defendant's conduct if the infringing device has a different function or result than the patented invention. The doctrine is applied when the allegedly infringing device performs the same function in a substantially different way.

Sequence listing. An attachment to a patent application used if a biotech invention includes a sequence listing of a nucleotide or amino acid sequence. The applicant attaches this information on separate sheets of paper and refers to the sequence listing in the application (see 37 CFR 1.77). If there is no sequence listing, the applicant states "Nonapplicable."

Small entity. A status that enables small businesses and nonprofit companies to pay a reduced application fee.

Species. One of a group of related individual items collectively subordinate to a genus.

Specification. A patent application disclosure made by the inventor and drafted so that an individual skilled in the art to which the invention pertains could, when reading the patent, make and use the invention without needing further experiment. A **specification** is constructed of several sections. Collectively, these sections form a narrative that describes and distinguishes the invention. If it can later be proved that the inventor knew of a better way (or "best mode") and failed to disclose it, that failure could result in the loss of patent rights.

Statute of limitations. The legally prescribed time limit in which a lawsuit must be filed. In patent law there is no time limit (statute of limitations) for filing a patent infringement lawsuit, but monetary damages can only be recovered for infringements committed during the six years prior to the filing the lawsuit. For example, if a patent owner sues after ten years of infringement, the owner cannot recover monetary damages for the first four years of infringement. Despite the fact that there is no law setting a time limit, courts will not permit a patent owner to sue for infringement if the owner has waited an unreasonable time to file the lawsuit ("laches").

Statutory subject matter. An invention that falls into one of the five statutory classes: process (method), machine, article of manufacture, composition, or a "new use" of one of the first four.

Substitute application. Essentially a duplicate of an abandoned patent application. (See MPEP 201.09.) The disadvantage of a substitute application is that the applicant doesn't get the benefit of the filing date of the previously abandoned patent application, which could be useful, because any prior art occurring after the filing date of the earlier case can be used against the substitute case. If the applicant's substitute application issues into a patent, the patent will expire 20 years from the filing date of the substitute.

Successor liability. Responsibility for infringement that is borne by a company that has purchased another company that is liable for infringements. In order for successor liability to occur, there must be an agreement between the companies to assume liability, a merger between the companies, or the purchaser must be a "continuation" of the purchased business. If the sale is made to escape liability and lacks any of the foregoing characteristics, liability will still attach.

Summons. A document served with the complaint that tells the defendant he has been sued, has a certain time limit in which to respond, and must appear in court on a stated date.

Temporary restraining order (TRO). A court order that tells one party to do or stop doing something—for example to stop infringing. A TRO is issued after the aggrieved party appears before a judge. Once the TRO is issued, the court holds a second hearing where the other side can tell its story and the court can decide whether to make the TRO permanent by issuing an injunction. The TRO is often granted ex parte (without allowing the other side to respond), and for that reason is short in duration and only remains in effect until the court has an opportunity to schedule a hearing for the preliminary injunction.

Traverse. To argue against.

Tying. A form of patent misuse in which, as a condition of a transaction, the buyer of a patented device must also purchase an additional product in an anti-competitive manner. For example, in one case a company had a patent on a machine that deposited salt tablets in canned food. Purchasers of the machine were also required to buy salt tablets from the patent owner, even though salt is a commodity that was sold by many others. A party that commits patent misuse may have its patent invalidated, may have to pay monetary damages, or both.

Utility patent. The main type of patent, which covers inventions that function in a unique manner to produce a utilitarian result.

Verified statement. A statement made under oath or a declaration. A false verified statement is punishable as perjury.

Vicarious liability. Legal responsibility that results when a business such as a corporation or partnership is liable for infringements committed by employees or agents. This liability attaches when the agent acts under the authority or direction of the business, an employee acts within the scope of employment, or the business benefits from, or adopts or approves the infringing activity.

***Voir dire* (Latin: "speak the truth").** A process by which attorneys and judges question potential jurors in order to determine whether they may be fair and impartial.

APPENDIX

4

Fee Schedule

CAUTION

The following table provides some relevant patent-related PTO fees as of the date of publication of this edition. As fees may have changed since publication, visit the PTO website (www.uspto.gov/learning-and-resources/fees-and-payment). The PTO usually raises its fees every October 1. If you underpay any fee, the PTO imposes a stiff surcharge.

37 CFR	Description	Large Entity Fee	Small Entity Fee	Micro Entity Fee
Patent Application Filing Fees				
1.16(a)	Basic filing fee—Utility (paper filing—also requires nonelectronic filing fee under 1.16(t))	350	140	70
1.16(a)	Basic filing fee—Utility (electronic filing for small entities)	n/a	70	n/a
1.16(b)	Basic filing fee—Design	300	120	60
1.16(b)	Basic filing fee—Design (CPA)	300	120	60
1.16(c)	Basic filing fee—Plant	240	96	48
1.16(d)	Provisional application filing fee	325	130	65
1.16(e)	Basic filing fee—Reissue	350	140	70
1.16(e)	Basic filing fee—Reissue (Design CPA)	350	140	70
1.16(f)	Surcharge—Late filing fee, search fee, examination fee or oath or declaration, or application filed without at least one claim or by reference	170	68	34
1.16(g)	Surcharge—Late provisional filing fee or cover sheet	65	26	13
1.16(h)	Independent claims in excess of three	600	240	120
1.16(h)	Reissue independent claims in excess of three	600	240	120
1.16(i)	Claims in excess of 20	200	80	40
1.16(i)	Reissue claims in excess of 20	200	80	40
1.16(j)	Multiple dependent claim	925	370	185
1.16(s)	Utility Application Size Fee—for each additional 50 sheets that exceeds 100 sheets	450	180	90
1.16(s)	Design Application Size Fee—for each additional 50 sheets that exceeds 100 sheets	450	180	90
1.16(s)	Plant Application Size Fee—for each additional 50 sheets that exceeds 100 sheets	450	180	90

522 | PATENT IT YOURSELF

37 CFR	Description	Large Entity Fee	Small Entity Fee	Micro Entity Fee
Patent Application Filing Fees (continued)				
1.16(s)	Reissue Application Size Fee—for each additional 50 sheets that exceed 100 sheets	450	180	90
1.16(s)	Provisional Application Size Fee—for each additional 50 sheets that exceed 100 sheets	450	180	90
1.16(t)	Nonelectronic filing fee—Utility (additional fee for applications filed in paper)	400	200	200
1.17(i)(1)	Non-English translation	150	60	30
Patent Search Fees				
1.16(k)	Utility Search Fee	770	308	154
1.16(l)	Design Search Fee	300	120	60
1.16(m)	Plant Search Fee	485	194	97
1.16(n)	Reissue Search Fee	770	308	154
Patent Examination Fees				
1.16(o)	Utility Examination Fee	880	352	196
1.16(p)	Design Examination Fee	700	280	140
1.16(q)	Plant Examination Fee	725	290	145
1.16(r)	Reissue Examination Fee	2550	1,020	510
Patent Post-Allowance Fees				
1.18(a)(1)	Utility issue fee	1,290	516	258
1.18(a)(1)	Reissue issue fee	1290	516	258
1.18(b)(1)	Design issue fee	1,300	520	260
1.18(c)(1)	Plant issue fee	905	362	181
1.18(d)(1)	Publication fee for early, voluntary, or normal publication	0	0	0
1.18(d)(3)	Publication fee for republication	344	344	344
1.17(a)(1)	Extension for response within first month	235	94	47
1.17(a)(2)	Extension for response within second month	690	276	138
1.17(a)(3)	Extension for response within third month	1,590	636	318
1.17(a)(4)	Extension for response within fourth month	2,495	998	499
1.17(a)(5)	Extension for response within fifth month	3,395	1,358	679
Patent Maintenance Fees				
1.20(e)	Due at 3.5 years	2,150	860	430
1.20(f)	Due at 7.5 years	4,040	1,616	808
1.20(g)	Due at 11.5 years	8,280	3,312	1,656
1.20(h)	Surcharge—3.5 years—Late payment within 6 months	540	216	108
1.20(h)	Surcharge—7.5 years—Late payment within 6 months	540	216	108
1.20(h)	Surcharge—11.5 years—Late payment within 6 months	540	216	108
1.17(m)	Petition for the delayed payment of the fee for maintaining a patent in force	2,260	904	452

APPENDIX
5

Mail, Telephone, Fax, and Email Communications With the PTO

A. Patent and Trademark Office Mail Addresses..524

B. Patent and Trademark Office Telephones and Faxes...525

A. Patent and Trademark Office Mail Addresses

Special Boxes for Patent Mail

If you are sending mail in any of the "Type of Mail" categories below to the PTO, add the appropriate Mail Stop below as the first line of your address as indicated. If your mail does not fall into one of these categories; for example, an amendment with a fee for extra claims, simply address it using just the last three lines of the address below.

> Mail Stop _____
> Commissioner for Patents
> P.O. Box 1450
> Alexandria, VA 22313-1450

For the most current listing of PTO mail stops, visit: www.uspto.gov/patents/contact-patents/mailing-and-hand-carry-addresses-united-states-patent-and-trademark-office.

Mail Stop	Type of Mail
Mail Stop AF	Amendments and other responses after final rejection, other than an appeal brief.
Mail Stop Amendment	Information Disclosure Statements, drawings, Notices of Appeal, and replies to Office Actions in patent applications.
Mail Stop Appeal Brief—Patents	Appeal briefs.
Mail Stop Assignment Recordation Services	Assignments (with cover sheets).
Mail Stop Post Issue	Requests for Certificates of Correction and changes in patent files.
Mail Stop EBC	Mail for the Electronic Business Center.

Mail Stop	Type of Mail
Mail Stop Expedited Design	Initial filing of design applications accompanied by a request for expedited examination ("Rocket Docket").
Mail Stop Express Abandonment	Requests for abandonment of a patent application.
Mail Stop Issue Fee	All communications following the receipt of a Notice of Allowance and Fee(s) Due, and prior to the issuance of a patent.
Mail Stop Missing Parts	Mail related to international applications filed under the Patent Cooperation Treaty.
Mail Stop Petition	Petitions to be decided by the Office of Petitions including petitions to revive and petitions to accept late payment of issue or maintenance fees.
Mail Stop PGPUB	Correspondence regarding publication of patent applications, including request for early publication and rescission of nonpublication request.
Mail Stop Post Issue	Requests for Certificates of Correction and changes in patent files.
Mail Stop RCE	Requests for continued examination under 37 CFR 1.114.
Mail Stop Ex Parte Reexam	Requests for Reexamination for original request papers only.
Mail Stop Inter Partes Reexam	Requests for Inter Partes Reexamination.
Mail Stop Reissue	All new and continuing reissue application filings.
Mail Stop Sequence	Submission of computer-readable form (CRF) for applications with sequence listings, when the CRF is not being filed with the application.

Assignments and Maintenance Fee Payments.
Assignments should preferably be filed online: go to assignmentcenter.uspto.gov. If filing by mail and paying with a credit card or deposit account, mail to:

> Director of the U.S. Patent and Trademark
> Mail Stop Assignment Recordation Services
> P.O. Box 1450
> Alexandria, VA 22313-1450

Maintenance fee payments should preferably be submitted online: go to www.uspto.gov/patents/maintain.

If paying by mail with a credit card or deposit account, or by hand-delivery, mail to:

> Director of the U.S. Patent and Trademark Office
> Mail Stop Maintenance Fee
> P.O. Box 1450
> Alexandria, VA 22313-1450

PTO Is Closed for 10 Holidays. The PTO is closed on weekends and the following holidays: New Year's Day, Martin Luther King, Jr. Day, Presidents' Day, Memorial Day, Independence Day, Labor Day, Columbus Day, Veterans' Day, Thanksgiving, and Christmas. If any action falls due on a holiday or weekend, it is due on the next open-for-business day. If there is a disaster or service interruption or a mail strike, the PTO will publish a notice postponing the due dates for everyone (or just those in a particular geographical area if applicable).

B. Patent and Trademark Office Telephones and Faxes

PTO phones and fax numbers change frequently. For that reason we have not provided a complete listing. Generally, PTO telephone numbers can be located by the following methods:

- A complete current listing of all PTO phones and faxes can be found by going to www.uspto.gov and searching for "telephone directory" in the search box and then clicking "Alphabetical List of PTO Organizations."
- Alternatively, to reach a specific person or department, call the PTO's main number, 800-786-9199.
- If you have received an Office Action, the examiner's phone number will be listed at the end.
- To send a fax to the PTO, all faxed communications should be sent to the PTO's central fax number, 571-273-8300, except for (a) corrected filing receipt papers, (b) responses to a requirement to file missing parts of a patent application, (c) PCT papers, (d) issue fee transmittals, (e) express abandonments, (f) electronic business center communications, (g) assignments, (h) reexamination and interference papers, (i) communications to the PTO's general counsel and solicitor, (j) communications to Licensing and Review, and (k) Petitions to withdraw an application from issue.
- If you need help with electronic filing, call the PTO's Electronic Business Center at 866-217-9197 from 6 a.m. to midnight Eastern time.
- If you need help and don't know where else to call, call the Patents Ombudsman's office at 571-272-5555 or 855-559-8589.

APPENDIX

Quick-Reference Timing Chart

The following is a summary of some of the more important timing intervals that apply in intangible property law. This list is not intended to be comprehensive, and certain exceptions may be applicable, so check the pertinent parts of this book, or with a patent attorney, if you have a special situation or need more precise advice.

A patent application must be filed before any public disclosure of the invention, unless the disclosure was made by the inventor or another who obtained the subject matter directly or indirectly from the inventor.

A PPA, to get the benefit of its filing date, one must file a utility patent application and corresponding foreign applications within **1 year.**

To preserve foreign-filing rights in Paris Convention Countries, one must not sell or publicly disclose details of an invention until **after U.S. filing date.**

To preserve foreign-filing rights in Non-Convention Countries, one must not publicly disclose or sell invention until **after filing in that country.**

From the PTO's mailing date, unless an extension is purchased, or unless a shorter date is set, one must file a response to most Office Actions within **3 months.**

From the PTO's mailing date of a Notice of Allowance, one must pay the issue fee within a nonextendable period of **3 months.**

The maximum statutory time to reply to an Office Action, provided extensions are bought, is **6 months.**

Unless a nonpublication request has been filed, or unless it has issued or is abandoned, every patent application is published **18 months after filing.**

The full term of a utility or plant patent is measured from the filing date of its patent application, or from any earlier domestic nonprovisional (regular) application from which it claims priority, and is **20 years, plus any adjustment (extension) granted by the PTO.**

The full term of a design patent is measured from the issue date and is **15 years.**

From the date of issue (grant) the issue fee will keep a utility patent in force for the first **4 years.**

From the issue date of a patent, the patentee must file a reissue application that attempts to broaden the claims within **2 years.**

From the issue date of a patent, an applicant in a pending application who wants to get into interference with the patent must copy the patent's claims in their application within **1 year.**

Timely payment of Maintenance Fee I (between year 3.0 and 3.5, or 3.5 and 4.0 with late charge) will keep a utility patent in force for another **4 years.**

Timely payment of Maintenance Fee II (between year 7.0 and 7.5, or 7.5 and 8.0 with late charge) will keep a utility patent in force for another **4 years.**

Timely payment of Maintenance Fee III (between year 11.0 and 11.5, or 11.5 and 12.0 with late charge) will keep a utility patent in force until expiration, which occurs **20 years after filing.**

Unless a foreign-filing license has been granted on your filing receipt or you request an expedited license, after filing a U.S. patent application, before foreign-filing a patent application, you must wait **6 months.**

From the U.S. filing date (priority date), to obtain priority of a utility patent application, one must file a foreign Convention application (PCT, EPO, or industrial countries) within **1 year.**

From the U.S. filing date (priority date), to obtain priority of a design patent application, one must file a foreign Convention application (PCT, EPO, or industrial countries) within **6 months.**

One must file a foreign Non-Convention application (most nonindustrial countries) **before invention becomes publicly known.**

From the U.S. filing date, after filing a PCT application, if a patent in a foreign jurisdiction is desired, one must file abroad within **30 months.**

From the U.S. filing date, after filing a PCT application, if examination in the USPTO or the European Patent Office is desired (Chapter II), one must file a request within **22 months or 3 months from search report.**

APPENDIX

7

Downloadable Forms

A. Editing RTFs 530

B. List of Forms 530

530 | PATENT IT YOURSELF

This book comes with forms that you can access online at:

www.nolo.com/back-of-book/PAT.html

To use the files, your computer must have specific software programs installed. Here is a list of types of files provided by this book, as well as the software programs you'll need to access them:

- **RTF.** You can open, edit, print, and save these form files with most word processing programs such as Microsoft *Word*, Windows *WordPad*, and recent versions of *WordPerfect*. On a Mac, you can use Apple *TextEdit* or Apple *Pages*. You can also work with the forms through a word processing app such as Google Docs.
- **PDF.** You can view these files with Adobe *Reader*, free software from www.adobe.com.

A. Editing RTFs

Here are some general instructions about editing RTF forms. Refer to the book's instructions for assistance in completing the forms.

Underlines. Underlines indicate where to enter information. After filling in the needed text, delete the underline.

Bracketed and italicized text. Bracketed and italicized text indicates instructions. Be sure to remove all instructional text before you finalize your document.

Optional text. Optional text gives you the choice to include or exclude text. Delete any optional text you don't want to use. Renumber numbered items, if necessary.

Alternative text. Alternative text gives you the choice between two or more text options. Delete those options you don't want to use. Renumber numbered items, if necessary.

Signature lines. Signature lines should appear on a page with at least some text from the document itself.

Every word processing program uses different commands to open, format, save, and print documents, so refer to your software's help documents for help using your program. Nolo cannot provide technical support for questions about how to use your computer or your software.

! CAUTION

In accordance with U.S. copyright laws, the RTF forms provided are for your personal use only.

B. List of Forms

To download any of the files listed here go to:

www.nolo.com/back-of-book/PAT.html

The following files are in Portable Document Format (PDF):

Form	File Name
Invention Disclosure	Form3-2.pdf
Provisional Application for Patent Cover Sheet	Form3-3.pdf
Application Data Sheet—PTO AIA/14	Form3-4.pdf
Declaration for Utility or Design Patent Application Using an Application Data Sheet	Form10-1A.pdf
Declaration for Utility or Design Patent Application	Form10-1A2.pdf
Supplemental Sheet for Declaration	Form10-1B.pdf
Utility Patent Application Transmittal	Form10-2.pdf
Fee Transmittal	Form10-3.pdf
Credit Card Payment Form	Form10-4.pdf

PDF files continued

Form	File Name
Information Disclosure Statement by Applicant	Form10-6AB.pdf
Information Disclosure Statement	Form10-6C.pdf
Nonpublication Request	Form10-7.pdf
Design Patent Application Transmittal	Form10-11.pdf
Petition for Extension of Time	Form13-4.pdf
Pre-Appeal Brief Request for Review	Form13-5.pdf
Request for Continued Examination (RCE) Transmittal	Form14-1.pdf
Certificate of Correction	Form15-2.pdf
Maintenance Fee Transmittal Form	Form15-4.pdf
Recordation Form Cover Sheet	Form16-4.pdf

The following files are in Rich Text Format (RTF):

Form	File Name
Nondisclosure Agreement	Form3-1.rtf
Positive and Negative Factors Evaluation	Form4-1.rtf
Positive and Negative Factors Summary	Form4-2.rtf
Consultant's Work Agreement	Form4-3.rtf
Searcher's Worksheet	Form6-1.rtf
Drawing Reference Numerals Worksheet	Form8-1.rtf
Information Disclosure Statement Cover Letter	Form10-5.rtf
Request Under MPEP 707.07(j)	Form10-8.rtf
Petition to Make Special	Form10-9.rtf
Design Patent Application	Form10-10.rtf
Amendment	Form13-1.rtf
Submission of Corrected Drawings	Form13-2.rtf
Supplemental Declaration	Form13-3.rtf
Request for Certificate of Correction	Form15-1.rtf
Maintenance Fee Reminder Sheet	Form15-3.rtf
Joint Applicants—Statement of Respective Contributions	Form16-1.rtf
Joint Owners' Agreement	Form16-2.rtf
Assignment of Invention and Patent Application	Form16-3.rtf
Universal License Agreement	Form16-5.rtf

Index

A

Abandonment of invention
    defensive publication, 435, 453, 455
    intention to abandon vs. intent to resume work, 178
    right to patent, 113, 178

Abandonment of patent application
    as after-final option, 434
    application not published, 177
    automatic abandonment if no reply to final action, 434
    choosing to keep as trade secret, 29, 177–178
    defensive publication, 435, 453
    defined, 514
    for failure to respond to PTO, 370, 377, 381, 388, 434, 437
    if prior-art reference makes invention unpatentable, 360, 381, 435
    intentional, do not refer to in applications, 178
    NPR not rescinded after foreign filing, 299, 364, 438
    petition to revive if delay unintentional, 437–438
    public access to, 178
    substitute application must be filed, 454, 455
    supplemental applications can be filed, 444–445, 448, 451–452
    Universal License Agreement, 497

Abbreviations used in the book, 501–502

Abstract
    overview, 186, 214–215
    in assembly order of specification, 186
    careful review of, 215
    defined, 514
    drafted after claims, 214
    optional requirement by PPA, 63, 76–77
    as part of the Specification, 167, 186–187
    patentability searches, 166
    prior-art examples, caution in using, 215
    samples, 11, 229
    utility patents, 10–11
    See also Specification

Abstract ideas
    claim rejections, 401
    computer software, 104, 243
    human organization, 13, 105, 401
    mathematical concepts, 13, 401
    pure mental steps as, 104
    as unpatentable, 12–13, 25, 103–104, 106, 240

Accelerated Examination Program (AEP), 324, 326

Actual damages (compensatory), 514

Address changes, 467

Advantages of invention
    in description of alternate embodiments, 215, 227
    disadvantages of prior art carefully noted, 191, 204–205, 236
    listing, in preliminary RPA work, 191
    in operation section, 213–214
    Positive and Negative Factors Summary, 191, 342
    in PPA, 63
    in specification, 205, 207
    whereby clause pointing out, 240, 243–244, 259, 414
    working model demonstrating, 342

Advertising
    availability of patent, 461
    copyright and, 23
    marketing and distributing inventions, 344–345
    media and publicity, 8, 344–346
    patent misconceptions, 19
    public relations firms, 345
    social media, 345, 459
    trademark law, 8, 22
    traditional media, 345
    unfair competition law, 8, 32–33

AEP. *See* Accelerated Examination Program (AEP)

Aesthetics. *See* Design and aesthetics

African Intellectual Property Organization (OAPI), 349, 356

African Regional Industrial Property Organization (ARIPO), 349, 356

Age
    Accelerated Examination Program (AEP), 322, 324
    irrelevance of inventor, 126
    patent applicants, 10
    PTMS filing, 322, 324
    PTO form SB/130, 322, 324

Agents, foreign filing
    European Patent Office (EPO), 353, 355, 358, 361–362, 364
    expedited through PPH, 326
    for individual Paris Convention countries, 355, 359
    non-Convention countries, 355
    for PCT individual countries, 355, 358–359
    power of attorney for, 361
    resources for finding, 364–365
    timely preparation, 356

534 | PATENT IT YOURSELF

Agents, patent (licensed by PTO)
  defined, 514
  fees for, 15, 248
  finding "discount," 139
  how to use, 138
  juristic entities require ADS signing, 311
  limitations of knowledge, 139
  locating, 138–139
  patentability searches, 150
  patent attorney preferable to, 137
  preparation of drawings, 279
  review of work, 215
  technical training for, 137
  tips for working with, 137
Akamai v. Limelight, 257
Algorithms
  copyright law protections, 13, 25
  as "significantly more," 402–403
  trade secret protections, 13
  as unpatentable, 104–105, 107, 241
Alice Corp. v. CLS Bank International, 104, 241, 401
Alice/Mayo test (statutory vs. nonstatutory subject matter)
  business processes and methods, 241
  prima facie rejections, 400–401
  software processes, 104, 241
  Step 1: eligibility for one of five statutory classes, 104, 401
  Step 2A: determined as judicial exception, 104, 401
  Step 2B: search for inventive concept, 104, 401–403
  See also Nonstatutory subject matter (judicial exceptions to patentability)
Allowance of patent (approval)
  formal drawings submitted, 388, 429
  issue fee checklist, 429
  issue fee not paid to prevent issuance, 29
  issue fee payment, 376, 428–429
  NASA Declarations, 436
  Notice of Allowability, 376, 428
  Notice of Allowance, 376, 428
  "Reasons for Allowance" section, reading carefully, 428
  Request for Continued Examination (RCE) for IDS, 429
  review applications and drawing carefully, 428
  Supplemental Declaration for substantial changes, 428
  See also Issue of patent
Amendments
  overview, 188
  after allowance, 426, 428
  after final OA, 384, 425, 429, 431
  brevity in, 387
  Certificate of Mailing, 427
  checklist for, 423
  to claim PPA, 301
  complying with examiner requirements, 430

conditional request for constructive assistance, 412
continuation-in-part filing, 414
correction of errors in application, 298, 370, 378
deadlines for responses, 376, 377
do your best job, 370, 419, 425
for drawings, 405, 409, 415, 418, 425–426
filed by fax or email, 381, 427–428
filing before first OA, 384
formatting to show changes, 415–417
interviews with examiner to help with, 379, 382, 394, 403–404
never get personal with examiner, 417–418
Notice of Allowability, 376, 428
Notice of Allowance, 376, 428
outlining response, 415
paper filing of, 381, 427
paragraph numbering for, 291
Patent Center filing, 309, 370, 381, 427, 431, 439
Preliminary, 384
sample "regular," 405–413
signatures, 427
of Specification, 415–416, 428
Supplemental, 384
typing and filing, 426–427
without narrowing scope of claim, 404
  See also Claim amendments
Amendments, remarks section
  argue Sections 102/103, 420–421, 437
  authorities to cite, 385
  case law (not recommended for), 385
  conclusion, 425
  Declaration under Rule 132, 424
  discussion of changes after allowable application, 428
  drafting remarks, 417–425
  general rules for drafting remarks, 417–418
  refute improper combination of references, 421–422
  refuting technical points raised by examiner, 424
  request for reconsideration, 424
  restate first rejection, 420
  review of references, 420
  sample, 410–412
  secondary factors of nonobviousness, 422
  Sections 102/103 approach, 418, 420–421
America Invents Act (AIA)
  derivation hearings, 515
  First-Inventor-To-File (FITF), 118
  inventor's assignee may file, 485
  reduced fees for micro entities, 16
  tax avoidance schemes prohibited, 109
American Arbitration Association, 480
American Intellectual Property Law Association, 2, 471
Amgen Inc. v. Sanofi et al., 193

ANSI (American National Standards Institute), 198

Answer, 514

Antecedents (proper use of articles), 211, 249, 259, 260, 271

Anticipation by prior invention
  defined, 156
  infringement versus, 156
  as lack of novelty, 114
  obviousness determinations, 116–117, 119

Anticybersquatting Consumer Protection Act (ACPA), 20

Antitrust law, 462–463, 480

Appeals
  overview, 431–432
  after rejection of appeal, 430
  arbitration cannot be appealed, 480
  attorney recommended for, 432–433
  civil lawsuit in the U.S. District Court, 432
  court appeals, 480
  electronic filing, 431–432
  Examiner's Answer, 432
  fee for, 432
  Focused Set of Arguments, 431
  free legal assistance for, 432–433
  for maximum term possible due to delays, 433
  Notice of Appeal, 431–432
  oral hearing request, 432
  patent expiration date extended if delayed by, 432–433
  Pre-Appeal Request for Review, 430, 431
  to the Supreme Court, 432
  See also PTAB (Patent Trial and Appeal Board)

Applicants, defined, 484

Application Data Sheet (ADS)
  advice from PTO Patent Ombudsman office, 311
  Authorization/Opt out of Authorization to Permit Access, 311
  continuation applications, 445–446
  design patents, 329
  for electronic filing, 79, 185, 187, 310–312
  filing by mail, 80, 299
  juristic entity as applicant, 311
  Patent Center filing, 309–311
  PPA claimed in, 65, 77, 79, 187, 298
  Request not to publish, 292, 299, 310
  for RPA, 185, 292–293, 310–312
  signing scenarios, 311
  simpler PAD (form AIA/01) if included, 185, 292, 293

Application Holding Folder, 78–79, 310, 312

Arbitration, 479–480

Articles, proper use of antecedents, 211, 249, 259, 260, 271

Articles of manufacture. *See* Manufactures (articles of manufacture)

Artificial intelligence (AI)
  drafting specification with, 215–216
  introduction of alternative embodiments or ramifications, 216
  large language models (LLMs), 269
  privately-hosted "in-house" systems, 269
  public disclosure destroying rights (no grace period), 269
  restrictions on use of, 269
  unreliability of, 269
  use to draft claims, 269–270

ArXiv, 453

ASMR (autonomous sensory meridian response), 45

Assignee
  Application Data Sheet (ADS) signing, 311
  common (Joint Research Agreement), 113
  defined, 514
  employed inventors, 490
  micro entities, 76
  as patent applicant, 485
  recorded in PTO, 492
  transfer to, 79, 320

Assignments
  overview, 320
  on Application Data Sheet for PPA, 79
  Assignment of Invention and Patent Application (Form 16-3), 97, 490, 491, 492
  in Consultant's work agreement, 97
  defined, 292, 514
  electronic filing, 313, 492
  employed inventors, 490
  filed after RPA, 320, 322
  filed with RPA, 322
  filing date of application on, 320
  issue fee transmittal form, 322
  Joint Owners' Agreement (Form 16-2), 97, 322
  licensing, 494
  ownership vs. inventorship, 320
  paper filing of, 320, 322, 492
  partial, for financing, 490
  PTO Mail Stops, 525
  Recordation Form Cover Sheet, 320, 322, 492
  recorded after filing RPA (recommended), 313
  record with PTO (highly recommended), 320, 490, 492
  title to provisional applications, 490
  transfer of ownership, 292, 320, 484, 490
  witnesses and, 492

Assignor, 514

Association for Molecular Pathology v. Myriad Genetics, Inc., 106

Attorneys
  infringer payment of fees, 17, 24, 28
  intellectual property, 8, 138
  licensed by the PTO, 8

NDA violations, 54
protection of trade secrets, 28
PTO examiners, 155
Attorneys, patent (PTO licensed)
overview, 8
avoidance of patent profanity, 202
confidential requirements, 139
consultation during prosecution period, 377–378
deciding whether to use, 2, 4
defined, 514
"discount" professionals, 139, 377
drafting claims, 184
fees charged by, 248
finding, 138–139
foreign filings, recommended for, 348
inability to witness lab notebooks, 59
licensing requirements, 137–138
negative opinions of patentability, 150
nonobviousness determinations, 116–117
patent litigators, 471
patent searches, 133, 137–139
reviewing work of, 215
terminology, 260
tips on using, 138
Attorneys, patent (PTO licensed), fees
overview, 2
contingency-fee litigators, 54, 468, 471, 481
damages and infringement cases, 17, 28
Patent Pro Bono Program (PPBP), 377
patent searches, 138–139
Attorneys, patent (PTO licensed), help from
assignment of invention and patent rights, 490
changing examiners, 446
divisional applications, 450
filing a passive citation against patent application, 478
infringement lawsuits, 471
invalidation of patents, 477
for Joint Owners Agreements, 487
negotiating licensing agreements, 495, 499
patentability searches, 137–139, 150
Request for Continued Examination (RCE), 447
requesting *ex parte* reexamination of patent, 478
requesting *inter partes* review of patent, 479
Autonomous sensory meridian response (ASMR), 45

B

Berkheimer v. HP Inc., 402
Best mode
court may limit invention, 191
courts no longer invalidate for failure to disclose, 191, 387
defined, 514
embodiment, 515

PPA and, 77
in Specification, 387
Bilski v. Kappos, 103, 105, 241
Biotechnology
deposit required for biological materials, 194
lawsuits for infringement, 463
prior art determinations, 135
sequence listing (nucleotide/amino acid sequences), 194, 214
Boolean logic, 168, 171, 245, 261
Boolean searches. *See* Keyword searching
Brain, creative vs. logical, 45
Brainstorming, 46, 48
Building and testing inventions
confidentiality of, 53–54
documentation of, 51, 53
lab notebooks documenting, 54–60
lab notebook witnesses, 58
nondisclosure agreements, 53–54
PPA alternative, 62–64
reduction to practice, 110
virtual prototypes, 96
working models (prototypes), 96–97
Business plans, 344
Business processes and methods
claims for, 240–242
patentability requirements, 105
specifications and disclosure requirements, 195, 197
as trade secrets, 105
as unpatentable, 13, 105, 240–242

C

California
Consumer's Legal Remedies Act, 32
Employment Agreement regulations, 489
unfair competition law, 32
Case law
distinguishing claims directed to judicial exception, 238
not recommended for amendments, 385
Cease and desist letter, 514
Certificate of Correction, 460, 482
Certificate of Mailing (paper filing)
amendments, filing, 427–428
do not use to file Continuation Application, 433
do not use to file RPA, 307
IDS, filing after application filed, 319
IDS, filing with application, 320
Maintenance fees, 467
PTMS filed after application, 324
Request for Continued Examination (RCE), 433
rescission of nonpublication request, 364
Certification marks, 19

Certification of Micro Entity Status, 62

Challenges to patents
computer software disclosure, 193, 195
domain names, 20
foreign patent offices and PPA, 82
hardware-based claims, 195
incomplete disclosure, 193
realistic uses for utility patents, 107
third-party submission of prior art, 384, 436, 478
unenforceability, 480

Chemical formulas
intellectual property laws, 7
lab notebook witnesses, 59
preliminary sketches, 198, 201
as trade secrets, 28, 36

Chemicals
compositions of matter, 106
conventional processes, 104
flowchart drawings of, 198, 201, 284
generally recognized as safe, 108
plant-based patents, 102
synergism, 123
trademarked chemical notes, 194
trademarks, 21
as trade secrets, 28–30
utility patents, 107–108

Chief Technology Officer (CTO), 486

CIP. *See* Continuation-in-part application (CIP)

Citation of Prior Art, 436

Claim(s), 235–270
overview, 235–236, 270
allotment of 3/20, 263, 268, 304, 386, 428
assembly order in application, 185
central, 358
classification searching, 167
closed vs. open, 260
defined, 235
defining scope of invention, 203, 210, 244
defining scope of offensive rights, 167
definitions not in specification may limit, 210
design patents, 329
details of full scope of, 167, 193, 235
DoE broadening of amended claims, 384–385
drafting before specification and drawings, 184
effect of prior art on, 247–248
examiner determining patentability with, 235, 247, 397
filing date, 236, 248
in foreign filings, 239
infringement boundaries defined by, 235, 475
infringement requires all elements to be met, 245, 257, 467
legal requirements for, 236–238
linking, 435

narrow (as weakening patent), 126
nonobviousness determinations, 247–248
novelty determinations, 247
as part of the Specification, 166, 186–187
peripheral, 358
PPA not required to present (but recommended), 65, 76–77
prior-art search and "claims trap," 167, 395
prohibitions on numerous, 239
PTO drafting assistance, 424–425
reissue to revise, 442, 452
restriction of application, 435–436
rules of practice, 238–239
samples, 240–244, 272–274
specific features in, 203, 210, 244–245
See also Claim amendments; Claim rejections; Claims, dependent; Claims, independent; Claims, technical requirements of; Claims and statutory classes of inventions; Means-plus-function claims (means claims); Preamble of a claim; Scope of the invention, claims as determining; Specification

Claim amendments
after final action, 427–428, 431
approaches to, 414–415
arguments to never use, 415, 417–418
arguments to use, 403–404
calling and visiting examiner, 403–404
canceling claims, 384, 396, 397, 404, 414
checklist for, 423
continuation-in-part filing, 386, 414
distinguishing physical novelty, 414
DoE used to broaden, 384–385
do your best job, 425
drafting remarks, 417–425
for drawings, 425–426
format for, 415
formatting to show changes, 415–417, 423, 428
insignificant, for examiner's sake, 404
narrowing claims, 397, 398, 414
number of claims, watching, 427, 428
outlining response, 415
Preliminary amendments, 384
reason for amendment must be stated, 385
Request for Continued Examination (RCE), 446–447
sample "regular," 405–413
Sections 102/103 approach, 418, 420, 421
"standing pat" (response), 404
Supplementary amendments, 384
typing and filing, 426–427
when you agree with examiner, 404, 414
without narrowing scope of claim, 404, 414
See also Amendments; Claim rejections

538 | PATENT IT YOURSELF

Claims and statutory classes of inventions
  overview, 235
  article-of-manufacture claims, 243, 270
  compositions of matter claims, 235, 243–244, 270
  inventive concepts beyond judicial exception, 238
  legal requirements for, 237–238
  machine claims, 235, 242–243, 270
  new-use claims, 235, 244, 270
  process (method) claims, 235, 240–242, 270
  rejections as judicial exceptions, 400–404
Claim rejections
  abstract ideas, 401
  ambiguous or missing references, 249
  consultation with patent attorney, 377
  defined, 385
  design patents, 437
  don't take it personally, 379
  for double patenting, 384
  European Patent Office suggestions for, 379
  first Office Action, 375, 376, 383
  improper use of articles, 249
  for incomplete disclosure of embodiments, 193, 195, 202, 215, 387
  multiple interpretations of claim wording, 247–248, 397
  nonstatutory subject matter, 238
  prima facie obviousness, 400, 411, 421–422
  for prolixity, 383
  request for reconsideration, 424
  Section 101 (judicial exception), 400–404
  Section 112 (inadequate specifications), 388, 400, 424
  "shoot-from-the-hip" rejections, 394
  technical reasons, 250
  technical rejection, 248, 424
  using means clause to avoid functionality of claim, 250
  Whack-a-Mole rejections (piecemeal prosecution), 386
  See also Claims, technical requirements of
Claim rejections, prior art
  arguments against obviousness, 395, 396
  combination of references, analyzing, 395, 396, 400
  compare broadest claim with novelty references, 397
  comparison chart of invention features, 395
  error correction after, 386, 394–395
  flowchart for, 395–396
  foreign patents and nonpatent references sent, 394
  general arguments against obviousness, 398–399
  nonobviousness (Section 103), 247, 397, 400, 404, 420–421
  novelty (Section 102), 247, 397, 404, 420–421
  reading carefully, 395
  response to OA, 383–384
  U.S. patent references must be located, 394

Claims, dependent
  overview, 261
  as adding additional or defining elements more narrowly, 255, 261, 263–264, 267
  allowance of 20 claims before fee, 263, 268, 304, 386, 428
  antecedents for terms, 249
  apparatus claims, 261, 264, 435
  as backup in case of broader-claim invalidation, 262
  canceling claims, 414
  checklist for drafting, 271
  connective expressions, proper use of, 252
  dependent on dependent claims (not recommended), 264–265
  dependent on independent claims, 264–265, 266
  descriptive recitations provided by, 263
  differentiation of broad claims, 262, 265, 266
  drafting, 263–266
  drafting additional claims on same invention, 267–268
  formatting, 240–241, 254, 256
  infringement damages, broader base for, 262
  infringement of, 255, 265–267
  infringing device must have all elements plus elements of incorporated claim, 266, 267
  litigator preference for, 263
  method claims, 261, 264, 435
  multiple dependent claims (not recommended), 236, 237, 265
  must include all features of referent claim, 266
  numbering of, 264–265
  physical structure to support, 264–266
  prevention of premature final action, 262
  reification of broad claims, 262
  request for reconsideration, 424
  right to rely on doctrine of equivalents, 263
  scope of independent claim not narrowed by, 262–263, 267
  Section 112 law, 244
  significant limitations, 265
  specific features in, 266, 267
  spectrum of coverage by, 262
  subsidiary feature permutations, 265
  third-level, 267
Claims, independent, 255–258
  overview, 255
  allowance of 3 claims before fee, 268, 304, 386, 428
  anticipating infringer attacks on patent, 246
  apparatus claims, 268
  broadening by maximizing scope of elements, 245–248, 258
  broadening by minimizing number of elements, 245, 247, 258
  broadening by using means-plus-function, 237, 250, 255, 261

checklist for drafting, 271

defined as standing alone, 255, 261, 267, 268

dependent claims on, 264–265

drafting additional claims on same invention, 267–268

improving on part names in, 255

infringement of, 255

method claims, 257, 268

nonmeans claims as alternative to means claims, 237

physical structure to support, 258, 259

prior art, defining novelty and nonobviousness over, 247–248, 258, 414

prior art patents as examples for, 255

process claims, 255

Section 112 law, 244

software processes, 268

specific features in, 266, 267

use of artificial intelligence (AI) to draft, 269–270

Claims, independent, four-step method for drafting

Step 1: Preamble, 255–256, 258, 259

Step 2: Elements, 255–256, 258, 259

Step 3: Interconnections, 255–256, 258, 259

Step 4: Broaden the claims, 255, 258

technical requirements, 248

See also Preamble of a claim

Claims, technical requirements of, 248–254

overview, 248

overview of the law (Section 112(b)), 248–250

affirmative recital of each element as subject of its clause, 253

affirmative recitation of each element followed by shape or function, 254

aggregation, 251

all elements must logically interrelate and interconnect, 251

articles, proper use and precision of antecedents, 249, 259

avoiding too many claims, 252

claims must correspond with disclosure, 252

claims supported by drawings, 252–253

completeness of elements, 251

connective expressions, proper use of, 252

Declaration under Rule 132, 424

format of, 254

functions preceded by affirmative recitation of element performing functions, 254

Jepson claim style (rarely enforced), 239, 259

language straightforward and simple (avoid prolixity), 251

logical interrelation and interconnections of all elements, 251, 255, 256, 258

means clause to avoid functionality of claim, 250

means must be supported, 251, 253

positive limitations requirement, 251–252

prior art, defining novelty and nonobviousness over, 245, 247–248, 258

punctuation requirements, 249

rejection of claims, 248, 424

relative terms, ensuring no ambiguity in, 254

software-as-means trap, avoiding, 253

structural support in recitation of operation, 254

Claims, writing tips for

antecedents for terms, 249, 259

Boolean less is more rule, 245, 261

checklist for drafting, 271

connective expressions, proper use of, 252

consisting vs. comprising, 260

drafting additional claims on same invention, 267–268

drafting dependent, 263–266

format of, 254

formatting and arrangement of, 239

gerund (--ing words) to begin, 240, 261

Jepson-type claims (not recommended), 239, 259

language straightforward and simple (avoid prolixity), 251

Markush group, 252

"means" labeling and wording, 237, 246, 261

method claims, 257, 261

as objects of words "I (we) claim," 235

padding a too-short claim, 261

patent attorney words, 260

"plurality" terminology, 258, 260

"predetermined" and "given" terms, 259

prior-art search and tailoring of, 135

reciting of additional features, 263–264

reference numerals, 259

as sentence fragments, 235

sketchability, 261

structural (nonmeans) clauses, 246

use of artificial intelligence (AI) to draft, 269–270

use of special terms, 261

whereby clause, 240, 243–244, 259

Classification searches, 158–168

overview, 158

Cooperative Patent Classification (CPC) Definitions, 158–160, 165–166

Cooperative Patent Classification (CPC) Scheme, 158–160, 165

examiner assistance, noting in comments, 161, 166

flowchart of, 159

low-tech inventions require, 170

Patent Public Search (PPS) system, 170–171

sample of search results, 162

sample pages from CDC, 163–164

Searcher's Worksheet, 160–161

Step 1: writing out nature and essence of invention, 158–160

Step 2: finding potentially relevant classifications, 158, 160, 165

540 | PATENT IT YOURSELF

Step 3: checking relevancy of classification, 159, 165
Step 4: retrieving U.S. patents, 159, 165–166
Step 5: reviewing patents in-depth, 159, 166–167
Step 6: checking U.S. pre-grant application publications, 159, 167–168
Step 7: checking References Cited, 159, 168
using with keyword searches, 158, 169
See also Keyword searching; Searches of patentability, do-it-yourself (DIY)

Clear and convincing proof, 514
Closed vs. open claims, 260
Code of Federal Regulations (CFR), 4, 238
Combination inventions
impossible to combine, 124
nonobviousness determinations, 123–125
prior-art references would not operate, 125
synergism, 123–124
unsuggested combinations, 124

Commands (patent searches), 157
Commercial potential, evaluation for
building and testing prototypes, 51, 96–97
confidentiality safeguards, 94–97
consultation and research, 94–96
decision to drop invention, 174, 182
demonstrating working models, 383
Five Ps factors influencing, 87
for foreign filings, 348–349
licensing or selling invention, 179–180
literature searches, 95
marketability factors, 88–93
misconceptions about profitability, 86–87
model makers and, 96–97
nondisclosure agreements, 96
overview, 86–87
patentability decisions, 383
patentability versus, 98, 101, 117
positive and negative factors test, 87–94
prior art searches, 98
protection against misappropriation, 95–96
small scale prototyping, 86–87, 98
test marketing, 86
trademarks and, 87
See also Marketing your invention

Commercial use
copyright protections, 24
foreign filing prior to, 15, 86
patentability and, 122, 134
patent applications prior to, 15
patent value through, 18, 38, 333
postponement of monopoly period, 177
prior-user rights, 31, 178
problem recognition and solution, 39–41

regulatory review, 16
secondary factors of nonobviousness in amendment, 422
trade secrets and patent filing, 29–30, 36
See also Marketing your invention

Commissioner of Patents and Trademarks, 434
Common law
trademarks rights, 21–22
unfair competition and offensive rights, 34

Compensatory damages, 461, 514
Competition
commodities, 92
entrenched, 92
manufacturer head start on, 345
as marketability factor, 90, 92
patent royalties, 499
potential, 90
See also Unfair competition

Complaint, 514
Components. *See* Parts
Compositions of matter (statutory subject class)
claims for, 235, 243–244
defined, 106, 514
patentability, 106
sample claim for, 243

Computer-aided design (CAD)
DIY drawings, 279, 288
drawings for PPA, 76
drawings for RPA, 281, 284, 288, 330
online availability, 288
tracing a photo, 288
virtual prototypes, creating, 338

Computer software
overview, 13
abstract ideas, 104, 243
bugs in, 195
challenged for incomplete disclosure, 193, 195
claims for, 240–241, 243, 268
copyright and, 23, 25
copyright notice in patent application, 197
creative problem solving, 46
electronic filing, 195, 212
enabling use flowchart, 194
flowchart drawings of, 201, 284
flowchart for disclosure of, 194–196, 198, 212
hardware basis of, 195
inventive concepts beyond judicial exception, 238
as machine, 105–106, 243
offensive rights, 25
patent protection, 25, 104–105
as process, 104–105
process inventions must be hardware-based, 195
programming language disclosure, 195

software-as means-trap, 253
source/object code listing of program, 194
special-purpose computers, 105
as trade secrets, 13
unconventional processes, 105–106
as unpatentable, per se, 13, 25, 104, 107
Computer software for inventors
CAD (computer-aided design), 76, 279, 281, 284, 288
CAT (computer-aided thinking), 46
group brainstorming, 46, 48
virtual prototypes, 86, 96
Conception, 39, 52–53, 55, 58, 60, 514
Conclusion section, 186, 213–214
Confidentiality, during patenting process
overview, 94
building and testing activity confidential, 53–54
Lab notebook witnesses, 60, 95–96
model makers and consultant agreements, 97, 337
patent attorneys, 139
recording conception, 60
send confirming letter, 96
trustworthy reviewers of application, 202, 215
See also Nondisclosure agreements (NDAs)
Confidentiality, situations requiring
marketing while patent pending, 340
patentability searches by professionals, 137
patent searches at PTO Public Search Facility, 153
showing invention and references for amendments, 414
See also Consultants
Confidentiality agreement, 514
See also Nondisclosure agreements (NDAs)
Connector words/operators (patent searches), 158
Constructive reduction to practice, 110
Consultants
Assignment of Invention and Patent Application, 97
commercial potential evaluation, 94–95
Consultant's Work Agreement, 97, 289, 337
independent invention evaluation services, 95
Joint Owners' Agreement, 97
model makers, 96–97
ownership of inventions by, 97
precautions to take, 95–97
Consumer's Legal Remedies Act (Calif.), 32
Contingent-fee invention brokers (CFIBs), 334, 336
Continuation applications
overview, 433, 442, 444
Accelerated Examination Program (AEP) filing, 326
as after-final option, 433, 444
Application Data Sheet (ADS), 445–446
attorney recommended for, 446, 447
changing examiners through, 446
CIP for, 451

continuations of continuations allowed, 445
deadline for filing, 374, 376
defined, 514
defined in MPEP, 444, 445
deletion of inventors form, 445
filed after final OA, 442, 444
filed before end of three-month period, 433, 444
filed before patent issues, 444, 459
filing date based on original application, 110, 442, 445, 448, 449
filing dates due to delay, 16
filing receipts, 445
Information Disclosure Statement (IDS), 446
parent application can issue or be abandoned, 445
Priority Mail Express filing, 433
priority through previous applications, 445
RCE as better option, 446, 447
revision of claims after final action, 386, 430, 445
serial number, 445
terminal disclaimer for, 444
Continuation-in-part application (CIP)
overview, 442, 450
claim amendments, 414
continuation applications, 451
defined, 514
defined by MPEP, 450, 451
deletion of inventors form, 452
divisional application, 451
electronic filing, 452
for embodiment changes, 378, 414
filing date based on original application, 450–452
filing date of CIP if unique matter included, 450–452
new matter added after filing, 370, 383, 442
new matter can't be added after filing, 450
paper filing of, 451
protection of improvements, 450
terminal disclaimer for, 450
Contributory infringement, 469, 471, 514, 516
Copyright, 24–28
overview, 8, 23, 27, 36
advertising, 23
computer software, 25, 197
defined, 23–24, 515
design patent comparisons, 26–27
duration of, 24, 26
exclusions from, 23
expiration of, 24
expressive content, 23, 26–27
fair use, for submission of prior art, 188
infringement of, 28
label wording, 181
notice of, 24, 28

542 | PATENT IT YOURSELF

offensive rights, 23–26, 34
original authorship, 24, 27
patent law overlap, 25–27
registration of, 28
registration of patent drawings, 188
separability requirement for aesthetic features of
  functional article, 26
on shapes and designs, 25–26
specifications, 211
for surface ornamentation, 26
trademark overlap, 27
utility patent comparison, 24–26
on work-made-for-hire, 24
Copyright Act, 23
Copyright Office, 4, 24, 27, 28, 36, 188, 504
Counterclaims, 515
Court appeals, 480
Court of Appeals for the Federal Circuit (CAFC), 480,
  482, 515
Court of Claims (Washington, D.C.), 472
Creativity problems, solving
  overview, 44
  ASMR, 45
  computerized, 46
  dreams and, 45–46
  engaging the creative (vs. logical) brain, 45
  flash of genius, 44
  framing problems differently, 44–45
  group brainstorming, 46
  hot tub method, 46
  idea tools, 46–47
  increase self-confidence, 46
  letting go of assumptions, 45
  meditation and, 45, 48
  20 questions, 46
  unstructured fanaticism, 46
Cross-licensing, 18, 156, 462, 467
Cross-reference to related applications (PPA or prior
  applications), 186, 203–204
Customer Number (PTO), 78, 79, 298, 310

D

Damages
  copyright and, 8, 24, 28
  for false marking of products, 461
  trademark infringement, 21
  unfair competition, 32
  unrecoverable under UDRP, 20
Damages for infringement of patents
  actual damages (compensatory), 514
  attorney fees, 17, 28, 468, 471
  bad faith and triple (treble), 17, 468, 471

copyright protections, 8, 24, 28
  dependent claims broadening basis for, 262, 263, 265
  illegally obtained trade secrets, 14
  profits of infringer, 468
  royalty based on sales, 17
  trademark infringement, 21
  unfair competition law, 32
  willful infringement, minimizing risk in copying
    products, 476–477
Date of invention, 515
Deadlines
  of critical importance in patent prosecution, 377
  PTO publication of postponement due to disaster, 525
  Quick-Reference Timing Chart, 527–528
  See also Abandonment of patent application; Weekends
    or holidays, filing dates falling on
"Deceived purchaser" test, 474
Declaration under Rule 132, 424
Declaratory judgment (DJ) actions, 472, 515
Deed (patent), 515
  See also Patent deed
Defensive publication of patent, 435, 453
Delayed-issue patents, 473
Deposit date, 515
Deposition, 515
Derivation proceedings
  overview, 434
  building and testing documentation, 53
  defined, 515
  documentation in case of theft, 52
  first-inventor-to-file law, 15
  prior art overcome by, 110, 386, 434–435
  PTO may read PPA if depending on earlier date, 185
  publication before filing may lead to, 96
Derwent Innovation, 154
Description (detailed)
  overview, 185–186
  of alternative embodiments, 213
  assembly order within specification, 187
  avoidance of negative or restrictive statements, 202
  avoiding legalese, 201
  avoiding patent profanity, 202
  avoiding technical terms, 211
  checklist for, 218
  classification searching, 160
  clear and understandable writing, 201, 210
  common-sense limits on, 209–210
  consider audience, 201
  copious subheadings in, 202
  defining terms, 212
  detailed discussion of each aspect, 208
  drafting claims prior to writing, 184

drafting tips, 201–203
Drawing Reference Numerals Worksheet used, 209
embodiments in, 186–187, 191, 208, 387
enabling disclosures to build and use invention, 133, 191, 193–194
figure numbers, discussions of, 208
interconnections between parts, 209
must comply with full disclosure rules, 77, 191, 193–194, 209
part names in, 208–209
patent claims, 167, 193
for PPA, 62–65, 77
preparing an outline, 203
prior art providing names for components, 133–134, 193
for prior-art searches, 139
reference numerals in text, 207–209
reference numerals list at end of, 207–208
references to trademarked products, 212
for RPA, 133–134, 191, 193–194
use of articles, 211
See also Embodiments; Ramifications; Specification
Design and aesthetics
design vs. utility patents, 10, 12, 109, 328
functional, overlapping utility or copyright, 25–26
marketability factors, 89, 91
surface ornamentation copyright, 26
surface ornamentation excluded from patents, 27, 33, 35, 180
as trademarks, 19
Designing around a patent
as choice, 476
defined, 151
improvements to inventions, 44
in-force patents are applicable, 476
scope of patent coverage and protection from, 125, 151–152
trade secrets as protection, 30
Design patents
overview, 10, 12, 27, 35, 328
address for application submission, 329
for aesthetic appeal, 33, 107, 328
as after-final option to try, 434
as alternative for invention failing to qualify for utility patent, 182
on appearance of utility inventions, 328
Application Data Sheet (ADS), 329
application for, 328–329
argue Sections 102/103, 437
article-of-manufacture requirement, 329
claims for, 329
compared to copyright, 26–27
compared to unfair competition law, 33
computer-generated symbols, 329

converted to utility application, 437
costs of, 26
deceived purchaser test, 474
defined, 515
Design Patent Application Transmittal, 328
drawings for, 328–329
duration of, 16
embodiments in, 329
examination fees, 522
Fee Transmittal Form, 328, 329
filing by mail, 328–329
Hague Agreement filing, 349, 356–357
ineligibility of PPA for, 62, 65
in-force period, 14
infringement of, 474
inventive appearance, 10, 12
issue fee payment, 437
maintenance fees not required, 14, 35, 437
narrowing claims, 437
nonobviousness, 102, 121, 437
no priority of PPA for, 437
novelty tests, 102, 121
offensive rights, 34
patentability searches, 136
Patent Application Declaration (PAD), 328, 329
Patent Center filing, 313, 329
post-allowance fees, 522
postcard receipt, 328, 329
prosecution of applications, 437
"Rocket Docket" (expedited examination), 136, 524
sample, 321, 323
single embodiments only, 329
specification for, 328
term of patent, 527
timing schedule, 528
title of invention, 329
Diamond v. Diehr, 13, 253
Digital Certificate, 311–312
Digital Millennium Copyright Act (1998), 23
Diluting marks, 20
Disclosure rules. *See* Specification, compliance with full disclosure rules
Disclosures by inventor
claims must correspond with, 252
discovery of relevant prior art, 373–375, 378, 383
duty to disclose material information, 380–381, 383
first-inventor-to-file, 15, 110–111
keeping a paper trail, 139
for RPA, 189, 191, 193–194
search information and literature, 381
witnesses and, 59
See also Invention Disclosure; Lab notebooks

544 | PATENT IT YOURSELF

Divisional application
    overview, 442, 448
    attorney recommended for, 448
    CIP for, 451
    defined, 515
    defined by MPEP, 449
    deletion of inventors form, 449
    divisional claims must relate directly, 448
    drawings for, 449
    electronic filing, 449
    filed before patent issues, 376, 459
    filing as soon as possible, 435
    filing date based on original application, 110, 190, 433, 435, 448, 449
    if multiple embodiments of design, 329
    Information Disclosure Statement (IDS), 449
    maintenance fees, 190, 448
    multiple inventions on RPA and use of, 190
    for nonelected claims if PTO restricts, 435–436, 442
    paper filing of, 448
    parent application can issue or be abandoned, 448
    priority through previous applications, 449
    serial number for, 448
    Utility Patent Application Transmittal, 449
Doctrine of Equivalents (DoE)
    ability to use in infringement lawsuit, 470
    copyright and, 27
    defined, 515
    dependent claims preserving, 263
    design patents and, 27
    Festo v. Shoketsu, 263, 384, 470
    file wrapper estoppel limiting, 470
    negative (reverse) doctrine, 470, 519
    structural (nonmeans) clauses, 246
    used to broaden claims, 384–385
Documentation of the invention
    overview, 51
    analysis stimulus, 51
    avoidance of ownership disputes, 52
    building and testing, 53–60, 83
    creative invention process, 51
    digital documents, 58–59, 62
    good engineering practice, 51
    Invention Disclosure form, 55, 60
    lab notebooks, 54–60
    legal implications of, 52
    nondisclosure agreements, 53–54
    Post Office Patent warning, 62
    as proof of inventorship, 52, 53, 58
    psychological stimulus, 51
    recording conception, 53, 58, 60, 83, 180
    recording inventions, 54–58
    saving paperwork, 58
    supporting tax deductions, 52
    witnesses and, 58–60
DOCX format, 78, 310, 312–313
Domain names, 20
Double patenting (DP)
    cause for invalidation of patents, 450, 454
    continuation application must have different scope, 442, 444
    defined, 515
    divisional application on nonelected inventions allowed, 450
    immunity if examiner required restriction, 454
    non-statutory (obviousness-type), 384, 454
    statutory, 454
    terminal disclaimer for, 384, 444, 450, 454, 455
Drawing Reference Numerals Worksheet, 209
Drawings
    amendments, 425–426
    assembly order of application, 185
    claiming copyright, 211
    claims drafted prior to, 184
    claims supported by, 252–253
    computer software submitted as, 211–212
    copying as prior art, copyright fair use, 188, 189
    in the Lab notebook, 59
    objections by examiner, 383–384, 385, 388, 390, 392, 425–426
    in the PPA, 76–77
    reference numerals, 186, 192, 207–209
    in specification, brief description, 186, 207
    in specification, list of reference numerals, 186, 207–209
    using computer-aided drafting (CAD), 279, 284, 288, 330
    using pen and ruler, 279
Drawings, final
    overview, 277
    amendment and replacement sheets for, 425–426
    black and white photos, petition required, 277
    CAD (computer-aided design), 284, 288, 330
    color photos or drawings, petition and fee, 277
    comprehensiveness of, 284
    conversion to PDF, 310
    deficiencies and examiner objections, 187, 277
    descriptive matter, 282
    design patents, 328–329
    divisional application, 449
    DIY drawings, 279, 281, 284–288
    drafting professionals and confidentiality, 279, 289
    filing formats, 277, 281–282
    flowcharts and, 281–282, 284
    foreign filings, 277

formal or informal, 280
format of, 277, 280, 281–283
improvements to inventions, 281
invisible margins, 280, 281
issuance with submission of formal, 376, 388, 429
manual methods, 284–288
must show features claimed, 281
PTO drawing inspector objections, 277, 278, 279
PTO rules for (37 CFR), 277, 279, 281–283, 289
reference numerals and lead lines, 282
size requirements, 277, 280
suitable for inclusion in *Official Gazette*, 198, 283
views, 282–283
Drawings, manual methods
drawing to scale, 284, 287
pen and ruler, 279
sketching from scratch, 284, 285
tracing a photo, 284, 286, 289
tracing a photo on a computer, 287
tracing three-dimensional objects, 284, 286
Drawings, preliminary sketches
as basis for drawings in RPA, 197
checklist for, 217
for chemical compositions, 198
for computer, chemical, or mechanical processes, 201
cross-section lines, 198, 200
decoding legends, 198
exploded views for complicated machines, 197–199
filed separately from patent application, 197
hidden lines shown as broken lines, 197–198
hiring a drafting professional, 198
inclusion in *Official Gazette*, 198
for machines, 198
numbering figures, 197
parts reference numbers, 197
perspective or isometric views, 197
prior-art devices, 198
prior to preparing specification, 197
reduced and compiled during finaling process, 197
software flowcharts, 198
symbols for parts, 198
Dreams, creative problem solving, 45–46
Drugs
foreign countries will not patent, 358
future profitability, 63
generally recognized as safe, 108
lawsuits for infringement, 463
Orphan Drug Act, 34
product liability risk, 91
proof of efficacy, 213
regulatory review, 16, 213
unpatentability of unsafe, 108

E

Ease of production
marketability factors, 89
as nonobviousness factor, 121
Economic Espionage Act, 32
EFilers. *See* Registered eFiler program
EFS Application Data Sheet (ADS) (PTO Form AIA/14), 310
Electronic filing
advantages of, 65, 185, 276
computer software listing, 195
filing fees, 276
filing formats, 78
Patentin program for nucleotide/amino acid sequences, 194
PPA and, 62, 65, 78, 81, 187
registered eFilers, 78
trademark registration, 22
Training Mode dry run, 79
See also Patent Center (PTO)
Elements of a claim, 255, 256, 258–259
Embodiments
in advantages (narrative), 205, 207
AI development of must be disclosed, 216, 270
alternative, description and operation of, 213–215
broadening claims with multiple, 184, 203
CIP for, 378, 414
defined, 515
design patents, 329
in detailed description, 186–187, 191, 208, 387
disadvantages of PPA, 64
disclosure of all for patent searches, 139
do not indicate best mode, 184, 191, 203
drawings must show all views, 197, 207–208
including all in PPA, 77
"knocked out" by prior art, 43
means claims, 237
operation described, 212–213
ramifications of, 189–190
as separate inventions, 435
specification must provide details of all, 193, 210
Employees
illegally obtained trade secrets, 31
know-how and, 495
nondisclosure agreements, 31–32, 181
Employees as inventors
overview, 487
assignment of rights to employers, 489–490
Chief Technology Officer (CTO) listed as inventor, 486
disclosure of inventions to employer, 489
disputes over ownership, 484, 487, 489–490
"employed to invent" doctrine, 489
Employment Agreement (EA), 488, 489–490
inventions made on own time, 489

negotiation of rights to invention, 490

records of inventions, 490

supervisor claims to invention, 52

Employers

claims for participation in invention, 52

nondisclosure agreements for confidentiality of trade
secrets, 31, 181

PCT applications, 76

rights to inventions made on employee's own time, 489

"shop rights," 489

trade secret theft, 31

Employment Agreement (EA), 488, 489–490

Energy conservation

defining for PTMS, 324

government research grants, 344

PTMS filing, 322, 324, 326

See also Perpetual-motion/-energy machines

Enhanced damages (triple/treble), 516

Environment

claims for invention, 239

defining for PTMS, 324

PTMS filing, 322, 324, 326

ramifications list, 189

technological, 238

E-Office Action, 309

Errors in printed patent, checking for

overview, 453, 455, 482

insignificant (filing "make-of-record" letter), 459

significant (filing Certificate of Correction), 460, 482

Estoppel, 470, 472

Eurasian Patent Organization (EAPO), 349, 356

Europatents, 354, 365

European Patent Convention (EPC), 349, 353, 504

European Patent Office (EPO)

overview, 349–350, 353

application based on PCT application, 349, 361–362

commercial potential strong or someone else paying, 353

Europatents, 354

European agent requirement, 353, 358, 361–362, 364

fees and annuities required, 353, 358, 361–362

filed before PPA, 363

filing in individual countries, 353, 359, 362

implementation of European Patent Convention, 504

member countries, 352

membership in Global PPH, 326

one-year deadline to file, 353, 359

patentability searches, 153–154, 170, 360–362, 505

patent prosecution costs, 353, 362

PCT and, 356

PPA priority dates, 82

priority date of original U.S date, 353

Unitary Patent system, 354, 365

validating the patent in each country, 353–354

Examiners (PTO)

as attorneys, 155

bureaucratic objections, 378–379

calling and visiting, 382, 394, 403–404

claim written by, if patentable (by request), 236, 248,
376–377, 439

contact information for, 525

continuation application to change, 446

demonstrating working models to, 383

Examiner's Answer, 432

interpretation of claims, 247, 397

interview with, 328, 362, 379, 382, 394, 403–404

job pressures of, 386, 394

keeping your composure, 386

negotiating with, 430–431

nonobviousness determinations, 116–118, 125–126

operability testing, 109

overruled by Commissioner of Patents and Trademarks, 434

patentability searches, 135–136

patent examination fees, 522

petitions to overrule, 434

prima facie obviousness, 400, 411, 421–422

qualifications of, 109

rejection of claims, don't take personally, 379, 394

rejections vs. objections, 385

responsive brief to appeals, 432

standards of patentability, 379, 403

statutes and rules followed, 385

technical points raised by, 424

Whack-a-Mole rejections (piecemeal prosecution), 386

working model furnished to, 189, 382

See also Office Actions (OA); Prosecution of patent
application (PTO process)

Examiner's Answer, 516

Exceptions to patentability. *See* Alice/Mayo test (statutory
vs. nonstatutory subject matter); Nonstatutory subject
matter (judicial exceptions to patentability)

Exclusive jurisdiction, 516

Exhaustion. *See* First sale doctrine (exhaustion doctrine)

Ex parte review of patent, 477–478

Expiration of patents

appealing to extend, 433

date of, 14, 17

double patenting, 454

end of monopoly, 17, 35

extending through PPA filing, 63–64

for failure to pay maintenance fees, 10, 14, 16–17, 466, 481

Google Patents information, 463

infringement lawsuits, 472

reasons for, 17

Expired patents
  infringer intervening rights, 466
  making and selling unpatentable inventions, 152
  marketability factors, 92
  as prior art, 14, 112, 156
  for unpaid maintenance fees, 14, 466
Exploitation of your invention
  caution not to ignore, 62
  employers, 490
  Joint Owners' Agreement, 487
  owner control of, 484, 487
  pursuit of commercial, 101, 332–333, 487
  RESAM flowchart for, 35, 36
  See also Commercial potential, evaluation for; Licensing;
    Marketing your invention; Sale of invention

F

Facebook, 345
Fair use of copyright, 188
Fax
  Certificate of Facsimile Transmission, 427–428
  for discussion of amendments, 428
  do not use to file application or drawings, 307
  PTO telephone numbers, 525
  Recordation Form Cover Sheet, 492
  Request for Continued Examination (RCE), 433, 447
  responses and amendments filed by, 381, 427–428
FBIEs (Fee-Based Inventor Exploiters), 334, 335
Federal government
  apply for intent to use trademark, 36
  invention made under contract with, 204, 328
  lawsuits for false marking, 461
  lawsuits for infringement by contractors, 472
  marketing your invention to, 344
  review of applications for national security classification,
    357
  See also PTO (Patent and Trademark Office)
Federal government publications
  no copyright on, 23
  resource list, 504
Federally-sponsored research or development
  contracts for inventions, 36, 204
  Department of Energy, 344
  design patents, 328
  specification section, 186, 192, 204
Federal patent laws
  overview, 4
  patent infringement, 10
  Section 101 (statutory/nonstatutory subject matter), 103,
    237–238, 240, 400, 454
  Section 102 (novelty), 110–111, 113, 114, 115–116, 118,
    125, 128, 152, 247, 265, 386, 388, 393, 397, 419–420, 425

Section 102/103 (argument technique), 421
Section 103 (nonobvioiusness), 116–118, 118, 126, 152,
  247, 265, 384, 393, 397, 420–422, 425
Section 112 (technical), 190–191, 193, 236–238, 246,
  248–250, 254, 258, 261, 387–388, 400, 421, 424, 479
trade-name infringement, 20
U.S. Constitution as basis, 13, 103
See also Manual of Patent Examining Procedure (MPEP)
Fee-Based Inventor Exploiters (FBIEs), 334, 335
Fees (PTO)
  overview, 15–16
  additional fees for excess claims, 263, 268, 304, 428
  for appeals, 432
  Application Size Fee, 304
  for bounced checks, 306
  design patents, 26
  excess claims, 263, 268, 304
  Fee schedule, 521–522
  Fee Transmittal Form, 299, 301, 304
  IDS size fee, 312, 313, 314, 319, 373
  Issue Fee, 16, 29, 376, 428–429, 437
  licensing invention, 495–496
  maintenance fees, 16
  micro entities, 16, 62, 76, 306, 312
  Multiple dependent claiming (MDC), 304
  paper-filing surcharge, 16, 304
  Petitions to make special (PTMS), 304, 324, 326
  PPA and, 62, 65
  provisional filing, 16
  PTO authority to set, 15–16
  reduced fees for electronic filing, 309
  Request for Continued Examination, 446–447
  RPA filing, 16, 80, 312–313
  small entities, 16, 76, 81, 306, 312
  Track 1 examination, 326, 328
Fee Transmittal Form, 185, 292
Feist Publications, Inc. v. Rural Telephone Service, 24
Festo v. Shoketsu, 263, 384, 470
Fields (patent searches), 157
Files (patent searches), 157
File wrapper estoppel (prosecution history estoppel), 470
Filing date
  appeals will extend patent term, 433
  commercial use of trade secrets, 29–30
  confidentiality of, 370
  foreign filings in non-Convention countries, 356
  instant, through Patent Center, 309, 313
  instant, through Priority Mail Express, 81, 307
  one claim (minimum) required to obtain, 236, 248
  Paris Convention countries allowing priority date, 82,
    309, 354
  patent deadlines, 15

548 | PATENT IT YOURSELF

postponement of monopoly period, 177
   for PPA, 62–63, 110
   prior-art reference established by, 14–15, 110–111, 385–386
   priority date, claimed by earlier application, 110, 360, 386, 528
   received by PTO, 383
   for RPA, 110, 309
   term of plant patents, 16
   term of utility patents, 16
Filing receipts
   confirmation number on, 370
   continuation applications, 445
   correction of errors on, 371, 439
   foreign-filing license on, 81, 348, 356, 357, 371
   official mailing of, 370–371
   patent pending status officially begins with, 309, 370–371
   PPA and, 81
   serial/application number on, 370
   See also Postcard receipt (paper filing)
Finaling of patent application
   overview, 276
   design patents, 328–329
   drawings for, 197, 277–289
   specification, paper filing, 289–308
   specification, Patent Center filing, 309–313
   See also Paper filing of patent application; Patent Center (PTO)
Final Office Actions. *See* Office Actions (OA), second/final
First-Inventor-To-File (FITF)
   overview, 15
   exception for derived inventions, 14
   prior-art reference established by, 110
   reduction to practice, 110
First Office Action. *See* Office Actions (OA), first
First sale doctrine (exhaustion doctrine), 516
Flowcharts
   foreign-filing routes, 355
   Patentability Flowchart, 126–129, 149
   Patent Application chart, 192
   patent exploitation, 35–36
   for prior-art rejections, 395–396
   PTO drawing rules, 281–282
   supplemental applications, 443
Flowcharts for processes
   chemical compositions, 198, 201, 284
   mechanical processes, 201
   software processes, 194, 195, 196, 197, 198, 201, 212, 216, 284
Food and Drug Administration (FDA), 108

Foreign filings, 348–365
   overview, 348–350
   alternate routes for filing, 358–364
   application under treaties, 277, 348, 349, 350, 353–365
   attorney recommended for, 81, 348, 357, 364
   central claiming, 358
   citing new references, 360, 361, 373–375
   claiming priority to original application, 350
   claims for, 239, 358
   commercial potential strong or someone else paying, 348–349, 353, 382
   costs and annual maintenance fees required, 349, 353–354, 357–358, 359, 365, 382
   deadlines for, 356, 363
   drawings for, 277
   election of PCT Chapter II for examination within 19 months, 354, 358–359, 361–362
   EPO/non-EPO filing, 359–362
   Europatents, 354
   expedited handling, petition for, 357
   expedited through PPH, 326, 363
   filing receipt permission, 81, 348, 356, 357, 371
   flowchart of routes, 355
   foreign-filing license (PTO issued), 348
   foreign patent agents, 359, 361–364
   formatting for, 277, 290
   incorporation by reference may not be accepted, 204
   in individual countries, 359, 362–363
   interval between patent application filing and, 332
   maintenance fees, 349, 353, 357–358, 361
   mandatory six-month delay, 357
   non-Convention/Convention PCT application, 358, 359–361
   nonpublication request (NPR) may not be made if also filing, 29, 185, 292, 350
   nonpublication request (NPR) rescinded within 45 days for, 29, 292, 350, 363–364, 438
   novelty examinations not conducted in small countries, 358
   Office Actions during, 371
   opposition proceedings, 353, 358
   patent laws, 357–358
   patent prosecution and practice costs, 348, 353, 362
   peripheral claiming, 358
   postcard receipt for, 306
   PPA priority allowed, 64, 76, 82, 348, 350, 354, 359, 363
   to prevent overseas manufacturing of invention, 336
   prior art established by, 112, 386
   public disclosure destroying rights (no grace period), 15, 86, 96, 269, 358
   regional patent associations, 356

resources for, 364–365

restricted for national security reasons, 81, 357

timing of, 356

timing schedule, 527–528

translation fees, 358, 359, 361

Unitary Patent system, 354

U.S. patents prevent knock-off importation, but can't prevent foreign manufacture, 336, 348

utility patents, 356, 365

within a year of earliest filing date, 63, 81, 348, 349, 350, 358

See also European Patent Office (EPO); Hague Agreement; Paris Convention; Patent Cooperation Treaty (PCT)

Foreign filings, non-Convention countries

overview, 356

countries involved, 82

file before publishing/offering invention for sale, 82, 348, 356, 358, 371

foreign-filing license or six months from filing date, 356

no priority date for patents, 82, 350, 356

patent pending does not provide rights, 372

timing schedule, 527–528

Trade-Related Aspects of Intellectual Property Rights (TRIPS) treaty, 350

World Trade Organization (WTO) members, 350

Foreign licensing, 348, 382, 439, 497

Foreign patents

can't be infringed by U.S. activity, 156

cited against international application, 360

copies sent with OA, 394

country codes, 319

expedited through PPH if held, 326

IDS must include, 313–314, 319

in-force patents only apply in country or origin, 393

marketing rights to manufacturers, 332

as prior art, 111, 156, 205, 319, 393

as prior art to owner of patent, 112

searches for, 154, 170

search reports on, 148

Formatting

abstract page, 214

amendment documents, 415–417

claims and claim section, 240–241, 254

computer programs, 212

Declaration under Rule 132, 424

final drawings, 277, 280, 281–282, 283

foreign filings, 277, 290

for paper filing, 290–291

PCT application, 360

Forms

downloading, 530

editing RTFs, 530

list of, 530–531

PTO downloads, 291

saving fillable PDFs, 299, 310

See also PDF documents

Formulas, in specification, 194

Fraud on the PTO

deception in application, 387

improper claim of small or micro entity status, 76

loss of patent rights, 17

nondisclosure of prior art in IDS, 275, 319, 320, 387

Free Patents Online, 154

Functionality

exclusion from design patents, 13

overlap of utility patents and copyright, 25–26

plant patents, 12

using means clause to avoid functionality of claim, 250

utility patents, 10–12, 328

G

G.E. v. Wabash, 237

Generic (genus), 516

Genetically altered organisms, 106

Genetic material, as unpatentable, 13

Glossary of Legal Terms, 514–520

Glossary of Useful Technical Terms, 508–513

Google, 21, 154

Google *Docs*, 310

Google Patents

classification searching, 168

patentability searches, 154, 168–170, 505

patent expiration dates, 463

source of patent references, 375

Google Scholar, 154

Gottschalk v. Benson, 12

Government Publishing Office, 504

Grace period, 111, 269, 319, 466–467, 516

Graham v. John Deere, 117, 121

H

Hague Agreement

overview, 356

design (industrial) patents, 349, 356–357

International Register and enforceability, 357

mandatory examination under, 356–357

member countries, 353

renewal fees, 357

six months of priority, 357

WIPO administration of, 356–357

550 | PATENT IT YOURSELF

Halliburton v. Walker, 237

Health
  abandonment of invention, 113
  defining for PTMS, 324
  irrelevance of inventor, 126
  marketability factors, 88
  PTMS filing, 322, 324
Higher Education Institutions, 76, 77, 81
Hot tub creative method, 46
Human organisms, as unpatentable, 13, 110
Human organization, as unpatentable, 13, 105, 401

I

Iancu v. Brunetti, 23
ICANN, 20
IDS. *See* Information Disclosure Statement (IDS)
Imported goods
  manufacture of your invention, 336
  patent prevents knock-offs imported but can't prevent
    oversea sales, 336, 348
  patent rights to exclude infringing, 9, 10, 462
  stopping importation of infringing devices, 472
  trademark infringement, 35
Improvement patents
  cross-licenses, 18, 156
  defined, 9
  disclosing embodiments to block others, 44, 191
  trade secrets, 10
  utility patents, 10
  withholding for later exploitation, 463
Improvements to inventions
  aesthetic appeal, 12
  benefits to exploring, 43–44
  prior-art search for technical information, 134
  problem recognition, 39, 41
  refiling of PPA, 63–65
Independent application, 444, 452, 455
Indirect infringement, 516
In-force patent, 14, 16, 18, 393
Information Disclosure Statement (IDS)
  overview, 314
  Certificate of Mailing filed with, 319, 320
  continuation applications, 446
  disclosure of material information (non prior-art), 320
  discovery of new references, 373–375, 378, 383
  divisional application, 449
  download form, 313
  duty to disclose material information, 380–381
  filed within three months, 313–314, 319, 373–374
  filed with RPA, 319
  foreign filings providing new references, 360, 361,
    373–375

Foreign Patent Documents section, 313–314, 319
fraud on the PTO if knowledge of relevant prior art, 320
IDS cover letter, 314
if no prior art found or no search, do not file, 314, 320
intervening rights, 466
irrelevant references, do not list, 314, 319
late filing and fees, 375
non-Convention/Convention PCT application, 359, 361
non-English-language references explained, 319–320
non-patent literature in, 188, 299, 313
Notice of Allowance, 373–375
paper filing of, 320, 373–375
Patent Center filing, 313, 373–375
petition for late filing, 374–375
postcard receipt, 320
prior art on References Cited in patent, 314
QPIDS program, 374, 429
Request for Continued Examination (RCE), 429
for RPA, 185–186, 205, 292, 312–314
sample, 315–318
size fees, 312, 313, 314, 319, 373
sources of prior art to list on, 314, 319
Infringement
  overview of legal options for, 467–468
  accrual of royalties before issuance (patent pending
    period), 16–17, 371, 436, 462, 474
  anticipation (by prior art) versus, 156
  avoiding liability, 479
  claim charts for determining, 468, 469
  conditions of, 167
  deceived purchaser test, 474
  defined, 156, 516
  dependent claims, 255, 265–266
  design patents, 474
  determined by claims, 235, 475
  direct, 257
  by direction or control of actions of other actors, 257
  divided, 257
  doctrine of contributory, 471
  forfeiting of rights, 480–481
  government contracts, 472
  health care activities, 463
  independent claims, 255
  in-force patent claims, 393
  injunctions, 156, 467–468, 472, 476, 477, 479
  insurance for, 481
  intervening rights, 466, 481–482
  literal, 517
  notice of published application, 371
  NPR allows during patent pending period, 371–372
  patent trolls (nonpracticing entities), 473

product clearance, 474–477

PTO plays no role in, 467, 482

publicly verifiable, 265

requires all elements of claims to be met, 245, 257, 467

search for potential, 135

successor liability, 520

use of method/patent before filing date, 477

vicarious liability, 520

See also Lawsuits for patent infringement

Infringement steps to take

compensation/royalties requested, 467, 471–472

declaratory judgment (DJ) action, 472

exchanging licenses with manufacturer, 467, 472

Step 1: obtain details of infringement, 467

Step 2: compare broadest claim with infringing device, 467

Step 3: determining extent of infringement and ability of infringer to pay damages, 469–470

Step 4: apply DoE if possible, 470

Step 5: consider whether a contributory infringement has occurred, 471

Step 6: find a patent attorney, 471

Step 7: write a letter requesting royalties, 471–472

Step 8: act promptly, 472

Step 9: who should be sued, 472–473

Step 10: stop importation of infringing devices, 473

suing for damages and injunctions, 467–468

Injunctions

contempt-of-court sanctions, 468

copyright violations, 23

defined, 516

for infringement, 156, 467–468, 472, 476, 477, 479

offer of license will void, 472

patent owner shows balance of equity, 479

permanent, 17, 475, 476, 518

temporary restraining orders, 516, 520

unfair competition law, 32

InnovationQ+™, 154

Instagram, 345

Intellectual property (IP)

overview, 7–9

defined, 7, 516

legal remedies for misappropriation, 33, 35

Nolo resources on, 505

offensive rights (not protection), 9–10, 24–27, 33–34

online resources, 504–505

ownership of, 7–9

subcategories of, 7–8

See also Copyright; Patent(s); Trademarks

Intellectual property attorneys, 8, 517

Intellectual Property Insurance Services Corp., 481

Intellectual Property Owners Association (IPO), 504

Intellectual Ventures, 461

Interconnections in a claim, 255, 256, 258, 259

Interference, 517

International Searching Authority, 354, 359, 374

Internet

advertising inventions on, 461

Digital Millennium Copyright Act, 23

patent resources via, 504–505

patent searches, 169, 505

process inventions must be hardware-based, 195

safe harbor for access to copyright infringement, 23

trademark registration, 22

utility patents for improvements, 10, 104

See also Patent Center (PTO)

Inter partes review of patent, 477–479, 517

Interrogatories, 517

Intervening rights of infringers, 466, 481–482

Invalidation of patents

Accelerated Examination Program (AEP) and, 326

antitrust law violations, 17, 463, 480

attorney recommended for, 471

claims too vague and indefinite (Section 112), 479

dependent claims as backup in case of, 262–263

double patenting, 450

for failure to enable PHOSITA to make, 149, 387, 479

for false marking, 480

false statements on PAD, 293

fraud on the PTO, 480

inoperability of machine, 479

inventorship on application incorrect, 479

misuse of patent, 480

public use or sale prior to filing date, 480

relevant prior art not previously uncovered, 17, 473, 477, 478, 479

validity search, 476

See also Challenges to patents; Fraud on the PTO; Unenforceability of patents

Invention(s)

common misconceptions, 39

defined, 9, 38–39, 517

documentation of, 51–54

embodiment changes, 378

four "rights" periods in life of, 14

models of, 189

never make negative admissions about, 370, 380

offensive rights, 9–10, 34, 53

proprietary rights, 180–181

RESAM flowchart, 35–36

scope determined by claims, 203, 210

secrecy orders, 357

statutory classes of, 235

552 | PATENT IT YOURSELF

as trade secrets, 30
types of patents, 10–12
unpatentable, 12–13
use of trademarked components, 194, 212
See also Inventors and inventing
Invention Decision Chart (exploring alternatives)
chart details, 175
commercial potential evaluation, 174, 179, 182
file RPA and manufacture and distribute yourself, 176–179
filing application and selling or licensing, 176–177
non-trade-secret protectable, manufacture and distribute yourself, 179
overview, 174
sell to manufacturer before RPA (possible PPA), 179
trade secret instead of patent, manufacturing and distributing yourself, 177–178
trade-secret protectable, manufacturing and distributing yourself, 178
unpatentable, license or sell to manufacturer without filing, 179–181
unpatentable, make and sell yourself, 182
Invention Disclosure
alternative to lab notebook, 55, 60
building and testing, 60–62, 83
conception documentation, 60–62, 83
contents of, 60
description of invention, 60
digital document copies, 62
PPA and, 77
reviewing prior to drafting RPA, 184, 192
sample form, 61
witnesses and, 60, 83
InventNet Forum, 504
Inventors and inventing
overview, 7
assignments, 490
attorneys and, 2, 4
clever trademarks, 180
consultants, 97
defined, 484
don't give up your day job, 179
employed inventors, 487
fee-based invention developers, avoiding, 334, 335
first-inventor-to-file law, 15
in-force period, 16–17
KISS (Keep it Simple, Stupid!), 42
life of inventions, 14
by magic (accident and flash of genius), 42–44, 48
micro entity fees, 16
networking with other inventors, 47

novice PGL Syndrome, 47–48
offensive rights and, 9
patent applications, 2, 4, 10, 17, 485–486
perseverance and, 41, 44, 48
problem recognition and solution, 38–42, 48
ramifications and improvements, 43
recording conception, 180
solving creativity problems, 44–47
status and personal qualification irrelevancy, 126
tax deductions, 52–53
trade secrets, 30–31
See also Creativity problems, solving; Documentation of the invention; Inventorship; Joint inventors
Inventor's Commandments
1: intellectual property familiarity, 7
2: problem recognition and solution, 38
3: documentation of conception, 51
4: documentation of building and testing, 51
5: evaluating for salability, 86
6: One-Year Rule, 101
7: evaluation of patentability, 101, 418
8: patentability searches, 133
9: consider alternatives, 174
10: avoid statements that could limit claims, 184
11: full description of invention, 184
12: "sell" the invention to the examiner or reader, 184
13: writing an independent claim, 235
14: writing alternative independent claims, 235
15: claims should be referenced in description, 235
16: signing after careful reading, 276, 293
17: avoiding fraud on the PTO, 276, 314
18: web-filing / mailing receipt postcards, 276, 306
19: prepare orderly files, 276
20: market your invention as soon as possible, 332
21: pursue commercial exploitation fully, 332
22: hiring invention developers with successful track records, 332
23: foreign filing only if strong commercial potential, 348
24: never make negative admissions about invention, 370
25: timely response to all Office Actions, 370
26: new matter cannot be added to application, 370
27: respond to all points in Office Actions, 370
28: do best job of responding to first Office Action, 370
29: supplemental applications and double-patenting trap, 439
30: check for errors, patent marking, maintenance fees, 459
31: ownership of patent, 484
32: joint ownership permits all to practice, 484
Inventors Digest Online, 47, 504
Inventors Groups of America, 47

Inventorship
    Assignment of Invention and Patent Application, 97
    assignments, 97, 320
    confusion of, 52
    consultants and, 97
    documentation as proof of, 51–52, 97
    Joint Owners' Agreement, 97
    ownership versus, 320
    trade secrets, 52
        See also Inventors and inventing
IRS Schedule C, 52
IRS Schedule E, 52
Issue Fee, 29, 376, 428–429, 437, 459
Issue Notification
    forthcoming issue date and number, 376, 459
    payment of issue fee, 376
Issue of patent
    Certificate of Correction, 460, 482
    conditional application must be filed before, 444, 459
    divisional application must be filed before, 376, 459
    formal drawings submitted, 388, 429
    issue fee payment, 376, 428–429
    Issue Notification, 376, 429, 459
    make-of-record letter for errors, 459
    with NPR, prevention of issuance, 29
    Official Gazette prints highlights, 459, 464
    patent deed, 376, 439, 453, 459
    patent number given, 429
    patent number marking, 460–461
    payment of issue fee, 376, 429, 459
    press release and marketing, 459, 461
    proofread for errors, 459–460
    scams and offers appearing after, 464, 466
    timeline for, 429
        See also Allowance of patent (approval); Patent rights

J

Japanese Patent Office, 358
Jepson claim style, 239, 259
Joint inventors
    amendments signed by all, 423, 425
    any owner can practice invention without accounting to
        others, 484
    avoiding disputes, 485–487
    Chief Technology Officer (CTO) listed as, 486
    consultant inventors becoming, 97
    contribution of inventive concepts, 291, 485–486
    correction of wrong inventor(s), 486
    defined, 291
    degrees of inventorship not recognized, 291, 485
    documenting respective contributions, 485–486

    first-named, 485
    Lab notebooks kept by each, 486
    PPA must name all, 64
    removal from supplemental applications, 445, 449, 452
    RPA must name all and only, 291, 320, 485–486
    supervisor claims to invention, 52
    witness to conception named as, 55
Joint Owners' Agreement (JOA), 97, 322, 484, 487, 490
Joint Research Agreements, 113, 186, 204
Judicial exceptions to patentability. *See* Alice/Mayo test
    (statutory vs. nonstatutory subject matter); Nonstatutory
    subject matter (judicial exceptions to patentability)
Jury instructions, 517
Jury trials, 473, 479

K

Keyword searching, 168–169
    overview, 158
    Boolean searches, 168
    broadening searches, 168–169
    narrowing searches, 168
    operators (connector words), 158
    proximity symbols (operators), 158
    PTO Patent Public Search (PPS) system, 170
    qualifiers, 157
    stop words, 158
    using with classification searches, 158, 169
    wild card symbols, 157
        See also Classification searches; Searches of patentability,
        do-it-yourself (DIY)
KSR International Co. v. Teleflex Inc., 117, 124

L

Lab notebooks
    overview of features in, 54–55
    attaching large documents, 59
    blank spaces, avoiding or crossing out, 55
    defined, 517
    digital document printing and attaching, 58
    entering technical information, 55–58
    entries from notes, 55
    entries signed at later date, 54–55
    entries signed in real time, 54–55
    information to include, 55, 58
    kept by each joint inventor, 486
    notarization of, 59
    notation of errors, 55
    permanent adhesive, 59
    photo insertion in, 58
    preservation of, 60
    as proof of inventorship, 53, 58

554 | PATENT IT YOURSELF

recording conception, 58
recording factual data, 58
recording inventions, 54–55
referring to adjacent pages, 59
sample pages, 56–57
saving paperwork, 58
signing and dating, 58
as technical diary, 55
use of ink, 55
Lab notebook witnesses
building and testing record, 58, 60
digital document copies, 58
large documents, 59
photos, 58
recording conception, 58, 60
selection of impartial and competent, 59
signatures of, 60, 95–96
Large language models (LLMs), 269
Laws of nature
claims involving, 401
as unpatentable, 107, 237, 400
Lawsuits
copyright infringement, 23
false patent marking, 461
litigation insurance, 481
negative statements can be used against you, 150, 370, 380
nondisclosure agreements and, 54
theft of inventions, 52, 54
trademark infringement, 35
trade secret, 35
Lawsuits for patent infringement
overview, 10, 17, 467–468
arbitration, 479–480
attorney fees awarded, 468
consultant inventions, 97
contingency-fee litigators, 468, 471, 481
court appeals, 480
against customers of retailers, 472
dependent claims facilitating, 263
enhanced damages awarded, 468
estoppel, 472
expired patents, 14, 472
file wrapper estoppel, 470
financing, 481
government contractors as infringers, 472
in-force period, 14, 475–477, 482
inventor credibility through patent improvements, 44
jury trials, 473, 479
laches defense, 472
against manufacturers, 467, 472

misappropriation of intellectual property, 35
multiple embodiments/ramifications as influence in, 213
nonobviousness as issue, 125–126
as offensive weapon, 17, 18
patent litigators for, 471
prior art citations, 477–479, 482
prior public use as defense, 112
against retailers, 472
stopping importation of infringing devices, 473
suing for damages and injunctions, 467–468
as weapons for offensive rights, 17–18
withheld prior art, 320
See also Infringement steps to take
Lawsuits for patent infringement, defenses to
intervening rights, 466
negative written opinion on patentability, 150, 380
prior-art citation, 473
prior-user rights, 31, 178
public-use-and-knowledge category of prior art, 112
reverse doctrine of equivalents, 469
Legal Information Institute, 504
Legality of the invention
documentation and, 52
illegal purposes, unpatentable, 108
as marketability factor, 91
LexisNexis Total Patent One, 154
Libraries and librarians
federal distribution of patents to, 156
marketability factor assistance, 95
Patent and Trademark Resources Centers (PTRCs), 156
patent searches assistance, 153–154
prior printed publications as prior art in, 111
researching manufacturers, 338
specialized, 154
LibreOffice, 288, 310
Licensing
overview, 17, 492, 494
advertising for sale, 461
antitrust laws, 463
assignments, 494
attorney recommended for, 495
compulsory for government contracts, 472
compulsory package, 463
cross-licenses, 18, 156, 462, 467
defined, 485
entity size change, 378
exclusive rights, 492, 494
fees for, 495–496
filing RPA prior to, 176
for in-force patents, 476
foreign filings, 348, 382, 439, 497

illegal practices and loss of, 480, 494

illegal tying arrangements, 481, 494

infringers as potential licensees, 462, 472

infringers offered, 467, 472

inventor must sign, 492

know-how and, 495–496

manufacturing without, 476

nonexclusive rights, 494

patentability searches for facilitating, 135

patent number marking, 460–461

perpetual royalties not allowed due to expiration of patent, 494

PPA and, 64

royalty rates, 499–500

sale vs. license, 494

single lump-sum payment, 498

terms and considerations for, 492, 494–495

Universal License Agreement, 493, 495–499

unpatentable inventions, 179–180

Literal infringement, 517

Lloyd's of London, 481

M

Machine-or-transformation test prohibition, 241

Machines (statutory subject class)

claims for, 235, 242–243

computer software as, 105–106

conventional, 242–243

defined, 105, 517

drawings for, 198, 200

examples of, 105

patentability, 105–106

as processes, 105

sample claim for conventional, 242

sample claims for software, 243

software, 243

Magic-type trade secrets, 28

Magistrate, 517

Mail. *See* Priority Mail Express; U.S. Postal Service

Maintenance fees

overview, 466–467

Certificate of Mailing, 467

design patents do not require, 14, 35, 437

divisional applications, 190, 448

foreign filings, 349, 353, 357–358, 361

grace period (with penalty), 466, 467

loss of patent rights for failure to pay, 10, 14, 16–17, 466

Maintenance Fee Reminder Sheet, 465, 531

Maintenance Fee Statement, 467

payment of, 467

petition for unintentional nonpayment, 466

petition to accept delayed payment, 438

plant patents do not require, 14, 35

PTO Mail Stops, 525

Reminder sheet, 465, 466

small entity status, 306

surcharges, 522

timing chart for, 464

timing schedule, 16, 35, 466, 482, 522, 527

Make-of-Record Letter for Errors in Printed Patent, 459

Manual of Patent Examining Procedure (MPEP)

overview, 4, 380, 504

attorney recommended if situation not covered in, 378

as authority for amendments, 385

biotechnology deposits, 194

claim drafted by examiner (by request), 236, 292

claim rejection examples, 401

on continuation applications, 444, 445

on continuation-in-part applications, 450, 451

on divisional applications, 449

guidance on patentable subject matter, 238

guidelines for patent examiners, 103

Incorporation by Reference Statement, 186

linking claims, 435

non-limiting factors for claims, 193

Patent Cooperation Treaty (PCT) and, 354

Patentin program for nucleotide/amino acid sequences, 194

patent rules and statutes in, 380

on reissue applications, 453

on substitute applications, 454

technical requirements of claims, 248

Manual of U.S. Classification, 155

Manufacturers

approaching with unpatentable inventions, 179–181

distribution systems, 338

fear of being sued, 339–341

head start on competition, 332, 345

infringement of patents, 467, 472

licenses for in-force patents, 476

online research for, 338–339

overseas knock-offs, 336

patent applications prior to approaching, 176, 182, 337

proprietary rights, 180

Proprietary Submission Agreement as alternative to waiver, 340–341

purposeful infringement, 476

seeking new inventions, 339

specialty gadgets, 339

trade secrets, 177

waivers required by, 176, 182, 338–342

See also Marketing your invention; Sale of invention

Manufactures (articles of manufacture)
claims for, 235, 243
defined, 106, 517
design patents, 329
patentability, 106
sample claim, 243

Marketing your invention
overview, 332, 345
advantages of U.S. market, 349
advertising invention for sale after patent issue, 461
alternative ways to profit from, 333–337
celebrity endorsement, 346
confidentiality concerns, 332, 334
contingent-fee intermediary brokers, 334, 336
distributing it yourself, 336
doing your own drawings, 279
factors affecting commercial potential, 88–93
fee-based invention developers, avoiding, 334, 335, 346
manufacturing it yourself, 336
offering as premium, 345–346
partial use of an intermediary, 336
patent pending status as advantage, 64, 332, 371
perseverance and patience are essential, 333
press release and, 459
prior to filing ends patent rights if done by anyone else, 113, 174
prior to foreign filing, 332
project team approach, 332
in the RESAM flowchart, 35–36
as soon as possible after filing, 332, 346
working model demonstration and sales pitch, 174, 337, 341–342, 346
writing specification with an eye to audience, 201
See also Commercial use; Licensing; Waiver of rights

Marketing your invention, finding a manufacturer/distributor yourself
agreements to sell invention, 343
all the benefits will be yours, 334, 336
confidentiality concerns, 339–340
copyrightable labeling, 181
correspondence, presentation by, 343
evaluation of manufacturers, 342–343
finding prospective manufacturers, 338–339
giant companies, avoiding, 338
letters and phone calls, 341–343
local manufacturers, 338
local stores with similar products, 338
manufacturing and distribution done for you, 336
as most favored pursuit, 337
networking for, 338
NIH (Not Invented Here) syndrome, as impediment, 339

patent pending application, 341
researching for, 338–339
respect in the marketplace, 334
simultaneous submissions, 343
"Three Fs"—Form, Fit, and Function in presentation, 342
trade dress distinctiveness, 181
trademark design, 180
trade secret protection, 181
unique patentable designs, 180–181
unpatentable inventions, 179–180
virtual prototypes, 338
waivers and loss of legal rights, 338–342
working model demonstration and sales pitch, 174, 337, 341–342
working models, development of, 337–338

Marketing your invention, manufacturing/distributing yourself
all the benefits will be yours, 336–337
business knowledge, acquiring, 343
business plan preparation, 344
financing manufacturing, 344
government services utilization, 344
publicity, 344–345
unpatentable inventions, 182
venture capitalists (VC) and, 344

Market penetration, 90

Matal v. Tam, 23

Mathematical concepts
as "significantly more," 403
as unpatentable, 13, 107, 401, 403

Mayo Collaborative Services v. Prometheus Labs., Inc., 12–13

Means-plus-function claims (means claims)
broadening claims with, 237, 250, 255
combination required for, 246, 250
defined, 264, 517
dependent claims, 266
disadvantages of, 250
functionality avoided with, 250
labeling and wording of "means," 237
limited to structure disclosed in application, 237
Section 112(f) law governing, 246, 250
supported in claim, 251, 253, 254

Media and publicity, 8, 344–346
See also Social media

Medical devices, 105, 213
See also Drugs

Medical procedure exemption, 104, 463

Meditation, creative problem solving, 45, 48

Mental processes, as unpatentable, 13, 104, 105

Metaphysical-energy converters, 108

Methods. *See* Processes (methods)

Micro entities (ME)
Certification of Micro Entity Status, 62, 65, 78
defined, 517
fee reduction, 16, 62, 76, 306
free legal assistance for, 433
PPA and, 76–78, 81
qualifying as, 76, 78
RPA and, 306, 312
Microsoft *Word*, 78, 194, 240, 310
Misuse of patent
defined, 518
false marking, 480
forfeiting of rights, 480
illegal licensing, 480
supplemental examination requested to correct, 478
third-party submission of prior art, 478, 482
tying, 463, 481, 494, 520
See also Challenges to patents; Invalidation of patents
Model makers
changes to scope of work, 97
confidentiality safeguards, 337
Consultant's Work Agreement, 96–97, 337
locating, 337
nondisclosure agreements, 53
protection of confidentiality, 97
working models for potential customers, 337
Monopoly provided by a patent, 348, 365, 454, 462–463, 482
Multiple dependent claiming (MDC), 265, 304

N

NASA Declarations, 436
National Bureau of Standards, 109
National Institute of Standards and Technology (NIST), 109
National security
infringement by government contractors, 472
NASA Declarations, 436
nuclear weapons unpatentable, 109
restriction of inventions for, 81, 357
Natural phenomena as unpatentable
overview, 12, 106
compositions of matter as altering, 106
DNA gene process, 13
human organisms, 13, 110
manufactures as altering, 106
Natural shapes, design patents excluded from, 12
Network Solutions, 21
New matter may not be added to RPA after filing
amendments may not contain new matter, 416
continuation-in-part application to add, 370, 383
defined, 517

definition of new matter, 383
design patents must convert unclaimed lines, 437
distinguished from newly discovered prior art, 383
drawings may be corrected, 426
filing drawings, 280
getting it right the first time, 193, 246, 439
New-use inventions
claims for, 235, 244
defined, 106–107, 517
nonobvious use, 119
novelty requirement, 114–115
sample claim for, 244
Nolo's Legal Encyclopedia, 505
Non-Convention countries. *See* Foreign filings, non-Convention countries
Nondisclosure agreements (NDAs)
advising receiving party of, 53–54
building and testing inventions, 53–54
defined, 514
employee signing of, 34, 177
lawsuits for theft, 54
model makers and machine shops, 53
precautions during consultation, 95–96
trade secrets, 32, 34, 177, 181, 414
venture capitalists (VC) and, 344
Nonobvious requirement
overview, 15, 115–116
claims must define, 247–248, 397
defined, 116, 517
design patents, 102, 121, 437
disposability, 120–121
duplication of a part, 120
examiner determinations, 125–126
examples of, 118–121
general arguments against obviousness, 398–399
in lawsuits, 125–126
limits on specific features, 152
new-use inventions, 106–107
novelty and, 115
obviousness determinations, 116–118
patentability, 102, 115–121, 386
in Patentability Flowchart, 127–128
patentability searches for proof of, 134
physical differences, 119–120
Positive and Negative Factors Summary, 94
prior art determinations, 116–117, 236
secondary factors, 422
Section 103 text, 116
substitution of element in known combination, 119–120
See also Advantages of invention; Claim amendments; Claim rejections, prior art; Patentability

558 | PATENT IT YOURSELF

Nonobvious requirement, secondary factors
  overview, 117, 121
  in amendment of Declaration, 422
  commercial success, 117, 122, 383
  contrary to prior art's teaching, 123
  crowded art, 122
  omission of element, 122
  previous failure of others, 122
  solution of long-felt need, 123
  solves an insoluble problem, 122
  solves an unrecognized problem, 122
  solves prior inoperability, 122
  successful implementation of ancient idea, 122–123
  unappreciated advantage, 122
  unsuggested modification, 122
Nonobvious requirement, secondary factors of combination
inventions
  overview, 123
  awkward, involved combinations, 125
  combinations unsuggested, 124
  different combinations, 125
  easier assembly or manufacture, 125
  general arguments against obviousness, 399, 400
  impossible to combine, 124
  prior-art references would not operate, 125
  references are from a different field, 125
  references teach away from combining, 125
  subject matter of broadest claim disclosed, 400
  synergism, 123–124
  unsuggested combinations, 124
Non-patent literature (NPL)
  copyright claims in, 189
  databases and services, 153–154
  defined, 154
  in Information Disclosure Statement (IDS), 188, 299, 313
  prior printed publications as prior art, 111, 154
  for submission as prior art, fair use of copyrighted
    material, 188
Nonpublication request (NPR)
  overview, 292
  assembly order of application, 185
  Certificate of Mailing, 364
  check box on ADS, 292
  check box on transmittal, 300
  foreign filing not allowed with, 29, 185, 292, 350
  if foreign filing made, must be rescinded within 45 days,
    29, 292, 310, 350, 363–364
  PPA and, 64
  prior art determinations, 111
  rescind for royalties before issuance, 474
  for RPA, 185, 188, 292, 299, 301

trade secrets maintained by, 29, 177–178, 181
unpublished pending applications as prior art, 111
unpublished pending applications do not accrue
  provisional royalties, 371, 474
unpublished pending applications not searchable, 136, 475
Nonstatutory subject matter (judicial exceptions to
patentability)
  overview, 12–13
  abstract ideas, 12–13, 25, 103–104, 106, 240, 401
  aesthetic purpose, 109
  computer software, per se, 13, 25, 104, 107, 241
  DNA gene process, 13
  electrical signals, 107, 268
  human organisms, 13, 110
  ideas, per se, 107
  illegal purposes, 108
  laws of nature, 240
  mathematical concepts, 13
  medical procedures, 104, 463, 482
  mental processes, 12–13, 104, 107
  methods of organizing human activity, 13, 105
  naturally occurring DNA, 106
  natural phenomena, 240
  nonoperable inventions, 108–109
  nuclear weapons, 109
  perpetual-motion/-energy machines, 108–109
  printed matter, per se, 107
  tax avoidance schemes, 13, 108–109
  theoretical phenomena, 109
  unsafe new drugs, 108
  whimsical inventions, 108
  See also Alice/Mayo test (statutory vs. nonstatutory
    subject matter)
Notice of Abandonment, 434
Notice of Allowability, 376, 428
Notice of Allowance (NOA), 188, 373–376, 428, 436, 442,
  444, 517, 527
Notice of Appeal, 431–432
Notice of Incomplete Application Parts, 187
Notice of Patent Term Adjustment, 428
Notice of References Cited, 383, 388, 391, 394
Notice to File Corrected Application Papers, 309, 393
Notice to File Missing Parts, 187, 309
Novelty
  copyright and, 24, 26
  marketability factors, 89
  unpatentable inventions, 179–180
Novelty requirement
  overview, 13, 15
  anticipation by prior invention (lack of novelty), 114
  claims defining, 247, 258

claims must define, 247, 397
common assignee or joint research agreement, 113
defined, 101, 110
examiner approach to analyzing, 135
new combinations, 114–115
new uses, 114–115
nonobviousness and, 115
objections by examiner, 383
patentability, 15, 101, 113–116, 386
in Patentability Flowchart, 128
patentability searches for expedited prosecution, 135
physical differences, 114, 414
prior art determinations, 110–114, 236
processes, 114
rejections by examiner, 383
scope of coverage, 151–152
sources of supply for exotic/uncommon materials, 190
unpatentable inventions, 180
utility patents, 101
See also Claim amendments
Nuclear weapons, unpatentability, 109
Nucleotide sequences
incorporation by reference statement, 186
Patentin program, 194
sequence listing, 186, 194, 214

O

OA. *See* Office Actions (OA)
OAPI (Organisation Africaine de la Propriété Intellectuelle), 349, 356
Objection vs. Rejection, defined, 385, 517
Objects and advantages, 517
Ocean Tomo, 481
Offensive rights
alternative and supplementary, 9–10
of copyright, 23–26, 34
defined, 9
inventions, 9–10, 34, 53
licensing or selling protections, 176
of trademarks, 20–23, 34
of trade secrets, 29, 34
unfair competition creation of, 32, 34
Offensive rights provided by patent
computer software, 25
defined, 9
design patents, 26, 27, 34
distinction from protection, 9
distinguished from "protection," 9, 18
exclusion from copyright, 24
lawsuits as weapons, 17–18

licensing/sale of invention improved by, 176
litigation costs and inequities in patent enforcement, 468
litigation insurance, 481
plant patents, 34
utility patents, 25–26, 34
writing specification for judge and jury, 201
Office Actions (OA)
overview, 375
attorney, routine suggestion to hire, 394
be available to respond to, 381–382
buying extensions, 437–438
calendar entries and due date reminders, 394
contact information for examiner, 525
deadline extensions, 381, 430, 431
deadline for response, 376–377, 381–383, 385, 437–438
defined, 517
disagreement responses, 419
drawings, objections to, 277, 383–384, 385, 388, 390, 392, 425
errors in, approach to, 378, 417, 418
during foreign filing period, 371
form paragraphs, 384, 394
IDS filing, 373, 375
issue fee, 376
Issue Notification, 376
missing or extending deadlines, 437–438
nonapplied references, 425
nonresponsive status, 383–384
Notice of Allowability, 376
Notice of Allowance, 376, 436
Notice of References Cited, 388, 391, 393, 394
PTMS filing, 324
for PTO mistakes, 378
references cited, 375, 382, 388, 393
references cited, checking for errors, 378, 385–386, 418
references cited, downloading U.S. patents, 394
references cited but not applied, 425
rejection vs. objection of examiner, 385, 517, 519
request for extraordinary relief, 438
rereading appropriate chapters before responding, 383
respond to each and every point, 370, 383–384, 418–419
scope of what is wrong with application, 375
specifications, objections to, 385, 387, 388, 390
three-date entries for response, 376, 394
timely response to, 385, 439
timing schedule, 527
Track 1 applications, 328
See also Claim amendments; Claim rejections; Claim rejections, prior art; Examiners (PTO); Prosecution of patent application (PTO process)

560 | PATENT IT YOURSELF

Office Actions (OA), first
overview, 187–188
amendment or response, 376, 439
claim rejections, 375, 376, 383, 388, 394–395
defined, 516
electing claims to one species, 435–436
filing Preliminary amendments before, 384
filing Supplementary amendments after, 384
First Office Action Estimator, 386
IDS filing, 373, 375
objections, 375–376, 378, 383, 385, 388
prior-art references cited, 394
references cited, 425
response to judicial exceptions rejection, 402–404
sample OA and analysis, 388–393
scope of response to, 376
timing of, 376
Office Actions (OA), second/final
overview, 376, 429
abandonment of application, 434
advisory actions (denials) of after-final filings, 430
amendment complying with examiner's requirements, 430
amendment offering narrower claims, 428, 430
amendments after, 384, 425, 429–431
amendments if don't affect substance, 428
appealing to PTAB, 430–433
appeals for extension of patent term, 433
automatic abandonment if no reply to, 434
continuation filed after, 442, 444
deadline for response, 376–377, 431
defined, 516
"final" defined, 430
negotiation with examiner, 430–431
new references in amended claim, may not be final, 429
petitions to Commissioner, 434
RCE filed after, 444
restriction of application, 435
text of applicable law for options following, 429–430
timing of, 376
See also Appeals; Continuation Applications; Request for Continued Examination (RCE)
Office of Patent Application Processing (OPAP)
overview of initial process, 187
conversion of paper to electronic format by, 187, 289
drawing inspector objections, 277, 278, 279
drawings reviewed and approved by, 187, 277, 279
Notice of Incomplete Application Parts, 187
Notice to File Corrected Application Papers, 309, 393
Notice to File Missing Parts, 187, 309
official filing receipt, 187, 371
petitions to the Commissioner for rulings by, 434
postcard/online receipt, 187

Official Gazette (OG)
Accelerated Examination Program (AEP), 326
advertising patents for sale in, 461
date status information on patent applications, 376
declarations of extraordinary relief, 438
drawings suitable for inclusion in, 198, 283
foreign filing fees, 360
highlights of patents issued, 459, 464
monitoring applications, 435
PTO contact information, 376
as search tool at PSF, 155
One-year rule (must file application after public disclosure)
commercial sales or offer to sell, 113, 174
defined, 518
experimental public use doctrine, 112, 516
as prior art, 111
professional searchers do not start clock running, 137
public disclosure not recommended due to risks, 96, 98
test marketing as, 174
Online resources
Accelerated Examination Program (AEP) form, 324
advertising patents for sale, 461
Assignment Center, 313
business plans, 344
Data Visualization Center, 382
defensive publications, 453
domain name registration, 20
eFiler registration, 78, 310
e-Office Action, 309
EPO patent guide, 362
European Patent Office (EPO), 350
First Office Action Estimator, 386
foreign patent agents, 364
General Services Administration, 344
invention promoter complaints, 335
Inventors Digest Online, 47
Inventors Groups of America, 47
lab notebooks, 54
lay patent searchers, 137
Makinbacon story, 346
Manual of Patent Examining Procedure (MPEP), 4, 238, 380, 385
manufacturer resources, 338–339
non-patent literature in RPA, 188
Patent and Trademark Resources Centers, 47, 155, 157
patent attorneys (licensed by PTO), 139
patent databases, 154, 505
patent enforcement litigation, 481
patent websites, 504
PCT filing, 360
PTO fees, 15
PTO patent dashboard, 376

PTO Patent Public Search (PPS) system, 153, 170
PTO trademark registration, 22
PTO Trademark Search, 21
PTO Training Mode, 79
Request for Accelerated Examination, 326
scammer listing, 364
Small Business Administration, 343, 344
specialty gadget manufacturers, 339
Technology Center Ombudsman (TCO), 387
Track 1 applications, 328
U.S. Department of Energy, 344
Wisconsin Innovation Service Center, 95
Operability
building and testing, 86–87, 96
commercial feasibility, 87–88
marketability factors, 91
patentability searches for information on, 134
PPA and, 77
as utility requirement, 108–109
Operators (patent searches), 158
Opposition proceedings (foreign filings), 353, 358, 365
Optical character recognition (OCR), 170
Ordinary skills. *See* Person having ordinary skill in the art
(PHOSITA)
Ortho-McNeil-Janssen v. State of Arkansas, 252
Ownership of patents
overview, 484
assignment of, 292, 320, 490, 491, 492
attorney recommended for, 484, 487
claims determining offensive rights, 166–167, 235
defined, 484–485
Doctrine of Equivalents (DoE), 263
employed inventors, 484, 487, 489
intellectual property, 7–9
joint owners, 97, 322, 484, 485, 486
Joint Owners' Agreement, 97, 322, 484, 487
obtaining value from, 462, 485
patent rights granted by, 10
recorded in PTO, 463
terms of rights, 16
title report for, 463
transfer of, 292, 320, 484, 490
Ownership of patents, disputes
avoidance of, 52, 484–487
confusion of inventorship, 52
documentation as proof of, 52, 54
employed inventors, 484, 487, 489–490
expired patents, 14
illegal conduct and loss of rights, 17
in-force patents, 14, 18
infringement of patents, 17

Lab notebooks kept by each, 486
naming all inventors, 485–486

P

PAD. *See* Patent Application Declaration (PAD)
PAIR. *See* Patent Application Information Retrieval (PAIR)
Paper filing of patent application, 289–309
overview of advantages of Patent Center filing option, 78,
276, 289, 292, 309
overview of parts of application, 291–292
from abroad, 291, 309
addresses for, 308, 524–525
amendment filing, 427
Application Data Sheet (ADS), 80, 299
application postcard receipt, 292, 306
assembly and mailing, final checklist, 307–308
assignments, 320
bounced check fees, 306
Certificate of Mailing, 427
changes after final preparation, 290, 298
changes to text, 290
computer programs on CD-ROMs, 194
Credit Card Payment Form, 304, 305
Cross-reference to related applications (PPA or prior
applications), 298, 301
design patents, 328–329
disadvantages of, 289
do not use fax or private courier, 307
Fee Transmittal Form, 299, 301, 302–303
filing fees, 301, 304
foreign filings, 290
format of, 290–291
IDS form, 320, 373–375
maintaining an orderly file, 307
Nonpublication request (NPR), 299, 301
paper size (U.S. letter or A4), 290–291
paragraph numbering, 291
Patent Application Declaration (PAD), 290, 292–298
Patent Application Transmittal Letter, 306, 309
payment by check, money order, credit card, 301, 304, 306
PCT application, 360
postcard receipt, 185, 187, 292, 299, 306, 309, 370
PPA and, 80–81
prefiling review, 289–290
PTMS filing, 307, 324
PTO conversion to electronic, 187, 289
PTO Mail Stops, 524–525
surcharge for, 16
transmittal letter, 185, 298, 300
See also Finaling of patent application; Postcard receipt
(paper filing)

562 | PATENT IT YOURSELF

Paranoia of inventors (PGL Syndrome), 96, 339
Paris Convention
 overview, 349, 350, 365
 claiming priority to original application, 350
 EPO/non-EPO filing, 362
 filed within a year of PCT, 363
 filing in individual countries, 362–363
 foreign patent agents, 355, 359
 late filings become non-Convention application, 350
 member countries, 351
 one-year deadline from earliest U.S. filing (PPA or RPA),
  82, 348, 349, 350, 527
 Patent Cooperation Treaty (PCT) application, 82, 277,
  348–349
 PCT application filing, 358–361, 363
 priority for patent filing dates, 82, 309, 354, 365
 reciprocal filing rights through, 350
 TRIPS requirement for WTO member compliance, 350
Parlor games, 26, 262
Part names
 drafting and improving names in claims, 255
 Glossary of Legal Terms as resource, 509–513
 naming and labeling preliminary sketches, 197
 naming and numbering in detailed description, 208–209
 prior art providing, 134, 189–190
 repetition technique, 208
 using several equivalent names, then choosing and
  consistently using one name, 208
Parts
 consistent use of terminology and nomenclature, 208
 detailed description, 191
 detailing interconnections between, 209
 patentability searches for descriptions, 133–134
 sources of supply of exotic or uncommon materials, 190,
  209
 symbols used for, 198
Patent(s)
 overview, 10–19
 copyright of text and drawings of, 188, 189, 211
 copyright overlap, 25–27
 defined, 9–10, 518
 delayed-issue, 473
 "exchange theory" of, 191, 494
 in-force period, 14, 16, 18
 misconceptions about, 18–19
 nonpublication request (NPR), 29, 64
 number granted, 17, 153
 as personal property, 10, 463, 482, 484–485
 post-grant review of, 477–478
 as prior art as of filing and publication dates, 385
 privileged position, 176

 PTO publication of, 29, 52
 quality of, 2
 quick-start guide, 3
 relationship with trade secrets, 29–31
 term extended by PTO delays, 14, 16, 384
 types of, 10–12
 who can apply for, 485–486
 See also Design patents; Fees (PTO); Offensive rights;
  Patentability; Patent application (RPA); Plant patents;
  Utility patents
Patentability, 101–129
 overview, 101–103, 129
 commercial success evaluations, 383
 compared to commercial viability, 98, 101
 defined, 101
 disclosure of material information (non prior-art), 320
 flowchart of, 126–129
 International Searching Authority for, 354, 359, 361, 374
 legal requirements for, 101–103
 manner of inventions, 42–43, 126
 nonobviousness, 102, 115–126, 386
 novelty, 101, 110–115, 386
 prior art searches, 98
 PTO defining of, 319
 scope of patent (broad vs. narrow), 150–153
 standards of, 379
 statutory subject matter, 101, 103–107, 253
 two-step process, 101, 103
 use of claims to determine, 235
 utility, 101, 107–110
 weak vs. strong patents, 126
 See also Nonobvious requirement; Novelty requirement;
  Searches of patentability; Statutory subject matter;
  Utility, as patentability requirement
Patentability searches. *See* Searches of patentability
Patent and Trademark Resources Centers (PTRCs)
 overview, 156–157
 patentability searches, 156
 as resource for inventor groups, 47
 staff assistance at, 155, 166
Patent application (RPA)
 overview, 184–185
 advantages and disadvantages of filing early, 177
 artificial intelligence (AI) used to draft, 215–216, 269–270
 attorney not required for, 185
 attorney preparation of, 2, 215
 coinventor determinations, 485
 confidentiality of, 29
 confirmation number for, 370
 conversion of PPA, 184
 conversion to PPA, 63–64

defined, 9, 518
divisional application, 435
expedited through PPH, 326
expedited through PTMS, 322, 324, 326
expedited through Track 1 examination, 326, 328
filing deadlines, 15
filing fees, 15–16, 521–522
foreign filers, 291
inventor assignees and, 485
inventor from PPA must be named in, 64
linking claims, 435
models of inventions, 189
multiple embodiments of invention on, 190, 435
naming only and all true inventors, 291, 320, 485–486
Notice of Allowance, 188, 436
not yet filed period, 14
paragraph numbering, 291
patent pending period, 14
PPA filing date, 62–63, 82, 184, 298
prior art citations, 477–478
prior art determinations, 111
publication of, 188, 384
received by PTO, 187–189
related inventions, 190
restriction of, 435–436
sample application, 220–232
sample claims of, 272–274
Suggested Requirement for Restriction, 436
teachings in, 386
    See also Abandonment of patent application; Filing
    receipts; Finaling of patent application; Office Actions
    (OA); Prosecution of patent application (PTO process);
    Supplemental applications
Patent application (RPA), parts of
    overview of content and order of assembly, 185–186
    additional and optional parts, 292
    Application Data Sheet (ADS), 185, 292–293, 294
    assignment and transmittal, 292
    biotechnology deposits, 194
    computer software, 194
    drawings, 292
    Fee Transmittal Form, 185, 292
    glossary of useful technical terms, 189, 197, 211, 212
    Information Disclosure Statement (IDS), 185–186, 205,
    292
    minimal and necessary parts, 292
    nonpublication request (NPR), 185, 188, 292
    Patent Application Declaration (PAD), 185, 292–293,
    294, 298
    payment, 185, 292
    postcard receipt, 292, 306

Request for Claim Drafting by Examiner under MPEP,
    292
    specification, including claims and abstract, 292
    transmittal letter, 185, 298, 300
    Utility Patent Application Transmittal, 292
    written description, 191, 193
    See also Abstract; Application Data Sheet (ADS);
    Claim(s); Drawings, final; Nonpublication request
    (NPR); Patent Application Declaration (PAD);
    Specification
Patent application (RPA), preparation of
    advantages and disadvantages of prior-art, 191
    checklist for, 216–219
    compliance with regulations, 276
    Customer Number, 298, 301
    enabling disclosures, 193–194
    flowchart of, 191–192
    formula notes, 194
    new matter can't be added after filing, 191, 280
    nucleotide/amino acid sequence notes, 194, 214
    preliminary steps for, 189–191
    prior-art search for background information, 133–134, 191
    ramifications list, 189–190
    review of disclosure, 189
    sources of supply disclosures, 190
    written description must comply with full disclosure
    rules, 191, 193
Patent Application Declaration (PAD)
    overview, 292–293, 298
    assembly order of, 185
    careful review of, 293
    declaration submitted with initial filing, 293
    defined, 518
    design patents, 328
    each inventor signs and files separate, 293
    filed after RPA, 293, 295
    filed with RPA, 292–293
    first named inventor, 293, 298
    inventor(s) must sign (all and only), 291, 486
    making changes before signing, 290, 298
    Patent Center filing, 309–310
    PTO Form AIA/08, 185, 292, 293, 295–296, 298
    samples, 294–297
    signed only after application completed, 298
    simpler declaration if ADS included (Form AIA/01), 185,
    292, 293, 294, 310
    statement of invalidation for false statements, 298
    supplemental sheet for joint inventors, 297–298
    title of invention, 293
Patent Application Information Retrieval (PAIR), 299, 476
Patent attorneys. See Attorneys, patent (PTO licensed)

564 | PATENT IT YOURSELF

Patent Auction, 461

Patent Center (PTO)
Acknowledgment Receipt, 313
additional paperwork submission, 372
advantages over filing by mail (strongly recommended), 65, 185, 276, 309
AEP Form, 324
amendment filing, 309, 370, 381, 427, 431
Application Data Sheet (AIA/14), 79–80, 185, 187, 310–312
assignments filing, 313
Calculate fees page, 80, 312–313
continuation application filing, 433
defined, 518
design patents, 313, 329
detection and validation of file formats, 312
Digital Certificate, 311–312
DOCX format allowed, 78, 310, 312
drawings submission, 277, 313
e-Office Action, 309
filed as Microsoft Word documents, 78
filing computer programs, 194, 212
IDS filed with application, 319
IDS filed within three months, 313–314, 319, 373–375
instant filing date with, 309, 313, 370
new applications, 309–313
non-PCT applications, 361
Patent Application Declaration (PAD), 309–310
payment by credit card, 313
PCT application filing, 360–361
PDF documents, 310, 312–313, 360–361, 373
petition to make special filing, 322
PPA filing, 65, 78–80
Provisional Application for Patent Cover Sheet, 77
PTMS filing, 322, 324
public access to patent applications, 188
reduced filing fees, 309, 330
registered eFilers, 78, 276, 309, 372
RPA filing, 311–313
sequence listing or program filing, 204
signatures for electronic documents, 309–310
Training Mode, 79
uploading documents, 312
See also Registered eFiler program

Patent Cooperation Treaty (PCT)
overview, 354
agents required for individual countries, 358–359
application preparation, 360–361
beware of scammers, 364
election of Chapter II for examination within 19 months, 354, 358–359, 361–362

EPO searching authority, 360, 362
European Patent Office (EPO) countries, 349, 361–362
examination report (Chapter II) election, 354, 355, 356, 361, 362
examination requests for, 354, 356, 357
fees required, 360–362
filed before PPA, 363
filing a PCT first, 354, 363
filing a PPA before, 354, 363
filing receipt and serial number, 361
Information Disclosure Statement (IDS), 359, 361
international preliminary examination report, 356, 362
International Searching Authority for patentability, 354, 359, 361, 374
member countries, 352, 356
MPEP and, 354
one-year to file in non-PCT Convention countries, 356, 359
Paris Convention country filings, 82, 277, 348, 349
PCT-SAFE software, 360
priority of U.S. filing date, 82, 354, 359–361, 363
prosecution in individual countries, 359
publication of application 18 months from priority date, 361
search report (Chapter I), 356, 361
separate filings for specific jurisdictions, 354
single international filing in USPTO within one-year, 354, 358–359
30-month delay before filing, 349, 354, 356, 359, 3 61–362, 365
timing schedule, 528
TRIPS application, 363
utility patents, 349
WIPO administration of, 350, 356, 360–361

Patent deed, 376, 439, 453, 459, 515

Patent law
overview, 7
agent's exams, 8
on claims, 236
defining inventors, 484
determining scope of protection, 152
making assumptions, 129
on manufacturer waivers, 176, 340
in other countries, 357–358
on prior art, 110
relation to trademark law, 21
U.S. Constitution as basis, 103
See also Attorneys, patent (PTO licensed); Design patents; Nonobvious requirement; Novelty requirement; Plant patents; Statutory subject matter; Utility patents

Patent misuse, 518

Patent number
advantages and disadvantages of marking, 460–461
changing patent pending to, 460–461
lawsuits for false marking, 461
PTO Patent Public Search (PPS) system searching by, 170
USPAT database searching by, 153
Patent Ombuds Office (PTO), 387
Patent One, 505
Patent pending (pendency period)
defined, 518
design patents on unpatentable utility inventions, 328
deterrence of competitors, 178
filing receipt received and instant status of, 307, 371
inability to search applications, 136, 476
inventor rights, 14
as marketing tool, 64, 332, 371
marking devices to show notice given, 371–372
monitoring applications, 435
notice of, as warning to competitors, 14, 178, 372
notice of, criminal offense to use without official status, 371
NPR allows infringement during, 371–372
PPA providing, 14, 64, 83, 371
product marking with, 460–461
protection of trade secrets, 178
publication and accrual of royalties from infringement, 16–17, 371, 436, 462, 474
publication and loss of rights in non-Convention countries, 372
publication without loss of rights, 372
public citing of prior art, 436
royalties from infringement, 14, 16–17, 371, 436, 462, 474
working models (prototypes), 337
Patent Pro Bono Program (PPBP), 377
Patent prosecution. See Prosecution of patent application (PTO process)
Patent Prosecution Highway (PPH)
countries with bilateral agreements with USPTO, 326
foreign filings, 326, 363
Global PPH, 326
intellectual property offices, 326
reciprocal procedures, 326
Patent Public Search (PPS)
classification searching, 170–171
defined, 518
keyword searching, 170
optical character recognition (OCR), 170
patentability searches, 153, 170–172

Patent rights
overview, 16–17
assignment of, 292, 320, 490
expiration dates, 463
expiration if maintenance fees not paid, 10, 14, 16–17, 466, 481
extending effectiveness with improvements, 463
extending monopoly and violating antitrust law, 463
forfeiting of, 480–481
loss of, 17
medical procedure exemption, 104, 463
monopoly period, 16–17, 176, 462
obtaining value from, 462–463
as offensive weapon, 17–18
as prior-art reference, 17–18
property rights, 463
publication and loss of, 96
See also Abandonment of patent application; Challenges to patents; Invalidation of patents
Patent Rules of Practice. See Rules of Practice (PTO, Title 37 CFR)
Patent Trial and Appeal Board (PTAB). See PTAB (Patent Trial and Appeal Board)
Patent trolls, 473
PCT. See Patent Cooperation Treaty (PCT)
PCT Applicant's Guide, 504
PDF documents
Application Data Sheet (ADS), 79
conversion of drawings to, 310
filing surcharges, 313
fillable forms, 530–531
non-U.S. patent references and non-patent publications, 373
Patent Center filing, 310, 312–313, 360
PCT filing, 360–361

Permanent injunction, 17, 475, 476, 518
Perpetual-motion/-energy machines, 108–109, 189
Personal property, patents as, 10, 463, 482
Person having ordinary skill in the art (PHOSITA)
defined, 116
nonobviousness determinations standard, 116, 118, 125
Person having ordinary skill in the art (PHOSITA), specifications
ability to sketch invention after reading claim, 261
detailed description for, 209–210
easily inferred dimensions and materials need not be provided, 133–134, 193
exchange theory of patents, 191

566 | PATENT IT YOURSELF

invalidation for incomplete disclosure, 193, 195, 202, 215, 387

obviousness of claimed invention as a whole, 422

for PPA, 63, 77

relative terms in claim are understood, 254

Section 112(a) text, 190, 191

sources of supply of exotic or uncommon materials, 190

See also Specification, compliance with full disclosure rules

Petitions to make special (PTMS)

overview, 322

Accelerated Examination Program (AEP), 324, 326

continuation applications, 326

Declaration in Support (DS), 325, 327

defined, 518

expedited examination of application, 322, 324, 326

fees for, 304, 324, 326

Office Actions (OA), 324

paper filing of, 307, 324

Patent Center filing, 324

PTMS Form 10-9, 322, 324

restrictive statements and admissions on, 326

"Rocket Docket" (design patents), 136, 524

RPA filing, 357

samples, 325, 327

simple filings based on health, age, environment, energy, terrorism, 322, 324, 326

Petitions to PTO

to accept delayed of issue or maintenance fees, 438, 524

for black and white photos, 277

for color photos or drawings, 277

to Commissioner of Patents for nonsubstantive matters, 434

conversion of RPA to PPA, 63

delayed maintenance fees, 438, 466

expedited handling of foreign filings, 357

for extension of time from OA, 437–438

final rejection, 429–430

IDS late filing, 374–375

objections that cannot be overcome, 385

overruling of examiner, 434

Petition to Revive, 437–438

to revive abandoned application, 377, 454

to revive due to unintentional delay, 437, 438, 439, 466

PGL (paranoia, greed, laziness) Syndrome, 47–48, 96, 339

PHOSITA. *See* Person having ordinary skill in the art (PHOSITA)

Photographs

black and white for drawings, petition required, 277

copyright and, 23, 27, 36

in Lab notebook, 58

PTO rules for (37 CFR), 279

tracing from, 284, 286, 289

tracing from a computer, 287

See also Drawings, final

Pinterest, 345

Plant patents

overview, 12, 35

application for, 330

defined, 518

duration of, 16

examination fees, 522

in-force period, 14

legal requirements for, 102

maintenance fees not required, 14, 35

offensive rights, 34

plant cultivation, 12

post-allowance fees, 522

term of patent, 527

Plants, protection of

Plant Variety Protection Act, 12, 34, 102

utility patents, 102

Plurality, as term in claims, 258, 260, 397

Positive and Negative Factors Evaluation Sheet, 87–88, 342

Positive and Negative Factors Summary, 94, 191

Postcard receipt (paper filing)

for amendment filing, 427

conspicuous color for, 306

design patents, 328, 329

for foreign filings, 306

IDS form, 320

including sufficient postage, 306

for PPA, 62, 65, 78, 80–81, 187

for RPA, 185, 187, 292, 299, 306, 309, 370

sample text for, 81, 306

Post-grant review (PGR), 477–478

Post Office Patent documentation, warning against, 62

Power of attorney, 361, 518

PPA. *See* Provisional Patent Application (PPA)

PPH. *See* Patent Prosecution Highway (PPH)

Preamble of a claim

defined in PTO's Rules of Practice, 238

in four-step method for drafting a claim, 248, 255, 258

may not name the invention, 240, 255

names purpose of invention, 240

statutory class, 255–256

Prima facie, 518

Printed patent

copied for reissue applications, 453

corrections to, 460

first-named inventor on, 485

format of, 254

photo quality for, 277

PTO adds additional data, 187
PTO issues for fee, 376, 463
References Cited on, 393
Prior art (previously existing inventions)
overview, 110, 113
age of reference is irrelevant, 394
background section of specification, discussion of, 186, 204–205, 209
challenges to patents via citation, 436, 477, 482
claims defined by, 134, 247
"claims trap," 167, 395
commercial offers to sell exception, 113
commercial potential evaluation, 98
common assignee or joint research agreement exception, 113
comparison of patent claims to determine infringement, 393
date established by foreign patents, 110, 111, 112
date established by PPA or RPA, 64, 110, 385–386
defined, 110, 518
derivation proceeding to overcome, 113
discovery of new references, 373–375, 378, 383
established by application publication, 14, 111, 385–386
as example for preliminary sketches, 197–198, 201
ex parte review, 477–478
experimental exception, 112
expired patents, 14, 112, 156
facilitation of prosecution, 134
failure to operate in combination, 125
first-inventor-to-file disclosures, 15, 110, 112–113
flowchart for claim rejections, 395–396
inter partes review, 477–479
"knocking" in patent applications, 191, 205
listing advantages and disadvantages of, 191, 205
loss of patent rights through failure to reveal (fraud on the PTO), 275, 319, 320, 387
loss of patent rights through relevant and undisclosed, 17, 360, 381, 397, 435
misconceptions about in-force patents, 112
nonobviousness determinations, 116–117, 236, 247–248
novelty determinations, 110–114, 236, 247
passive citation against patent application, 477–478
passive citation against patents, 477–478
patentability searches, 133–134
patents filed by others before you, 14–15, 17, 111
printed publications as, 111
prior use and on-sale activities, 110, 112–113
PTO mistakes, 378
public citing of, 436, 439
public vs. PTO knowledge, 110–112
reproduced in patent application, 188
reviewed in patent application, 185–186, 189

supplemental examination to correct, 477–478
supplemental IDS for relevant, 435
unpublished pending applications as, 111–112
See also Information Disclosure Statement (IDS)
Priority, 350, 518
Priority Mail Express (PME)
continuation application filing, 433
instant filing date with, 81, 307
paper filing of patent application, 78, 81, 299, 307
for PPA, 78, 81
PTO Rule 10 (37 CFR), 307
Prior-user rights for commercial use, 31, 178
Processes (methods)
business processes and methods, 13, 105, 240–241
claims for, 235, 240, 255, 257, 261, 264, 268
conventional, 104, 240
defined, 104, 518
divided infringement, 257
drawings for, 201
increased scrutiny of, 240
machines as, 105
manual methods, 242
new uses of, 106–107
novelty determinations, 114
offensive rights, 34
sample claim for business process, 242
sample claim for conventional process, 240
sample claim for manual method, 242
sample claim for software process, 241
software processes, 104–105, 240–241
statutory subject matter, 104–107
unconventional computers, 105–106
unpatentability of mental, 13
unpatentable, 107
See also Business processes and methods; Computer software; Flowcharts for processes; New-use inventions
Product clearance (legally copying an invention), 474–477
claims interpreted by patent description, 474
determining applicability of in-force patents, 475–476
do not copy features with secondary meaning, 474
do not infringe in-force patents, 474, 482
extended validity searches, 476–477
home, personal, charity infringement is actionable, 474–475
if no in-force patent applicable, 477
infringement determined by patent claims, 475
method/process preceding filing date, 477
patented products may not be marked as patented, 474
pending patent applications, 476
relevant prior art, 477
review claims and design around them, 476

Property rights
  licensing and, 485
  patents and, 463, 482, 484–485
  See also Intellectual property (IP)
Proprietary Submission Agreement, 340
Pro se (no lawyer) applicants
  Application Data Sheet (ADS), 79
  assistance program for, 2
  calling and visiting examiner, 403–404
  examiner drafts claims for, 248
  examiner interviews and assistance, 403–404
  PTO allows to correct nondate errors, 377
Prosecution of patent application (foreign process)
  European Patent Office (EPO), 353, 356
  expedited through PPH, 326, 363
  foreign patent agents, 353, 359, 364
  individual countries, 359, 362
  non-Convention countries, 356
  PCT and, 356, 359, 361
  substantial fees for, 348, 362
Prosecution of patent application (PTO process)
  overview, 187–188, 437
  attorney recommended for, 377
  bureaucratic objections, 378–379
  commercial success arguments, 117
  date received (official date) of responses, 383
  deadlines for responses, 376–377
  defined, 518
  defined as entire process of correspondence with the
    PTO, 376, 518
  delays caused by PTO or appeals, term extended, 14, 16,
    384, 428, 432
  design patents, 437
  discovery of new prior-art references, 378
  embodiment changes, 378
  foreign filings and, 375
  general considerations during, 376–387
  in-force period extensions to compensate for delays, 14, 16
  initial processing of application, 187, 371
  interviewing and visiting examiner, 382, 394
  know who has the ball, 383
  never make negative admissions about invention, 370,
    380, 439
  new matter can't be added after filing, 370, 383, 439
  offensive copyright rights, 24
  official filing date, 383
  Patentability Flowchart for, 126
  patentability searches for novelty, 135
  patent attorney consultation, 377–378
  prior art deficiencies, 134
  PTO can request search information and literature, 381

request examiner write claims, 376–377, 439
technical error corrections, 377
timeline, checking on, 377
timeline of, 187–188, 370–371
  See also Allowance of patent (approval); Amendments;
    Claim rejections; Examiners (PTO); Office Actions (OA)
Provisional Patent Application (PPA)
  overview, 15, 62
  advantages and disadvantages of, 62–64
  as alternative to building and testing, 62–64
  constructive reduction to practice, 110
  conversion of RPA to, 63–64
  conversion to RPA, 184
  defined, 518–519
  design patents unable to use, 62, 65
  early filing date, 62–63, 298, 527
  effective extension of patent expiration date, 63–64
  effective filing date, 63, 65, 111
  expiration if RPA is not filed, 63, 65, 83, 101
  filing fees, 16, 65, 80
  filing PCT application before, 363
  filing RPA incorporates PPA (cross-reference to related
    applications), 186, 192, 203–204, 206, 220
  filing separate RPA, 184
  foreign filings allow priority one year after filing, 64, 76,
    82, 348, 350, 354
  misconceptions about, 65
  multiple inventions on, 64, 77, 83
  patent pending status, 14, 64, 83, 371
  prior-art reference established by, 64
  PTO cautions regarding, 64–65
  PTO may read if depending on early date, 65, 77, 83, 185
  refiling for improvements to invention, 63–65, 82
  selling to manufacturer, 179
  timing schedule, 527
Provisional Patent Application (PPA), preparation and filing
  overview, 65, 76–77, 187
  Acknowledgment Receipt, 80
  Application Data Sheet (ADS), 65, 77, 79, 187
  bare-bones vs. embellished application, 77
  checklist for, 81–82
  Cover Sheet download and completion, 77–78
  disclosure requirements, 77
  drafting claims in, 65, 76–77
  drawings and, 76
  electronic filing, 65, 78–80
  filing by mail, 80–81
  full description of invention, 76–77, 80
  including embodiments of invention, 77
  micro entity qualification, 76–78, 81
  multiple inventions on, 64, 77

official filing receipt, 81
postcard receipt, 62, 65, 78, 80–81, 187
recommendation to model after RPA, 65, 76
sample application with embellishments, 69–75
sample application without embellishments, 66–68
small entity qualification, 62, 76, 78, 81
statutory class, 77
Proximity operations (patent searches), 158
PTAB (Patent Trial and Appeal Board), appeal of patent rejection
defined, 518
Focused Set of Arguments, 431
inter partes review, 479
jurisdiction over rejections and objections, 434
Notice of Appeal, 431
oral hearing request, 432
patent expiration date extended if delayed by, 432
Pre-Appeal Request for Review, 430, 431
Pro Bono Program, 432–433
PTAB Bar Association, 433
PTMS. *See* Petitions to make special (PTMS)
PTO (Patent and Trademark Office)
Assignment fee payment addresses, 525
attorney licensing, 8
attorneys and patent agents registered, 138, 504
claim-drafting assistance from, 424–425
confidentiality of patent applications, 29
electronic patent grant, 376
e-Office Action, 309
frustrating and unfair experiences, 379–380
holiday closures, 525
in-force period extensions, 14
loss of pre-1836 patents in fire, 155
Mail Stops for, 524
operation of, 155
organization and history, 155
patentability searches, 133, 155
Patent Ombuds Office, 387
patent rights granted by, 10, 35
policies and duties to Office, 216
PPA cautions, 64–65
subject matter eligibility guidelines, 13
telephone and fax numbers, 525
trademark registration, 22
Trademark Search, 21
Training Mode, 79
unpatentable inventions, 13
website for, 504, 505
PTO (Patent and Trademark Office) publications
Annual Indexes of Inventors, 155
Cooperative Patent Classification (CPC) Definitions, 155, 158–160, 165–166, 504

Cooperative Patent Classification (CPC) Scheme, 155, 158–160, 165, 504
Manual of U.S. Classification, 155
Rules of Practice, 103, 380, 385, 432, 504
U.S. Patents Quarterly (USPQ), 155
See also Manual of Patent Examining Procedure (MPEP); *Official Gazette* (OG)
PTO (Patent and Trademark Office) resources
compliance with regulations, 4
databases and services, 153–154
Data Visualization Center, 382
digitization of records, 153
Electronic Business Center, 312
First Office Action Estimator, 386
government publications, 504
Inventor Assistance Center, 357
Patent and Trademark Resources Centers (PTRCs), 47, 155–157
Patent Related Notices, 438
Patents Ombudsman's office, 311, 387, 525
patent statutes, 380
PCT Help Desk, 360
Public Search Facility (PSF), 155
researching patent agents and attorneys, 138
staff assistance at, 155, 157
Training Mode for electronic filing, 79
Publication of patent applications (PTO)
accrual of royalties for infringement during pendency period, 16, 371, 436
after 18-month period, 29, 301, 364, 384, 527
citing prior art against another pending application, 436
effective filing date, 384
following rescinding of NPR, 364
Official Gazette (OG) publication of, 459, 464
patentability not guaranteed in, 301, 384
prior-art reference established by, 14, 111, 385–386
prior art searches, 151, 166–167
public citing of prior art, 436, 439
trade secrets lost (use NPR), 29, 52
unpublished pending applications as prior art, 111–112
unpublished pending applications not searchable, 136, 475
See also Nonpublication request (NPR)
Public disclosure of invention prior to filing, patent rights ended
Consultant's Work Agreement to prevent, 289
file PPA or RPA before, 15, 527
foreign filings, 15, 86, 96, 269, 358
test marketing, 98, 174, 179
trade secrets, 29, 139

570 | PATENT IT YOURSELF

Public knowledge
  experimental exception, 112
  prevention of obtaining foreign patent, 15, 86, 269
  prior art established by, 110–112
  trade secrets, 29
Public Search Facility (PSF)
  classification searching, 170
  patentability searches, 155, 157, 170
  staff assistance at, 157, 166
Public-use-and-knowledge category of prior art, 112, 156

Q

QPIDS. See Quick Path Information Disclosure Statement (QPIDS)
Qualifiers (patent searches), 157
Quality
  environmental, 322, 324, 326, 330
  marketability factors, 90
  patentability searches, 136–137, 166
  photographs and drawings, 277, 281, 284, 337, 345
  predetermined and given terminology, 259
Questel, 154
Quick Path Information Disclosure Statement (QPIDS), 374, 429
Quirky.com, 181, 339

R

Ramifications
  as alternative is first RPA rejected, 189
  broadness of patent claims, 189–190
  comprehensive listing for broad claims, 213–214
  defined, 519
  holding back for later exploitation, 43
  introduced by artificial intelligence, 216
  inventions and, 43–44
  listing for RPA preparation, 189–190, 213–214
  multiple embodiments, 189–190, 213
  recordation of conception and thoroughness of naming, 55, 58
  subsections for each, 186
Recesses (holes, voids), reciting of, 252, 259
Recordation Form Cover Sheet, 320, 322, 492
Recordkeeping for patent application
  Correspondence folders, 276, 307, 338
  dates noted on all communications, 276, 376–377, 394
  documentation of invention, 51–54, 58, 62, 83
  employed inventors, 490
  no IDS required, memo for, 314
  nonofficial papers folders, 307
  Official Papers folders, 138, 276

original signatures, retaining documents, 427
  PTO official file (file wrapper), 380
  three-date entries for OAs, 376, 394
Records (patent searches), 157
Reduction to practice, 110, 519
Reference numerals
  in claims, 259
  in Description text, 186, 207–209
  Drawing Reference Numerals Worksheet, 209
  in drawings, 186, 192, 207, 282
  listing at end of Description, 207–208
  no duplication of, 282
  in prior-art figures, 205
References Cited
  importance of Information Disclosure Statement, 314, 374–375
  Notice of References Cited (OA), 388, 391, 393, 394
  working backward to get additional relevant references, 159, 168
Registered eFiler program
  amendment filing, 381
  batch downloading of patent references, 375
  Certificate of Correction submission, 460
  confirmation number for, 370
  continuation application filing, 433
  Digital Certificate, 311–312
  electronic filing, 78, 80, 276, 309–311, 372
  e-Office Action, 309
  filing additional paperwork, 372
  IDS submission, 373
  online IDS filing, 313
  PTMS filing, 324
  RCE filing, 447
  registering as, 78, 276, 310
  viewing docket sheet for application, 377, 382
  See also Patent Center (PTO)
Regular Patent Application (RPA). See Patent application (RPA)
Reissue application
  attorney recommended for, 453
  broadening of claims, 452
  defined, 519
  defined by MPEP, 453
  original patent claims will be examined, 453
  overview, 442, 453
Rejection vs. Objection, 385, 519
Reliability
  marketability factors, 89
  simplicity and, 337
Repairability, marketability factors, 89

INDEX | 571

Repair doctrine, 519
Reply, 519
Request for admission, 519
Request for Claim Drafting by Examiner under MPEP, 292
Request for Continued Examination (RCE), 429
  overview, 433
  after final action, 430, 433, 442, 446–447
  as better option than continuation, 446, 447
  Certificate of Mailing for, 433
  defined, 519
  electronic filing, 447
  fees for, 433, 446–447
  filing date based on original application, 448, 449
  paper or fax filing of, 433, 447
  utility patents, 447
Request for production of documents, 519
RESAM (Record it, Evaluate commercial potential, Search it, Apply for a patent, and Market it), invention exploitation flowchart, 35–36
Research and development, 113, 186
Restriction of application, 435–436
Reverse doctrine of equivalents, 470, 519
Reverse engineering
  copying of successful products, 177
  patent protection from, 36, 177
  recording conception, 180
  trade secrecy if difficult to, 181, 182
  uncovering of trade secrets, 30–31, 36, 177
Royalties
  damages due to infringement, 17, 467, 471–472
  employee inventors receiving share of, 490
  expiration of, 494
  from infringer during patent pending period, 14, 16–17, 371, 436, 462, 474
  joint owners, 487
  licensing invention, 484, 492, 494
  lump-sum payment for, 498
  Patent Royalty Rate, 495
  rates for, 499–500
  Universal License Agreement, 493, 495–498
Rozenblat v. Sandia Corp, 188
RPA. *See* Patent application (RPA)
RTF (Rich Text Format) forms, 530–531
Rules of Practice (PTO, Title 37 CFR)
  appeal process in, 432
  attorney recommended if situation not covered in, 378
  claims requirements, 238–239
  consulting during patent prosecution, 380, 385
  defined, 518
  patent statutes, 103

S

Safety/health
  marketability factors, 88
  medical devices, 213
  unsafe drugs not patentable, 108
Sale of invention
  advertising availability patent after issue, 461
  agreements for, 343
  evaluating for commercial potential, 86
  filing RPA prior to, 176
  innovative inventions, selling without RPA, 63, 177
  internet auction sites, 461, 481
  licensing vs., 494
  monopoly value, 176, 462
  non-Convention countries, 82
  offensive rights hold value for, 176
  patent monopoly term, 63, 176
  on PPA basis, 63
  presenting to manufacturers, 341–343
  prior art search facilitating, 135
  test marketing, 86
  See also Marketing your invention
Scams and scammers
  appearing after patent issue, 464, 466
  foreign patent filing, 364
  WIPO naming of, 364
Scope of the invention (broad vs. narrow)
  commercial potential evaluation, 150
  determined by claims, 203, 210, 245
  marketability factors, 93
  novelty determinations, 151–152
  offensive rights, 20, 27
  patent laws, 152
  search report on, 151–153
  title of invention, 203
Scope of the invention, claims as determining
  overview, 235
  Boolean less is more rule, 245
  maximizing by reciting elements broadly, 245–246
  means claims limited to structure disclosed, 237, 246, 250–251
  minimizing number of elements, 245
  multiple embodiments and ramifications to broaden, 184, 189, 191, 203, 210
  reissue application and broadening of claims, 452
  specific features as limiting, 203, 210, 244
  specific features do not limit, 209, 245
  wording of claims vs. number of claims, 244
  See also Claims, independent, four-step method for drafting

572 | PATENT IT YOURSELF

Sculptural works, 23, 24, 26, 27, 35
Searches of patentability
   overview, 86, 133
   design patents, 136
   fees for, 522
   importance of searching before filing, 136
   inability to search paper patents, 136
   novelty rarely disproved in, 114
   potential savings of time and money, 133
   PTO examiners, 135–136
   quality of search can vary, 136–137
   reasons for making, 133–135
   search shock, 135
   unpublished pending applications not searchable, 136,
     475
   when not to search, 135–136
Searches of patentability, do-it-yourself (DIY)
   overview, 136, 153
   overview of resources, 153–154
   anticipation vs. infringement, 156
   classification searching, 158–168
   databases and services, 153–154
   European Patent Office (EPO), 153–154
   Google Patents, 154, 168–170
   important searching tips, 171
   keyword searching, 158, 168–169
   limitations of PTO, 170–171
   nonpatent literature, 153
   at Patent and Trademark Resources Centers (PTRCs), 47,
     155–157
   Patent Public Search (PPS) system, 153, 170, 172
   PTO can request search information and literature, 381
   at PTO Public Search Facility, 155, 157
   vocabulary associated with, 157–158
   See also Classification searches
Searches of patentability, professional
   overview, 136–137
   analyzing the search report, 139, 148
   confidentiality safeguards, 139
   example of search report results, 144–147
   example of search request, 140–143
   fee-based databases, 154
   finding and working with lay searchers, 137
   non-patent literature (NPL), 154
   patent agents (licensed by PTO), 137
   patent attorneys (licensed by PTO), 133, 137–139
   preparing agents for search, 139, 172
Search report
   overview of four parts of, 139
   analysis of, 139, 148–151
   inability to provide opinions on patentability, 150

   Patentability Flowchart used in analysis of, 149
   sample report, 144–147
   scope of patent (broad vs. narrow), 150–153
Secrecy Order (PTO), 16, 357, 462
Sequence listing or program, 186–187, 204, 214, 519
Serial number (application number)
   assignments requiring, 313, 320
   PCT, 361
   PPA, 78, 80, 81, 187, 301
   RPA, on receipt, 292, 306, 309, 370
Service marks, 19
Shapes
   copyright/utility patent decisions, 25–26
   design patents, 10
   exclusion of patents on natural, 13
   functional purposes for utility patents, 109
   plant patents, 12
   as trademarks, 19
Shark Tank, 345
Signatures
   on amendments, 425, 427
   on Certificate of Mailing, 427
   copies are acceptable, 427
   on each application page, 276
   on Invention Disclosure, 60
   on Lab notebook pages, 54, 60
   on Patent Application Declaration (PAD), 298
   "S" (slash-sandwiched), 78, 79, 310
   by witnesses, 59, 62
Small Business Administration (SBA), 343, 344
Small entities (SE)
   change in status, 378
   defined, 519
   fee reduction, 16, 76, 81, 306
   issue fees, 306
   maintenance fees, 306
   PPA and, 62, 76, 78, 81
   qualifying as, 76
   RPA and, 306, 312
Social media, 345, 459
Species, 519
Specification
   overview, 184
   additional headings, 186
   amendments to, 415–416, 428
   assembly order of application, 185–186
   careful review of, 215
   checklist for, 218–219
   claiming copyright, 211
   claims drafted prior to, 184
   common misconceptions on detailing specific features,
     203, 210

data elements added by PTO, 187

defined, 519–520

full description of invention, 184, 246

"knocks" on prior art disadvantages, 205

means claims supported and identifiable, 237, 246, 250–251

not applicable rules, 186

preparing sketches prior to, 197–198

sources of supply of exotic or uncommon materials, 190

statutory definition of, 187, 387

terms in claims must appear in, 208, 212, 216

use of artificial intelligence (AI) to draft, 215–216

writing with an eye to commercial audience, 201

See also Paper filing of patent application; Patent Center (PTO)

Specification, compliance with full disclosure rules

best mode identification, 191

biotechnology deposits, 194

clear and understandable writing, 201

detailed description, 190–191, 193

formula notes, 194

nucleotide/amino acid sequence notes, 194

Section 112(a) text, 190, 191

software, computer-related inventions, business methods, 195–197

software notes, 194, 212

trademarked chemical notes, 194

written description compliance, 191–192

Specification sections

Abstract, 186–187, 214–215

Advantages (narrative section), 191, 205, 207

Background, discussion of prior art, 186, 204–205, 209

claims, 186–187

Conclusion, 186, 213–214

Cross-reference to related applications (PPA or prior applications), 186, 203–204, 298

Description and operation of alternative embodiments, 213

Detailed description, 186–187, 193, 201–203, 208–212

Drawings--brief descriptions, 186, 207

Drawings--reference numerals list (optional but recommended), 186, 207–209

Federally-sponsored research or development, 186, 204

incorporation by reference statement, 186

Joint Research Agreement, names of parties to, 186, 204

Operation, 212–213

Ramifications, 213–214

Scope, 213–214

Sequence listing, 186–187, 204, 214

skeleton patent application, 206

Summary, 186, 207, 216

Technical field, 204

Title, 186, 203

See also Description (detailed)

Specification writing tips

articles, proper use of indefinite, 211

avoid grammatical and spelling errors, 202

avoiding legalese, 201

avoid negative statements, 202

avoid "patent profanity," 202

checklist for, 218

consider the audiences, 201

Glossary of Legal Terms, 514–520

Glossary of Technical Terms, 509–513

repetition technique, 208

selecting and arranging words, 210

short and simple sentences, 201–202

trademarked product references, 194, 211

use copious headings, 202

State law

limits on Employment Agreement terms, 489

theft of trade secrets, 32

trademark registration, 22

trademarks, 20

Statute of limitations, 472, 520

Statutory subject matter

overview, 103–104

business processes and methods, 105

claims for, 235, 237–238

conventional processes, 104

defined, 520

legal requirements for, 237–238

machines, 105–106

patentability, 101, 103–107, 253

in Patentability Flowchart, 126, 128

PPA and, 77

software processes, 104–105

unpatentable, 107

See also Compositions of matter (statutory subject class); Machines (statutory subject class); Manufactures (articles of manufacture); New-use inventions; Nonstatutory subject matter (judicial exceptions to patentability); Processes (methods)

Stop words (patent searches), 158

Submarine patents, 473

Substitute application, 444, 454, 455, 520

Successor liability, 520

Suggested Requirement for Restriction, 436

Summons, 520

Supervising Patent Examiner (SPE), 387

574 | PATENT IT YOURSELF

Supplemental applications
 overview, 442, 443, 444, 455
 attorney recommended for, 444
 flowchart of relationships, 443, 444
 independent applications, 444, 452, 455
 substitute applications, 444, 454–455
 See also Continuation applications; Continuation-in-
  part application (CIP); Divisional application; Reissue
  application; Request for Continued Examination (RCE)
Supplemental examination, 477, 478, 482
Synergism, 123–124

T

Tax-avoidance schemes, as unpatentable, 13, 108–109
Tax deductions and income, 52–53, 481
Technical Disclosure Commons, 453
Technology Center Ombudsman (TCO), 387
Temporary restraining order, 520
Terminal disclaimer (TD), 384, 444, 450, 454, 455
Terms (patent searches), 157
Terms of patents
 overview, 14, 16–17
 delays caused by PTO or appeals, 14, 16, 384, 428,
  432–433
 European Patent Office (EPO), 353
 PPA effectively extends, 63
Terrorism
 defining for PTMS, 324
 marketability factors, 91
 PTMS filing, 322, 324, 326
Theft of invention
 after commercial success, 96, 117
 contingent-fee intermediary brokers, 334
 documenting proof of invention, 52
 patent pending protection, 14
 test marketing increases possibility, 174
 trade secrets, 31–32
 waivers before filing patent application, 341
TikTok, 345
Timing schedule, 527–528
Toys and games, 34, 205, 499
Track 1 examination, 326, 328
Trade dress
 alternative to patent, 181
 defined, 33
 distinctive appearances, 181
 surface ornamentation, 33
 unfair competition law, 32–33
Trademarks, 19–23
 overview, 19, 36
 advertising, 8, 22

certification marks, 19
commercial potential, 87
copyright overlap, 27
defined, 19–20
design/logos, 19
diluting marks, 20
domain name protection, 20
federal registration, 22
generic words and loss of, 21, 23
intent-to-use (ITU) application, 22, 180
law of, 8
as marketing tool, 180
monopoly rights, 20
nonqualifying registrations, 23
offensive rights, 20–23
ownership of, 8, 20–22
proper use of, 22–23
references to inventions using, 212
relationship to patent law, 21
searches of registered/unregistered, 21
secondary meaning and, 19
service marks, 19
shape of objects, 19
strong/weak marks, 20–21
trade group registration, 22
trade names, 19–20
as trade secrets, 21
unregistered (common law), 21–22
use of generic name, 194, 212
word trademarks, 19, 22–23
Trade names
 defined, 19–20
 infringement as false designation of origin, 20
Trade-Related Aspects of Intellectual Property Rights
 (TRIPS). *See* TRIPS
Trade secrets, 28–32
 overview, 8, 28, 36
 acquiring and maintaining rights, 31–32
 advantages of protection, 30
 commercial use filing dates, 29–30
 computer program protections, 13
 defined, 28
 disadvantages versus patenting, 30–31
 documentation as proof of invention, 52
 employee nondisclosure agreements, 31–32
 illegally obtained, 14, 31–32
 immediate rights to, 30
 improvements to inventions, 10
 infringement of patents, 31
 magic-type, 28
 maintained by nonpublication request, 29, 177–178, 181

maintaining confidentiality, 29–31, 178
not discoverable from final product, 177–178
offensive rights, 29
ownership of, 8, 29–31, 52
patent application confidentiality, 29
patent pending status, 178
perpetual protection, 30
prior-user rights, 31
proof of existence, 31
public disclosure, 29–31
relationship with patents, 29–31
reverse engineering, 30–31, 36, 177
sale to manufacturer, 177
technical information, 28–29
trademarks preserved as, 21
Trade secret status chosen instead of patenting
advantages and disadvantages of, 30–31, 177–178
for business processes and methods, 105
coverage of complicated information, 30
immediate obtaining of, 30
maintaining confidentiality, 30–31
manufacture and distributing yourself, 177–178
potential of perpetual protection, 30
prior user's rights, 31, 178
public reverse engineering, 30–31
sale to manufacturer, 177
Training Mode, 79
Traverse, 520
TRIPS (Trade-Related Aspects of Intellectual Property
Rights)
filed within a year of PCT, 363
Paris Convention provisions applied to, 350
patent expiration date, 432
patent law differences, 357–358
priority for patent filing dates, 354, 365
WTO countries governed by, 350
Twitter (X), 345
Tying, 463, 481, 494, 520

U

Unenforceability of patents, 387, 461, 480, 494
Unfair competition, 32–33
overview, 8, 32, 36
advertising and, 8, 32–33
creation of offensive rights, 32, 34
design patent comparisons, 33
distinctive appearances, 32–33
injunctions, 32
trade dress, 32–33
Unified Patent Court (UPC), 354

Uniform Commercial Code, 472, 477
Uniform Dispute Resolution Policy (UDRP), 20
Uniform Trade Secrets Act, 32
Unitary Patents, 354
Unitary Patent system, 365
United Inventors Association (UIA), 504
United States Code (U.S.C.), 4
United States International Trade Commission (USITC),
473
United States Patent and Trademark Office (PTO). *See*
PTO
Universal License Agreement, 495–499
Unpatentable inventions
business processes and methods, 13, 105, 240–242
judicial exceptions, 12–13
licensing or selling to manufacturer, 179–181
misconceptions that it can't be made and sold, 152
prima facie case, 319
subject matter eligibility guidelines, 13, 103
submission to Quirky.com, 181, 339
unsafe new drugs, 108
utility patents, 328
See also Nonstatutory subject matter (judicial exceptions
to patentability)
Unstructured fanaticism, 46
U.S. Congress
intellectual property laws, 4
patent laws, 13–14, 101, 103
plant patents, 12
statutory class, 101
U.S. Constitution, 103
U.S. Copyright Office, 4, 24, 27–28
U.S. Customs and Border Protection, 35, 473
USOCR database, 153
USPAT database, 153
US-PGPUB database, 153
U.S. Postal Service
filing by mail (not recommended), 80, 289, 306
Post Office Patent misconception, 62, 83, 244
See also Certificate of Mailing; Postcard receipt; Priority
Mail Express (PME)
U.S. Supreme Court
Akamai v. Limelight, 257
Alice Corp. v. CLS Bank International, 104, 241
Alice v. CLS Bank, 401
Amgen Inc. v. Sanofi et al., 193
*Association for Molecular Pathology v. Myriad Genetics,
Inc.*, 106
Berkheimer v. HP Inc., 402
Bilski v. Kappos, 103, 105, 241

576 | PATENT IT YOURSELF

on commercial success and patentability, 383

court appeals, 480

Diamond v. Diehr, 253

Feist Publications, Inc. v. Rural Telephone Service, 24

Festo v. Shoketsu, 263, 384, 470

G.E. v. Wabash, 237

Gottschalk v. Benson, 12

Graham v. John Deere, 117, 121

Halliburton v. Walker, 237

Iancu v. Brunetti, 23

KSR International Co. v. Teleflex Inc., 117, 124

Matal v. Tam, 23

Mayo Collaborative Services v. Prometheus Labs., Inc., 12

Ortho-McNeil-Janssen v. State of Arkansas, 252

patent appeals, 432

on patent claims, 106, 193, 238

Rozenblat v. Sandia Corp, 188

Utility, as patentability requirement

legal requirements for, 101–102

operability requirement, 108–109

patentability, 107–110

in Patentability Flowchart, 128

safe new drugs, 108

unpatentability, 108–110

usefulness and, 107–108

Utility Patent Application Transmittal, 292

Utility patents

overview, 10, 35

compared to copyright, 24–26

converted to design patent, 437

defined, 520

duration of, 16

examination fees, 522

foreign filing dates, 356, 365

functionality, 10–12, 328

maintenance fees, 16, 35

nonobviousness tests, 102

novelty tests, 102

offensive rights, 25–26, 34

plants and, 102

post-allowance fees, 522

Request for Continued Examination (RCE), 447

shapes and, 25–26

term of patent, 527

timing schedule, 527–528

V

Venture capitalists (VC), 344

Verified statement, 520

Vicarious liability, 520

Voir dire, 520

W

Waiver of rights

attorney review of, 341

avoid signing if possible, 340–341

likelihood with giant companies, 338, 340

manufacturer requests for, 176, 182, 339–342

patent rights retained after signing, 176, 341

Proprietary Submission Agreement as alternative to, 340–341

Washpat, 154

Websites

distributing content, 257

ghost servers, 257

printed publications as prior art, 111

sending content, 257

tagging page content, 257

See also Internet; Online resources

Weekends or holidays, filing dates falling on

any action due on next open-for-business day, 394, 467, 525

Maintenance fees, 467

Office Actions date moved to next business day, 394

PPA anniversary and RPA filing, 184

PTO holiday closings, 525

Whimsical inventions, 108

Wikipedia, 154

Wild card symbols (patent searches), 157

WIPO. *See* World Intellectual Property Organization (WIPO)

Witnesses

building and testing, 51, 58

confusion of inventorship, 52

consultation on invention potential, 96

digital documents, 58, 62

documentation of the invention, 58–60, 62

Invention Disclosure, 60

recording conception, 58

See also Lab notebook witnesses

Working models (prototypes)

demonstrating to examiner, 383

demonstration and sales pitch to manufacturers, 174, 337, 341–342, 346

examiner requests for, 189

getting opinions on invention, 94–95

marketability factors, 91, 94

professional model makers, 337–338

reasons for making, 96

virtual prototypes, 96, 338

Work-made-for-hire, copyright on, 24

World Intellectual Property Organization (WIPO), 350, 356–357, 360–361, 364

World Trade Organization (WTO), 350, 365 ●

More from Nolo

Nolo.com offers a large library of legal solutions and forms, created by Nolo's in-house legal editors. These reliable documents can be prepared in minutes.

Create a Document Online

Incorporation. Incorporate your business in any state.

LLC Formation. Gain asset protection and pass-through tax status in any state.

Will. Nolo has helped people make over 2 million wills. Is it time to make or revise yours?

Living Trust (avoid probate). Plan now to save your family the cost, delays, and hassle of probate.

Download Useful Legal Forms

Nolo.com has hundreds of top quality legal forms available for download:

- bill of sale
- promissory note
- nondisclosure agreement
- LLC operating agreement
- corporate minutes
- commercial lease and sublease
- motor vehicle bill of sale
- consignment agreement
- and many more.

Nolo's Bestselling Books

Patent Pending in 24 Hours

Patent, Copyright & Trademark
An Intellectual Property Desk Reference

Nolo's Patents for Beginners

Profit From Your Idea
How to Make Smart Licensing Deals

Trademark
Legal Care for Your Brand

Every Nolo title is available in print and for download at Nolo.com.

www.nolo.com

Register your Nolo purchase, and we'll send you a **coupon for 15% off** your next Nolo.com order!

Nolo.com/customer-support/productregistration

On Nolo.com you'll also find:

Books & Software
Nolo publishes hundreds of great books and software programs for consumers and business owners. Order a copy, or download an ebook version instantly, at Nolo.com.

Online Forms
You can quickly and easily make a will or living trust, form an LLC or corporation, or make hundreds of other forms—online.

Free Legal Information
Thousands of articles answer common questions about everyday legal issues, including wills, bankruptcy, small business formation, divorce, patents, employment, and much more.

Plain-English Legal Dictionary
Stumped by jargon? Look it up in America's most up-to-date source for definitions of legal terms, free at Nolo.com.

Lawyer Directory
Nolo's consumer-friendly lawyer directory provides in-depth profiles of lawyers all over America. You'll find information you need to choose the right lawyer.

PAT22